CW01651980

Bad Painting
good art

Bibliografische Information der Deutschen Bibliothek
Die Deutsche Bibliothek verzeichnet diese Publikation
in der Deutschen Nationalbibliografie;
detaillierte bibliografische Daten sind im Internet über http://dnb.ddb.de abrufbar.
Bibliographic information published by Die Deutsche Bibliothek
Die Deutsche Bibliothek lists this publication in the Deutsche Nationalbibliografie;
detailed bibliographic data is available in the Internet at http://dnb.ddb.de

MUMOK
Museum
Moderner
Kunst
Stiftung
Ludwig
Wien

Bad Painting
good art

Herausgegeben von / published by
Museum Moderner Kunst Stiftung Ludwig Wien
Eva Badura-Triska, Susanne Neuburger

DUMONT

Inhalt / Contents

Foreword

Pronounced dead at regular intervals, painting remains the medium in which the public displays the greatest interest and for which it harbors the most intense affection. The painted picture is still a synonym for the artwork per se. Shaped by its history, the MUMOK collection focuses more on socially-engaged, object-based, and performative art, and on new media. In spite of this, not only on account of its nonetheless respectable collection of painting from 1900 to the present, but also as a matter of principle, it remains an important task of the museum to follow and contribute to the discourse on painting in exhibitions and in symposiums.

Bad Painting is a theme that fits MUMOK's self-image as an active participant in critical discourse. The exhibition attempts an alternative history that pointedly addresses the question of the quality and relevance of painting. The open-ended formulation "Bad Painting—good art," based on a quotation from Neil Jenney (whose work is featured in the show), approaches the question controversially, and is likely to be perceived as a provocation. This is not against the intentions of the show.

Bad Painting—good art is the first major historical overview of a phenomena which has undeservedly received little attention to date, offering a new, differentiated view on the history of Modern and Postmodern painting. Seen from the perspective of Bad Painting, famous and less well-known works—by artists including Francis Picabia, René Magritte, Asger Jorn, Georg Baselitz, Philip Guston, Neil Jenney, Albert Oehlen, and Julian Schnabel—appear in a new light. With selected works by twenty-one artists, the exhibition spans a period from the 1920s to the present.

Vorwort

Die in regelmäßigen Abständen totgesagte Malerei ist bis heute das Medium, dem das größte Interesse und die intensivste Zuneigung des Publikums entgegengebracht werden. Das Tafelbild gilt immer noch als Synonym für das Kunstwerk an sich. Der Sammlungsgeschichte des MUMOK entsprechend, sind die Schwerpunkte seiner Sammlung aber eher im Bereich der gesellschafts-, objektbezogenen und performativen Kunst beziehungsweise in den neuen Medien zu finden. Nicht nur aufgrund seiner dennoch durchaus respektablen Bestände an Malerei von zirka 1900 bis heute, sondern auch aus prinzipiellen Überlegungen ist es eine der wichtigen Aufgaben des Museums, sowohl in Ausstellungen als auch in Symposien den Diskurs über Malerei zu verfolgen und zu diesem eigene Beiträge zu leisten.

Bad Painting ist ein Thema, das dem kritisch-diskursiven Selbstverständnis des MUMOK entspricht. Versucht wird eine Parallelgeschichte der Malerei, die pointiert die Frage nach Qualität und Relevanz von Malerei stellt. In der offenen Formulierung „Bad Painting – good art", einem Zitat nach dem (in der Ausstellung vertretenen) Künstler Neil Jenney, wird diese Frage kontroversiell gestellt und wohl auch als Provokation wahrgenommen werden. Das liegt durchaus auch in der Absicht des Projekts.

Bad Painting – good art beleuchtet erstmals in einem groß angelegten historischen Überblick ein bislang zu Unrecht kaum wahrgenommenes Phänomen, das eine neue differenzierte Sichtweise auf die Geschichte der Malerei von Moderne und Postmoderne eröffnet. Berühmte wie auch bislang weniger beachtete malerische Werke – wie jene von Francis Picabia, René Magritte, Asger Jorn, Georg Baselitz, Philip Guston, Neil Jenney, Albert Oehlen oder Julian Schnabel – erscheinen unter dem Blickwinkel von Bad Painting in einem neuen Licht. Anhand ausgewählter Werke von 21 Künstlern spannt die Ausstellung einen Bogen von den 1920er-Jahren bis in die Gegenwart.

Bad Painters bekennen sich eindeutig zur Malerei. Sie fordern dieses Medium aber neu heraus, indem sie es mittels verschiedenster Formen eines „unkorrekten", „schlechten", „hässlichen" oder „bösen" Malens mit seinen ureigensten Mitteln kritisieren und angreifen. Bad Painting ist eine Strategie, die letztlich bei keinem Künstler das gesamte Schaffen betrifft, sondern meist nur in bestimmten Phasen zum Einsatz kommt, um dem Medium neue Möglichkeiten zu eröffnen. Im Grunde richtet

Bad Painters are unequivocally committed to the medium. But they challenge this medium afresh by criticizing and attacking it with its own means, by using a range of "incorrect," "bad," or "ugly" styles and techniques of painting. Bad Painting is a strategy that no artist has followed consistently throughout his entire career, but rather deployed during specific phases as a way of opening up new possibilities for the medium. It is directed against all manner of rigid canons, not only against those of the traditionalists, but also against the precepts and dogmas of the avant-gardes of the twentieth century. As such, Bad Painting is ultimately also a critique of the utopian claims and promises of Modernism, whose untenability it aims to lay bare.

In accordance with the exhibition's historical approach, this catalog contains essays that trace connections and lines of development, and others that explore Bad Painting in the work of individual artists. It thus offers an unprecedented opportunity to explore the subject in depth.

The idea for this project came from Susanne Neuburger, who then developed the exhibition together with Eva Badura-Triska. I owe both curators my sincere thanks for this innovative, complex, and courageous project. I would like to thank all the staff at MUMOK, and in particular Dagmar Steyrer and Nina Krick, for organizing the show and producing the catalog.

Special thanks are due to all those who loaned works, without whose generous support this project would not have been possible.

Edelbert Köb, Director
Museum Moderner Kunst Stiftung Ludwig Wien

es sich gegen erstarrte Kanons aller Art, also nicht nur gegen jene der Traditionalisten, sondern auch gegen die Vorschriften und Dogmen der Avantgarden des 20. Jahrhunderts. Bad Painting ist damit nicht zuletzt auch eine Kritik an den utopischen Ansprüchen und Versprechungen der Moderne, deren Uneinlösbarkeit aufgedeckt werden soll.

Dem historischen Ansatz der Ausstellung entsprechend, enthält dieser Katalog sowohl Aufsätze, die Zusammenhänge und Entwicklungslinien aufspüren, als auch solche, die Bad Painting bei einzelnen Künstlern näher beleuchten. Er bietet damit erstmals eine Möglichkeit, sich mit dem Thema in umfassender Weise auseinander zu setzen.

Die Idee zu diesem Projekt stammt von Susanne Neuburger, die die Ausstellung dann zusammen mit Eva Badura-Triska erarbeitet hat. Beiden Kuratorinnen gilt mein aufrichtiger Dank für dieses innovative, komplexe und mutige Projekt. Dagmar Steyrer und Nina Krick danke ich stellvertretend für alle Mitarbeiter des Hauses für die Organisation der Ausstellung beziehungsweise die Realisierung des Kataloges.

Mein ganz besonderer Dank gebührt den zahlreichen Leihgebern, ohne deren großzügige Bereitschaft, sich von wertvollen Werken zu trennen, dieses Projekt nicht zustande gekommen wäre.

Edelbert Köb, Direktor
Museum Moderner Kunst Stiftung Ludwig Wien

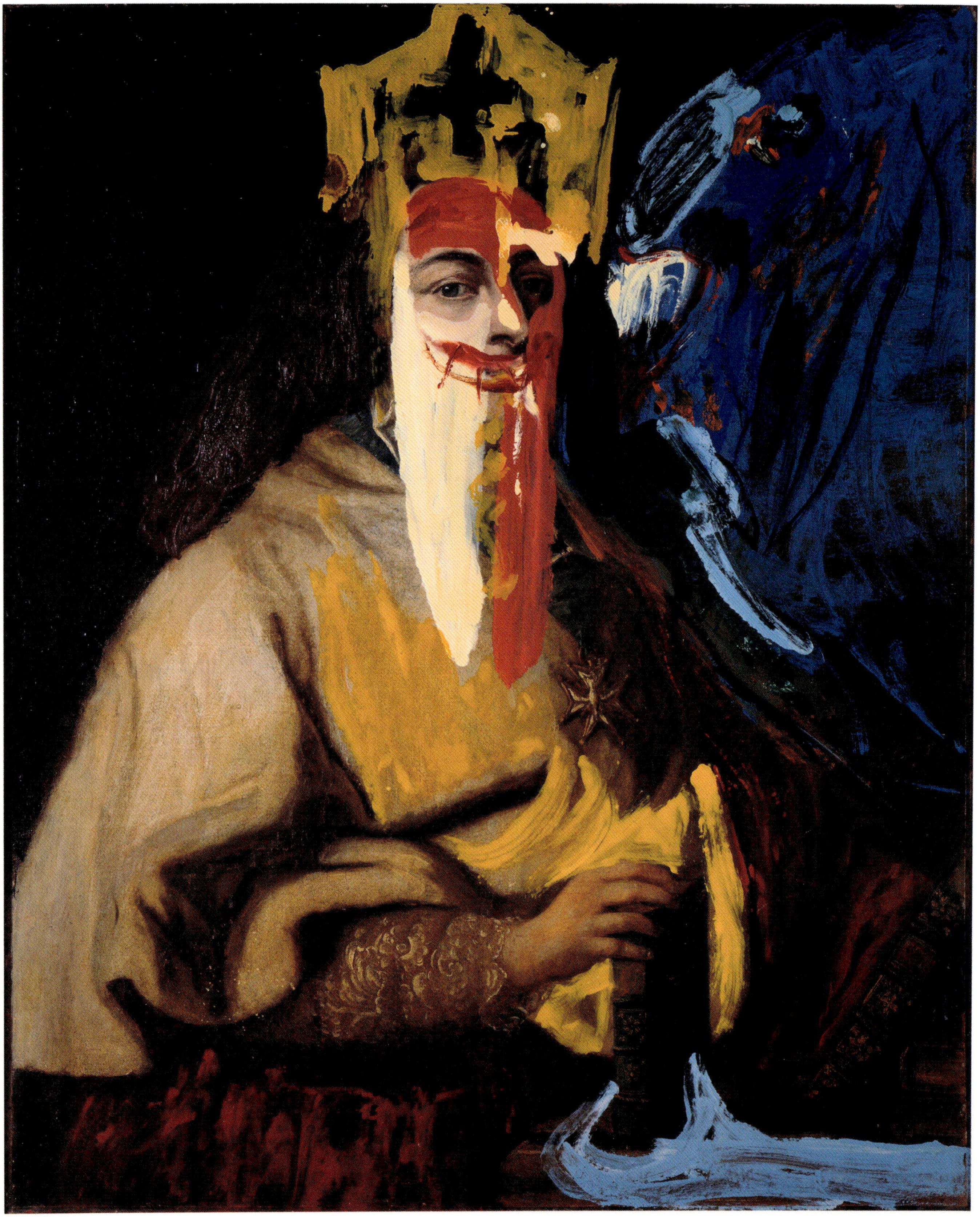

001 **Asger Jorn**
Grand Baiser au Cardinal d'Amerique, 1962
(Dicker Kuss an den Kardinal von Amerika /
Big Kiss to the Cardinal of America)

Öl auf Leinwand / oil on canvas, 92 x 73 cm
Pierre et Micky Alechinsky, Bougival

Das erste und das letzte Bild?

Eine Versuchsanordnung für Bad Painting

Susanne Neuburger

Seit den späten 1970er-Jahren scheint eine stille Übereinkunft über Bad Painting als Ware, Label oder „brand“ zu bestehen, an der die Koinzidenz zwischen der Verwendung des Begriffs und der Neuformierung des Kunstmarkts auffällig ist. Dennoch war keinerlei Definitionsmacht ausreichend, um „Bad Painting“ zu einem programmatischen Begriff aufzuwerten. Ein Pionierprojekt war die 1978 veranstaltete Ausstellung *“Bad” Painting* von Marcia Tucker im New-Yorker New Museum. Tucker verteidigte die damals unzeitgemäße „Figuration“ unter dem Vorzeichen von „bad“ in einer Gesamtdarstellung, in der auch einige Positionen von Frauen enthalten sind, die von nun an (und erst recht davor) von Bad Painting ausgeschlossen waren.

Bad Painting ist in kurzen Werkphasen und kurzen Zeiten zu finden und tatsächlich ein komplexes Phänomen, das einen großen Bogen von regressiver Wunschvorstellung zu kritischer Kulturanalyse spannt. Wenngleich der theoretische Unterbau fehlt, hat dies einer regen Praxis bei Picabia, Jorn oder Magritte, später dann bei Oehlen, Büttner oder Schnabel keinen Abbruch getan. Im Bad Painting wird die Malerei des 20. Jahrhunderts mit ihren Regeln der Avantgarden auf den Prüfstein gebracht, kritisiert und destabilisiert. Besonders deren Zeitgesetze von Entwicklung und Geschichtlichkeit, von „Irreversibilität und Retroaktion“, um mit Thierry de Duve[1] zu sprechen, scheinen Gegenreaktionen herauszufordern. Magrittes „période vache“ ist ein gutes Beispiel, wie im Bad Painting Normbrüche und kontrastive Wertmodelle angelegt sein können. Dass diese nicht nur von einem Ausbruch gekennzeichnet sind, sondern auch einen hohen Grad an Reflexivität in sich tragen, macht Bad Painting erst zu einer Denkfigur der Malerei. Diese aufzuzeigen und zu befragen ist Intention dieser Ausstellung, die mit exemplarischen Beispielen eine erste historisch motivierte Gesamtdarstellung des Phänomens versucht. Dabei soll weniger Vollständigkeit denn die Frage im Vordergrund stehen, ob Bad Painting auch als andere Malereigeschichte taugen kann, die sich – wenn auch mehr mental als linear – in schon bestehende einschreibt.

Bad Painting ist zwar Malerei, aber auch Projekt, Aktion und Text. Es hat nicht nur die Regeln, sondern auch das Reglement der Avantgarden im Auge und spekuliert vorauseilend mit Erfolg oder Misserfolg, mit Aufmerksamkeit oder Ablehnung. Mit dem Skandal von Manets *Olympia*, vor der das Publikum seine Kontrolle verlor, mag es begonnen haben.[2] Bad Painting hat ein großes

The First and the Last Painting?

An experimental set-up for Bad Painting

Susanne Neuburger

Since the late 1970s there seems to be a tacit agreement on Bad Painting being a commodity, label or brand name. It is quite remarkable how the use of the term coincided with the newly structured art market. Nonetheless, no defining power could sufficiently upgrade "Bad Painting" to a programmatic term. A pioneering project in this regard was the exhibition *"Bad" Painting* held in 1978 and curated by Marcia Tucker in the New Museum, New York. Tucker defended the then outmoded "figuration," subscribing to the designation of "bad" in a general overview, which also included several positions from female artists, who were thereafter (and hitherto even more so) excluded from Bad Painting.

Bad Painting is a product of brief working phases and confined within short periods of time. It definitely is a complex phenomenon, ranging from regressive wishful thinking to a critical analysis of culture. Even though the theoretical foundation is missing, Picabia, Jorn or Magritte avidly pursued it, and later it did not diminish the esteem Oehlen, Büttner or Schnabel enjoyed. In Bad Painting we find that twentieth-century painting with its avant-garde rules is put to the test, criticized and destabilized. Especially its zeitgeist of evolution and historicity, "irreversibility" and "retroaction"—to adopt Thierry de Duve's[1] terms—seems to provoke a counter-reaction. Magritte's "période vache" serves as a fitting example for how breaking with norms and contrasting value models can structure Bad Painting. It is primarily the fact that they are not only marked by breaking with patterns, but also inhere a high degree of reflexivity, that makes Bad Painting a figure of thought within the pictorial arts. The exhibition aims to show this and to question the same, in an attempt to give the first historically motivated overview of the phenomenon using paradigmatic artworks. In doing so, the focus is not so much on completeness, but rather on the issue of Bad Painting also being valid as an alternative history of painting that inscribes itself—even if mentally rather than linearly—in already existing art history.

Bad Painting may be painting, but it is also project, action and text. It not only questions rules, but also avant-garde dictates, and speculates ahead, either successfully or unsuccessfully, attracting attention or meeting with disapproval. Perhaps all this began with the scandal around Manet's *Olympia*, which made its viewing public lose control of itself.[2] Bad Painting's narrative potential is immense, and it can certainly take up the comparison of "ut pictura poesis" or vouch for the

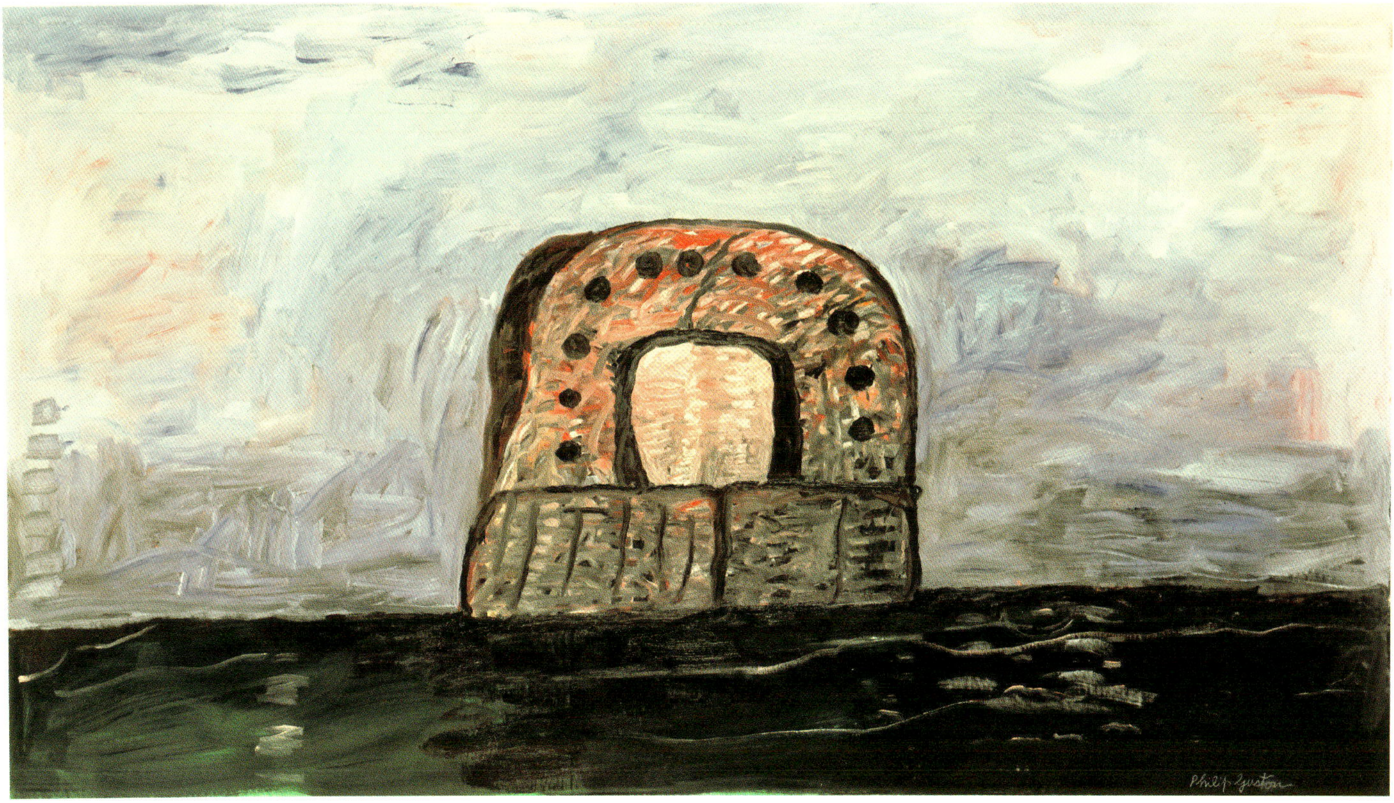

002 **Philip Guston**
Black Sea, 1977
(Schwarzes Meer)
Öl auf Leinwand / oil on canvas, 173 x 297 cm
Tate London

narratives Potenzial, das durchaus den Vergleich von „ut pictura poesis" aufnehmen kann. Eine prinzipiell transhistorische Struktur ist ebenso wichtig und präsent, wie sie verstoßen und malträtiert wird. Und insofern ist es gleichzeitig richtig und falsch, wenn Albert Oehlen sagt: „Bad Painting kann auf nichts aufbauen."[3] Tatsächlich baut es auf, muss aber gleich wieder vergessen, dass die Avantgarde sein eigentliches Movens war.

Eines seiner Gesetze jedenfalls ist sicher: Bad Painting folgt dem Wesen der Malerei, meint immer Bild und Piktoralität und kokettiert mit ihrem „apokalyptischen Mythos" (Yves-Alain Bois). Wenn Buren Malerei ist, sind auch Metapositionen als Malereikritik von Interesse und Ansätze wie die Kippenbergers nur scheinbare Standpunkte von außen. Jorns bekannter Ausspruch, dass „die Lieblingsnahrung der Malerei die Malerei ist",[4] richtet sich an das Wesen der Malerei, das auch den Rahmen seiner „Detourned Paintings" abgibt. Schon in seinem Text „Intime Banalitäten" wertete er den Kitsch auf, den Adorno und Greenberg bekanntlich in Opposition zum Modernismus sahen, und bezeichnete „diese Seen in den Wäldern und diese röhrenden Hirsche, die in tausenden von Wohnzimmern in Goldverzierung auf gemusterten Tapeten hängen", als „tiefsinnigste Eingebungen der Kunst".[5] Jetzt sei die „kitschige Generation an der Reihe", propagiert die Gruppe SPUR und fordert den Kitsch als „junge Tochter der alten Kunst".[6]

Bad Painting ist kaum formal fassbar, schon gar nicht durchgängig und ausschließlich, sondern behauptet sich vielmehr auch hier als eine Strategie, die das Potenzial der Moderne und ihrer

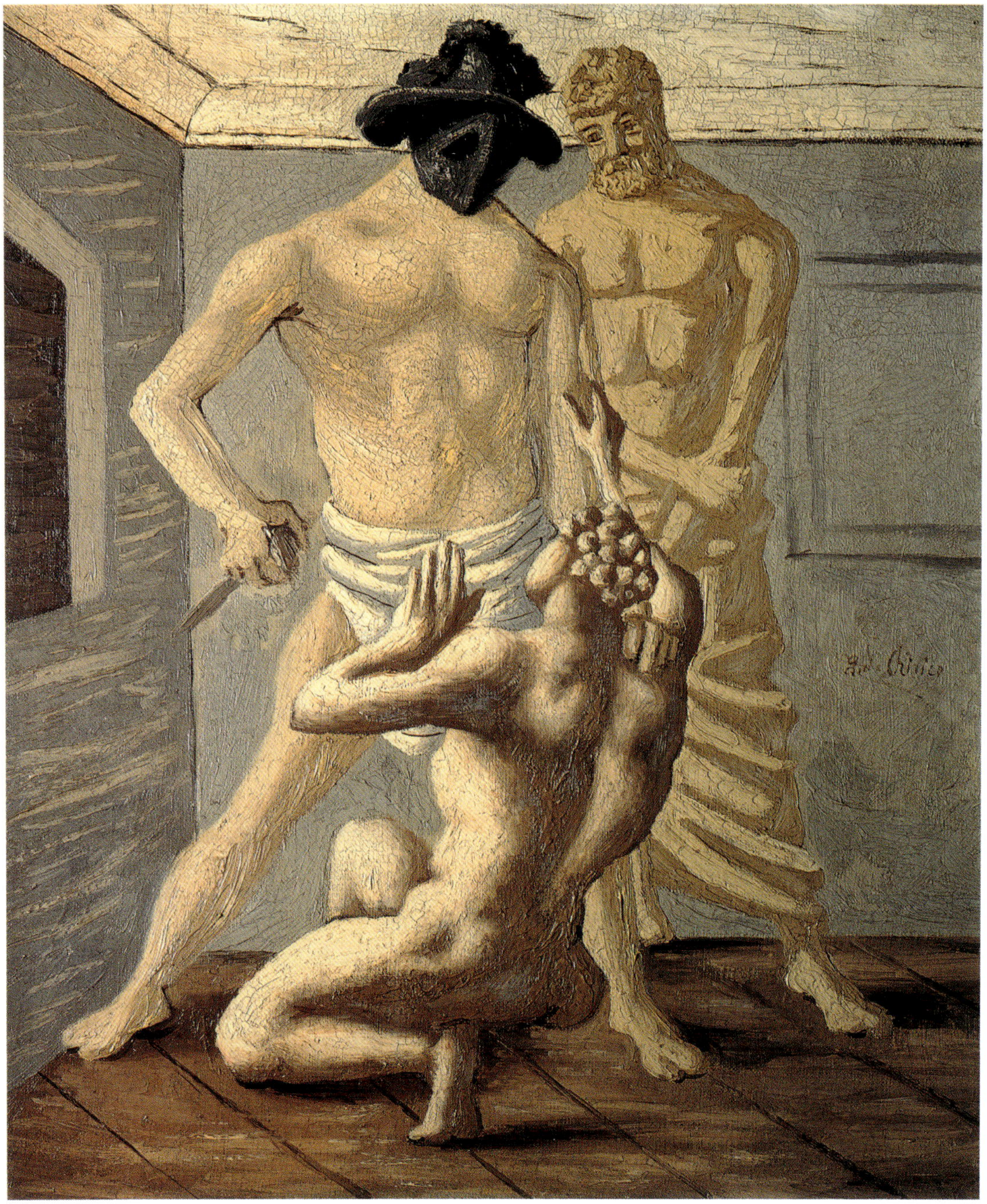

003
Giorgio de Chirico
Gladiateurs s'amusant à l'école, 1927 (Sich in der Schule amüsierende Gladiatoren / Gladiators Amusing Themselves at School)
Öl auf Leinwand / oil on canvas
55 x 46 cm
Privatsammlung, Venedig / Private Collection, Venice

espousal of the arts. A fundamentally transhistorical structure is equally important and must be present just as it must be rejected and maltreated. And in this respect, Albert Oehlen's statement that "Bad Painting has no foundation to build on" is simultaneously true and false.[3] It does in fact build something up, but must immediately forget that the avant-garde was its actual motive cause.

At any rate, one of its rules is certain: Bad Painting follows the essence of painting, always connotes image and pictoriality and flirts with its "apocalyptic myth" (Yves-Alain Bois). If Buren is painting, then also metapositions are interesting as criticisms of painting, and approaches such as Kippenberger's are only apparent external viewpoints. Jorn's renowned remark—"painting is painting's favorite food"[4]—refers to the essence of painting, which likewise furnishes the framework of his

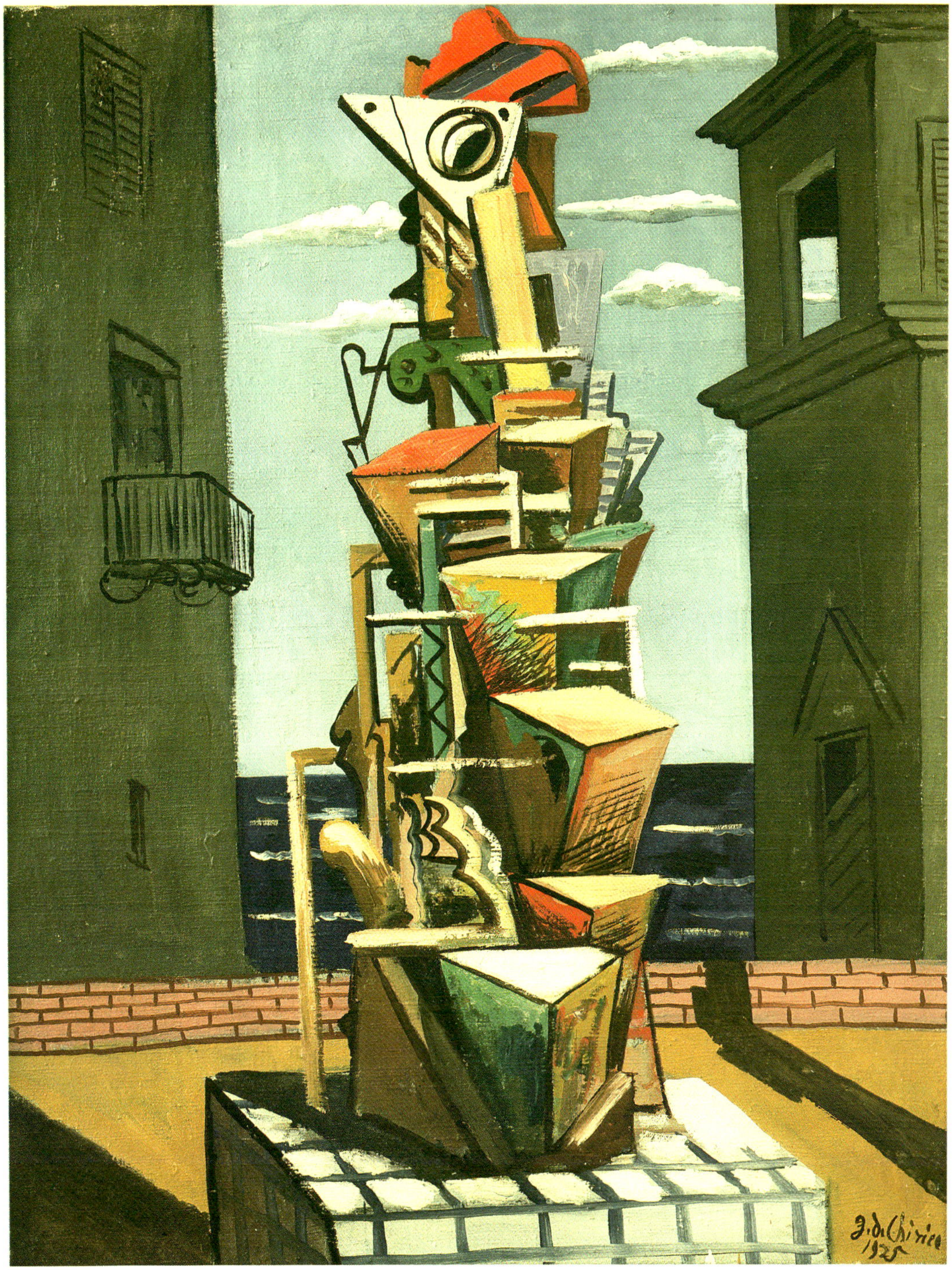

004 Giorgio de Chirico
Au bord de la mer, 1925
(Am Meer / At the Sea)
Öl auf Leinwand / oil on canvas
100 x 80 cm
Museum Moderner Kunst Stiftung Ludwig Wien, erworben / acquired 1985

Avantgarden regressiv unterläuft. Bad Painting muss ein antiklassizierender, antimodernistischer Ansatz implizit sein, der bisweilen an die Bataille'sche „opération" erinnert, und zwar genau in dem Maße, wie der Signifikant im „informe" über das Signifikat die Oberhand[7] gewinnt, obwohl generell Signifikant und Signifikat kaum voneinander zu trennen sind. Um indexalische Zeichen einzubauen, die oft Weltbezug und subversive Kritik einbringen, wird gelegentlich eine prinzipiell ikonische Repräsentation aufgebrochen. Die Gruppe SPUR hat den Index sogar als Namen gewählt, um programmatisch „den Kontakt mit der Geschichte und dem Ausland"[8] durchzuspielen. Eine weitere Strategie, Bildräume zu desituieren, lässt oft „abstrakt" in „figurativ" und umgekehrt übergehen, was durchaus auch ideologisch interpretierbar ist. Dass hier abermals das Signifikat gegenüber dem Signifikanten

"Detourned Paintings." Already in his text "Intimate Banalities" he enhances the status of kitsch, which in the eyes of Adorno and Greenberg opposed Modernism. He describes "the lakes in the forests and those roaring stags in golden, decorative frames hanging by thousands in living-rooms on walls with patterned wallpaper" as "the profoundest inspirations of art."[5] The Gruppe SPUR propagated that now the "kitsch generation" was to have its turn and claims that kitsch "is the young daughter of old art."[6]

It is almost impossible to comprehend Bad Painting in formal terms, for it is not at all consistent and certainly not exclusive. It holds its ground rather by strategic means, also here, regressively undermining the potential of Modernism and its avant-gardes. Bad Painting must subscribe to an implicit anti-classical, anti-modernist approach, reminding us now and then of the Bataillian "opération" and, indeed, precisely in the same measure the signifier in "informe" gains an upper hand over the signified[7], despite the fact that signifier and signified are practically indiscernible from one another. Occasionally, a fundamentally iconic representation is broken up in order to incorporate indexical signs that often introduce worldviews and subversive criticism. The Gruppe SPUR even chose the index as a name to programmatically go through "the contact with history and foreign countries."[8] Another strategy of de-situating pictorial spaces often turns "abstract" into "figurative" and vice versa—which can certainly be also interpreted as ideology. The fact that here the signified is repeatedly neglected in relation to the signifier typifies displacements that Bad Painters are well aware of. In addition to kitsch they utilize the means of parody, irony and humor as avidly as appropriation, citation or the pastiche. Albert Oehlen, by specifying Bad Painting as between "gravity and play,"[9] implemented a kind of ironical figure of speech that oscillates between distance and complicity. Here, complicity with the avant-garde stands in opposition to a regression, which demands from the "civilized," highly elaborate model of modern painting a step backward as an expedient or alternative. What Michael Krebber says on behalf of Philip Guston can likewise generally apply to Bad Painting: "[That] painters step backwards after opting out of the progressive (abstract) movement at the very moment in which it becomes established and academic. In this way anachronism can be revolutionary or even the very means of survival."[10] Psychoanalysis speaks of regression when the enlightened impetus of progressive developments is countered by other needs and longings.[11] Regressions are often displaced into

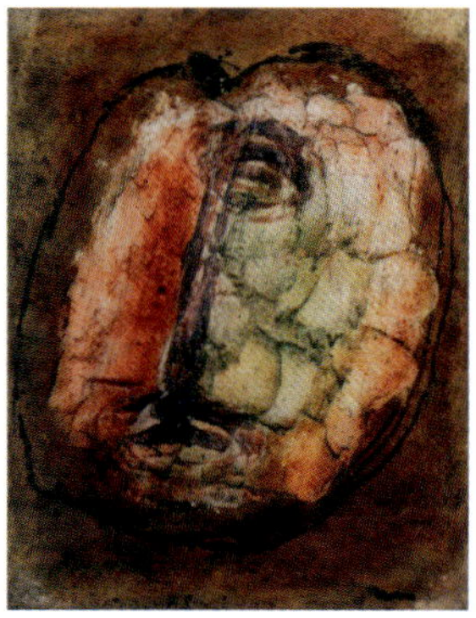

005 Jean Fautrier
Tête d'otage no.1, 1943
(Kopf einer Geisel Nr. 1 /
Head of Hostage No. 1)

Öl auf Papier kaschiert auf Leinwand /
oil on paper mounted on canvas
24 x 22 cm

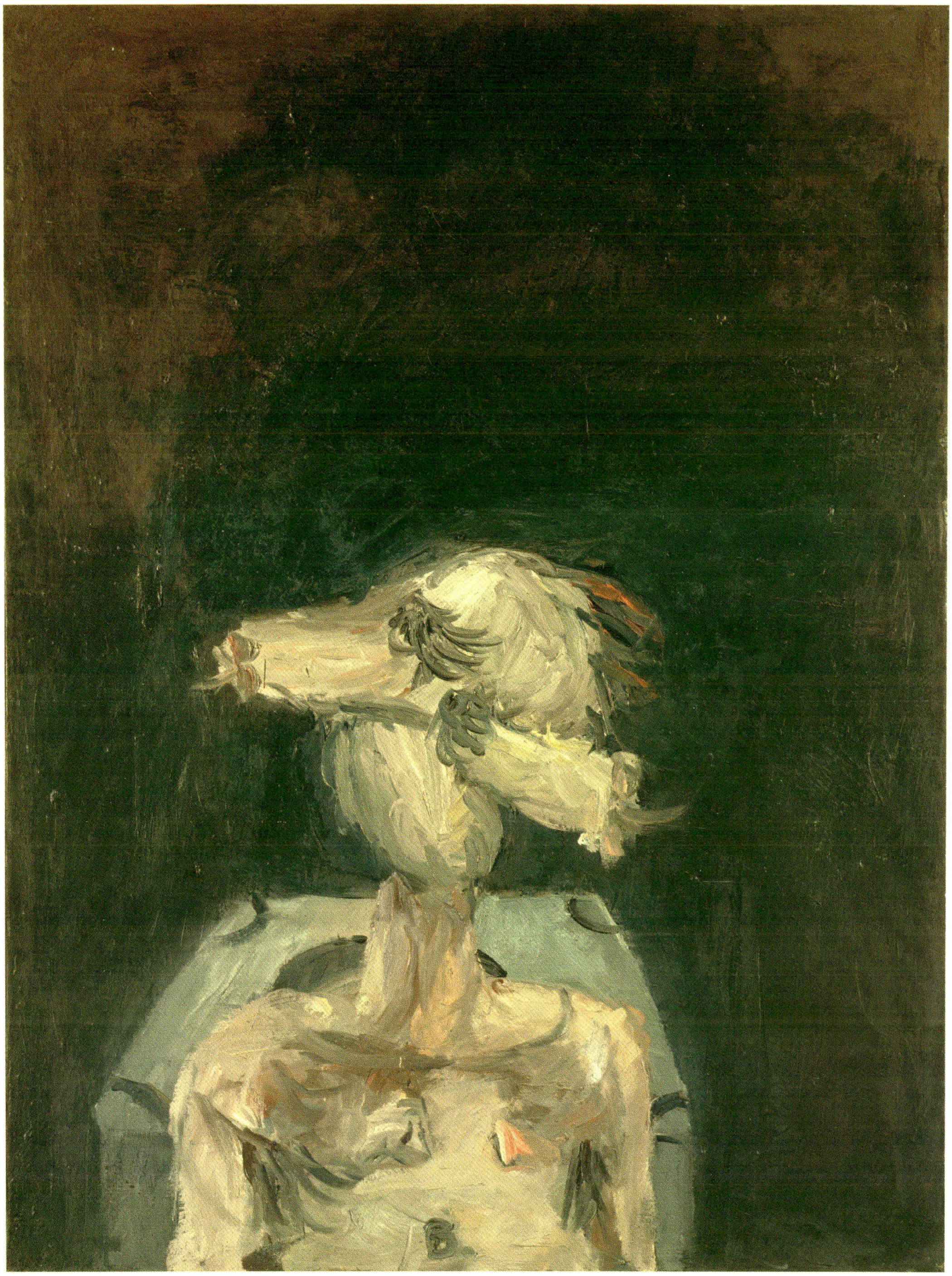

006 **Georg Baselitz**
Der Zwerg, 1962
(The Dwarf)
Öl auf Leinwand / oil on canvas, 136 x 101 cm
Bayerische Staatsgemäldesammlungen, München, Pinakothek der Moderne, WAF, Sammlung Prinz Franz von Bayern

vernachlässigt wird, sind Verschiebungen, um die Bad Painters Bescheid wissen. Neben dem Kitsch sind es Parodie, Ironie und Humor ebenso wie Appropriation, Zitat oder Pastiche, die eingesetzt werden. Zwischen „Ernst und Spaß"[9] benannte Albert Oehlen das Bad Painting mit einer Art von Ironiefigur, die bekanntlich zwischen Distanz und Komplizenschaft schwankt. Dabei steht die Komplizenschaft zur Avantgarde einer Regression gegenüber, die Rückschritte als Auswege und Alternativen dem „zivilisatorisch" hoch elaborierten Modell der Malerei der Moderne abverlangt. Was Michael Krebber für Philip Guston sagt, könnte auch für Bad Painting generell gelten: „Ein Rückwärtsgehen von Malern, die sich aus der fortschrittlichen (abstrakten) Bewegung ausgeklinkt haben, im Moment, in dem diese etabliert und akademisch geworden sei, sodass das Anachronistische das Revolutionäre sein konnte

the sphere of culture and aesthetics. Supposed freedom from inherited burdens and the "pressures of adapting to restrictive social norms"[12] can also collide with the claims of one's own superego. Werner Büttner summed this up as: "Finding in the very act of disregarding a homeland with culture,"[13] and being your own alternative. However, when he—in another context—calls this the "imitation of Christ,"[14] it can be seen how Bad Painting is geared to be a provocation—often in a very misogynistic way—in which failing just about manages to function.

This, too, could be a dictate of Bad Painting: Searching for the origins of painting by pursuing the original and anachronistic. A man with a bird's head and erect sexual organ: This is how Bataille describes a cave painting that he interprets as the earliest document revealing a yearning for the sacred.[15] Images by Baselitz exist that would fit this description, and also Picabia's *Noi* [ILL·016] has an element of atavism, of forgetting and dabbling frivolity, feigning a total lack of discrimination in order to appropriate earlier phases of development in civilization.

"To instigate something and to end something. To be the first and the last painting": In connection with Fautrier, Jutta Koether spoke of a "regressive turn."[16] Fautrier's simultaneously hollowed-out and refilled paintings seem to disappear beyond all form—as in the *Otages* (Hostages) [ILL·005], the anonymous portraits of the disfigured hostages of the German occupying power in France—to nevertheless establish profound references of meaning. "The first and the last painting" could also be a conceptual experimental set-up for a Bad Painting that adds a new and different way of viewing painting. Probably the one who comes closest to being a theoretician of Bad Painting is Bataille, who spoke of the "unfolding of a work as its withdrawal."[17] To comprehend the subject matter and framework of painting as "not going beyond something," meant for Merlin Carpenter "but likewise extending beyond something; that is, transgressing the notion of 'development.' In this way, a specificity of painting is opened up."[18] However, this does not refer to the discourse on the end of painting, on the (other) last image. Such a discourse could be a distant and already reinforced, theoretical counterpart, which perhaps shares revolutionary, subversive approaches with Bad Painting. What is Bad Painting then? Is it breaking the norm, is it attempting to come to terms with or even solving an underlying conflict? Certainly it is seriously concerned with breaking out, but it is equally an overwhelming acknowledgment of painting: Bad Painters as the "most obstinate and recalcitrant people."[19]

René Magritte and the Happy Revolt

Magritte's "période vache" [ILL·008·009·070–076] comprises a group of 30 oil paintings or gouaches that he executed in 1947/1948 for his first one-man exhibition at the Parisian Galerie Faubourg in 1948. Later he termed these sketchy and colorful artworks with grotesque and crude subject matter also as "peintures" or "gouaches fauves,"[20] so as to name his historically motivated regression during which he interimly suspended his expertise for the rawness and wildness of the

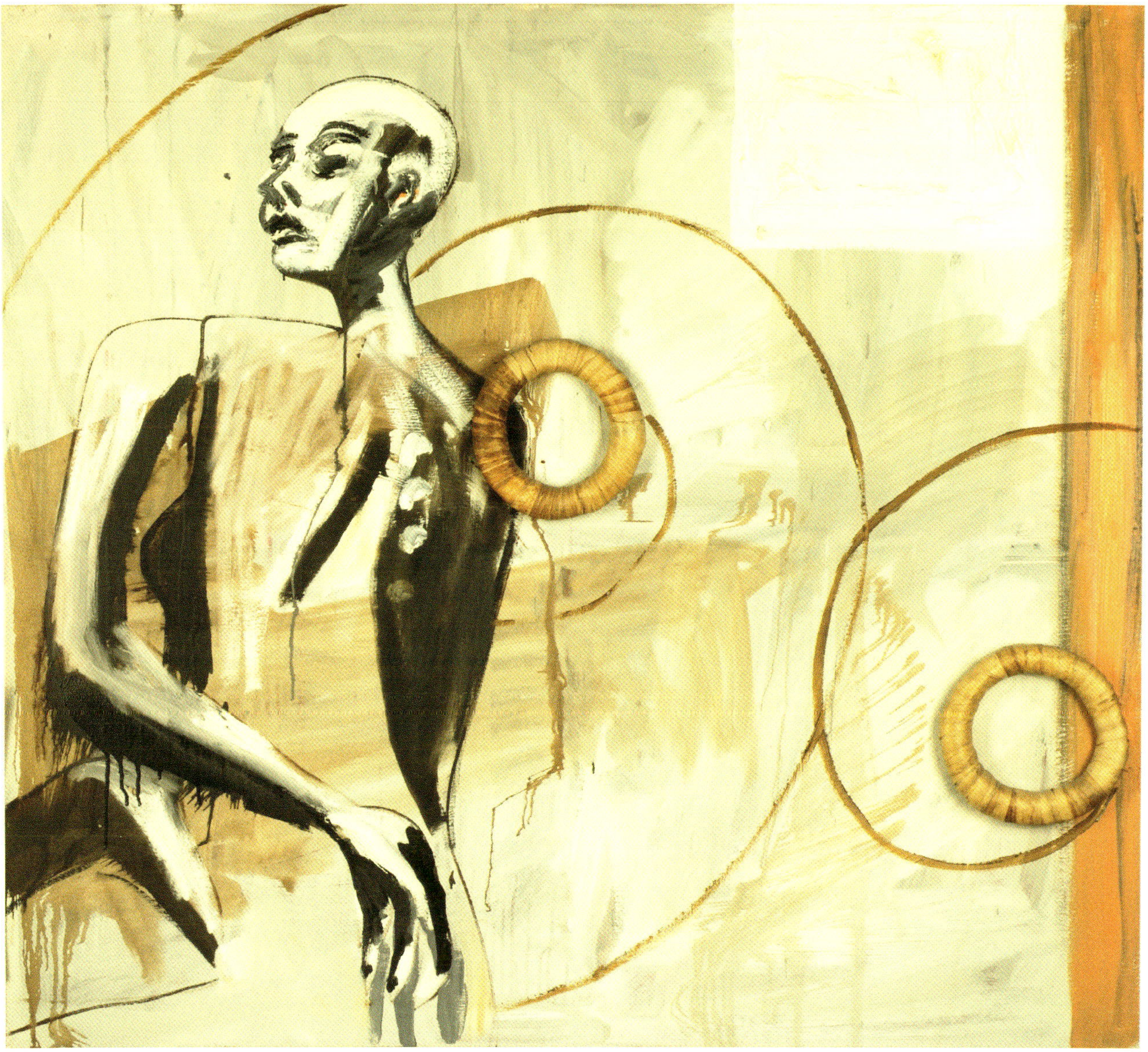

007 **Albert Oehlen**
Krefelder Appell, 1983
(Muster of Krefeld)

Öl, Bastringe auf Leinwand /
bast fiber coils, oil on canvas
122,20 x 133,40
Museum Moderner Kunst Stiftung Ludwig Wien,
Leihgabe der Österreichischen Ludwig Stiftung /
on loan from the Austrian Ludwig Foundation,
seit / since 2007

oder überhaupt Überlebensmöglichkeit."[10] In der Psychoanalyse wird von Regression gesprochen, wenn dem aufklärerischen Impetus progressiver Entwicklungen andere Bedürfnisse und Sehnsüchte entgegengesetzt werden.[11] Regressionen werden nicht selten in die Sphäre von Kultur und Ästhetik verschoben. Eine vermeintliche Befreiung von Altlasten und einem „Anpassungsdruck der restriktiven sozialen Normierungen"[12] kann auch mit den eigenen Über-Ich-Forderungen kollidieren. Werner Büttner nannte es: „In der Geste des Absehens eine Heimat mit Kultur zu finden"[13] und seine eigene Alternative zu sein. Wenn er diese aber – in anderem Zusammenhang – als „Imitation Christi" benennt,[14] zeigt sich, wie Bad Painting um eine – oft auch sehr frauenfeindliche – Provokation angelegt ist, in der ein Scheitern gerade noch funktionieren kann.

"Fauves." The preceding artistic phase was his "période Renoir," which was a reaction to the German occupation. It propagated "sun, joy and plenitude"[21] as the motto for a counter-offensive by an artist who believed in the strength of painting and poetry. In contrast, his exhibition in Paris programmatically aimed at causing a scandal.[22] Margritte sought to outrage the French taste in painting, in fact the Parisians found the Belgian artist's small group of works indeed vulgar. Even though he was well-disposed toward the artist, Paul Éluard did not want to have paintings of this kind hanging on his walls. What strategies does Magritte pursue in this group of works? Did he want to plunder high culture? Just like de Chirico, the artist he greatly admired, who was a "pictor optimus" or a Bad Painter "avant la lettre," Magritte, too, tended to portray banalities.[23] Both above-mentioned phases of his work express Magritte's figurative gratification of desires: Paint like Renoir for once? For once enjoy the swerve and flow of the line? Be a "true," a "born" artist for once?

"Magritte is a painter. Magritte is not a painter"[24]: Perhaps the "période vache" would not have developed into such a comprehensive initiative without Louis Scutenaire's collaboration. Working together with the poet must have been a major incentive for Magritte; especially the former's "incendiary preface" must have made a profound impact on the artist.[25] After the exhibition, which was unsuccessful with not a single painting sold, Scutenaire finished a second piece of writing. Magritte initially intended to illustrate this text. In this art-historical satire with 20 items Magritte is stylized as the better Parisian painter in an ironical way, and it is a more or less Belgian rejoinder, as can be seen in the statement: "Formerly, René Magritte arrived in Paris and enrolled himself at a school there. In this city he became very fashionable and monopolized the art market. [...] He is our first primitive. [...] [He] has a considerable impact on Matisse, Van Gogh, Bonnat, Renoir and Chabas."[26]

"...a Magritte can conceal a Magritte": One thesis is that Magritte never belied his old style, but concealed it within the "vache" paintings. He over paints his own work and transforms his iconical principle into indexical signs, a "simulacre appauvri"[27]: For instance, in *Le Contenu Pictural* [ILL·072] the content of painting comprises the traces of its own disintegration. Philippe Vergne placed the "période vache" in the 1980s context of Bad Painting and additionally called attention to "'le premier dans la décrépitude de [son] art'".[28] Baudelaire detected in *Olympia* that Manet deployed his later work

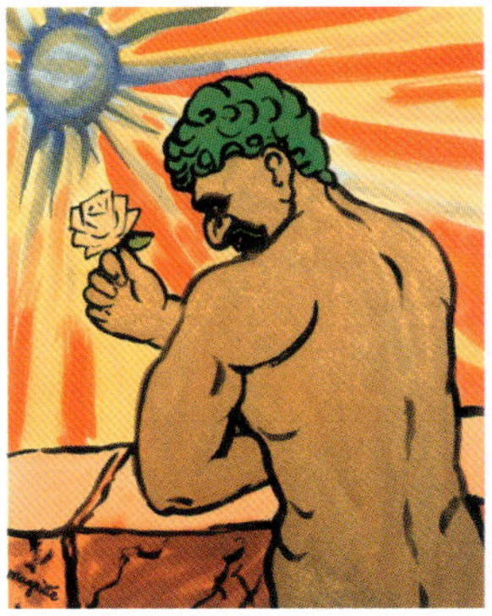

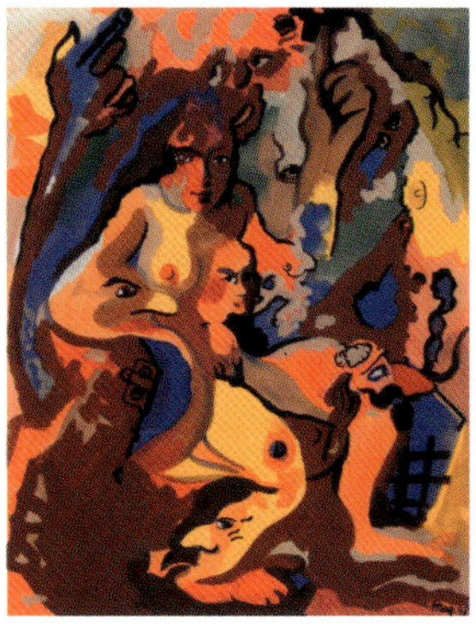

008 René Magritte
Le Psychologue, 1948
(Der Psychologe /
The Psychologist)
Gouache auf Papier /
Gouache on paper
40,7 x 32,8 cm

009 René Magritte
Titania, 1948
Gouache auf Papier /
Gouache on paper
81,3 x 64 cm

Auch das könnte ein Gesetz von Bad Painting sein: den Ursprung der Malerei zu suchen, indem es sich an das Ursprüngliche und Anachronistische anlehnt. „[E]in Mann mit Vogelkopf und aufgerichtetem Geschlecht": So beschreibt Bataille eine Höhlenmalerei, die er als frühestes Dokument einer Sehnsucht nach dem Sakralen deutet.[15] Es gibt Bilder von Baselitz, auf die diese Beschreibung passen würde, und auch Picabias *Noi* [ABB·016] hat Momente von Atavismus, Verlernen und Dilettieren in sich, legt eine vermeintliche Nichtkönnerschaft wie eine Maske an, um frühere zivilisatorische Entwicklungsstufen appropriieren zu können.

„Etwas anzustiften und etwas zu beenden. Das erste und das letzte Bild sein": In Zusammenhang mit Fautrier hat auch Jutta Koether von einem „regressive turn" gesprochen.[16] Seine zugleich ausgehöhlten wie wieder aufgeladenen Bilder scheinen hinter alle Form zurückzugehen, um dennoch – wie in den *Otages* (Geiseln) [ABB·005], die anonyme Porträts der verstümmelten Geiseln der deutschen Besatzungsmacht in Frankreich sind – starke inhaltliche Bezüge herzustellen. „Das erste und das letzte Bild" könnte auch eine konzeptuelle Versuchsanordnung für ein Bad Painting sein, das der Malerei eine neue und andere Sichtweise hinzufügt. Bataille, der einem Theoretiker des Bad Painting wohl am nächsten kommt, sprach von einer „Entfaltung des Werks, die eine Zurücknahme des Werks" sei.[17] Gegenstand und Rahmen der Malerei als „über etwas nicht hinausgehend" zu begreifen bedeutete für Merlin Carpenter „aber auch, darüber hinauszugehen; über den Begriff ‚Entwicklung' nämlich. So tut sich eine Bestimmtheit von Malerei auf."[18] Dennoch ist damit nicht der Diskurs vom Ende der Malerei, vom (anderen) letzten Bild, gemeint, der ein ferner und bereits in der Theorie verfestigter Gegenpart sein könnte, mit dem Bad Painting vielleicht revolutionäre umstürzlerische Ansätze teilt. Was also ist Bad Painting? Normbruch, Krise, Bewältigungsversuch oder sogar Lösung des dahinter stehenden Konflikts? Gewiss verhandelt es ernsthaft den Ausbruch, ist aber ebenso ein großes Bekenntnis zur Malerei: die Bad Painters als die „stursten Dranbleiber".[19]

René Magritte und die glückliche Revolte

Die „période vache" [ABB·008·009·070–076] umfasst eine Werkgruppe von 30 Ölbildern oder Gouachen, die 1947/1948 für Magrittes erste Einzelausstellung in Paris in der Galerie Faubourg 1948 entstanden sind. Später bezeichnete er diese skizzenhaften und buntfarbigen Arbeiten mit grotesk-derben Inhalten auch als „peintures" oder „gouaches fauves"[20], um seine historisch motivierte Regression zu benennen, mit der er kurze Zeit seine Könnerschaft im Rohen und Wilden der „fauves" aufhob. Vorangegangen war die „période Renoir", die eine Reaktion auf die deutsche Besatzung war und „sun, joy and plenitude"[21] als Motto einer Gegenoffensive eines Künstlers propagierte, der an die Kraft von Malerei und Dichtung glaubte. Für seine Ausstellung in Paris hingegen galt programmatisch „scandaliser"[22]. Er wollte den „Peinture"-Geschmack der Franzosen treffen, und tatsächlich empfand das Pariser Publikum die kleine Werkgruppe des Belgiers als vulgär. Sogar der Magritte wohlgesinnte Éluard wollte sich ein solches Bild nicht an die Wand hängen.

strategically. Such a procedure may have also been significant in Magritte's case, as his style remains essentially the same after 1926.

What subsequent Bad Painters can learn is: The fortune of a "manifestation du plaisir" (manifestation of pleasure)[29] and the danger of flirting with failure. According to Bataille, Manet's ultimate goal was to disappoint the expectations of his viewers.[30] Similarly, Magritte too opposed his own success. We are supposed to be silent about such creative phases in an artist's life as if they were a sickness (regression). Magritte announced that further phases were pending, reverted, however, to the "peinture d'antan" (painting of previous times). But for his wife's sake he promised: "I'll certainly find some way to slip in a big fat incongruity from time to time."[31]

Roaring Stags: Asger Jorn and Gerhard Richter

With an interval of three years, two paintings were executed by Jorn and Richter focusing on a centrally placed stag. The two paintings differ immensely and can both currently be viewed in Berlin's National Gallery. But in fact both bear a resemblance in their reaction to the "totally depleted ontological project of modern art."[32] Despite Jorn having explicitly declared that he was a Bad Painter, Richter can by no means be comprehended as such. However, this context appears to give his early work a certain logic, and seems to open the way for Gerhard Richter to leave Modernist "art-painting" behind. Executed in 1960, Jorn's *Hirschbrunft am Wilden Kaiser* (Stag Rut at the Wilder Kaiser) is the older of the two paintings and stems from the series "Modifications" or "Défigurations." Otto van de Loo gifted the painting to the National Gallery, Berlin. In these series the artist painted over images he bought from the flea market. His comment on working in this way was "why reject the old if one can modernize it with a few strokes of the brush?" This comment was printed in his programmatic text "Detourned Painting," which outlines his situationist concept of transvaluation.[33] Like Magritte he exhibited the paintings in Paris. As in Magritte's case the exhibition comprised a small series of his oeuvre on which he had reportedly elaborated for quite a while. Already in 1939 he had wished to pay tribute to "humdrum and pompous painting." But only in 1959, at the age of sixty, was he strong enough to bear the full responsibility of putting it into practice.[34]

Richter's *Hirsch* (Deer) of 1963 from the Onnasch collection (currently on loan to the National Gallery) is number 7 in his œuvre catalogue and, together with *Neuschwanstein Castle* with which it is often exhibited, is the largest of his first paintings. Both artworks were—together with *Mund* (Mouth) and *Papst* (Pope)—part of a performance *Leben mit Pop – Eine Demonstration für den Kapitalistischen Realismus* (Living with Pop—a demonstration for Capitalist Realism), which he organized together with Konrad Lueg and which took place on October 11, 1963 in the Berges furniture store in Düsseldorf.[35] Together with those of Lueg, Polke and Kuttner, both of Richter's paintings were formerly amongst those works exhibited in 1964 in Jährling's front garden in order

Welche Strategien verfolgt Magritte mit diesen Werkgruppen? Wollte er die Hochkultur ausrauben? Wie der von ihm verehrte de Chirico, der als „Pictor Optimus" ein Bad Painter „avant la lettre" ist, tendiert auch Magritte zum Banalen.[23] Beide Werkphasen lassen ein piktorales Wunschdenken Magrittes zum Ausdruck kommen: Einmal so malen wie Renoir? Einmal die Gestik der Linie auskosten? Einmal ein „richtiger", ein „geborener" Maler sein?

„Magritte ist ein Maler. Magritte ist kein Maler"[24]: Ohne die Zusammenarbeit mit Louis Scutenaire wäre die „période vache" vielleicht zu keiner so umfassenden Aktion geworden. Die Gemeinschaftsarbeit mit dem Dichter, dessen „incendiary preface" essenzieller Bestandteil war,[25] muss ihn angespornt haben. Nach der erfolglosen Ausstellung, in der kein einziges Werk verkauft wurde, schrieb Scutenaire einen zweiten Text, den Magritte ursprünglich illustrieren wollte. In dieser kunsthistorischen Persiflage in 20 Punkten wird auf ironische Weise und quasi als belgische Retourkutsche Magritte zum besseren Pariser Maler stilisiert, wenn es etwa heißt: „René Magritte von ehedem kommt nach Paris, schreibt sich an der Schule dieser Stadt ein, wo er große Mode wird, und monopolisiert den Markt. [...] Er ist unser erster Primitiver. [...] [Er] übt tief gehenden Einfluss auf Matisse, van Gogh, Bonnat, Renoir und Chabas aus."[26]

„... ein Magritte kann einen Magritte verbergen": Eine These ist auch die, dass Magritte seinen alten Stil nicht verleugnet, sondern unter den „Vache"-Bildern verborgen hält. Er übermalt sich selbst und wandelt sein ikonisches Prinzip in indexalische Zeichen, ein „simulacre appauvri"[27]: In *Le Contenu Pictural* [ABB·072] etwa wird der Inhalt der Malerei zur Spur ihres Zerrinnens. Philippe Vergne, der die „période vache" in den Kontext des Bad Painting der 1980er-Jahre stellt, hat außerdem noch auf „‚le premier dans la décrépitude de [son] art'"[28] aufmerksam gemacht. Was Baudelaire Manets *Olympia* konstatierte, nämlich das Alterswerk strategisch einzusetzen, mag auch für Magritte Bedeutung haben, dessen Stil sich seit 1926 tatsächlich nicht wesentlich änderte.

Was spätere Bad Painters lernen können: das Glück einer „manifestation du plaisir"[29] und die Gefahr eines Kokettierens mit dem Misserfolg. Nach Bataille war es Manets eigentliches Ziel, Erwartung zu enttäuschen.[30] Auch Magritte widersteht seinem eigenen Erfolg. Wie eine Krankheit (Regression!) sollte diese Werkphase verschwiegen werden. Magritte kündigte weitere an, kehrte jedoch zur „peinture d'antan" zurück, seiner Frau zuliebe, versprach aber: „Ich werde sicher immer wieder einen Weg finden, von Zeit zu Zeit dicke Inkongruenzen einzubauen."[31]

Röhrende Hirsche: Asger Jorn und Gerhard Richter

Im Abstand von drei Jahren entstanden zwei Bilder von Jorn und Richter mit einem zentralen Hirsch, die derzeit in der Berliner Nationalgalerie zu sehen sind und unterschiedlicher nicht sein könnten. Dennoch reagieren beide nicht unähnlich auf das „völlig erschöpfte ontologische Projekt der Moderne".[32] Hat Jorn sich als Bad Painter dezidiert deklariert, soll Richter hier keineswegs als solcher vereinnahmt werden, dennoch macht dieser Kontext in seinem Frühwerk Sinn und scheint auf

to effect an exhibition. Robert Storr describes the two paintings as proto-photorealistic[36], which, however, disregards their specific position in Richter's early work.

In 1962 Richter produced greatly differing paintings such as *Party*, which he resolutely judged as "bad,"[37] or *Hitler* [ILL·013]. When Jorn wrote of the "roaring stags" in living rooms, Richter took his stag into a furniture store. There, together with Lueg, he wandered through the model rooms in which the pictures hung. Here, more or less "functioning" living rooms were on display and combined, by interlinking macro- and microstructures, a domestic situation with a backdrop of world politics.[38] Did he paint the picture specially for this performance?[39] For, after all, the roaring stag decorating the living-room wall is synonymous for kitsch. This is particularly true for an amateur photograph, which Richter transferred into painting by mechanically overpainting or, respectively, copying, and for a picture from a junk market, such as Jorn used.

Both paintings employ the method of overpainting, retaining, to an extent, the original image whilst also transforming it. The two artists confront the analytical and enlightened course taken by Modernism and its "de-stratification"[40] with overlaying, which could also be comprehended as a critical comment on Informal art. Claire Gilman explains for Jorn that overpainting can be positioned between collage and negation,[41] whilst Richter transforms a kitschy and trivial photo—similar examples can be found in his *Atlas*—into a sort of "picture puzzle"[42] that dodges the apparent spatial logic of the image. The branches function as drawing or grid and support first and foremost—together with the tree trunk that divides the image into two—the oscillation between abstraction and figuration. Nevertheless, Richter does not answer the certainly ideological question concerning abstraction and figuration, and the choice between the two options remains undecided, much as it does in Jorn's case as well.

In this period, Richter often referred to kitsch and banality as a means of questioning the image. He even speaks of the "banality of evil."[43] In 1962 he executed his painting *Hitler*. In this context one must not forget that, since 1961, "bad" meaning "evil" and "banal" permeated the discussion around the Eichmann process, as reported by Hannah Arendt in 1964.[44] Richter's 1966 performance *Volker Bradtke* counts as a "hommage to banality"[45] and makes evident the power of the normal and

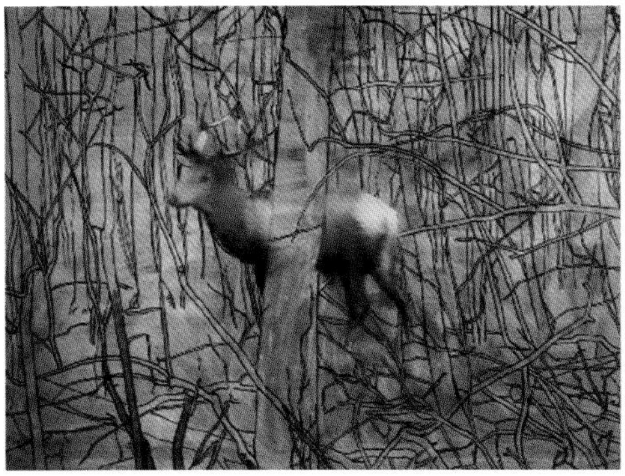

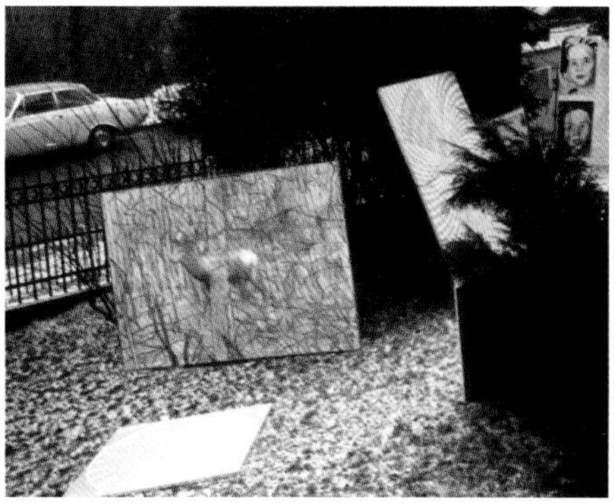

010 Gerhard Richter
Hirsch, 1963, (Deer)
Öl auf Leinwand / oil on paper
150 x 200 cm
Staatliche Museen zu
Berlin, Nationalgalerie

011
Richters Hirsch in der
Vorgartenausstellung
der Galerie Parnass / Richter's
Deer at the front garden exhibition of Parnass gallery,
Wuppertal, 1964

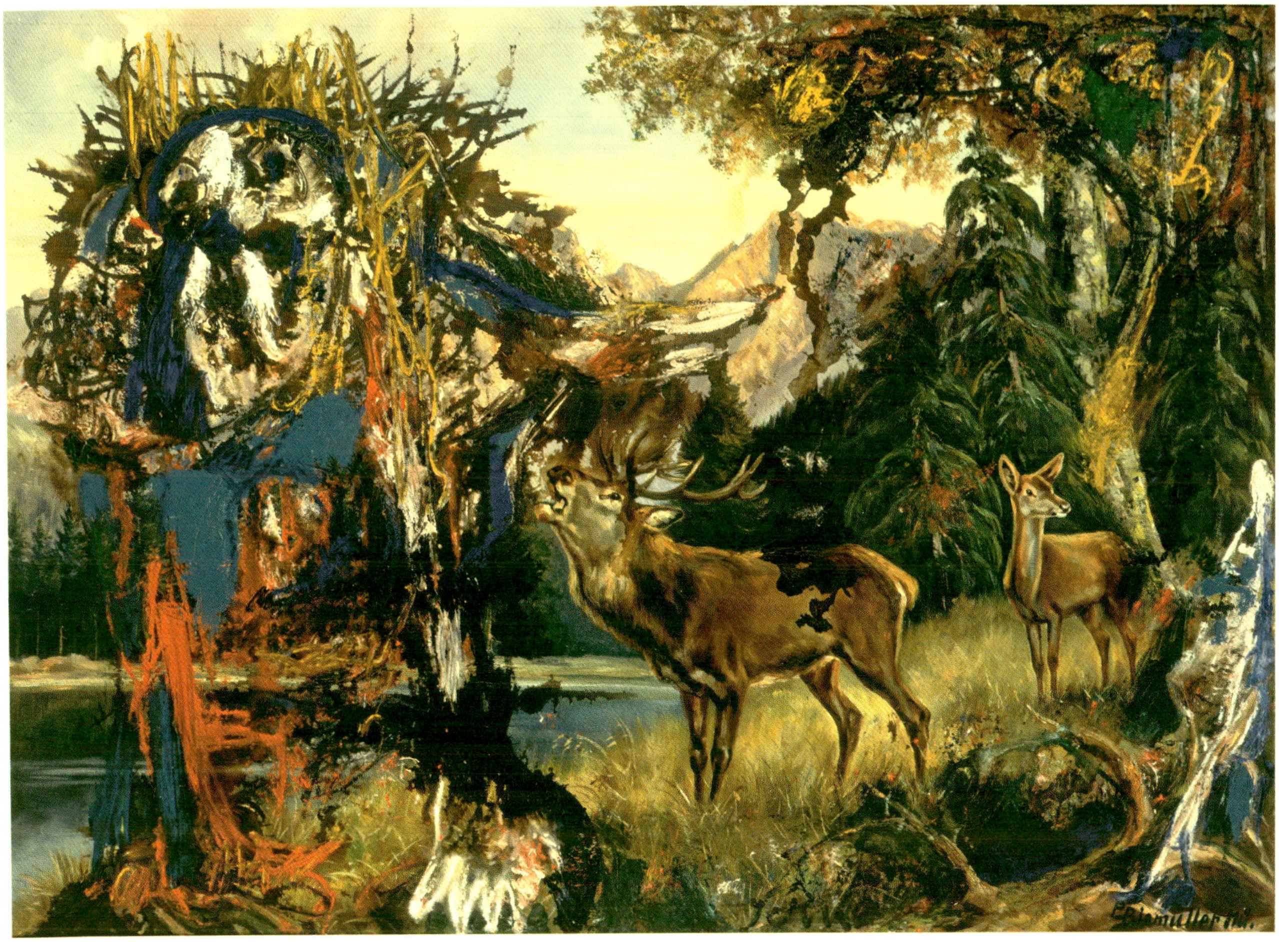

012 **Asger Jorn**
Hirschbrunft im Wilden Kaiser, 1960 (Stag Rut at the Wilder Kaiser)
Öl auf Leinwand / oil on canvas, 90 x 120 cm
Staatliche Museen zu Berlin, Nationalgalerie

seinem Weg zu liegen, die modernistische „Peinture-Kunst“ (Gerhard Richter) hinter sich zu lassen. Das ältere, 1960 entstandene ist Jorns *Hirschbrunft am Wilden Kaiser*, das als Schenkung Otto van de Loos an die Berliner Nationalgalerie kam und aus seiner Werkgruppe der „Modifications“ beziehungsweise „Défigurations“ stammt. In diesen Serien übermalte er Bilder vom Flohmarkt. „Warum das Alte verwerfen, wenn es mit ein paar Pinselstrichen modernisiert werden kann?“, sagt er dazu in seinem programmatischen Text „Detourned Painting“, der sein situationistisches Konzept der „Umwertung“ umreißt.[33] Wie bei Magritte zeigte er die Bilder in einer Ausstellung in Paris, und wie bei Magritte handelt es sich um eine kleine Werkgruppe in seinem Œuvre, die Jorn nach eigenen Angaben länger elaboriert hat. Bereits 1939 wollte er dem „humdrum und pompous painting“ Hommage zollen, fand tatsächlich aber erst 1959 – 60 Jahre alt – die Kraft, dies in voller Verantwortung umzusetzen.[34]

Richters *Hirsch* von 1963 aus der Sammlung Onnasch (und derzeit als Leihgabe in der Nationalgalerie) hat die Nummer 7 in seinem Œuvre-Verzeichnis und ist mit *Schloss Neuschwanstein*, mit dem er oft gemeinsam gesehen wird, das größte unter den ersten Bildern. Beide Werke waren – gemeinsam mit *Mund* und *Papst* – Teil seiner Aktion *Leben mit Pop – Eine Demonstration für den Kapitalistischen Realismus*, die er mit Konrad Lueg am 11. Oktober 1963 im Düsseldorfer Möbelhaus Berges veranstaltete.[35] Beide Bilder waren unter den Werken, die er gemeinsam mit Lueg, Polke und Kuttner 1964 bei Jährling im Vorgarten aufstellte, um dort eine Ausstellung zu erwirken.

ordinary reigning at the time. The fact that this had a counterpart in the suppressed history of the National Socialist era took on meaning for Richter when he encountered an often veiled history articulated in the photographs he used: "at those locations to where it had been shifted after the end of the Third Reich."[46] Also in the case of *Deer*, where a playing card with a Hitler portrait is found on the reverse,[47] the connection between kitsch, banality or normality with history is relevant, even though it remains hidden to the viewer.

Sigmar Polke and the "Back-Breeding" of the Avant-garde

Unfortunately Polke did not participate in the performance in the Berges furniture store. Obviously Richter and Lueg did not wish him to participate. However, he was just the man to dispose over a location freighted with middle-class consumer culture more or less in situ. In February 1964 the loosely knit group comprising Polke, Richter, Lueg and Kuttner once again pursued the prospect of an exhibition. In order to procure an exhibition at Jährling's in Wuppertal, they arrived there with their paintings and set them up in his front garden.[48] Those objects that are now worth millions and in leading German collections, could be viewed in a wintry open-air museum. Among them were Richter's *Hirsch* (Deer) and *Hitler*, Polke's *Wurstesser* (Sausage Eater), *Doppelportrait Fabiola* (Double Portrait of Fabiola) [ILL·011·013·014] and many other works. To be rejected or accepted? The experiment was successful, as the "authority" Jährling consented to an exhibition, which took place in the autumn of 1964.

The *Vitrinenstück* (Showcase Piece) of 1966, the most iconoclastic of Polke's works, critiqued the presentation and production conditions of the art market, as probably experienced by Polke himself. It was conceived as a demonstration object with a wall display and a showcase, above all, as critique of painting, questioning authorship as an ideologically motivated artistic approach. Here one of his image sequences has its origins, settling the old score between triviality and middle-class kitsch: the "flamingos" that later became "herons."[49] These were commissions from "higher beings," as the wall text reads, who had "commanded" Polke to paint flamingos instead of a bunch of flowers.

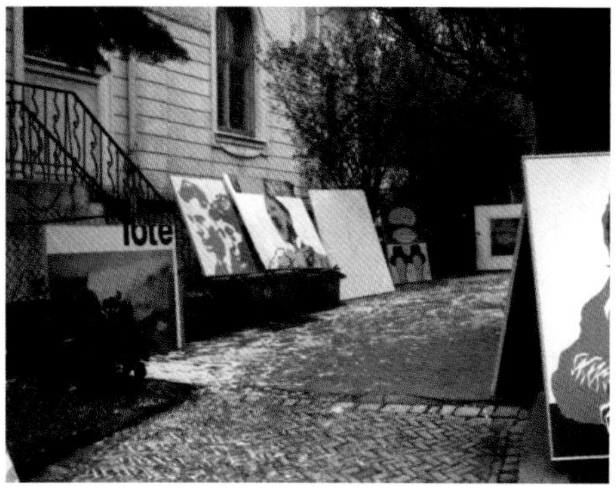

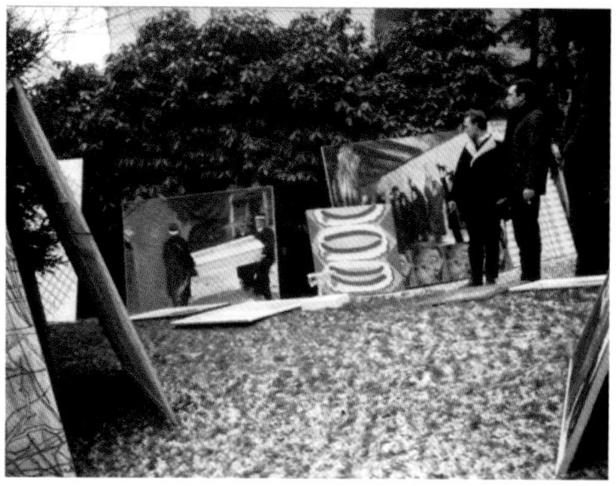

013
Vorgartenausstellung der Galerie Parnass / front garden exhibition of Parnass gallery, Wuppertal, 1964

014
Manfred Kuttner, Gerhard Richter, Konrad Lueg in der Vorgartenausstellung der Galerie Parnass / at the front garden exhibition of Parnass gallery, Wuppertal, 1964

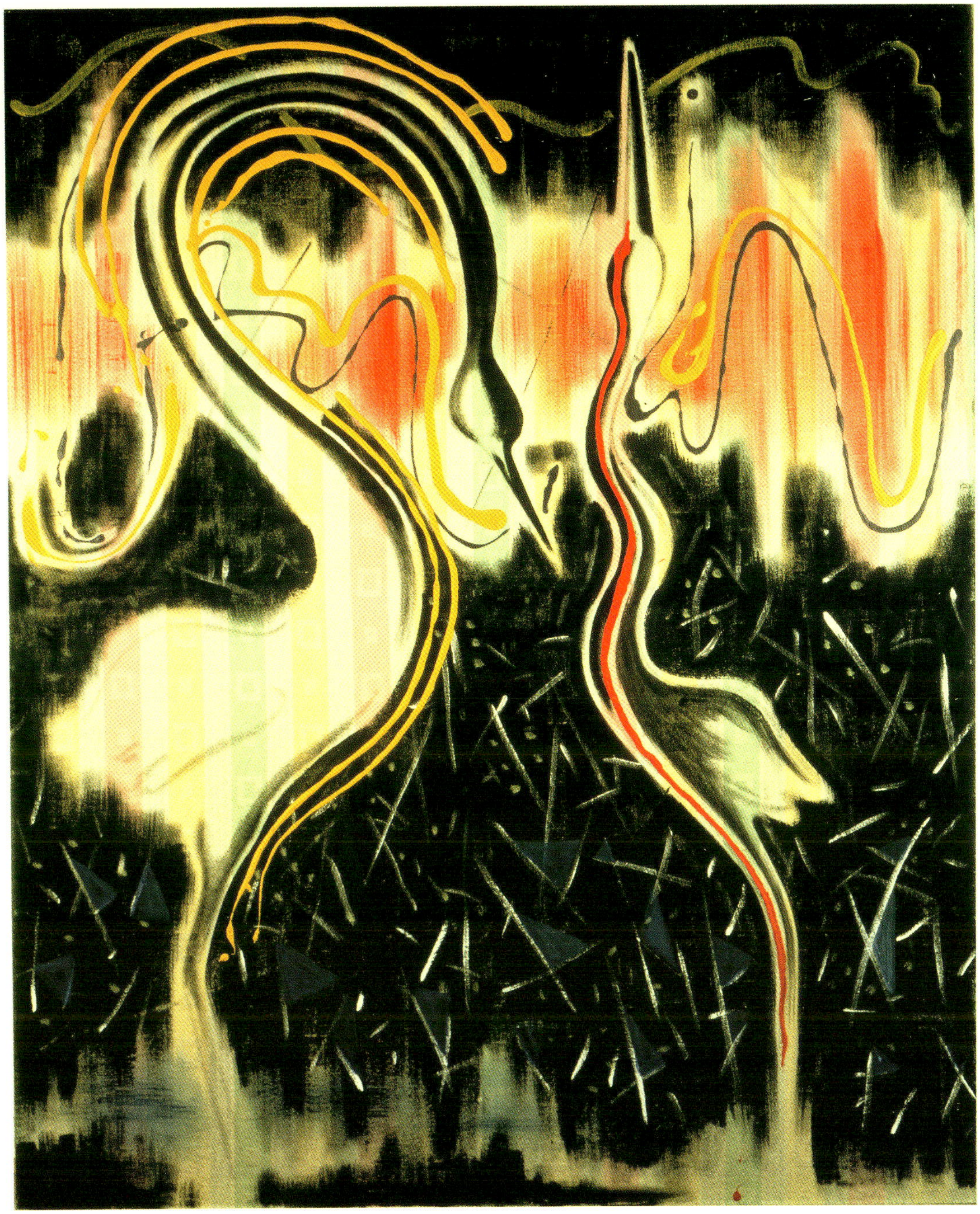

015 **Sigmar Polke**
Reiherbild IV, 1969
(Heron Painting IV)

Dispersion auf Biber-
tuch / emulsion
on flannelette
190 x 150 cm
Städtische Galerie
Karlsruhe, Sammlung
Garnatz

Robert Storr beschreibt die beiden Bilder als protofotorealistisch[36], was den Bildern jedoch ihre spezifische Stellung im Frühwerk Richters nimmt. 1962 etwa waren nebeneinander so unterschiedliche Werke wie *Party* – ein Bild, das Richter dezidiert als „schlecht"[37] bezeichnete – oder *Hitler* [ABB·013] entstanden. Wenn Jorn von den „röhrenden Hirschen" im Wohnzimmer schrieb, brachte Richter seinen Hirsch in ein Möbelhaus, wo er mit Lueg vor dem Rundgang durch die Modellzimmer, in die die Bilder gehängt waren, ein Wohnzimmer quasi „in Funktion" vorführte und in einer Verknüpfung von Makro- und Mikrostrukturen eine häusliche Situation mit dem weltpolitischen Hintergrund verband.[38] War das Bild extra für diese Aktion entstanden?[39] Schließlich sind röhrende Hirsche an der Wohnzimmerwand das Synonym für Kitsch, zumal in einer Amateurfotografie, die

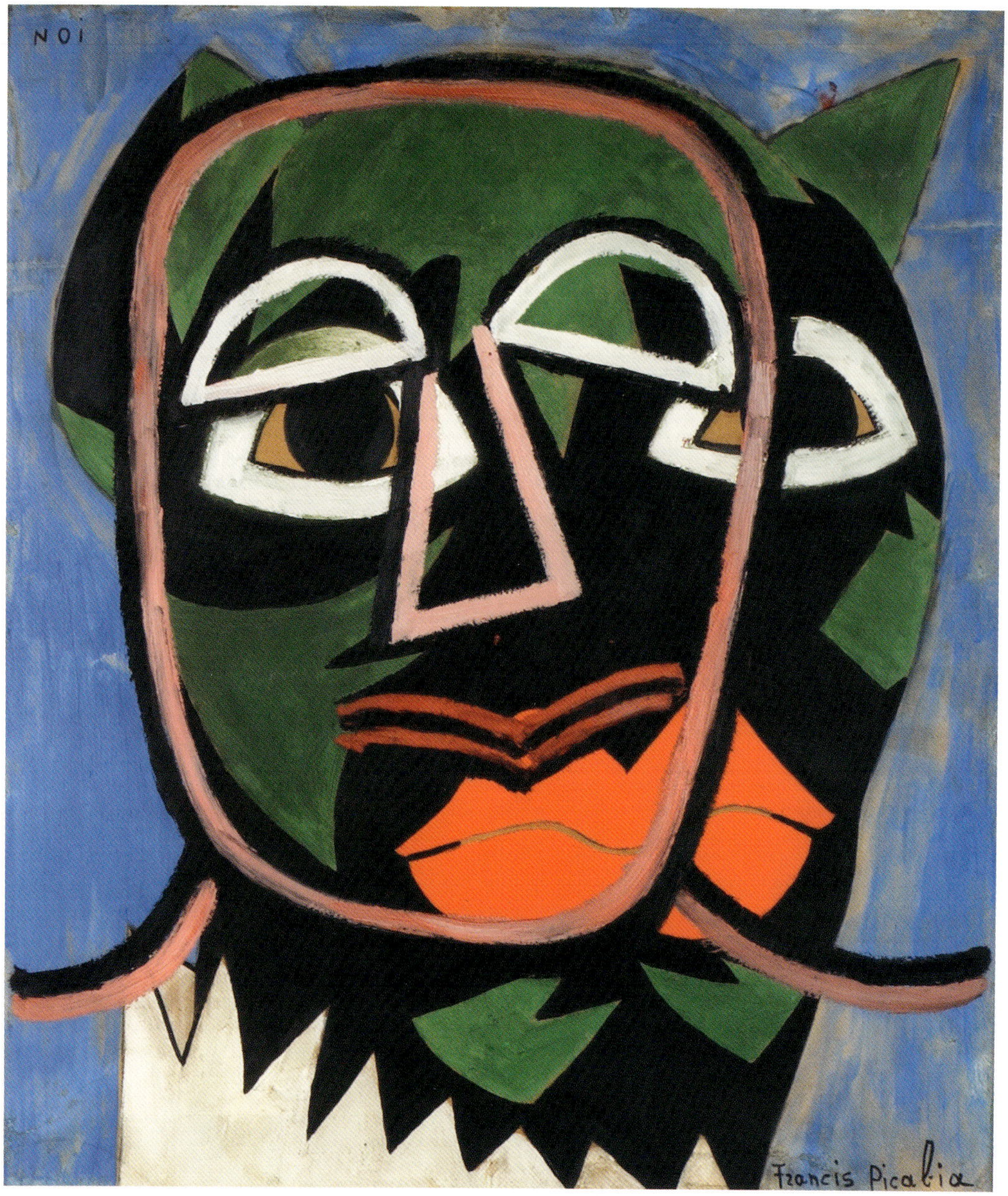

016 **Francis Picabia**
Noi, 1938

Öl auf Leinwand / oil on canvas
80 x 60 cm
Privatsammlung, Wien /
Private Collection, Vienna

Polke frees himself of unnecessary burdens, thereby, however, taking on others. He transfers the problem of pictorial innovation to that of the cultural production of images. Polke's attitude fundamentally differs from "traditional terms such as productivity, invention or spontaneity."[50] Images of flamingos are kitsch as much as roaring stags, and now they are more or less raised to the status of "high art," where Polke launches a strategic experiment using them. In the name of the authority of a "jury," Polke breaks the avant-garde's will to innovation with its complicated temporal structures, thereby also curtailing the formation of an aesthetic judgment in the usual retroactive order.[51] He calls the system of dissent and consent toward art into question: of being accepted or rejected, of being regarded as good or bad. He applies parody and irony as his means of criticism and questioning

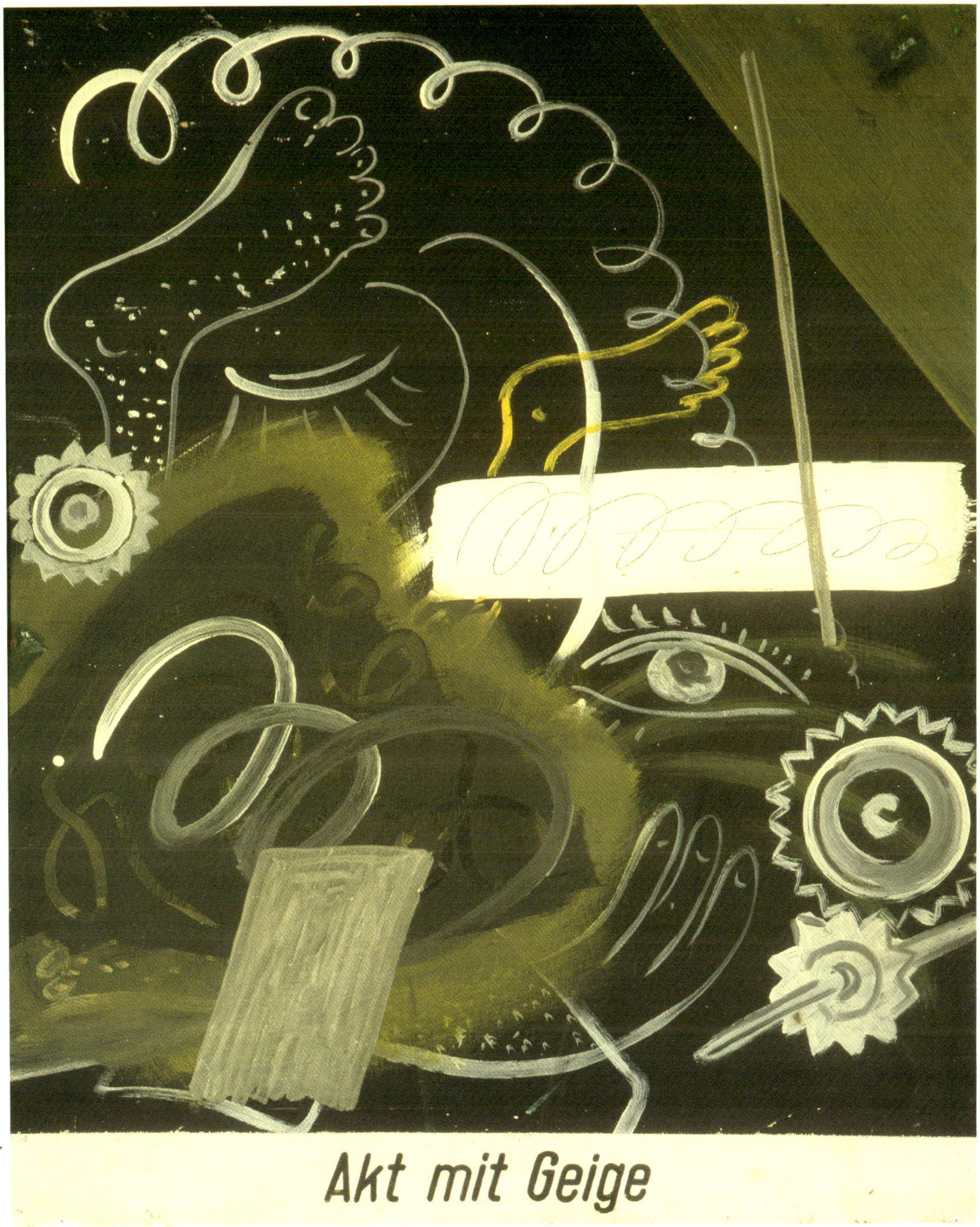

017 **Sigmar Polke**
Akt mit Geige, 1968
(Nude with Violin)

Dispersion auf Holzfaserplatte / emulsion on particleboard, 100,1 x 79,8 cm
Bayerische Staatsgemäldesammlungen, München, Pinakothek der Moderne, WAF Sammlung Prinz Franz von Bayern

Richter nach dem Prinzip der mechanischen beziehungsweise kopierenden Übermalung überträgt, und in einem Bild vom Trödelmarkt, das Jorn verwendet.

Beide Bilder sind eine Übermalung, die die Vorlagen gewissermaßen bewahrt, wenn auch verändert. Dem analytischen aufklärerischen Gang der Moderne und seiner „Entschichtung“[40] setzen beide Künstler eine Überlagerung entgegen, die auch als kritischer Beitrag zum Informel gelesen werden kann. Für Jorn beantwortet Claire Gilman die Frage der Übermalung zwischen Collage und Negation,[41] während Richter ein kitschiges und triviales Foto – ähnliche sind im *Atlas* – in eine Art „Vexierbild“[42] umsetzt, das dem Bildraum seine scheinbare Logik entzieht: Das Geäst fungiert als Zeichnung oder Raster und unterstützt erst – gemeinsam mit dem das Bild zweiteilenden Baumstamm – ein

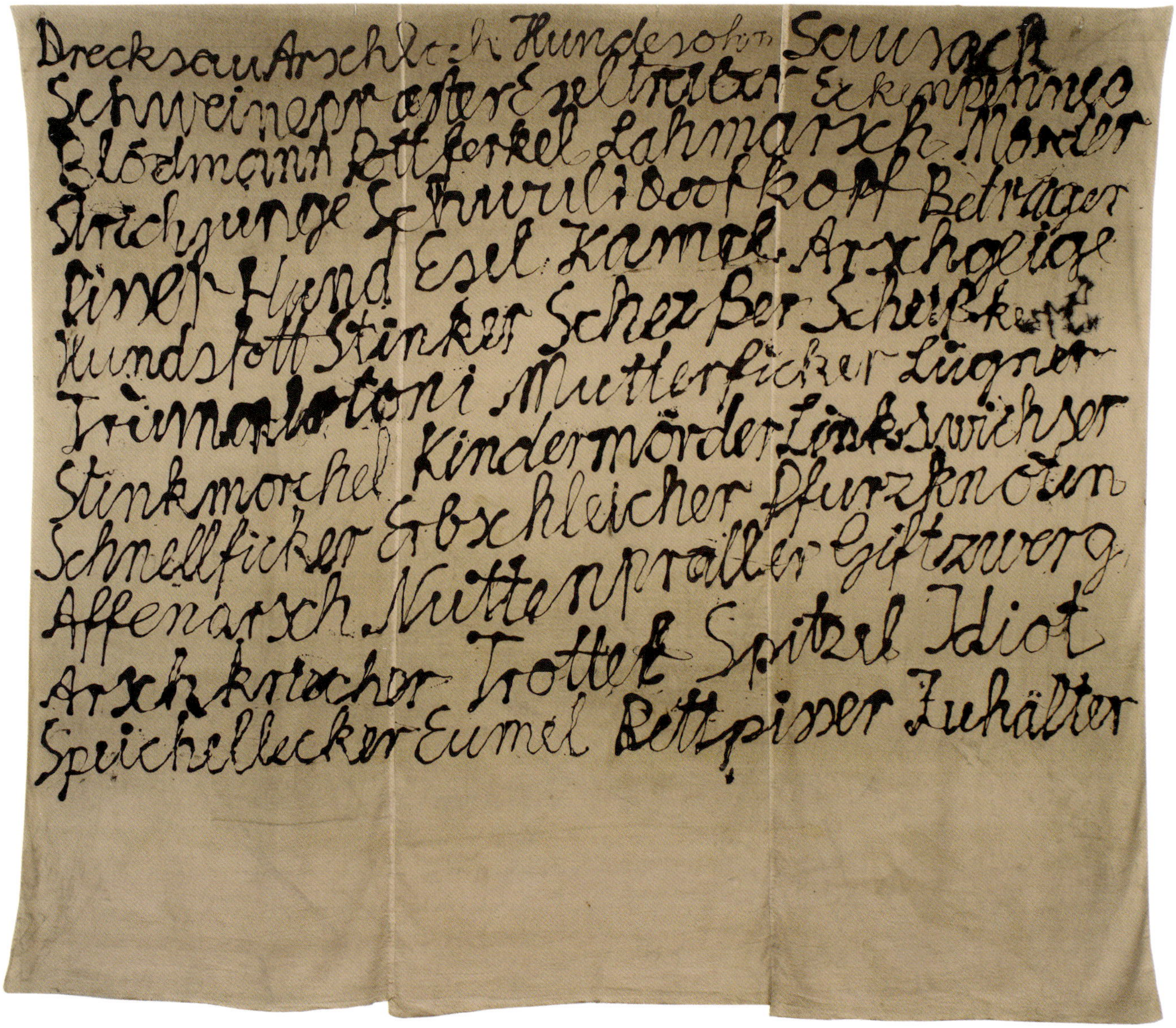

018 **Sigmar Polke**
Schimpftuch, 1968 (Cloth of Abuse)
Acryl auf Bibertuch / acrylic on flannelette
400 x 437 cm
Daros Collection, Zürich

the nature of things. "So in its very essence my painting is by commission, and I flatter myself to think that I have always used templates."[52] Polke insists that the initial driving force behind his thoughts and deliberations was the "innovative leap in printing errors" (Sigmar Polke).

Additionally he uses irony in his "art-historical" works, such as *Moderne Kunst* (Modern Art) [ILL·083] or *Akt mit Geige* (Nude with Violin) [ILL·017], in order to free modern art from its status of isms, just as Breton and Picabia as well as the Situationists before him. Polke creates pictures that comprise parodistic language of signs, and which only manage by a narrow margin to maintain an indexical relationship to historic Modern art. In *Moderne Kunst* the white frame of Malevich's *Black Square* is cited so as to emphasize the frame once again and to comprend the rejection of avant-garde

Changieren zwischen Abstraktion und Figuration. Dennoch beantwortet Richter die durchaus ideologisch zu wertende Frage zwischen Abstraktion und Figuration nicht und lässt sie unentschieden, wie auch Jorn sie letztendlich offen lässt.

Kitsch und Banalität hat Richter in diesen Jahren öfters als Bildbefragung herangezogen. Er spricht selbst von der „Banalität des Bösen“[43]. 1962 war sein Bild *Hitler* entstanden. Schließlich darf nicht vergessen werden, dass „bad“ im Sinne von „böse“ und „banal“ seit 1961 eine Diskussion um den Eichmann-Prozess bildete, wie es Hannah Arendt 1964 darlegte.[44] Als „Hommage an die Banalität“[45] gilt Richters Aktion *Volker Bradtke* von 1966, die auch die große Macht des Normalen in dieser Zeit deutlich hervorhebt. Dass diese in der verdrängten NS-Zeit einen Gegenpart hatte, war für Richter dann von Bedeutung, wenn er Geschichte oft verdeckt in den Fotografien, die er verwendete, begegnete: „an den Orten, an die man es nach dem Ende des Dritten Reiches verschoben hatte.“[46] Auch für den *Hirsch*, der auf der Rückseite eine Spielkarte mit einem Hitler-Porträt aufweist,[47] ist diese Verbindung von Kitsch, Banalität oder Normalität mit Geschichte relevant, die gleichwohl dem Betrachter verborgen bleibt.

Sigmar Polke und die „Rückzüchtung“ der Avantgarde

Leider war Polke, weil offensichtlich von Richter und Lueg ausgeschlossen, nicht an der Aktion im Möbelhaus Berges beteiligt, wäre er doch prädestiniert gewesen, an einem Ort bürgerlicher Konsumkultur quasi in situ zu walten. Im Februar 1964 war die lose Gruppe von Polke, Richter, Lueg und Kuttner dann wieder gemeinsam auf der Suche nach Ausstellungsmöglichkeiten: Um bei Jährling in Wuppertal eine Ausstellung zu erwirken, reisten sie mit ihren Bildern an und stellten sie in Jährlings Vorgarten auf.[48] Was heute eine millionenschwere Angelegenheit ist und sich in großen deutschen Sammlungen befindet, war damals als winterliches Freilichtmuseum zu bewundern. Da haben wir etwa Richters *Hirsch* und seinen *Hitler*, Polkes *Wurstesser*, sein *Doppelportrait Fabiola* [ABB·011·013·014] und andere mehr. Ablehnen oder annehmen? Die „Entscheidungsinstanz“ Jährling sagte zu, das Experiment gelang, und die Ausstellung fand im Herbst 1964 statt.

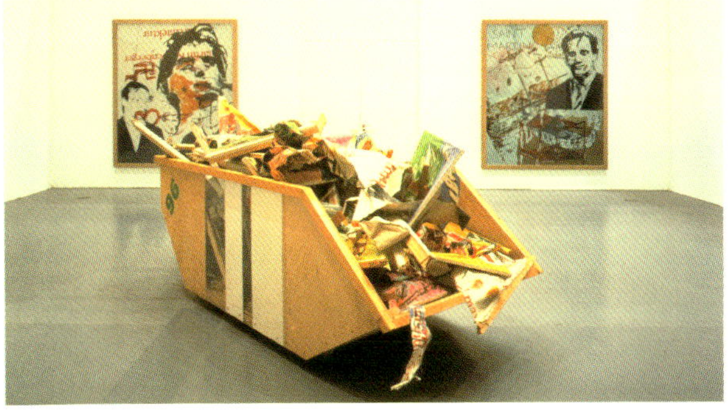

019 **Martin Kippenberger**
Heavy Burschi, 1989/90
(Heavy Guy)
Installationsansicht
installation view
Tate London, 2006

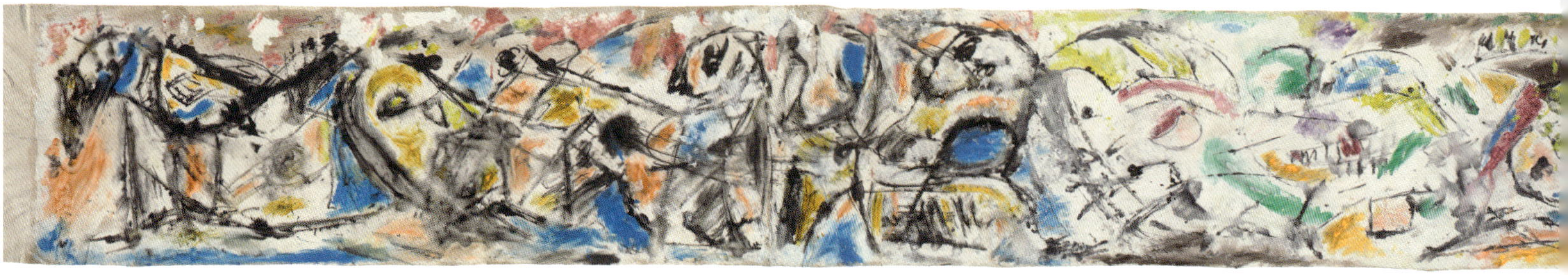

020 **Pinot Gallizio**
Il muro della mia casa, 1958
(Die Wand meines Hauses / The Wall of my House)
Öl auf Leinwand / oil on canvas
95 x 1073 cm
Galerie van de Loo, München

mental space. The text is included instead, which parodies, using citations, talk on modern art. Additionally, these pictures of Polke are not marked by innovation but by recapitulation. He operates receptively, yet ambiguously with "[...] an active and undisguised passivity toward images and the self-motivated emergence of images, an active receptivity towards images that already exist."[53] He reduces the life cycle of the avant-gardes and, by doing so, likewise reduces one of their most fundamental laws into empty signs. Why is Polke preoccupied with Bad Painting, but nevertheless not a Bad Painter? Because he doesn't stage himself within this concept as the other, but focuses on the system, thereby pursuing a kind of "back breeding,"[54] alternatively also called "bad breeding."

The Bad Painting Monument and its Inscriptions

Jorn explicitly erected a "monument in honour of Bad Painting,"[55] Polke abused it, Guston set an alienated object in the landscape [ILL·002] or in *Monument* [ILL·040] superimposed it over indeterminate formations. Are there specific indications in Bad Painting pointing to a mnemonic function, particularly one specific to painting?

Polke's *Schimpftuch* (Cloth of Abuse) [ILL·018] of 1968 is a unique document of "ut pictura poesis" narration in the twentieth century. According to Buchloh, it contains the "necessity of outspoken clarity" and, alongside the "question concerning the expressive ability of painting," also asks "why [it] should submit to the tolerated verdict of only being a language of signs and forms, and

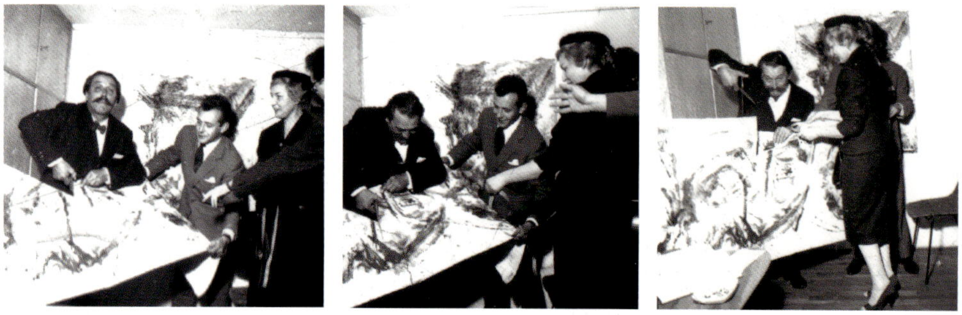

021–023
Versteigerung der „pittura industriale" Pinot Gallizios in der Galerie van de Loo, München / Auction of Pinot Gallizio's „pittura industriale" at Galerie van de Loo, Munich 15. April 1959

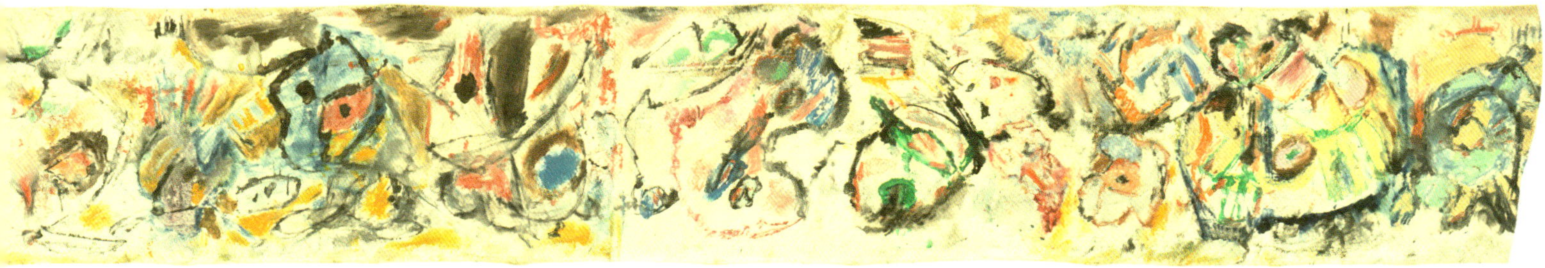

Gerade die ikonoklastischste von Polkes frühen Arbeiten, das *Vitrinenstück* von 1966, kritisiert den Kunstbetrieb mit seinen Produktions- und Präsentationsbedingungen, so wie Polke ihn vermutlich selbst erlebt hat. Als Demonstrationsobjekt mit Wanddisplay und Vitrine konzipiert, ist es vor allem eine Malereikritik, die Autorschaft als ideologisch motivierte künstlerische Setzung hinterfragt. Hier hat eine seiner Bilderserien ihren Ursprung, die mit Trivialität und bürgerlichem Kitsch abrechnet: die „Flamingos", die später zu „Reihern" wurden.[49] Diese waren eine Auftragsarbeit „höherer Wesen", wie in einem Wandtext zu lesen ist, der eben besagt, dass „höhere Wesen" Polke „befohlen" hätten, Flamingos statt Blumenstrauß zu malen.

Polke wirft Ballast ab, nimmt aber anderen wieder auf: Das Problem pikturaler Innovationen verschiebt er in jenes kultureller Bildproduktion. Polkes Haltung unterschiedet sich grundsätzlich von „traditionellen Begriffen wie Produktivität, Erfindung oder Spontaneität".[50] Bilder von Flamingos sind ebenso Kitsch wie von röhrenden Hirschen und werden nun quasi zu „Hochkunst", wo sie Polke zu einem strategischen Experiment einsetzt. Denn Polke bricht im Namen der Autorität einer „Jury" den Innovationswillen der Avantgarden mit ihren verwickelten Zeitstrukturen und kürzt damit auch die Bildung eines ästhetischen Urteils in der üblichen retroaktiven Ordnung[51] ab. Er stellt das System von Dissens und Konsens über Kunst – hier angenommen, dort abgelehnt, hier gut, dort schlecht – infrage und kritisiert es mit den Mitteln von Parodie und Ironie. „So ist meine Malerei in ihrem tiefsten Wesen eine Auftragsmalerei, und ich schmeichle mir, immer nach Vorlage gearbeitet zu haben."[52] Polke insistiert auf dem „innovativen Sprung im Druckfehler" (Sigmar Polke), der erst der Motor seiner Überlegungen ist.

Auch in seinen „kunsthistorischen" Arbeiten wie *Moderne Kunst* [ABB·083] oder *Akt mit Geige* [ABB·017] setzt er Ironie ein, um die Moderne aus ihrem Status der Ismen zu befreien, wie dies vor ihm Breton, Picabia, aber auch die Situationisten angestrebt haben. Bei Polke entstehen nun Bilder, die aus einer parodierenden Zeichensprache bestehen, die gerade noch eine indexalische Beziehung zur historischen Moderne aufrechterhalten können. *Moderne Kunst* zitiert den weißen Rand von Malewitschs *Schwarzem Quadrat*, um noch einmal den Rahmen zu betonen und die Abkehr vom mentalen Raum der Avantgarde mitzudenken. Stattdessen ist der Text eingefügt, der ein Sprechen über

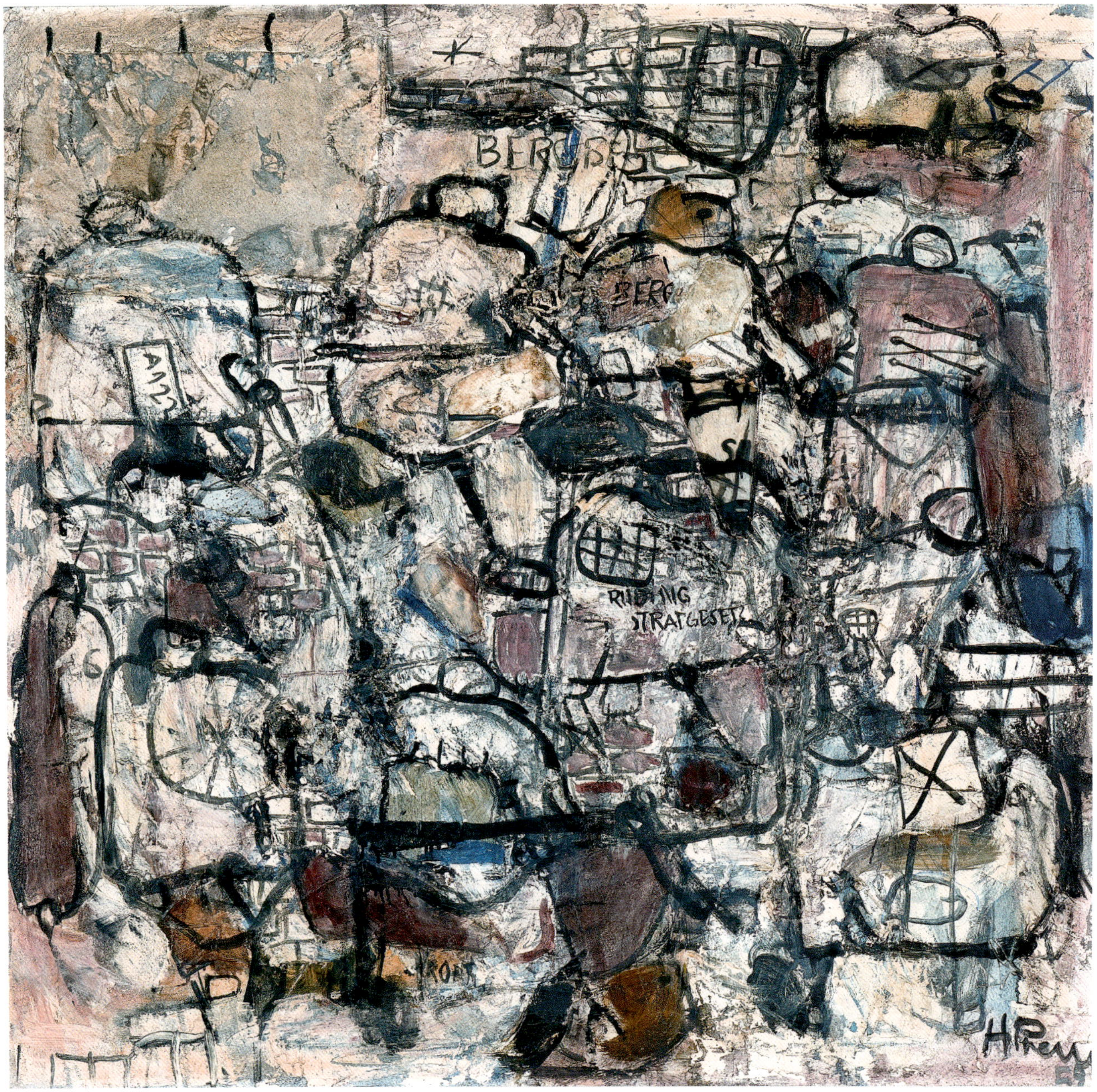

024 **Heimrad Prem**
Roding. Strafgesetz (Weg-Männer), 1959
(Roding. Penal Law)
Öl, verschiedene Materialien auf Leinwand /
oil, various materials on canvas, 100 x 100 cm
Museum Lothar Fischer, Neumarkt i.d.OPf

forever relinquish verbal language without a thought and without a fight?"[56] But what is a *Schimpftuch* exactly? Painting or text? Buchloh states that it is an "abuse of the public at the level of painting." Could it have possibly originated as painting, similar to what was claimed about Ed Ruscha's painting *Liquid Words* to thereby raise a fundamental question of status: whether it is about painting or text?[57] Was the *Schimpftuch* originally liquid and color with which words were then written? This thesis infers that painting was transformed into language. By personally wearing it, Polke has actually taken the cloth out of the horizontal mode of writing and script. Although not vertically fixed to the wall, the cloth is draped over the body to confront the viewer as an abusive tableau vivant. However, it definitely addresses a masculine and in no way feminine painting. In Bad Painting, painting is otherwise always

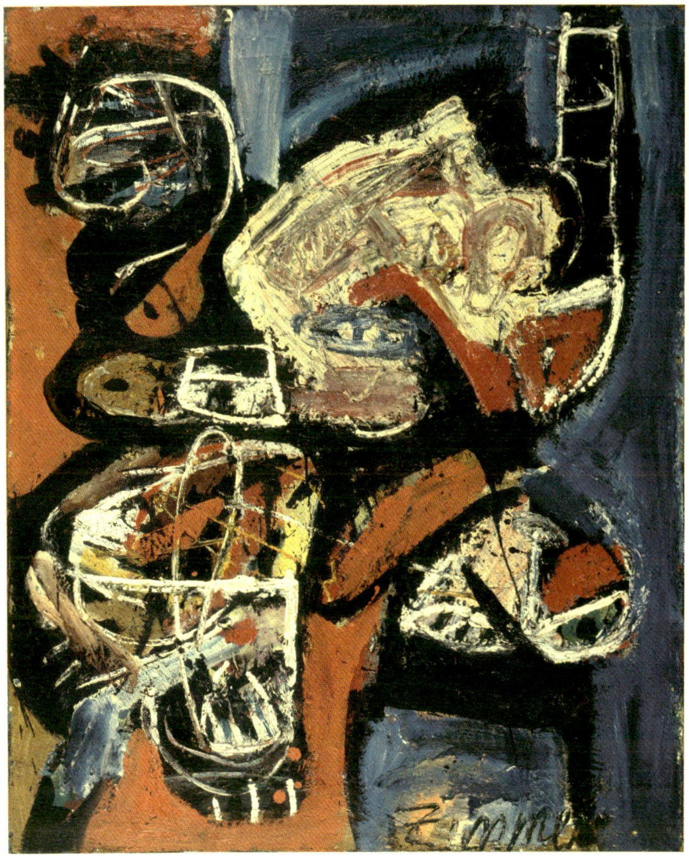

025 **HP Zimmer**
Die behaarte Pforte der Sehnsucht, 1961/62
(Hairy Gate of Desire)
Öl auf Leinwand / oil on canvas
140 x 100 cm
Galerie van de Loo, München

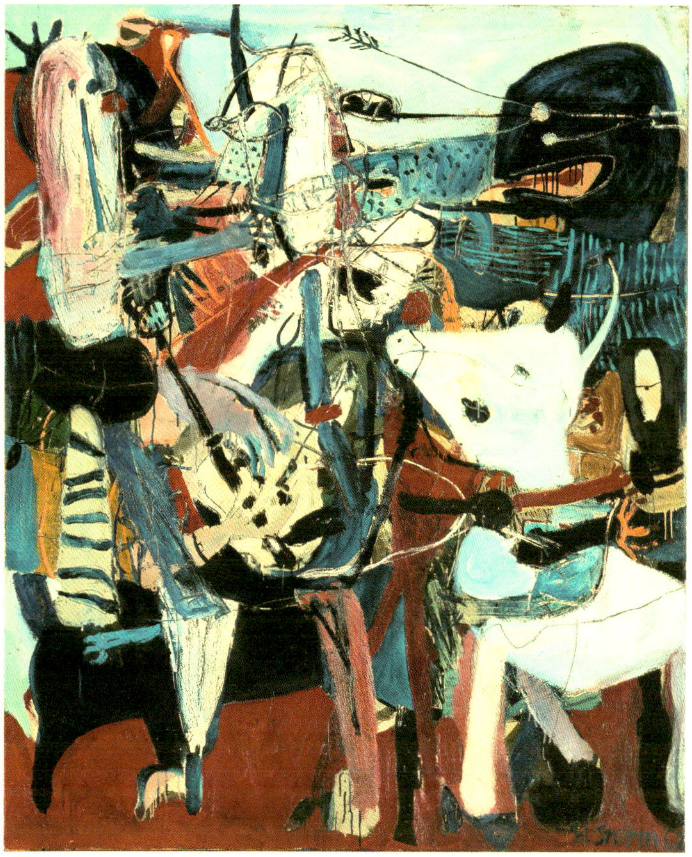

026 **Helmut Sturm**
Ländlicher Konflikt (Ländliches Scharmützel), 1962
(Rural Conflict – Rural Skirmish)
Öl auf Leinwand / oil on canvas
150 x 120 cm
Sammlung Niggl, Feldafing

die Moderne zitierend parodiert. Auch diese Bilder Polkes sind nicht innovativ, sondern rekapitulierend. Er verhält sich selbst – auf eine doppeldeutige Weise – rezeptiv: „[...] eine aktive offene Passivität gegenüber Bildern und der selbsttätigen Entstehung von Bildern, eine aktive Rezeptivität gegenüber den schon existierenden Bildern [...].“[53] Den Kreislauf der Avantgarden und damit eines ihrer fundamentalsten Gesetze löst er in leere Zeichen auf. Warum Polke sich zwar im Bad Painting bewegt, aber dennoch kein Bad Painter ist: weil er sich nicht als der andere in diesem Konzept inszeniert, sondern am System arbeitet und eine Art von „Rückzüchtung“[54] betreibt, auch „bad breeding“ genannt.

Das Denkmal Bad Painting und seine Inschriften

Jorn hat dem Bad Painting explizit ein Denkmal – das „Monument zu Ehren der schlechten Malerei“[55] – gesetzt, Polke hat es beschimpft, Guston ein zweckentfremdetes Gebilde in eine Landschaft [ABB·002] positioniert oder in *Monument* [ABB·040] unbestimmte Formationen überlagert. Gibt es im Bad Painting besondere Hinweise auf eine Gedächtnisfunktion, zumal eine der Malerei?

Polkes *Schimpftuch* [ABB·018] von 1968 ist ein einmaliges Dokument einer „Ut pictura poesis“-Narration im 20. Jahrhundert: Nach Buchloh enthält es die „Notwendigkeit zum ausgesprochenen Deutlichen“ und neben der „Frage nach der Ausdrucksfähigkeit der Malerei“ auch die, „warum sie ihrem ertragenen Verdikt, nur Zeichen- und Formensprache sein zu können und auf Wortsprache ewig verzichten zu müssen, sich gedanken- und widerstandslos fügen sollte“.[56] Was aber ist das *Schimpftuch*?

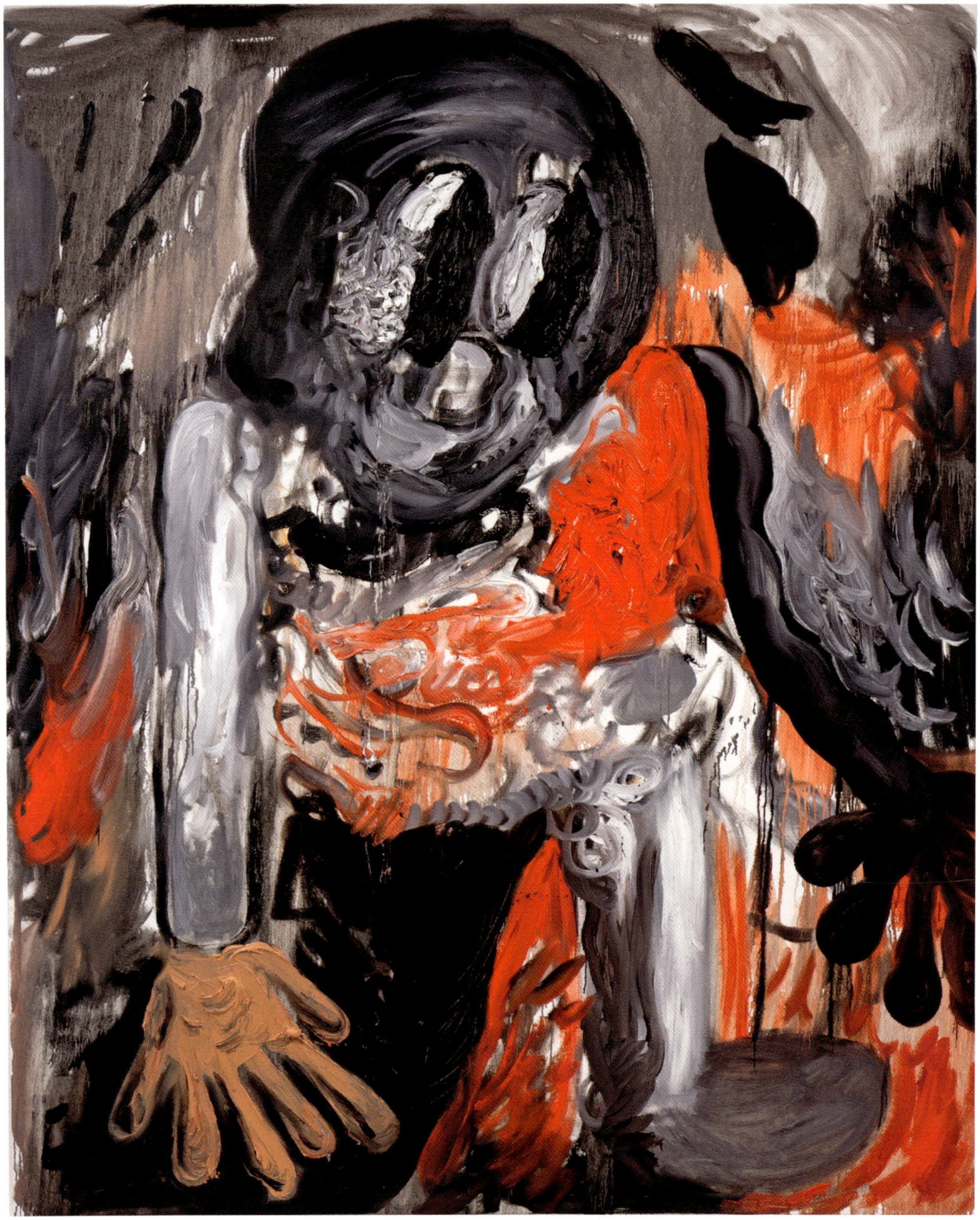

027
André Butzer
Pluton, 2002
Öl auf Leinwand / oil on canvas
250 x 200 cm
Privatsammlung / Private Collection

a woman, as in Jorn's *Choux* (Cabbage) [ILL·078]. The crude inscriptions certainly deviate from *Moderne Kunst* and *Akt mit Geige*. Scutenaire and Magritte would have appreciated them greatly, as they already knew then that good taste leads to powerlessness and impotence. Nonetheless, in this work Polke deconstructs male subjectivity as it was built up by Picabia and the Bad Painters of the 1980s using the very means of painting.[58] Already in this regard it denoted a break with tradition, even though it remained without consequences, and Polke never again staged such an outburst at the interface between painting and language.

In relation to text and painting two related systems of signs confront each other: those of Polke and Picabia, who said the lie was the most beautiful thing life had to offer.[59] His texts

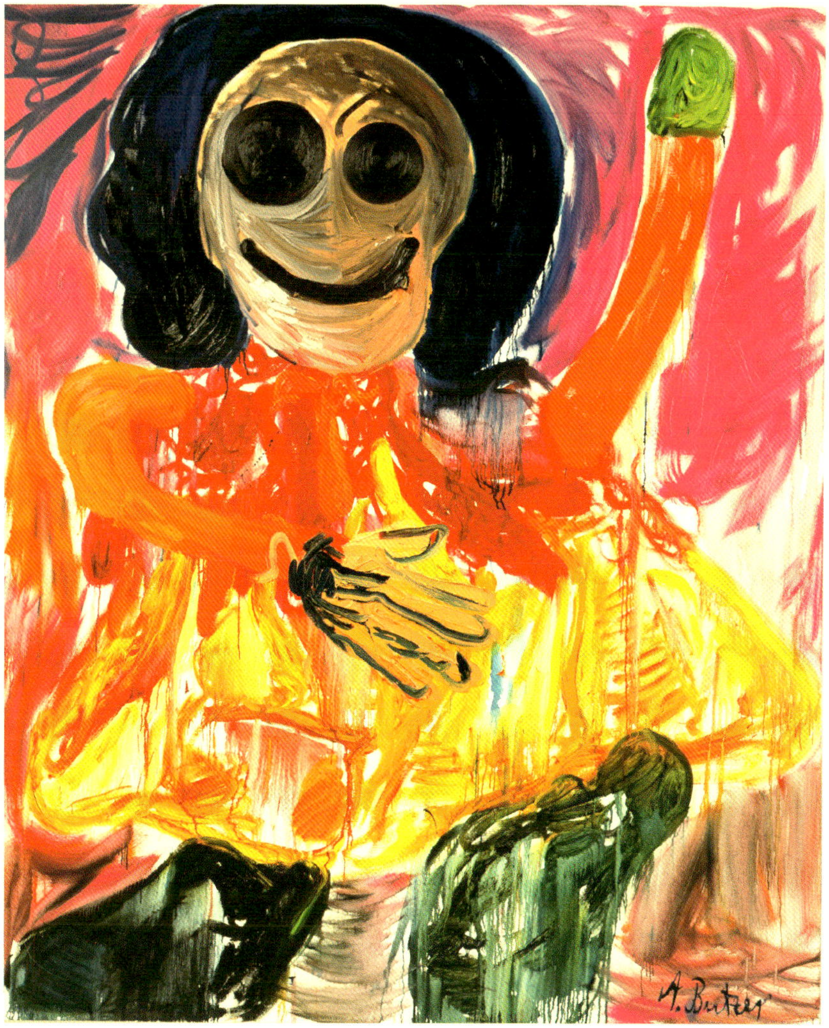

028 **André Butzer**
Frau, 2002
(Woman)
Öl auf Leinwand /
oil on canvas
250 x 200 cm
Privatsammlung /
Private Collection

Malerei oder Text? Buchloh nennt es „eine Publikumsbeschimpfung auf der Ebene der Malerei". Ist es möglicherweise als Malerei entstanden, ähnlich wie dies für Ed Ruschas *Liquid Words* beschrieben wurde, um eine prinzipielle Statusfrage zu stellen, ob es sich dabei um Malerei oder um Sprache handle?[57] War das *Schimpftuch* ursprünglich Flüssigkeit und Farbe, aus denen dann Wörter geschrieben wurden? Diese These beinhaltet, dass Malerei in Sprache verwandelt wurde. Tatsächlich hat Polke es, indem er es selbst trägt, aus der Horizontalität von Schreiben und Schrift genommen. Es ist zwar nicht vertikal an der Wand, liegt aber als Tuch am Körper, um als schimpfendes Tableau vivant auf den Betrachter zu treffen. Dieser ist allerdings eindeutig männlich adressiert und keineswegs *die* Malerei, die immer wie Jorns *Choux* [ABB·078] im Bad Painting eine Frau ist. Die Derbheit der Inschriften weicht gewiss von *Moderne Kunst* und *Akt mit Geige* ab. Sie hätten Scutenaire und Magritte gefallen, die schließlich schon früher wussten, dass der gute Geschmack zur Machtlosigkeit und Impotenz führe. Dennoch dekonstruiert Polke in diesem Werk männliche Subjektivität, wie sie Picabia und die Bad Painters der 1980er-Jahre mit den Mitteln der Malerei aufbauen.[58] Schon in dieser Hinsicht bedeutet es einen Bruch, wenngleich er keine Konsequenzen hatte und Polke keinen solchen Ausbruch mehr an der Schnittstelle von Malerei und Sprache inszenierte.

In Text und Malerei stehen sich ihre Zeichensysteme verwandt gegenüber: Polke und Picabia, der die Lüge als das Schönste im Leben bezeichnete.[59] Seine Texte surren dahin wie seine Werkphasen. „Weil Literatur Malerei ist", „alles dekorativ ist", er „nicht nur eine Gussform" sein will,

seem to drone along, resembling the way he goes through his artistic phases. "Because literature is painting," because "everything is decorative," he did not want to be "just a casting mold" or classified as some "-ist," but rather execute "Francis Picabia paintings" as the "most beautiful nonsensical painting" that was ever produced.[60] While Picabia stoked up the temporality of the avant-garde, which he traversed like a "nomad," "roamed through ideas as if through countries and cities,"[61] Polke put an end to it altogether. As Picabia proclaimed, "I regard every image as a drama going through all the stages of development of my antecedent productions—forming, transparency, stratification etc.—in order to be continued."[62] Stratification and overlaying connect Picabia and Polke to the alchemists just like Fautrier or Pinot Gallizio. As artistic practice—even if not under the banner of the new but by addressing memory—it also determined the character of the Gruppe SPUR, which supported a reassessment of painting as an experimental domain. The members of the group considered the avant-garde as a "movement distinguished by moronic progressiveness," which they wanted to transform to the extent that it "unites all the significant schools in a single system. We produce not only abstract but also figurative art."[63] Their method comprised associatively "layering lines, old figures and old rooms one over the other"[64] and thereby suspending the discrimination between "abstract" and "figurative," whilst Pinot Gallizio introduced the regulation of the "pittura industriale," that is, the industrial painting to be sold by the meter.[65]

Renowned for a view on painting that is characterized by an ambivalent metaposition, Kippenberger once again went through the motions of setting up a monument to Bad Painting in his *Heavy Guy* [ILL·019] before artists such as André Butzer in the 1990s declared that Bad Painting was no longer an issue.[66] *Heavy Guy*, just like Manet's *Olympia*, is an attack on painting. It leaves behind a container of destroyed images, whilst the images hang on the walls as photographs. Also in this case Kippenberger utilized for his work appropriation and transvaluation as well as a change of media, which he often applied when appropriating critically Breton's crown of thorns, Polke's watch-towers, Richter's painting in *Modell Interconti*, and Picabia's criticism of middle-class Sundays. The images in *Heavy Guy* were executed by Merlin Carpenter, who adopted from his own and those of others, exhausting image potential and abundantly integrating text. The container as the memory of painting forms a monument that equally runs aground or elevates such painting, which is dead and yet lives on. However, while memory ceases, it still—as Nora claimed for his "lieux de mémoire" (places of memory)—releases enough "to raise questions concerning its embodiment."[67] Kippenberger seems to have performed the sacrifice announced by Jorn, who spoke of "sacrificing the past."[68] What would Picabia's comment have been on this issue, having feared that silverware would tire the domestics?[69]

1 Thierry de Duve, *Pikturaler Nominalismus. Die Malerei und die Moderne*, (Munich: Schreiber, 1987), p. 131.

2 See Yves-Alain Bois, "The Use Value of the 'Formless'," in ibid., Rosalind E. Krauss, *Formless. A User's Guide* (New York: Zone Books, 1997), p. 13.

3 Taken from a conversation with Albert Oehlen, November 14, 2007.

„nicht ‚...istisch' klassifiziert" werden will, sondern „Francis-Picabia-Bilder" als die „schönstmögliche schwachsinnige Malerei"[60] machen wollte. Picabia hat die Zeitlichkeit der Avantgarde angeheizt, die er wie ein „Nomade" durchzog – „durch die Ideen wie durch Länder und Städte gehen"[61] –, Polke hat sie gestoppt. „Jedes Bild", so Picabia, „ist für mich ein Drama, das durch alle Entwicklungsstufen meiner vorausgegangenen Produktion – Formen, Transparenz, Schichtung usw. – hindurchgeht, um fortgesetzt zu werden [...]."[62] Dieses Überlagern und Schichten verbindet Picabia und Polke mit den Alchemisten wie Fautrier oder Pinot Gallizio. Als künstlerische Praxis, wenngleich nicht unter dem Zeichen des Neuen, sondern unter jenem des Gedächtnisses, bestimmt es auch die Gruppe SPUR, die für eine Aufwertung der Malerei als Experimentierfeld eintrat. Die Avantgarde sahen ihre Mitglieder als „stupide Fortschrittsbewegung", die sie so weit verändern wollten, dass sie „alle wesentlichen Strömungen in einem System zusammenfassten. Wir sind nicht nur abstrakt, sondern auch gegenständlich."[63] Ihre Methode war die einer assoziativen „Übereinanderschichtung von Linien, alten Figuren und alten Räumen",[64] die „abstrakt" und „gegenständlich" aufhob, während Pinot Gallizio die „pittura industriale", die per Quadratmeter verkauft wird, als Regulativ einführte.[65]

Ein Denkmal des Bad Painting hat Kippenberger, der die Malerei bekanntlich aus einer ambivalenten Metaposition beobachtete, noch einmal im *Heavy Burschi* durchexerziert, bevor die 1990er-Jahre, wie etwa André Butzer, sagen werden, dass Bad Painting kein Thema mehr sei.[66] *Heavy Burschi* [ABB·019] ist wie Manets *Olympia* eine Attacke auf die Malerei, die nun einen Container von zerstörten Bildern zurücklässt, während die Bilder als Fotos an der Wand hängen. Kippenberger arbeitet auch hier mit Aneignung und Umwertung sowie mit einem Medienwechsel, den er oft einsetzt, wenn er kritisch appropriiert: die Dornenkrone von Breton, die Wachtürme von Polke, das Bild von Richter im *Modell Interconti*, die Kritik an den bürgerlichen Sonntagen von Picabia. Die Bilder im *Heavy Burschi* hatte Merlin Carpenter ausgeführt, der sie aus eigenen und anderen übernahm, die Bildkapazitäten ausreizte und viel Text integrierte. Der Container als Gedächtnis der Malerei ist ein ebenso gestrandetes wie erhebendes Denkmal einer Malerei, die tot ist und weiterlebt. Das Gedächtnis reißt ab, setzt aber noch – wie Nora dies für seine „lieux de mémoire" sagte – so viel frei, „dass sich die Frage nach dessen Verkörperung stellen kann".[67] Kippenberger scheint die Opferung vollzogen zu haben, die Jorn angekündigt hat, als er von einem „Opfern der Vergangenheit" sprach.[68] Was hätte wohl Picabia dazu gesagt, der doch befürchtete, dass das Silbergeschirr die Dienerschaft ermüden würde?[69]

1 Thierry de Duve, *Pikturaler Nominalismus. Marcel Duchamp. Die Malerei und die Moderne*, München 1987, S. 131.

2 Vgl. Yves-Alain Bois, „The Use Value of the 'Formless'", in: ders., Rosalind E. Krauss, *Formless. A User's Guide*, New York 1997, S. 13.

3 Aus einem Gespräch mit Albert Oehlen, 14. November 2007.

4 Zit. n. Roberto Ohrt (Hg.), *Asger Jorn, Heringe in Acryl. Heftige Gedanken zu Kunst und Gesellschaft*, Hamburg 1993 (1987), S. 49.

4 Cited after Roberto Ohrt (ed.), *Asger Jorn, Heringe in Acryl. Heftige Gedanken zu Kunst und Gesellschaft*, (Hamburg: Edition Nautilus, 1993) (1987), p. 49.

5 Ibid., p. 48.

6 In the first manifesto of the artists' group; see Jo-Anne Birnie Danzker, Pia Dornacher (eds.), *Gruppe SPUR*, (Ostfildern: Hatje Cantz, 2006), p. 16.

7 See Bois (see note 2), p. 14.

8 Diedrich Diederichsen, "Verfolgung und Selbstverfolgung. Die Künstler und ihr 'psychischer Mehrwert,'" in *Gruppe SPUR* (see note 6), p. 47.

9 See note 3.

10 Michael Krebber, "Wo die Liebe hinfällt," in *Texte zur Kunst*, 36 (December 1999), p. 223.

11 On the definition of regression see Lars Heiler, *Regression und Kulturkritik im britischen Gegenwartsroman* (Tübingen: Narr, 2004), pp. 1ff. (Pagination stems from a partial internet publication in the Google book search).

12 Ibid., citation p. 1

13 Cited from Harald Falckenberg, "Auf Wiedersehen. Zur Rolle der Groteske in der Gegenwartskunst," in Pamela Kort (ed.), *Grotesk! 130 Jahre Kunst der Frechheit*, exhib. cat. (Frankfurt/M: Prestel, 2003), p. 188.

14 Werner Büttner in "Die 80er Jahre sind unter uns. Roundtable-Gespräch mit John M. Armleder, Benjamin H. D. Buchloh, Werner Büttner, Isabelle Graw, Philipp Kaiser, Kaspar König, Jutta Koether und Thomas Ruff," in exhib. cat. *Flashback. Eine Revision der Kunst der 80er Jahre* (Ostfildern: Hatje Cantz, 2005), p. 91.

15 Georges Bataille, *The Tears of Eros* (San Francisco: City Lights Books, 1989), pp. 50, 51. See also ibid., *Prehistoric Painting: Lascaux or the Birth of Art* (Lausanne: Skira 1955), as well as Hans-Jürgen Heinrichs, *Der Wunsch nach einer souveränen Existenz*, (Graz, Vienna: Literaturverlag Droschl, 1999), p. 101.

16 Jutta Koether, "All Alone (1957). Fautrier in den Vereinigten Staaten," in *Texte zur Kunst*, 50 (June 2003), p. 60, citations p. 60.

17 See Heinrichs (see note 15), p. 110.

18 Merlin Carpenter, "The Sound of Bamboo," in Michael Krebber, *Apothekerman*, (Cologne: Walther König, 2001), p. 32.

19 Krebber on Guston (see note 10), p. 223.

20 See David Sylvester (ed.), *René Magritte. Catalogue Raisonné*, vol. 2 (London: Wilson, 1993), p. 160.

21 Cited from Suzi Gablik, *Magritte* (London: Thames and Hudson, 1985), pp. 145, 146, citation p. 145.

22 From a letter written by Louis Scutenaire, cited from Sylvester (see note 20), p. 160.

23 See Philippe Vergne, "Petit voyage au pays de la régression picturale," in exhib. cat. *René Magritte. La période « vache »* (Marseille: Musées de Marseille et al., 1992), pp. 57f.

24 See Bernard Blistène's contribution to this volume.

25 See Sylvester (see note 20), p. 162

26 Cited from Laszlo Glozer, exhib. cat. *Westkunst. Zeitgenössische Kunst seit 1939* (Cologne: DuMont, 1981), p. 161.

27 Vergne (see note 23), p. 56.

28 Ibid.

29 See Sylvester (see note 20), p. 159, 162.

30 Cited in Bois (see note 2), p. 15

31 See Sylvester (see note 20), p. 167

32 Johannes Meinhardt, *Ende der Malerei und Malerei nach dem Ende der Malerei*, (Ostfildern-Ruit: Cantz, 1997), p. 178.

33 See exhib. cat. *Asger Jorn. Modifications* (Antwerp: Ronny Van de Velde 1998), unpaginated.

34 Ibid.

35 See Susanne Küper, *Konrad Lueg und Gerhard Richter: "Leben mit Pop – Eine Demonstration für den Kapitalistischen Realismus" 1963 in Düsseldorf*, Master's Thesis, Munich University, 1990.

36 See Robert Storr, "Anfänge," in ibid., *Gerhard Richter. Malerei*, exhib. cat. Museum of Modern Art (New York, Ostfildern-Ruit: Hatje Cantz, 2002), p. 32.

5 Ebd., S. 48.

6 Aus dem ersten Manifest der Gruppe, in: Jo-Anne Birnie Danzker, Pia Dornacher (Hg.), *Gruppe SPUR*, Ostfildern 2006, S. 16.

7 Vgl. Bois (zit. Anm. 2), S. 14.

8 Diedrich Diederichsen, „Verfolgung und Selbstverfolgung. Die Künstler und ihr ‚psychischer Mehrwert'", in: *Gruppe SPUR* (zit. Anm. 6), S. 47.

9 Wie Anm. 3.

10 Michael Krebber, „Wo die Liebe hinfällt", in: *Texte zur Kunst*, 36 (Dezember 1999), S. 223.

11 Zur Definition der Regression vgl. Lars Heiler, *Regression und Kulturkritik im britischen Gegenwartsroman*, Tübingen 2004, S. 1 ff. (Seitenangaben beziehen sich auf die Teilwiedergabe in „Google Buchsuche").

12 Ebd., Zitat S. 1.

13 Zit. n. Harald Falckenberg, „Auf Wiedersehen. Zur Rolle der Groteske in der Gegenwartskunst", in: Pamela Kort (Hg.), *Grotesk! 130 Jahre Kunst der Frechheit*, Ausst.-Kat., Frankfurt/M. 2003, S. 188.

14 Werner Büttner in: „Die 80er Jahre sind unter uns. Roundtable-Gespräch mit John M. Armleder, Benjamin H. D. Buchloh, Werner Büttner, Isabelle Graw, Philipp Kaiser, Kaspar König, Jutta Koether und Thomas Ruff", in: Ausst.-Kat. *Flashback. Eine Revision der Kunst der 80er Jahre*, Ostfildern 2005, S. 91.

15 Georges Bataille, *Die Tränen des Eros*, München 1981, S. 37. Vgl. dazu auch: ders., *Lascaux oder die Geburt der Kunst*, Genf 1955, sowie Hans-Jürgen Heinrichs, *Der Wunsch nach einer souveränen Existenz*, Graz, Wien 1999, S. 101.

16 Jutta Koether, „All Alone (1957). Fautrier in den Vereinigten Staaten", in: *Texte zur Kunst*, 50 (Juni 2003), S. 60, Zitate S. 60.

17 Vgl. Heinrichs (zit. Anm. 15), S. 110.

18 Merlin Carpenter, „The Sound of Bamboo", in: Michael Krebber, *Apothekerman*, Köln 2001, S. 32.

19 So Krebber über Guston (zit. Anm. 10), S. 223.

20 Vgl. David Sylvester (Hg.), *René Magritte. Catalogue Raisonné*, Bd. 2, London 1993, S. 160.

21 Zit. n. Suzi Gablik, *Magritte*, London 1985, S. 145 u. 146, Zitat S. 145.

22 Aus einem Brief von Louis Scutenaire, zit. n. Sylvester (zit. Anm. 20), S. 160.

23 Vgl. Philippe Vergne, „Petit voyage au pays de la régression picturale", in: Ausst.-Kat. *René Magritte. La période « vache »*, Marseille 1992, S. 57 f.

24 Siehe den Beitrag von Bernard Blistène in diesem Band.

25 Vgl. Sylvester (zit. Anm. 20), S. 162.

26 Zit. n. Laszlo Glozer, Ausst.-Kat. *Westkunst. Zeitgenössische Kunst seit 1939*, Köln 1981, S. 161.

27 Vergne (zit. Anm. 23), S. 56.

28 Ebd.

29 Sylvester (zit. Anm. 20), S. 159 u. 162.

30 Zit. n. Bois (zit. Anm. 2), S. 15.

31 Sylvester (zit. Anm. 20), S. 167.

32 Johannes Meinhardt, *Ende der Malerei und Malerei nach dem Ende der Malerei*, Ostfildern-Ruit 1997, S. 178.

33 Siehe Ausst.-Kat. *Asger Jorn. Modifications*, Antwerpen 1998, o. S.

34 Ebd.

35 Siehe Susanne Küper, *Konrad Lueg und Gerhard Richter: „Leben mit Pop – Eine Demonstration für den Kapitalistischen Realismus" 1963 in Düsseldorf*, Magisterarbeit, München 1990.

36 Vgl. Robert Storr, „Anfänge", in: ders., *Gerhard Richter. Malerei*, Ausst.-Kat. Museum of Modern Art, New York, Ostfildern-Ruit 2002, S. 32.

37 Vgl. Küper (zit. Anm. 35), S. 67: „Dieses schlechte Bild vom Dez. 1962 vermache ich G. Uecker – G. Richter – 13.4.68".

38 Siehe Küper (zit. Anm. 35), S. 30 u. 34.

39 Dass drei der Bilder dieselbe Größe haben, würde dafür sprechen.

40 Meinhardt (zit. Anm. 32), S. 19.

37 See Küper (see note 35), p. 67 "I bequeath this bad painting from Dec. 1962 to G. Uecker – G. Richter – 13/4/68."

38 See Küper (see note 35), pp. 30, 34.

39 The fact that three of the paintings are equal in size speaks for this.

40 Meinhardt (see note 32), p. 19.

41 See Gilman's contribution in this catalog.

42 See Küper (see note 35), p. 59.

43 Gerhard Richter in an interview with Robert Storr, in Storr (see note 36), p. 294.

44 See Paul B. Jaskot, "Gerhard Richter and Adolf Eichmann," *Oxford Art Journal*, vol. 28, no. 1 (2005), pp. 457 ff.

45 Dietmar Elger, *Gerhard Richter, Maler* (Cologne: DuMont Literatur und Kunst, 2002), p. 150.

46 Stefan Germer, "Die Wiederkehr des Verdrängten," cited from Jaskot (see note 44), p. 457, note 1.

47 See ibid, p. 47, note 35.

48 Documented in *Ganz am Anfang/How It All Began. Richter, Polke, Lueg & Kuttner* (= *sediment. Mitteilungen zur Geschichte des Kunsthandels*, no. 7, (2004), esp. pp. 80–87.

49 On the *Vitrinenstück* and the "heron" pictures see Martin Hentschel, "Solve et Coagula. Zum Werk Sigmar Polkes," in exhib. cat. *Die drei Lügen der Malerei* (Ostfildern-Ruit: Hatje Cantz 1997), pp. 47 ff.

50 Meinhardt (see note 32), p. 208.

51 See de Duve (see note 1), p. 59.

52 Sigmar Polke, "Sigmar Polke – frühe Einflüsse, späte Folgen oder: Wie kamen die Affen in mein Schaffen? und andere ikono-biographische Fragen," in exhib. cat. *Sigmar Polke. Bilder, Tücher, Objekte. Werkauswahl 1962–1971* (Tübingen, Düsseldorf, Eindhoven: Kunsthalle et al., 1976), p. 130.

53 Meinhardt (see note 32), p. 208.

54 *Rückzüchtung* is the title of a work by Polke executed in 1983.

55 Jorn, cited from Ohrt (see note 4), p. 49.

56 Benjamin Buchloh, "Polke und das große Triviale," in *Sigmar Polke. Bilder, Tücher, Objekte* (see note 52), pp. 150.

57 See Yves-Alain Bois, "Liquid Words," in *Formless. A User's Guide* (see note 2), p. 124ff.

58 See Buchloh, in *Flashback* (see note 14), p. 74.

59 Francis Picabia, *Schneckenbisse der Unvernunft* (Hamburg: Nautilus, 1997), p. 98.

60 Ibid, pp. 102, 99, 97, 26.

61 Ibid., p. 34.

62 Ibid., p. 111.

63 *Ein kultureller Putsch. Manifeste, Pamphlete und Provokationen der Gruppe SPUR* (Hamburg: Edition Nautilus, 1991), p. 27.

64 Ibid., p. 33.

65 See Selima Niggl, *Pinot Gallizio. Malerei am laufenden Meter* (Hamburg: Edition Nautilus, 2007), pp. 58ff. and 73ff.

66 In a conversation between the author and André Butzer, January 28, 2008.

67 Pierre Nora, *Zwischen Geschichte und Gedächtnis* (Frankfurt/M: Fischer, 1998), p. 11.

68 Jorn, cited from Ohrt (see note 4), p. 48.

69 Picabia (see note 59), p. 11.

41 Siehe Gilmans Beitrag in diesem Katalog.

42 Küper (zit. Anm. 35), S. 59.

43 Gerhard Richter in einem Interview mit Robert Storr, in: Robert Storr, *Gerhard Richter. Malerei*, Ausst.-Kat. Museum of Modern Art, New York, Ostfildern-Ruit 2002, S. 294.

44 Vgl. Paul B. Jaskot, „Gerhard Richter and Adolf Eichmann", in: *Oxford Art Journal*, Bd. 28, Nr. 1, 2005, S. 457 ff.

45 Dietmar Elger, *Gerhard Richter, Maler*, Köln 2002, S. 150.

46 Stefan Germer, „Die Wiederkehr des Verdrängten", zit. n. Jaskot (zit. Anm. 44), S. 457, Anm. 1.

47 Siehe ebd., S. 472, Anm. 35.

48 Dokumentiert in: *Ganz am Anfang/How It All Began. Richter, Polke, Lueg & Kuttner (= sediment. Mitteilungen zur Geschichte des Kunsthandels*, Heft 7, 2004), bes. S. 80–87.

49 Zum *Vitrinenstück* und den „Reiher"-Bildern vgl. Martin Hentschel, „Solve et Coagula. Zum Werk Sigmar Polkes", in: Ausst.-Kat. *Die drei Lügen der Malerei*, Bonn, Berlin, Ostfildern 1997, S. 47 ff.

50 Meinhardt (zit. Anm. 32), S. 208.

51 Siehe de Duve (zit. Anm. 1), S. 59.

52 Sigmar Polke, „Sigmar Polke – frühe Einflüsse, späte Folgen oder: Wie kamen die Affen in mein Schaffen? und andere ikono-biographische Fragen", in: Ausst.-Kat. *Sigmar Polke. Bilder, Tücher, Objekte. Werkauswahl 1962–1971*, Tübingen, Düsseldorf, Eindhoven 1976, S. 130.

53 Meinhardt (zit. Anm. 32), S. 208.

54 *Rückzüchtung* ist ein Werktitel von Polke von 1983.

55 Jorn, zit. n. Ohrt (zit. Anm. 4), S. 49.

56 Benjamin Buchloh, „Polke und das große Triviale", in: *Sigmar Polke. Bilder, Tücher, Objekte* (zit. Anm. 52), S. 150.

57 Vgl. Yves-Alain Bois, „Liquid Words", in: *Formless. A User's Guide* (zit. Anm. 2), S. 124 ff.

58 Vgl. Buchloh, in: *Flashback* (zit. Anm. 14), S. 74.

59 Francis Picabia, *Schneckenbisse der Unvernunft*, Hamburg 1997, S. 98.

60 Ebd., S. 102, 99, 97, 26.

61 Ebd., S. 34.

62 Ebd., S. 111.

63 *Ein kultureller Putsch. Manifeste, Pamphlete und Provokationen der Gruppe SPUR*, Hamburg 1991, S. 27.

64 Ebd., S. 33.

65 Vgl. Selima Niggl, *Pinot Gallizio. Malerei am laufenden Meter*, Hamburg 2007, S. 58 ff. u. 73 ff.

66 In einem Gespräch der Autorin mit André Butzer, 28. Jänner 2008.

67 Pierre Nora, *Zwischen Geschichte und Gedächtnis*, Frankfurt/M. 1998, S. 11.

68 Jorn, zit. n. Ohrt (zit. Anm. 4), S .48.

69 Picabia (zit. Anm. 59), S. 11.

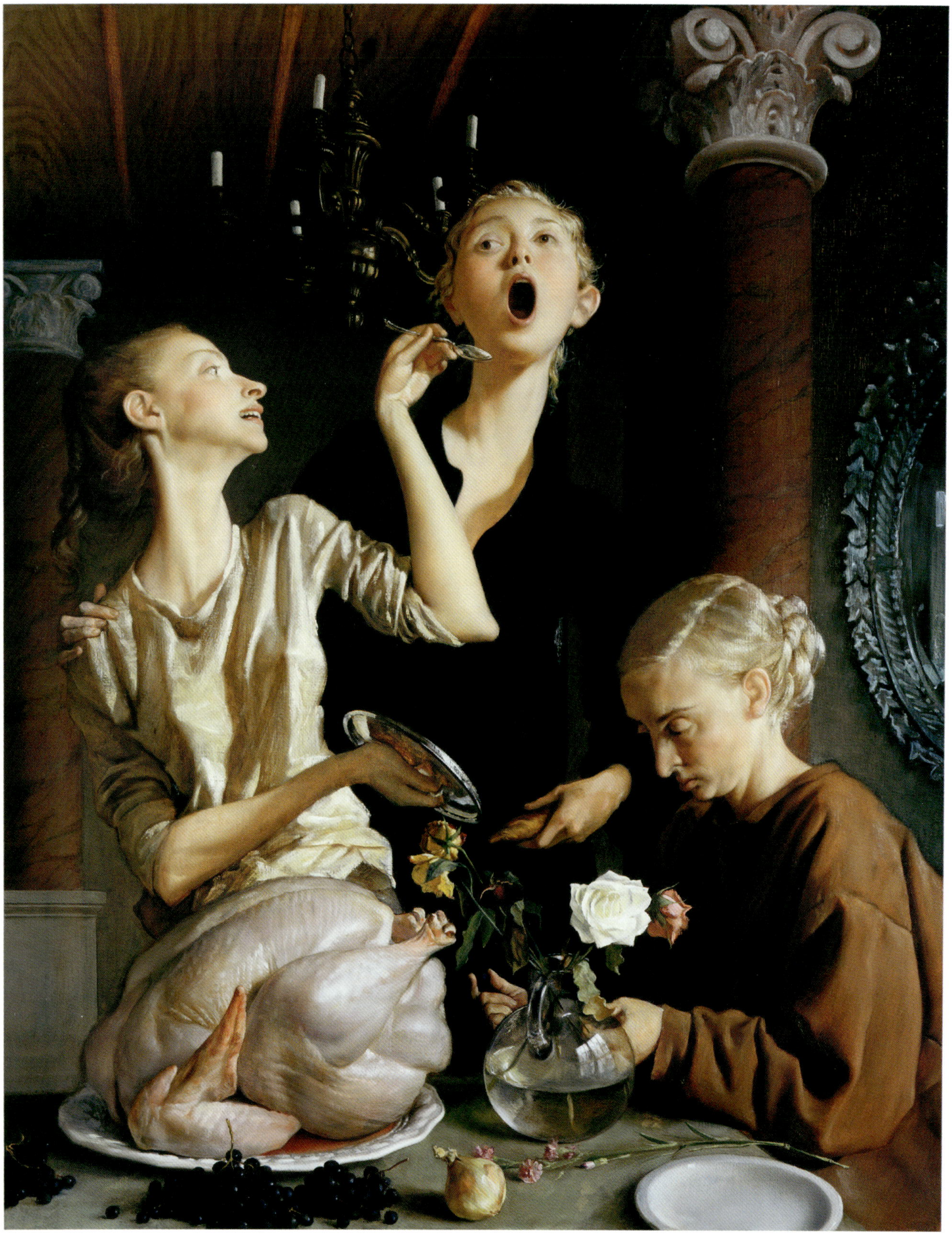

029 **John Currin**
Thanksgiving, 2003
(Erntedankfest)

Öl auf Leinwand / oil on canvas
172,9 x 132,3 cm
Tate London, Leihgabe / on loan from American Fund for the Tate Gallery, courtesy of Marc Jacobs

Wer wird wann, warum und inwiefern zum Bad Painter?

Eva Badura-Triska

Wie kann man Bad Painting definieren beziehungsweise ist so ein Unterfangen überhaupt sinnvoll – und nötig? Ebenso komplex wie verfänglich ist dieser Begriff, der nie programmatisch festgelegt wurde, aber insbesondere seit den 1980er-Jahren verstärkt durch die Kunstdiskussion geistert und mittlerweile fast schon zu einem Modeausdruck geworden ist. Allein aufgrund der zahlreichen Übersetzungsmöglichkeiten des englischen Adjektivs „bad" – im breiten Spektrum von „qualitativ schlecht" über „ungezogen", „schlimm", „unmoralisch", „unkorrekt" oder sogar „pervers", „hässlich" und „böse" bis hin zu „geil" (im amerikanischen Slang) – lässt sich der Begriff nicht auf eine Bedeutung festnageln, noch dazu, wo schon im Umgangssprachlichen, dort, wo er verwendet wird, oft mehrere Bedeutungsaspekte gleichzeitig zutreffen. Man ist also wohl gut beraten, von vornherein anzuerkennen, dass dieser Begriff – nicht zuletzt auch zeit- und kontextabhängig – mehrere Bedeutungen haben kann.

Dennoch nimmt diese Ausstellung natürlich eine Position ein beziehungsweise folgt einer Arbeitshypothese, die bestimmte Bedeutungsaspekte von Bad Painting schwerpunktmäßig herausgreift und beleuchtet. Ja, sie skizziert sogar eine mögliche Sichtweise des Phänomens, aus der sich nicht zuletzt im Hinblick auf Wertschätzungen Akzentverschiebungen und somit eine alternative oder zumindest differenzierte Lesart der Geschichte der Kunst des 20. Jahrhunderts ergeben kann.

Fangen wir aber zunächst damit an, worum es hier nicht gehen soll: Fast müßig erscheint es zu sagen, dass es nicht darum geht, „tatsächlich schlechte" Bilder zu zeigen. Nicht dass Derartiges in Museen nicht laufend passieren würde, doch das Unterfangen, dies – mit welcher Begründung auch immer – bewusst zum Konzept zu erklären, also absichtlich zu tun, führt unweigerlich bald auf schlüpfriges Terrain, selbst dann, wenn es aus soziokulturellen respektive historischen Interessen erfolgt (wie beispielsweise im Falle faschistischer Malerei). Man gelangt unvermeidlich zur ebenso facettenreichen wie banalen Frage der Relativität von Werturteilen wie „gut" und „schlecht" und begibt sich in ein weites und letztlich nie klärbares Gebiet, das jedenfalls hier ganz sicher nicht Thema sein soll.

Es geht auch nicht um „bad subject matter", also um die Darstellung böser, unkorrekter, schlimmer oder hässlicher Sujets – zumindest nicht primär, da sich nämlich doch zeigen wird, dass

Who Becomes a Bad Painter, When, Why, and in What Sense?

Eva Badura-Triska

How can one define Bad Painting? Does it even make sense to try? And is it necessary? The term, as complex as it is slippery, has never been fixed in programmatic terms, but since the 1980s in particular it has been popping up more and more frequently in art debate and has by now become almost fashionable. The broad semantic range of the adjective "bad"—poor quality, naughty, nasty, immoral, incorrect, perverse, ugly, evil, and even (in American slang) very good—prevents it from being pinned down to a single definition, especially as several of these aspects often apply at the same time. One is thus well advised to accept from the outset that the term has several (time and context-specific) meanings.

In spite of this, of course, the exhibition adopts a position, working with a hypothesis that focuses on and highlights particular aspects. In fact, it even sketches out a way of seeing the phenomenon that may lead to a shift in terms of appreciation, and thus to an alternative or at least newly differentiated reading of the history of twentieth-century art.

But let us begin by establishing what we are *not* talking about here. First, it almost goes without saying that it's not about showing pictures that are "actually bad." Not that this never happens in museums, but the notion of doing so deliberately, as a concept—for whatever reason—is bound to quickly end up on thin ice, even if it is motivated by sociocultural or historical interests (as, for example, in the case of fascist painting). Such an approach cannot but lead to the many-facetted and banal question of the relative nature of value judgments such as "good" and "bad," a broad and ultimately irresolvable issue that we certainly won't be dealing with here.

Second, we are not talking about "bad subject matter," the choice of evil, incorrect, nasty, or ugly motifs—at least not primarily, because, as we will see, Bad Painting of the kind we are talking about here actually often goes hand in hand with "bad subject matter."

Third, we are not talking about those works resulting from an "aesthetic of ugliness," [1] including the numerous artistic positions of the twentieth century that aimed to widen the circle of what is acceptable by emphasizing aesthetic qualities until then unjustly dismissed as negative, pointing to the "beauty" in things and human products previously considered ugly or "not worthy of art," the kind of intentions associated in the field of painting with Art Brut, among others.

Bad Painting, so wie es hier verstanden werden soll, zumindest immer wieder auch mit „bad subject matter" einhergeht.

Ebenfalls nicht gemeint sind sämtliche Werke, die einer „Ästhetik des Hässlichen"[1] verpflichtet sind, somit auch nicht jene in der Kunst des 20. Jahrhunderts zahlreich anzutreffenden künstlerischen Positionen, die im Sinne einer Erweiterung des Akzeptierten auf bislang zu Unrecht als negativ bewertete ästhetische Qualitäten verweisen wollen, also auf die „Schönheit" in Dingen und menschlichen Erzeugnissen, die bislang als hässlich oder „nicht kunstwürdig" galten, so wie es im Bereich der Malerei unter anderem das Anliegen des Art brut war.

Und schließlich sollen auch jene im 20. Jahrhundert ebenfalls zahlreichen Positionen kein Thema sein, die über die Malerei hinausgehen, indem sie das Tafelbild und damit auch „die Malerei" de facto attackieren, überschreiten oder gar verlassen, um sie dann von außen – sprich: unter Einsatz anderer künstlerischer Medien – zu kritisieren oder zumindest zu thematisieren und dabei als „bad" zu brandmarken.

Ganz im Gegenteil: Bad Painters, wie sie hier verstanden werden sollen, sind überzeugte Maler und bekennen sich eindeutig zu ihrem Medium. Sie stehen zu ihm auch oder sogar erst recht dann, wenn es im Verständnis des jeweils aktuellen dominanten Kunstgeschehens einer Zeit gerade desavouiert wird, weil man ihm vorwirft, für die aktuellen Fragestellungen und Anliegen nicht mehr adäquat und daher veraltet zu sein. Schon allein deshalb gelten sie oft als „bad". Doch auch über derartige zu gewissen Zeiten von den Avantgarden ausgesprochene Malverbote hinaus, sind Bad Painters nicht bereit, irgendwelche Benimmgebote zu akzeptieren. Sie verweigern generell die Unterordnung unter künstlerische Kanons und opponieren – und das ist entscheidend – nicht nur gegen traditionell-akademische, sondern auch gegen dogmatische (oder dogmatisch gewordene) Konzepte und Vorschriften der Avantgarden und Ismen des 20. Jahrhunderts, die ja im Grunde alte Dogmen immer nur über Bord werfen, um sie durch neue zu ersetzen.

Auf diese Weise kämpfen Bad Painters immer an mehreren Fronten zugleich: Unreflektiert konservative Kanons akademischer Traditionalisten lehnen sie sowieso vornweg ab, wobei aber eine besondere Pikanterie darin liegt, dass viele von ihnen aufgrund der Tatsache, dass sie meist figurativ und in einigen Fällen sogar in traditioneller bis altmeisterlicher Manier malen, selbst immer wieder dem Vorwurf ausgesetzt sind, Traditionalisten zu sein. Das bedeutet, dass sie im Endeffekt gegen den akademischen Traditionalismus ebenso kämpfen wie gegen den Vorwurf, selbst traditionalistisch-konservativ zu sein (der sich natürlich bei genauerer Analyse ihrer Werke nie halten lässt). Die radikalsten Reibepunkte der Bad Painters aber sind die grundsätzlichen Ansprüche der Avantgarden und Ismen des 20. Jahrhunderts. Sie hegen eine prinzipielle Skepsis gegenüber deren Glauben an Fortschritt durch Überwindung des Alten wie auch gegen deren Erlösungskonzepte, die entweder ein gesellschaftsveränderndes Potenzial der Kunst postulieren und/oder der Kunst eine Ersatzfunktion für ein transzendentes

And finally, we are not talking about those many twentieth-century positions that went beyond painting by attacking, exceeding, or abandoning easel painting and with it "painting as a whole," before criticizing or at least focusing attention on it from outside (i.e., using other artistic means) and stigmatizing it as "bad."

On the contrary: Bad Painters, in the sense we are talking about here, are convinced painters who clearly declare their commitment to the medium. They stand by it even (or especially) in times when it is repudiated by the dominant movements in art, accused of being unsuited to the issues of the day and thus outdated. For this reason alone, such artists are often considered "bad." But even beyond such bans on painting occasionally proclaimed by the avant-gardes, Bad Painters reject all rules of conduct. They generally refuse to submit to artistic canons and oppose not only traditional academic concepts and rules, but also—and this is crucial here—the concepts and rules established by the avant-gardes and isms of the twentieth century, which ultimately threw old dogmas overboard only to replace them with new ones.

In this way, Bad Painters are always fighting on several fronts at once: it goes without saying that they reject the unreflected conservative canons of the academic traditionalists, although, ironically, many of them are accused of being traditionalists themselves due to the fact that they mostly paint figuratively, sometimes even using traditional or Old Masterly styles. Finally, then, they find themselves fighting both against academic traditionalism and against accusations of being conservative traditionalists themselves (even if, in the light of a close analysis of their works, this charge never sticks). But the most radical points of friction for the Bad Painters are the fundamental claims of the avant-gardes and isms of the twentieth century—their belief in progress by overcoming the old, their notions of redemption that credit art with the potential to change society and/or the function of a substitute for some transcendental deficit. In this light, Bad Painting is not least a critique of the utopias of Modernism, whose untenable claims and promises it wishes to rigorously unmask.

But it is not only about the ideas and expectations of twentieth-century movements. Bad Painters reflect on and criticize the ability of painting, and ultimately of art in general, in a far more fundamental sense, and thus, logically enough, their attention is focused on the history of painting as a whole. In many cases, their own painting is a reflection on the potential and possibilities of the medium, but instead of entertaining illusions, they aim to ruthlessly reveal the incapacity of painting and the impossibility of the expectations placed in it—which are in fact the weaknesses and limits of all art. Consequently, they also see no sense in switching to a different medium, as this would be of no use. The realization that all such claims are futile can be expressed just as well in the medium of painting and is in fact often a key theme of their work.

One might consider it a schizophrenic strategy to use a medium to criticize that same medium. But one could just as well call it ruthless and logically consistent honesty when an artist's

Defizit zuschreiben. Bad Painting ist somit nicht zuletzt eine Kritik an den Utopien der Moderne, deren uneinlösbare Ansprüche und Versprechungen es schonungslos aufdecken will.

Es geht aber nicht allein um die Vorstellungen und Erwartungshaltungen der Bewegungen des 20. Jahrhunderts. Bad Painters reflektieren und kritisieren das Vermögen der Malerei und damit letztlich der Kunst überhaupt in einem viel grundsätzlicheren Sinne und haben daher nicht von ungefähr die Geschichte der Malerei als Ganzes im Blickwinkel. In vielen Fällen ist ihre eigene Malerei eine Reflexion über das Potenzial und die Möglichkeiten des Mediums, wobei sie sich keinen Illusionen hingeben, sondern schonungslos das Unvermögen der Malerei und die Unerfüllbarkeit der in sie gesetzten Erwartungshaltungen aufzeigen, die im Grunde ja die Schwächen und Grenzen der Kunst überhaupt sind. Demnach sehen sie auch keinen Sinn darin, das Medium zu wechseln, da dies nichts nützen würde. Die Erkenntnis des unvermeidlichen Scheiterns jeglicher Ansprüche kann auch im Medium der Malerei zum Ausdruck gebracht werden und ist sehr oft ein zentraler Inhalt ihrer Arbeit.

Man mag es eine schizophrene Strategie nennen, ein Medium zu benützen, um dieses zu kritisieren. Ebenso gut könnte man aber auch von schonungslos und konsequent bis ans Äußerste gehender Ehrlichkeit sprechen, wenn man die Zweifel und die Kritik an der Kunst im Allgemeinen und an der Malerei im Besonderen, die man ja beide nicht ernsthaft aufgeben will, mit den Mitteln der Kunst formuliert – und weshalb dann nicht auch in einem ihrer traditionellsten Medien? Neil Jenney jedenfalls beantwortete die Frage, wie man seine Malerei bezeichnen könnte, einmal mit „honest art“[2], und Albert Oehlen meinte, „wenn man etwas gegen die Kunst ausrichten will, dann muss man genau den Kern treffen. Das sind großformatige Gemälde.“[3]

In diesem Sinne entwickeln Bad Painters formal wie inhaltlich unterschiedlichste „Bad“-Strategien, um ihre Kritik der Malerei im gemalten Bild – „mit den Mitteln der Malerei“[4] – zu formulieren. Diese reichen vom schon erwähnten, oft als Provokation empfundenen Rückgriff auf „überwunden“ geglaubte Malweisen und -techniken der Kunstgeschichte über ein bewusst „fehlerhaftes“ oder grobes Malen, das Einbringen diverser Störfaktoren in Bilder oder ihre Überfrachtung mit formalen wie inhaltlichen Elementen und Bedeutungsträgern bis hin zur Entwicklung diverser idiosynkratischer, als unpassend oder ungelenk empfundener Idiome oder der Aufwertung von Kitsch. Dabei steht es schon im Einklang mit der Missachtung modernistischer Reinheitsgebote, dass Bad Painters sehr oft auf die Relativität beziehungsweise letztlich Irrelevanz des Unterschiedes von „gegenständlich“ und „abstrakt“ verweisen und diesem in ihrer Malerei keinerlei Bedeutung beimessen.

Schließlich ist noch eine weitere Front nicht zu unterschätzen, an der die Bad Painters konstant kämpfen: nämlich gegen sich selbst, gegen jegliche Bequemlichkeit, Nichthinterfragung und Erstarrung ihres eigenen Vorgehens, wie sie etwa mit der Beibehaltung und Perpetuierung eines einmal erreichten – und gar akzeptieren und kommerziell erfolgreichen – „signature style“ verbunden sind. Auch in dieser Hinsicht huldigen sie einer radikalen Unangepasstheit und Denkfreiheit, die etwa Arbeitsmodellen und Schemata sowie deren Begründungen kritisch gegenüberstehen: „Ich würde die

doubts and criticism concerning art in general and painting in particular, neither of which that artist seriously wishes to abandon, are formulated using the means of art—and why not in one of its most traditional media? Asked for a description of his painting, Neil Jenney once suggested "honest art."[2] And Albert Oehlen once said, "[...] if you want to achieve anything against art, you have to go right to the core of it. Which means large-format paintings."[3]

Along these lines, Bad Painters develop various "bad" strategies, in terms of both form and content, to formulate their critique of painting in painted pictures—"with the means of painting."[4] These strategies range from the above-mentioned recourse to supposedly "outmoded" painting styles and techniques from art history (often seen as a provocation), to deliberately "imperfect" or crude painting, the introduction of various disruptive factors, and/or overloading with elements of form and content/meaning, through to the development of idiosyncratic, "inappropriate," or clumsy idioms and an appreciation of kitsch. In keeping with their disregard for Modernism's purist dictates, Bad Painters very often point to the relativity and ultimate irrelevance of the distinction between figurative and abstract, according it no importance in their work.

Finally, one should not underestimate another front on which Bad Painters are constantly fighting: that is, against themselves, against all forms of complacency, non-questioning, and ossification linked to the perpetuation of a "signature style" once it has been accepted, let alone established as commercially successful. Here, too, the Bad Painters adhere to a brand of radical nonconformism and freedom of thought that is critically at odds with model-based or schematic working methods and the arguments used to justify them: "I wouldn't overestimate the importance of working models," says Albert Oehlen, refusing to see the "clarity" supposedly achieved by many artists as a positive goal: "They talk about clarity: the more schematic their work becomes, the more clarity they think they've gained."[5] In the most basic terms, Bad Painting is a method of expressing a general distrust of and opposition to the concept of the successful, harmonious, "correct" artwork.

Such a claim or concept of Bad Painting cannot meaningfully be maintained in every picture throughout an artist's life, and very often this strategy is only deployed during specific (more or less prolonged) phases—as a way of opening up new spaces for the medium.

This essay now asks: When does Bad Painting occur? In what historical situations? When, why, and in what sense does one become a Bad Painter? And the answer is: Ever since the demise of the golden age of the early twentieth-century avant-gardes, their various claims have repeatedly been questioned and ironized by forms of Bad Painting, most especially when these avant-gardes had become pale, feeble, and frozen; or during periods when the medium of painting found itself repudi-ated by these avant-gardes. This essay thus takes an alternative look at the history of twentieth-century art, or at least suggests new ways of assessing it. In order not to further expand this already extensive and complex subject (and for this reason only) it does not pursue the undoubtedly

Bedeutung von Arbeitsmodellen nicht überbewerten", sagt etwa Albert Oehlen und weigert sich auch, das, was viele Künstler als erreichte „Klarheit" sehen, als positives Ziel zu begreifen: „Sie sprechen von Klarheit: Je schematischer ihre Arbeit wird, umso mehr Klarheit glauben sie erreicht zu haben."[5] Ganz grundsätzlich ist Bad Painting eine Methode des Ausdrucks eines Misstrauens respektive der Opposition gegen das Konzept des gelungenen, in sich stimmigen, „richtigen" Kunstwerks.

So ein Anspruch oder Konzept des Bad Painting lässt sich sinnvollerweise nicht ein Leben lang bei jedem Bild durchhalten, und sehr oft sind es nur bestimmte (längere oder kürzere) Phasen, in denen sich Künstler dieser Strategie verschreiben, letztlich um dem Medium neue Freiräume zu eröffnen.

Dieser Text fragt nun, wann, in welchen historischen Situationen Bad Painting auftritt beziehungsweise wer, wann, warum und inwiefern zum Bad Painter wird. Die Antwort lautet, dass, sobald die Hochphase der Avantgarden des frühen 20. Jahrhunderts vorbei ist, deren Ansprüche immer wieder durch Formen von Bad Painting hinterfragt und gebrochen werden, ganz besonders dann, wenn die jeweiligen Avantgarden fahl, kraftlos und erstarrt geworden sind; oder eben in jenen Zeiten, wenn das Medium Malerei durch diese Avantgarden gerade desavouiert wird. In diesem Sinne wirft dieser Text einen alternativen Blick auf die Geschichte der Kunst des 20. Jahrhunderts respektive propagiert neue Akzentsetzungen. Ausgeklammert bleibt damit – und dies einzig und allein, um das ohnehin schon sehr umfangreiche und komplexe Thema nicht noch mehr auszuweiten – die ohne Zweifel lohnenswerte und wohl zu bejahende Frage, ob und inwiefern Strategien eines Bad Painting auch in der historischen Kunst sowie insbesondere in der Malerei des späten 19. Jahrhunderts – etwa bei Courbet – auszumachen sind.

Wie bei jeder Ausstellung erhebt die Liste der einbezogenen Künstler keinerlei Anspruch auf Vollständigkeit, sondern greift lediglich einige besonders markante Positionen heraus. Bezeichnenderweise gibt es aber insofern schon so etwas wie eine (lose) „Familie" beziehungsweise eine Genealogie von Bad Painters, als man feststellen kann, dass sehr oft jene, deren Schaffen dem Bad Painting im Sinne der hier genannten Kriterien entspricht, ihre Bewunderung für andere aussprechen, deren Schaffen ebenfalls diesen Kriterien entspricht. Dass Baselitz schon sehr früh von Picabia begeistert war,[6] Oehlen von Jorn[7] oder Currin sich mit Picabia, Polke und Guston auseinander gesetzt hat,[8] sind nur einige Beispiele dafür.

Von Dada und Surrealismus zu Bad Painting

Die aus heutiger Sicht markanteste Figur, die nach der Blütezeit der Avantgarden der klassischen Moderne deren grundlegende Prämissen infrage gestellt und dabei zu Formen von Bad Painting gefunden hat, ist Francis Picabia. Zunächst dem innersten Kreis der Dadaisten und Surrealisten angehörend, schert er ab Mitte der 1920er-Jahre aus und verweigert dem Denken und den Ansprüchen

worthwhile question of whether and to what extent strategies of Bad Painting might also be identified elsewhere in art history, in particular in the work of late nineteenth-century painters like, for instance, Courbet.

As with any exhibition, the list of featured artists makes no claim to completeness, merely picking out several especially striking positions. Significantly, however, there is something akin to a (loose-knit) "family" or genealogy of Bad Painters insofar as those whose work fulfills the criteria for Bad Painting named here very often express their admiration for others whose work also fulfills these criteria. Baselitz's early enthusiasm for Picabia,[6] Oehlen's for Jorn,[7] and Currin's interest in Picabia, Polke, and Guston[8] are just a few examples.

From Dada and Surrealism to Bad Painting

From today's point of view, the most striking figure to question the fundamental premises of the Modernist avant-gardes once their golden age had passed, and to arrive via this questioning at forms of Bad Painting, is Francis Picabia. Initially a member of the Dadaist and Surrealist inner circle, he broke free in the mid 1920s, henceforth refusing any form of allegiance to the thinking and claims of the avant-gardes. Granting himself a radical painterly freedom and changing styles repeatedly—thus foregoing any kind of "signature style"—he used and freely combined styles and motifs from the whole of art history, including the "progressive painting" of the early twentieth century, as well as cultivating a seemingly unscrupulous proximity to kitsch or even the painting of fascism. In the early 1920s his dada-surrealist machine pictures were already interspersed with women in traditional Spanish dress [ILL·063·065], while the "Monstres" from the middle of the same decade [ILL·058] used elements of the vocabulary of Modernism in heretically disrespectful or even satirical form, in pictures whose motifs were mostly borrowed from photographs of Old Masters.[9] And finally, in the "Transparences" [ILL·031·056] painted from around the same time, quotations from the entire history of art are layered so as to be hard to unravel, giving the impression of everything being melded together. In the 1930s, Picabia painted themes from Christianity and classical antiquity, among others, but also banal motifs (a fisherman on the shore, for example) in a crude, deliberately course manner [ILL·062], the figures edged with thick, black contours recalling the lead in stained glass windows. And at the end of the decade,[10] he began painting mostly female nudes, based on erotic photographs from magazines, thereby coming dangerously close to kitsch and to the tastes prevailing in the fascist painting of the period [ILL·030·068].

Long rejected by critics as regressive aberrations of a former avant-gardist, in the late 1950s these works experienced a first reevaluation "thanks to several far-sighted critics and art collectors such as Lawrence Alloway, William Copley and Enrico Baj"[11] and later, in the 1980s, a radical new appreciation. It is no mere coincidence that this occurred at precisely this moment in time. The questioning of the achievements and claims of Modernism that set in on a broad scale for the first time

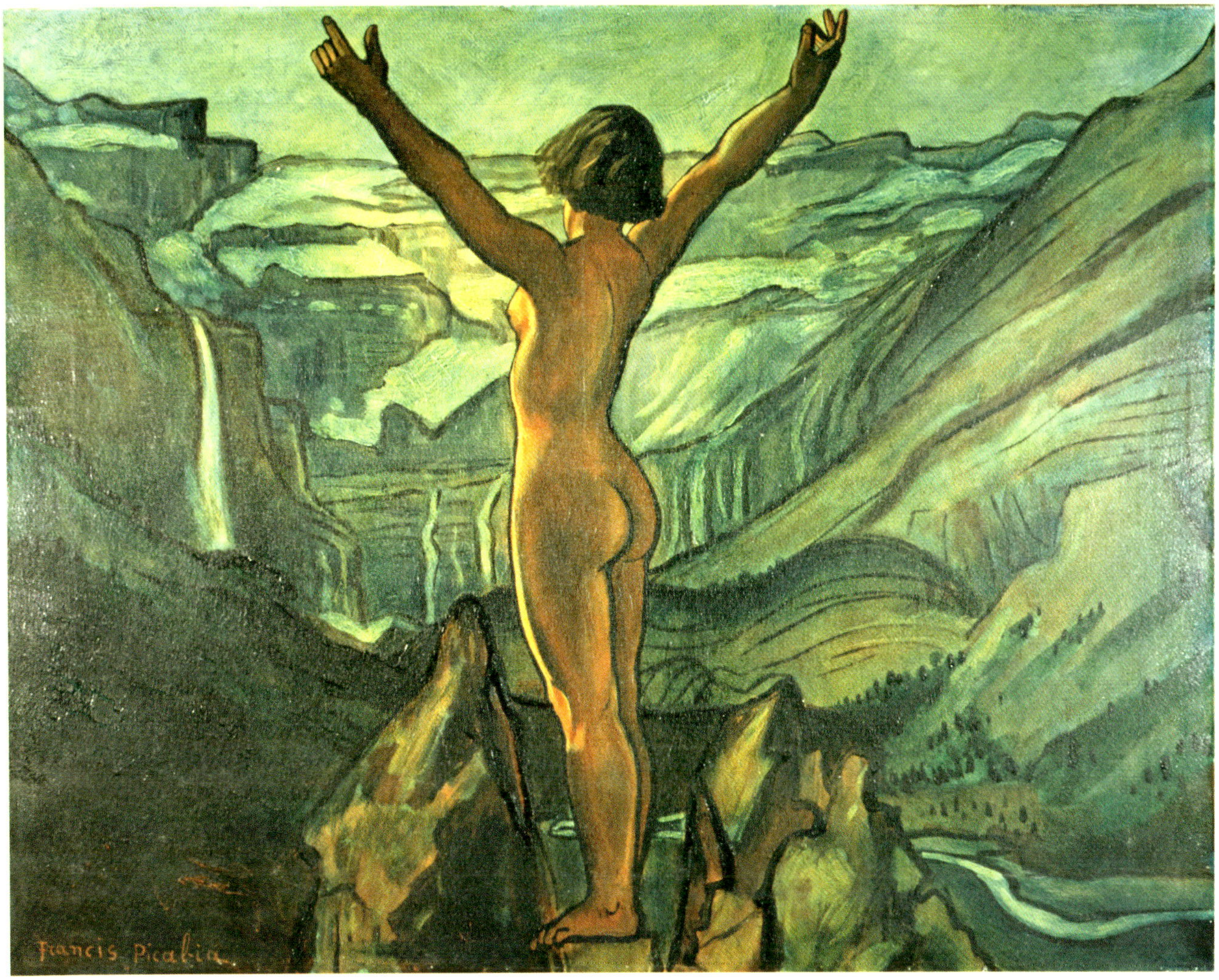

030 **Francis Picabia**
Nu devant un paysage, 1938
(Akt vor einer Landschaft / Nude in Front of a Landscape)
Öl auf Leinwand / oil on canvas
81 x 100 cm
Musée Magnelli, musée de la céramique, Vallauris

der Avantgarden jegliche Gefolgschaft. Er gestattet sich eine radikale malerische Freiheit, die bei wiederholtem Stilwechsel – und somit Verzicht auf einen „signature style“ – das Aufgreifen und freie Kombinieren von Stilen und Motiven der gesamten Kunstgeschichte, inklusive jener der „progressiven Malerei“ des frühen 20. Jahrhunderts, ebenso einschließt wie die scheinbar skrupellose Annäherung an den Kitsch oder gar die Malerei des Faschismus. Hat er schon Anfang der 1920er-Jahre Frauen in spanischer Folklore [ABB·063·065] zwischen seine dadaistisch-surrealen Maschinenbilder gemischt, werden in seinen ab Mitte dieser Dekade entstehenden „Monstres“ [ABB·058] Elemente des Vokabulars der Moderne in häretisch-respektloser bis persiflierender Form eingesetzt, wobei die Sujets dieser Bilder Fotografien alter Meister entlehnt sind.[9] In den ab etwa der gleichen Zeit entstehenden

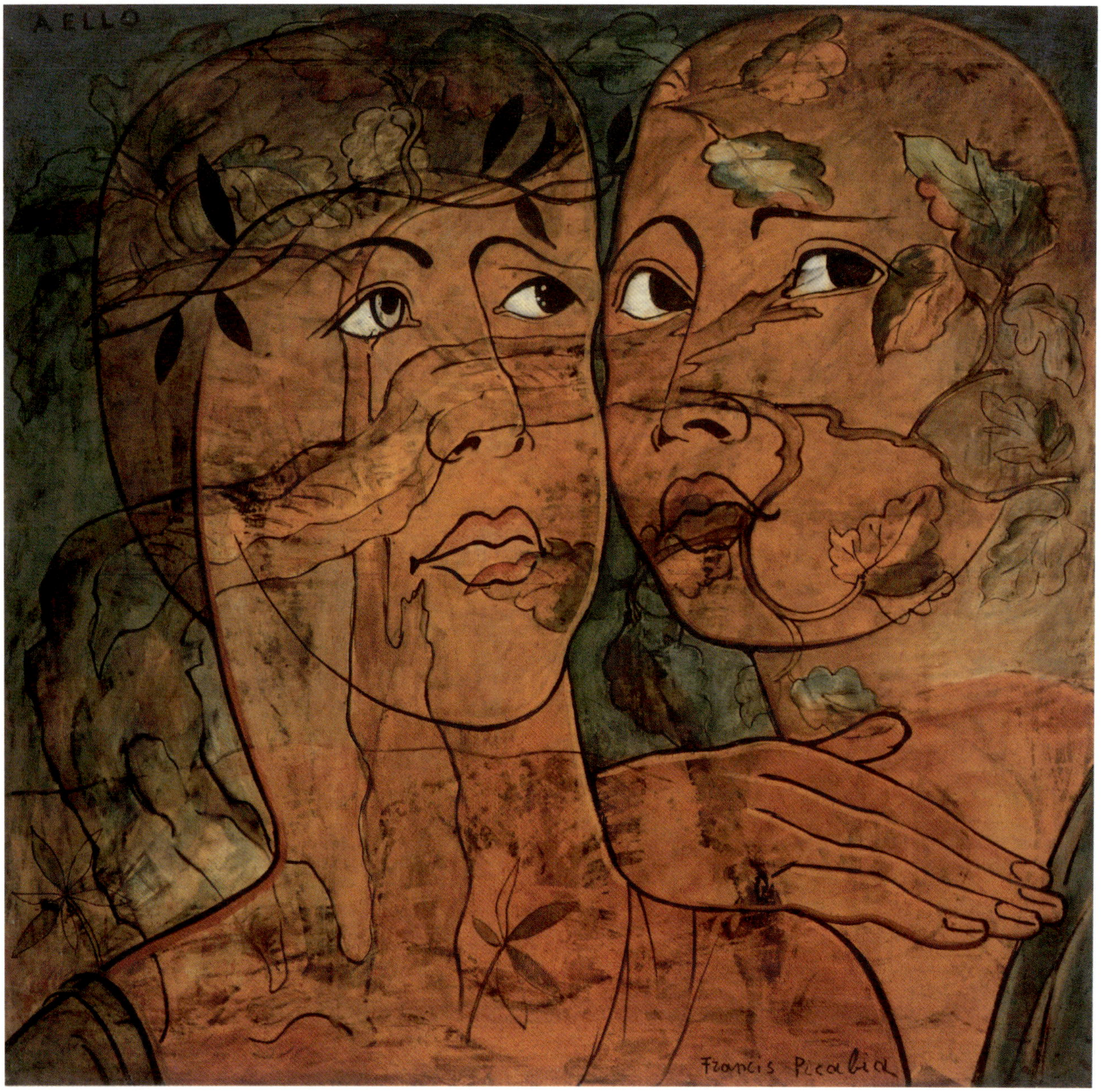

031 **Francis Picabia**
Aello, 1930
Öl auf Leinwand / oil on canvas
169 x 169 cm
Privatsammlung / Private Collection, Paris

in the 1980s was bound to focus attention on earlier proponents of such a questioning. And Picabia was the foremost such figure. What in the age of avant-garde thinking was viewed as inconsistent and retrograde could now be understood—from an altered point of view—as a positive attitude: the refusal to believe in closed heroic-utopian models bound to the concept of purposeful progress by overcoming the old, and often coupled with a belief in the potential of art to change society or even to offer spiritual experiences. "Picabia found convictions, and especially the need to convince other people, totally suspect. [...] Ideological justifications and aesthetic theories [...] restricted and bored [him]."[12] Our heads are round, he said, "to allow our thoughts to change direction,"[13] and he was just as dubious about the concept of good taste: "We say someone has taste, when he has the taste of others."[14]

„Transparences“ [ABB·031·056] werden schließlich Bildzitate aus der gesamten Weltkunstgeschichte in bisweilen nur schwer entwirrbarer Weise so übereinander gelegt, dass alles mit allem vereint scheint. In den 1930er-Jahren malt Picabia unter anderem christliche wie antike Themen, aber auch banale Sujets (wie etwa einen Fischer am Meeresstrand) in grober, absichtlich derber Manier [ABB·062], die Figuren mit dicken, schwarzen, an Bleistege von Glasfenstern erinnernden Linien umrandet, und beginnt Ende des Jahrzehnts[10] nach erotischen Fotografien aus Illustrierten vor allem weibliche Nackte zu malen, die gefährlich nahe an den Kitsch wie auch den Geschmack der faschistischen Malerei dieser Jahre herangehen [ABB·030·068].

Von der Rezeption lange als regressive Verirrungen eines vormaligen Avantgardisten desavouiert, erfuhren diese Werke bereits in den späten 1950er-Jahren „durch einige weitsichtige Kritiker und Künstlersammler wie Lawrence Alloway, William Copley und Enrico Baj“[11] eine erste Neubewertung und vor allem ab den 1980er-Jahren eine radikale neue Wertschätzung. Es ist kein Zufall, dass dies gerade zu jenem Zeitpunkt geschah. Die in den 1980er-Jahren erstmals auf breiter Ebene einsetzende Relativierung der Errungenschaften und Postulate der Moderne musste den Blick auf jene Figuren lenken, die diese Relativierung schon früher vertreten hatten. Picabia steht hierbei an vorderster Front. Was im Zeitalter des Avantgardedenkens als inkonsequent und rückschrittlich gesehen wurde, konnte nun – aus verändertem Blickwinkel – als positive Haltung verstanden werden: die Verweigerung des Glaubens an in sich geschlossene heroisch-utopische Denkmodelle, die dem Konzept eines zielgerichteten Fortschritts durch Überwindung des Alten huldigen und noch dazu oft mit dem Glauben an ein gesellschaftsveränderndes Potenzial der Kunst oder gar an spirituelle Erfahrungsmöglichkeiten verbunden sind. „Überzeugungen und vor allem das Bedürfnis, andere zu überzeugen, waren Picabia total suspekt. [...] Ideologische Rechtfertigungen und ästhetische Theorien [...] beengten und langweilten [ihn].“[12] Der Kopf sei rund, „damit die Gedanken ihre Richtung ändern können“,[13] und ebenso suspekt war ihm auch das Konzept eines guten Geschmacks: „Man sagt, jemand habe Geschmack, wenn er den Geschmack von anderen hat.“[14]

Für unseren Zusammenhang entscheidend ist, dass sich diese Haltung auch an den formalen Lösungen seiner Bilder festmachen lässt, ja, Anliegen und Thema dieser Malerei ist. Zu Recht verweist Roberto Ohrt auf Picabias Fähigkeit, „den Weg zu Widersprüchen zu finden, ohne sie zu einer Klärung hin aufzulösen“[15] – ein Prinzip, dem viele seiner späten Bilder unterliegen. So unterscheiden sich etwa seine Werke von den in den 1920er- und 1930er-Jahren ja zahlreichen Rückgriffen auf klassische figurative Malerei – sei es bei Picasso oder der Neuen Sachlichkeit – nicht nur durch eine oftmals bewusst grobe, ungelenke Malweise, sondern vor allem durch kompositorische Modi wie auch verschiedene, teils nur sehr subtile ins Bild eingebaute Störfaktoren, die es verunmöglichen, das Bild als in sich stimmiges kohärentes und gar einer bestimmten Stilrichtung zuschreibbares Ganzes wahrzunehmen. Weder bei den „Monstres“ noch bei den „Transparences“ führt die Überlagerung der Sujets und Bildelemente zu einer Auflösung. Ganz im Gegenteil, die Arbeiten werden oft derart überfrachtet, dass

Significantly for our context, this attitude is also evident in Picabia's formal solutions, actually constituting a concern and theme of his painting. Roberto Ohrt rightly points out Picabia's ability "to find an approach to contradictions without resolving them towards clarity"[15]—a principle that applies to many of his late pictures. This sets his works apart, for example, from all the work of the 1920s and 1930s that returned to classical figurative painting—be it Picasso, or New Objectivity. His paintings are different not only because of their often deliberately crude, clumsy technique, but above all due to Picabia's choice of compositional modes and his sometimes very subtle inclusion of disruptive factors that make it impossible to perceive a given picture as a harmonious, coherent whole that might be assigned to a particular stylistic category. In the "Monstres" and "Transparences" series, the layering of motifs and pictorial elements never leads to resolution. On the contrary, the works are often overloaded to such a degree that the individual elements become mutually disruptive, preventing coherence and causing the pictures to implode in both formal and semantic terms. Picabia's so-called "kitsch pictures," his nudes of the 1930s and 1940s, are also characterized not only by a crude technique, but also by their search for stylistic discord. On closer inspection, a broad range of often only very subtle nuances and details distinguish them from the straightforwardness, the one-dimensionality, and the quest for perfection that characterized both the fascist codes of beauty and the kind of "unironic" erotic painting with which they are so often over-hastily associated. For example, the cold, frozen-looking landscape that provides the backdrop for the sun worshipper in Picabia's *Nu devant un paysage* (1938) [ILL·030] hardly corresponds to the code of propagandist glorification and rapturous enthusiasm for nature. It is also doubtful whether in his nudes, the bold contrasts between cold, glaring studio lighting and dark backgrounds, the sharp body outlines, or the angular skin folds that often give his figures a lifeless, artificial quality are always conducive to undiminished enjoyment of nakedness and eroticism.[16] Importantly, these pictures also contain a variety of inconsistencies and errors related to the transfer of photographs into painting. Distortions of human proportions caused by the camera angle in the originals are ruthlessly retained by Picabia in his painted versions, where they cease to make any sense and become clumsy mistakes.[17] It is hard to believe that these errors were all made inadvertently; rather, they seem to be a deliberate reference to the difference not only between the two media, but also between the claims made by the respective pictures in terms of both form and content. As provocations in the sense of dangerous flirtation and resistance at the same time, these pictures ultimately refuse to be co-opted by any ideology or program. They are Bad Painting.

Turning away from what he saw as Dada's fruitless questioning of art, then, Picabia expressed his lack of faith in ideologies and, ultimately, in the potential of art in general within the medium of painting.

During and after World War II, related doubts concerning the meaningfulness of coherent movements and ideologies also led René Magritte to break away from the Surrealist program—

die einzelnen Elemente zu sich gegenseitig störenden Faktoren werden, die Kohärenz vereiteln und diese Bilder formal wie semantisch letztlich in sich implodieren lassen. Auch Picabias so genannte „Kitschbilder", also die Nackten der 1930er- und 1940er-Jahre, zeichnen sich nicht nur durch eine grobe Malweise aus, sondern suchen den stilistischen Dissens. Bei genauerer Betrachtung stehen sie aufgrund verschiedenster, oft nur subtiler Nuancen und Details in Differenz zur Geradlinigkeit und Eindimensionalität sowie dem Vollkommenheitsstreben sowohl des faschistischen Verherrlichungskodex als auch einer „straighten" erotischen Malerei, mit denen sie so oft vorschnell in Verbindung gebracht werden. Die kalte, vereist und erstarrt wirkende Landschaft etwa, vor der die Sonnenanbeterin in Picabias *Nu devant un paysage* (1938) [ABB·030] steht, entspricht kaum dem Kodex propagandistischer Verherrlichung und Naturschwärmerei. Ebenso mag man bezweifeln, ob die oft plakativ-groben Kontraste zwischen kalter, grellster Studiobeleuchtung und dunklen Hintergründen, die scharfen Körperumrisse oder die kantige Herausarbeitung von Hautfalten, die Picabias nackte Körper sehr oft ins Artifizielle und Leblose erstarren lassen, einem ungebrochenen Genuss von Nacktheit und Erotik immer entgegenkommen.[16] Nicht zuletzt finden sich in diesen Bildern verschiedentlich Ungereimtheiten und Fehler, die mit der Übertragung von Fotografien in Malerei in Zusammenhang stehen. Beispielsweise werden durch den fotografischen Blickwinkel bedingte Verzerrungen der menschlichen Proportionen in den Vorlagen von Picabia gnadenlos in die Malerei übernommen, wo sie jegliche Nachvollziehbarkeit verlieren und zu Ungeschicklichkeiten werden,[17] die dem Maler wohl kaum nur „passiert" sind. Viel eher verweisen sie bewusst auf eine Differenz nicht nur zwischen den beiden Medien, sondern auch im formalen wie inhaltlichen Anspruch der Bilder. Als Provokationen im Sinne von gefährlicher Annäherung und Widerstand zugleich verweigern sich diese Bilder letztlich der Indienstnahme durch jegliche Ideologie und Programmatik. Sie sind Bad Painting.

Picabia hat sich also von der in seinen Augen fruchtlosen Infragestellung der Kunst durch Dada abgewandt, um nicht nur seine Zweifel an Ideologien, sondern auch an den Möglichkeiten der Kunst überhaupt letztlich malereiimmanent zum Ausdruck zu bringen.

Verwandte Zweifel an der Sinnhaftigkeit kohärenter Bewegungen und Ideologien führen während und nach dem Zweiten Weltkrieg auch René Magritte zum Ausscheren aus der Programmatik des Surrealismus – allerdings nur für kurze Zeit. Aus Sehnsucht nach einer anderen Gefühlslage schlüpft er 1943 neben seiner bisherigen in eine dieser weitgehend entgegengesetzte Malweise. Er entwickelt den „Surrealismus im vollen Sonnenlicht" („Le Surréalisme en plein soleil"), auch seine „période Renoir" genannt, in der er jedoch keineswegs nur Renoir „imitiert". [ABB·032] „Ich male Bilder im Stil von Renoir, Ingres, Rubens usw., aber ohne speziell die Technik Renoirs zu verwenden, sondern vielmehr die des Impressionismus – Renoir, Seurat und weitere inbegriffen."[18] Magritte verlässt dabei aber mehr als seinen zu diesem Zeitpunkt bereits sehr erfolgreichen Stil. Er gibt vor allem auch das Konzept einer einheitlichen in sich stimmigen Bildidee auf und versucht eine „Verbindung

even if only for a short time. In 1943, his desire for a different feel led him to a style of painting that was essentially the antithesis of what had gone before. He developed "Surrealism in full sunlight" ("Le Surréalisme en plein soleil"), also known as his "Renoir period" [ILL·032], during which, however, he did not merely "imitate" Renoir. "I paint pictures in the style of Renoir, Ingres, Rubens etc., not making particular use of Renoir's technique, but rather that of Impressionism—Renoir, Seurat, and others included."[18] By doing so, Magritte did more than just move beyond his by then highly successful style. He also abandoned the concept of a unified pictorial concept and tried to "join together two mutually exclusive things: 1) a feeling of levity, intoxication, happiness, which depends on [...] an atmosphere that [...] Impressionism [...] has managed to render in painting. [...] and 2) a feeling of the mysterious existence of objects [...] which is experienced only by means of a certain objective clarity."[19]

His fellow Surrealists held both against him, denying him "permission" to use Impressionist techniques to paint Surrealist pictures.[20] In 1946, the resulting dispute caused Magritte to reject his colleagues' dogmatism and to criticize their perpetuation of their own movement: "This sense of chaos, of panic, which Surrealism hoped to foster so that everything might be called into question was achieved much more successfully by those idiots the Nazis."[21] "It's time to leave the safe path, a path leveled by Surrealism for its many adherents over 20 years and which they now diligently tread."[22] "Otherwise people will be bored stiff in Surrealist museums just as much as in any others."[23]

On the occasion of an international Surrealist exhibition at Galerie Maeght in Paris in July 1947, André Breton publicly condemned "Surrealism in full sunlight." Magritte was "excommunicated,"[24] making him even less inclined to bend to the dictates of the Paris "headquarters". In 1948, having just turned 50, he used his first solo show in Paris[25] to take things to new extremes. He presented a series of works very different to each other that appear in their entirety as a critically satirical inventory of the styles—and thus also the claims in terms of content—of (French) Modernism, calling this his "période vache."[26] [ILL·008·009·070–076] In these pictures, as well as parodying the expressive, classicist, and even abstract idioms of (French) Modernism, Magritte also referred in a range of grotesques and caricatures to phenomena from popular culture. Elements of his own "former" style also appear in corrupted form in this medley, such as the famous pipe in the coded self-portrait

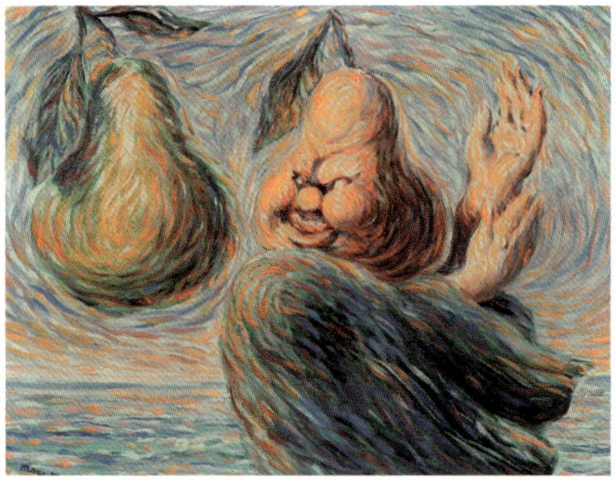

032 René Magritte
Le Lyrisme, 1948,
(Die Lyrik / The Lyricism)

Gouache auf Papier /
Gouache on paper,
50 x 65 cm

zweier Dinge, die [einander] ausschließen: 1.) Gefühle der Leichtigkeit, des Rausches, des Glücks, die nur [...] in einer Atmosphäre, wie [...] der Impressionismus [...] sie in der Malerei zu vergegenwärtigen wusste, [möglich sind]. [...] 2.) Das Gefühl von der geheimnisvollen Existenz der Dinge [...], das sich nur mit einer gewissen objektiven Klarheit wahrnehmen lässt."[19]

Die Surrealistenkollegen nahmen ihm beides übel und verweigerten die „Erlaubnis", sich beim Malen surrealistischer Bilder impressionistischer Techniken zu bedienen.[20] 1946 kommt es zum Streit, der nun Magritte zur Ablehnung der Dogmatik seiner Künstlerkollegen wie auch zur Kritik an deren Perpetuierung ihrer Bewegung führt: „Dieses Durcheinander, diese Panik, die der Surrealismus schaffen wollte, um alles infrage zu stellen: Die Nazi-Idioten haben das viel besser gemacht als wir."[21] „Es ist an der Zeit, den abgesicherten Weg zu verlassen: einen Weg, den der Surrealismus seinen zahlreichen Anhängern in 20 Jahren geebnet hat und den sie jetzt brav gehen."[22] „Andernfalls wird man sich langweilen – in den surrealistischen Museen genauso wie in den anderen."[23]

Anlässlich einer internationalen Surrealistenausstellung in der Pariser Galerie Maeght kommt es dann im Juli 1947 zur offenen Verdammung des „Surréalisme en plein soleil" durch André Breton. Magritte wird „exkommuniziert"[24] und will sich nun erst recht von der Pariser „Zentrale" nichts mehr vorschreiben lassen. 1948, gerade 50-jährig, treibt er es bei seiner ersten Einzelausstellung in Paris[25] jetzt wirklich auf die Spitze. Er präsentiert eine Reihe untereinander äußerst unterschiedlicher Werke, die zusammen ein kritisch-persiflierendes Inventar der Stile – und damit auch der inhaltlichen Ansprüche – der (französischen) Moderne ergeben, und spricht von seiner „période vache"[26]. In parodistischer Weise spielt Magritte in diesen Bildern die expressiven, klassizistischen und teilweise auch die abstrakten Idiome ebenso durch, wie er in Form verschiedenster Grotesken und Karikaturen auf populärkulturelle Phänomene verweist [ABB·008·009·070–076]. In diesem bunten Reigen tauchen auch verschiedentlich Elemente seines eigenen „vormaligen" – und von seinen Surrealistenkollegen als „richtig" akzeptierten – Stils in verballhornter Form auf, so beispielsweise die berühmte Pfeife in dem als kodiertes Selbstporträt geltenden, expressiv gemalten Bild *Le Stropiat*, für dessen Titel Magritte aus „estropier" („verstümmeln") ein Substantiv kreiert hat [ABB·070]. Der Dogmatik seiner Surrealistenkollegen antwortet Magritte also mit einer kritischen Relativierung sämtlicher Postulate der Avantgarden, wobei die humorigen Inhalte dieser Bilder selbst das ins Ironische ziehen, womit er sich in seinem eigenen Schaffen bislang sehr ernsthaft auseinander gesetzt hatte, nämlich die erkenntnistheoretischen beziehungsweise linguistischen Fragen nach der Realität eines Bildes respektive der Nichtidentität von Zeichen und Bezeichnetem. Der Inhalt der Malerei – *Le Contenu Pictural* [ABB·072] – ist nun eine tragikomisch-bankrotte Figur, ein mit Clown- und Vogelköpfen gehörnter Mann, der mit ebenso aggressiven wie lächerlichen Waffen in den Händen, leeren Taschen und zerschlissenen Kleidern auf undefiniertem Grund vor den Wolken steht.

Wie jener von Picabia wird auch Magrittes Vorgriff auf den Stilbruch und die dekonstruktiven Methoden der 1980er-Jahre vom Nachkriegsparis, das sich (noch) als Nabel und

painted in an expressive style and entitled *Le Stropiat* [ILL·070], a neologism based on the verb " estropier" (to mangle). Magritte thus responded to the dogmatism of his Surrealist colleagues with a critical relativization of all the postulates of the avant-gardes, whereby the humorous content of these pictures even comments ironically on what Magritte himself had dealt with very seriously in his work up to this point, i.e., epistemological and linguistic questions pertaining to the reality of images and the discrepancy between signifier and signified. The content of painting, *Le Contenu Pictural* [ILL·072], is now a tragicomically bankrupt figure, a man with horns consisting of clown's and bird's heads, holding weapons as aggressive as they are ridiculous, with empty pockets and torn clothes, standing in front of clouds on an undefined ground.

As in Picabia's case, Magritte's anticipation of the stylistic inconsistency and deconstructive methods of the 1980s was not appreciated at all by postwar Paris, which (still) considered itself the hub and nerve center of the art world. The exhibition was a total failure in every respect.[27] After this debacle, Magritte gave in to pressure from his wife and returned to his familiar style, although not without reserving the right to future "incongruities."[28]

Bad Painting in the spirit of Situationism

A similar skepticism was behind Asger Jorn's series of "Modifications" and "Défigurations" [ILL·001·033·077–080]. They were painted between 1959 and 1962,[29] on the threshold to the period of the neo-avant-gardes which, over the following twenty years, were to radically question and even proscribe the traditional form of painting on canvas—or at least the type dedicated to figurative or subjective expression. In these works, Jorn professes his faith in painting at the same time as using the medium to articulate his doubts concerning its possibilities, linking this in turn to a critique of the claims of the avant-gardes.

He, too, positions himself within the broader framework of artistic production in painting—both in historical terms and with regard to what is accepted as art. As his point of departure he took old pictures purchased at fleamarkets, generally viewed as kitsch, against whose condemnation he had already appealed in 1939: "Anyone who tries to fight against the production of these bright, appealing, carefully executed pictures is an enemy of the best contemporary art. [...] The lakes in the forests and those roaring stags in golden, decorative frames hanging by thousands in living-rooms on walls with patterned wallpaper are among the most profound products of artistic inspiration. It is always a little tiring to see people setting about sawing through the branch on which they are sitting."[30]

Jorn's figurative and abstract reworking of these old and kitschy pictures left the original motif essentially legible; it is neither attacked nor destroyed, but simply—as Jorn put it—"modified." "If you have old paintings, do not despair," he wrote in the catalog for an exhibition of these pictures at Galerie Rive Gauche in Paris in May 1959: "Retain your memories, but detourn them, so that they correspond with your era. Why reject the old if one can modernize it with a few strokes of

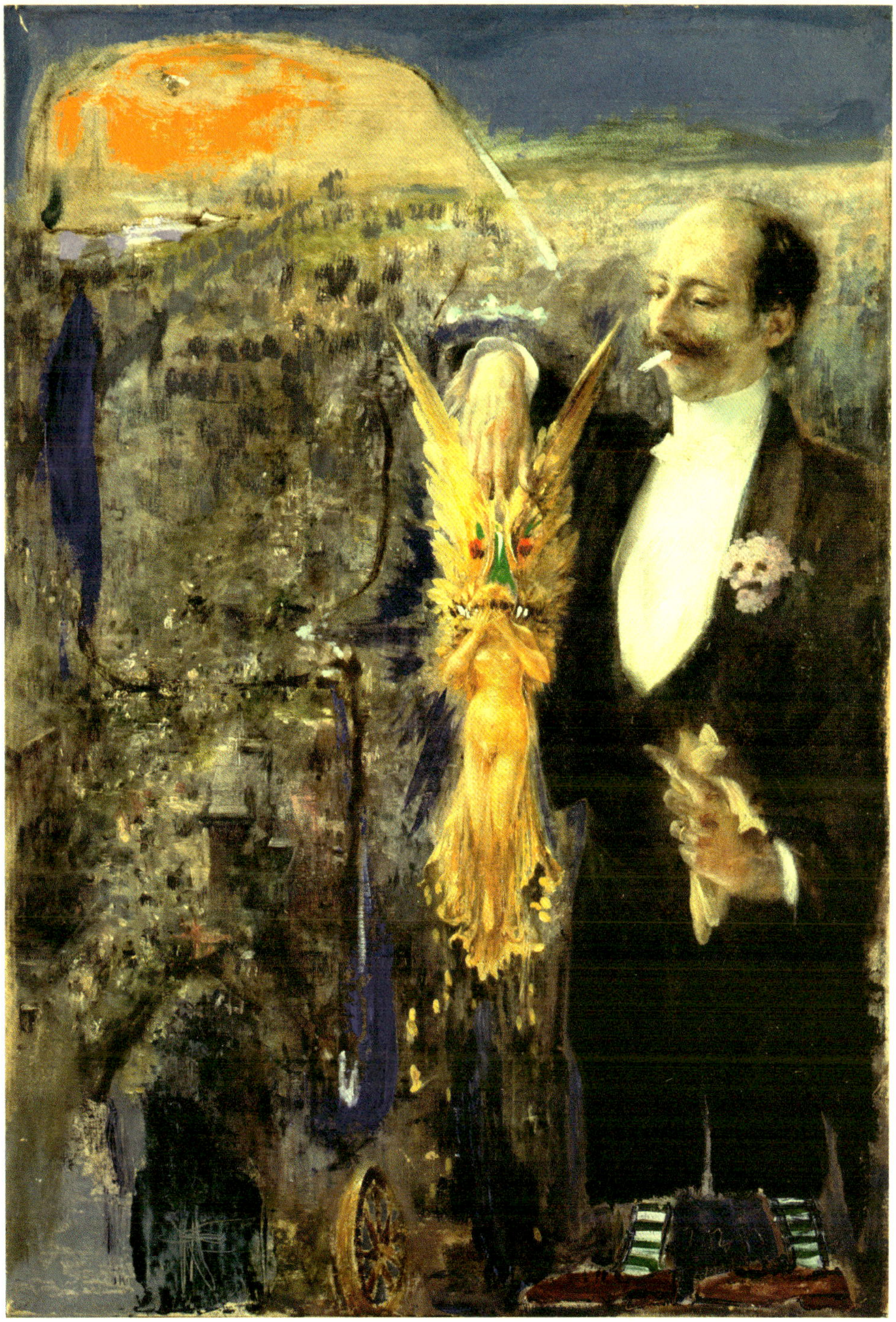

033 Asger Jorn
Il faut porter la fortune du bonheur, 1962
(Wir müssen die Zufälligkeit des Glücks ertragen / We Have to Carry the Fortuity of Bliss)
Öl auf Leinwand / oil on canvas
81 x 55 cm
Pierre et Micky Alechinsky, Bougival

Schaltzentrale der Kunstwelt fühlt, absolut nicht goutiert. Die Ausstellung wird in jeder Hinsicht ein totaler Misserfolg.[27] Dem Drängen seiner Frau Folge leistend, kehrt Magritte nach diesem Desaster schließlich doch wieder zu seinem bekannten Stil zurück, nicht aber ohne sich weitere „Ungereimtheiten" vorzubehalten.[28]

Bad Painting im Geist des Situationismus

Eine ähnliche Skepsis steht hinter Asger Jorns Bildserien der „Modifications" und „Défigurations" [ABB·001·033·077–080]. Diese entstanden zwischen 1959 und 1962[29], also an der Schwelle zur Zeit der Neoavantgarden, die in den beiden folgenden Jahrzehnten die traditionelle Form der

the brush? This casts a bit of contemporaneity on your old culture. Be up to date, and distinguished at the same time. Painting is over, you might as well finish it off. Detourn. Long live painting."[31]

This method of "modification" or "détournement" (diversion, rerouting) of existing pictures is to be seen in the context of the thinking of the Situationist International led by Guy Debord, to which Jorn belonged from 1957 to 1961. According to Debord's analysis, capitalist society is one in which individuals subjugated by the "spectacle" of an "economic realm developing for itself"[32] are reduced to passive observers of their own lives. The Situationist concept of change did not envisage toppling this system in favor of one dictated by themselves and thus inevitably leading back to unfreedom. Instead, they advocated the "détournement" of the conditions of life under capitalism by the people themselves through the creation of situations, "moment[s] of life constructed concretely and deliberately"[33] to enable "the realization of a superior game [...] of human presence"[34] in all areas of life.

It is in this spirit that Jorn acts with his "Modifications," merely "adapting" existing artworks without attacking or even destroying their form or content. A crucial factor here is his indifference towards the original work. If any claim to "rightness" that might be imposed on an individual from outside is to be rejected, then any artistic work one accepts without intervening (in the form of "détournement" or "modification") is ultimately a cultural product of no significance to one's own life—and by extension to society as a whole. But this also means the choice of works adapted is of no importance. Any creative product can provide the basis for a "détournement." Besides an indifference towards historical works, this naturally also results in contempt for the claims of the avant-gardes, while facilitating an acceptance of kitsch as an artistic expression. "L'avant-garde se rend pas" (the avant-garde doesn't give up) writes Jorn with fitting cynicism in the background of one "Modification" [ILL·077], the portrait of a bourgeois girl to which he has added, among other things, a mustache—a gesture identifiable to anyone in the know as a comment on Duchamp's aggressive Dadaist reworking of a postcard of the Mona Lisa (an iconic masterpiece in the eyes of the bourgeois). In the eyes of the Situationists, the questioning of art by Dada, like any radically subversive gesture, had ended up as just another style accepted by culture, and thus of no relevance to life.

Of particular interest for us here is the resulting positive revaluation of kitsch, which Jorn calls Bad Painting. The "Modifications" exhibition was explicitly intended to "honor" kitsch, and the above-quoted catalog text praised it as banality brought to perfection and named bad taste as an important source of inspiration. "The great masterpieces are nothing but accomplished banalities, and the deficiency of the majority of banalities is that they are not complete. These works do not push banality to the limits of its profundity, they fail to explore the full extent of its consequences; instead they rest on a foundation of aestheticism and spirituality. [...] Nowhere else but in Paris does one find gathered together so many things of bad taste. This is the very secret which explains why Paris remains the place where artistic inspiration is alive."[35]

Malerei auf Leinwand – oder zumindest deren figürliche oder einem subjektiven Ausdruck verschriebene Varianten – radikal infrage stellen bis ächten sollten. Jorn legt in diesen Bildern ein Bekenntnis zur Malerei ab, um gleichzeitig dieses Medium zur Formulierung seiner Zweifel an dessen Möglichkeiten einzusetzen, was wiederum mit einer Kritik an den Ansprüchen der Avantgarden einhergeht.

Auch er verortet sich dafür im größeren Gefüge einer malerischen Bildproduktion – sowohl im zeitlich-historischen Sinne als auch hinsichtlich dessen, was als Kunst Akzeptanz findet. Ausgangspunkt sind auf Trödelmärkten erstandene, gemeinhin als Kitsch gewertete, alte Bilder, gegen deren Verdammung er schon 1939 ein Plädoyer formuliert hatte: „Wer gegen die Produktion der schönen, grellen, sorgfältig ausgeführten Bilder zu kämpfen versucht, ist der Gegner der besten zeitgenössischen Kunst. […] Diese Seen in den Wäldern und diese röhrenden Hirsche, die in tausenden von Wohnzimmern in goldenen Rahmen auf gemusterten Tapeten hängen, gehören zu den tiefsinnigsten Eingebungen der Kunst. Es ist immer ein wenig ermüdend zu sehen, wie die Menschen darangehen, den Ast, auf dem sie sitzen, abzusägen.“[30]

Diese alten Kitschbilder werden von Jorn in gegenständlicher wie abstrakter Manier jeweils so überarbeitet, dass das originale Sujet weitgehend lesbar bleibt. Es wird weder angegriffen noch zerstört, sondern nur – wie Jorn selbst sagt – „modifiziert“. „Verzweifeln Sie nicht, wenn Sie alte Bilder haben. Behalten Sie Ihre Erinnerungen, aber leiten Sie sie um, sodass sie Ihrer Zeit entsprechen. Warum das Alte verwerfen, wenn es mit ein paar Pinselstrichen modernisiert werden kann? Das bringt Aktualität in Ihre alte Kultur. Gehen Sie mit der Zeit und seien Sie gleichzeitig distinguiert. Die Malerei ist am Ende. Man kann ihr gleich den Gnadenstoß versetzen. Leiten Sie sie um. Es lebe die Malerei“, schreibt er im Vorwort des Katalogs seiner Ausstellung dieser Bilder im Mai 1959 in der Pariser Galerie Rive Gauche.[31]

Die Methode der „modification“ oder des „détournement“, also der Umgestaltung beziehungsweise Umleitung bestehender Bildwerke, ist vor dem Hintergrund des Denkens der Situationistischen Internationale um Guy Debord zu sehen, der Jorn zwischen 1957 und 1961 angehörte. Dieses basierte auf der Reflexion über die kapitalistische Gesellschaft, die die Situationisten als eine begriffen, in der vom „Spektakel“ einer „sich für sich selbst entwickelnden Wirtschaft“[32] unterjochte Subjekte in ihrem eigenen Leben nur mehr passive Zuschauer sind. Ihr Konzept der Veränderung sah aber nicht einen Umsturz dieses Systems zugunsten eines von ihnen diktierten und damit unweigerlich wieder zur Unfreiheit führenden vor. Die kapitalistischen Lebensbedingungen sollten vielmehr von den Menschen selbst durch das Schaffen von Situationen „konkret und mit voller Absicht konstruierter Momente“[33] „umgeleitet“ werden in „die Verwirklichung eines höheren Spiels […] der menschlichen Anwesenheit“[34] in allen Bereichen des Lebens.

Genau in diesem Sinne agiert Jorn, wenn er in seinen „Modifications“ bestehende Kunstwerke lediglich „anpasst“, ohne sie physisch oder inhaltlich zu attackieren oder gar zu zerstören.

While Debord notoriously ended up expelling most of his collaborators from the movement, Jorn left the Situationist International in 1961 of his own accord, soon returning in his painting to the line which he had been pursuing before the "Modifications" and which he had never fully abandoned while making them. In this way, he stood by his practice of painting, a practice he was to pursue throughout his life. Within his œuvre as a whole, the series of "Modifications" and "Défigurations" can be seen as a pause for reflection during which he tried to gain clarity—within and by means of this medium—about his position as an artist and about the possibilities of art and of painting in particular, not least as a way of admitting to himself their inability to bring about revolutionary change and of rejecting the utopias of Modernism. Guy Debord, by contrast, eventually came to the conclusion that the artwork as a product separate from the practice of life would cease to be necessary as soon as people became the self-determined and thus creatively active makers of their own lives.

Painting when painting was outlawed—Bad Painting in the 1960s and 1970s

In the 1960s and 1970s, a high point in the rejection of painting by the dominant avant-gardes of the time, the very decision to paint was either "bad" or an act of resistance, depending on one's point of view. Those artists—like Georg Baselitz, Sigmar Polke, Gerhard Richter, Jörg Immendorff, and A. R. Penck in Germany—who remained true to painting and in particular to painting that was figurative or even permitted subjectivity, were especially liable to be accused of being traditionalists, and thus under increased pressure to position themselves—a situation that led to various strategies of Bad Painting.

For Georg Baselitz, who, at the end of the 1950s, had escaped the artistic dictates of Communist East Germany, there was no question of submitting to the dictate he saw in the western avant-gardes' rejection of figurative painting, nor to the subsequent proscription of painting as a whole. Significantly, this struggle against the dictates of East and West led him to deliberately choose bad painting: "I had no choice. As a young man, I wanted to paint with muck, with mud, with non-colors, with black and white, really bad pictures that got noticed. [...] To set something against beautiful things. This is only possible with a vehement approach, with aggression and with violent opposition. In other words, with all kinds of bad things."[36]

With paints mixed using his fellow students' leftovers scraped from the floor,[37] and with disregard for composition and harmony, he painted pictures with taboo-breaking "bad" subject matter: miserable-looking figures including masturbating boys and grossly priapic men, isolated crooked penises, women with sagging breasts, monstrous-looking people whose noses and ears can often be read as genitals [ILL·006·034–039]. In prudish postwar Germany, it was no wonder that two of these pictures were confiscated from an exhibition.

Entscheidend dabei ist seine Gleichgültigkeit dem Ursprungswerk gegenüber. Wenn jeglicher von außen an das Individuum herangetragene Anspruch auf „Richtigkeit“ abzulehnen ist, stellt auch jegliche künstlerische Hervorbringung, die man ohne eigenes Zutun, also ohne „détournement“ oder „modification“, akzeptiert, für das eigene Leben – und in weiterer Folge für die Gesellschaft – letztlich bedeutungsloses Kulturgut dar. Demnach ist es aber auch egal, welches Werk überarbeitet wird. Jede Hervorbringung kann Basis eines „détournement“ sein. Neben einer Indifferenz gegenüber historischen Werken ergibt sich daraus natürlich auch eine Geringschätzung bis Verachtung der Ansprüche der Avantgarde, während andererseits Kitsch als künstlerische Äußerung akzeptiert werden kann. „L'avant-garde se rend pas“ (Die Avantgarde gibt nicht auf) schreibt Jorn dementsprechend zynisch in den Hintergrund einer „Modification“ [ABB·077], bei der er ein bürgerliches Mädchenbildnis unter anderem mit einem Schnurrbart versehen hat – eine Geste, die jeder Eingeweihte unweigerlich als Kommentar zu Duchamps im aggressiven Geiste von Dada erfolgter Überarbeitung einer Postkarte der Mona Lisa (als Meisterwerk par excellence im bürgerlichen Kunstverständnis) lesen muss. Wie jegliche radikal umstürzlerische Geste wurde auch die Infragestellung der Kunst durch Dada in den Augen der Situationisten zu nichts anderem als einem weiteren kulturell akzeptierten und daher für das Leben bedeutungslosen Stil.

Von besonderem Interesse für unseren Zusammenhang ist natürlich die sich aus diesem Konzept ergebende Aufwertung des Kitschs, den Jorn als Bad Painting apostrophiert. Mit seiner Ausstellung der „Modifications“ will er diesem ausdrücklich seine „Ehre“ erweisen und preist im schon erwähnten Katalogvorwort den Kitsch als Banalität in ihrer vollendeten Form sowie den schlechten Geschmack als wesentliche Quelle der Inspiration. „Die großen Meisterwerke sind nichts als vollendete Banalitäten, und die Unzulänglichkeit der meisten Banalitäten ist, dass sie nicht komplett sind. Diese Werke treiben die Banalität nicht bis an die Grenzen ihrer Tiefe, sie schöpfen nicht den vollen Gehalt ihrer Konsequenzen aus, sondern bleiben auf einem Fundament des Ästhetizismus und der Spiritualität. […] Nirgendwo anders als in Paris findet man so viele Dinge von schlechtem Geschmack versammelt. Das ist aber auch das Geheimnis, das erklärt, warum Paris der Platz bleibt, wo die künstlerische Inspiration lebendig ist.“[35]

Während Debord dafür bekannt war, die meisten seiner Mitstreiter irgendwann wieder aus seiner Bewegung auszuschließen, sollte Jorn die Situationistische Internationale 1961 aus eigenen Stücken verlassen, um bald in seiner Malerei im Wesentlichen wieder in jener Linie weiterzuarbeiten, die er vor den „Modifications“ gepflegt und auch während deren Entstehung nie ganz aufgegeben hatte. Er stand somit voll zu seiner Praxis des Malens und verfolgte sie zeitlebens. Die Serien der „Modifications“ und „Défigurations“ sind in seinem Gesamtschaffen als reflektierendes Intermezzo zu sehen, in dem er sich – anhand des Mediums und in diesem – über seinen Standort als Künstler sowie über die Möglichkeiten der Kunst und insbesondere der Malerei Klarheit zu verschaffen sucht, nicht zuletzt um sich ihre Unfähigkeit, revolutionär etwas bewirken zu können, einzugestehen und

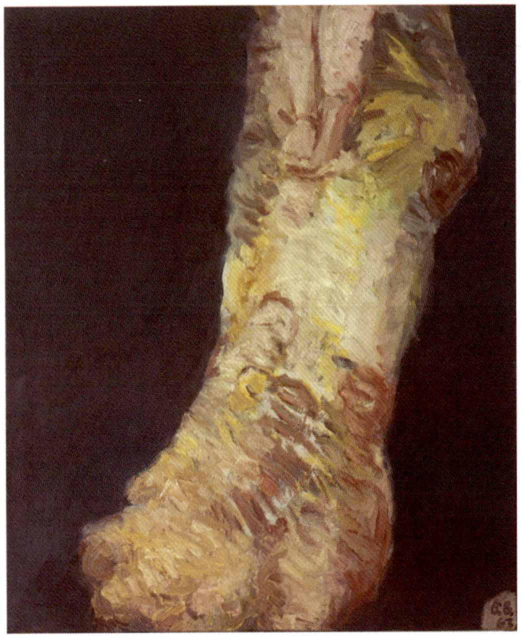

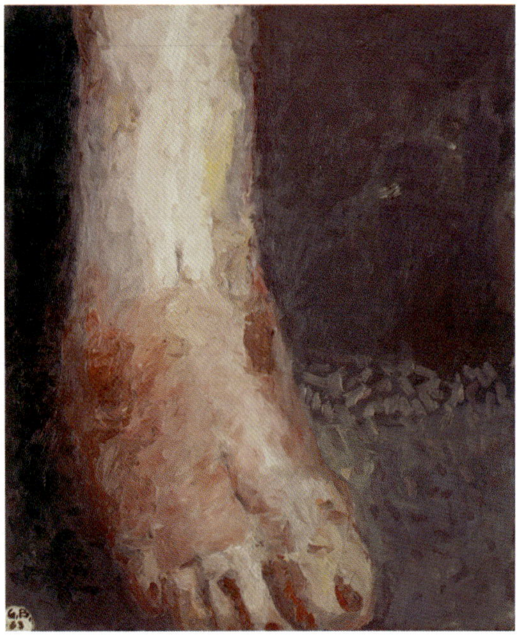

034
Georg Baselitz
Achter P.D. – Die Hand, 1963
(Eighth P.D. –The Hand)
Öl auf Leinwand /
oil on canvas
100,9 x 82,1 cm
Sammlung Crex, Zürich

035
Georg Baselitz
Erster P.D. – Der Fuß, 1963
(First P.D. – The Foot)
Öl auf Leinwand /
oil on canvas
101 x 82 cm
Sammlung Crex, Zürich

Sigmar Polke and Gerhard Richter—both of whom relocated from the East to the West—also refused to participate in the general rejection of painting, although in their cases the resulting "bad" strategies are far more conceptual and in some instances more analytical. Polke's ironico-cynical deconstruction of the heroic claims of Modernism, for example, is not unrelated to that practiced by Picabia with his "Monstres." In pictures like *Moderne Kunst* (Modern Art) [ILL·083·017], he declared his aversion to ideologies and styles, and to the coupling of the two, by satirically cobbling together "typical" elements from the formal idioms of Modernism.

And even Jörg Immendorff, always far more directly political in his work, stuck with the traditional medium of painting when he wished to express his skepticism with regard to its potential impact, above all in socio-political terms. "Hört auf zu malen" (Stop Painting) he wrote on one of his pictures in 1966 [ILL·110], thus attacking painting as a commodity and bourgeois status symbol that is ultimately incapable of making an effective critical impact. But this attack was made without so much as contemplating turning his back on the medium. He was mocked by Beuys for always stating his critique of painting in the medium of painting itself.[38] He himself saw this positively, as a constructive strategy, a brand of Bad Painting that adopted a critical position with regard to art in general and which equally doubted the potential effectiveness of the actionist art forms for which Beuys, amongst others, stood: "[...] for me, painting was always a schizophrenic undertaking. Working in a medium while at the same time fighting it, there's something about that which I always call constructive schizophrenia."[39]

In the United States, Philip Guston was the first prominent painter to rebel against the "rules of correctness" of the then "official" brand of modernism. In his case, this meant Abstract Expressionism, the first major independent and internationally successful manifestation of American artistic production which was, as we now know, even used to political ends in the ideological Cold War between East and West. Following the revaluation of his long-dismissed late works—a revaluation which, significantly, took place in the 1980s—he was celebrated by young painters as a father figure of Bad Painting in the same way Picabia and Jorn were in Europe.

036 **Georg Baselitz**
Sechster P.D. Fuß, 1963
(Sixth P.D. Foot)

Öl auf Leinwand /
oil on canvas
100,7 x 82 cm
Sammlung Crex, Zürich

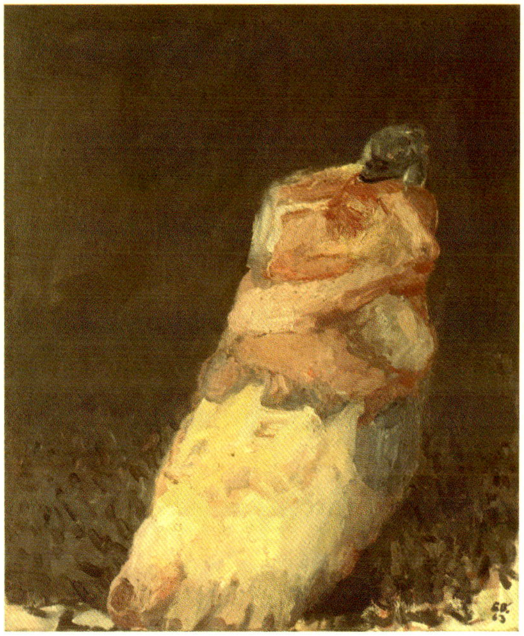

037 **Georg Baselitz**
P.D. Fuß – Kelte, 1963
(P.D. Foot – Celt)

Öl auf Leinwand /
oil on canvas
100 x 82,2 cm
Sammlung Crex, Zürich

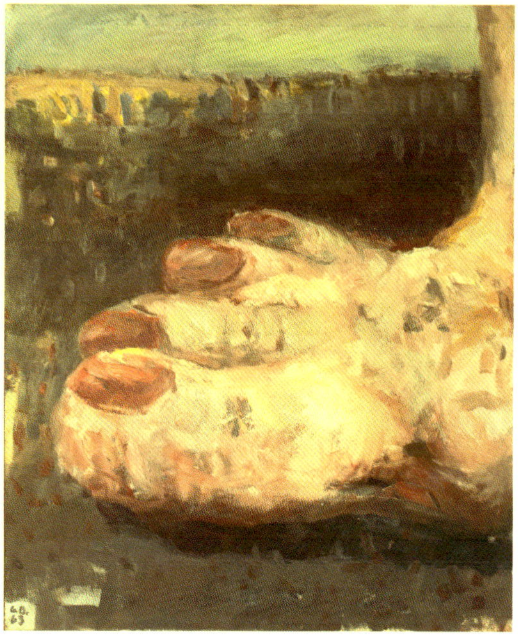

auch den Utopien des Modernismus eine Absage zu erteilen. Guy Debord hingegen sollte à la longue überhaupt zu dem Schluss kommen, dass für das Kunstwerk als von der Lebenspraxis getrennte Hervorbringung keine Notwendigkeit mehr bestehe, sobald die Menschen selbstbestimmt und damit kreativ ihr eigenes Leben gestalten würden.

Malen zur Zeit der Ächtung der Malerei – Bad Painting in den 1960er- und 1970er-Jahren

In den 1960er- und 1970er-Jahren als einer Hochphase der Ächtung der Malerei durch weite Teile der damals dominanten Avantgarden war allein schon die Entscheidung zu malen „bad" oder ein Akt des Widerstandes, je nachdem von welchem Blickwinkel aus man es betrachtet. Jene Künstler, die – wie in Deutschland Georg Baselitz, Sigmar Polke, Gerhard Richter, Jörg Immendorff oder A. R. Penck – damals der Malerei und im Speziellen einer figurativen oder gar Subjektivität zulassenden treu blieben, waren in besonderer Weise dem Vorwurf ausgesetzt, Traditionalisten zu sein, und dementsprechend verschärft gefordert, sich zu positionieren – eine Situation, die zu verschiedenen Strategien eines Bad Painting führte.

Für Georg Baselitz, der Ende der 1950er-Jahre den Kunstdiktaten des kommunistischen Deutschlands durch Übersiedlung in den Westen eben erst entkommen war, kam es in keinster Weise infrage, sich wieder einem Diktat zu unterwerfen, als welches er zunächst die Ächtung gegenständlicher Malerei und später das Malverbot der westlichen Avantgarden der 1960er-Jahre empfand. Der Kampf gegen die Diktate von Ost und West führt bezeichnenderweise zur Entscheidung für das bewusst schlechte Malen:„Ich konnte wohl nicht anders. Als junger Mann wollte ich mit Mist, mit Schlamm, mit Unfarben, mit Schwarz-Weiß wirklich schlechte Bilder machen, die auffallen. [...] Also [...] gegen die schönen Dinge etwas setzen. Das können sie eigentlich nur vehement, mit Aggression und mit heftigem Widerspruch. Also mit allen schlechten Sachen."[36]

Mit Farben, die er aus den vom Boden aufgesammelten Farbresten seiner Mitstudenten zusammengemischt hat,[37] malt er unter Geringschätzung von Komposition und Harmonie Bilder mit tabubrechend „bösen" Inhalten: elendig erscheinende Figuren, darunter onanierende Jungen sowie

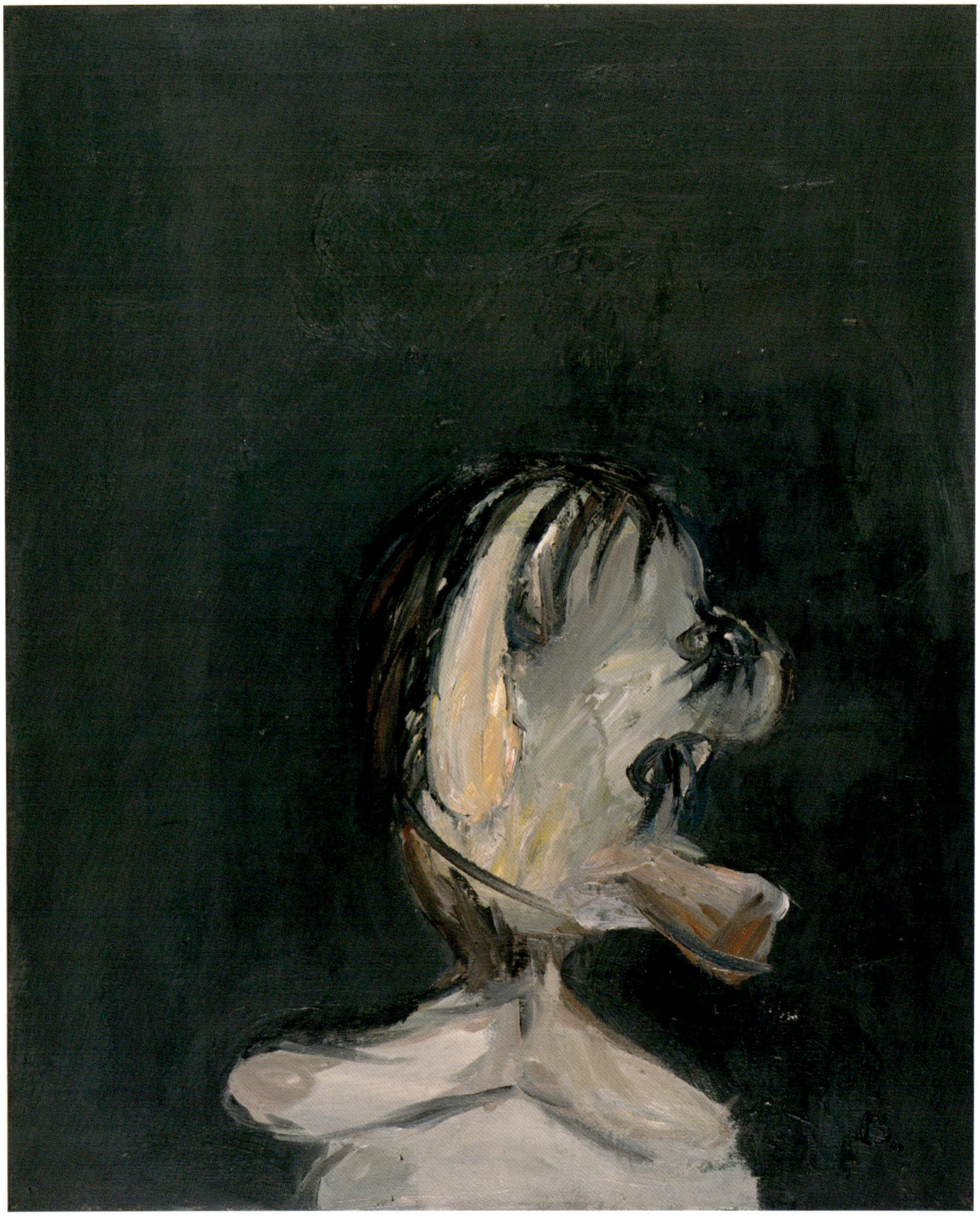

038
Georg Baselitz
Der Kummerkopf, 1962
(Sorrow Head)
Öl auf Leinwand /
oil on canvas
100 x 80 cm
Privatsammlung /
Private Collection, Berlin

Himself a successful practitioner of Abstract Expressionism, the second half of the 1960s saw him abandon it, and thus his own "signature style," turning instead to an almost comic-like, idiosyncratically figurative mode of painting. These pictures, not always easy to decipher at first glance and often disturbing, show objects and body parts in isolation or in peculiar clusters or tangles [ILL·002·040], as well as mostly strange situations and scenes, including explicit references to the dark sides of (American) society, like people in Ku Klux Klan hoods. And significantly, they also repeatedly address the role and possibilities of painting via the figure of the painter and his utensils.

For Guston, abstraction, celebrated as the epitome of the humanist ideal of freedom, with all its claims and its purism, had become a prison: "I got sick and tired of that purity! I wanted to

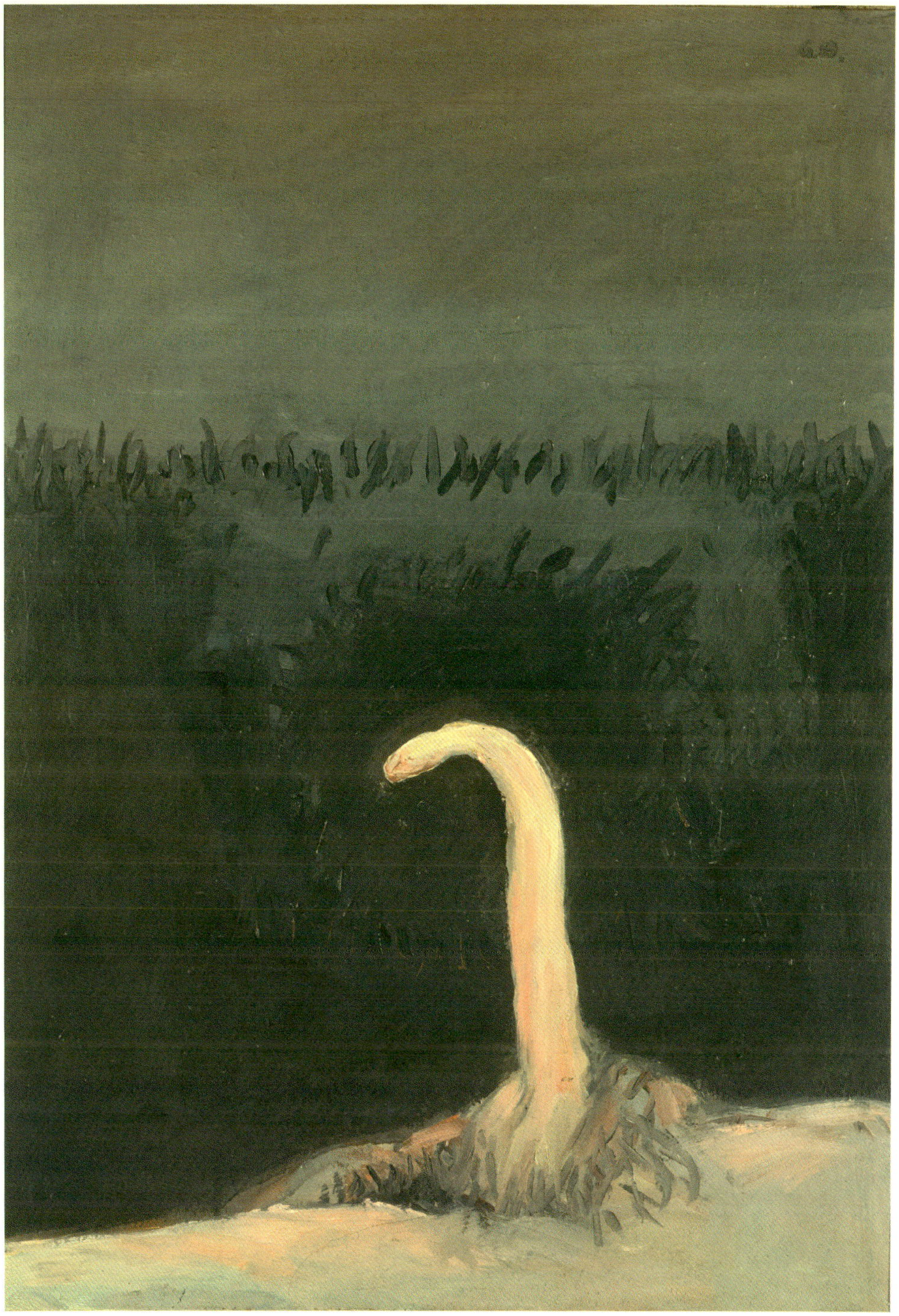

039 **Georg Baselitz**
P.D. Stengel, 1963 (P.D. Stem)
Öl auf Leinwand / oil on canvas
130 x 90 cm
Sammlung Schmidt-Drenhaus,
Köln • Dresden

Männer mit überdimensionierten Penissen, isoliert stehende, geknickte Penisse, Frauen mit Hängebusen, Menschen, die wie Monster wirken und deren Nasen oder Ohren oft als Penisse lesbar sind [ABB·006·034-039]. Es verwundert nicht, dass zwei dieser Bilder im prüden Nachkriegsdeutschland bei einer Ausstellung beschlagnahmt wurden.

Auch Sigmar Polke und Gerhard Richter – die übrigens beide wie Baselitz aus dem Osten in den Westen übersiedelt beziehungsweise geflohen sind – verweigern ihre Teilnahme an der allgemeinen Ablehnung der Malerei, wobei ihre daraus resultierenden „Bad"-Strategien wesentlich konzeptueller und teilweise auch analytischer sind. Polkes zynisch-ironische Dekonstruktion der

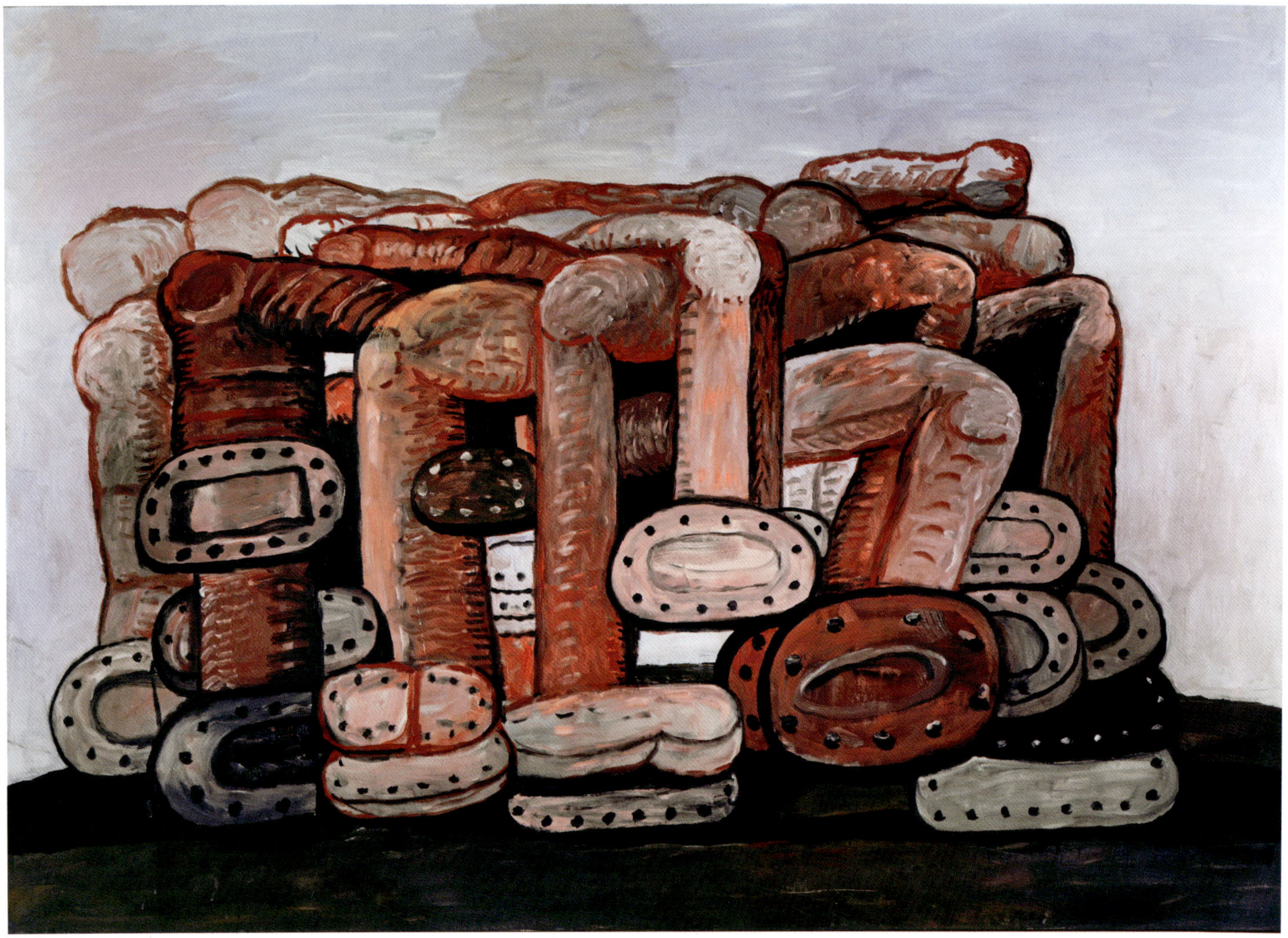

040 **Philip Guston**
Monument, 1976
Öl auf Leinwand / oil on canvas
203,2 x 279,4 cm
Tate London, erworben mit Unterstützung des / purchased with assistance of American Fund

tell stories"[40]—an explanation often given by American Bad Painters in particular. Although in a different form, this "purity" also characterized (with very few exceptions) the dominant American avant-gardes of the 1960s like Pop and Minimal art, which were generally less radical in their rejection of panel pictures and painting than their European counterparts. "Regarding the general situation in art today [...] it is so insured against failure, against bad painting, against risking. But something must be wrong somewhere, because there is this overwhelming success and at the same time this overwhelming apathy. [...] We don't really recognize the extent to which we are victims of the institutionalized art which is all around us,"[41] said Guston in 1978 in a lecture, going on to quote an ironic address by Isaak Babel to the Union of Soviet Writers: "'The party and the government have given us everything but

heroischen Ansprüche der Moderne ist etwa jener nicht unverwandt, die seinerzeit Picabia in seinen „Monstres" praktiziert hatte. In Bildern wie *Moderne Kunst* [ABB·083·017] bekundet er seine Aversion gegen Ideologien und Stilbildungen respektive die Koppelung der beiden durch persiflierendes Zusammenwürfeln „typischer" Elemente aus den Formensprachen der Moderne.

Und selbst der in seinem Schaffen immer viel unmittelbarer politisch engagierte Jörg Immendorff bleibt beim traditionellen Medium der Malerei, wenn er seine Skepsis darüber zum Ausdruck bringen will, was diese – vor allem in politisch-sozialer Hinsicht – bewirken kann. „Hört auf zu malen" schreibt er 1966 auf eines seiner Bilder [ABB·110] und beschimpft so die Malerei als Gebrauchsartikel und Statussymbol der Bourgeoisie, das letztlich keine effektive kritische Wirkung entfalten kann – ohne aber auch nur im Geringsten selbst daran zu denken, diesem Medium den Rücken zu kehren. Von Beuys wurde er dafür verspottet, dass er seine Kritik an der Malerei immer wieder im Medium der Malerei vorgetragen hat.[38] Er selbst sieht es positiv, als konstruktive Strategie im Sinne eines Bad Painting, das der Kunst generell kritisch gegenübersteht und gleichermaßen an den Wirkungsmöglichkeiten aktionistischer Kunstformen, für die Beuys steht, zweifelt: „[...] für mich war die Malerei ja immer ein schizophrenes Unterfangen. Gleichzeitig eine Kunstform installieren mit dem Aspekt des Bekämpfens dieser Kunstform, da steckt schon was drinnen, was ich immer die konstruktive Schizophrenie nenne."[39]

In Amerika ist Philip Guston jener prominente Maler, der sich als Erster gegen die „Korrektheitsgebote" der damals „offiziellen" Moderne aufgelehnt hat – in seinem Fall noch dazu gegen den abstrakten Expressionismus, der als erste große eigenständige und international erfolgreiche Manifestation amerikanischen Kunstschaffens gefeiert und, wie man heute weiß, im Kalten Krieg der Ideologien von Ost und West sogar realpolitisch implementiert wurde. Mit seinem lange geächteten und bezeichnenderweise in den 1980er-Jahren wiederentdeckten Spätwerk wird er seither von den jungen Malern in ähnlicher Weise als eine Vaterfigur des Bad Painting gefeiert wie Picabia oder Jorn in Europa.

Selbst ein erfolgreicher Vertreter des abstrakten Expressionismus, wendet er sich in der zweiten Hälfte der 1960er-Jahre radikal von diesem – und damit auch von seinem eigenen „signature style" – ab, zugunsten einer fast comichaften, idiosynkratisch-figürlichen Malerei. Seine auf den ersten Blick nicht immer leicht entzifferbaren und vielfach verstörenden Bilder zeigen Gegenstände und Körperteile in Vereinzelung oder in eigenartigen Anhäufungen beziehungsweise Verknotungen [ABB·002·040] sowie meist befremdliche Situationen und Szenen, darunter ganz explizite Verweise auf die Schattenseiten und Abgründe der (amerikanischen) Gesellschaft, wie Menschen in Ku-Klux-Klan-Kapuzen. Und bezeichnenderweise thematisieren sie auch immer wieder Rolle und Möglichkeiten der Malerei anhand der Figur des Malers und seiner Utensilien.

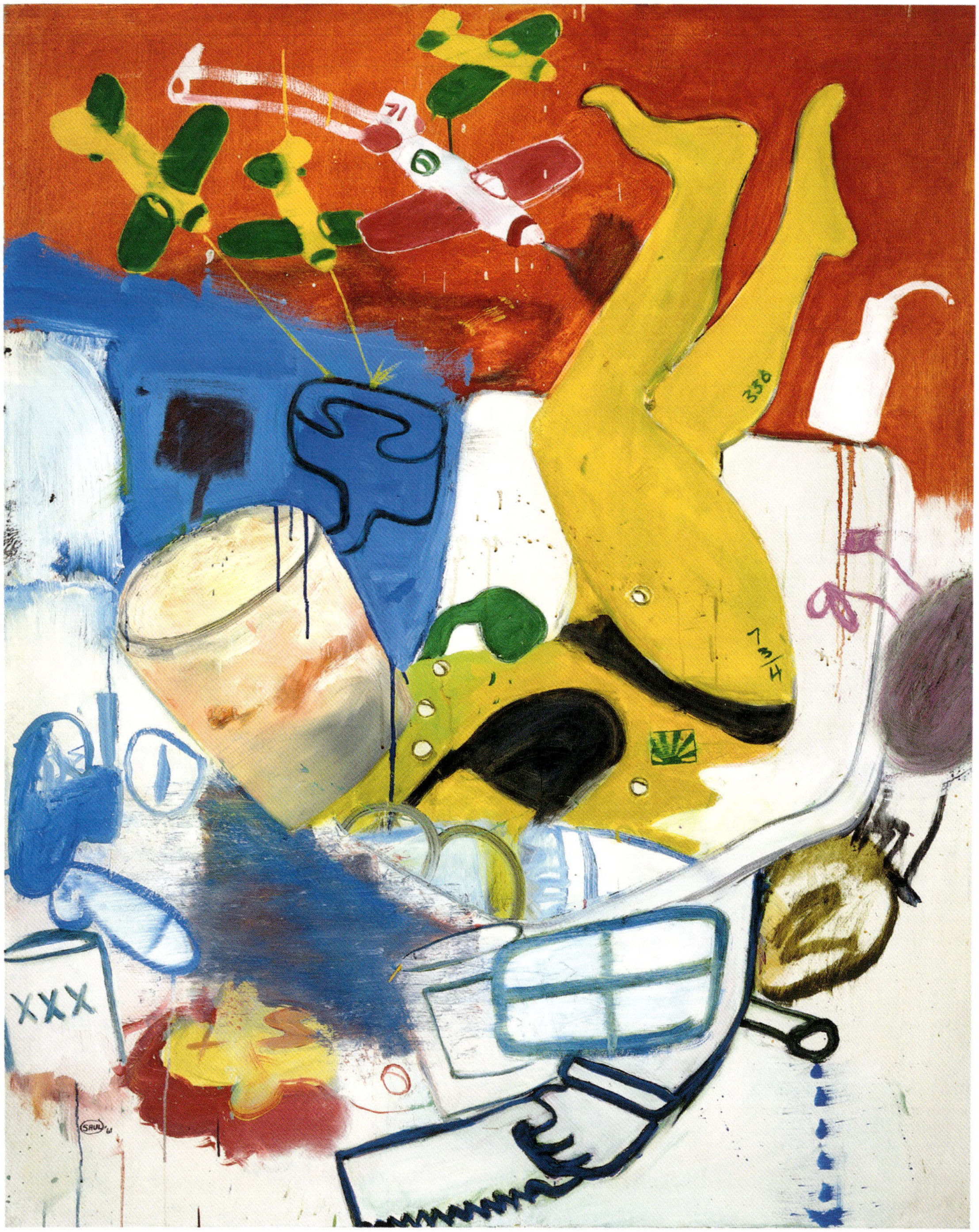

041
Peter Saul
Tokyo Rose, 1961
(Rose von Tokio)

Öl auf Leinwand /
oil on canvas
140 x 109 cm
BAM, Collection de la Communauté française de Belgique, Mons, Donation Maurice Duvivier

have deprived us of one privilege. A very important privilege, comrades […], that of writing badly.'" And he added: "Isn't that wonderful? […] Doesn't anybody want to paint badly?"[42]

Guston's first exhibition of his new pictures—in 1970 at Marlborough Gallery in New York—was a total failure, and Guston was despised as a painter for the rest of his life. But for him it was "such a relief not to have anything to do with modern art. It felt as if a big boulder had been taken off my shoulders."[43]

Barely noticed by a wider art public, Peter Saul had begun before Guston to question the values of American art and society with their puritanical striving for "purity," observing that "the

Die als Inbegriff des humanistischen Freiheitsideals gefeierte Abstraktion mit all ihren Ansprüchen und Reinheitsgeboten war für Guston zum Gefängnis geworden: „Diese Reinheit widerte mich an! Ich wollte Geschichten erzählen“[40] – eine Begründung, die insbesondere die amerikanischen Bad Painters sehr oft als Motiv nennen sollten. Wenngleich in anderer Form prägte jene „Reinheit“ ja – von wenigen Ausnahmen abgesehen – auch die dominanten amerikanischen Avantgarden der 1960er-Jahre wie Pop- und Minimal Art, die im Prinzip das Tafelbild und auch die Malerei weniger radikal ablehnten, als dies zeitgleich in Europa der Fall war. „Was generell die Situation in der Kunst heute betrifft [...], sie ist so abgesichert gegen Fehlschläge, gegen schlechtes Malen, gegen Risiken. Aber irgendetwas muss da irgendwo falsch sein, weil es einerseits diesen überwältigenden Erfolg gibt und gleichzeitig diese überwältigende Teilnahmslosigkeit. [...] Uns ist ja gar nicht bewusst, in welchem Ausmaß wir Opfer dieser institutionalisierten Kunst rund um uns sind“,[41] sagt Philip Guston 1978 in einem Vortrag und zitiert weiters eine ironische Ansprache von Isaak Babel vor der sowjetischen Schriftstellervereinigung: „‚Die Partei und die Regierung haben uns alles gegeben, aber sie haben uns eines Privileges beraubt. Eines sehr wichtigen Privileges, Genossen [...], nämlich schlecht zu schreiben.‘“ Und er fügt hinzu: „Ist das nicht wunderbar? [...] Will nicht jemand schlecht malen?“[42]

Gustons erste Ausstellung seiner neuen Bilder – 1970 in der Marlborough Gallery in New York – war ein totaler Misserfolg, und Guston sollte für den Rest seines Lebens als Maler geächtet sein. Für ihn aber war es „so eine Erleichterung, nichts mit moderner Kunst zu tun zu haben. Es war, als hätte man eine große Last von meinen Schultern genommen.“[43]

Von einer breiteren Kunstöffentlichkeit lange kaum wahrgenommen, hatte Peter Saul schon vor Guston begonnen, das vom puritanisches Streben nach „Reinheit“ geprägte Wertesystem der amerikanischen Kunst und Gesellschaft infrage zu stellen: „Die Vereinigten Staaten waren immer auf ‚good‘ fokussiert.“[44] Schon Anfang der 1960er-Jahre – als er im Übrigen aus privaten Gründen in Paris lebte – entwickelte er einen äußerst idiosynkratischen Stil, in dem er seine bitterböse Kritik an Konsumgesellschaft und puritanischer Heuchelei formulierte [ABB·041·042], in etwa zeitgleich mit Georg Baselitz’ frühen bösen Bildern. Philip Guston hat Sauls frühe Ausstellungen besucht und soll von dessen Unorthodoxie wesentliche Impulse für seinen Bruch mit dem abstrakten Expressionismus erhalten haben.

Etwa zur gleichen Zeit, als Guston mit dem abstrakten Expressionismus bricht, entstehen Neil Jenneys Bad Paintings. Eine Generation jünger als Guston, ist jene dominierende und in seinen Augen versteinerte respektive „vorhersehbare“[45] Avantgarde, gegen die er opponiert, nicht mehr der abstrakte Expressionismus, sondern vor allem „hard-edged color-field painting“ beziehungsweise die minimalistische Skulptur, die er in seinen Art-College-Jahren selbst noch praktiziert hatte.[46] Als er sich im Dezember 1968[47] entschließt, figürlich zu malen – was damals absolut nicht angesagt war –, folgt er wie Guston einem Bedürfnis nach einer Wiederanbindung an konkrete Inhalte.

United States have always focused on 'good.'"[44] In the early 1960s (by which time he was living in Paris for private reasons), he had already developed a highly individual idiom in which he formulated his mordant critique of consumer society and puritanical hypocrisy [ILL·041·042], at roughly the same time that Georg Baselitz was painting his early "bad" pictures. Philip Guston visited Saul's early exhibitions and reportedly derived important stimuli from the latter's unorthodox approach for his own break with Abstract Expressionism.

Neil Jenney's Bad Paintings date from the late 1960s, which is about the same time Guston abandoned his successful signature style. A generation younger, the dominant and (as he saw it) ossified or "predictable"[45] avant-garde against which Jenney rebelled was no longer Abstract Expressionism but rather the hard-edged color-field painting and Minimalist sculpture that he had practiced himself in his art college years.[46] When he decided in December 1968[47] to take up figurative painting—which at the time was far from the done thing—he was driven, like Guston, by a desire to reconnect with specific content.

Against extremely reduced backgrounds, painted in crude brushstrokes with clichéd color coding—green for fields and woods, brown for earth, blue for water—Jenney set simple figures and objects in relation to one another, leaving it up to the viewer to exploit the potential for often highly emotional content that lies in these combinations. He himself lays no traces, withdrawing instead to a position of "literalness." An integral part of these works are their titles, which simply name either the figures and objects—*Girl and Doll* [ILL·044], *Man and Mirage* [ILL·043], *Husband and Wife*—or elementary emotional and moral relations—*Admonition and Inexperience*, *Apprehension and Approval*, *Aggression and Reinforcement*. Initially, Jenney wrote these titles on labels hung next to the pictures, and later on self-adhesive strips that he attached directly onto the lower areas of the painted surface, before deciding in 1971 to give his pictures heavy black frames on which he then placed the titles.[48]

In his own way, then, Jenney transfers the concept of "literalness" from the abstractness of Minimal Art into figurative motifs that are selected to rule out any abstract or unemotional reading. This, again, points to a critique of the dogmas and claims of an avant-garde which, in the case of Minimal art, postulates the utopia of a Platonic abstractness and non-referentiality that in practical terms appears neither tenable nor relevant, but which is nonetheless understood as a model for a new and ideal social order. Like the Minimalists, Jenney saw his art as a philosophical activity—"the true artist is a philosophical craftsman"[49]—but one which, within the framework of a classical inquiry into the "ideas of truth and good,"[50] was to deal with concrete lived reality and which thus needed to be realistic: "Art is a social science."[51] Whereas Minimal art postulated abstract theories without addressing their untenability or their unfitness for transfer into the realm of the concrete, Jenney's pictures highlight these irreconcilable contradictions, the discrepancy between abstract relations and individual perception of specific cases. To achieve this, he turns to painting as a medium accused of antiquated

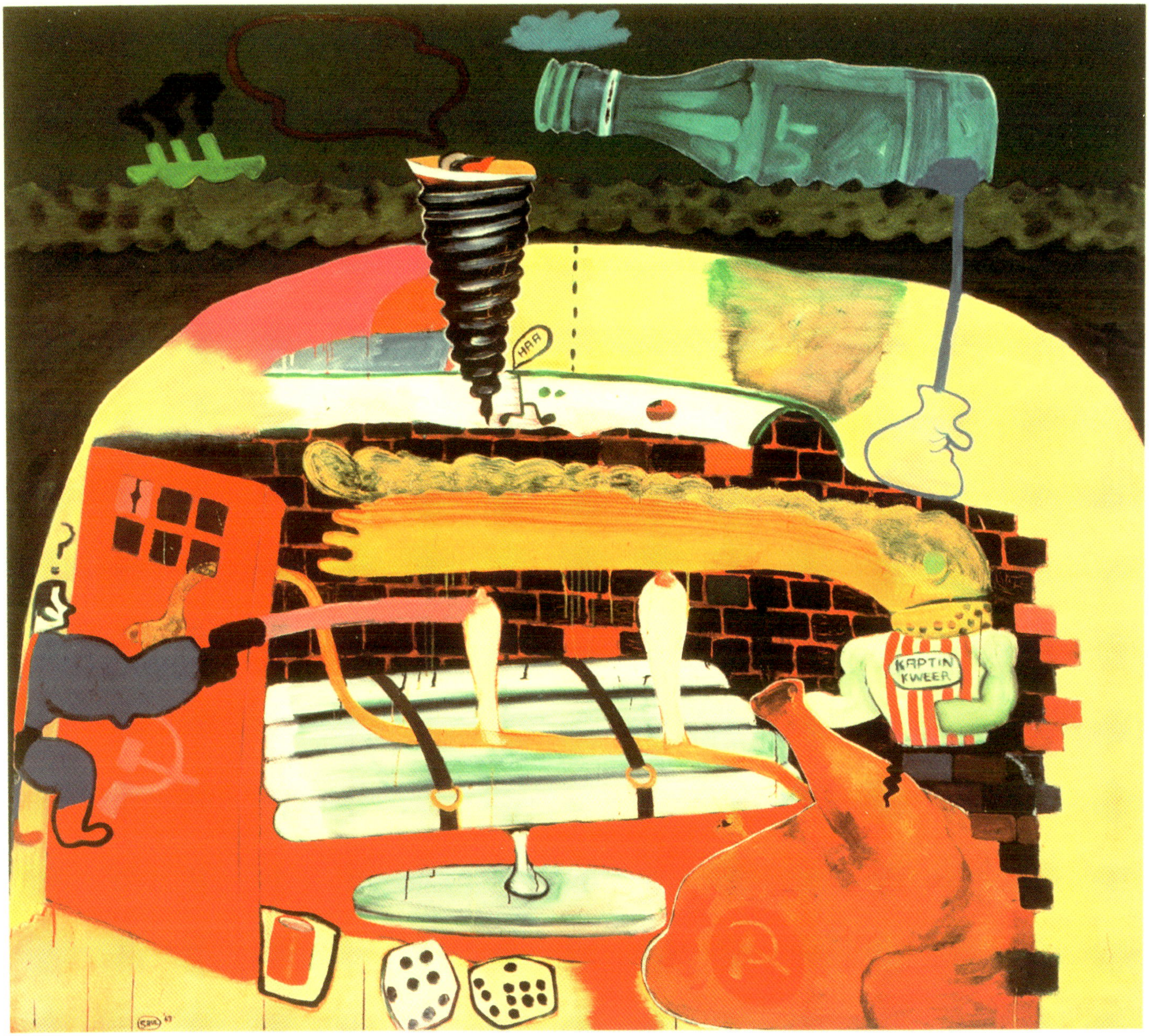

042 **Peter Saul**
Communist Hideout, 1963
(Kommunistisches Versteck)
Öl auf Leinwand / oil on canvas
160 x 120 cm
Museum Ludwig, Köln

Vor sehr reduzierte, durch grobe Pinselstriche klischeehaft farblich markierte Hintergründe – Grün für Wiese und Wald, Braun für Erde, Blau für Wasser – stellt Jenney einfache Figuren und Objekte zueinander in Relation und überlässt es dem Betrachter, das in seinen Kombinationen liegende Potenzial an oft hochemotioneller Inhaltlichkeit auszuschöpfen. Er selbst legt keine Spuren, sondern zieht sich auf die Position der „literalness“ zurück. Grundlegende Bestandteile dieser Bilder sind Titel, die entweder lediglich die Figuren und Objekte – wie *Girl and Doll* [ABB·044], *Man and Mirage* [ABB·043] oder *Husband and Wife* – benennen oder elementare emotionale wie moralische Relationen – *Admonition and Inexperience*, *Apprehension and Approval* oder *Aggression and Reinforcement*. Jenney schrieb diese zunächst auf neben die Bilder gehängte Schilder und später auf

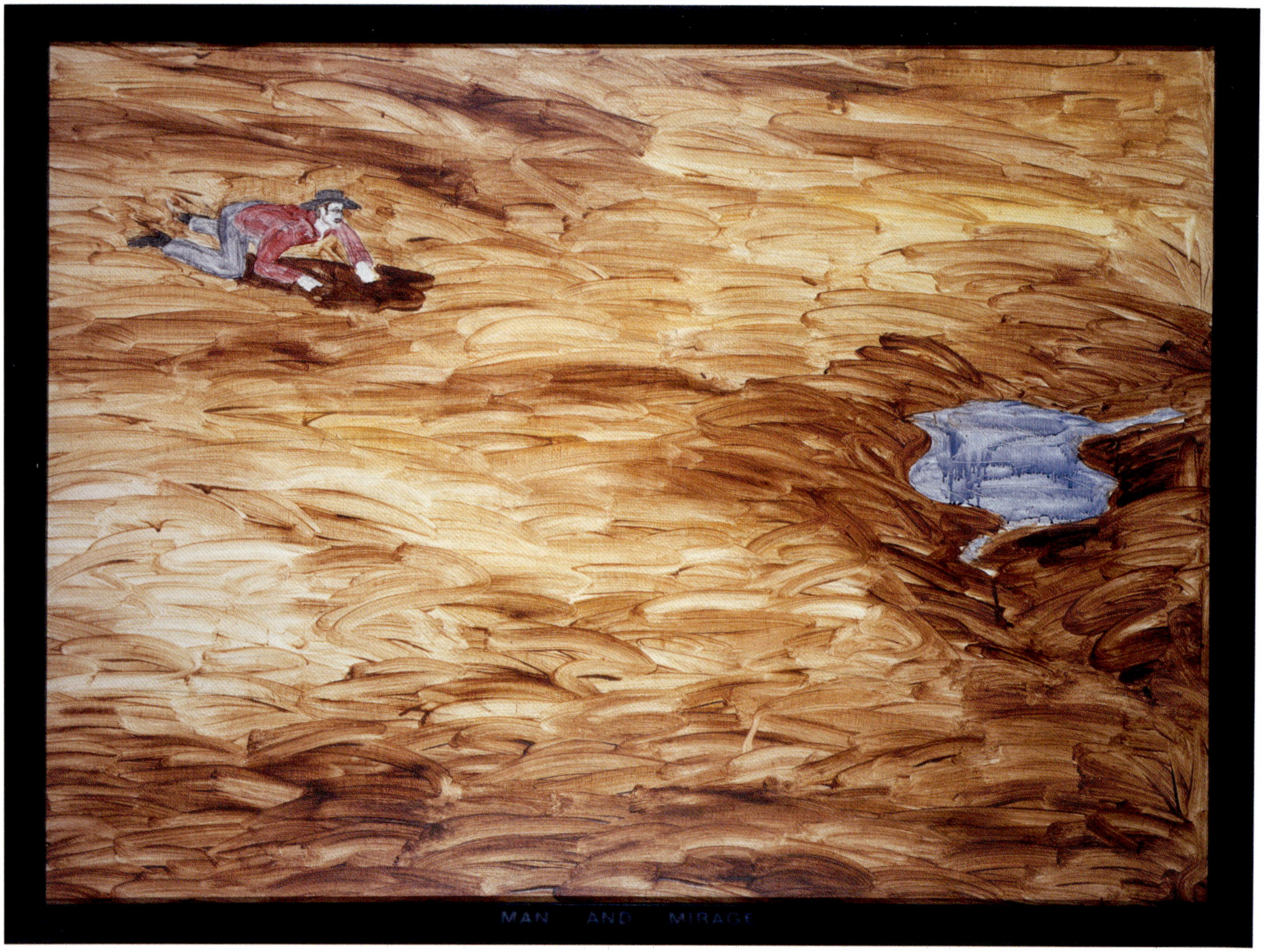

043 **Neil Jenney**
Man and Mirage, 1969 (Mann und Fata Morgana)
Öl auf Leinwand, gerahmt / oil on canvas, framed
147,5 x 193 cm
Privatsammlung / Private Collection

044 **Neil Jenney**
Girl and Doll, 1969 (Mädchen und Puppe)
Acryl auf Leinwand, gerahmt /
acrylic on canvas, framed 147,5 x 193 cm
Privatsammlung / Private Collection

subjectivism, as he considers demands for purity and the scorning of signature styles irrelevant and unacceptable. On the other hand, what he termed his "unconcerned" approach to painting was intended to avoid the trap of becoming devoted to painterly "refinement" or even Expressionism. His pictures from the years 1969 and 1970, the "unconcerned" works that he later renamed as his "Bad Paintings," are characterized by their preliminary sketching on the canvas remaining visible in the finished work, their deliberately course brushwork, and their emphatically simple color schemes coupled with an equally simple portrayal of figures and objects. Interestingly, Jenney has also reflected on the ultimate irrelevance of the distinction between realism and abstraction: "There is actually no distinction between abstraction and realism. All realism must resolve abstract complications, because you are

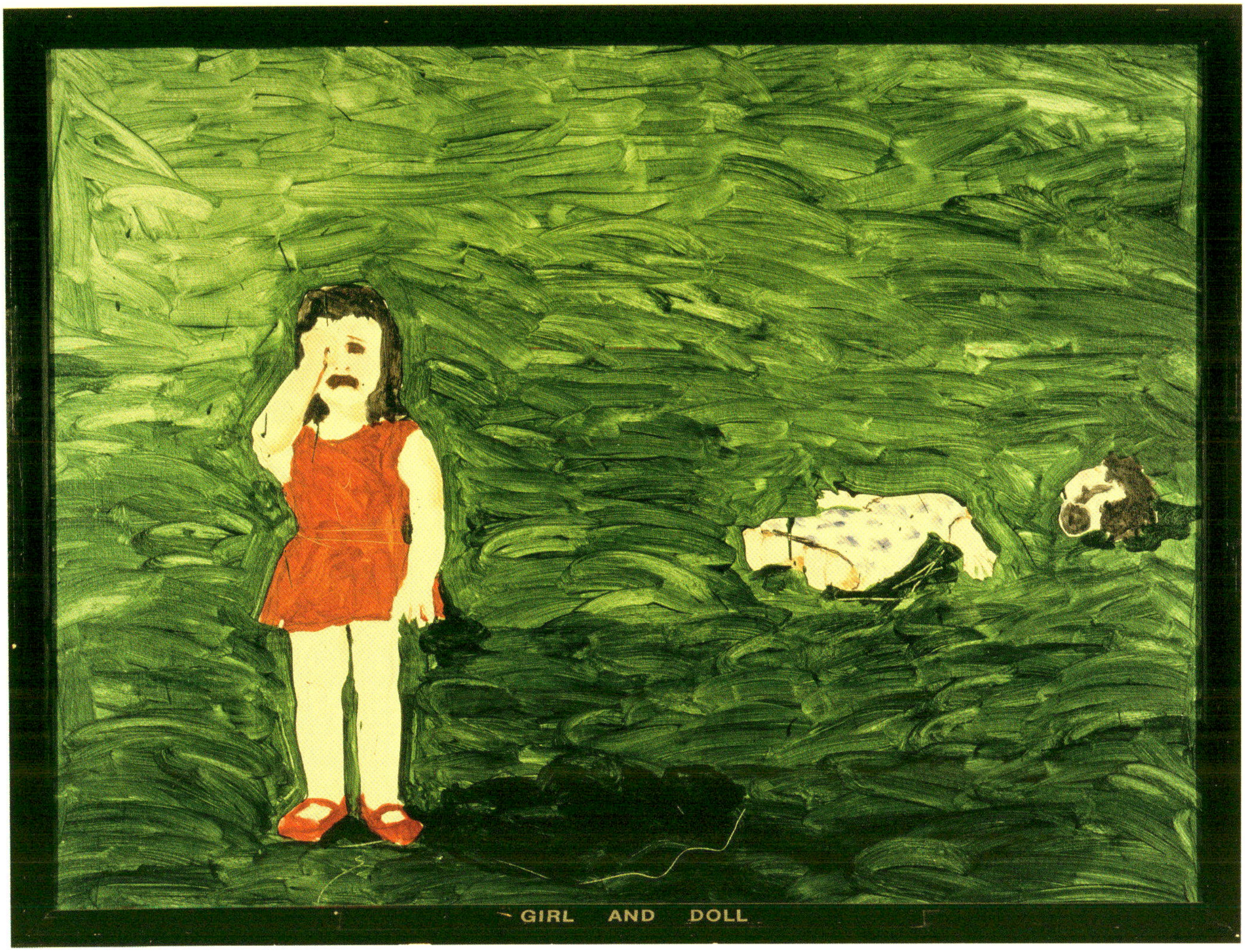

Klebestreifen, die er am unteren Rand sogar direkt im Bild befestigte, bevor er sich 1971 entschloss, seine Bilder mit massiven schwarzen Holzrahmen zu versehen, auf die er auch die Titel setzte.[48]

Auf seine Weise überträgt also Jenney das Konzept der „literalness" von der Abstraktheit des Minimal in gegenständliche Sujets, die so ausgewählt sind, dass sie sicher keine abstrakt-unemotionale Lesart zulassen. Man kann daran wieder eine Kritik an den Ansprüchen und Dogmen einer Avantgarde festmachen, die im Falle der Minimal Art die Utopie einer platonischen Abstraktheit und Referenzlosigkeit postuliert, die in der Praxis weder erfüllbar ist noch relevant erscheint, aber dennoch als Modell für eine neue und ideale Gesellschaftsordnung verstanden wird. Wie die Minimalisten begreift auch Jenney seine Kunst als philosophische Aktivität – „der wahre Künstler ist ein philosophischer Handwerker"[49] –, die sich aber im Rahmen der klassischen Fragen nach der „Wahrheit und dem Guten"[50] mit der konkreten Lebensrealität auseinander zu setzen und daher realistisch zu sein habe: „Kunst ist eine Sozialwissenschaft."[51] Während die Minimal Art abstrakte Thesen postuliert, deren Uneinlösbarkeit und vor allem Unübertragbarkeit in den konkreten Bereich sie nicht thematisiert, stellt Jenney gerade die unüberbrückbaren Widersprüche, also die Diskrepanz zwischen abstrakten Relationen und der individuellen Wahrnehmung konkreter Einzelfälle im Bild zur Schau. Er greift dafür zur Malerei als einem des antiquierten Subjektivismus bezichtigten Medium, da ihm Reinheitsgebote wie die Verpönung einer subjektiven Handschrift irrelevant und unakzeptabel erscheinen. Andererseits will er aber durch eine, wie er zunächst sagt, „unconcerned", also unbekümmert-

involved with space and balance and harmony. Realism is a higher art form because it is more precise—it not only solves all abstract concerns, but it involves precise philosophical interpretation."[52]

As early as 1971, however, he dropped his "unconcerned" style and turned instead to the "Masterful Series," which he later also referred to as "concerned" or "good style."[53] Here, he actually emphasized the importance of skilled execution, having realized "1) that even if I produced the worst paintings possible, they would not be good enough, and 2) that Idealism is unavoidable."[54] Interestingly, and characteristically, this led him back to an approach directly opposed to the avant-gardisms of the twentieth century and one often found in Bad Painting, i.e., the use of illusionistic techniques[55] and the associated positioning of his painting in the content of the entire history of the medium,[56] as well as the use of Old Masterly techniques.[57]

"Bad" Painting—an exhibition on the eve of the painting hype of the 1980s

In early 1978, it was Jenney's "unconcerned paintings" that curator Marcia Tucker selected for her exhibition *"Bad" Painting* at New York's New Museum, and it was only then that Jenney renamed this group of works "Bad Paintings."

As the organizer of this exhibition, Marcia Tucker was the first to use the term from the position of curators and theorists—in her case with "bad" in inverted commas. Her show included only American artists who had not only resisted the dictates of the avant-gardes of the 1960s and 1970s by painting figuratively in highly personal idioms, but who generally rejected all canons of painting and refused to develop a signature style. "It is figurative work that defies, either deliberately or by virtue of disinterest, the classic canons of good taste, draftsmanship, acceptable source material, rendering or illusionistic representation."[58] Many of the featured works also criticized puritanical American values and addressed taboos.

Although its scope was far narrower in terms of both time and place, the exhibition thus addressed concerns that are not unrelated to the current MUMOK show. Of the fourteen featured artists,[59] few went on to become well-known, but through them Marcia Tucker pointed very early on to issues and positions that were to be of crucial importance to a generation of artists that emerged shortly thereafter. With hindsight, her exhibition foreshadowed the renewed vigor and acceptance of (especially figurative) painting in the 1980s, as well as this period's questioning of the avant-gardes' belief in progress and the acceptance of artistic pluralism.

After the end of the avant-gardes

In the late 1970s and early 1980s, as the avant-gardes came to an end, a whole generation of young artists began to actively oppose what they saw as the diluted and bloodless mainly performative and conceptual tendencies of the 1960s and 1970s, turning instead to a medium that had been widely scorned during these decades—painting. These artists began to paint figuratively, giving

gleichgültige Malweise der Falle einer Hingabe an ein malerisches „refinement" oder gar einen Expressionismus entgehen. Seine Bilder der Jahre 1969 und 1970, die er später auch seine „Bad Paintings" nennen sollte, zeichnen sich durch eine im Endprodukt sichtbar bleibende Vorzeichnung auf der Leinwand, eine bewusst grobe Pinselführung sowie eine betont einfache Farbgebung und eine ebenso bewusst simple Darstellung der Figuren und Objekte aus. Bezeichnenderweise reflektiert Jenney auch die letztliche Irrelevanz der Unterscheidung zwischen Realismus und Abstraktion. „Es gibt eigentlich keinen Unterschied zwischen Abstraktion und Realismus. Jeglicher Realismus muss abstrakte Probleme lösen, weil man mit Raum, Balance und Harmonie zu tun hat. Der Realismus ist eine höhere Kunstform, weil er präziser ist – er löst nicht nur alle abstrakten Angelegenheiten, sondern bedingt auch präzise philosophische Interpretation."[52]

Seine „unconcerned" Malweise gab er allerdings schon 1971 wieder auf zugunsten seiner „Masterful Series", die er später auch „concerned" oder „good style" nannte.[53] In dieser legte er sogar besonderen Wert auf handwerkliche Ausführung, nachdem ihm bewusst geworden war, „1. dass, selbst wenn ich die schlechtestmöglichen Bilder produzierte, sie nicht gut genug wären; und 2. dass Idealismus unvermeidbar ist".[54] Interessanter- und bezeichnenderweise sollte ihn dies aber unter anderem wieder zu einem den Avantgardismen des 20. Jahrhunderts entgegengesetzten und im Bad Painting oft anzutreffenden Verhalten führen, nämlich zur Entscheidung für illusionistische Malweisen[55] und der damit verbundenen Verortung seiner Malerei im Kontext der gesamten Geschichte der Malerei[56] wie auch zum Einsatz altmeisterlicher Techniken[57].

"Bad" Painting – eine Ausstellung am Vorabend des Malereihypes der 1980er-Jahre

Es waren Jenneys „unconcerned paintings", die die Kuratorin Marcia Tucker für ihre Anfang 1978 im New Museum in New York gezeigte Ausstellung *"Bad" Painting* wählen sollte, und Jenney hat diese Werkgruppe auch erst aus diesem Anlass in „Bad Paintings" umbenannt.

Marcia Tucker verwendet den Begriff „Bad Painting" also erstmals von theoretischer beziehungsweise kuratorischer Seite her an prominenter Stelle – in ihrem Falle mit „bad" in Anführungszeichen. In ihrer Ausstellung zeigte sie ausschließlich amerikanische Künstler, die sich nicht nur den Diktaten der Avantgarden der 1960er- und 1970er-Jahre widersetzt hatten, indem sie in sehr individuellen Idiomen figurativ malten, sondern überhaupt die Unterordnung unter Kanons der Malerei ablehnten und sich auch der Ausbildung eines „signature style" verweigerten. „Es sind figurative Arbeiten, die sich entweder bewusst oder aus Desinteresse an den klassischen Kanons von gutem Geschmack, Zeichenkunst, akzeptablem Quellenmaterial, Gestaltung oder illusionistischer Darstellung hinwegsetzen."[58] Viele der gezeigten Werke üben auch Kritik an amerikanisch-puritanischen Wertvorstellungen beziehungsweise sprechen Tabus an.

Wenngleich in einem zeitlich wie räumlich wesentlich engeren Rahmen verfolgte diese Schau also bereits Überlegungen, die jenen der Ausstellung im MUMOK nicht unverwandt sind.

free rein to their subjectivity and positioning themselves within the broader context of the history of painting.

Within this current, however, there soon emerged artists who rejected this "wild" and often casually irreverent approach (with its emphasis on the sensual pleasure of painting and its references to traditions), but without wishing to reject painting itself. Instead, they approached this medium in an attitude of critically reflecting its potential, thus again deploying the strategy of a "critique of painting in the medium of painting."[60] Consequently, they too found themselves in the situation of fighting on several fronts—not just against the traditionalists and the preceding generations, but also against the type of painting produced by certain of their contemporaries, which they saw as insufficiently reflected while considering itself progressive and, of course, also against the ever present threat of getting stuck in a rut themselves. An often analytically deconstructive approach became an essential strain of Bad Painting.

A striking case in point is the work of German painter Albert Oehlen who, from the late 1970s and into the 1980s, had close artistic ties with Werner Büttner and Martin Kippenberger. A perfect example of their deconstructive approach and the resulting conclusions is the long text co-authored by the three artists in the catalog for their joint exhibition *Wahrheit ist Arbeit* (Truth Is Work, 1984) at the Folkwang Museum in Essen. In ironic terms, it articulates a critical rejection of all models for establishing truth in philosophy, art, and society, seeing "failure" and the productive use of contradictions and mistakes as the only viable options.[61]

Of the three, it is Albert Oehlen who has pursued this deconstructive approach with the greatest rigor in painting, making its inevitable failure manifest itself in his pictures: "Because we now refuse to deny the direct dependence and responsibility of art vis-à-vis reality, and on the other hand see no chance for art as we know it to have an effect, there is only one possibility left: failure."[62]

Among others, he addresses, in an ironic and sometimes pseudo-analytically systematic form the functioning of the traditional means of painting and their capacity for generating meaning, focusing in particular on color, which throughout the history of painting has always been considered the most "ungraspable" and incomprehensible means at the artist's disposal and which has accordingly often been endowed with mystico-spiritual connotations. In his "Color Theory" cycles painted in the mid 1980s, Oehlen addresses the question of color's potential and its possible systematics, in some cases via provocatively chosen subject matter including biblical dignitaries or motifs linked to problematic aspects of German history, painting among others portraits of Adolf Hitler, or the *Hitlerbrücke in Krefeld* (Hitler Bridge in Krefeld) in the three primary colors red, yellow, and blue. The conclusion he draws is pragmatic and free of illusions: "Pictures consist to a large extent of color/paint," which however "cannot be trusted." One can only "believe [...] what's written on the tube."[63] "Just as the word, either spoken or written, stands in no real relation to the object it is supposed to denote, so

Von den 14 gezeigten Künstlern[59] haben allerdings nur wenige Bekanntheit erlangt. Marcia Tucker verwies anhand dieser Künstler aber schon zu einem sehr frühen Zeitpunkt auf Fragestellungen und Haltungen, die für die kurz danach auf den Plan tretende Künstlergeneration von essenzieller Bedeutung sein sollten. Im Rückblick gesehen, war ihre Ausstellung eine Vorbotin der Wiederbelebung und -akzeptanz der Malerei – insbesondere auch einer figürlichen –, der in den 1980er-Jahren ebenfalls erfolgten Relativierung des Fortschrittsglaubens der Avantgarden sowie der Akzeptanz eines künstlerischen Pluralismus.

Nach dem Ende der Avantgarden

Ende der 1970er-, Anfang der 1980er-Jahre, also am Ende der Avantgarden, vollzieht eine ganze Generation junger Künstler den Schritt der Opposition gegen die in ihren Augen ausgedünnt und blutlos gewordenen, überwiegend performativen und konzeptuellen Tendenzen der 1960er- und 1970er-Jahre mittels Rückgriff auf das in diesen beiden Jahrzehnten weitgehend verpönte alte Medium der Malerei. Sie beginnt, figurativ zu malen, lässt ihrer Subjektivität freien Lauf und verortet sich im großen Ganzen der Geschichte der Malerei.

Innerhalb dieser Entwicklung finden sich aber bald auch Künstler, die sich dieser meist „wilden", in vielen Fällen unbekümmert frechen Herangehensweise, die oft eine sinnlich lustvolle Freude am Malen propagiert und sich gerne auf Traditionen beruft, verweigern, ohne deswegen mit dem Malen aufhören zu wollen. Sie beginnen, die Malerei wieder als sich selbst kritisch reflektierendes Medium einzusetzen, und praktizieren damit einmal mehr die Strategie einer „Kritik der Malerei im Medium der Malerei".[60] Dabei finden sie sich wiederum in der klassischen Situation des Kampfes an mehreren Fronten – nicht nur gegen die Traditionalisten (das sowieso) und die vorangegangene Generation, sondern auch gegen eine in ihren Augen zu wenig reflektierte, sich aber als progressiv begreifende zeitgenössische Malereiproduktion und selbstverständlich gegen die Gefahr der eigenen Routine. Ein teilweise analytisch dekonstruktiver Ansatz wird nun zu einer wesentlichen Spielvariante des Bad Painting.

Ein markantes Beispiel hierfür ist das Werk des deutschen Malers Albert Oehlen, der insbesondere in den späten 1970er- sowie den 1980er-Jahren in engem künstlerischem Austausch mit Werner Büttner und Martin Kippenberger stand. Geradezu ein Paradebeispiel für deren dekonstruktive Herangehensweise und die daraus entwickelten Schlüsse ist der von den dreien verfasste, lange Katalogtext zu ihrer gemeinsamen Ausstellung *Wahrheit ist Arbeit* (1984) im Essener Museum Folkwang. Er formuliert eine kritisch-ironische Absage an alle Modelle einer Wahrheitsfindung in Philosophie, Kunst und Gesellschaft und sieht als einzige Option das „Scheitern" respektive den produktiven Einsatz von Widersprüchen und Fehlern.[61]

Albert Oehlen ist derjenige, der diesen dekonstruktiven Ansatz am konsequentesten im Medium der Malerei verfolgt, um deren unvermeidliches Scheitern im Bild offenbar werden zu

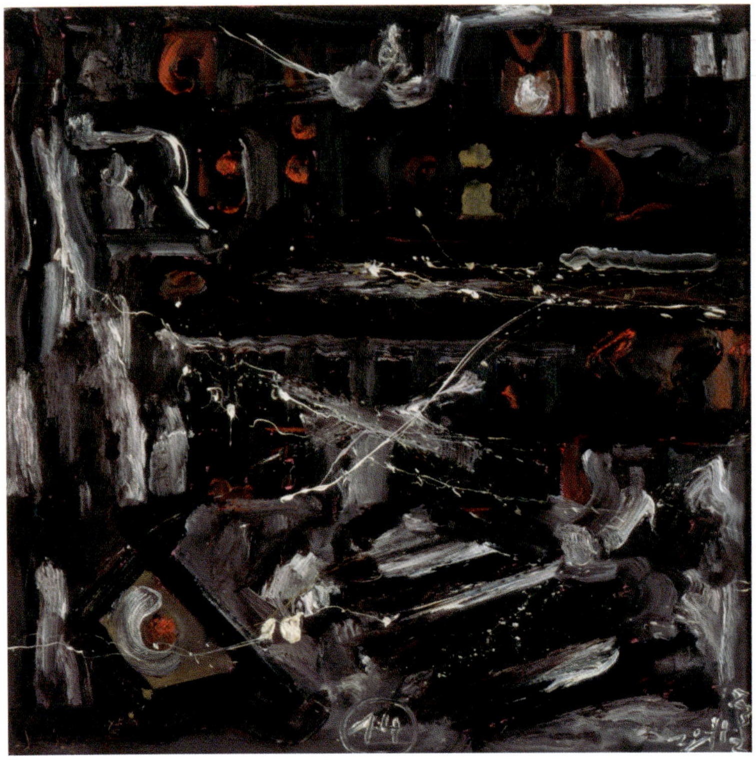

045 Werner Büttner
Die Paarung des Grundgesetzes mit Farbe ergibt kein Grundgesetz sondern Farbe (Art. 14: Das Erbrecht und das Eigentum werden gewährleistet), 1983
(The Copulation of Basic Law with Color Totals no Basic Law but Color [art. 14: Property and the Right of Inheritance Shall be Guaranteed])
Öl auf Leinwand / oil on canvas
120 x 120 cm
Sammlung Grässlin, St. Georgen

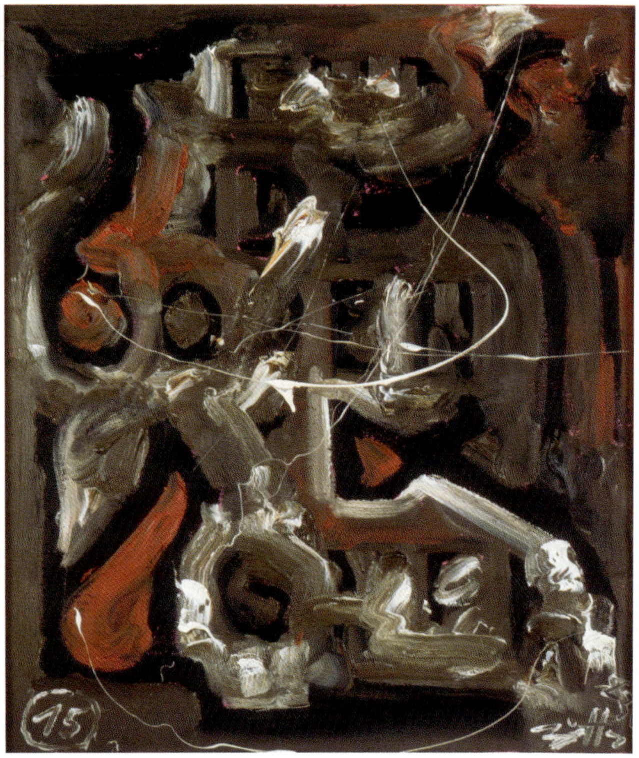

046 Werner Büttner
Die Paarung des Grundgesetzes mit Farbe ergibt kein Grundgesetz sondern Farbe (Art. 15: Grund und Boden anderes könnten), 1983
(The Copulation of Basic Law with Color Totals no Basic Law but Color [art. 15: Land, Natural Resources, and Others May])
Öl auf Leinwand / oil on canvas
90 x 75 cm
Sammlung Grässlin, St. Georgen

color/paint, [...] applied to canvas or in the tube, stands in no relation to reality beyond its own existence, to which it draws attention by costing money."[64]

In the field of the portrayal of three-dimensionality, too—the primary domain of illusionism and thus an age-old concern of painting—the false propositions made by the medium are mercilessly exposed. Oehlen constructs spaces seemingly governed by perspective but rendered illegible by layering and overloading with disruptive elements including lines and shading. To increase the disruptive potential of these layered and woven structures, mirrors are also included, and in some cases painted over are even [ILL·050·112·113]. In the (supposedly) illusionistic world of the picture, then, mirrors—the most blatant instrument for the creation of illusions—become a disruptive factor at the same time as being disrupted themselves by painting. Thus, the failure of the picture is addressed within the picture itself by attacking and overloading it with "incorrect" elements such as "wrong" and "wrongly used" artistic means, to the point of implosion. Instead of resolving contradictions, Oehlen highlights them. Diedrich Diederichsen once aptly described this method as "using and destroying a given code."[65]

Ruthless exposure, without self-deception, is Oehlen's motto: "Whether they are good or bad, pretty or ugly, paintings should maintain themselves without excuses. No magic, no science, no excuses."[66] From this, he has derived a definition of autonomy[67] which ultimately leads back to a kind of literalness: "In the last few years I have been particularly concerned with evidence—with not seeing

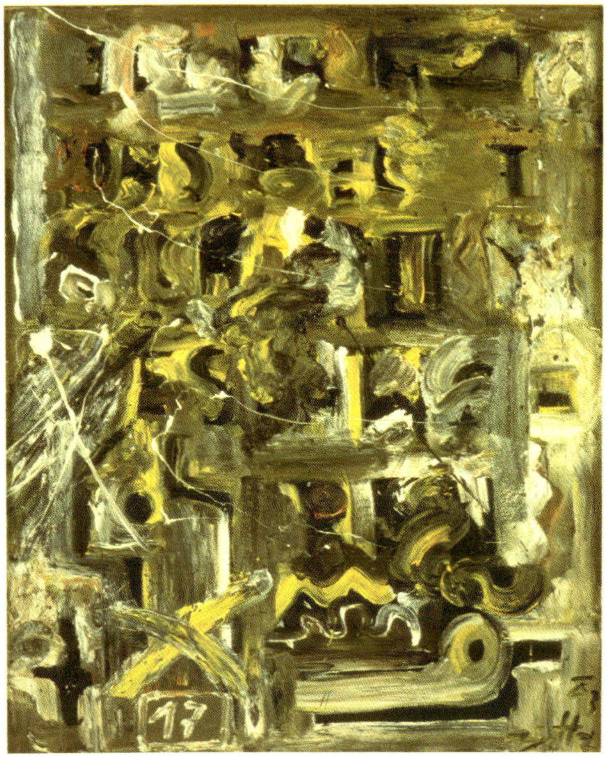

047 **Werner Büttner**
Die Paarung des Grundgesetzes mit Farbe ergibt kein Grundgesetz sondern Farbe (Art. 17: Jeder Deutsche hat das Recht, sich zu beschweren), 1983
(The Copulation of Basic Law with Color Totals no Basic Law but Color [art. 17: Every German Shall Have the Right to Address Complaints])

Öl auf Leinwand / oil on canvas
100 x 79 cm
Sammlung Grässlin, St. Georgen

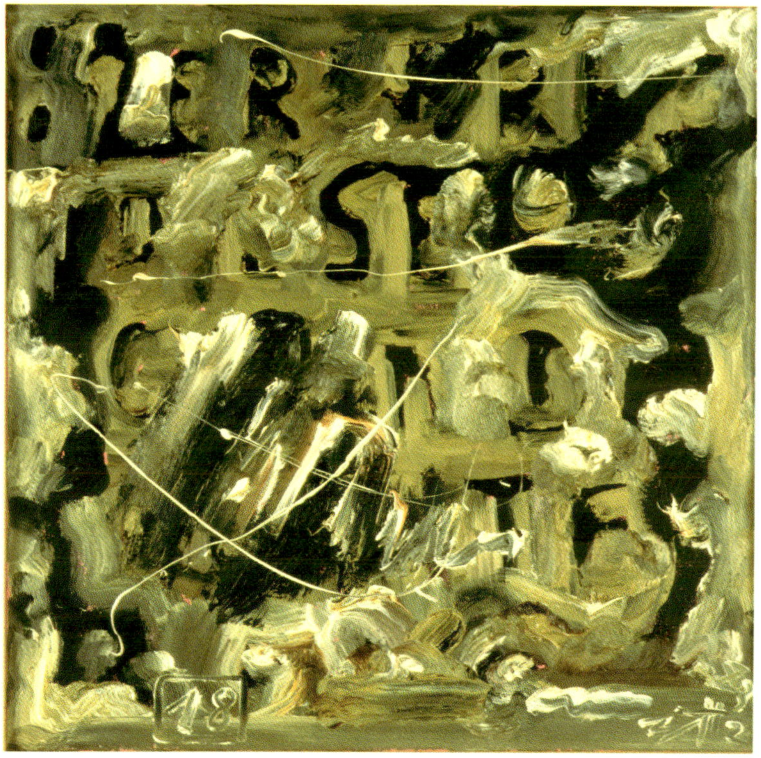

048 **Werner Büttner**
Die Paarung des Grundgesetzes mit Farbe ergibt kein Grundgesetz sondern Farbe (Art. 18: Wer die Grundordnung missbraucht, verwirkt dieselbe), 1983
(The Copulation of Basic Law with Color Totals no Basic Law but Color [art. 18: Whoever Abuses the Freedom of Expression, Shall Forfeit these Basic Rights])

Öl auf Leinwand / oil on canvas
75 x 75 cm
Sammlung Grässlin, St. Georgen

lassen: „Da wir nun aber die unbedingte Abhängigkeit und Verantwortung der Kunst gegenüber der Realität zu leugnen verbieten, andererseits aber keine Möglichkeit sehen, die Kunst in unserem Sinne wirken zu lassen, gibt es nur noch eine Möglichkeit: zu versagen.“[62]

Unter anderem thematisiert er in ironischer und bisweilen pseudoanalytisch-systematischer Form die Wirkweise der traditionellen malerischen Mittel und ihrer Möglichkeiten der Bedeutungsgenerierung insbesondere anhand der Farbe, die ja in der Geschichte der Malerei immer als „ungreifbarstes“ und unfassbarstes bildnerisches Mittel galt und dementsprechend oft mit mystisch-spirituellen Bedeutungen belegt wurde. In seinen Mitte der 1980er-Jahre entstandenen Bildserien der „Farbenlehre“ wird die Frage nach deren Potenzial wie auch ihrer möglichen Systematik unter anderem anhand provokant gewählter Sujets abgehandelt, wie etwa biblischen Würdenträgern oder Sujets mit Bezügen zu den problematischen Aspekten der deutschen Vergangenheit. So malt Oehlen Porträts von Adolf Hitler oder die *Hitlerbrücke in Krefeld* in der Trias der klassischen Grundfarben Rot, Gelb und Blau. Sein Schluss ist illusionslos-pragmatisch: „Bilder bestehen zu einem guten Teil aus Farbe.“ Dieser ist jedoch „nicht zu trauen“. Man könne nur „glauben […], was auf der Tube steht“.[63] „So wie das Wort, gesprochen oder geschrieben, in keiner wirklichen Beziehung zum Gegenstand, den es bezeichnen soll, steht, […] so steht die Farbe, gemalt oder in der Tube, in keiner Beziehung zur Wirklichkeit außerhalb ihrer eigenen Existenz, die sie dadurch hervorhebt, dass sie Geld kostet.“[64]

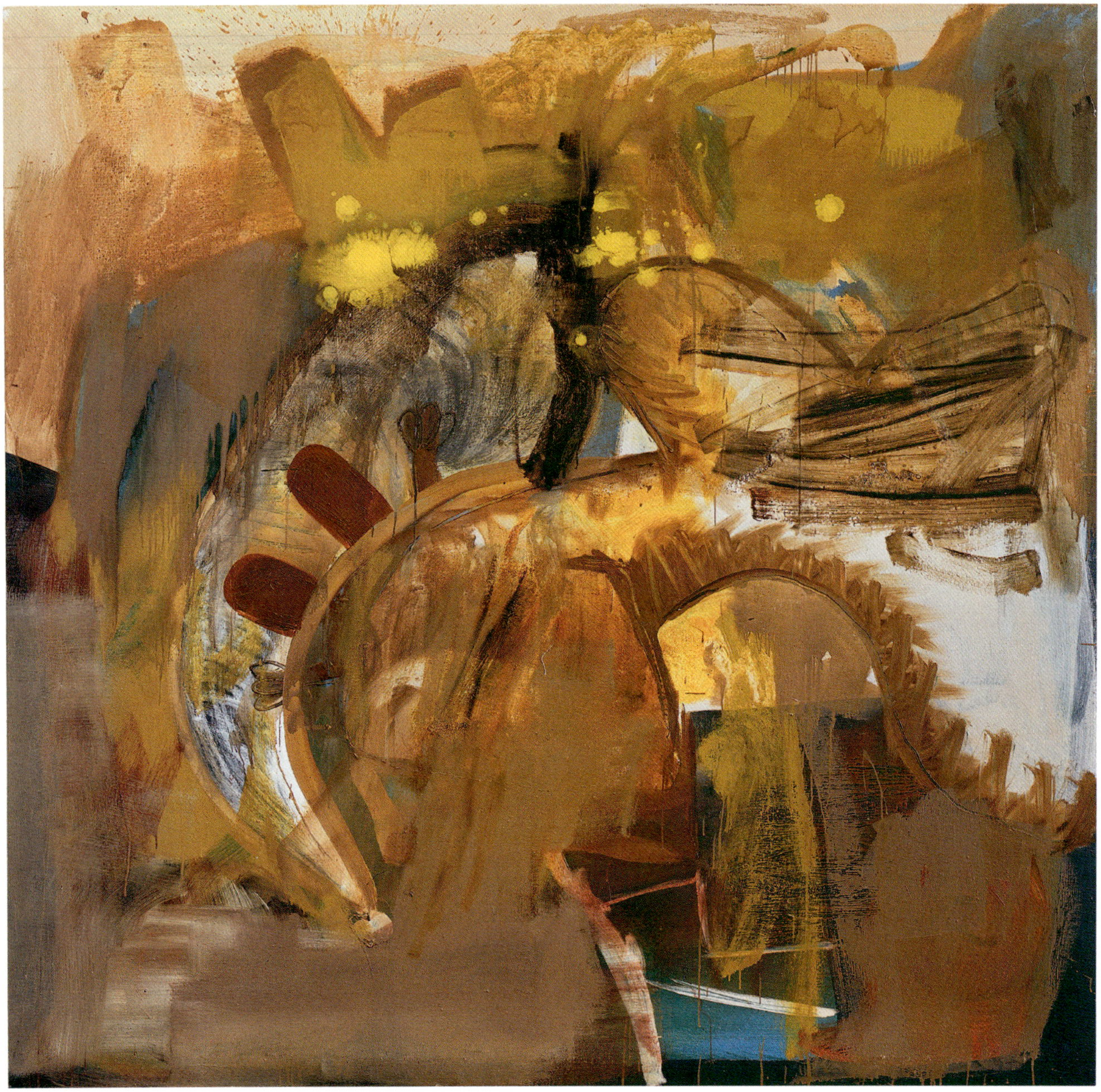

049 **Albert Oehlen**
Ohne Titel, 1992 (Untitled)
Öl auf Leinwand / oil on canvas
200 x 200 cm
Essl Museum Klosterneuburg/Wien

anything in the painting other than what is actually there. Nothing is codified—a mess is just a mess."[68] After 1988, Oehlen's work also became more abstract [ILL·049], although seldom really non-figurative. In any case—and this is a position typical of Bad Painting—he considers the distinction between abstract and non-abstract painting irrelevant.[69]

Oehlen has on occasion used the term "Bad Painting" himself,[70] but not without underlining its ultimate indefinability, contradictoriness, and untenability. In 2006, he called his show at London's Whitechapel Gallery *I will always champion good painting*; but at the second venue in Bristol, he retitled it *I will always champion bad painting*.

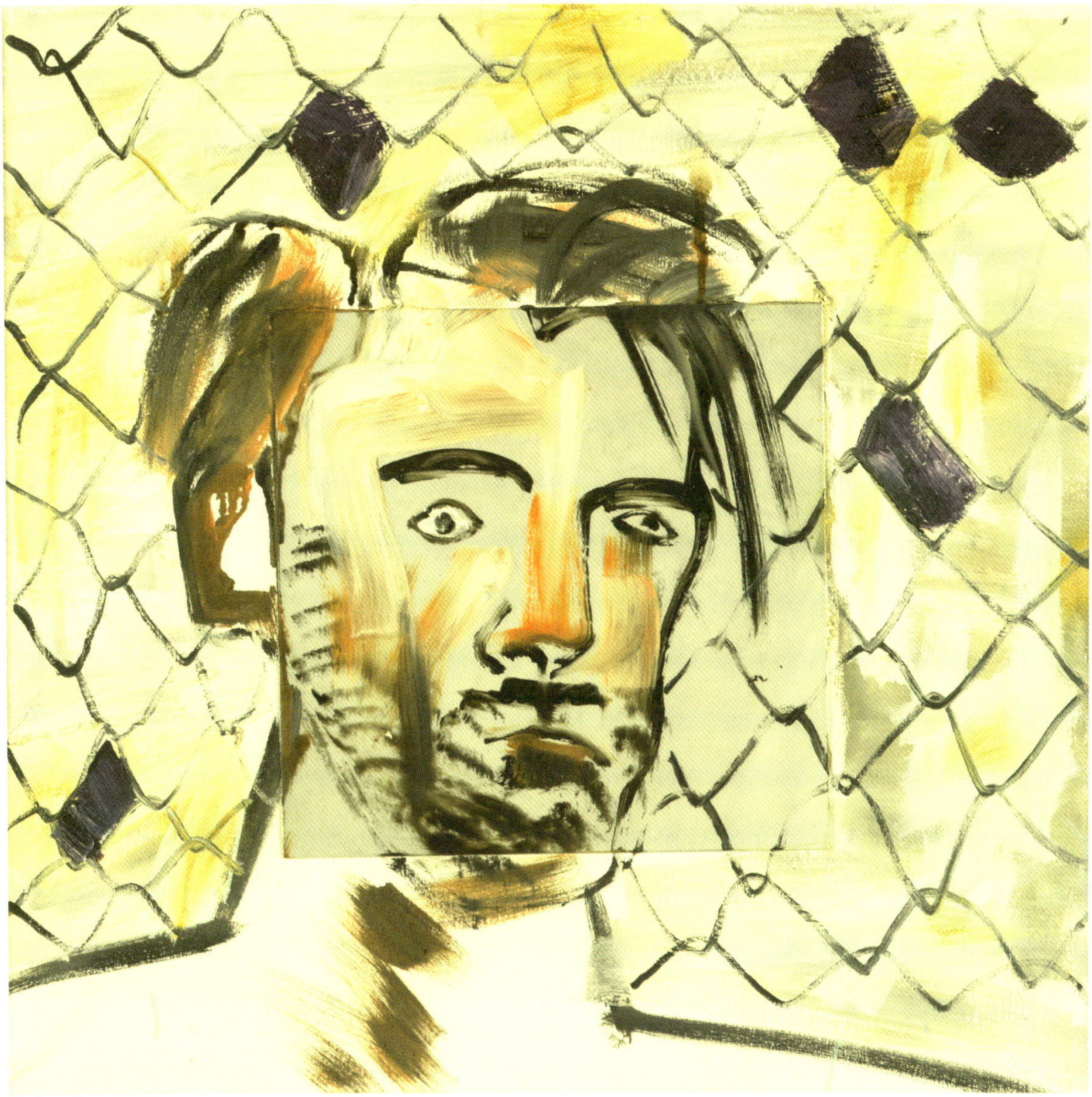

050 **Albert Oehlen**
Ohne Titel, 1982 (Untitled)
Öl, Spiegel auf Leinwand / oil, mirror on canvas
60 x 60 cm
Sammlung Stolitzka, Graz

Auch im Bereich der Raumdarstellung, primäre Domäne des Illusionismus und somit uraltes Anliegen der Malerei, werden die falschen Angebote des Mediums gnadenlos vor Augen geführt. Oehlen konstruiert scheinbar perspektivische Räume, die durch Überlagerung und auch Überfrachtung mit Störfaktoren wie Linien und Schraffuren wieder unlesbar gemacht werden. In derartige Geflechte werden auch Spiegel als weitere Störfaktoren integriert, die wiederum teilweise übermalt werden [ABB·050·112·113]. Der Spiegel als plattestes Instrument der Illusionserzeugung wird in der (scheinbar) illusionistischen Welt des Bildes zum Störfaktor, während er gleichzeitig von der Malerei selbst gestört wird. Das Scheitern des Bildes wird im Bild abgehandelt, indem es mit „unkorrekten" Vorgangsweisen wie „falschen" und „falsch eingesetzten" Mittel angegriffen beziehungsweise überfrachtet wird, bis

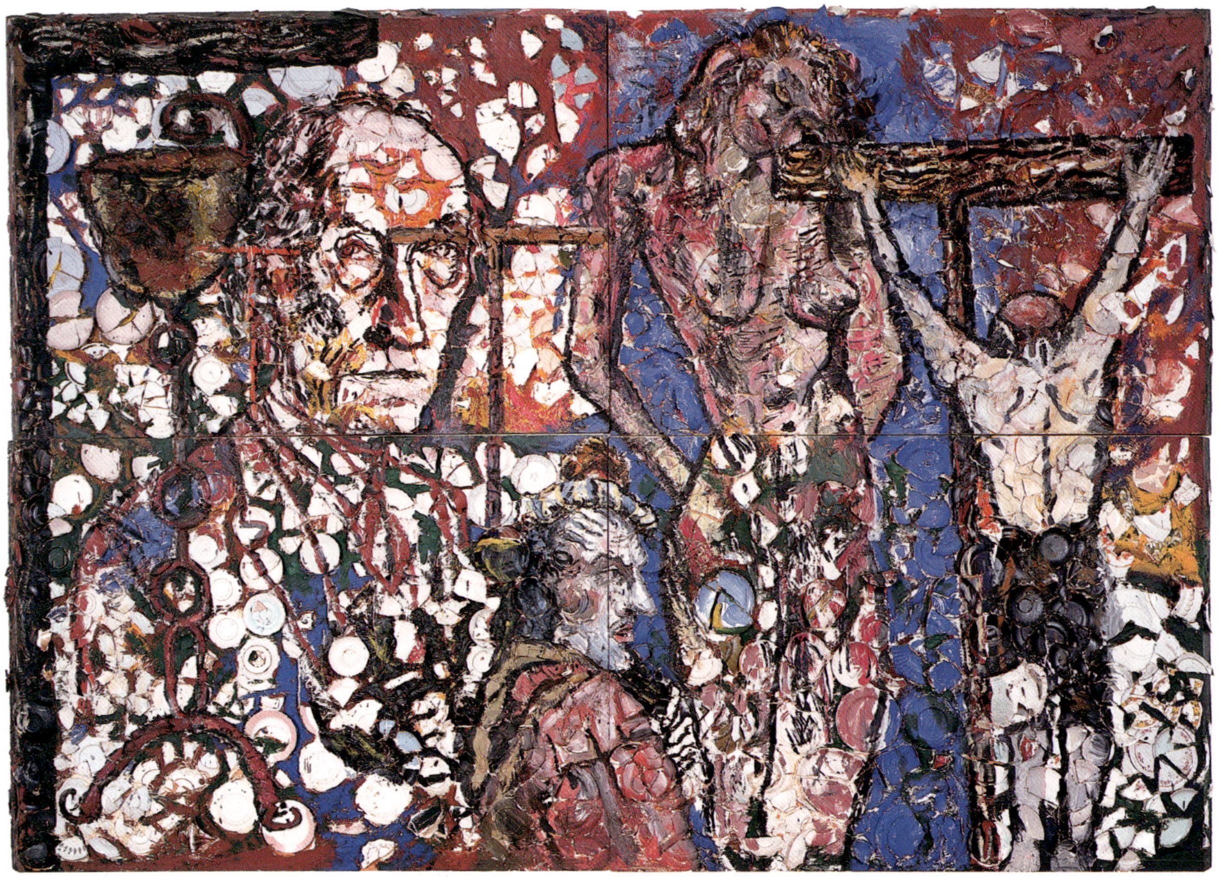

051 **Julian Schnabel**
Painting without Mercy, 1981, (Malerei ohne Erbarmen)

Teller, Kitt, Ölfarbe, Wachs, Epoxy, auf Holz / Plates, plaster, oil paint, wax, epoxy on wood
240 x 336 cm
Museum Moderner Kunst Stiftung Ludwig Wien, Leihgabe der Österreichischen Ludwig Stiftung / on loan from Austrian Ludwig Foundation, seit / since 1981

Compared to that of Oehlen, Büttner, or Kippenberger, the approach of American painter Julian Schnabel is less analytical. But his refusal to develop and remain true to a signature style springs from a similar spirit of rejecting all rules and obligations. His free use of existing pictures, overpainting them in different ways [ILL·115·116] and often—especially in his early work— also breaking the surface with materials including smashed plates [ILL·051], reflects an approach that is consciously grounded in a broader historical and cultural perspective, but which doesn't believe in holistic frames of thought, choosing instead to accept many things while simultaneously relativizing them. As such, it is not unrelated to the approach of Picabia, Magritte, Jorn, or Polke. "What these things can give to the viewer is the sensation of freedom, the sensation of being able to say something or the sensation of not necessarily having to believe certain things, or the sense of a dichotomy in one simultaneous reality."[71]

Following the end of the avant-gardes, and the deconstruction of the claims of art in general that took place in the 1980s and 1990s, major sources of friction that gave rise to Bad Painting seemed to have been removed. In times where (seemingly) anything goes, "badness" becomes a fashionable name for positions that seek subversion and breaches of taboo, but which are usually co-opted all too swiftly and gladly by the booming art market and by an art world hungry for sensation.[72] Approaches that swim against the tide for more principled reasons—and which elicit a genuinely indignant "This really isn't acceptable!"—are becoming rare.

es in sich selbst implodiert. Widersprüche werden nicht aufgelöst, sondern im Gegenteil hervorgehoben. Mit „einen bestehenden Kode benützen und zerstören“ hat Diedrich Diederichsen diese Methode einmal trefflich beschrieben.[65]

Schonungslose Offenlegung, kein „Drüberschwindeln“ ist Oehlens Devise: „Ob sie nun gut oder schlecht, hübsch oder hässlich sind, Bilder sollten sich ohne Ausreden behaupten. Kein Zauber, keine Wissenschaft, keine Ausreden.“[66] Daraus entwickelt er einen Autonomiebegriff[67], der wieder zu einer Art von „literalness“ führt: „In den letzten paar Jahren war ich besonders um Augenscheinlichkeit bemüht – darum, im Bild nichts anderes zu sehen als das, was tatsächlich da ist. Nichts ist kodifiziert – ein Durcheinander ist einfach ein Durcheinander.“[68] Ab 1988 werden Oehlens Bilder auch abstrakter [ABB·049], wenngleich selten wirklich ungegenständlich, wobei er aber in für Bad Painting typischer Weise die Unterscheidung in abstrakte und nicht abstrakte Malerei für irrelevant hält.[69]

Albert Oehlen hat den Begriff „Bad Painting“ selbst immer wieder verwendet,[70] nicht aber ohne auch auf dessen letztliche Undefinierbarkeit, Widersprüchlichkeit und Uneinlösbarkeit zu verweisen: So nannte er 2006 seine Schau in der Londoner Whitechapel Gallery *I will always champion good painting*, während er der anschließenden zweite Station derselben Ausstellung in Bristol den Titel *I will always champion bad painting* gab.

Der Ansatz des Amerikaners Julian Schnabel ist im Vergleich zu jenem von Oehlen, Büttner oder Kippenberger weniger analytisch. Doch auch seine Weigerung, einen Stil zu entwickeln und diesem treu zu bleiben, entspringt dem Geist der Ablehnung jeglicher Regeln und Verbindlichkeiten. Sein freier Umgang mit bestehenden Bildern, die er verschiedentlich überlagert und übermalt [ABB·115·116], wobei er – speziell in seiner Frühzeit – oft noch die Bildoberfläche unter anderem mit zerschlagenen Tellern bricht [ABB·051], ist Ausdruck eines Denkens in größeren geschichtlichen und kulturellen Zusammenhängen, das Ansprüche auf Ganzheitlichkeit ablehnt und vieles akzeptiert, um es gleichzeitig zu relativieren. Es ist damit jenem von Picabia, Magritte, Jorn oder Polke nicht unverwandt. „Was diese Dinge dem Betrachter vermitteln können, ist das Empfinden von Freiheit, das Gefühl, etwas sagen zu können, oder das Gefühl, bestimmte Dinge nicht unbedingt glauben zu müssen, oder das Empfinden einer Dichotomie in einer simultanen Realität.“[71]

Nach dem Ende der Avantgarden und der in den 1980er- und 1990er-Jahren erfolgten Dekonstruktion der Ansprüche der Kunst überhaupt scheinen wesentliche Reibepunkte, die in Bad Painting resultieren, beseitigt. In Zeiten eines (scheinbaren) „anything goes“ wird „badness“ zu einem Modewort für Positionen, die Subversion und Tabubrüche suchen, vom boomenden Kunstmarkt und einer nach Sensationen gierenden Kunstwelt aber in der Regel nur allzu gerne und schnell vereinnahmt werden.[72] Aus grundsätzlicheren Überlegungen gegen den Strom schwimmende Ansätze, die ein ehrlich entrüstetes: „Das geht aber nun doch nicht!“, hervorrufen, werden selten.

In the field of painting, John Currin and Lisa Yuskavage are artists who have developed such positions. When they emerged with their specific approaches in the early 1990s, painting, and especially the figurative kind they practiced, which in Currin's case includes portraits (painted after photographic material) [ILL·054], was passing through another phase of rejection while politically correct, socially engaged art was in vogue. "At the time [...] the feeling was that figurative painting was the equivalent of lying. [...] The idea of a freestanding subject that sprays out meaning was under attack. The whole 'French theory' attack on authorship was the accepted truth. [...] My whole life, I thought 'I want to be an author' and when I got to [art] school I learned that this was a bad thing. It was like being a Nazi or a Fascist."[73] Both artists' "badness" consists of linking supposedly provocative subject matter with strategic formal subversion of the "good" picture, often applying the principle of over-freighting a picture with "badness" in terms of both form and content.

Lisa Yuskavage's subject matter has from the outset always been images of woman and female (homo-)sexuality. In her work, feminine attributes and portrayals of desiring and being desired are exaggerated in terms of both form and content in a way that puts all norms of acceptance and beauty to the test [ILL·052·053]. She is not afraid of going very close to what is usually considered kitsch, working with sugary sweet and extremely bright colors and placing her figures in fairytale settings or scenes laden with attributes such as flowers, fruit, and pearls whose sensuality seems to be borrowed from the world of the Baroque. And indeed, an engagement with the entire history of painting is a key aspect of Yuskavage's work, which explores the potential of the medium in a permanent balancing act, always treading the fine line between beauty and ugliness, decadence, or even morbidity, between good taste and bad, between desire and revulsion, innocence and pornography, feminism and misogyny—whatever these terms may mean.

In the case of John Currin, who, like Yuskavage, soon "simply stopped caring what Modernity would think of [him],"[74] it was above all the way his motifs attacked the canonical American-Puritan values of decency, correctness, "good taste," and beauty that was vilified in the 1990s as shocking, sensationalistic, "politically incorrect," and "reactionary." He paints menopausal woman engaged in an ultimately pitiful quest for youthfulness, ailing or even crippled beautiful young women, and especially women with unnaturally large breasts, but also miserably unconfident men who fall victim to embarrassment while trying to perform ideal male roles [ILL·055·106·107]. These are figures from those same urban middle and upper classes which, among other things, constitute the supporting strata of the art world—the museum and gallery visitors, the trustees and patrons, and, not least, the buyers. For Currin as an outcast from this world at the time, they came to embody his own misery: "These women mirrored my situation as a painter and the political problem of being a painter. [...] When I was making these paintings my validity as an artist was greatly challenged."[75] The surfaces of these pictures are often heterogeneous, often including sections that have been treated roughly with a pallet knife, causing "damage" to faces in particular.

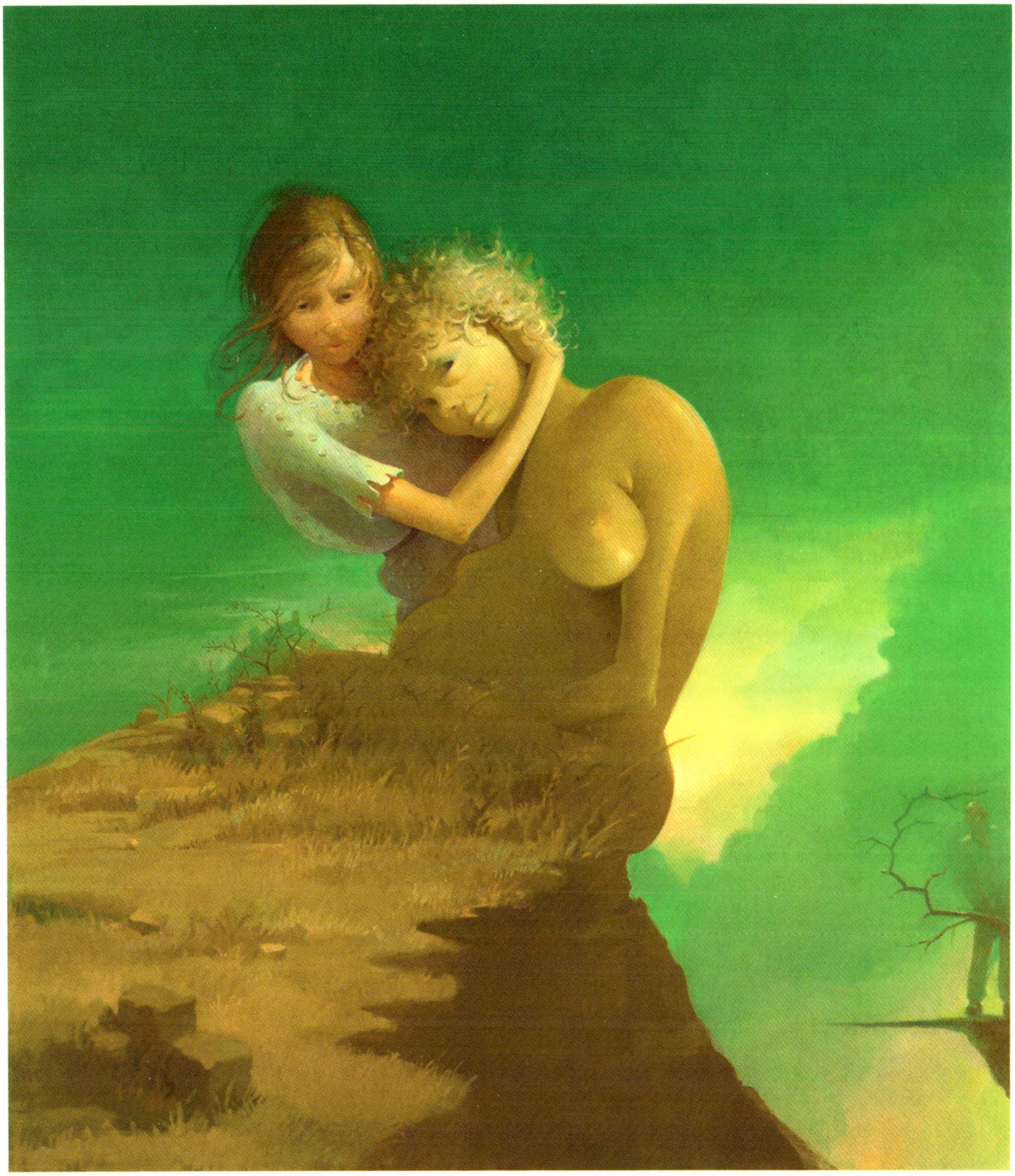

052 **Lisa Yuskavage**
Cliff, 2007 (Klippe)
Öl auf Leinwand / oil on canvas
195,6 x 157,5 cm
Sammlung Titze

Im Bereich der Malerei sind John Currin und Lisa Yuskavage derartige Fälle. Als sie Anfang der 1990er-Jahre mit ihren spezifischen malerischen Ansätzen auf den Plan traten, war gerade wieder einmal die Malerei, erst recht in der von ihnen praktizierten figürlichen Form, die bei Currin sogar (nach Vorlagen gemalte) Porträts [ABB·054] einschloss, von der damals angesagten politisch korrekten, sozial engagierten Kunst verpönt. „Damals herrschte die Ansicht, malen sei wie lügen", sagt John Currin. „Die Idee eines frei stehenden Subjekts, das von einem zentralen Ursprung aus Bedeutung verströmt, stand unter Beschuss. Die ganze Attacke der ‚französischen Theorie' gegen die Autorschaft war die anerkannte Wahrheit. […] Mein ganzes Leben lang hatte ich gedacht: ‚Ich will ein Autor sein', und als ich auf die Akademie kam, erfuhr ich, dass das etwa Schlimmes sei. Es war, als wäre man Faschist

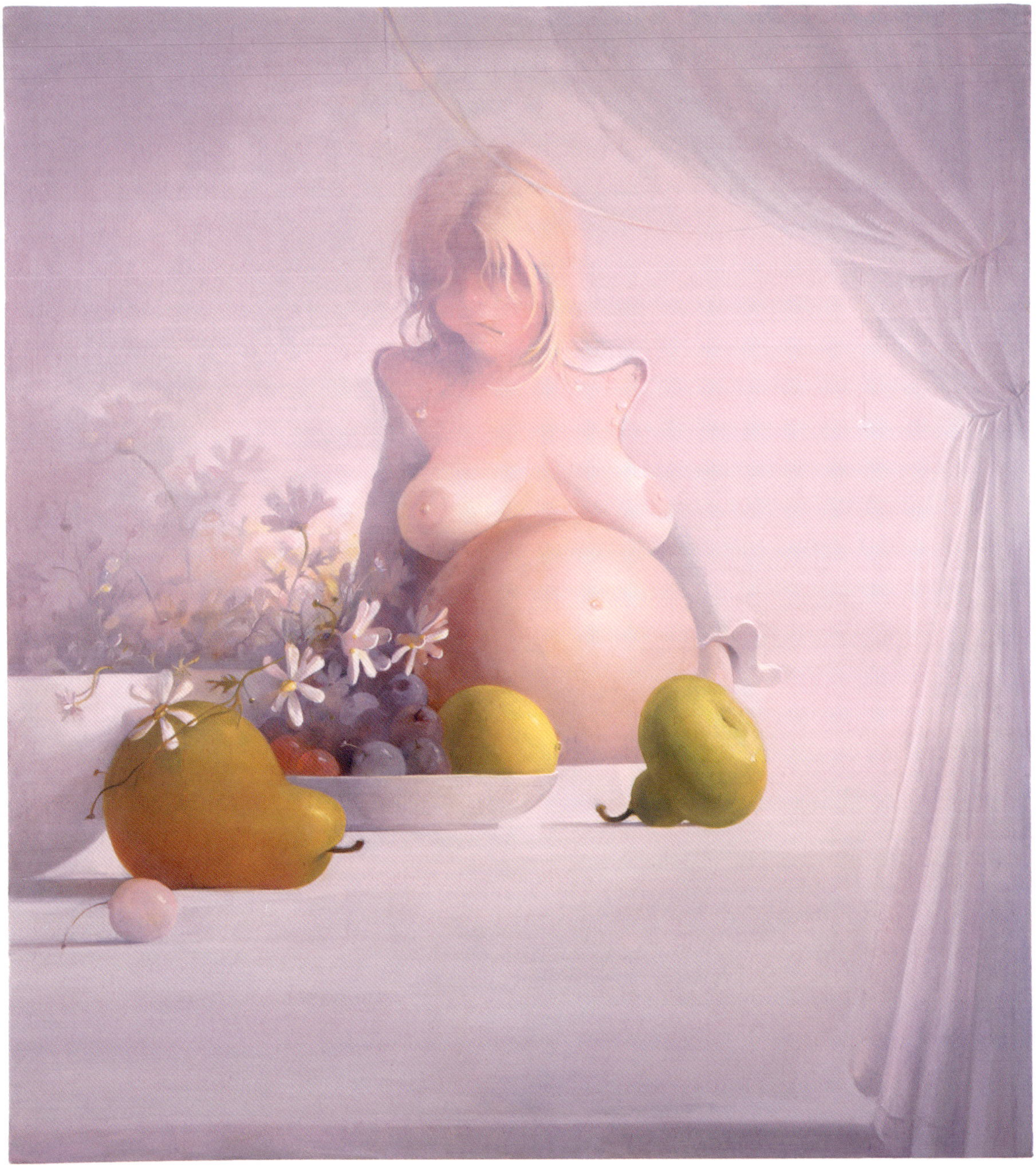

053
Lisa Yuskavage
Brood, 2005–2006
(Brut)
Öl auf Leinwand /
Oil on canvas
190,5 x 175 cm
Sammlung / Collection
of Mr. Alberto Cortina

Around 1998/1999, after art's evolution had brought forth a new wave of painting and renewed acceptance of figurative painting, robbing Currin of his outer enemy, so to speak, he shifted the emphasis in his work, focusing now on the potential of the medium itself. This led him to engage increasingly with the Old Masters as the historical roots of his own figurative painting and to use their styles and techniques in his own work—which earned him fresh accusations of being "conservative." Significantly, he was especially inspired by the formal principles of artists who—like the Mannerists—opposed the "classical" canon of beauty [ILL·029]. He has also revived techniques that are no longer practiced, such as that of underpainting, always aware of the fact that he was damned to be "bad" insofar as he would never approach the mastery of the Old Masters.[76] Conversely, he is worried

oder Nazi."[73] Beider „badness" besteht wiederum in der Verschränkung als provokant empfundener Inhalte mit formalen Strategien der Subversion des „guten" Bildes, wobei sie in formaler wie inhaltlicher Hinsicht sehr oft mit dem Prinzip der Überfrachtung eines Bildes mit „badness" operieren.

Bei Lisa Yuskavage ist es von Anfang an eine Auseinandersetzung mit dem Bild der Frau und weiblicher (Homo-)Sexualität, wobei Weiblichkeitsmerkmale sowie die Darstellung von Begehren und Begehrtwerden von ihr formal wie inhaltlich in einer Weise übersteigert werden, die alle Normen von Akzeptanz und Schönheit auf den Prüfstand stellt. [ABB·052·053] Unerschrocken nahe geht sie dabei an das heran, was man gemeinhin unter Kitsch einreiht. Sie arbeitet mit zuckersüßen und denkbar grellen Farben, stellt ihre Figuren in märchenhafte Umgebungen beziehungsweise stattet sie überreich mit Attributen wie Blumen, Früchten und Perlen aus, deren Sinnlichkeit der Welt des Barock entnommen scheint. Tatsächlich ist die Auseinandersetzung mit der gesamten Geschichte der Malerei ein wesentlicher Aspekt von Yuskavages Arbeit, die unter Ausschöpfung des Potenzials dieses Mediums eine permanente Gratwanderung unternimmt. Immer am Punkt des Umkippens von Schönheit in Hässlichkeit, Dekadenz oder gar Morbidität, von gutem in schlechten Geschmack, vom Begehren ins Abgestoßenwerden, von Unschuld in Pornografie oder von Feminismus in Frauenfeindlichkeit – was immer diese Begriffe bedeuten mögen.

Bei John Currin, der sich wie Yuskavage sehr bald „einfach nicht mehr darum geschert [hat], was die Moderne von [ihm] halten würde",[74] wurde in den 1990er-Jahren vor allem die Art, wie seine Sujets den amerikanisch-puritanischen Wertekanon von Anstand, Korrektheit, „gutem Geschmack" und Schönheit angreifen, als schockierend, sensationalistisch, „politically incorrect" und „reaktionär" beschimpft. Er malt in den Wechseljahren stehende und in letztlich Mitleid erregender Weise nach Jugendlichkeit strebende Frauen, kränkelnde oder gar verkrüppelte schöne junge Frauen sowie insbesondere Frauen mit unnatürlich überproportionalen Brüsten, ebenso aber auch erbärmlich unsichere Männer, die in der Performance ihres Rollenideals der Peinlichkeit verfallen [ABB·055·106·107]. Es sind Figuren jener urbanen Middle- und Upperclass, die unter anderem die Trägerschicht des Kunstbetriebs stellt – also die Museums- und Galeriebesucher, die „trustees" und „patrons" sowie nicht zuletzt die Käufer. Für Currin als damaligen Outcast dieses Betriebes werden sie zur Verkörperung seines eigenes Elends: „Diese Frauenbilder spiegelten meine Situation als Maler wider und das politische Problem, Maler zu sein. Als ich diese Bilder machte, wurde mein Wert als Künstler heftig infrage gestellt."[75] Die Oberflächen dieser Bilder sind oft heterogen, wobei immer wieder Partien grob gespachtelt und auf diese Weise speziell Gesichter „beschädigt" sein können.

Um 1998/1999, nachdem die Entwicklung der Kunst wieder eine neue Malereiwelle und auch eine Wiederakzeptanz figürlicher Malerei gebracht hatte, womit Currin sozusagen seinen äußeren Feind verloren hatte, verlegte er den Schwerpunkt seiner Arbeit in die Auseinandersetzung mit dem Potenzial des Mediums selbst. Dies führt ihn zur zunehmenden Beschäftigung mit den alten Meistern als den historischen Wurzeln der von ihm praktizierten figurativen Malerei und zur Anwendung

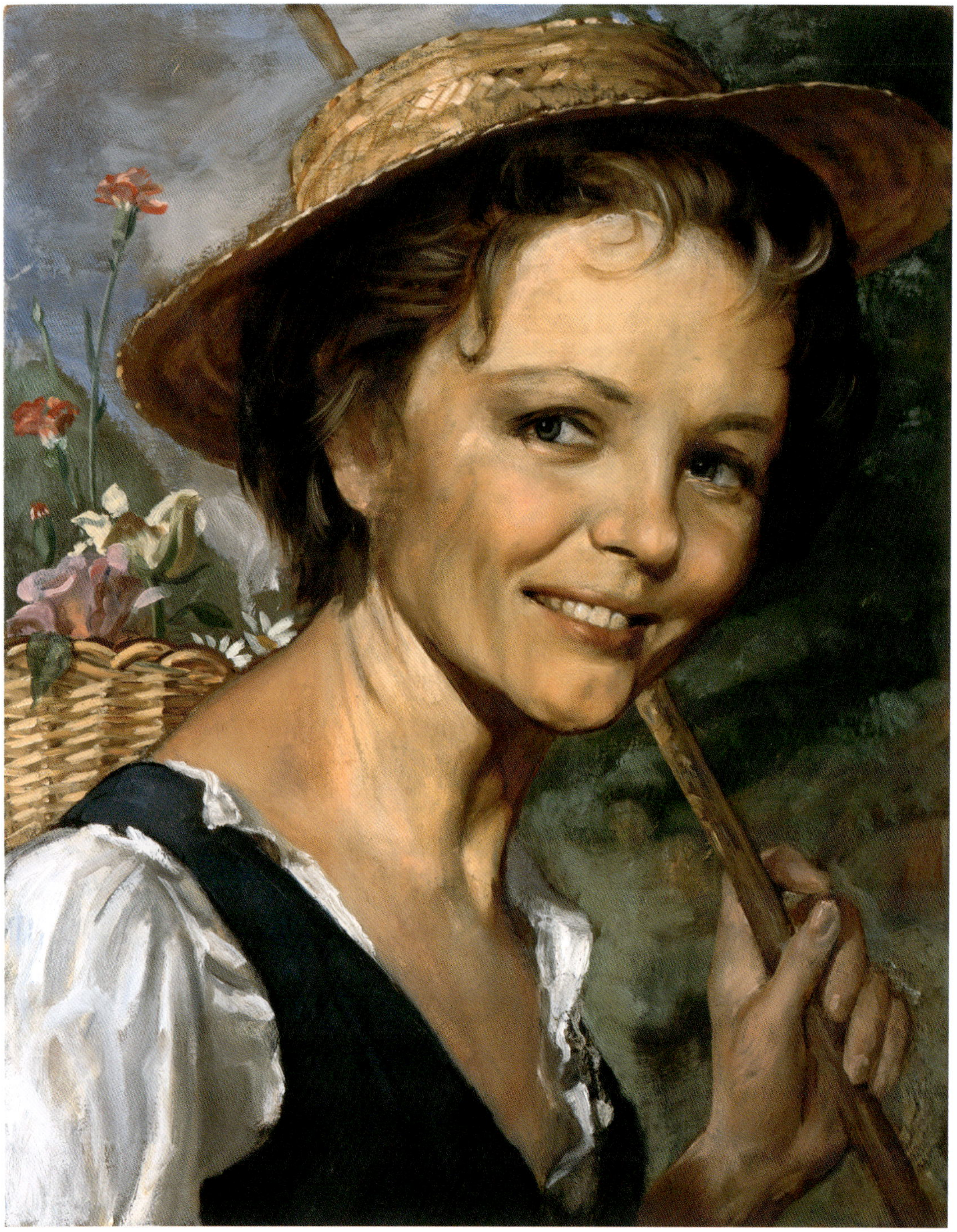

054
John Currin
Sheree North, 2003
Öl auf Leinwand / oil on canvas
66 x 50,8 cm
Courtesy Sadie Coles HQ, London

about getting too good or even settled into a routine: "It is getting technically really good at it that makes me more uncomfortable."[77] In terms of form and content, then, Currin's pictures, too, oscillate, Janus-like, between perfection and inadequacy, between the ideal and the grotesque, between attraction and repulsion, beauty and ugliness, pleasant feelings and feelings of guilt. They refuse to see "good" and "bad" as mutually exclusive opposites, refuse even to believe in the possibility of an unproblematically "good" picture.

It is no coincidence that during his years at art school, Currin was already drawn to artists who did not submit to the dictates of good taste and correctness (including those laid down by the avant-gardes) and who were consequently often attacked and marginalized—artists like Picabia,

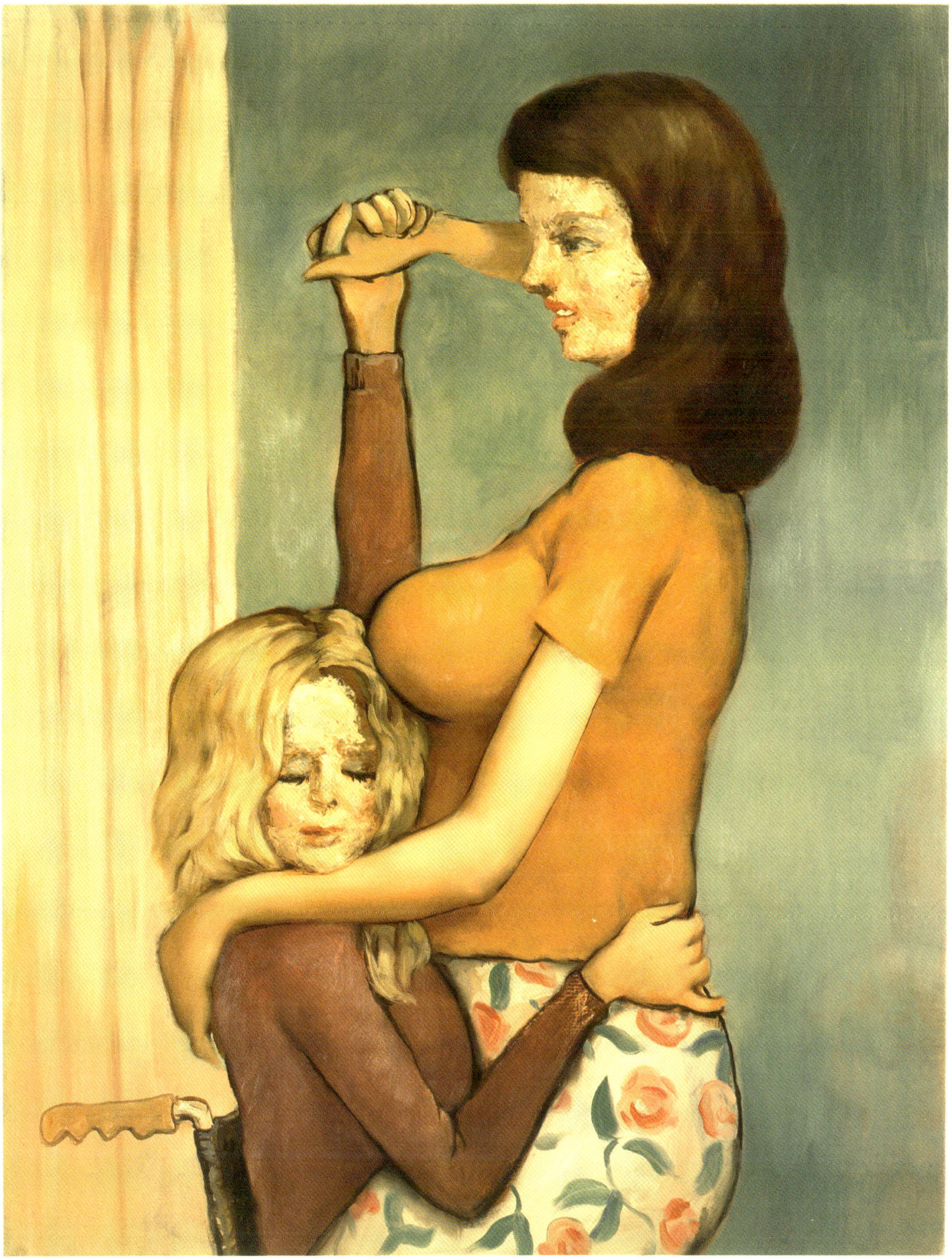

055 **John Currin**
The Invalids, 1997
(Die Invaliden)
Öl auf Leinwand / oil on canvas
121,9 x 91,4 cm
Hauser & Wirth, Zürich / London

von deren Malweisen und -techniken in seiner eigenen Arbeit – was ihm erneut den Vorwurf einbringt, „konservativ" zu sein. Bezeichnenderweise inspirierten ihn dabei in besonderer Weise die formalen Prinzipien jener Künstler, die sich – wie die Manieristen – dem „klassischen" Schönheitskanon widersetzten [ABB·029]. Zudem greift er nicht mehr praktizierte Techniken auf, wie beispielsweise jene des Untermalens, wobei ihm bewusst wird, dass er insofern dazu verdammt sei, „bad" zu sein, als er an die Meisterschaft der Alten nie herankommen würde.[76] Andererseits beunruhigt es ihn, zu gut oder gar routiniert zu werden: „Mehr Kopfzerbrechen macht es mir, dass ich wirklich gut darin werde."[77]
In formaler wie inhaltlicher Hinsicht oszillieren also auch Currins Bilder immer wieder janusköpfig zwischen Perfektion und Ungenügen, dem Idealen und dem Grotesken, dem Anziehenden und dem

Polke, and Guston. Which brings us full circle, with the Bad Painters proving themselves to be the loose-knit family mentioned above, consisting of non-conformists and loners who defy classification and who subject everything—including their own thinking and their activity as painters—to constant, in-depth questioning.

1 This concept emerged in the nineteenth century; see in particular the work of the same name published in 1853 by the German Hegelian philosopher Karl Rosenkranz.

2 Undated quotation from Neil Jenney, from "Statements by Neil Jenney," *Neil Jenney*, exhib. cat., University Art Museum Berkeley, 1981, p. 50.

3 *Tiefe Blicke. Kunst der Achtziger Jahre aus der BRD, der DDR, Österreich und der Schweiz*, exhib. cat. (Cologne: Hessisches Landesmuseum Darmstadt, 1985), p. 56 f.

4 Friedrich Petzel, *Die Theorie des Bad Painting am Beispiel von Albert Oehlen*, masters dissertation, Philosophy Faculty of Cologne University, 1990, p. 9.

5 Albert Oehlen interviewed by Diedrich Diederichsen, "The rules of the game," in *Artforum*, Nov. 1994, p. 71.

6 Interview with the author, Munich, 28 January 2008.

7 A biography written by Albert Oehlen himself explicitly mentions his early purchase of a Jorn catalog. *Albert Oehlen, Peintures / Malerei 1980–2004*, exhib. cat., Musée Cantonal des Beaux-Arts de Lausanne; Domus Artium, Salamanca (2002); Kunsthalle Nürnberg (2004/2005), p. 121.

8 See Alison M. Gingeras, "John Currin, Pictor Vulgaris," in *John Currin*, exhib. cat. (New York: Gargosian Gallery, 2006), p. 34.

9 See, among others, Maria Lluïsa Borràs, *Picabia* (London: Thames and Hudson, 1985), p. 321–330.

10 Contrary to the view long upheld in the literature, that Picabia began his series of nudes in the winter of 1941/1942 as commissioned works for the Algerian businessman André Romanet, Sara Cochran comes to the conclusion, based on study of sources, "that Picabia began painting his realistic nudes based on erotic photographs at the end of the 1930s, i.e., before the war and before he met Romanet." See Sara Cochran, "Zur Malerei von Francis Picabia während des Zweiten Weltkrieges," in Zdenek Felix (ed.), *Francis Picabia. Das Spätwerk 1933–1953*, exhib. cat. (Hamburg: Deichtorhallen,; Rotterdam: Museum Boijmans Van Beuningen, Ostfildern-Ruit: Hatje-Cantz, 1997), p.19.

11 Robert Rosenblum, "Picabia: Das Spätwerk," in *Picabia 1879–1953*, exhib. cat., Galerie Neuendorf, Frankfurt/M., Scottish National Gallery of Modern Art, Edinburgh 1988, p. 47.

12 Katharina Hegewisch, "Die Kunst ist ein Spiel wie Liebe und Sport. Picabia und die Postmoderne," in *Picabia 1879–1953* (see note 11), p. 48.

13 Francis Picabia, 1922, in "The Pine Cone," February 1922, quoted from Francis Picabia, *I Am a Beautiful Monster. Poetry, Prose and Provocation*, trans. Marc Lowenthal (Cambridge, MA: MIT Press, 2007), p. 283.

14 Francis Picabia, May 1921, ibid. p. 264.

15 Roberto Ohrt, "Avantgardistische Falten und realistisches Kunstlicht," in *Francis Picabia. Das Spätwerk 1933–1953* (see note 10), p. 15.

16 See ibid. p. 14 ff.

17 See, among others, Sara Cochran (see note 10), p. 19–22.

18 René Magritte, letter to André Breton, 24 June 1946, translated after: Harry Torczyner, *René Magritte, Zeichen und Bilder* (Cologne: DuMont) 1977, p.187

19 René Magritte, letter to Gaston Puel, March 8, 1955, translated after: Harry Torczyner, René Magritte (see note 18), p.186

20 "They talk about the clumsiness of my posthumous use of Impressionist technique as the reason for their rejection." René Magritte, "La Querelle du Soleil," "They talk about the clumsiness of my posthumous use of Impressionist technique as the reason for their rejection." René Magritte, "La Querelle du Soleil." translated after: Harry Torczyner,

Abstoßenden, dem Schönen und dem Hässlichen, dem Angenehmen und Schuldgefühlen. Sie weigern sich, „gut“ und „schlecht“ als einander ausschließende Gegensätze zu sehen, ja, überhaupt an die Möglichkeit eines problemlos „guten“ Bildes zu glauben.

Nicht von ungefähr haben Currin schon in seiner Akademiezeit Künstler anzogen, die sich den Diktaten von „good taste“ und Korrektheit auch im Sinne der jeweiligen Avantgarden nicht unterwarfen und dafür oft angegriffen sowie marginalisiert wurden, darunter Picabia, Polke und Guston. Womit sich der Kreis schließt und die Bad Painters sich als die schon eingangs angesprochene lose Familie erweisen, bestehend aus Unangepassten und oft Einzelgängern, die sich nirgends einordnen und alles – inklusive ihres eigenen Denkens und ihrer Tätigkeit als Maler – permanent und grundsätzlich infrage stellen.

1 Der Begriff kommt im 19. Jahrhundert auf; vgl. insbesondere das 1853 erschienene, gleichnamige Werk des Hegel-Schülers Karl Rosenkranz.

2 Undatiertes Zitat von Neil Jenney, zit. n. „Statements by Neil Jenney“, Ausst.-Kat. *Neil Jenney*, University Art Museum Berkeley, 1981, S. 50.

3 Ausst.-Kat. *Tiefe Blicke. Kunst der achtziger Jahre aus der BRD, der DDR, Österreich und der Schweiz*, Hessisches Landesmuseum Darmstadt, Köln 1985, S. 56 f.

4 Friedrich Petzel, *Die Theorie des Bad Painting am Beispiel von Albert Oehlen*, Magisterarbeit, Philosophische Fakultät der Universität Köln, 1990, S. 9.

5 Albert Oehlen im Interview mit Diedrich Diederichsen, „The rules of the game“, in: *Artforum*, Nov. 1994, S. 71.

6 Gespräch mit der Autorin, München, 28. Jänner 2008.

7 In einer von Albert Oehlen selbst verfassten Biografie wird der frühe Erwerb eines Jorn-Kataloges ausdrücklich erwähnt. Ausst.-Kat. *Albert Oehlen, Peintures / Malerei 1980–2004*, Musée Cantonal des Beaux-Arts de Lausanne/Domus Artium 2002, Salamanca, Kunsthalle Nürnberg, 2004/2005, S. 121.

8 Vgl. Alison M. Gingeras, „John Currin, Pictor Vulgaris“, in: Ausst.-Kat. *John Currin*, Gargosian Gallery, New York 2006, S. 34.

9 Vgl. dazu u. a. Maria Lluïsa Borràs, *Picabia*, London 1985, S. 321–330.

10 Entgegen der in der Literatur lange gängigen Auffassung, Picabia habe seine Werkgruppe der Akte im Winter 1941/1942 als Auftragswerke für den algerischen Kaufmann André Romanet begonnen, kommt Sara Cochran durch Quellenstudium zu dem Schluss, „dass Picabia seine realistischen Aktbilder am Ende der Dreißigerjahre nach Vorlagen erotischer Fotografien zu malen begann, also noch vor dem Krieg und seiner Begegnung mit Romanet“. Vgl. Sara Cochran, „Zur Malerei von Francis Picabia während des Zweiten Weltkrieges“, in: Ausst.-Kat. *Francis Picabia. Das Spätwerk 1933–1953*, hg. v. Zdenek Felix, Deichtorhallen, Hamburg; Museum Boijmans Van Beuningen, Rotterdam, Ostfildern-Ruit 1997, S.19.

11 Robert Rosenblum, „Picabia: Das Spätwerk“, in: Ausst.-Kat. *Picabia 1879–1953*, Galerie Neuendorf, Frankfurt/M., Scottish National Gallery of Modern Art, Edinburgh 1988, S. 47.

12 Katharina Hegewisch, „Die Kunst ist ein Spiel wie Liebe und Sport. Picabia und die Postmoderne“, in: Ausst.-Kat *Picabia 1879–1953* (zit. Anm. 11), S. 48.

13 Francis Picabia, 1922, aus: „La Pomme de Pins“, Februar 1922, zit. n. *Funny Guy and Dada, Picabias Schriften, Band 1*, Hamburg 1983, S. 63.

14 Francis Picabia, Mai 1921, ebd., S. 59.

15 Roberto Ohrt, „Avantgardistische Falten und realistisches Kunstlicht“, in: *Francis Picabia. Das Spätwerk 1933–1953* (zit. Anm. 10), S. 15.

16 Vgl. dazu auch ebd., S. 14 ff.

René Magritte (see note 18), p.186

21 René Magritte, letter to André Breton, June 24, 1946, translated after: Harry Torczyner, René Magritte (see note 18), p.187

22 René Magritte, letter to André Breton, August 11, 1946, translated after: Harry Torczyner, René Magritte (see note 18), p.188

23 René Magritte, letter to André Breton, June 24, 1946, translated after: Harry Torczyner, René Magritte (see note 18), p.187

24 See Gisèle Ollinger-Zinque, Frederik Leen (eds.), *Magritte 1898–1998* [sic!] (Stuttgart, Zurich: Belser, 1998), p. 332.

25 At Galerie Faubourg, May 11–June 5, 1948.

26 "Vache," actually meaning "cow," is a slang adjective for "nasty" or "hard-hearted," and in this context Magritte is also using it as a parody on the word "fauve" ("wild animal") and the corresponding ism.

27 By this, Louis Scutenaire, Magritte's poet friend from the circle of the Belgian Surrealists, who had already penned the catalog foreword "Les pieds plats" (The Flat Feet), felt obliged to further outdo himself: In his text "The life and acts of the Magritte of yore. Universal and Parisian painter," he rails with great cynicism against every system of thought in the world from Descartes to NATO to Mayan magic and most especially against Parisian painting, all the while celebrating the "Magritte of yore" (so longed for by the Surrealists) as the great modish painter who holds aloft "the grating banner of Parisian decency." See Laszlo Glozer, *Westkunst. Zeitgenössische Kunst seit 1939*, exhib. cat. (Cologne: DuMont Verlag, 1981), p. 161 f.

28 See René Magritte, letter to Louis Scutenaire, June 7, 1948, in David Sylvester (ed.), *René Magritte. Catalogue Raisonné*, vol. 2 (London: Philip Wilson, 1994), p. 167.

29 See also the text by Claire Gilman in this catalog, especially note 2.

30 Asger Jorn, "Intimer banaliteter," in *Helhesten*, May 1941. In the foreword to the catalog for his exhibition *Vingt peintures modifiées par Asger Jorn* at Galerie Rive Gauche, Paris, May 1959, Jorn mentions having written this text in 1939.

31 "Si vous avez des peintures anciennes, ne désespérez pas. Gardez vos souvenirs, mais détournez-les pour qu'ils correspondent à votre époque. Pourquoi rejeter l'ancien si on peut le moderniser avec quelques traits de pinceau ? Ca jette de l'actualité sur votre vieille culture. Soyez à la page, et distingués du même coup. La peinture, c'est fini. Autant donner le coup de grâce. Détournez. Vive la peinture. » Asger Jorn, "Peinture, détournée," in: *Vingt peintures modifiées par Asger Jorn*, exhib. cat., Galerie Rive Gauche, Paris 1959.

32 "l'économie se développant pour elle-même," Guy Debord, *La Societé du Spectacle* (Paris: Gallimard, 1967), §16; *The Society of the Spectacle*, trans. Donald Nicholson-Smith (New York: Zone Books, 1994), online at: http://situationist.cjb.net/

33 "Situation construite: Moment de la vie, concrètement et délibérément construit par l'organisation collective d'une ambiance unitaire et j'un jeu d'évènements." in "Définitions," in *Situationist International* Vol. 1, 1958, in *internationale situationniste*, édition augmentée, (Paris: Librairie Arthème Fayard, 1997), p. 13; English translation online at http://situationist.cjb.net/

34 "C'est la réalisation d'un jeu supérieure, plus exactement la provocation à ce jeu qu'est la présence humaine," *Manifeste*, in: SI Vol. 4 (1960), in *internationale situationniste* (see note 33, p. 144). English translation online at: http://situationist.cjb.net/

35 From "Peinture, détournée" (see note 31).

36 Interview with Georg Baselitz, "Ich bin ein renitenter Typ," in *Der Spiegel*, No. 33, August 13, 2007, p. 131.

37 Interview with the author, Munich, Jan. 28, 2008.

38 Peter-Klaus Schuster, "Raphael ohne Hände. Über Immendorffs verwirrende Strategien zur Kunst," in *Jörg Immendorff*, exhib. cat., Neue Nationalgalerie Berlin, 2005/2006, p. 24.

39 Jörg Immendorff interviewed by Walter Grasskamp, in *Arbeit in Geschichte – Geschichte in Arbeit*, exhib. cat., Kunsthaus Hamburg 1988, p. 157, quoted from Petzel (see note 4), p. 45.

40 Philip Guston quoted from Norbert Lynton, "An Obverse Decorum," in *Philip Guston, Paintings, 1969–1980*,

17 Vgl. dazu u. a. Cochran (zit. Anm. 10), S. 19–22.

18 René Magritte, Brief an André Breton, 24. Juni 1946, zit. n. Harry Torczyner, *René Magritte. Zeichen und Bilder*, Köln 1977, S. 187.

19 René Magritte, Brief an Gaston Puel, 8. März 1955, zit. n. Torczyner (zit. Anm. 18), S. 186.

20 „Die Ablehnung wird mit der ungeschickten Verwendung beim posthumen Gebrauch impressionistischer Technik begründet." René Magritte, „La Querelle du Soleil", zit. n. Torczyner (zit. Anm. 18), S. 186.

21 René Magritte, Brief an André Breton, 24. Juni 1946 (zit. Anm. 18), S. 187.

22 René Magritte, Brief an André Breton, 11. August 1946, zit. n. Torczyner (zit. Anm. 18), S. 188.

23 René Magritte, Brief an André Breton, 24. Juni 1946 (zit. Anm. 18), S. 187.

24 Vgl. Gisèle Ollinger-Zinque, Frederik Leen (Hg.), *Magritte 1898–1998* [sic!], Stuttgart, Zürich 1998, S. 332.

25 In der Galerie Faubourg, 11. Mai bis 5. Juni 1948.

26 „Vache", eigentlich „Kuh", bedeutet als umgangssprachliches Adjektiv „gemein", „hartherzig" und gilt in diesem Zusammenhang auch als Parodie Magrittes auf das Wort „fauve" („wildes Tier") und die entsprechende Kunstrichtung.

27 Louis Scutenaire, Magrittes Dichterfreund aus dem Kreis der belgischen Surrealisten, der schon das Katalogvorwort „Les pieds plats" („Die Plattfüße") verfasst hat, fühlt sich dadurch veranlasst, noch eins draufzusetzen: In seinem Text „Leben und Taten des Magritte von ehedem. Universeller und Pariser Maler" zieht er gegen sämtliche Gedankensysteme dieser Welt von Descartes über die Nato bis zum Mayazauber und ganz besonders gegen die Pariser Malerei mit vollem Zynismus zu Felde, um dabei den (von den Surrealisten so herbeigesehnten) „Magritte von ehedem" als größten Modemaler zu feiern, der „das knarrende Banner des Pariser Anstands hoch[hält]". Vgl. Laszlo Glozer, Ausst.-Kat. *Westkunst. Zeitgenössische Kunst seit 1939*, Köln 1981, S. 161 f.

28 Vgl. René Magritte, Brief an Louis Scutenaire, 7. Juni 1948, in: David Sylvester (Hg.), *René Magritte. Catalogue Raisonné*, Bd. 2, London 1993, S. 167.

29 Siehe dazu auch den Text von Claire Gilman in diesem Katalog, insbesondere die dortige Anm. 2.

30 Asger Jorn, „Intimer banaliteter", in: *Helhesten*, Mai 1941, auf Deutsch in: Asger Jorn, *Heringe in Acryl*, Hamburg 1987, S. 13 ff. Im Vorwort seines Kataloges seiner Ausstellung *Vingt peintures modifiées par Asger Jorn* in der Galerie Rive Gauche, Paris, Mai 1959, spricht Jorn davon, diesen Text 1939 verfasst zu haben.

31 « Si vous avez des peintures anciennes, ne désespérez pas. Gardez vos souvenirs, mais détournez-les pour qu'ils correspondent à votre époque. Pourquoi rejeter l'ancien si on peut le moderniser avec quelques traits de pinceau ? Ca jette de l'actualité sur votre vielle culture. Soyez à la page, et distingués du même coup. La peinture, c'est fini. Autant donner le coup de grâce. Détournez. Vive la peinture. » Asger Jorn, „Peinture, detournée", in: Ausst.-Kat. *Vingt peintures modifiées par Asger Jorn*, Galerie Rive Gauche, Paris 1959.

32 Guy Debord, *Die Gesellschaft des Spektakels*, übers. v. Jean-Jacques Raspaud, Luzern 1994, o. S., § 16.

33 „Definitionen", in: Heft 1 (1958), in: *Situationistische Internationale 1958–1969. Gesammelte Ausgaben des Organs der Situationistischen Internationale, Bd. 1*, Hamburg 1976, S. 18.

34 „Manifest", in: Heft 4 (1960), in: ebd., S. 152.

35 Asger Jorn, „Peinture, detournée" (zit. Anm. 31), Anm. 1.

36 Georg Baselitz im „Spiegel-Gespräch", „Ich bin ein renitenter Typ", in: *Der Spiegel*, Nr. 33, 13.08.2007, S. 131.

37 Gespräch mit der Autorin, München, 28. Jänner 2008.

38 Peter-Klaus Schuster, „Raphael ohne Hände. Über Immendorffs verwirrende Strategien zur Kunst", in: Ausst.-Kat. *Jörg Immendorff*, Neue Nationalgalerie Berlin, 2005/2006, S. 24.

39 Jörg Immendorff im Gespräch mit Walter Grasskamp, in: Ausst.-Kat. *Arbeit in Geschichte – Geschichte in Arbeit*, Kunsthaus Hamburg 1988, S. 157, zit. n. Petzel (zit. Anm. 4), S. 45.

40 Philip Guston zit. n. Norbert Lynton, „An Obverse Decorum", in: Ausst.-Kat. *Philip Guston, Paintings, 1969–1980*, Whitechapel Art Gallery, London 1982, S. 11.

41 „Philip Guston talking. A lecture given by Philip Guston at the University of Minnesota in March 1978, edited by Renée McKee", in: ebd., S. 50.

42 Ebd., S. 53.

exhib. cat., (London: Whitechapel Art Gallery, 1982), p. 11.

41 "Philip Guston talking. A lecture given by Philip Guston at the University of Minnesota in March 1978, edited by Renée McKee," ibid., p. 50.

42 Ibid., p. 53.

43 Ibid., p. 52.

44 Peter Saul, interview with the author, New York, Jan. 25, 2008.

45 Mark Rosenthal, "Neil Jenney, Paintings and Sculpture 1967–1980," in *Neil Jenney* (see note 2), p. 7.

46 See ibid, pp. 7 f., on Jenney's early and very earliest production, which included work oriented towards Abstract Expressionism as well a phase of "hard-edged color-field painting" and Minimalist and Post-Minimalist sculpture. See also account therein of a group of artist friends to which Jenney belonged around 1967 who, among other things, defined idiosyncrasy as an elevated value that opposed the predictability of Minimal Art. In an interview with the author, Jenney also underlined that the realism in his painting of the late 1960s was a reaction to that of Photorealism, which he detested.

47 See "Statements by Neil Jenney," in *Neil Jenney* (see note 2), p. 48.

48 Telephone interview with the author, April 7, 2008.

49 Undated quotation from Neil Jenney, from "Statements by Neil Jenney" (see note 2), p. 50.

50 Neil Jenney quoted from Rosenthal (see note 45), p. 11.

51 Neil Jenney 1969, in *"Bad" Painting*, exhib. cat., The New Museum, New York 1978, p. 22.

52 Neil Jenney 1978, in: "Statements by Neil Jenney" (see note 2), p. 49.

53 See Rosenthal, note 45, p. 10, and interview with the author, New York, Jan. 24, 2008.

54 See *"Bad" Painting*, exhib. cat. (see note 51), p. 22, and Rosenthal (see note 45), p. 10, and, in the same catalog (see note 2), p. 48. Although Jenney referred in interviews with the author on Jan. 14 and April 7, 2008, to his "bad period" as lasting until 1970, in this quotation he speaks of a transition to the "concerned paintings" from October 1969. See also the pictures dated 1970 in *Neil Jenney. The Bad Years 1969–70*, exhib. cat., Gargosian Gallery, New York 2001.

55 The realization that realistic painting is ultimately always illusionistic, and his concurrent decision to paint in an illusionistic style, led Jenney to retrofit his pictures with heavy frames that would strengthen this illusionistic character.

56 Interview with the author, New York, Jan. 24, 2008.

57 On these pictures, see Rosenthal, (see note 45), p. 13 ff.

58 Marcia Tucker, *"Bad" Painting* (see note 51), p. 5.

59 The show featured: James Albertson, Joan Brown, Eduardo Carrillo, James Chatelain, CPLY, Charles Garabedian, Robert Chambless Hendon, Joseph Hilton, Neil Jenney, Judith Linhares, P. Walter Siler, Earl Staley, Shari Urquhart, and William Wegman.

60 See Petzel (see note 4).

61 On this, see, among others: "Die Suche nach der Wahrheit ist eine der vornehmsten Aufgaben des Menschen, umso mehr, als es gar keine Wahrheit gibt [...]," or: "Das Wissen erweitern durch Scheitern," in *Werner Büttner, Martin Kippenberger, Albert Oehlen, Wahrheit ist Arbeit*, exhib. cat., Folkwang Museum, Essen, p. 28 f. See also the reflection on this show in the exhibition curated by Helmut Draxler at Kunstverein München in 1992 entitled *Malen ist Wahlen*, especially Diedrich Diederichsen's text "Virtueller Maoismus: Das Wissen von 1984“, p. 36 ff in the catalog to this show.

62 Albert Oehlen interviewed by Diedrich Diederichsen, in Diedrich Diederichsen, *Elektra. Schriften zur Kunst* (Hamburg: Meterverlag, 1987), p. 16.

63 Albert Oehlen, "Das Ende bringt die Wende," in Kasper König (ed.), *Von hier aus. 2 Monate neue deutsche Kunst in Düsseldorf*, exhib. cat., Gesellschaft für aktuelle Kunst, Düsseldorf 1984, pp. 210, 212.

64 Albert Oehlen, "You Take the Blue One and I Take a New One. (Farbenlehre II)," in *Wolkenkratzer Art Journal*, No. 8 (1985), p. 44–47, quoted here from Petzel (see note 4), p. 55.

65 "The rules of the game," (see note 5), p. 67.

43 Ebd., S. 52.

44 Peter Saul im Gespräch mit der Autorin, New York, 25. Jänner 2008.

45 Mark Rosenthal, „Neil Jenney, Paintings and Sculpture 1967–1980", in: Ausst.-Kat. *Neil Jenney* (zit. Anm. 2), S. 7.

46 Vgl. ebd., S. 7 f., zu Jenneys frühem und frühestem Schaffen, das am abstrakten Expressionismus orientierte Werke ebenso umfasst wie eine Phase von „hard-edged color-field painting" sowie minimalistische und postminimalistische Skulptur. Siehe dort auch zu einer Gruppe von Künstlerfreunden, der Jenney um 1967 angehörte, die unter anderem Idiosynkrasie als hohen, der Vorhersehbarkeit des Minimal entgegentretenden Wert definierte. Im Gespräch mit der Autorin hat Jenney weiters herausgestrichen, dass er Ende der 1960er-Jahre mit seinem Realismus in der Malerei auf jenen des von ihm gehassten Fotorealismus reagiert habe.

47 Vgl. „Statements by Neil Jenney", in: Ausst.-Kat. *Neil Jenney* (zit. Anm. 2), S. 48.

48 Telefonat mit der Autorin, 7. April 2008.

49 Undatiertes Zitat von Neil Jenney, zit. n. „Statements by Neil Jenney" (zit. Anm. 2), S. 50.

50 Neil Jenney zit. n. Rosenthal (zit. Anm. 45), S. 11.

51 Neil Jenney 1969, in: Ausst.-Kat. *"Bad" Painting*, The New Museum, New York 1978, S. 22.

52 Neil Jenney 1978, in: „Statements by Neil Jenney" (zit. Anm. 2), S. 49.

53 Vgl. Rosenthal (zit. Anm. 45), S. 10, und Gespräch mit der Autorin, New York, 24. Jänner 2008.

54 Vgl. Ausst.-Kat. *"Bad" Painting* (zit. Anm. 51), S. 22, und Rosenthal (zit. Anm. 45), S. 10, sowie im selben Katalog S. 48. Obwohl Jenney in Gesprächen mit der Autorin am 14. Jänner und 7. April 2008 seine „bad period" als bis 1970 gehend bezeichnete, spricht er in diesem Zitat vom Übergang zu den „Concerned Paintings" ab Oktober 1969. Vgl. dazu auch die mit 1970 datierten Bilder in: Ausst.-Kat. *Neil Jenney. The Bad Years 1969–70*, Gargosian Gallery, New York 2001.

55 Die Entscheidung für illusionistische Malweisen beziehungsweise die Erkenntnis des letztlich immer illusionistischen Charakters realistischer Malerei führt Jenney zum Entschluss, seine Bilder nachträglich mit schweren, die Illusion verstärkenden Rahmen zu versehen.

56 Gespräch mit der Autorin, New York, 24. Jänner 2008.

57 Zu diesen Bildern siehe Rosenthal (zit. Anm. 45), S. 13 ff.

58 Marcia Tucker, „'Bad' Painting", in: Ausst.-Kat. *"Bad" Painting* (zit. Anm. 51), S. 5.

59 Die gezeigten Künstler waren: James Albertson, Joan Brown, Eduardo Carrillo, James Chatelain, CPLY, Charles Garabedian, Robert Chambless Hendon, Joseph Hilton, Neil Jenney, Judith Linhares, P. Walter Siler, Earl Staley, Shari Urquhart und William Wegman.

60 Vgl. Petzel (zit. Anm. 4).

61 Vgl. dazu u. a.: „Die Suche nach der Wahrheit ist eine der vornehmsten Aufgaben des Menschen, umso mehr, als es gar keine Wahrheit gibt […]", oder: „Das Wissen erweitern durch Scheitern", in: Ausst.-Kat. *Werner Büttner, Martin Kippenberger, Albert Oehlen, Wahrheit ist Arbeit*, Museum Folkwang, Essen, S. 28 f. Vgl. auch die Reflexion dieser Ausstellung im Rahmen der von Helmut Draxler 1992 im Kunstverein München veranstalteten Ausstellung *Malen ist Wahlen*, insbesondere im dort publizierten Text von Diedrich Diederichsen, „Virtueller Maoismus: Das Wissen von 1984", S. 36 ff.

62 Albert Oehlen, Interview mit Diedrich Diederichsen, in: Diedrich Diederichsen, *Elektra. Schriften zur Kunst*, Hamburg 1987, S. 16.

63 Albert Oehlen, „Das Ende bringt die Wende", in: Kasper König (Hg.), Ausst.-Kat. *Von hier aus. 2 Monate neue deutsche Kunst in Düsseldorf*, Gesellschaft für aktuelle Kunst, Düsseldorf 1984, S. 210, 212.

64 Albert Oehlen, „You Take the Blue One and I Take a New One. (Farbenlehre II)", in: *Wolkenkratzer Art Journal*, Nr. 8 (1985), S. 44–47, hier zit. n. Petzel (zit. Anm. 4), S. 55.

65 „The rules of the game" (zit. Anm. 5), S. 67.

66 Ebd., S. 71.

67 Die Frage der „Autonomie des Bildes" wird von Oehlen im Interview mit Diederichsen (zit. Anm. 5), S. 66 ff., wiederholt angesprochen.

68 Ebd., S. 100.

66 Ibid., p. 71.

67 The question of the "autonomy of the picture" is referred to repeatedly by Oehlen in the interview with Diederichsen, ibid., p. 66 ff.

68 Ibid., p. 100.

69 Ibid., p. 69.

70 See, among others, ibid., p. 104.

71 Julian Schnabel, in Amnon Barzel, "With Schnabel, About Schnabel. An Introduction and Excerpts from an Interview," in *Julian Schnabel*, exhib. cat., Museo d'arte contemporanea Prato, 1989, p. 20.

72 In an interview with Susanne Neuburger and the author (Vienna, Nov. 20, 2007), Jutta Koether called Bad Painting a "brand" controlled by the art market.

73 John Currin interviewed by Alison M. Gingeras, Feb. 26, 2002, quoted from Alison M. Gingeras, "John Currin, Pictor Vulgaris" (see note 8), p. 33.

74 Ibid., p. 75.

75 Ibid., p. 39.

76 "My technique is in no way comparable to that of an average European painter." Quoted from: Calvin Thomas, "Lifting the veil. Old masters, pornography and the work of John Currin," in *The New Yorker*, Jan. 28, 2008, p. 60.

77 John Currin interviewed by Alison M. Gingeras, Feb. 26, 2002 (see note 8, p. 43).

69 Ebd., S. 69.

70 Vgl. u. a. ebd., S. 104.

71 Julian Schnabel, in: Amnon Barzel, „With Schnabel, About Schnabel. And Introduction and Excerpts from an Interview“, in: Ausst.-Kat. *Julian Schnabel*, Museo d'arte contemporanea Prato, 1989, S. 20.

72 Im Gespräch mit Susanne Neuburger und der Autorin (Wien, 20. November 2007) nannte Jutta Koether Bad Painting eine kunstmarktgesteuerte „brand“.

73 Alison M. Gingeras, „Interview mit John Currin“, in: Ausst.-Kat. *Lieber Maler, male mir. Radikaler Realismus nach Picabia*, Centre Pompidou, Kunsthalle Wien, Schirn Kunsthalle Frankfurt, 2002, S. 76.

74 Ebd., S. 75.

75 Ebd., S. 76.

76 „Meine Technik ist in keinster Weise mit der eines durchschnittlichen europäischen Malers des 19. Jahrhunderts vergleichbar.“ Zit. n. Calvin Thomas, „Lifting the veil. Old masters, pornography and the work of John Currin“, in: *The New Yorker*, 28. Januar 2008, S. 60.

77 Gingeras (zit. Anm. 73), S. 77.

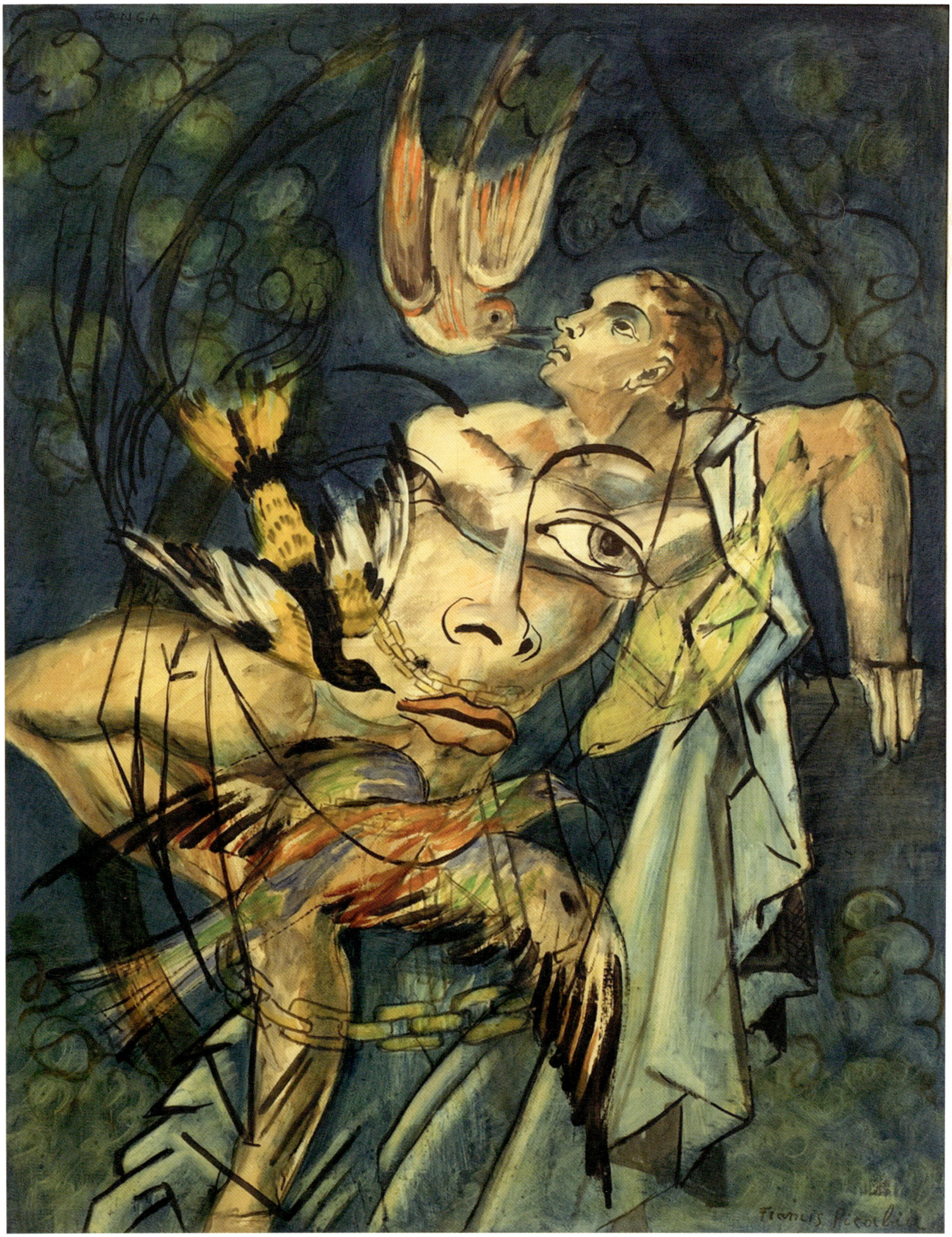

056 Francis Picabia
Ganga, 1927

Öl auf Leinwand / oil on canvas, 116,5 x 87 cm
Museum Moderner Kunst Stiftung Ludwig Wien,
Leihgabe der Österreichischen Ludwig Stiftung /
on loan from the Austrian Ludwig Foundation,
seit / since 1988

Picabias Konzept der Ironie

Stefan Neuner

Allerdings war im zwanzigsten Jahrhundert noch kein Künstler imstande, bis an seinen Tod immer neue Abnormitäten zu erzeugen: der Umschlag in Norm, Konvention, Affirmation droht allen, und manchmal fangen die Spätwerke heute außerordentlich früh an. Sie waren einmal, und das ist lang her, die besten […]; in neuerer Zeit sind sie meist Abfall.
Heinz-Klaus Metzger

[A]nhand welcher textlichen Kennzeichen, Hilfsmittel, Hinweise oder Signale können wir entscheiden, ob ein Text ironisch ist oder nicht?
Paul de Man

I.

Jemand könnte kommen – sagen wir: der „Mann von der Straße" – und die naive Frage stellen: „Warum sollte ich mich für ‚schlechte Malerei' interessieren?" Jemand anders – sagen wir: jemand, der die Malerei eines Albert Oehlen oder eines Martin Kippenberger zu schätzen weiß – könnte darauf antworten, dass „schlechte Malerei" noch lange keine „schlechte Kunst" zu sein brauche. Dieser Jemand würde dann wahrscheinlich versuchen, seinem Gegenüber verständlich zu machen, dass es einen Unterschied gebe zwischen misslungenen oder dilettantischen Bildern und solchen, die im vollen Bewusstsein „schlecht" gemalt worden seien. Der „Mann von der Straße" würde womöglich immer noch nicht verstehen, was daran „gut" und interessant sein sollte. Ich stelle mir vor, dass man ihm dann erklären würde, dass die Qualität solcher Malerei darin bestehe, etablierte Normen des Geschmacks in kritischer Absicht infrage zu stellen und andere, nicht konforme Qualitäten bildnerischer Gestaltung zu erkunden und auszuarbeiten.

Das wäre eine ziemlich theoretische Antwort und wahrscheinlich die einzige, die man dem „Mann von der Straße" geben können wird. Ich glaube aber, dass eine solche Erklärung – zumindest wenn sie von jemandem kommt, der beim Betrachten „schlechter Malerei" ein ehrliches Vergnügen empfindet – nicht ganz aufrichtig wäre. Denn ich kann mir auf der einen Seite kaum vorstellen, dass man den „kritischen Gehalt" solcher Kunst genießt. Würde, wer solche Präferenzen setzt und in erster Linie an einer kritischen Auseinandersetzung mit ästhetischen Wertzuschreibungen interessiert

Picabia's Concept of Irony

Stefan Neuner

In the twentieth century no artist has yet been able to create ever new abnormities right through to his death: the turn to norms, conventions, and affirmation threatens them all, and sometimes the later period sets in remarkably early.
Once—a long time ago—they were the best [...]; but in recent years they are mainly just trash.
Heinz-Klaus Metzger

[B]y what markers, by what devices, by what indications or signals in the text can we decide that a text is ironic or is not?
Paul de Man

I.

Someone might come along—perhaps the "man in the street"—and ask a naive question: "Why should I take any interest in 'bad painting'?" Someone else, perhaps someone who appreciates the painting of artists like Albert Oehlen or Martin Kippenberger, might answer that "bad painting" is not by definition "bad art." This second someone would then probably try to explain that there is a difference between failed or amateurish pictures and pictures that have been very deliberately painted as "bad." The "man in the street" might then still not understand what it was that was supposed to be "good" and interesting. I guess that then the explanation would be that the quality of this kind of painting rests in its critical questioning of established norms of taste and in its exploration and testing of other, nonconformist qualities of painting and form.

That would be a fairly theoretical answer and perhaps the only answer one would be able to give the "man in the street." But I believe that this explanation is not quite right, at least when it comes from someone who feels a sincere pleasure when looking at "bad painting." For one, I find it hard to believe that it is possible to enjoy the "critical content" of this art. Would it not be the case that a person who sets such a priority and is interested in a critical approach to aesthetic value judgments would prefer conceptual art practices and be excited about forms like Appropriation Art or institutional critique? On the other hand, I also do not believe that the pleasure in "badly" painted pictures can have anything to do with a conviction that this kind of painting can develop a new and positive basis for

ist, sich nicht eher an konzeptuelle Kunstpraktiken halten und sich etwa an Appropriation-Art oder Institutional Critique begeistern? Auf der anderen Seite glaube ich auch nicht, dass der Genuss an „schlecht" gemalten Bildern irgendetwas mit der Überzeugung zu tun haben kann, dass diese Malerei neue, positiv bestimmbare Grundlagen des Bildermachens entwickelt, auf denen man dereinst eine Akademie errichten wird. Wer sich für Bad Painting ernstlich erwärmt, so viel ist sicher, der genießt gerade die Differenz zu dem, was *andere* für „gute" Malerei halten.

Hinter einem derartigen Genuss steht freilich ein recht sophistizierter Geschmack. Ich vermute, dass wir alle, Leser und Autoren dieses Kataloges, mit ihm gut vertraut sind. Er ist in einem bestimmten urbanen intellektuellen Milieu verbreitet, in dem ein Lebensstil gepflogen wird, der aus dem Unauthentischen einen Kult macht. Vielleicht gehören wir selbst zu Menschen, die ihre Klamotten im Gebrauchtwarenladen kaufen, ohne dazu finanziell gezwungen zu sein. Es könnte auch sein, dass wir unsere Wohnung mit Kitschaccessoire ausgestattet haben, das wir am Flohmarkt zusammengesucht haben. Und möglicherweise frequentieren wir Bars, in denen zwischen elektronischer Tanzmusik auch aus der Mode gekommene Schlager aufgelegt werden. Vielleicht kennen wir also den sekundären Genuss, den man aus dem Gebrauch von Stilelementen ziehen kann, die anderen ein unmittelbares Vergnügen bereiten. Eine derartige ästhetische Wertschätzung hegt ein tiefes Misstrauen gegenüber der Vorstellung authentischen Ausdrucks. Überdies dient dieser Geschmack – wie alles, was mit Fragen des Lebensstils zu tun hat – einer sozialen Unterscheidung, und zwar von jenen Menschen, denen solches ästhetisches Raffinement nicht zugänglich ist. Wir sehen jetzt auch, weshalb unser Aficionado des Bad Painting dem „Mann von der Straße" keine ehrliche Antwort geben wird: Denn sein Geschmack am Sekundären entzündet sich an der Tatsache, dass er dem „Mann von der Straße" unterstellt, an die Möglichkeit authentischen Ausdrucks zu glauben und die von ihm aufgegriffenen Stilelemente auf unmittelbare – will heißen: naive – Weise zu genießen.

Man könnte einen solchen unkompliziert empfindenden Menschen mit einem Subjektivierungstyp in Verbindung bringen, den Richard Rorty „Metaphysiker" genannt und von einem anderen, den er als „Ironikerin" bezeichnet, unterschieden hat.[1] Rortys „Metaphysiker" ist davon überzeugt, dass der Diskurs, in dem er seine Überzeugungen zum Ausdruck bringt, sich auf Tatsachen bezieht, die in der Realität wirklich existieren. Er glaubt an den gesunden Menschenverstand und besteht darauf, dass es in diesem Diskurs nicht auf die Sprache ankommt, sondern nur auf Wahrheit. Demgegenüber zweifelt die „Ironikerin" an diesem Diskurs. Für sie besteht er nur aus Begriffen, und sie glaubt nicht daran, dass diese sich auf etwas real Existierendes beziehen (sie ist „Nominalistin"). Ihre Überzeugung ist vielmehr, dass diese Begriffe kontingent sind und über keine zeitlose Bedeutung verfügen (sie ist „Historistin"). Und deshalb geht sie davon aus, dass es in diesem Diskurs vor allem auf die Sprache ankommt. Da die Begriffe, deren sich die „Ironikerin" bedient, für sie kontingent sind, hält sie sie auch für austauschbar. Sie ist bemüht, alternative Sprechweisen kennen zu lernen, und versteht die Arbeit am Diskurs über ihre Ansichten als an eine Arbeit an sich selbst. Sprache ist ihr ein Mittel

making pictures, such as might some day be good enough to justify the foundation of an academy. If you are interested in Bad Painting, then—and this is for sure—it is because you enjoy the difference to what *others* see as "good" painting.

Admittedly, this kind of pleasure is based on a pretty sophisticated taste, which I am fairly sure that all of us, the readers and authors of this catalog, will be quite familiar with. It is common in a certain urban intellectual milieu that fosters a preference for a lifestyle that makes a cult of the inauthentic. Maybe we buy our clothes in second-hand stores, without being financially bound to do so. Perhaps we have furnished our apartments with all sorts of kitsch that we have collected at flea markets. And maybe we frequent bars where electronic dance music is punctuated by old-fashioned pop songs. Perhaps we know the vicarious pleasure that can be derived from using styles which have provided others with a more direct form of pleasure. This approach to aesthetic values involves a deep-rooted distrust of the idea of authentic expression. And this taste also serves a function of social distinction—like all other questions of lifestyle—from those people who are not capable of such refined aesthetics. We can therefore also see now why our aficionado of Bad Painting will not give the "man in the street" an honest answer. His taste for the vicarious is based on the fact that he assumes the "man in the street" believes in the possibility of authentic expression and is therefore able to directly, that is, naively enjoy the styles others select second-hand.

It would be possible to see this kind of person with straightforward sentiments as the type of subject Richard Rorty called the "metaphysician," to be distinguished from the ones he termed "ironist."[1] Rorty's "metaphysician" is convinced that the discourse he uses to express his views is based on hard facts that really exist. He believes in common sense and insists that this discourse is not about language but about truth alone. By contrast, the "ironist" doubts the validity of this discourse, seeing it as consisting only of terms that do not refer to anything that really exists (the "ironist" is a "nominalist"). The "ironist" rather believes that all terms are contingent and have no timeless meaning; she is also a "historicist." Therefore, she assumes that the discourse is primarily about language. As the ideas that the "ironist" draws on are contingent they are also exchangeable. She makes an effort to learn alternative ways of speaking, and she understands her work on the discourse about her ideas as work on her own person. Language is a means of creating the self, and subjectivity is formable. The "ironist" sees the creation of her own self as a process that will never lead to a final result free from doubt. Therefore she keeps her distance to everything that she herself says. This is what makes her an "ironist": her way of speaking is a mask.

In aesthetic questions, I imagine that Rorty's "ironist" will prefer vicarious pleasure. From the trash that she collects from the paraphernalia of capitalist consumer culture, she puts together a "style" in which she can clothe herself as if behind a mask. The contingency of this "individual style" is highlighted by the historical index that its elements carry like phased-out fashion articles. The "bad guys" of new painting are in fact her sisters. They too are "ironists" who create themselves from used

der Selbsterschaffung, und Subjektivität versteht sie als formbar. Ihre Selbsterschaffung begreift sie als einen Prozess, der nie zu einem abschließenden und nicht weiter bezweifelbaren Ergebnis führen kann. Daher wahrt sie auch Distanz zu allem, was sie behauptet. Eben darin ist sie „Ironikerin": Ihre Sprechweise ist eine Maske.

In ästhetischen Fragen, stelle ich mir vor, wird Rortys „Ironikerin" eine Vorliebe für das sekundäre Genießen zeigen. Aus dem Plunder, den sie unter den Abfällen der kapitalistischen Konsumkultur zusammensucht, bastelt sie sich einen „Stil" zusammen, in den sie sich wie in eine Larve hüllen kann. Die Kontingenz dieses „Individualstils" wird durch den historischen Index hervorgehoben, den seine Elemente als ausrangierte Modeartikel tragen. Die „bad guys" der neuen Malerei sind eigentlich ihre Schwestern. Auch sie sind „Ironikerinnen", die sich aus Verbrauchtem selbst erschaffen. Sie greifen dabei auf zwei Malweisen zurück, die in den 1980er-Jahren längst obsolet geworden waren; nicht zuletzt weil diese auf die „metaphysische" Grundannahme bauten, ein Gemälde sei auf Reales bezogen – entweder indem es die Erscheinung der wirklichen Welt wiedergibt oder subjektives Erleben und Empfinden zum Ausdruck bringt: Figuration und Expressionismus. Diese herabgekommenen Versatzstücke haben die „bösen Mädels" zu ihren pointiert unauthentischen „Individualstilen" verschmolzen.

II.

Francis Picabias künstlerische Entwicklung ist so unstet wie die der allermeisten Maler in der ersten Hälfte des 20. Jahrhunderts. Kaum ein Künstler, der in den ersten beiden Jahrzehnten des vergangenen Jahrhunderts zu jenen Innovationsschüben beigetragen hätte, die wir mit dem Begriff der klassischen Avantgarde verbinden, der in den 1920er- und 1930er-Jahren dem Vorstoß in die Abstraktion die Treue gewahrt oder die Experimente mit radikalen Verfahrenstechniken wie Collage oder Assemblage weitergetrieben hätte. Picassos Rückzug aus dem Kubismus während der Kriegsjahre ist ein Präzedenzfall. In den 1920er-Jahren verlassen immer weitere Teile der Avantgarde die Frontstellungen und kehren ins gesicherte Lager der figurativen Tradition zurück.[2] Die Diskontinuitäten, denen man im Œuvre von Künstlern wie André Derain, Carlo Carrà, Gino Severini, Kasimir Malewitsch und vielen anderen begegnet, lassen es zweifelhaft erscheinen, ob von so etwas wie einer „stilistischen" Entwicklung, geschweige denn vom „Reifen" eines individuellen malerischen Idioms überhaupt noch gesprochen werden kann. Nur wenigen Malern gelingt es, über die Brüche hinweg ein Werk von gleich bleibendem Interesse hervorzubringen. Mäßigung und qualitativer Verfall sind oft gleichbedeutend. Die Fallhöhe ist mitunter beträchtlich. Giorgio de Chirico ist der Schulfall eines Künstlers, der nach einem radikalen und historisch folgenreichen Schaffensmoment in die völlige Bedeutungslosigkeit zurücksank.

Lange Zeit wollte es scheinen, dass es bei Picabia sich nicht anders verhält. So haben wir auf der einen Seite den Picabia zwischen 1912 und 1922, einen frühen Vorkämpfer der Abstraktion, einen Picabia, der mit Bild-Text-Montagen experimentierte, den Picabia der „Mechanomorphe", der an

goods. In doing so they draw on two painting styles that had become long obsolete by the 1980s, not least because these rested on the metaphysical assumption that a painting refers to something real, either by reproducing the appearance of the real world or by expressing subjective experience and sentiment: Figuration and Expressionism. The "bad girls" transformed elements of these out-of-fashion approaches into their accentuated "individual styles."

II.

Francis Picabia's artistic development is as unstable as that of most painters in the first half of the twentieth century. Of all the artists of the classical avant-garde who contributed to the great drive to innovate in the first decades of the century, there are only few who remained faithful to their abstract principles in the 1920s and 1930s, or even developed them further with radical methods like collage or assemblage. Picasso's retreat from Cubism during the war years set a precedent. In the 1920s more and more avant-garde artists abandoned the front lines and returned to the snug camp of the figurative tradition.[2] The discontinuities encountered in the œuvre of artists like André Derain, Carlo Carrà, Gino Severini, Kasimir Malevich, and many more, raise the question as to whether it is even possible to still speak of something like a "stylistic" development, let alone of a "maturation" of an individual painterly idiom. Only few artists are able to produce a consistently interesting œuvre across all the disruption. Moderation often amounts to a loss of quality, and this loss is sometimes very considerable. Giorgio de Chirico is the classic case of an artist who sank into complete obscurity after a radical and historically influential productive period.

For a long time it seemed as if the same was true of Picabia. On the one hand, there is the Picabia of 1912 through 1922, an early proponent of abstraction, a Picabia who experimented with image-text montage, the Picabia of the "mechanomorphs," working on a new pictorial syntax that drew on the diagram and engineering drawing. And then we have Picabia, as a close friend and partner in artistic dialog with Marcel Duchamp, who translated the latter's readymade method into the pictorial and provided an artistic commentary on the complex of ideas associated with *The Large Glass*. Finally Picabia as an impresario and protagonist of the Paris Dada scene, whose iconoclastic pranks are mentioned in all guidebooks of the classical avant-gardes.[3] On the other hand, we have Picabia after Dada. An artist who seems to waver between two different variations on figuration, a maker of pastiche and a plagiarist, plundering all of art history, copying photographs as paintings, and seemingly unable to paint a single stroke without having an already existing image as an (unacknowledged) model. This is a Picabia who again and again painfully shows that he was once an innovative thinker, but never a good painter.

For a long time the work of this second Picabia was paid only scant attention. Picabia after Dada was Picabia *after* Picabia. In the 1980s, this appraisal fundamentally changed. Picabia's work of the 1920s, 1930s and 1940s suddenly became interesting again. It seemed to intersect with key themes

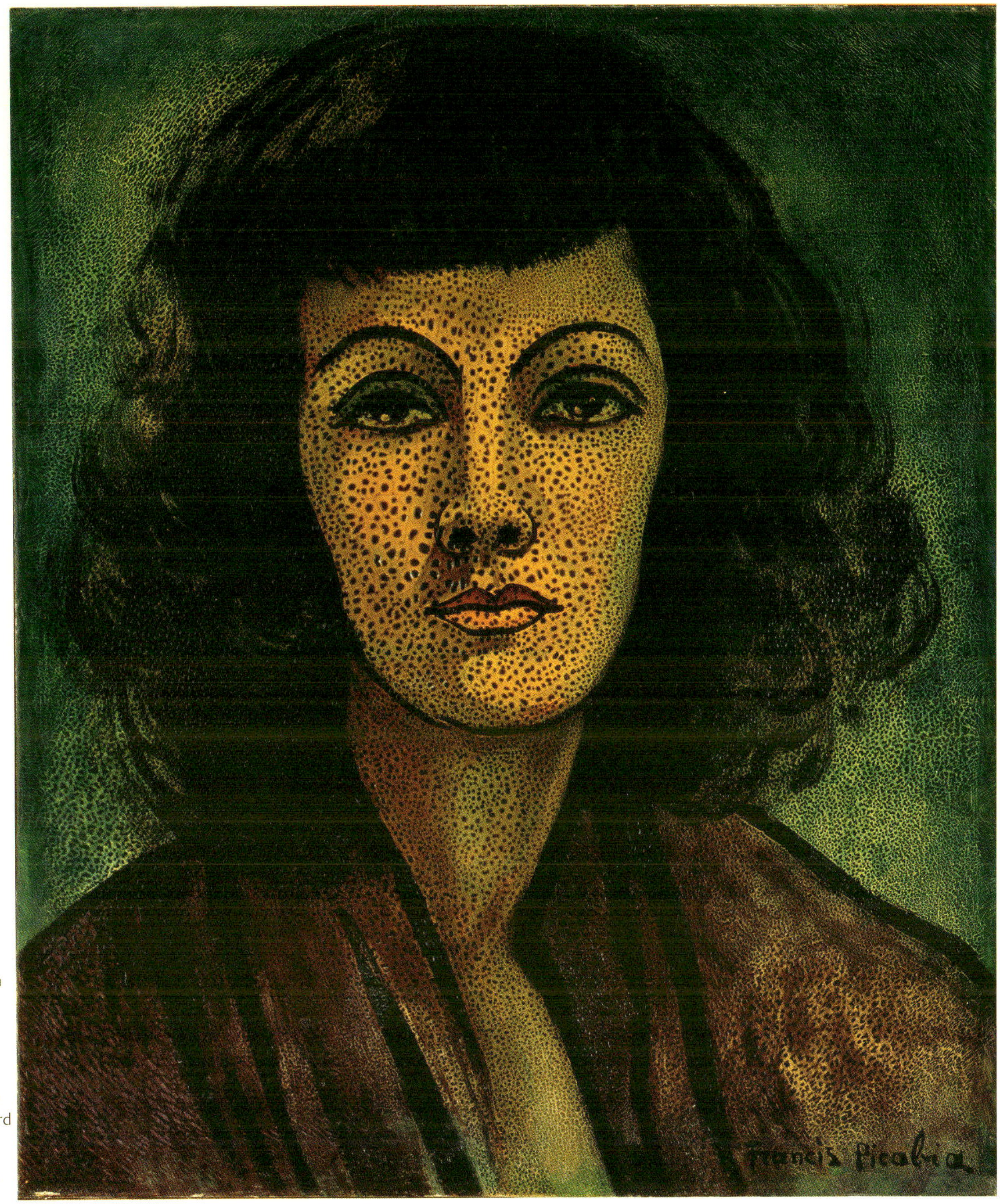

057 **Francis Picabia**
Portrait de Femme, 1935 (Porträt einer Frau / Portrait of a Woman)
Öl auf Karton / oil on cardboard
73 x 60 cm
Galerie Bruno Bischofberger, Zürich

einer neuen, am Diagramm und der Ingenieurszeichnung orientierten Bildsyntax arbeitete. Wir haben den Intimus und künstlerischen Dialogpartner Marcel Duchamps, der das Readymade-Verfahren ins Bildliche transponierte und den Ideenkomplex um das *Große Glas* künstlerisch kommentierte. Schließlich den Picabia als Impresario und Protagonisten der Pariser Dada-Szene, dessen ikonoklastische Pranken sich in allen Res gestae der klassischen Avantgarden verzeichnet finden.[3] Auf der anderen Seite haben wir aber den Picabia nach Dada. Einen Künstler, der scheinbar unentschlossen zwischen verschiedenen Spielarten der Figuration schwankt, einen Pasticheur und Plagiator, der die gesamte Kunstgeschichte plündert, Fotografien abmalt und keinen Strich hervorbringen zu können scheint, ohne sich an einer (unausgewiesenen) Bildvorlage zu orientieren – einen Picabia, der bis zur Unerträglichkeit

in contemporary debate. For one, the discussion of a postmodern plurality of styles elevated pastiche to the status of a relevant aesthetic category, and for another the New Painting context saw a new "taste for the tasteless," partly deriving from the punk movement. Clever and subtle games with quotations on the one hand, trash on the other: two poles within an aesthetics of the secondary. The "late" Picabia became interesting as an "ancestor" of and point of contact between both of these trends.[4] His art historical pasticci and his transgression of all the standards of good taste seemed to recommend him as a model figure in a "postmodern" and "post-avant-gardist" art practice. Picabia was now recognized as an ironist and as the supreme "bad guy" in modern art history.[5] The perspective on his work shifted fundamentally in the 1980s. Picabia after Dada now seemed more and more to reveal Picabia *as* Picabia. A period which prioritized the demystification of the "myth" of originality[6] now discovered in the early Picabia an artist who had made quotation and copy key principles of his work.[7]

This leads to the question whether the rediscovered Picabia was accorded the role of a subject or of an object of secondary aesthetic pleasures. Was he in his later years a naive "metaphysicist," whose dubious painterly production could be recycled as trash? Or was he himself already an "ironist," whose paintings made second-hand use of outmoded painterly idioms? Is the inauthentic a strategy or the fate of Picabia's painting?

III.

There is no simple answer to these questions. I suspect that we can only get closer to an answer if we take a step backwards and reexamine in greater depth the structural status of "bad" painting within Modernism. There is good reason to argue that all great modernist painting was once "bad" painting. This is not merely to say that an audience bound by its own prejudices and that conservative critics thought this painting was "bad," whilst it was in fact always as great as we see it today. When it was said of Courbet in the 1850s, of Manet in the 1860s, of the Impressionists, and later of Cézanne, Matisse, and Picasso that they could not paint, this was not just a philistine reaction; strictly speaking it was the truth, simply because the standards we employ today to define these painters as "good" were first established by the painters themselves. To take the example of Impressionism: Measured against the norms of pictorial representation, a painting that showed a landscape without using the available technical methods of producing spatial depth could only be seen as a failure, and the same was true of a picture of a human body that was not made plastic by means of shading. In the nineteenth century, the new textures created by unmixed and bright colors set directly adjacent to each other, which are so popular today, still looked as if their creators were unable to master an identifiable painting technique.[8] A positive assessment of canvases like these required a totally new consensus on the aims of painting. It was necessary to accept the ephemeral and superficial instead of the permanent and weighty, and to accept that the aim of representation was an optical impression in place of the embodiment of something real, and also to see subjectivity and originality

immer von neuem den Beweis antritt, dass er zwar einmal ein innovativer Kopf gewesen ist, nie aber ein guter Maler.

Lange Zeit hat das Werk dieses zweiten Picabia wenig Aufmerksamkeit auf sich gezogen. Picabia nach Dada: Das war Picabia *nach* Picabia. Diese Situation sollte sich indes in den 1980er-Jahren grundlegend ändern. Picabias Werk der 1920er-, der 1930er- und 1940er-Jahre rückte in den Fokus des Interesses. Es kommunizierte mit Zentralthemen der zeitgenössischen Diskussion. Zum einen wertete die Debatte um den postmodernen Stilpluralismus den Pastiche zu einer relevanten ästhetischen Kategorie auf, zum anderen kam im Kontext der Neuen Malerei, angestoßen von Impulsen aus der Punkbewegung, ein „Geschmack am Geschmacklosen" auf. Das raffinierte Spiel mit Zitaten auf der einen, Trash auf der anderen Seite: zwei Pole innerhalb einer Ästhetik des Sekundären. Der „späte" Picabia geriet als „Ahnherr" und Kreuzungspunkt beider Tendenzen ins Blickfeld.[4] Seine kunsthistorischen Pasticci, seine Unterbietungen aller Standards des guten Geschmacks schienen ihn nun als Leitbild einer „postmodernen" und „postavantgardistischen" Kunstpraxis zu empfehlen. Picabia schien sich nun erkennen zu geben als Ironiker und „bad guy" der modernen Kunstgeschichte par excellence.[5] Die Perspektive auf Picabias Werk verschob sich in den 1980er-Jahren grundlegend. Picabia nach Dada schien nun immer mehr Picabia *als* Picabia zu enthüllen. Eine Zeit, die sich an nichts so sehr wie der Entzauberung des „Mythos" der „Originalität" abarbeitete,[6] entdeckte nun immer mehr auch im frühen Picabia einen Künstler, der das Zitat und die Kopie zum Prinzip erhoben hatte.[7]

Allerdings erhebt sich die Frage, ob Picabia im Szenario seiner Wiederentdeckung die Rolle eines Subjekts oder Objekts sekundärer ästhetischer Genüsse zufiel. War er in seinen späten Jahren ein naiver „Metaphysiker", dessen zweifelhafte malerische Produktion sich als Trash recyceln ließ? Oder war er selbst schon eine „Ironikerin", die in ihren Gemälden verbrauchte malerische Idiome einem Gebrauch von zweiter Hand zuführte? Ist das Unauthentische Strategie oder Schicksal der Malerei Picabias?

III.

Auf diese Fragen gibt es keine einfache Antwort. Ich denke, dass wir uns ihnen nur annähern können, wenn wir einen Schritt zurückgehen und noch einmal etwas grundsätzlicher nach dem strukturellen Ort des „schlechten" Malens in der Moderne fragen. Mit guten Gründen ließe sich die Behauptung vertreten, dass alle große Malerei in der Moderne einmal „schlechte" gewesen ist. Damit wäre nicht einfach gesagt, dass sie von einem in Vorurteilen befangenen Publikum und konservativen Kritikern dafür gehalten wurde, während sie immer schon so großartig gewesen ist, wie wir sie heute einschätzen. Wer in den 1850er-Jahren von Courbet, in den 1860ern von Manet und den Impressionisten, später von Cézanne, Matisse oder Picasso behauptete, sie könnten nicht malen, war nicht einfach verbohrt, sondern sprach – streng genommen – eine Wahrheit aus. Das hat den einfachen Grund darin, dass die Standards, nach denen wir diese Künstler heute als „gute" Maler zu beurteilen

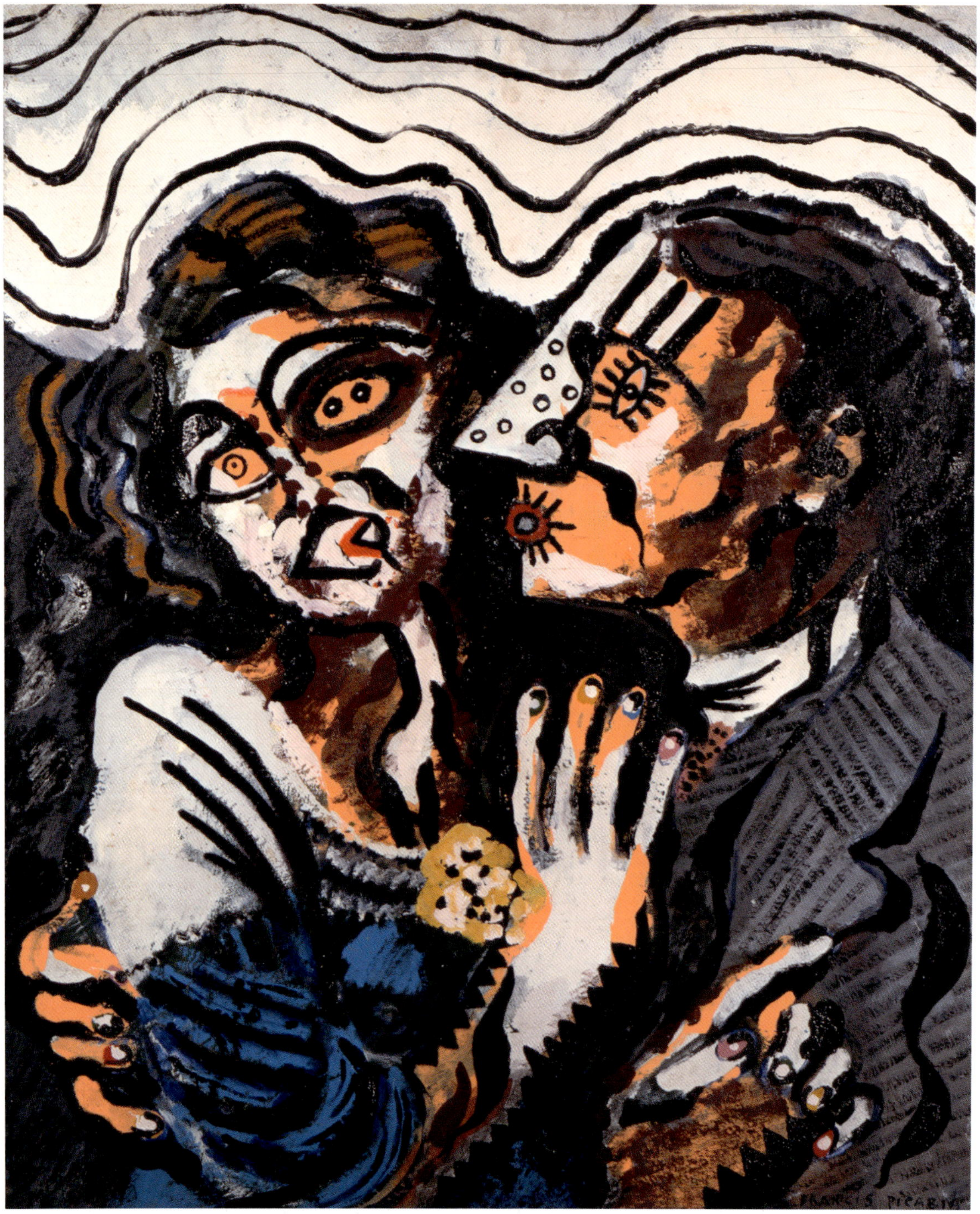

058
Francis Picabia
Première rencontre (Les Amoureux), 1925–1926 (Erste Begegnung [Die Liebenden] / First Encounter [The Lovers])
Öl, Lack auf Weichfaserplatte / oil, lacquer on fiber board
93 x 73 cm
Moderna Museet Stockholm

as primary aesthetic values. Only when this consensus was achieved was it possible to see positive qualities in the new painting. Innovation in Modernism, under the sign of originality, always meant first and foremost abandoning painterly skills. This is why the "bad" occupies a structurally essential place in the history of Classical Modernism. In other words: The logic of this history implies moments of a *structural irony*. These are those moments when the new, in so far as it shifts the categories of artistic quality, must define itself as deficient for a certain time—for as long as it takes for this shift in the definition of quality to achieve broad acceptance (if it does so at all). In brief: In Modernism the "good" can only appear on the historical stage in the guise of the "bad."

wissen, von ihnen erst etabliert wurden. Denken wir an den Impressionismus: Gemessen an den tradierten Normen bildlicher Darstellung, konnte man ein Gemälde nur als fehlgeschlagen beurteilen, das eine Landschaft wiedergab, ohne die verfügbaren technischen Mittel der Darstellung räumlicher Tiefe einzusetzen, oder einen Körper, ohne ihn durch Abschattierungen plastisch herauszumodellieren. Die Texturen aus ungemischten, leuchtkräftigen und unvermittelt nebeneinander gesetzten Farben , die heute so beliebt sind, sahen im 19. Jahrhundert noch so aus, als verfügten ihre Hersteller über gar keine identifizierbare Maltechnik.[8] Die Wertschätzung solcher Leinwände setzte eine ganz neue Übereinkunft über die Ziele des Malens voraus. Es hieß, das Flüchtige und Oberflächliche und nicht das Bleibende und Gehaltvolle, den optischen Eindruck und nicht die Verkörperung als Darstellungsziel akzeptieren zu können und Subjektivität und Originalität als primäre ästhetische Werte anzuerkennen. Erst auf der Grundlage einer solchen Übereinkunft war es möglich, positive Qualitäten in der neuen Malerei zu sehen. Innovation in der Moderne, Innovation unter dem Leitbild der Originalität bedeutete immer auch oder zuallererst Preisgabe malerischer Fertigkeiten. Man kann daher sagen, dass das „Schlechte" schon in der Geschichte der klassischen Moderne einen strukturell notwendigen Ort hatte. Man kann es aber auch so formulieren: Die Logik dieser Geschichte impliziert Momente einer *strukturellen Ironie*. Es sind jene Momente, in denen das Neue, insofern es die Maßstäbe künstlerischer Qualität verschiebt, eine bestimmte Zeit – und das heißt: die Zeitspanne, bis diese Verschiebung auf eine breitere Akzeptanz stößt (sofern sie das tut) – sich unvermeidlich als defizient bestimmen muss. Kurz: In der Moderne kann das „Gute" nur in der Maske des „Schlechten" die kunsthistorische Bühne betreten.

Mit Sicherheit sehen wir den jungen Picabia genau in diesem Sinne als „schlechten" Maler ins Rampenlicht treten. 1912 biegt seine Kubismusrezeption schnell in die Passage zur Abstraktion [ABB·059]. Picabia weiß sehr gut, in welche Richtung er die kubistische Ausdünnung der Malerei weitertreiben kann. In seinen Gemälden werden die ikonischen Versatzstücke (ein Schnurrbart, eine Brustwarze und so fort) eliminiert, die Picasso und Braque in das Facettengerüst ihrer Bilder eingepasst hatten; die Reminiszenzen an das Chiaroscuro werden noch weiter zurückgedrängt, und die Differenzierung zwischen Figur und Grund wird weiter abgeschwächt. Nahe an dem, was man später unter dem Eindruck der Pollock'schen Abstraktion als „all-over" bezeichnen wird (das Gemälde als ungebrochene, dekorative Textur, in der Figur und Grund koinzidieren), sind die besten Abstraktionen Picabias eine Herausforderung an den Bildbegriff der europäischen Malereitradition. Und Picabia ist ein Künstler, der die ironische Diskrepanz zwischen Anspruch und Geltung in der modernistischen Malerei besonders pointiert hervorzukehren weiß. Er gibt seinen Gemälden Titel – oft prangt er in großen Lettern direkt auf der Leinwand –, die ihnen ein traditionelles Sujet wie etwa „Kreuzigung" zuschreiben: wie um die Frage nach der Aussagefähigkeit seiner Abstraktion mit Dringlichkeit aufzuwerfen; wie um die ganze, lange, erhabene genealogische Reihe früherer Darstellungen dieses Themas zum Vergleich aufzurufen und zu unterstreichen, dass das Fleisch des inkarnierten Gottes in seiner Vision von Malerei nunmehr in diesen Farbflecken Bild werden kann.

There is no doubt that the young Picabia first entered the limelight as a "bad" painter in precisely this sense. In 1912 his reception of Cubism quickly turned to abstraction [ILL·059]. Picabia knew very well the direction in which he could push Cubism's reduction of painting. In his paintings he no longer used the iconic fragments that Picasso und Braque had inserted into the abstract ensembles of their pictures (a moustache, a nipple, etc.); remnants of chiaroscuro are used less and less, and the distinction between figure and background is blurred further. Close to what later would be called the "all-over" (in the wake of Jackson Pollock's abstract work), in which the painting is an unbroken decorative texture where figure and background run into one, Picabia's best abstract works are a challenge to the concept of the picture in the European painting tradition. And Picabia is an artist who very pointedly emphasized the ironic discrepancy within all the claims made to significance in modernist painting. He gave his paintings titles that suggested traditional subjects, such as "Crucifixion," often written in large letters across the canvas, as if he wanted urgently to raise the question of the meaning of his abstraction. This invokes the long and illustrious tradition of earlier depictions of this theme as a point of comparison, and it underlines that, in Picabia's vision of painting, the flesh of the incarnate God can now be represented in mere splashes of paint.

Picabia's undermining of painting achieves what is probably its ultimate highest level not in his abstraction, but in the "mechanomorphs." During World War I Picabia spent a long period in New York, and here he began to orient his pictorial language on construction drawings and technical diagrams [ILL·060]. These works quite clearly show machines and technical gadgets, but Picabia still insisted that they continued the figurative tradition. In one 1915 series, the titles, which were now consistently included in the picture along with further textual elements, indicate that the "mechanomorphs" are portraits. This is the culmination of the "excarnation" of the image. In the outlines, plans, diagrams, and schematic representations the image not only loses the power of showing a real body, but also its very own corporeality.[9] In this respect, Picabia's "mechanomorphs" are more "abstract" than his "abstract" works, for the latter still had their own sensuality that was linked to the medium of painting. It is no coincidence that Picabia turned to graphic art; he intended some of his most important works of this period to be reproducible and published them in magazines. The reduction

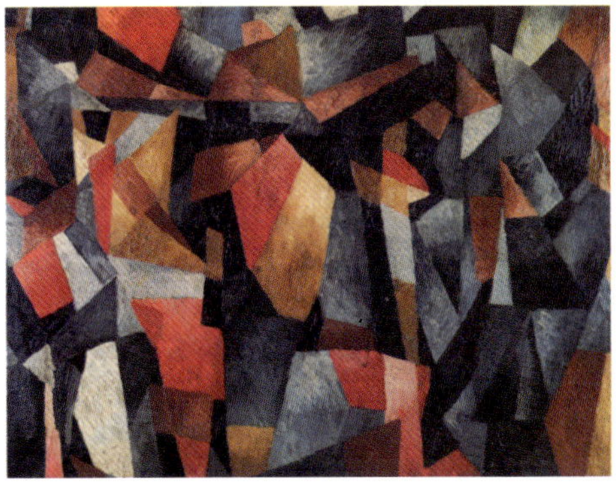

059 Francis Picabia
Crucifixion, 1912
(Kreuzigung)
Öl auf Leinwand /
oil on canvas
119 x 155 cm

Die Aushöhlung der Malerei erreicht bei Picabia aber nicht in der Abstraktion, sondern in seinen so genannten „Mechanomorphen" ein vielleicht ultimatives Niveau. In New York, wo Picabia sich während des Ersten Weltkriegs längere Zeit aufhielt, begann er seine Bildsprache an Konstruktionszeichnungen und technischen Diagrammen zu schulen [ABB·060]. Stellen diese Arbeiten auch offensichtlich Maschinen und technische Geräte dar, so insistiert Picabia dennoch weiterhin darauf, dass sie die figurative Tradition beerben. Die Titel, die zusammen mit anderen textuellen Beigaben jetzt konsequent ins Bildfeld eingetragen werden, weisen die „Mechanomorphe" im Falle einer berühmten Werkgruppe aus dem Jahr 1915 etwa als Porträts aus. Hier kulminiert die „Exkarnation" des Bildes: In den Umrisszeichnungen, Plänen, Diagrammen und schematischen Darstellungen verliert es nicht nur die Kraft, einen Leib zu vergegenwärtigen, sondern auch seine eigene Körperhaftigkeit.[9] Picabias „Mechanomorphe" sind in dieser Hinsicht „abstrakter" als seine „Abstraktionen", die noch eine an das malerische Medium gebundene Sinnlichkeit entfalteten. Es ist kein Zufall, dass Picabia sich der Grafik zuwendet und einige der wichtigsten Werke dieser Periode auf Reproduzierbarkeit hin anlegte und in Zeitschriften publizierte. Der Rückbau der künstlerischen Fertigkeiten gipfelt hier aber in der Tatsache, dass Picabias Maschinen größtenteils als Kopien technischer Zeichnungen identifiziert werden konnten. Mechanisierung ist nicht nur Sujet, sondern auch Verfahrensprinzip.

Bis an diesen Punkt in Picabias Entwicklung kann das Verlernen und Aushöhlen der Bildkunst noch im Horizont der „modernistischen Ironie" gesehen werden: Preisgabe im Dienste neuer ästhetischer Ziele. Die „Exkarnation" des Bildes ist hier verstehbar als positive Setzung, stellt man sie in den Horizont modernistischer Technikutopien. Sie ist nur die andere Seite einer Rationalisierung, Objektivierung und Mechanisierung pikturaler Verfahren. Die „Mechanomorphe" waren als Prototypen einer Malerei im Maschinenzeitalter gemeint.[10]

Spätestens mit Picabias Rückkehr nach Frankreich und dem Beginn der Pariser Dada-Aktivitäten kommt es aber zu einem qualitativen Sprung. Picabias pikturaler Radikalismus verliert jede positive Implikation. Es geht nicht mehr darum, die Grundlagen eines neuen pikturalen Idioms zu erarbeiten, sondern die Idee eines solchen Idioms selbst in Zweifel zu ziehen. Die Unterbietung des künstlerisch Akzeptablen erfährt eine ikonoklastische Zuspitzung, die zu einem Zweck in sich zu werden

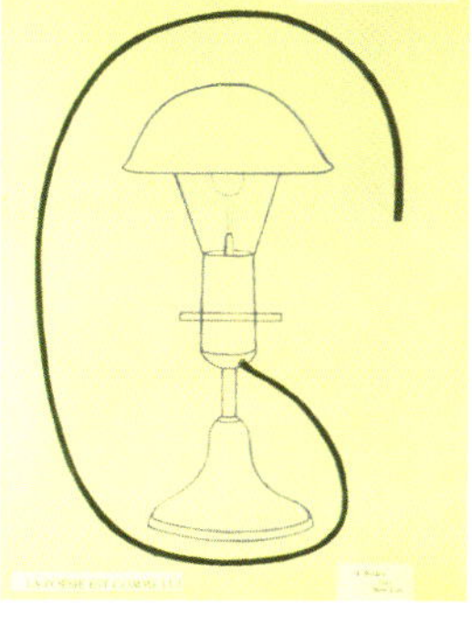

060 Francis Picabia
Voilà Haviland, 1915
Tinte, Bleistift auf Papier / ink, pencil on paper
65,5 x 47,7 cm

of artistic skill here reached its peak in the fact that Picabia's machines were largely copies of real technical drawings. Mechanization is not only a subject of these works, but also a method.

Up to this point in Picabia's development the "unlearning" and undermining of the art of painting can still be seen within the horizon of "modernist irony," as renouncement in the name of new aesthetic goals. Here, the "excarnation" of the image can be understood as a positive gesture, within the realm of modernist utopias of technology. It is just the other side of a rationalization, objectivation, and mechanization of pictorial methods. The "mechanomorphs" were intended to be prototypes of painting for the machine age.[10]

A new quality emerged (at the latest) when Picabia returned to France, and Paris Dada got under way. Picabia's pictorial radicalism loses all its positive implications. It is no longer a matter of working out the basis of a new pictorial idiom, but rather of questioning the idea of such an idiom itself. The aim of continually working outside the parameters of what was artistically acceptable is iconoclastically radicalized, and this radicalization seems to be an aim in itself. The most famous example from this period is probably the inkblot that Picabia published in 1920 in the twelfth issue of his *391* magazine under the title *La Sainte Vierge* [ILL·061].[11] It alludes to two factual levels: female biology and the means of representation. This blot that the artist placed onto his drawing paper performs a dual demystification: On the one hand, the Christian mystery is deflated, and on the other so is the act of aesthetic transfiguration, whereby applying paint to a white background would normally result in more than just making it dirty. The ironic disparity between the image and the claim to significance could not be any greater. Without the title the inkblot would be no more than a blot which no one would even think of seeing as a picture. More than that, the most banal form of graphic sign, such as otherwise only comes about by mistake and through clumsiness, is presented as the figuration of one of the most sublime subjects in the history of painting. But it is not merely the case that the thematic and semantic levels are ostentatiously left wanting, as Picabia also remorselessly drags the imaginative basis of Western iconography through the dirt. Strictly speaking, this is no longer an artistic maneuver at all, which might be understood as undermining certain artistic conventions. Rather Picabia's inkblot is based on the spirit of the readymade that declares something that is

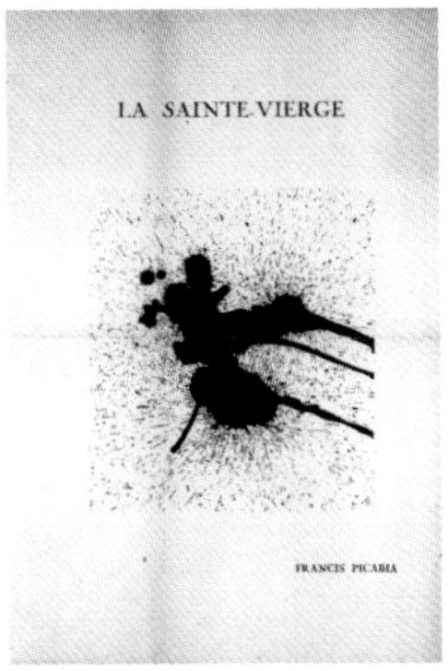

061 Francis Picabia
La Sainte Vierge, 1920
(Die Heilige Jungfrau / The Holy Virgin)
391, Nr. 12, März / March 1920

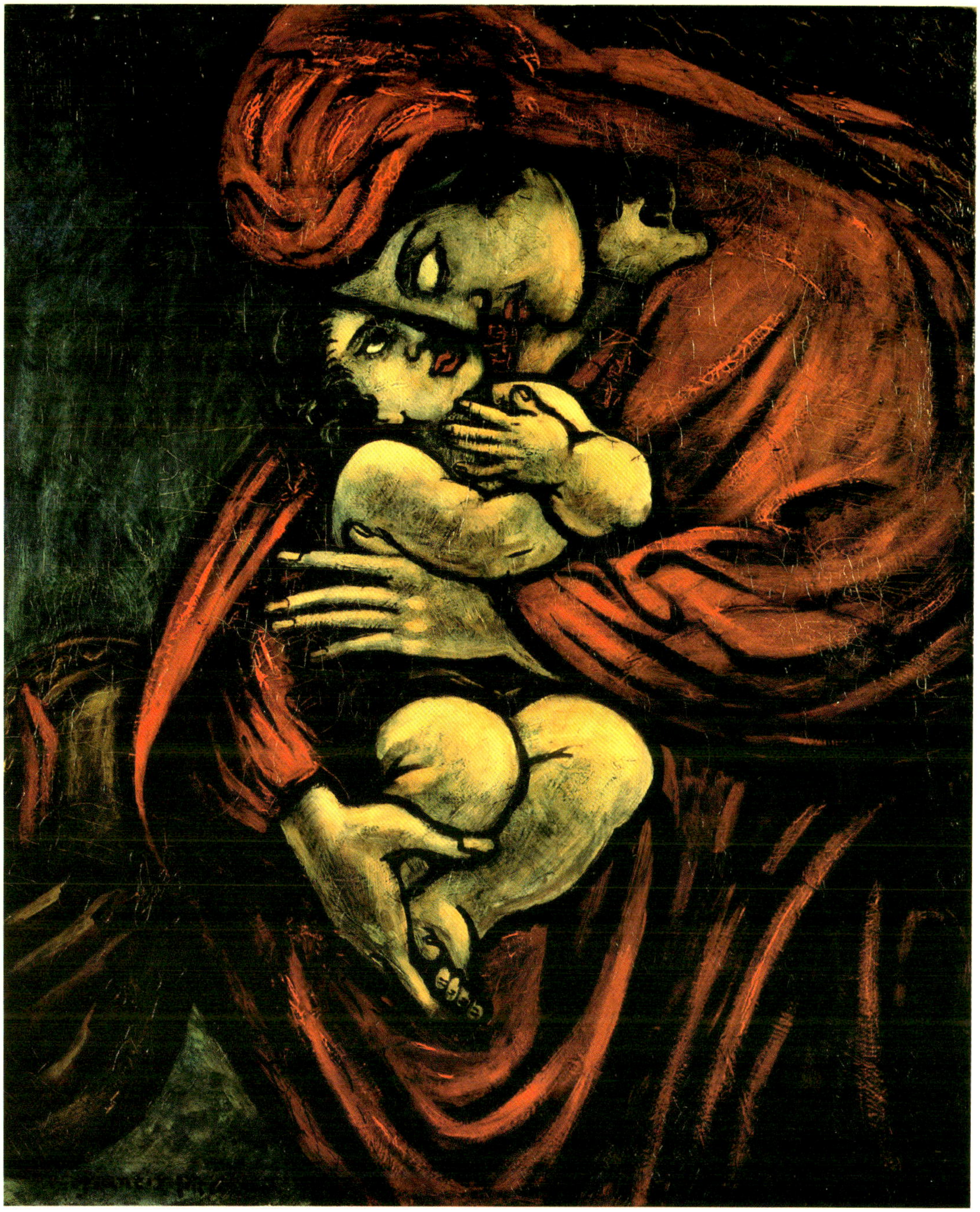

062 **Francis Picabia**
Maternité, 1935/36
(Mutterschaft /
Maternity)

Öl auf Leinwand /
oil on canvas
163 x 130,7 cm
Paris, musée national
d'Art moderne –
Centre Georges
Pompidou

scheint. Berühmtestes Beispiel aus dieser Periode ist wahrscheinlich jener Tintenklecks, den Picabia 1920 in der zwölften Nummer seiner Zeitschrift *391* unter dem Titel *La Sainte Vierge* publizierte [ABB·061].[11] Er indiziert eine zweifache Faktizität: die der weiblichen Biologie und die der Bildmittel, und dabei leistet der Fleck, den der Künstler auf sein Zeichenblatt gemacht hat, eine doppelte Entmystifikation: Während das christliche Mysterium an jener zuschanden wird, entzaubert diese die ästhetische Transfiguration, die das Aufbringen von Farbe auf eine weiße Unterlage in mehr resultieren ließ als ihrer bloßen Verunreinigung. Die ironische Kluft zwischen Bildgestalt und Bedeutungsanspruch könnte größer nicht mehr sein. Der Klecks wäre ohne den darübergestellten Titel nichts als einfach nur ein Klecks, den als Bild anzusehen niemand in den Sinn kommen würde. Zudem wird uns die banalste

fundamentally not art to be art. This same logic is seen in a series of "drawings" that were done in the same year. *L'Addition* is an artless, scribbled invoice; *Jeune Fille* a round hole cut into a piece of paper; *Francis Picabia* is a signed signature.[12] It is self-evident that none of these gestures, each of which ridicules traditional aesthetic norms, can become the basis of a new pictorial language. These works have no future. They are gestures that become obsolete in the act of making them.

But in spite of all their negativity, these works are highly original. If it would be fair to say that Picabia reduced painting to making inkblots, his destructive work still produced innovative pictorial forms. The second half of the twentieth century was to show that each of his ideas—the cutting, pouring, writing—not only had conceptual implications, but could also be taken up in practice and lead to productive methods, which in some cases even became the basis for an artist's entire œuvre (e.g. Gordon Matta-Clark, Jackson Pollock, Cy Twombly, and many more). In 1921, when the Paris Dada movement was at its height, Picabia announced that he was leaving Dada, and this led to a further new quality in his work. He had seen Dada as the epitome of nonconformity, nihilism, and individualism, but now he was sure that it was doing its best to become an art "ism," and—horribile dictu—a "serious" business: "Cubism was born one morning only to die the same evening and then Dada appeared, which was just as fleeting. Someone will always think the latest phenomenon already out-of-date, and so it goes on [...] Dada, you see, was never serious and for this very reason, being such a wildfire, it conquered the world. If anyone now takes it seriously it's because it's dead! [...] Thanks to Dada, art dealers will make their fortunes, editors will able to afford cars, authors will get the Legion of Honour and me...I'll stay *Francis Picabia*."[13]

How can you still be "Francis Picabia" when nonconformity has become a new doctrine? Picabia's answer was: by negating the negation. The only way of remaining true to the spirit that was attached to the word "Dada" was to betray it: "If you want to have proper ideas, change them as you would your shirts." [14] In 1922 Picabia showed a new series of "abstractions" at Galeries Dalmau in Barcelona, and here he also first exhibited his notorious "Spanish Women," cliché-ridden watercolors of Mediterranean beauties in the style of a hobby painter [ILL·057·062·065].[15] His exhibition in Galerie Danthon in Paris the next year contained only figurative works (primarily *Hispánica*) and was a clear provocation aimed at the Dada circle.[16] Picabia projected himself into a sublime outsider position that allowed him to direct his derision at all sides: at the avant-garde on the left-wing of Modernism and at Neo-Classicism on the right.[17]

This is the point in Picabia's career where the "late work" sets in. His work was never again to play such a significant role in the development of artistic positions as in the decade before. His painting was liked and exhibited by the Surrealists for a while, but it now remained an epiphenomenon. Its heyday was over. But Picabia seems to have developed an awareness of the fact that his neo-figurative "late work" might just be "trash." In the mid-1920s, he spent all his energy on vulgarizing his métier. He began to use industrial varnishes, painted his canvases in strident colors, enclosed his figures in

Form einer grafischen Spur, wie sie sonst nur durch den ungeschickten Gebrauch der Bildmittel zustande kommt, als Figuration eines der erhabensten Sujets der Malereigeschichte vorgeführt. Aber nicht genug damit, dass der thematische Anspruch ostentativ verfehlt wird, Picabia zieht die ganze Vorstellungswelt der abendländischen Ikonografie erbarmungslos in den Schmutz. Im strengen Verstande handelt es sich hier gar nicht mehr um ein künstlerisches Manöver, das man als Ausdünnung irgendwelcher künstlerischen Konventionen verstehen könnte. Vielmehr hat Picabia im Geiste des Readymade mit dem Tintenklecks etwas prinzipiell Kunstunwürdiges zum Bild erklärt. Der gleichen Logik folgt eine Reihe von „Zeichnungen", die im gleichen Jahr entstanden sind. *L'Addition* ist eine kunstlos hingekritzelte Rechnung, *Jeune Fille* ein kreisrundes Loch, das Picabia in einen Papierbogen geschnitten hat, *Francis Picabia* eine signierte Signatur.[12] Es versteht sich von selbst, dass keine dieser Gesten, die je auf ihre Weise tradierte ästhetische Wertvorstellungen aufs Korn nehmen, zur Basis einer neuen Bildsprache werden kann. Diese Arbeiten kennen keine Zukunft. Es sind Gesten, die sich im Akt, mit dem sie gesetzt werden, verbrauchen.

Aber aller Negativität zum Trotz sind diese Arbeiten im höchsten Maße originell. Wenn Picabia die Malerei auch gleichsam auf das Klecksen herabgebracht hat, seine Zersetzungsarbeit bringt immer noch innovative Bildformen hervor. Die zweite Hälfte des 20. Jahrhunderts wird beweisen, dass sich jeder dieser Einfälle, das Schneiden, Schütten, Schreiben (einmal ganz abgesehen von ihren konzeptuellen Implikationen) zu produktiven Verfahrenstechniken ausbauen ließen, die in manchen Fällen ein ganzes künstlerisches Œuvre tragen sollten (man denke an Gordon Matta-Clark, an Jackson Pollock, an Cy Twombly und viele andere). Zu einem neuerlichen qualitativen Sprung kommt es, als Picabia am Höhepunkt der Pariser Dada-Aktivitäten 1921 seinen Rückzug aus der Bewegung verkündet. Dada, für Picabia Inbegriff des Nonkonformismus, Nihilismus und Individualismus, war in seinen Augen auf dem besten Weg, sich zu einem Kunst-„Ismus" zu konsolidieren und dabei – horribile dictu – zu einer „ernsten" Sache zu werden: „Der Kubismus wurde eines Morgens geboren, um am Abend desselben Tages wieder zu sterben, und Dada tauchte auf, war aber übrigens ebenso vergänglich; die Entwicklung geht weiter, jemand wird den Namen des neuen Schmuckkästchens im Geiste des bereits Vergangenen finden – und so weiter. [...] Dada, müssen Sie wissen, war nicht ernsthaft, und genau deshalb hat er sich wie ein Lauffeuer verbreitet und die Welt für sich eingenommen; wenn ihn nun einige ernst nehmen, dann weil er tot ist! [...] Und dank Dada werden Bilderhändler Erfolg haben, Verleger sich Automobile leisten, Autoren Aufnahme in die Ehrenlegion finden, und ich ... ich werde *Francis Picabia* bleiben!"[13]

Wie aber bleibt man „Francis Picabia", wenn der Nonkonformismus zu einer neuen Doktrin geworden ist? Picabias Antwort lautete: durch Negation der Negation. Die einzige Möglichkeit, dem Geist, dem die Etikette „Dada" angeheftet wurde, die Treue zu halten, bestand darin, ihn zu verraten: „Wenn Sie saubere Ideen haben wollen, dann wechseln Sie sie wie die Hemden."[14] 1922 zeigt er bei Galeries Dalmau in Barcelona zusammen mit einer neuen Serie von „Abstraktionen" erstmals

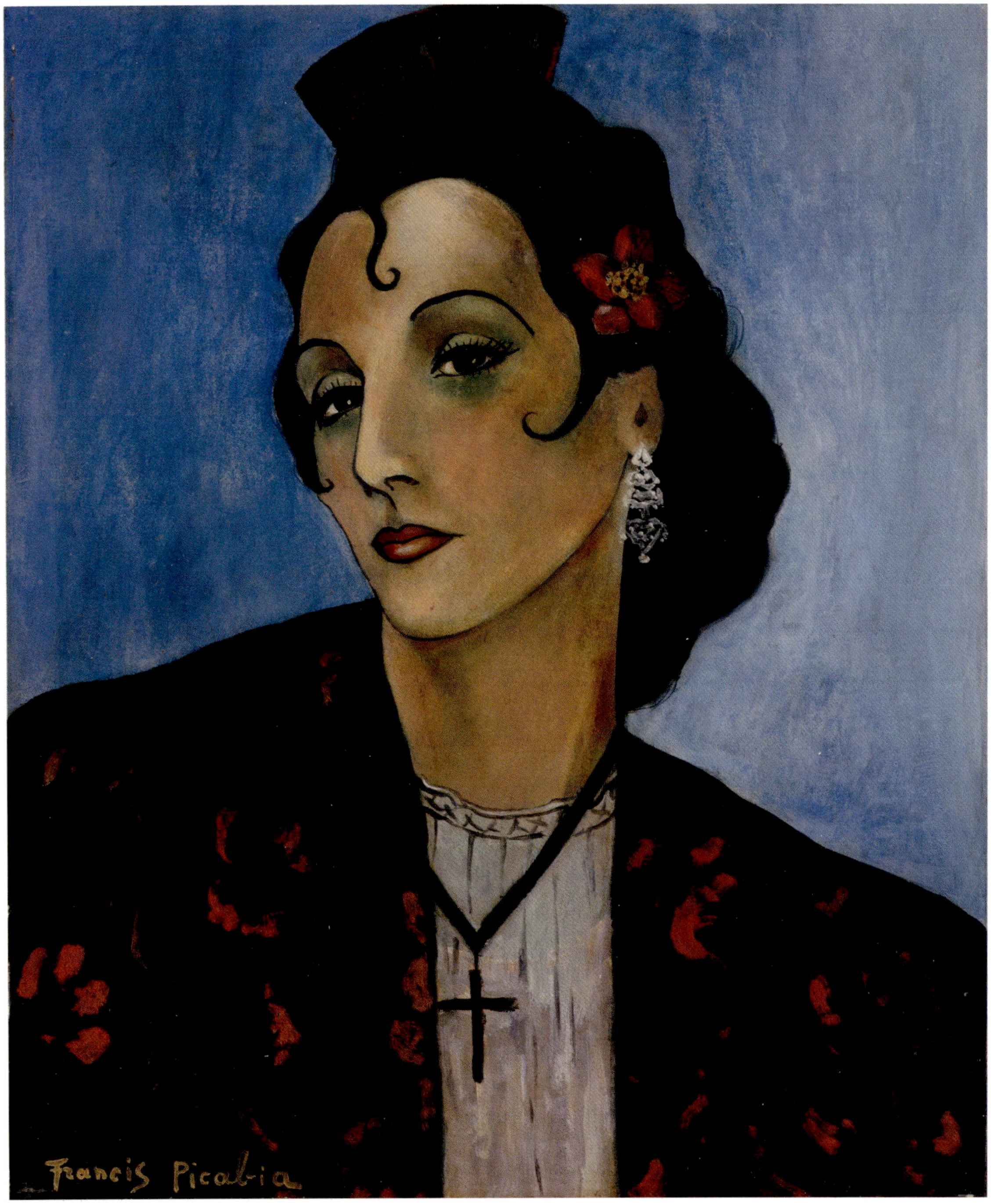

063
Francis Picabia
L'Espagnole, 1938
(Spanierin /
Spanish Woman)
Öl auf Leinwand /
oil on canvas
73 x 60 cm
Galerie Bruno
Bischofberger,
Zürich

thick dark contours, and did all he could to avoid anything that might be seen as painterly subtlety. He preferred using postcards as his model, and he exaggerated his stereotypical motifs until they became grotesque and monstrous: idylls in pink, in which young women with two pairs of eyes cast loving glances at their lovers and present four mouths ready for a kiss [ILL·058]. Picabia is now the Picabia who came to be loved in the 1980s: the provocateur of tastelessness, the cynic, the post-avant-gardist, relativizing all values. The genesis of his further work lacks all consistency whatsoever. Picabia borrowed from everything that art can offer, and he did not pursue any one artistic strategy for more than a few years. The only principle to which he remained true was inconsistency. Avoiding any kind of commitment and definition was meant as a statement of independence, but it also reveals a deep

seine berüchtigten „Spanierinnen“, im Stil des Sonntagsmalers aquarellierte Klischeebilder mediterraner Schönheiten [ABB·057·062·065].[15] Seine Ausstellung in der Galerie Danthon in Paris im folgenden Jahr, die er ausschließlich mit figurativen Arbeiten – in der Hauptsache *Hispánica* – bestritt, war eine gegen den Dada-Kreis gerichtete Provokation.[16] Picabia projiziert sich in eine erhabene Außenposition, die es ihm erlaubt, seinen Spott gegen alle Seiten hin zu richten: gegen den Avantgardismus am linken Rand des Modernismus wie gegen den Neoklassizismus am rechten.[17]

An diesem Punkt seiner Karriere beginnt Picabias „Spätwerk“: Nie mehr wird seine Produktion in der künstlerischen Entwicklung eine vergleichbare Rolle spielen wie in dem verstrichenen Jahrzehnt. Auch wenn seine Malerei eine gewisse Zeit lang von den Surrealisten geschätzt und ausgestellt wird, bleibt sie Epiphänomen. Ihr Kairos war vorüber. Aber Picabia schien ein Bewusstsein dafür entwickelt zu haben, dass sein neofiguratives „Spätwerk“ nur „Abfall“ sein konnte. Mitte der 1920er-Jahre gilt sein ganzer Ehrgeiz der Vulgarisierung seines Metiers. Er greift zu Industrielacken, bestreicht seine Leinwände in schrillen Farben, schließt seine Figuren in dicke schwarze Konturen und bemüht sich, auch sonst alles zu meiden, was als malerische Subtilität gewertet werden könnte. Mit Vorliebe wählt er Postkarten als Vorwurf und übersteigert seine stereotypen Motive ins Groteske und Monströse: Idyllen in Pink, auf denen junge Frauen ihren Erwählten gleich aus zwei Augenpaaren verliebte Blicke zuwerfen und vier Münder zum Kuss hinhalten [ABB·058]. Picabia ist nun der Picabia, den man in den 1980er-Jahren zu schätzen lernte: der Provokateur der Geschmacklosigkeit, der Zyniker, der Postavantgardist, der Relativist aller Werte. Die Genese seines weiteren Werks lässt jede Stringenz vermissen. Picabia borgt von allem, was in der Kunst aufkommt, und verfolgt keine künstlerische Strategie länger als ein paar Jahre. Das einzige Prinzip, das er getreulich verfolgt, scheint Ikonsequenz zu sein. Die Vermeidung jeder Festlegung, mag sie auch als Demonstration der Unabhängigkeit gemeint sein, verrät aber ein tiefes Misstrauen gegenüber den eigenen Hervorbringungen. Picabia scheint die Distanz, welche die „Ironikerin“ zwischen sich und ihre Worte geschaltet hat, wahren zu wollen. Man ist versucht, Picabia das Projekt zu unterstellen, die Malerei endgültig aus ihren „metaphysischen“ Verankerungen in Wirklichkeit und expressiver Subjektivität herauszulösen. Als Parodie, Kompilation, Zitat und Montage entfaltet sich die Malerei beim „späten“ Picabia als eine Oberfläche, die sich auf nichts

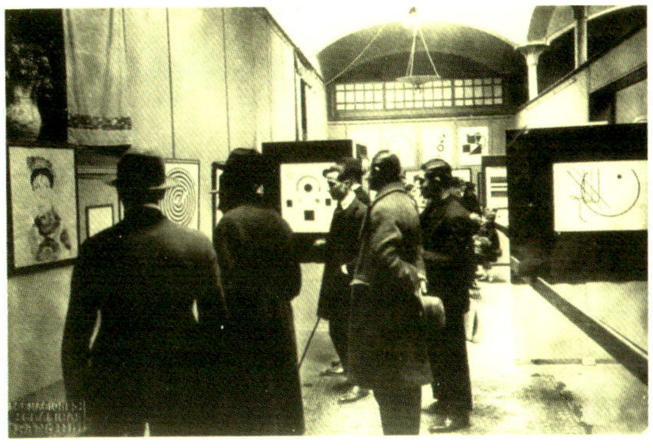

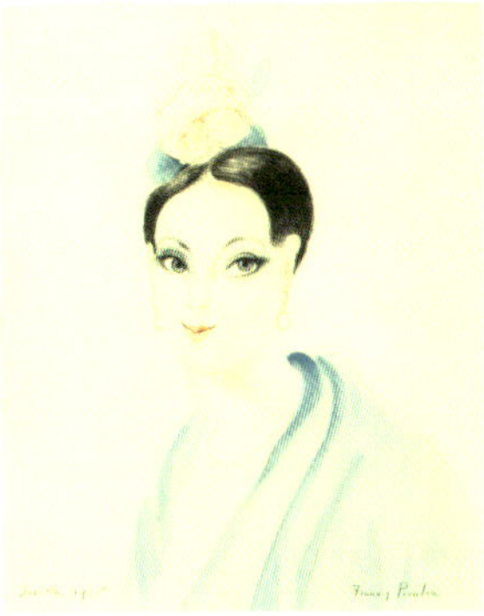

064
Eröffnung der Ausstellung / Exhibition opening Francis Picabia, Galerie Dalmau, Barcelona, 18. November 1922

065 Francis Picabia
Espagnole à la rose, 1916
(Spanierin mit Rose / Spanish Woman with Rose)
Aquarell, Bleistift auf Papier / watercolor, pencil on paper
54 x 42 cm

mistrust of his own creations. Picabia seemed to want to preserve the distance that the "ironist" has inserted between herself and her words. It is tempting to see Picabia as pursuing the project of finally freeing painting of its "metaphysical" roots in reality and in expressive subjectivity. As a parody, compilation, quotation and montage, Picabia's "late" painting is a surface that refers to nothing that has not itself already been a picture. And as Picabia's eclecticism does not distinguish between kitsch and great painting and stubbornly seeks to convert the one into the other, any question of "good" or "bad" seems to be pointless from the outset.

IV.

Of all of his later periods of creativity, Picabia seems to have pursued this kind of project with most determination in the period of the "Transparences." In the paintings in this group of works the canvases seems to have become projection screens showing a large number of pictorial quotations selected apparently arbitrarily from the whole of art history. They overlap each other to produce a graphical and iconographic cacophony. Picabia painted here from reproductions in art books and transferred his models onto the canvas in crude outline drawings and numerous transparent layers of paint (thus the name "Transparences"). In the case of the painting in the MUMOK collection, Picabia superimposed the features of Sandro Botticelli's *Madonna della melagrana* onto a nude boy which he took from a well-known presentation drawing by Michelangelo called *Il sogno* [ILL·056·066·067]. Picabia's picture was titled *Ganga*, presumably in allusion to the Indian river deity; it included birds and chains that Picabia laid around the male nude, and the ultimate effect is of a scene that vaguely refers to motifs from Christian, Classical, and Indian mythology. Interpretation is fraught with difficulty, and iconographers will capitulate in the face of the arbitrary combinations of these montages. It is tempting to read these "Transparences" as the apotheosis of the semantic depletion of a history of painting that has become available in reproductions.

But we should look more closely. In his painterly style, Picabia quite obviously attempted to achieve a Classical touch, and he placed his figures in front of a dark background. In the manner of an Old Master he painted in glazing layers and mixed a yellow varnish in with his

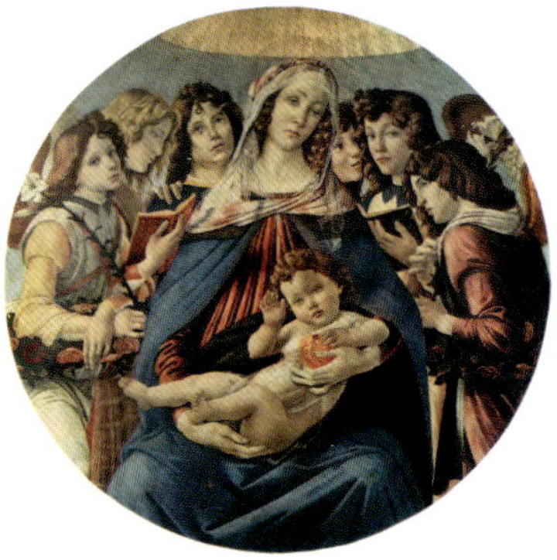

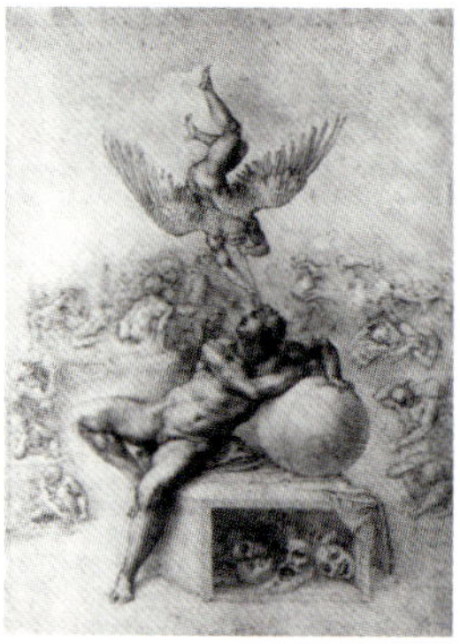

066 Sandro Botticelli
Madonna della melagrana, ca. 1487
Tempera auf Holz / tempera on wood
Durchmesser / diameter 143,5 cm

067 Michelangelo Buonarroti
Il sogno, ca. 1533
(Der Traum / The Dream)
Graphit auf Papier /
graphite on paper

bezieht, was nicht selbst schon Bild gewesen ist. Und da Picabias Eklektizismus keinen Unterschied macht zwischen Kitsch und großer Malerei und beharrlich das eine ins andere zu konvertieren sucht, scheint jede Frage nach „gut" oder „schlecht" a limine verfehlt.

IV.

In keiner seiner späteren Schaffensphasen scheint Picabia ein derartiges Projekt so konsequent zu verfolgen wie in der Periode der „Transparences". In den Gemälden dieser Werkgruppe scheint die Leinwand zu einem Projektionsschirm geworden zu sein, auf dem sich eine Vielzahl scheinbar wahllos aus der gesamten Kunstgeschichte herausgegriffener Bildzitate zu einer grafisch wie ikonografisch sinnbenebelnden Kakofonie überblenden. Picabia malte nach Reproduktionen in Kunstbänden und übertrug seine Vorlagen in kruden Umrisszeichnungen und vielen durchscheinenden Malschichten (von da die Bezeichnung „Transparences") auf seinen Bildträger. Im Falle des Gemäldes in der Sammlung des MUMOK legte Picabia die Züge von Sandro Botticellis *Madonna della melagrana* über einen nackten Jüngling, den er einer – unter dem Titel *Il sogno* bekannten – Präsentationszeichnung Michelangelos entnahm [ABB·056·066·067]. Das Ganze erhielt, vermutlich in Anspielung auf die indische Flussgöttin, den Titel *Ganga* und verschmilzt samt den Vögeln und den Ketten, in die Picabia die männliche Aktfigur legte, zu einer vage auf Motive aus der christlichen, antiken und indischen Mythologie bezogenen Szenerie. Es deute, wer da wolle. Vor der kombinatorischen Beliebigkeit dieser Montagen wird jeder Ikonograf in die Knie brechen. Man ist versucht, die „Transparences" als Apotheose der semantischen Entleerung einer in Reproduktionen verfügbar gewordenen Malereigeschichte zu lesen.

Wir müssen aber genauer hinsehen: In seinem malerischen Vortrag mühte sich Picabia offenkundig, eine klassische Tonlage anzuschlagen, und setzte seine Figuren vor einen dunklen Hintergrund. In altmeisterlicher Manier malte er in lasierenden Schichten und mengte seinen Farben einen gelblichen Firnis bei, als wollte er die Beschauer über das Alter des Werks täuschen. Die synthetisierende Oberflächenqualität der Ölmalerei, der Picabia so nachzuhelfen wusste, lässt die disparaten Quellen entnommenen, aber aller konkreten Attribute entkleideten Figuren zu einer illusorischen und bedeutungsschwangeren Einheit verschwimmen. Nach allem, was wir wissen, blieb dem zeitgenössischen Publikum der kompilatorische Charakter der „Transparences" verschlossen. Man darf nicht glauben, dass Picabia – hier wie auch sonst – irgendetwas unternommen hätte, seine Zitationspraxis offen zu legen. Die Deutung des Okkultisten Vivian du Mas, der die „Transparences" als „exakte Repräsentationen" einer „astralen Welt" verstehen wollte, erhielt Picabias Beifall.[18] 1930 präsentierte er Gemälde aus dieser Werkreihe in der Galerie Léonce Rosenberg, einem Forum der neoklassizistischen Strömungen der 1920er-Jahre. Im Vorwort des Katalogs erklärt er die Arbeiten zu Emanationen intimster innerer Regungen und beteuert, nach den kalkulierten Erfindungen seiner früheren Arbeiten zu einer Malerei vorgestoßen zu sein, in der sein Instinkt endlich freien Lauf hätte.[19]

paints, as if he wanted to trick the viewers about the age of the work. The synthetizing surface quality of oil painting, which Picabia was well able to reinforce, means that all the figures drawn from disparate sources and deprived of all concrete attributes appear as an illusory unity that seems to be laden with meaning. As far as we know, the contemporary audience had no access to the compilatory character of the "Transparences." There is no reason to believe that Picabia undertook anything to reveal his use of quotation—here or anywhere else. The interpretation given by the occultist Vivian du Mas, who understood the "Transparences" as "exact representations" of an "astral world" was applauded by Picabia.[18] In 1930 he presented paintings from this series in the Galerie Léonce Rosenberg, a forum for Neo-Classical movements in the 1920s. In the foreword to the catalog Picabia explained these works as emanations of the most intimate emotions and he asserted that, after all the calculated and rational earlier works, he had finally found a form of painting in which his instincts could roam free.[19]

The same is true of Picabia's notorious 1940s nudes, for which photographic models have since been discovered in 1930s pin-up magazines [ILL·001·001]. They were produced directly for sale through an art dealer in Algiers. This is of course paradoxical: Just before these pictures were discovered as the epitome and the very incunabulum of contemporary painting in the 1980s, and this precisely because they were boldly produced just for sale, in 1977 Gabrielle Buffet-Picabia still felt that she had to justify these rather lewd paintings as a lapse due to Picabia's need for money.[20] Picabia made no effort to erase the photographic arrangement of his motifs and presented the bodies in the bright light of a photo studio. Unimaginative, but "spiced up" with numerous drawing errors, these artificial poses are transferred verbatim to the canvas. These nudes seem to be proclaiming the total bankruptcy of realism in painting—loud and clear. How could one possibly appreciate these paintings that are corrupted by commerce and the mass media, if not from a Warholian perspective?

Around this time Picabia wrote to Gertrude Stein, and said that his painting had become "more and more" a "picture" of his "life" and of "life in general."[21] And visitors to his studio praised the fact that the nudes were so true to life, marveling in good faith at an "almost photographic" realism.[22] What are we to make of the fact that Picabia again and again demands that we accept the

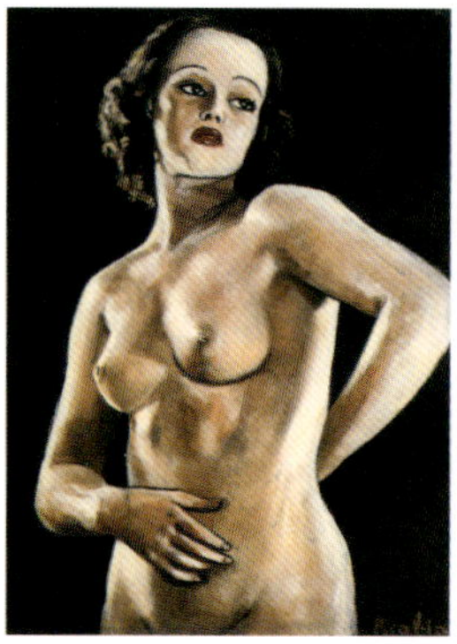

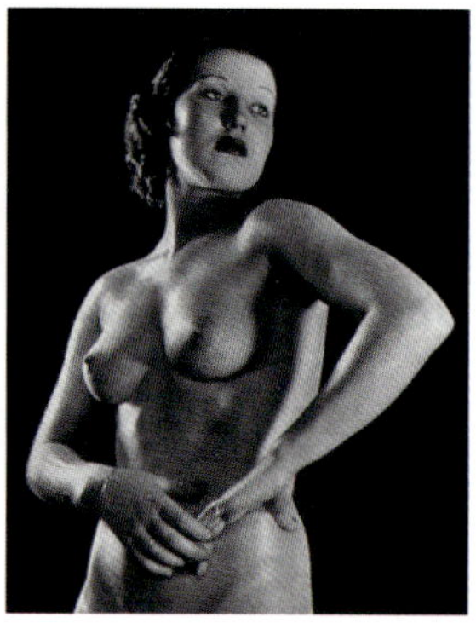

068 Francis Picabia
Nu, ca. 1942,
(Akt / Nude)
Öl auf Karton /
oil on cardboard
105 x 76 cm

069
Mon Paris, Nr. 5
März / March 1936

Nicht anders verhält es sich in den 1940er-Jahren mit Picabias notorischen Akten, deren fotografische Vorlagen inzwischen in Pin-up-Magazinen der 1930er-Jahre ausfindig gemacht werden konnten [ABB·068–069]. Sie wurden unmittelbar für den Vertrieb durch einen Kunsthändler in Algier produziert. Es ist freilich paradox: Bevor die 1980er-Jahre – gerade auch weil sie ganz unverblümt für den Verkauf gefertigt waren – in ihnen das Inbild und die Inkunabel der aktuellsten Malerei entdecken sollten, glaubte Gabrielle Buffet-Picabia noch 1977, die schlüpfrigen Gemälde als eine durch Picabias finanzielle Notlage erzwungene Entgleisung rechtfertigen zu müssen.[20] Picabia hat sich keine Mühe gegeben, die fotografische Zurichtung seiner Motive zu tilgen, und präsentiert die Körper im Scheinwerferlicht eines Fotoateliers. Fantasielos, aber mit zahlreichen Verzeichnungen „aufgewürzt", werden die gekünstelten Posen buchstäblich auf die Leinwand übertragen. Lautstark scheinen die Akte den endgültigen Bankrott des malerischen Realismus verkünden zu sollen. Wie anders denn in einer Warhol'schen Perspektive könnte man diese von Kommerz und Massenmedien korrumpierten Gemälde schätzen?

Picabia ließ in dieser Zeit Gertrude Stein in einem Brief wissen, dass seine Malerei „mehr und mehr" zum „Bild" seines „Lebens" und des „Lebens im Allgemeinen" geworden sei.[21] Und Besucher seines Atelier priesen die Lebensechtheit der Akte und bewunderten – offenkundig im guten Glauben – einen „beinahe fotografischen" Realismus.[22] Was ist davon zu halten, dass Picabia uns immer wieder aufnötigt, ihm den „metaphysischen" Glauben an eine „Wahrheit" in seiner Malerei abzunehmen, die abwechselnd aus der Quelle seiner „Imagination" und dem „Leben" schöpft? Dass er immer wieder die Ironie des Modernismus für seine Gemälde beanspruchte, wie um ihre malerischen Schwächen als eine Annäherung an Natur und subjektiven Ausdruck zu rechtfertigen? Sollte er tatsächlich geglaubt haben, dass er mit seinen notdürftig getarnten Pastiches am Prüfamt der Kunstgeschichte als Originalgenie durchkommen würde?

Es sieht jetzt so aus, als würde der spätere und späte Picabia sehr gut zum Objekt sekundärer ästhetischer Genüsse taugen, aber nicht als Subjekt solcher Ironien infrage kommen. Es spricht vieles dafür, dass Picabias postavantgardistische Figuration, die als ironische Überbietung avantgardistischer Positionen begonnen hat, sich mit der Zeit in ein ernstes Projekt verwandelt hat. Der biografische Kontext kann diese Annahme nur stützen. Nach dem Austritt aus Dada ging Picabia zunehmend auf Distanz zu seinen ehemaligen Mitstreitern. Bereits in der ersten Hälfte der 1920er-Jahre kehrte er Paris den Rücken, verlegte seinen Lebensmittelpunkt an die Côte d'Azur und fand in der High Society Südfrankreichs einen neuen sozialen Kontext für sein Wirken. Statt Dada-Soireen begann er dort Ballabende künstlerisch auszustatten. Es kann gut sein, dass sich Picabia irgendwann selbst für den Meistermaler hielt, den die Gesellschaftsschicht, in der er sich nun bewegte, zweifellos in ihm gesehen hat. Und spätestens als er verarmt während des Zweiten Weltkriegs gezwungen war, „suggestive Bilder" für „marokkanische Paläste" (Buffet-Picabia) zu malen, wurde aus der großen Komödie ein bitteres Drama.

"metaphysical" faith in a "truth" in his painting, which alternately derives from his imagination and from "life" itself? What are we to make of his claims for the modernist irony in his painting, as if he wanted to justify all their painterly shortcomings as an attempt to get close to nature and subjective expression? Did he really believe that he would be allowed to pass the art-historical test of originality with his scantily camouflaged pastiches?

Today it seems as if the later and late Picabia would certainly be a suitable object of secondary aesthetic pleasure, but not qualify as a subject of such irony. There is plenty of evidence that Picabia's post-avant-garde figuration, which began as an ironic exaggeration of avant-garde positions, gradually transformed into a serious project. The biographical context supports this assumption quite clearly. After he left the Dada movement Picabia kept more and more distance to his former colleagues. As early as 1925 he left Paris for the Côte d'Azur and found a new social context for his work in southern France's high society. Instead of for Dada soirées he began to provide the artistic decoration for society balls. It is certainly conceivable that Picabia came to view himself as the master painter that the people he now associated himself no doubt saw in him. And at the very latest, when he was living in poverty during World War II and was forced to paint "suggestive pictures" for "Moroccan palaces" (Buffet-Picabia), the great comedy had become a bitter drama.

V.

The above investigation of irony in late Picabia led to the question as to where the limits of an ironic reading of his work may be. Rhetoric and the literary studies teach us that this is the very nature of the beast: Irony is usually defined as a form of expression whose meaning contradicts what the words seem to say. This is how Quintilian sees it.[23] And his Classical text already points out that when using this rhetoric tool (which ultimately has no lesser effect than to transform a statement into its opposite) it is necessary to signal that it is being used and when listeners should be expected once again to stick to literal meanings.[24] Irony has the potential to become expansive—according to Quintilian it can spread to long passages of text and speeches, and there are also cases, like Socrates, where it begins to color a person's entire life.[25] To understand ironies thus initially means that you have to know where they are being applied.

The literary critic Wayne Booth devoted a whole chapter of his study of irony to this question. Whereas tone of voice can clearly signal what is meant as irony and what is not, for written texts we are not in possession of such simple aids to understanding. We can only presume that certain signals are being made. But as soon as we suspect that something is to be understood ironically, then we are faced with doubts that may set in motion a process of questioning meaning, a process that lacks any inherent reason to terminate. If I understand a statement in a text as an ironic attack on something, then I can just as well ask myself whether this irony is merely feigned, so as to lure me into a trap, and whether the real irony of the text—to the author's great pleasure—actually lies in provoking misleading

V.

Die Behandlung des Problems der Ironie beim späten Picabia ist in die Frage gemündet, wo die ironische Lektüre seines Werks enden muss. Rhetorik und Literaturwissenschaft lehren uns, dass dies in der Natur der Sache liegt. Ironie wird gewöhnlich als eine Ausdrucksweise definiert, deren Bedeutung im Gegensatz zu dem steht, was die Wörter zu sagen scheinen. So fasst es etwa die *Rhetorik* Quintilians.[23] Und schon dieser antike Text macht darauf aufmerksam, dass beim Einsatz dieses rhetorischen Mittels – das schließlich nichts Geringeres bewirkt, als eine Aussage in ihr Gegenteil zu verkehren – signalisiert werden muss, an welcher Stelle einer Rede man es verwendet und wo die Zuhörer sich wieder an den wörtlichen Sinn halten können.[24] Es ist eine Möglichkeitstendenz der Ironie, immer weiter um sich zu greifen. Nach Quintilian kann sie sich auf ganze Textpassagen, ja Reden ausbreiten, und schließlich gibt es auch Fälle – wie den des Sokrates –, wo sie das ganze Leben einer Person einzufärben beginnt.[25] Ironien zu verstehen heißt also in erster Instanz, ihren Geltungsbereich zu kennen.

Der Literaturwissenschaftler Wayne Booth hat in seiner Studie über die Ironie dieser Frage ein ganzes Kapitel gewidmet. Wenn uns bei einer Rede etwa der Tonfall unzweifelhaft bedeuten mag, was ironisch gemeint ist und was nicht, so sind uns im Fall gedruckter Texte keine so einfachen Hilfsmittel in die Hand gegeben. Wir können nur vermuten, dass uns Signale gegeben werden. Aber sobald wir einmal auf den Gedanken verfallen sind, dass etwas ironisch zu verstehen sein könnte, sind wir mit Zweifeln konfrontiert, die einen Prozess der Infragestellung von Bedeutung in Gang zu setzen vermögen, den wir aus keinem inhärenten Grund mehr aussetzen können. Verstehe ich eine Aussage in einem Text als ironischen Angriff auf irgendetwas, kann ich mich ebenso gut fragen, ob diese Ironie nur vorgetäuscht wurde, um mich in eine Falle zu locken, und die tatsächliche Ironie des Textes (zum höheren Vergnügen des Autors) darin bestehen könnte, falsche ironische Lektüren zu provozieren: „[B]is zum Ende geführt, kann eine ironische Verfasstheit alles auflösen – in einer endlosen Aneinanderreihung von ‚Lösungsmitteln'. Nicht die Ironie, sondern das Verlangen, sie zu verstehen, stoppt diesen Prozess."[26]

Picabias „Liebespaare" aus den 1920er-Jahren [ABB·058] sind relativ unkomplizierte Beispiele einer pikturalen Ironie. Niemand wird die groteske Entstellung der Figuren als Zeichen dafür übersehen, dass die Gemälde es mit der Gefälligkeit nicht ganz ernst meinen. Aber schon in der ersten Stunde von Picabias postavantgardistischer Figuration sind wir mit einer weitaus abgründigeren Form der Ironie konfrontiert. Als sich Picabia anschickte, seine „Spanierinnen" gegen die Pariser Avantgarde in Stellung zu bringen, verfasste er ein „Manifest des guten Geschmacks", in dem er seine neue Figuration als naiven Realismus anzupreisen schien:

„Nun bedenke ich, dass die Malerei sich hin zur Wiedergabe des *Lebens* entwickeln muss, ohne dabei unterwürfig die Fotografie zu imitieren. Ich habe vor, Männer und Frauen so zu malen, wie meine esoterische Vorstellungskraft mir das eingibt, ich beabsichtige, Malerei zu betreiben,

ironic readings: "[P]ursued to the end, an ironic temper can dissolve everything, in an infinite chain of solvents. It is not irony, but the desire to understand irony that brings such a chain to a stop."[26]

Picabia's "Lovers" from the 1920s [ILL·058] are relatively uncomplicated examples of pictorial irony. No one will overlook the fact that the grotesque disfigurement of the figures is a sign that the charm of these paintings is not really serious. But as early as the very beginnings of Picabia's post-avant-garde figuration we are confronted with a much more complex form of irony. When Picabia set about positioning his "Spanish Women" against the Paris avant-garde, he wrote a "Manifesto of Good Taste," in which he seemed to praise his new figurative style as naive realism: "Now I consider that painting has to evolve towards the reproduction of *life* without sticking to a servile imitation of photography. I aspire to paint men and women in the way in which my esoteric imagination pushes me. I paint in a way which I hope will never be classed as "-ist" but simply as a painting by Francis Picabia, *the prettiest possible*, a stupid painting likely to please my concierge just as much as sophisticated men, a painting which has no interest in being buried in a museum. A real Dada painting is one that everyone likes to make and the public likes to look at." [27]

This text clearly shows that Picabia's neo-figurative painting was not simply an ironic attack on the Dada circle, but was directed at two different addresses. At the end of the above excerpt Picabia says that his pictures should be liked just as much by a janitor as by an expert. And the manifesto itself also seems to want to say something to both of these types. It can be read as a commitment to agreeable painting that is true to nature, and yet half way down the passage quoted here we encounter a choice of words that has the potential to undermine the whole meaning of the text. "Peinture imbécile" is too strong an expression for it merely to refer to the ideal of naivety in naturalistic painting. This kind of self-depreciatory formulation is more like something we would expect in a Dada manifesto. Its effect is to make us unsure how genuine Picabia's manifesto really is. And the whole thing is turned on its head again when we read the last sentence, in which Picabia claims that his naive figurative work is the "true Dada painting." It is not just that a gesture that flatters bourgeois taste is a slap in the face of his Dada colleagues, but also that Picabia's gentle and pleasing figurative works are now to be understood as the avant-garde in disguise, and thus actually ridicule the tastes in art that they seem to want to accommodate. We can no longer decide at which point these twists and turns become unreliable.

This becomes all the more difficult when we look at Picabia's pictures. The "Spanish Women" do not even give us any clear marker that we should read them ironically. If we knew nothing of Picabia's own explanation, would we able to read the distorted faces as a subtle oscillation between the fresh and lively naivety of a hobby painter and the malice of a post- or meta-Dadaist? Or would we come to the conclusion that these paintings are simply "badly" done and that there is nothing to interpret? Or has Picabia perhaps brought his own artistic deficiencies quite deliberately into play here—in the name of some subversive effect? Would there then be a self-ironic level to his work? If so, would he

die, so hoffe ich, niemals mit einem Ismus klassifiziert werden kann, sondern ganz einfach die Malerei von Francis Picabia ist, *so hübsch wie möglich*, eine dumme Malerei, die meinem Hausmeister ebenso wie sehr gebildeten Menschen gefallen kann, eine Malerei, die nicht in den Museen zu finden sucht, was die Kuratoren dort begraben haben. Die wahre Dada-Malerei ist jene, die jeder gerne betreibt und deren Betrachtung dem Publikum Spaß macht."[27]

Dieser Text macht deutlich, dass Picabias neofigurative Malerei nicht einfach eine ironische Attacke gegen den Dada-Kreis gewesen ist, sondern an einen doppelten Adressaten gerichtet war. Picabia sagt am Ende des oben angeführten Zitats selbst, dass seine Bilder einem Hausmeister genauso gut gefallen sollten wie einem Kenner. Und auch das Manifest selbst scheint beiden etwas mitteilen zu wollen. Man kann das Statement als Bekenntnis zu Naturwahrheit und Gefälligkeit lesen. Doch wird man in dieser Passage auf halbem Wege über eine Formulierung stolpern, die die Kraft hat, den Sinn des Ganzen zu untergraben. „Dumme Malerei" („peinture imbécile") ist ein zu starker Ausdruck, um damit auf das Ideal der Naivität naturunmittelbarer Malerei anzuspielen. Diesen selbstdenunziatorischen Ausfall würden wir eher in einem Dada-Manifest erwarten. Es wird unklar, wie ernst es Picabia mit seinem Bekenntnis ist. Die Sache kehrt sich aber erneut um, wenn wir im letzten Satz zu lesen bekommen, dass Picabias naive Figuration als „wahre Dada-Malerei" verstanden werden will. Nicht lediglich gilt, dass die Geste, die dem bürgerlichen Geschmack schmeichelt, zugleich eine Ohrfeige ins Gesicht seiner Dada-Kollegen ist, sondern überdies, dass Picabias gefällige Figurationen als maskierte Avantgardemalerei verstanden sein wollen, die den Kunstgeschmack verhöhnen, dem sie scheinbar gefallen wollen. Wir haben keine Grundlage für eine Entscheidung, an welchem Punkt die Lektüre dieser Umkehrungen anhalten soll.

Die Sache wird nur schlimmer, wenn wir uns an Picabias Bilder selbst wenden. Die „Spanierinnen" geben nicht einmal einen eindeutigen Anhaltspunkt dafür, ob wir sie überhaupt ironisch lesen sollen. Wüssten wir nichts von Picabias Erklärung, wären wir in der Lage, in den verzeichneten Physiognomien ein hintersinniges Schwanken zwischen der herzerfrischenden Unbefangenheit eines Sonntagsmalers und der Böswilligkeit des Post- oder Metadadaisten zu sehen? Oder würden wir zu dem Urteil gelangen, dass sie einfach nur „schlecht" gemacht sind und es gar nichts zu interpretieren gibt? Oder hat Picabia gar seine künstlerischen Ungeschicklichkeiten mit Vorbedacht subversiv in Spiel gebracht? Gäbe es dann eine selbstironische Bezugsebene in seinem Werk? Dann hätte er nicht „bewusst" schlecht gemalt, sondern sich „bewusst" als „schlechter" Maler betätigt? Inwiefern wäre das aber „gute Kunst"? Könnte es überhaupt „gute" „schlechte Malerei" sein oder handelte es sich dann „lediglich" um „gute" Konzeptkunst? Und was bedeutet es, dass Picabia in die Ausstellung bei Danthon (figurative) Frühwerke einbezogen hat, von denen wir sicher sein können, dass ihr Realismus voll und ganz „ernst" gemeint war? Dass es bei Ironie nur auf den Kontext ankommt und keine Aussicht darauf besteht, irgendetwas in dem Werk selbst ausfindig zu machen, das seinen ironischen Sinn anzeigt? Und wenn das der Fall ist, wäre Picabias Œuvre als Kontext nicht stark genug, um alle bildnerischen

perhaps not have "deliberately" painted badly, but rather "deliberately" acted like a "bad" painter? To what degree would that then be "good art"? Could it really be "good" "bad painting" or would it just be "good" Conceptual art? And what is the significance of Picabia including (figurative) early works in the exhibition at Danthon, works whose realism we know for sure was meant quite sincerely? And what are we to make of the fact that irony is purely contextual and that there is no chance of finding anything in the work itself that proves its ironical intent? And if this is the case, would Picabia's own œuvre not be context enough to make it necessary to place all the pictorial statements it contains in inverted commas? Or should we be concerned that in his later periods the artist increasingly refrained from making relativizing comment? Or should we perhaps draw a line somewhere?

VI.

I took the title of this essay from Paul de Man, who had taken it from Søren Kierkegaard's dissertation entitled *The Concept of Irony*. Right at the beginning of his lecture, "The Concept of Irony," Paul de Man states that his choice of title is itself ironic, as he merely wishes to prove that there is no definable "concept" of irony.[28] I also believe that it is pointless to aim for a definitive explanation of what irony might mean for Picabia and where it is to be encountered in his work. But if there can be no immanent reason to halt the process of an ironic reading, there may still be extrinsic reasons. I think that there are such reasons that apply to the late Picabia, and that these reasons are political.

It would be possible to discuss Picabia's unpleasant anti-democratic views at length, and to include here a literary faux-pas in which he speculated on Mussolini's advantage over Lenin,[29] or to wonder even more about his questionable behavior under the Pétain regime, for which he was imprisoned for a short while after his country was liberated.[30] Some critics have discovered a problematic proximity to Nazi tastes in art in the canvases of the 1930s and 1940s. But this is not the issue here, and I am also not concerned with whether a picture like *Nu devant un paysage* (1938) [ILL-030] intentionally breaks with the aesthetic norms it applies.[31]

During this period Picabia simply painted too "badly" for him to be aligned with the official and very academic artistic norms associated with fascism. It is simply this: I refuse to understand or to applaud the masquerades of someone whose "need to contradict" brought him to behave like a "raving racist," and who was proud to be "pursued and persecuted" by the Résistance and collaborators at the same time.[32] Picabia did not understand where the limits to his ironic game of disguises should have been and at which point his heroic consistency of inconsistency would become unforgivable stupidity. His critics, however, should know better.

1 On the following see Richard Rorty, *Kontingenz, Ironie und Solidarität*, (Frankfurt/M.: Suhrkamp, 1992) chapter 4: "Private Ironie und liberale Hoffnung," pp. 127–161. Rorty uses "she" when referring to the "ironist" in the collective singular.

2 For a critical view of this see Benjamin H. Buchloh, "Figures of Authority, Ciphers of Regression. Notes on the

Aussagen, die in ihm stehen, unter Anführungsstriche zu setzen? Muss es uns dann nicht kümmern, dass der Künstler in späteren Schaffensphasen sich relativierender Kommentare zunehmend enthalten hat? Oder sollte man hier doch irgendwo eine Grenze ziehen?

VI.

Den Titel dieses Essays habe ich bei Paul de Man entlehnt, der ihn sich selbst von Søren Kierkegaard, dessen Dissertationsschrift *Über den Begriff der Ironie* überschrieben ist, geliehen hat. Gleich eingangs erklärt Paul de Man in seinem Vortrag „The Concept of Irony", dass es sich bei diesem Titel um eine ironische Setzung handle, da er nur den Beweis antreten wolle, dass ein definierbares „Konzept" der Ironie nicht existiere.[28] Auch ich halte den Versuch für aussichtslos, eine abschließende Erklärung davon zu geben, was Ironie bei Picabia genau bedeutet und wo sie am Werk ist und wo nicht. Wenn es aber keinen immanenten Grund geben kann, den Prozess einer ironischen Lektüre zu arretieren, so können doch äußere Gründe existieren. Ich denke, dass es beim späten Picabia solche Gründe gibt – und zwar Gründe, die politischer Natur sind.

Über Picabias unsympathische antidemokratische Ansichten wäre viel zu sagen, ebenso über eine literarische Entgleisung, in der er über die Vorzüge Mussolinis vor Lenin spekuliert,[29] und noch mehr über sein fragwürdiges Verhalten unter dem Pétain-Regime, das ihn nach der Befreiung seines Landes vorübergehend ins Gefängnis brachte.[30] Es gibt Interpreten, die in den Leinwänden der 1930er- und1940er-Jahre eine problematische Nähe zum nationalsozialistischen Kunstgeschmack entdeckt haben. Aber darum geht es nicht. Auch nicht darum, ob es in einem Bild wie *Nu devant un paysage* (1938) [ABB·030] einen intentionalen Bruch der Ästhetik gibt, deren es sich bedient.[31]

Picabia hat in dieser Zeit einfach zu „schlecht" gemalt, um ihm eine objektive Nähe zu den offiziellen, sehr akademischen Kunstvorstellungen der faschistischen Regimes nachzusagen. Es geht nur um dies: Ich weigere mich, die Maskeraden eines Mannes nachzuvollziehen oder ihnen gar Beifall zu schenken, den sein „Bedürfnis nach Widerspruch" dahin brachte, sich als „wütender Rassist" zu gebaren, und der darauf stolz gewesen ist, von Résistance und Kollaborateuren gleichermaßen „gesucht und verfolgt" zu werden.[32] Picabia hat nicht verstanden, wo sein ironisches Verstellungsspiel hätte enden müssen und die heroische Konsequenz der Inkonsequenz zu einer unverzeihlichen Dummheit wird. Umso mehr sollten es seine Interpreten wissen.

1 Zum Folgenden vgl. Richard Rorty, *Kontingenz, Ironie und Solidarität*, Frankfurt/M. 1992, Kap. 4: „Private Ironie und liberale Hoffnung", S. 127–161. Rorty verwendet „Ironikerin" als Kollektivsingular.

2 Dazu kritisch: Benjamin H. Buchloh, „Figures of Authority, Ciphers of Regression. Notes on the Return of Representation in European Painting", in: *Art After Modernism. Rethinking Representation*, hg. v. Brian Wallis, New York, Boston 1984, S. 107–135. Für eine Neubewertung der klassizistischen Tendenzen in der Moderne siehe: Ausst.-Kat. *Canto d'Amore. Klassizistische Moderne in Musik und bildender Kunst 1914–1935*, hg. v. Gottfried Boehm, Ulrich Mosch, Katharina Schmidt, Kunstmuseum Basel, Basel 1996.

3 Zum künstlerischen Dialog zwischen Picabia und Duchamp, zur diagrammatischen Syntax der „Mechanomorphe"

Return of Representation in European Painting," in *Art After Modernism. Rethinking Representation*, ed. Brian Wallis (New York, Boston: New Museum of Contemporary Art, 1984), pp. 107–135. For a reevaluation of the Classical trends in Modernism see *Canto d'Amore. Klassizistische Moderne in Musik und bildender Kunst 1914–1935*, exhib. cat., ed. Gottfried Boehm, Ulrich Mosch, Katharina Schmidt, Kunstmuseum Basel (Basel, 1996).

3 On the artistic dialog between Picabia and Duchamp, on the diagrammatic syntax of the "mechanomorphs" and on Picabia's reception of the readymade see George Baker, *The Artwork Caught by the Tail. Francis Picabia and Dada in Paris* (Cambridge/MA, London: MIT Press, 2007).

4 On Picabia reception in the 1980s see Katharina Hegewisch, "Die Kunst ist ein Spiel wie Liebe und Sport. Picabia und die Postmoderne," in *Picabia 1879–1953*, exhib. cat., Galerie Neuendorf (Frankfurt/M., Stuttgart, 1989), pp. 48–52.

5 In the 1980s scholarship begins to take an interest in kitsch and bad taste in Picabia's work. See for example Peter Winter, "Das Picabia-Syndrom oder die Lust an 'schlechter Malerei.' Notizen zu einem speziellen Aspekt der 'Westkunst'," in *Das Kunstwerk*, 6:24 (1981), pp. 34 ff.; Bernard Blistène, "Francis Picabia: in praise of the contemptible. Picabia's commitment to going farther than anyone else into the bad taste of his epoch," in *Flash Art*, 113 (1983), pp. 24–31; Robert Rosenblum, "Picabia in the Land of Kitsch," in *Francis Picabia. Nudes*, exhib. cat. (New York: Panicali Fine Arts, 1989), pp. 5 f.

6 Compare the influential collection of essays by Rosalind E. Krauss, which provided important ideas for a critical reappraisal of modernist art: *The Originality of the Avant-Garde and Other Modernist Myths* (Cambridge/MA, London: MIT Press, 1986).

7 This aspect is particularly emphasized by Schuldt: "Einführung: Francis Picabia," in *Francis Picabia*, exhib. cat., Städtische Kunsthalle Düsseldorf, Kunsthaus Zurich, (Cologne, Dumont, 1984), pp. X–XLIV.

8 Compare Richard Shiff, *Cézanne and the End of Impressionism. A Study of the Theory, Technique, and Critical Evaluation of Modern Art* (Chicago et al, 1984), pp. 108 ff.

9 On the reduced "realism" of post-Cubist painting as an "excarnation" and a reaction to the crisis in pictorial mimesis in the early twentieth century see Ralph Ubl, "Giorgio de Chirico: Exkarnation und Filiation der Malerei," in *Ikonologie des Zwischenraums. Der Schleier als Medium und Metapher*, ed. Johannes Endres, Barbara Wittmann and Gerhard Wolf (Munich, 2005), pp. 385–416.

10 When talking about himself at the time Picabia did not refer to the pictorial methods he used in his mechanistic art. In 1915 he said to a New Yorker reporter: "Almost immediately upon coming to America it flashed on me that the genius of the modern world is in machinery, and that through machinery art ought to find a most vivid expression," cited in William A. Camfield, *Francis Picabia, his art, life and times* (Princeton, 1979), p. 77.

11 On this work see David Hopkins, "Questioning Dada's Potency: Picabia's 'La Sainte Vierge' and the Dialogue with Duchamp," in *Art History*, 15:3 (1992), pp. 317–333; see Baker, *The Artwork* (see note 3), pp. 33 ff.

12 See *Francis Picabia. Singulier idéal*, exhib. cat., Musée d'Art moderne de la Ville de Paris (Paris, 2003), pp. 210, 213 and 217.

13 Francis Picabia, "Monsieur Picabia se sépare des dada" (1921), in *Écrits critiques*, ed. Carole Boulbès, Paris 2005, pp. 80 f. "Le cubisme naquit un matin pour mourir le soir même et Dada apparut, il fut d'ailleurs aussi éphémère ; l'évolution continue, un être trouvera le nom du nouvel écrin d'un esprit déjà passé, et ainsi de suite. [...] Dada, voyez-vous, n'était pas sérieux, et c'est pour cela que, telle une traînée de poudre, il a gagné le monde ; si quelques-uns maintenant le prennent au sérieux, c'est parce qu'il est mort ! [...] Et, grâce à lui, des marchands de tableaux feront fortune, des éditeurs s'offriront des automobiles, des auteurs auront la Légion d'honneur, et moi... je resterai *Francis Picabia*!"

14 Francis Picabia, "Tract pour le Salon d'Autonme" (1921), in *Picabia* (see note 12), p. 127. « Si vous voulez avoir les idées propres changez-en comme de chemises. »

15 These "abstractions" are in fact "mechanomorphs" that have been defamiliarized to the point of abstraction, and which, like Picabia's earlier machine pictures, are all based on technical drawings; see Baker, *The Artwork* (see note 3), pp. 210 ff. Picabia painted his "Spanish Women" throughout more or less all of his different periods, with the first dating back to a trip to Spain in 1902; see Maria Lluïsa Borràs, *Picabia* (New York, 1985), p. 16.

und zu Picabias Readymade-Rezeption siehe: George Baker, *The Artwork Caught by the Tail. Francis Picabia and Dada in Paris*, Cambridge/MA, London 2007.

4 Zur Picabia-Rezeption in den 1980er-Jahren siehe: Katharina Hegewisch, „Die Kunst ist ein Spiel wie Liebe und Sport. Picabia und die Postmoderne", in: Ausst.-Kat. *Picabia 1879–1953*, Galerie Neuendorf, Frankfurt/M., Stuttgart 1989, S. 48–52.

5 Die Literatur beginnt sich in den 1980er-Jahren für Kitsch und schlechten Geschmack bei Picabia zu interessieren, siehe z. B. Peter Winter, „Das Picabia-Syndrom oder die Lust an ‚schlechter Malerei'. Notizen zu einem speziellen Aspekt der ‚Westkunst'", in: *Das Kunstwerk*, 6:24 (1981), S. 34 ff.; Bernard Blistène, „Francis Picabia: in praise of the contemptible. Picabia's commitment to going farther than anyone else into the bad taste of his epoch", in: *Flash Art*, 113 (1983), S. 24–31; Robert Rosenblum, „Picabia in the Land of Kitsch", in: Ausst.-Kat. *Francis Picabia. Nudes*, Panicali Fine Arts, New York 1989, S. 5 f.

6 Vgl. die einflussreiche Aufsatzsammlung von Rosalind E. Krauss, von der wichtige Anstöße für eine kritische Revision der Kunst der Moderne ausgingen: *The Originality of the Avant-Garde and Other Modernist Myths*, Cambridge/MA, London 1986.

7 Diesen Aspekt hebt besonders Schuldt heraus: „Einführung: Francis Picabia", in: Ausst.-Kat. *Francis Picabia*, Städtische Kunsthalle Düsseldorf, Kunsthaus Zürich, Köln 1984, S. X–XLIV.

8 Vgl. Richard Shiff, *Cézanne and the End of Impressionism. A Study of the Theory, Technique, and Critical Evaluation of Modern Art*, Chicago u. a. 1984, S. 108 ff.

9 Zum ausgedünnten „Realismus" der nachkubistischen Malerei als „Exkarnation" und Verarbeitung der Krise der pikturalen Mimesis am Beginn des 20. Jahrhunderts siehe: Ralph Ubl, „Giorgio de Chirico: Exkarnation und Filiation der Malerei", in: *Ikonologie des Zwischenraums. Der Schleier als Medium und Metapher*, hg. v. Johannes Endres, Barbara Wittmann u. Gerhard Wolf, München 2005, S. 385–416.

10 In seinen Selbstaussagen aus dieser Zeit berührte Picabia die bildtechnische Frage seiner technizistischen Kunst nicht. Er erklärte einem New-Yorker Reporter 1915: „Als ich nach Amerika kam, schoss mir fast sofort ein, dass der Genius der modernen Welt in den Maschinen liegt und dass Kunst durch Maschinen einen höchst intensiven Ausdruck finden sollte", zit. n. William A. Camfield, *Francis Picabia, his art, life and times*, Princeton 1979, S. 77.

11 Zu dieser Arbeit siehe: David Hopkins, „Questioning Dada's Potency: Picabia's 'La Sainte Vierge' and the Dialogue with Duchamp", in: *Art History*, 15:3 (1992), S. 317–333; siehe: Baker, *The Artwork* (zit. Anm. 3), S. 33 ff.

12 Vgl. Ausst.-Kat. *Francis Picabia. Singulier idéal*, Musée d'Art moderne de la Ville de Paris, Paris 2003, S. 210, 213 u. 217.

13 Francis Picabia, „Monsieur Picabia se sépare des dada" (1921), in: ders., *Écrits critiques*, hg. v. Carole Boulbès, Paris 2005, S. 80 f. « Le cubisme naquit un matin pour mourir le soir même et Dada apparut, il fut d'ailleurs aussi éphémère ; l'évolution continue, un être trouvera le nom du nouvel écrin d'un esprit déjà passé, et ainsi de suite. […] Dada, voyez-vous, n'était pas sérieux, et c'est pour cela que, telle une traînée de poudre, il a gagné le monde ; si quelques-uns maintenant le prennent au sérieux, c'est parce qu'il est mort ! […] Et, grâce à lui, des marchands de tableaux feront fortune, des éditeurs s'offriront des automobiles, des auteurs auront la Légion d'honneur, et moi… je resterai *Francis Picabia* ! »

14 Francis Picabia, „Tract pour le Salon d'Autonme" (1921), in: Kat. *Picabia* (zit. Anm. 12), S. 127. « Si vous voulez avoir les idées propres changez-en comme de chemises. »

15 Diese „Abstraktionen" sind eigentlich bis zur Ungegenständlichkeit verfremdete „Mechanomorphe", denen – wie Picabias frühere Maschinenbilder – allesamt technische Illustrationen zugrunde liegen; vgl. Baker, *The Artwork* (zit. Anm. 3), S. 210 ff. Die „Spanierinnen" entstanden praktisch während allen Schaffensperioden Picabias, die ersten auf einer Spanienreise im Jahre 1902; vgl. Maria Lluïsa Borràs, *Picabia*, New York 1985, S. 16.

16 Und dies auch in sozialer Hinsicht: Das Publikum, das die Galerie bediente, konnte keinen Zweifel daran lassen, dass Picabias neuer Realismus als Umarmung der Bourgeoisie gemeint war; vgl. Borràs (zit. Anm. 15), S. 238 f.

17 Zu Picabias Auseinandersetzung mit dem Neoklassizismus siehe: Arnauld Pierre, „Picabia contre le retour à l'ordre", in: Ausst.-Kat. *Francis Picabia. Les Nus et la méthode*, Musée de Grenoble, Paris 1998, S. 8–19.

16 This in a social respect too: The audience that the gallery was aimed at could not doubt that Picabia's new realism was meant to accommodate the bourgeoisie; see Borràs (see note 15), p. 238 f.

17 On Picabia's interest in Neo-Classicism see Arnauld Pierre, "Picabia contre le retour à l'ordre," in *Francis Picabia. Les Nus et la méthode*, exhib. cat., Musée de Grenoble (Paris, 1998), pp. 8–19.

18 Camfield, *Picabia* (see note 10), p. 242.

19 Ibid., p. 239.

20 Gabrielle Buffet-Picabia, "Francis Picabia 1879–1953," in *Francis Picabia. Schriften*, vol. 2, translated by Pierre Gallissaires and Hirma Mittelstädt (Hamburg, 1983), p. 25.

21 Borràs (see note 15), p. 422.

22 Ibid., p. 423.

23 See Marcus Fabius Quintilianus, *Institutionis oratoriae libri XII / Ausbildung des Redners. Zwölf Bücher*, ed. and translated by Helmut Rahn, 2 vols., Darmstadt 1995, vol. 1, VI/2/15, pp. 702 ff.

24 Ibid., vol. 2, VIII/6/54, pp. 240 ff.; also ibid., IX/2/46, p. 288.

25 Ibid., vol. 2, IX/2/46, pp. 288 ff.

26 Wayne Booth, *A Rhetoric of Irony* (Chicago, 1974), p. 59 (see note 14).

27 Francis Picabia, "Manifeste du bon gout" (1923), in Picabia, *Écrits* (see note 13), p. 609. "Maintenant, je considère que la peinture doit évoluer vers la reproduction de la vie, sans pour cela s'en tenir à l'imitation servile de la photographie. J'ai l'ambition de peindre des hommes et des femmes de la façon dont mon imagination ésotérique m'y poussera, je compte faire de la peinture qui, je l'espère, ne sera jamais classée en " iste " mais sera tout simplement une peinture Francis Picabia, la plus jolie possible, une peinture imbécile, susceptible à plaire à mon concierge, aussi bien qu'à l'homme évolué, une peinture qui n'ira pas chercher dans les musées ce que les conservateurs y ont enterré. La vraie peinture Dada est celle qu'il plaît à chacun de faire et qu'il plaît au public de regarder." Picabia wrote this text for the catalog of the above-mentioned exhibition in Galerie Danthon, but instead that catalog contained a foreword by Germaine Everling.

28 See Paul de Man, "The Concept of Irony," in *Aesthetic Ideology*, ed. Andrzej Warminski, Minnesota, London 1996 (Theory and History of Literature, vol. 65), pp. 163 ff.

29 See Francis Picabia, "Une profession de foi de Picabia lumière froide" (1926), in Picabia, *Écrits* (see note 13), p. 230.

30 See Yve-Alain Bois, "Francis Picabia. From Dada to Pétain," in *October*, 30 (1984), pp. 120–127.

31 This is Roberto Ohrt's view: "Avantgardistische Falten und realistisches Kunstlicht," in *Francis Picabia. Das Spätwerk 1933–1953*, exhib. cat., ed. Zdenek Felix, Deichtorhallen, Hamburg; Museum Boijmans Van Beuningen, Rotterdam (Ostfildern-Ruit 1997), p. 16.

32 See Buffet-Picabia (see note 20), pp. 25 ff.

18 Vgl. Camfield, *Picabia* (zit. Anm. 10), S. 242.

19 Vgl. ebd., S. 239.

20 Vgl. Gabrielle Buffet-Picabia, „Francis Picabia 1879–1953", in: *Francis Picabia. Schriften*, Bd. 2, übers. v. Pierre Gallissaires u. Hirma Mittelstädt, Hamburg 1983, S. 25.

21 Vgl. Borràs (zit. Anm. 15), S. 422.

22 Vgl. ebd., S. 423.

23 Vgl. Marcus Fabius Quintilianus, *Institutionis oratoriae libri XII / Ausbildung des Redners. Zwölf Bücher*, hg. u. übers. v. Helmut Rahn, 2 Bde., Darmstadt 1995, Bd. 1, VI/2/15, S. 702 f.

24 Vgl. ebd., Bd. 2, VIII/6/54, S. 240 f.; vgl. auch ebd., IX/2/46, S. 288.

25 Vgl. ebd., Bd. 2, IX/2/46, S. 288 f.

26 Wayne Booth, *A Rhetoric of Irony*, Chicago 1974, S. 59, Anm. 14.

27 Francis Picabia, „Manifeste du bon goût" (1923), in: Picabia, *Écrits* (zit. Anm. 13), S. 609. « Maintenant, je considère que la peinture doit évoluer vers la reproduction de la *vie*, sans pour cela s'en tenir à l'imitation servile de la photographie. J'ai l'ambition de peindre des hommes et des femmes de la façon dont mon imagination ésotérique m'y poussera, je compte faire de la peinture qui, je l'espère, ne sera jamais classée en " iste " mais sera tout simplement une peinture Francis Picabia, *la plus jolie possible*, une peinture imbécile, susceptible à plaire à mon concierge, aussi bien qu'à l'homme évolué, une peinture qui n'ira pas chercher dans les musées ce que les conservateurs y ont enterré. La vraie peinture Dada est celle qu'il plaît à chacun de faire et qu'il plaît au public de regarder. » Den Text setzte Picabia für den Katalog der schon erwähnten Ausstellung in der Galerie Danthon auf. Veröffentlicht wurde aber schließlich ein Vorwort von Germaine Everling.

28 Vgl. Paul de Man, „The Concept of Irony", in: *Aesthetic Ideology*, hg. v. Andrzej Warminski, Minnesota, London 1996 (Theory and History of Literature, Bd. 65), S. 163 ff.

29 Vgl. Francis Picabia, „Une profession de foi de Picabia lumière froide" (1926), in: Picabia, *Écrits* (zit. Anm. 13), S. 230.

30 Siehe Yve-Alain Bois, „Francis Picabia. From Dada to Pétain", in: *October*, 30 (1984), S. 120–127.

31 Das nimmt Roberto Ohrt an: „Avantgardistische Falten und realistisches Kunstlicht", in: Ausst.-Kat. *Francis Picabia. Das Spätwerk 1933–1953*, hg. v. Zdenek Felix, Deichtorhallen, Hamburg; Museum Boijmans Van Beuningen, Rotterdam, Ostfildern-Ruit 1997, S. 16.

32 Vgl. Buffet-Picabia (zit. Anm. 20), S. 25 f.

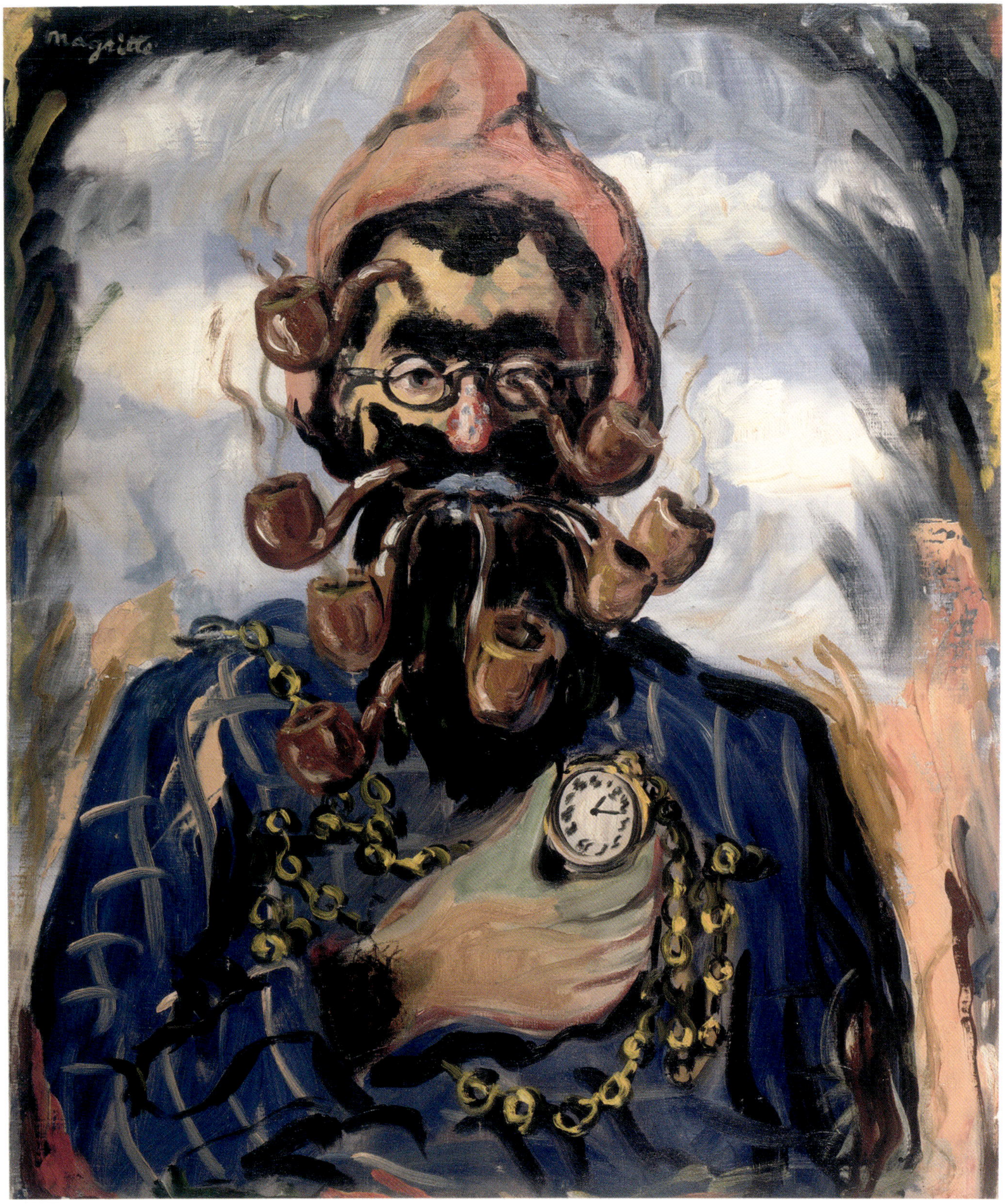

070 **René Magritte**
Le Stropiat, 1948
(Verkrüppelter / Mangled)

Öl auf Leinwand / oil on canvas
59,5 x 49,5 cm
Paris, musée national d'Art
moderne – Centre Georges Pompidou

Magrittes „Gaunersprache“

Bernard Blistène

René Magrittes „période vache“ entspringt zweifellos einer Stilabweichung und einem bewusst unternommenen Abweg, um all jene aus der Fassung zu bringen, die Marcel Duchamp seinerseits „les regardeurs“ (die „Anschauer“/„Blicker“) nannte. Das Werk Magrittes, das bis dahin ganz in reflexiver Pädagogik aufging, die alles Unruhige und Überraschende ablehnte, war durch Genauigkeit und Sorgfalt gekennzeichnet. Magritte war ein Verstandesmensch.

In den Jahren 1947 und 1948 schien er jedoch von den selbst auferlegten Regeln abzuweichen. Die Malereilektionen wichen einer ungenierten und ungehemmten Vorgehensweise. Von Sorgfalt keine Spur mehr. 15 Ölbilder und ebenso viele Gouachen setzten der glasklaren Ordnung von 20 Jahren ein plötzliches Ende. Die Malerei wurde zu einem Kuhfladen, das *Alphabet des révélations* (Alphabet der Offenbarungen) geistiger Vogelmist. Paul Éluard und André Breton, beide dogmatisch, waren damit gar nicht einverstanden.[1] Und Magritte, der die Gefahr wissentlich heraufbeschwor, nahm das Risiko „eines langsamen Suizids“ gern in Kauf.[2]

Denn hier ging es vor allem um den Streich, den Magritte sich selbst spielte. Seit langem schon hatte er sich keinerlei Abweichungen mehr gestattet. „Es [war] ein für alle Mal vorbei mit der Heftigkeit im Tun, die Übersteigerung [hatte] sich in ihr Haus zurückgezogen und die Tür für lange Zeit verschlossen.“[3] Was der Maler als „Figuren“ bezeichnete – in dem vielfachen Sinn, der dem Begriff zuzuweisen ist –, wurde in einem bis zum Äußersten beanspruchten Vokabular miteinander kombiniert. Die Kunst Magrittes glich dem „Requisitenfundus“ eines Illusionisten – und die Methode schien unabänderlich. „Magritte ist ein Maler, Magritte ist kein Maler“, hatte Scutenaire gesagt. Das war Urteil, Sinnspruch, Aphorismus, Apophthegma zugleich und trug zur gedanklichen Verwirrung und auf verbaler Ebene zur Intensivierung der *autistischen* Dimension der Arbeit seines Komplizen bei.

Denn Magritte hatte sich entschieden aus dem Gattungsstreit herausgehalten und deutlich zu verstehen gegeben, dass sich der Zweck der Malerei nicht einer „Terpentinvergiftung“ beugen sollte: Er selbst verzichtete auf Materialwirkungen, auf das „freizügige Gebaren“ seiner Zeitgenossen und schuf eine Kunst der *Konventionen*, bei der immer wieder darauf hingewiesen wurde, dass sie mehr als die der anderen Surrealisten Veränderung ablehnte, während alle anderen sie großzügig feilboten, dass sie auf Verzerrung verzichtete, als jeder darin malerische Freiheit sah, dass sie zur

The Roguish Language of Magritte's

Bernard Blistène

René Magritte's "vache" period undoubtedly arose from a deviation in style and a deliberate aberration intended to confound all those described by Marcel Duchamp as "regardeurs" ("spectators"). Magritte's work, until then consisting of an introspective pedagogy, which naturally repudiated the turbulent and the unexpected, had accustomed us to precision and diligence. Magritte was a man of the intellect.

Now, in 1947 and 1948, he seemed to be departing from the rule he himself had set. Lessons in painting gave way to uninhibited and unrestrained work. Diligence was entirely absent. Fifteen oils on canvas and another 15 gouaches disrupted the crystalline order of twenty years. Painting became a cowpat and the *Alphabet des révélations* (Alphabet of Revelations) the bird droppings of the mind. Paul Eluard and André Breton, both of them dogmatic, did not agree at all with it.[1] And with this, Magritte, deliberately courting danger, was risking "slow suicide."[2]

For the fundamental thing here was the trick Magritte was playing on himself. In fact, for a long time he had not allowed himself any aberrations. "Violence in creation was well and truly over, exaggeration had retreated behind a door in its house which it held shut for a very long time."[3] What the painter called "figures," in the multiple meanings we should assign to the word, were part of a lexicon created to do his bidding. Magritte's art resembled an illusionist's "collection of props" and the method appeared to be immutable. "Magritte is a painter, Magritte is not a painter," Scutenaire had said. This phrase was a judgment, an adage, an aphorism, an apothegm that added to the mental turmoil and, on the verbal level, intensified the *autistic* dimension of the works of his accomplice.

For Magritte had resolutely distanced himself from the quarrels over style, making it clear that the function of painting should not give way to "turpentine toxication." For him, there were to be no effects of material, nor the "laissez-faire" of his contemporaries. His was an art of *conventions* which, as has been recalled many times, far more than the art of the other Surrealists, opposed change when all the others were lavish with it, refused distortion when others saw in it painterly freedom, became the mentor of exactitude when those who might have been thought its followers rejected it. Magritte painted "in a closed circuit."[4]

Verfechterin der Genauigkeit wurde, als ihre vermeintlichen Anhänger sich dieser verweigerten. Magritte hatte „in einem geschlossenen Kreislauf"[4] gemalt.

Die „période vache" erscheint daher wie ein schlechter Scherz. Sie brüskiert und hat zugleich etwas von einem Schuljungenstreich. Ähnlich wie der Kalauer in seinem Verhältnis zur Sprache birgt sie Entspannung und Ausgelassenheit. Freilich gibt es eine Vorgeschichte, zu der etwa die rotznäsige Gauguin-Parodie aus dem Jahr 1924 gehört. Und freilich folgen die „Vache"-Bilder auf die der Renoir-Periode [ABB·032], von denen Magritte sagte, dass sie unmittelbar nach Kriegsende „den Surrealismus der grellen Sonne aussetzen" sollten. Aber etwas in diesen „Renoirs" gehört eher in den Bereich des Pasticcios und der Parodie. Der Maler der harmlosen *Baigneuses* (Badenden) dient dabei als *Alibi* für eine vor lauter perlmuttschillernder Sanftheit und vorgetäuschter Unterwerfung unter Stil und selbst Namen des von den Surrealisten so verabscheuten Malers fratzenhaft verzerrte Malerei.[5]

Die „période vache" ist hemmungslos und zerstörerisch. Magritte geht sogar das Risiko ein, sich bis zur Unkenntlichkeit zu verändern. Obschon es einige Ölgemälde und Gouachen gibt, von denen sich sagen lässt, dass hier bis in die Faktur hinein die Durchgängigkeit eines gewissen Stils und bestimmter Kompositionsprinzipien zu beobachten ist, drücken doch die meisten Werke dieser Schaffensphase und der Schock, den sie vermutlich *zusammen* auslösten, das aus, worin Scutenaire die ureigenste Definition des Humors sah: „Eine Art, sich aus der Klemme zu helfen, ohne sich aus der Affäre zu ziehen."[6] Man braucht sich nur die Kritik und die Marginalisierung dieser Werke in den verschiedenen nachfolgenden Ausstellungen vor Augen zu führen, um festzustellen, dass das Ziel erreicht war und dass Magritte hier dem Gesetz von Gattung und Art zuwiderhandelte. „Man würde schon sehen." Und in der Tat sah man es so klar, dass Magritte und Scutenaire am Ende in dieser düsteren Geschichte Täter und Opfer zugleich waren.

Kommen wir also noch einmal zu dieser vorangehenden Äußerung, denn sie zeigt mit offenkundigem Genuss, dass die beiden Komplizen bei dieser Gelegenheit beschlossen hatten, wie Pech und Schwefel zusammenzuhalten. Das waren die „Mittel und Wege", um es mit „Parure" (oder „Piras", wie Magritte von nun an wechselweise die Hauptstadt Frankreichs nannte) aufnehmen zu können. Diese freche Buchstabenverdreherei war gewissermaßen das sprachliche Pendant für die Bilder, denen

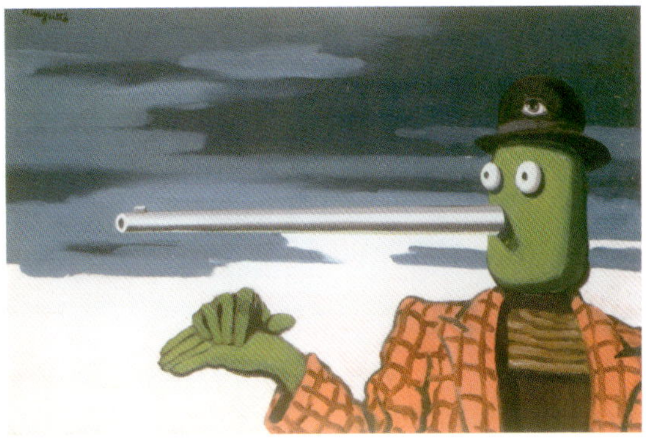

071 René Magritte
L'Ellipse, 1948
(Die Ellipse / Ellipse)
Öl auf Leinwand / oil on canvas
50 x 73 cm

The *vache* period thus had all the appeal of a bad joke. It was both something of a snub and a prank. It constituted both relaxation and turbulence, just as a corny pun does in relation to language. Certainly, there were antecedents, like his flippant parody of Gauguin dating from 1924. Certainly, the "vache" pictures followed those of the "Renoir" period [ILL·032], of which Magritte said that they were supposed, at the end of the war, to "expose Surrealism to bright sunlight." But something about those "Renoirs" belonged more to the sphere of pastiche and parody. The painter of the chocolate-box *Baigneuses* (Bathers) was an *alibi* for caricature-like, distorted painting by means of iridescent softness and feigned submission to the style and very name of the painter whom the Surrealists had held in contempt.[5]

Thus, the "vache" period was unrestrained and destructive. Magritte went as far as risking becoming unrecognizable. Certainly, there were a few oils and a few gouaches which it was possible to say retained a certain style, certain compositional principles in their technique, but most of the works which comprise this period, and the shock they were likely to produce *together*, express what was for Scutenaire the very definition of humor: "A way of avoiding embarrassment without getting out of the fix."[6] You only have to follow the criticism and marginalization of these works in the various exhibitions which followed to understand that the goal had been achieved and that Magritte was hereby departing from the law of genre and type. "You'll see what you see." And people did see it, so clearly that Magritte and Scutenaire were in the end both executioners and martyrs in this gloomy business.

So let's return to the aforementioned remark since it shows, with unconcealed enjoyment, that these two accomplices had on this occasion decided to be as thick as thieves. These were, in fact, the "ways and means" used to attack "Parure" (or "Piras" as Magritte subsequently referred to France's capital): the taste for spoonerisms being the linguistic corollary of the paintings we are interested in.

But it was also a way of proceeding quickly: responding to demand, with no time to lose. Three months to complete the project: a test of oneself in which the act of painting would know neither composure nor self-control, where things would no longer be subject to "the sweet delusion" of mastery, to a "beautiful hand," but deliberately distorted, trivial, of little virtue in the same way that one might say that they are of little taste; certainly, a cheeky and indecent joke, whose perverse effects would force connoisseurs to review their judgment of taste which, as we know, will never be a judgment based on knowledge.

However, this delinquent period appears to us today to be eminently moral, since painting once again resembled "the permanent revolt against the commonplaces of existence."[7] And that was well worth the sacrifice of some 15 paintings and 15 gouaches with which Magritte well knew that the Parisians (and others) would not concern themselves. It was well worth disgrace at the moment of recognition. Furthermore, this is one of the essential aspects of Magritte's art, which

wir uns hier zuwenden. Und so ging es auch schneller: Man wollte der Nachfrage entsprechen und keine Zeit verlieren. Drei Monate, um das Projekt zu Ende zu bringen. Eine Art Selbstprüfung, in der das Malen weder Beherrschung noch Zurückhaltung kennt, wo die Dinge nicht mehr dem „verlockenden Trugbild" der Meisterschaft, der „schönen Hand" unterworfen sind, sondern willentlich verzerrt, trivial, wenig tugend- und ebenso wenig geschmackvoll. Ein frecher und unanständiger Scherz, dessen Perversität den Kenner zwingt, sein Geschmacksurteil, das ja bekanntlich nie auf Erkenntnis basiert, zu revidieren.

Trotzdem erscheint uns diese Phase des Abwegs heute als höchst moralisch, denn die Malerei fungiert hier wieder einmal als „permanente Auflehnung gegen die Gemeinplätze der Existenz".[7] Und das war doch das Opfer der rund 15 Gemälde und ebenso vieler Gouachen wert, von denen Magritte sehr wohl wusste, dass die Pariser (und die anderen) sie kaum beachten würden. Ein Moment der Ungnade in einer Zeit allgemeiner Wertschätzung konnte dafür in Kauf genommen werden. Darin zeigt sich einer der wesentlichen Aspekte der Kunst Magrittes, der ihn hier einem Duchamp näher rückt als einem de Chirico, weil für diesen der Reiz eher im gleichzeitigen Ausdruck von Zeit und Gedächtnis besteht, während es Magritte vor allem um die unmittelbare Wirkung des Bildes geht. Des *Bildes* und nicht der Malerei.

Etwas philosophischer: Gilles Deleuze und Félix Guattari haben betont, dass „der Künstler weniger gegen das Chaos ankämpft (das er auf gewisse Weise sehnlich herbeiwünscht) als gegen die Klischees der öffentlichen Meinung. Gerade weil das Bild zunächst mit Klischees überdeckt ist", erläutern sie weiter, „muss sich der Künstler dem Chaos stellen und die Zerstörung vorantreiben, um eine Empfindung hervorzurufen, die (wie lange?) jeder öffentlichen Meinung und jedem Klischee standhält."[8]

In paradoxer Umkehrung wollte Magritte gegen den Automatismus beim Malen ankämpfen, der sich seiner bemächtigte, indem er zum Vollstrecker der Zerstörung seines eigenen Bildes wurde. In diesem Sinne ist sein Streich keinesfalls ein lustiger und eher dem zuzurechnen, was André Breton als „schwarzen Humor" bezeichnete. Wir haben es hier mit einer Ironie zu tun, die als schmerzliches Bewusstsein verstanden werden muss. Und die „période vache" zelebriert auf ihre Art die

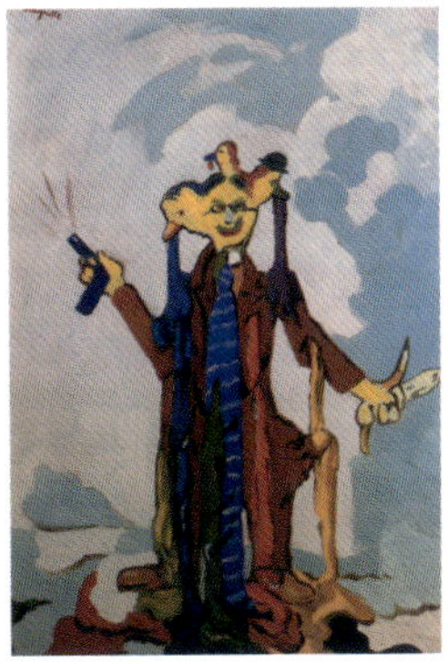

072 **René Magritte**
Le Contenu Pictural, 1947
(Der Inhalt der Malerei/ The Content of Painting)
Öl auf Leinwand / oil on canvas
73 x 50 cm

makes it more similar to a Duchamp than a de Chirico, who was tempted to create a simultaneous expression of time and memory, while Magritte remained above all preoccupied by the immediate impact of the image. Of the *image* and not of the painting.

Let's philosophize a little: Gilles Deleuze and Félix Guattari have made it clear that "the artist fights less against chaos (which, to an extent, he desires) than against the clichés of public opinion." They continue by saying that it is precisely because the painting starts off covered with clichés that "the painter must grapple with chaos and hasten destruction in order to produce a sensation which defies any opinion or any cliché (but for how long?)."[8]

Magritte, through a paradoxical reversal, wanted to fight the automatism in creation which was taking him over by becoming the executioner of the destruction of his own image. In this sense, the hoax is not a funny one but rather brinks on the realms of what André Breton called "black humor." This is a case of irony, which we must know is a painful awareness. And the "vache" period celebrates, in its own way, the whole problem of retaining a grip on one's thoughts and reason. By relinquishing his work to haphazardness, and at the same time holding it up to public obloquy, Magritte celebrates the humor of derision. "The invention which characterizes all true indignation is already a celebration in itself."[9]

Thus, the meaning he attributes to Georgette's words when he says that she urges him to return to "his earlier painting" makes of her less a muse than a guardian of orthodoxy. Georgette alone incarnates that bourgeois taste of which she feigns approval while Magritte himself feigns submission to it.

The practice of art is certainly far too much of an inner-moral concern for it not to be insubordinate. Once more, Magritte preferred repudiation and "joyous blasphemy" to recognition.

It was undoubtedly on such fertile soil that the complicity of Mag' and Scut' thrived. Raoul Vaneigem says that *Les Inscriptions* reveal "a fundamental disrespect for bourgeois, humanist, religious, artistic and moral values, which inspires them and makes them faithful to Surrealist negation, faithful to all negations."[10] And, about the "vache" period, we might say the same thing that Scutenaire was implying when asked why he wrote books: "I write for the same reasons which compel

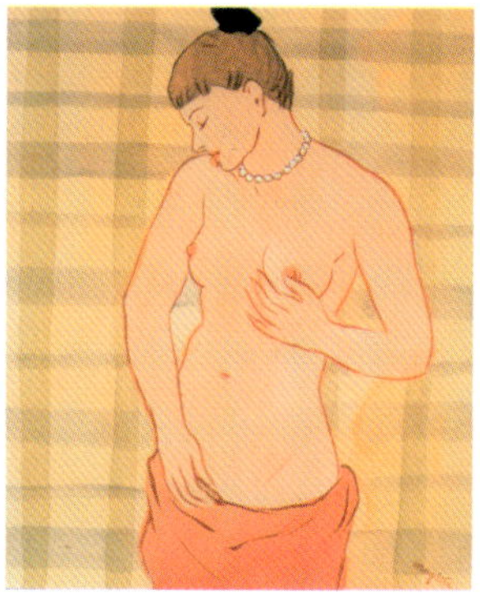

073 **René Magritte**
Le Galet, 1948
(Der Kiesel / The Pebble)
Gouache auf Papier / gouache on paper
39,5 x 31,5 cm

ganze Schwierigkeit, die darin liegt, an den eigenen Gedanken festzuhalten und Vernunft zu bewahren. Indem er sein Werk dem Geratewohl überlässt und damit der Schmach preisgibt, zelebriert Magritte die Komik des Hohns. „Die Erfindung, die jeder wahren Empörung anhaftet, ist an sich schon ein Fest."[9]

Der Sinn der Worte, die er Georgette in den Mund legt, wenn er von dieser sagt, dass sie ihn dazu anhalte, zur „Malerei von einst" zurückzukehren, macht sie also weniger zur Muse als zur Hüterin des Konformismus. Georgette allein verkörpert diesen bourgeoisen Geschmack, den gutzuheißen sie vorgibt, während Magritte seinerseits so tut, als fügte er sich ihm.

Die künstlerische Arbeit ist eine viel zu innerlich-moralische Angelegenheit, als dass sie ihr aufsässiges Wesen ablegen könnte. Einmal mehr waren dem Maler Ablehnung und „fröhliche Blasphemie" lieber als Anerkennung.

Auf solchem Boden konnte die Komplizenschaft zwischen Mag' und Scut' gedeihen. Von den *Inscriptions* sagt Raoul Vaneigem, sie zeugten „von einer grundlegenden Missachtung der bürgerlichen, humanistischen, religiösen, künstlerischen und moralischen Werte, die sie beseelen und mit der surrealistischen Negation wie überhaupt allen Negationen verbinden".[10] Für die „période vache" gilt das, was Scutenaire auf die Frage antwortete, warum er Bücher mache: „Ich schreibe aus den Gründen, die andere dazu bewegen, ein Postamt zu verwüsten, den Gendarmen oder seinen Herrn zu töten, eine soziale Ordnung zu zerstören. Weil mich etwas stört, eine Abscheu oder ein Verlangen."

Auch hier gibt es wieder Übereinstimmungen zwischen Magritte und Scutenaire. Ohne die Problematik des Malers und die des Schriftstellers unbedingt gleichsetzen zu wollen, kommt man doch nicht umhin, ihre gemeinsame Neigung zur Ablehnung und zum Aufbegehren zu bemerken, die nur durch eine immer während neue *Infragestellung* in Bewegung gehalten werden konnte. Das Projekt einer ersten Ausstellung in Paris kam hierbei gerade recht. Genau in dem Augenblick, wo die Erwartungen der Öffentlichkeit erfüllt werden sollten, entschied sich Magritte für die *Negation* und die *Satire* und stieß damit all jene vor den Kopf, die ihn zu kennen glaubten. Wieder einmal, nur auf andere Weise, wurde die *Repräsentation* als fehlerhaft entlarvt.

Und Magritte, dessen Werk sich jedem Akademismus entgegenstellt, in dem Sinne, dass es versucht, die Kräfte der Realität und der Illusion zu neutralisieren, um unbemerkt zum

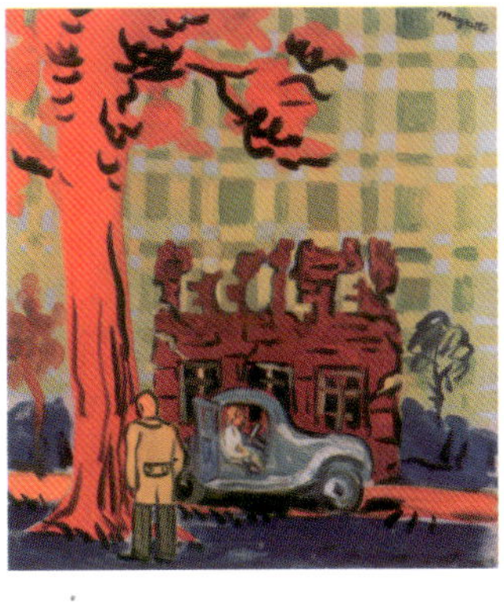

074 René Magritte
L'Etape, 1948
(Die Etappe / The Tour Stage)
Öl auf Leinwand / oil on canvas
64 x 54 cm

others to rob post offices, knock down a police officer or their boss, destroy a social order. Because something is bothering me: revulsion or desire."

And again, Magritte and Scutenaire found each other. And without taking the comparison between painterly and literary concerns to extremes, it is impossible to ignore their common taste for rebellion and insubordination which could only be kept in motion by a constant *replay*. The plan for a first exhibition in Paris came at just the right moment for this. At the moment when the public's expectations were to be fulfilled, Magritte opted for *negation* and *satire* and at the same time alienated those who believed they knew him. Once again, but in a different way, *representation* was revealed to be erroneous.

And Magritte, whose work was opposed to any kind of academicism in that it sought to neutralize the powers of reality and illusion, leading insidiously to the collapse of illusory representation, caricatured himself by ransacking with exquisite delight the codes and conventions he had perfected in his "earlier" work: "an excess in the true sense of the word, where eroticism mingles with low puns, gentleness with the unfathomable, boorishness with beauty, profundity with laughter, anger with the uncouth. One of the singular goals attained by the art of painting is the proud massacre of comfortableness of heart and mind, or indeed of mental stupor. Finally, subject and color were both given free rein to the point of having fun together in a way that robbed abstract painters of their basic arguments."[11] A bravado which revealed itself, beyond what Bataille elsewhere called "the disorder of prose," to be the weapon in a battle constantly replayed with his contemporaries, "in the face of a crowd of imitators who mend the holes in their parasols with a patch vaguely resembling a vision, and a crowd of annotators who fill up the cracks with opinions." With this act, Magritte toppled the optical system he had created in order to feed it to *opinion*: "For it is from opinion," add Deleuze and Guattari, "that human unhappiness arises."[12] Following the example of the caricaturists who "treated the human species with an almost delirious expressionistic virulence consisting of appalling deformations in atrocious colors,"[13] the trickles and dribbling colors of *Le Contenu Pictural* (The Content of Painting) [ILL·072], the slapdash stridence of *Mal de Mer* (Seasickness) [ILL·076] or the beaming grotesque of *La Famine* (The Famine) [ILL·075], and the painted paper backgrounds of *Jean-Marie* are as many fire-

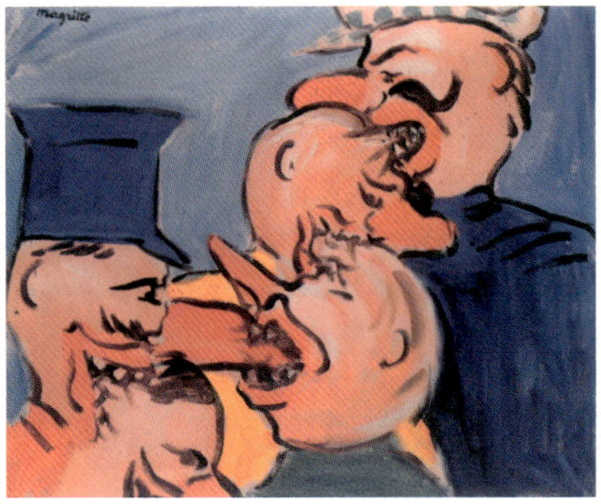

075 **René Magritte**
La Famine, 1948
(Die Hungersnot / The Famine)
Öl auf Leinwand / oil on canvas
46 x 55 cm

Zusammenbruch der illusionistischen Repräsentation zu führen, karikierte sich selbst, indem er genüsslich die Regeln und Konventionen, die er in seinem „einstigen“ Werk ausgeformt hatte, auf den Kopf stellte. Mit anderen Worten: „[...] ein Exzess im wahrsten Sinne des Wortes, wo sich Erotisches und Kalauer, Sanftes und Unergründliches, Flegelei und Schönheit, Tiefe und Lachen, Wut und Ungehörigkeit vermischen. Eines der besonderen Ziele, das die Malerei erreichte, ist der stolze Angriff auf die Bequemlichkeit des Herzens und des Geistes beziehungsweise auf den Stumpfsinn. Sujet und Farbe wurden ihrer Zügel entledigt und konnten sich nun frei vergnügen. Die Abstrakten wurden so ihrer grundlegenden Argumente beraubt.“[11] Eine Provokation, die sich neben dem, was Bataille an anderer Stelle „die Unordnung der Prosa“ nennt, als Waffe in einem immer währenden Kampf gegenüber seinen Zeitgenossen herausstellt, gegenüber der „Masse der Nachahmer, die den Schirm mit einem Stück flicken, das vage der Vision ähnelt, und die der Glossenschreiber, die den Schlitz mit Meinungen füllen“. Magritte brachte das optische System, das er errichtet hatte, ins Wanken, um es der *öffentlichen Meinung* zum Fraß vorzuwerfen. „Denn es ist die öffentliche Meinung“, so Deleuze und Guattari, „von der das Übel der Menschen ausgeht.“[12] Ganz nach dem Beispiel der Karikaturisten, die „den Menschen mit einer nahezu unbändigen expressionistischen Virulenz in grauenhaften Deformierungen und abscheulichen Farben behandelten“,[13] bringen die hinunterklecksenden und -sabbernden Farben des *Le Contenu Pictural* (Der Inhalt der Malerei) [ABB·072], die hingeschluderte grelle Schärfe des *Mal de mer* (Seekrankheit) [ABB·076] die heitere Groteske von *La Famine* (Die Hungersnot) [ABB·075] oder der Tapetenhintergrund von *Jean-Marie* allesamt das Feuer, mit dem ein unterkühltes Werk entzündet und in lodernden Brand gesetzt werden soll. Die „période vache“ war ein befreiender *Durchfall*, der die Malerei von Erstarrung und Verkrampfung erlöste. Und weit mehr. Sie fungierte auch als *Kontradiktionsprinzip*[14] in einem Werk, in dem es an Widersprüchen nicht mangelte. Sie stellt das einzige Moment im Werk Magrittes dar, das entschieden von der Kunst der *Ähnlichkeit* abrückt.

Es sei denn, der Mensch fand sich hier sogar viel wahrhaftiger als in Wirklichkeit wieder. Dann hätte die einzige Innovation innerhalb dieses Werkes, das eine solche bis dahin konsequent ablehnte, aus dieser „Gaunersprache“ eine Sprache der Wahrheit gemacht.

Wie sagte doch Scutenaire: « Il y en a maints et maints qui réfléchient. »[15]

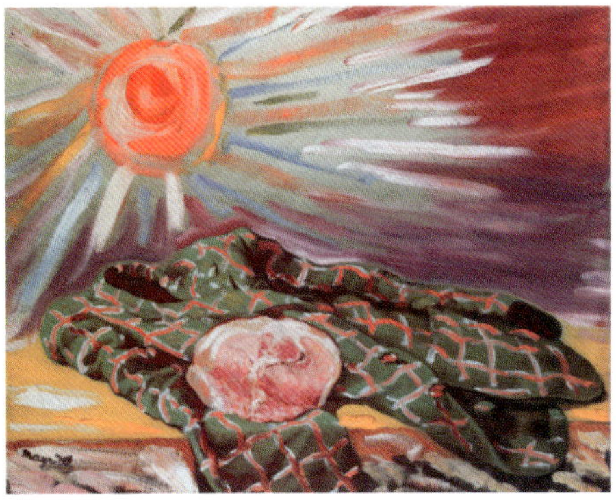

076 René Magritte
Le mal de mer, 1947
(Die Seekrankheit / The Seasickness)
Öl auf Leinwand / oil on canvas
53,5 x 65 cm

brands who have come to stir up and set on fire a resolutely cold work. The "pèriode vache" is a memorable case of *the runs* which liberated painting from stupefaction and torpor. Even better, this time it also acted as a *principle of contradiction*[14] in a canon of work which is by no means lacking in this; it is the only moment in Magritte's work that resolutely distances itself from the art of *resemblance*.

Unless the human species can be found here more accurately than in nature; unless this single innovation within an *œuvre* whose principle had, until then, been to refuse innovations has once again allowed this "slang" to become a language of truth.

To cite Scutenaire again: "Il y en a maints et maints qui réfléchient."[15]

1 It is well known how strongly Breton and Eluard repudiated this snub. The oft-cited expression by Eluard, an excerpt from the Golden Book at the Faubourg gallery, « Rira bien qui rira le dernier. » (He who laughs last laughs longest.), should not, as some believe, be taken as a compliment. Rather, it is a lively expression of the disapproval of the poet, who was offended by this impertinence. Even more offended was Breton, who thought that since the appearance of *Surrealisme en plein soleil*, Magritte's arguments « étaient cousus de fil blanc » (had become spurious) (see Jose Pierre, *Magritte*, Paris: Editions Aimery Somogy, 1984, pp. 63–67), and who also attacked the works from the Renoir period and the political commitment of Magritte and his friends (with the notable exception of Marcel Lecomte) who had joined the Belgian Communist Party in 1945.

2 On June 7, 1948, Magritte wrote to Scutenaire and Irene Hamoir from Paris: « [...] J'aimerais assez continuer en plus fort la ‹ démarche › expérimentée à Paris. C'est ma tendance : celle du suicide lent. Mais il y a Georgette et le dégoût que je connais d'être ‹ sincère › [...]. » ("[...] I should quite like to push further the 'process' I tried out in Paris. This is a tendency I have: that of slow suicide. But there is Georgette, and the distaste I have of being 'sincere' [...].")

3 French original: « C'en [était] bien fini de la violence dans le faire, l'outrance [était] rentrée dans sa maison et [avait] fermé la porte pour longtemps. » In Louis Scutenaire, *L'Invention de la Vie*, Magritte retrospective catalog (Brussels: Palais de Beaux Arts, 1978, Paris: Centres Georges Pompidou, 1979), p.16.

4 French original: « en circuit fermé, » idem., p.15.

5 The "Renoir" period was, in many ways, a forerunner of the "vache" period. As well as preceding it, Magritte's intentions, which he clarified in a letter to Scutenaire in 1945, are significant: « Mossieu le Minisse, Donc il y a peut-être une idée, encore lavaire, que tu pourrais former et formuler. Somm' tout', j'ai toujours représenté avec *netteté* les choses, affaires, objets, gens et animaux, même si ces choses et affaires étaient mystérieuses. De là à désirer éclairer plus vivement encore, il n'y a pas décision malheureuse de ma part, me semble-t-il? [...] » ("Dear Minister, I may have an idea, still embryonic, that you could develop and formulate. When all is said and done, I have always represented things, matters, objects, people, animals, with *clarity*, even if these things and matters were mysterious. Hence, to wish to illustrate more clearly still cannot be a bad decision on my part, can it? [...]").

6 French original: « Une façon de se tirer de l'embarras sans se tirer d'affaire. » In Raoul Vaneigem, *Louis Scutenaire* (Paris: ed. Seghers, 1991), p.103.

7 French original: « la révolte permanente contre les lieux communs de l'existence ». In Suzi Gablik, *Magritte* (Brussels 1978), translated from the English by Evelyn Deknop-Kornelis.

8 French original: « l'artiste se bat moins contre le chaos (qu'il appelle de ses vœux d'une certaine manière) que contre les clichés de l'opinion. C'est même parce que le tableau est d'abord recouvert de clichés que le peintre doit affronter le chaos et hâter les destructions pour produire une sensation qui défie toute opinion, tout cliché (combien de temps?), » in Gilles Deleuze, Felix Guattari, *Qu'est-ce que la Philosophie?* Paris, ed. Minuit, 1991, pp. 191–192.

9 French original: « L'invention qui caractérise toute indignation vraie est une fête déjà. » idem., p. 6.

10 French original: « [...] d'un irrespect fundamental des valeurs bourgeoises, humanistes, religieuses, artistiques et

1 Es ist bekannt, wie sehr Breton und Éluard diese mutwillige Brüskierung ablehnten. Der häufig zitierte Satz von Éluard aus dem Gästebuch der Galerie du Faubourg: « Rira bien qui rira le dernier » („Wer zuletzt lacht, lacht am besten"), ist nicht, wie viele meinen, als Kompliment zu verstehen. Er ist der lebhafte Ausdruck des Widerwillens, den der Dichter angesichts dieser Anmaßung empfand. Breton, der der Auffassung war, dass Magrittes Argumente seit Erscheinen des *Surréalisme en plein soleil* „fadenscheinig waren" (« étaient cousus de fil blanc » [vgl. José Pierre, *Magritte*, Somogy 1984, S. 63–67]), griff die Werke der Renoir-Periode noch schärfer an und kritisierte das politische Engagement Magrittes und seiner Freunde (mit Ausnahme von Marcel Lecomte), die 1945 in die kommunistische Partei Belgiens eingetreten waren.

2 Am 7. Juni 1948 schrieb Magritte aus Paris an Scutenaire und Irène Hamoir: « J'aimerais assez continuer en plus fort la "démarche" expérimentée à Paris. C'est ma tendance : celle du suicide lent. Mais il y a Georgette et le dégoût que je connais d'être "sincère" [...]. » („Ich würde die in Paris erprobte ‚Vorgehensweise' gern noch etwas stärker ausweiten. Meine Neigung liegt eben im langsamen Selbstmord. Aber da ist ja Georgette und die mir wohl bekannte Abscheu davor, ‚ehrlich' zu sein [...].")

3 Originalzitat: « C'en [était] bien fini de la violence dans le faire, l'outrance [était] rentrée dans sa maison et [avait] fermé la porte pour longtemps. » In: Louis Scutenaire, *L'invention de la vie*, Katalog zur Magritte-Retrospektive, Brüssel, Paris, 1978–1979, S. 16.

4 Originalzitat: « en circuit fermé », ebd., S. 15.

5 Die Renoir-Periode steht in vielerlei Hinsicht am Beginn der „période vache". Davon abgesehen, dass sie dieser zeitlich vorangeht, sind die Absichten Magrittes, die aus einem Brief an Scutenaire aus dem Jahr 1945 hervorgehen, recht deutlich: « Mossieu le Minisse, Donc il y a peut-être une idée, encore lavaire, que tu pourrais former et formuler. Somm' tout', j'ai toujours représenté avec *netteté* les choses, affaires, objets, gens et animaux, même si ces choses et affaires étaient mystérieuses. De là à désirer éclairer plus vivement encore, il n'y a pas décision malheureuse de ma part, me semble-t-il ? » („Lieber Herr Minister, da ist vielleicht eine Idee, noch nicht vollständig ausgereift, die du formen und formulieren könntest. Alles in allem habe ich ja die Dinge, Angelegenheiten, Gegenstände, Menschen und Tiere immer sehr *deutlich* dargestellt, auch wenn diese Dinge und Angelegenheiten geheimnisvoll waren. Darüber hinaus noch größere Klarheit schaffen zu wollen scheint mir doch nicht gerade eine unpassende Entscheidung zu sein.")

6 Originalzitat: « Une façon de se tirer d'embarras sans se tirer d'affaire. » In: Raoul Vaneigem, *Louis Scutenaire*, Paris 1991, S. 103.

7 Originalzitat: « la révolte permanente contre les lieux communs de l'existence », in: Suzi Gablik, *Magritte*, Brüssel 1978.

8 Originalzitat: « [...] l'artiste se bat moins contre le chaos (qu'il appelle de ses vœux d'une certaine manière) que contre les clichés de l'opinion. C'est même parce que le tableau est d'abord recouvert de clichés que le peintre doit affronter le chaos et hâter les destructions pour produire une sensation qui défie toute opinion, tout cliché (combien de temps ?). » In: Gilles Deleuze, Félix Guattari, *Qu'est-ce que la philosophie ?*, Paris 1991, S. 191 f.

9 Originalzitat: « L'invention qui caractérise toute indignation vraie est une fête déjà. » Vaneigem (zit. Anm. 6).

10 Originalzitat: « [...] d'un irrespect fondamental des valeurs bourgeoises, humanistes, religieuses, artistiques et morales, qui les anime et les place dans la fidélité de la négation surréaliste, dans la fidélité de toutes les négations. » In: Vaneigem (zit. Anm. 6), S. 65–70.

11 Originalzitat: « [...] un débordement à l'état pur, où l'érotisme se mêle au calembour, la douleur à l'insondable, la goujaterie à la beauté, la profondeur au rire, la colère à l'incongru. L'un des buts singuliers qu'ai touché l'art de peindre : le fier massacre des conforts du cœur et de l'esprit ou bien de l'hébétude. Enfin le sujet et la couleur sont l'un et l'autre laissés bride sur le cou, au point de pouvoir s'amuser ensemble, de la sorte enlevant aux abstraits leurs arguments de base. » In: Louis Scutenaire, *Magritte*, Antwerpen 1948. Es handelt sich hierbei um eine kurze Monografie über Magritte. Allerdings wird man feststellen, dass Scutenaire in diesem recht bündigen Text bereits sein Augenmerk auf die „période vache" lenkt, die Magritte eben erst vorgestellt hatte. Scutenaire bleibt übrigens der Einzige, der diese mutwillige Ausfälligkeit unterstützt.

12 Originalzitat: « Car c'est de l'opinion que vient le malheur de l'homme. » Deleuze, Guattari (zit. Anm. 8).

13 Originalzitat: « [...] traitent l'espèce humaine avec une virulence expressionniste quasi délirante, d'épouventables

morales, qui les anime et les place dans la fidélité de la négation surréaliste, dans la fidélité de toutes les négations. » In Raoul Vaneigem, *Louis Scutenaire*, Paris, ed. Seghers, 1991, pp. 65–70.

11 French original: « [...] un débordement à l'état pur, où l'érotisme se mêle au calembour, la douceur à l'insondable, la goujaterie à la beauté, la profondeur au rire, la colère à l'incongru. L'un des buts singuliers qu'ait touché l'art de peindre: le fier massacre des confort du cœur et de l'esprit ou bien de l'hébétude. Enfin le sujet et la couleur sont l'un et l'autre laissés la bride sur le cou, au point de pouvoir s'amuser ensemble, de la sorte enlevant aux abstraits leurs arguments de base. » In Scutenaire, *Magritte* (Antwerp: De Sikkel, 1948). This is a short monograph on Magritte but it must be said that Scutenaire, even in this short text, gives the lion's share to the "vache" period Magritte had just exhibited. Scutenaire would remain the only one to support this snub.

12 French original: « Car c'est de l'opinion que vient le malheur des hommes. » Ibid., p. 8.

13 French original: « [...& traitaient l'espèce humaine avec une virulence expressioniste quasi délirante, d'épouvantables déformations dans des coloris atroces. » In her monograph of Magritte, Suzi Gablik quoted a postcard tract (p. 149) in which Magritte wrote: « La bêtise éternelle se manifeste notamment ces temps derniers en prétendant venu le moment où l'art de peindre est remplacé par un soi-disant art ‹ abstrait ›, non figuratif ou ‹ informel › qui consiste à déposer de la ‹ matière › sur une surface plus ou moins de fantaisie et de conviction. » ("Eternal stupidity has been manifested particularly in recent times by the claim that the moment has arrived where the art of painting has been replaced by so-called 'abstract,' non-figurative or 'informal' art which consists of depositing 'material' on a surface more or less consisting of fantasy or conviction.") The "material" of the "vache" period here gains its excremental connotation and critical dimension in relation to the situation of painting in post-war Paris.

14 Vincent Bounoure, *La Theme de la Contradiction chez Magritte* in *L'Oeil*, February/March 1972, no. 206–207, pp. 5–11. Vincent Bounoure, although not referring to the "vache" period, denounces the danger of the catalog produced by Suzi Gablik in an attempt to classify the different procedures of Magritte's invention. It is clear that the "vache" period, by its very nature, departs from the principle of any classification since it contains all the classifications and evades them at the same time.

15 Louis Scutenaire, *Mes Inscriptions, 1945–1963* ed. Allia, Paris, 1984, p. 121. English translation: "There are a great many who shit with their minds." ("Réfléchient" is formed with "réfléchir" [to reflect] and "chier" [to shit].)

déformations dans des coloris atroces […]. » In ihrer Magritte-Monografie (zit. Anm. 7) zitiert Suzi Gablik ein Postkartenflugblatt (S. 149), auf das Magritte schrieb: « La bêtise éternelle se manifeste notamment ces temps derniers en prétendant venu le moment où l'art de peindre est remplacé par un soi-disant art "abstrait", non figuratif ou "informel" qui consiste à déposer de la "matière" sur une surface plus ou moins de fantaisie et de conviction. » („Die endlose Dummheit tritt in letzter Zeit insbesondere in der Ansicht zutage, der Augenblick sei gekommen, wo die Kunst des Malens durch eine so genannte ‚abstrakte', nicht gegenständliche oder ‚informelle' Kunst ersetzt wird, die darin besteht, ‚Material' auf einer mehr oder weniger ernst gemeinten oder willkürlich erdachten Fläche zu hinterlassen.") Das „Material" der „période vache" erhält hier seine Konnotation bezüglich Exkrementen und seine kritische Dimension im Hinblick auf die Situation der Malerei im Paris der Nachkriegszeit.

14 Vincent Bounoure, „Le Thème de la contradiction chez Magritte", in: *L'Œil*, Februar/März 1972, Nr. 206–207, S. 5–11. Vincent Bounoure weist, ohne jedoch von der „période vache" zu sprechen, auf die Gefahr eines Verzeichnisses hin, wie es Suzi Gablik in dem Versuch anlegte, die verschiedenen Verfahren der Magritte'schen Erfindungswelt zu klassifizieren. Fest steht, dass die „période vache" sich in ihrem Wesen selbst jeder Art von Klassifizierung entzieht, da sie gleichzeitig alle Verfahren umfasst und sich doch keinem zuordnen lässt.

15 Louis Scutenaire, *Mes inscriptions, 1945–1963*, Paris 1984, S. 121. Auf Deutsch in etwa: „Es sind derer viele, die denkacken." („Réfléchient" ist gebildet aus „réfléchir" [„nachdenken"] und „chier" [„scheißen"].)

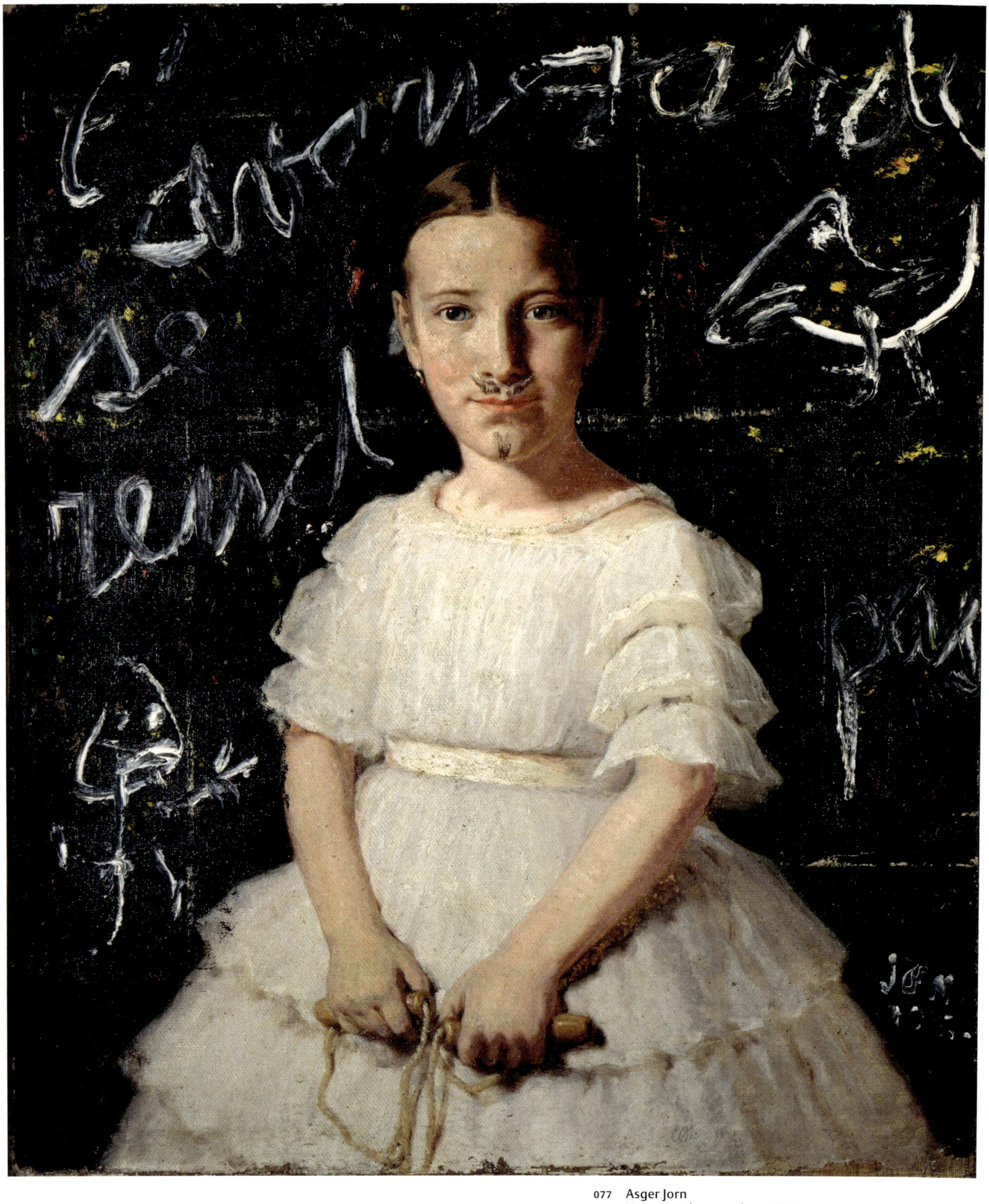

077 **Asger Jorn**
L'Avantgarde se rend pas, 1962
(Die Avantgarde gibt nicht auf /
The Avant-garde Does not Give up)

Öl auf Leinwand / oil on canvas, 73 x 60 cm
Pierre et Micky Alechinsky, Bougival

Schlechte Malerei? Asger Jorns „Modifications“

Claire Gilman

Im Mai 1959 stellte der dänische Künstler Asger Jorn in der Pariser Galerie Rive Gauche eine neue Werkgruppe vor. Es handelte sich um eine Serie von acht Leinwandbildern, die er unbekümmert als „Kitsch“ bezeichnete (erst später wurden sie als „Modifications“ bekannt). Bestehend aus zweitklassigen Bildern, die Jorn auf Flohmärkten erstanden und danach mit „drips“ im Stile Pollocks und Figuren im Stil Dubuffets versehen hatte, erinnerten sie nur vage an die expressiven, dicht gearbeiteten Bilder, die er seit den frühen 1940er-Jahren gemacht hatte und zu denen er in späteren Jahren wieder zurückkehrte. [ABB·001·012·033·077–080] Im Vorwort zum Ausstellungskatalog spielte Jorn die Arbeiten geradewegs und jubelnd herunter: „Mit dieser Ausstellung errichte ich ein Denkmal zu Ehren der schlechten Malerei. Ich persönlich mag sie lieber als gute Malerei. Vor allem aber ist dieses Denkmal unerlässlich – für mich und wen auch immer. Die Malerei wird geopfert … Feierlich ziehe ich meinen Hut und lasse das Blut meiner Opfer fließen, während ich Baudelaires Hymne an die Schönheit anstimme.“[1]

Einerseits wäre es verführerisch, Jorns modifizierte Gemälde als eine Art Schabernack zu nehmen, als kurze Verschnaufpause in einem sonst so engagierten malerischen Werk. Diese Sichtweise erscheint angesichts der am öftesten reproduzierten „Modifikation“ gerechtfertigt – des vorgefundenen Gemäldes eines Mädchens, das wie bei Duchamps *L.H.O.O.Q.* mit einem Bart versehen und provokant *L'Avant-garde se rend pas* (Die Avantgarde gibt nicht auf, 1962) [ABB·077] betitelt wurde.[2] Während Duchamps Aktion neu war, weil er eine bürgerliche Ikone stürzte und als fotografische Reproduktion abwertete, ist Jorns Eingriff nachgeahmt – er übernimmt die bestehende Negation Duchamps und wärmt sie als Witz neu auf.

Andererseits begann Jorn die „Modifications“ am Höhepunkt seines Engagements in der Situationistischen Internationale, das von 1957 bis zu seinem Austritt im April 1961 währte. Sie beschließen eine intensive Phase der Zusammenarbeit mit Guy Debord, dem Aushängeschild der Situationisten (deren zweites und letztes gemeinsames Buchprojekt, *Mémoires*, wurde Anfang 1959 veröffentlicht).[3] Dieser Umstand verlangt für sich genommen schon eine tiefer gehende Auseinandersetzung mit dieser Werkgruppe. Und in der Tat: Situationistische Schriften führen die Abwandlung von Gemälden als Musterbeispiel für ein „détournement“ (eine „Umleitung“, ein „Ablenken“, eine

Bad Painting? Asger Jorn's "Modifications"

Claire Gilman

In May 1959, at Galerie Rive Gauche, Paris, Danish artist Asger Jorn unveiled a new body of work: a series of eight canvases that he blithely labeled "kitsch" (they would later come to be known as the „Modifications"). Comprising second-rate canvases that the artist found in flea markets and decorated with Pollock-like drips and Dubuffet-style figures, the new work was a far cry from the expressive, densely worked images that Jorn had been making since the early 1940s and to which he returned in later years [ILL·001·012·033·077–080]. The artist's preface to the exhibition catalog was straightforward in its jubilant dismissal of the paintings: "In this exhibition I erect a monument in honor of bad painting. Personally, I like it better than good painting. But above all, this monument is indispensable, both for me and for everyone else. It is painting sacrificed.... I solemnly tip my hat and let the blood of my victims flow while intoning Baudelaire's hymn to beauty."[1]

It is tempting to take Jorn's modified paintings as a kind of prank—a brief respite from the artist's otherwise intensely committed painterly production. Such a response appears justified by Jorn's most frequently reproduced modification, a found painting of a young girl inscribed with a mustache and beard a la Duchamp's *L.H.O.O.Q.* provocatively titled *L'Avantgarde se rend pas* (The Avant-Garde Does not Give Up, 1962) [ILL·077].[2] If Duchamp's act is primary—overturning the bourgeois icon, which is further undone by its status as photo reproduction—Jorn's mark is necessarily secondary—a received gesture that reads as a humorous rehashing of Duchampian negation after the fact.

But Jorn began the „Modifications" during the height of his involvement with the Situationist International, which lasted from 1957 until his resignation in April 1961, and concludes an intense period of collaboration with Situationist front man Guy Debord (the second of two joint book projects, *Mémoires,* was published in early 1959).[3] In and of itself, this circumstance encourages a more serious reading of the work. Indeed, Situationist texts cite the modification paintings as primary examples of "détournement," the principal tactic of the SI's anything-but-insincere effort to undermine capitalist alienation and restore authentic human meaning within what Guy Debord termed "the society of the spectacle."[4] The relevant question is less whether or not Jorn's paintings should be taken seriously, than *how* they support the SI's committed agenda given their self-consciously trivial appea-

„Entwendung") an – jene Hauptmethode der alles andere als unernsten Bemühungen der SI, die kapitalistische Entfremdung zu unterwandern und damit die authentische menschliche Bedeutung in einer Gesellschaft wiederherzustellen, die Guy Debord „die Gesellschaft des Spektakels" genannt hat.[4] Die entscheidende Frage ist nicht, ob man Jorns Bilder ernst nehmen sollte, sondern *wie* sie in ihrer absichtlich trivialen Erscheinung der von der SI festgelegten Agenda dienen. Anders gefragt: Gibt es eine Art, Jorns selbst so bezeichnete „schlechte Malerei" in einer Weise zu sehen, die etwas Wertvolles, ja „Unerlässliches" in diesen scheinbar oberflächlichen Gesten erkennen kann?

Wörtlich definiert als „Einbeziehung gegenwärtiger und vergangener Kunstwerke in die übergeordnete Konstruktion einer Situation", kann man „détournement" als Sabotage mit kritischem Anspruch und damit ähnlich den Collagemethoden von Dada und Surrealismus verstehen. Isoliert betrachtet, sprechen zahlreiche Verlautbarungen der SI für diese Sichtweise. Im Aufsatz „Die Zweckentfremdung als Negation und als Vorspiel" zum Beispiel wird „détournement" als Spiel erklärt, das von der „Fähigkeit der Entwertung abhängt", mit der „alle Elemente der kulturellen Vergangenheit entweder ‚reinvestiert' werden oder verschwinden müssen". Der nächste Punkt jedoch ist überraschender und verweist auf einen Blickwinkel, der, von Kritikern beinahe vergessen, besonders für Jorns Werk wichtig ist. Die Autoren schließen nämlich: „[E]s ist nötig, ein parodistisch-ernstes Stadium ins Auge zu fassen, in dem die Anhäufung zweckentfremdeter Elemente, weit davon entfernt, durch den Bezug auf ein Originalwerk Lachen oder Empörung zu provozieren, unsere *Gleichgültigkeit* gegenüber einem sinnentleerten und vergessenen Original deutlich macht und sich darum bemüht, eine gewisse Erhabenheit auszudrücken."[5] – „Eine solche recht gemäßigte Zweckentfremdung ist letzten Endes nur das moralische Äquivalent der Restauration alter Gemälde in Museen."[6]

Kurz gesagt: Anstatt das zweckentfremdete Kunstwerk im Dienste einer politischen Aussage zu demontieren, wird es durch die Aneignung *konserviert*, wenn auch als toter Gegenstand. Es wird durch keine neue, bessere Bedeutung ersetzt, sondern als bloßes Museumsobjekt definiert. „Dass die Sprache der Kommunikation verloren wurde, dies wird *positiv* durch die moderne Auflösungsbewegung aller Kunst", schreibt Debord in der *Gesellschaft des Spektakels*. „Was diese Bewegung *negativ* ausdrückt, ist die Tatsache, dass eine gemeinsame Sprache wiedergefunden werden muss."[7] Und weiter: „Malt eine neue, unabhängige Kunst ihre Welt in bunten Farben, dann muss ein Moment des wirklichen Lebens alt geworden sein. Die bunten Farben können diesen Moment nicht wieder jung, sondern nur auf ihn aufmerksam machen. Große Kunst entsteht erst dann, wenn sich Staub auf das Leben senkt."[8] Der Kunstgegenstand kann das Leben nur reflektieren – ein Leben, das bereits alt ist, wenn es im Kunstwerk erscheint. Das Kunstwerk spricht keine wirkungsvoll kritische Sprache. Mit seinen „bunten", aber machtlosen Formen kann es nichts produzieren, nichts in Bewegung setzen, sondern nur bekräftigen. Und doch, das alleine hat bereits einen Wert. In Debords Denken ist das einzig Positive an der modernen Kultur, dass ihre Trägheit selbst ihren Zerfall beweist, ihr „Verwelken, ihre Zeugenschaft gegen sich selbst".[9]

rance. More generally, is there a way of approaching Jorn's self-proclaimed "bad painting" that locates something valuable, even "indispensable," in an apparently superficial gesture?

Literally defined as "the integration of present or past artistic production into a superior construction of a milieu," détournement is typically understood as a form of critical sabotage, parallel, in this sense, to Dada and Surrealist collage tactics. Taken in isolation, many SI statements support this view. For instance, the 1959 essay "Détournement as Negation and Prelude" explains that "*détournement* is a game made possible by the capacity of 'devaluation' [...] all the elements of the cultural past must be 'reinvested' or disappear." However, the next point is more surprising and suggests a dimension, all but ignored by critics, that assumes particular significance when applied to Jorn's work. The authors conclude: "'it is necessary [...] to conceive of a parodic-serious stage where the accumulation of detourned elements, far from aiming at arousing indignation or laughter by alluding to some original work, will express our *indifference* toward a meaningless and forgotten original, and concern itself with rendering a certain sublimity [italics mine].'"[5] "Such a detournement —a very moderate one—is in the final analysis nothing more than the moral equivalent of the restoration of old paintings in museums."[6]

In short, instead of dismantling the original work of art to make an effective political statement, appropriation *preserves* the work, albeit as inert artifact. The work is not superseded by a new, enlightened meaning, but reconfirmed as a mere object suitable for the museum. "The fact that the language of real communication has been lost is what the modern movement of art's decay expresses *positively*," explains Debord in *The Society of the Spectacle.* "What it expresses *negatively* is that a new common language has yet to be found.[7] And again: "When a newly independent art paints its world in brilliant colors, then a moment of life has grown old. By art's brilliant colors, it cannot be rejuvenated but only called to mind. The greatness of art makes its appearance only as dusk begins to fall over life."[8] The art object is capable only of reflecting life, a life grown old as soon as it is registered on the work's surface. It cannot produce or activate—it does not speak a viable critical language—but only solidifies with its "brilliant," impotent forms. And yet, in this alone it possesses some value. In Debord's thinking, the only positive thing about modern culture is that its very inertia testifies to its own disintegration, to "its withering away, its witness against itself."[9]

What Debord describes here is nothing less than a new artistic strategy, one physicalized in Jorn's overlaid surfaces, which differ from avant-garde collage in their express departure from previous structures of visuality and spatiality. Unlike Dada's propagandistic collage tactics (as in, for example, *L.H.O.O.Q.*'s overturning of the bourgeois art object *par excellence* or John Heartfield's assault on Nazi German politics) in which disjunction and fragmentation, shock and simultaneity, ultimately combine in new, synthetic configurations, Jorn's painting functions as a sort of neutral collection from which meaning has not been overturned but evacuated. Indeed, on closer look, Jorn's girl proves to be one motif among others, which include his scrawled title and childlike forms painted on

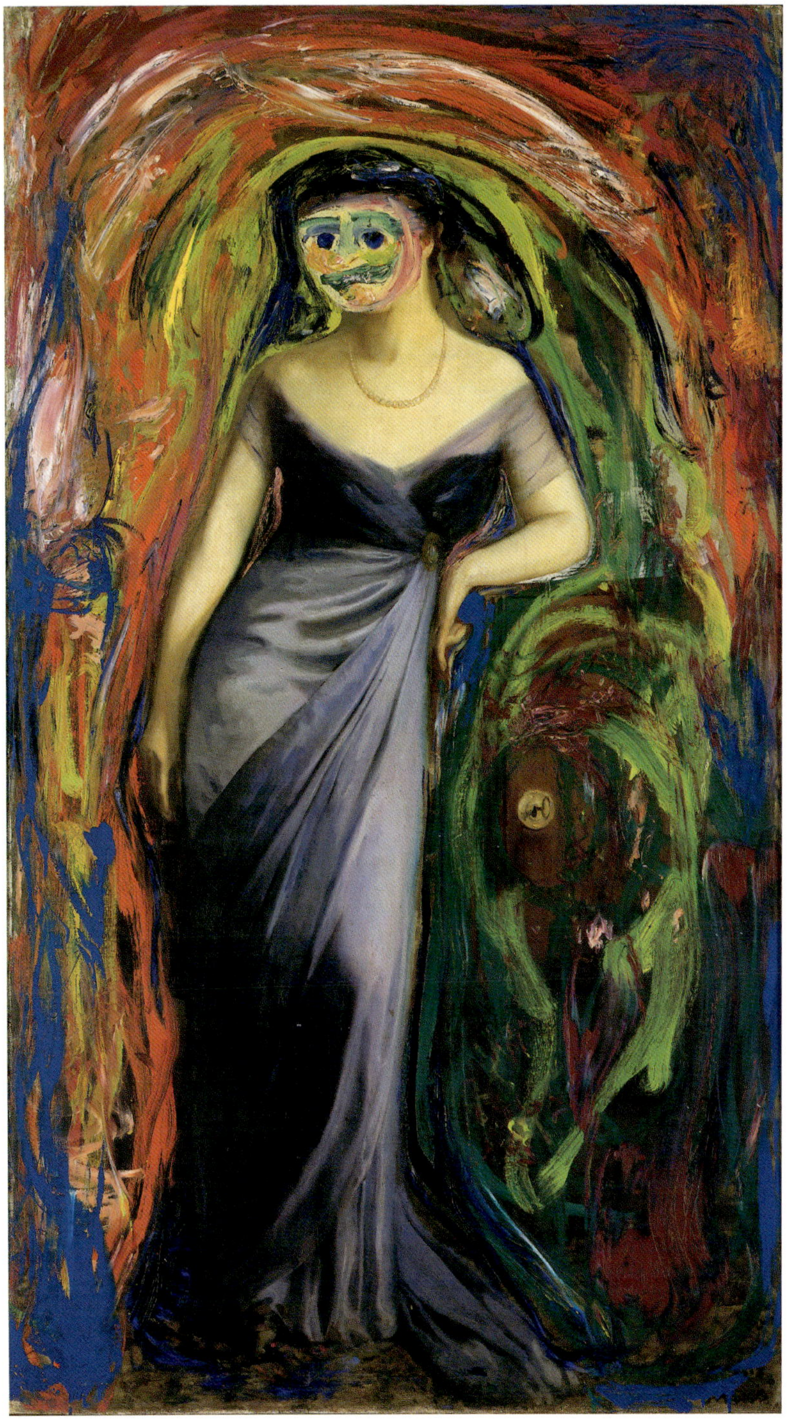

078 Asger Jorn
Choux, 1961
(Kohlkopf / Cabbage)
Öl auf Leinwand / oil on canvas
210 x 117 cm
Kunsthalle zu Kiel, Dauerleihgabe Stifterkreis

Debord beschreibt hier nichts Geringeres als eine künstlerische Strategie, materialisiert in Jorns übermalten Bildern, die sich von avantgardistischen Collagen durch ihr Abweichen von alten Strukturen der Sichtbarkeit und Räumlichkeit unterscheiden. Anders als die propagandistischen Collagetechniken von Dada (wie zum Beispiel *L.H.O.O.Q.*, das den bürgerlichen Kunstgegenstand par excellence stürzte, oder John Heartfields Angriffe auf die Politik der Nazis), mit denen Zitat und Fragment, Schock und Simultanität letztlich zu neuen synthetischen Konfigurationen verbunden werden, fungiert Jorns Malerei als eine Art von neutraler Ansammlung, deren Bedeutung nicht gestürzt, sondern entleert wird. Und wirklich: Bei genauerer Betrachtung entpuppt sich Jorns Mädchen als ein Sujet unter vielen, auch der hingekritzelte Titel und die kindlichen Formen auf schwarzem Grund. Dieses

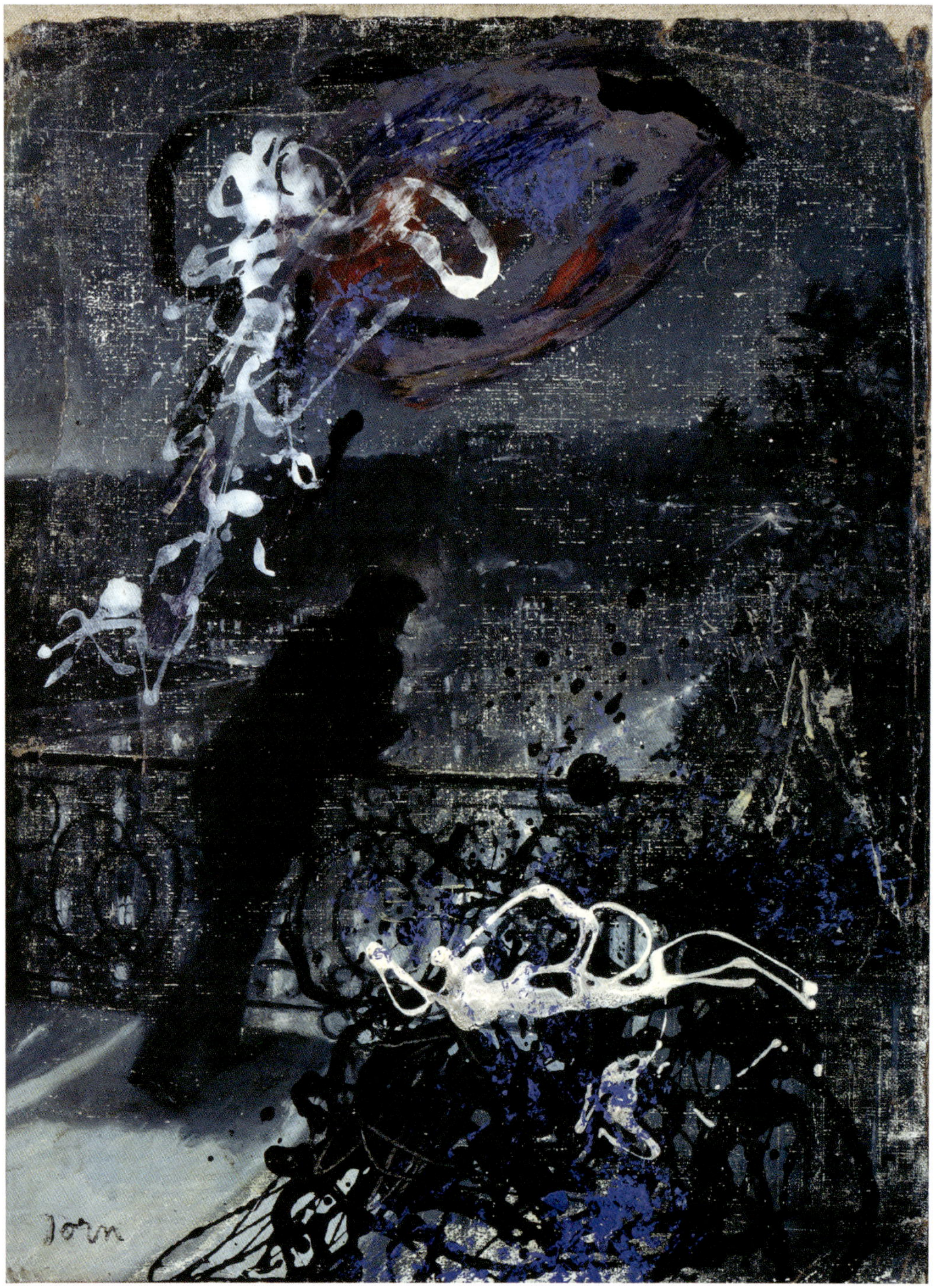

079
Asger Jorn
Paris by Night, 1959
(Paris bei Nacht)
Öl auf Leinwand /
oil on canvas
53 x 37 cm
Pierre et Micky
Alechinsky, Bougival

the black ground. This work is not a reference to Duchamp so much as a reflection on several previous artistic strategies (the graffito, the readymade, appropriation, gestural painting, *Art Brut*), which come together with no apparent rhyme or reason. It is a kind of archive of the avant-garde; a recollection of earlier artistic forays, which, registered on the surface alongside each other, become distinct, borrowed styles, made equivalent with all other artistic interventions and preserved, albeit as mere trace, for posterity. In other words, instead of employing internal rupture to critically provide meaning, Jorn's banal image quotations offer a view from a place where such gestures are no longer thought possible.

Consider, in this context, *Paris by Night* (1959) [ILL·079], a found painting of a man leaning over a balcony looking down over the city of Paris, which Jorn has overlaid with paint in the

Bild bezieht sich nicht auf Duchamp, sondern ist eine Reflexion mehrerer künstlerischer Strategien der Vergangenheit (Graffito, Readymade, Aneignung, gestische Malerei, Art brut), die ohne offensichtlichen Reim oder Grund nebeneinander gestellt werden. Es handelt sich um eine Art Archiv der Avantgarde, um einen Nachgeschmack künstlerischer Heldentaten der Vergangenheit, die, auf einer einzigen Leinwand nebeneinander festgehalten, ihrerseits zu eigenen, geklauten Stilen werden. Damit werden sie allen früheren künstlerischen Neuerungen gleichgestellt und für die Nachwelt konserviert, wenn auch nur als bloße Spur. Mit anderen Worten: Es wird kein neuer Bruch behauptet, der eine neue Kritik ermöglicht. Jorns banale Bildzitate verraten eine Sichtweise, in der Neuerungen in der Kunst nicht mehr für möglich gehalten werden.

Man betrachte diesbezüglich *Paris by Night* (1959) [ABB·079], ein gefundenes Gemälde von einem Mann, der sich über einen Balkon lehnt und über Paris blickt, das Jorn in der rechten unteren und der linken oberen Ecke übermalt hat. Oben erkennt man schematisch ein eiförmiges Gesicht, während sich die figurativen Ansätze unten in einem Netz wirrer Linien und vereinzelter Farbtropfen verlaufen. Die dunklen Blautöne schaffen eine bedeutsame Stille, die Jorns Eingriffe trotz ihrer bemühten Kühnheit nicht beleben können. Anstatt in die kontemplative Einsamkeit des Mannes einzugreifen oder den Bildraum signifikant zu verändern, sind Jorns Eingriffe genau das, was sie zu sein scheinen: ohnmächtige Farbkleckse, die auf der Leinwand verkrusten. Anstatt die Bildebene zu „vandalisieren“ oder „aufzubrechen“, belegen Jorns *Nicht*-Eingriffe die Undurchdringlichkeit der stummen Leinwand und das Scheitern jeder immanenten dekonstruktiven Methode. Man betrachte auch das eklatant witzige *Ainsi on s'ensor* (1962), ein seltsam prosaisches Gemälde eines Mannes, der sich in seinem Wohnzimmer erhängt hat. Jorns einzige Eingriffe sind eine grüne Maske mit Hakennase und ein Kommentar, den er auf das Blatt Papier gekritzelt hat, das im Vordergrund auf dem Tisch liegt: „Merde au Monde“ („Scheiß auf die Welt“). Seltsam ist an diesem Bild nicht die vulgäre Aggressivität des Kommentars, sondern dass der Künstler hier bloß einen bereits existierenden Eindruck verstärkt hat. Jorns Modifikationen verändern nicht das Original, sondern entsprechen dem vorhandenen düsteren Eindruck, der sichtlich von der Unmöglichkeit jeder positiven Handlung in einer hoffnungslos verderbten Welt herrührt.

Die Abwertung des Kunstobjekts durch Jorn und Debord bis hin zu einer Irrelevanz, die an dessen „Selbstliquidierung“ grenzt, hat eine überraschende Parallele in den Schriften Theodor Adornos, jenes Kämpfers für das radikal autonome Kunstwerk. In seiner *Ästhetischen Theorie* rühmt er Baudelaire dafür, als Erster erkannt zu haben, dass die Kunst in einer entwickelten Warengesellschaft nichts tun kann als zuzusehen, wie diese Gesellschaft ihren Lauf nimmt. Die Kunst kann die Herrschaft der kapitalistischen Gesellschaft nur transzendieren, wenn sie ihre Autonomie den Bildern dieser Gesellschaft anpasst. „Moderne ist Kunst durch Mimesis ans Verhärtete und Entfremdete; dadurch, und nicht durch Verleugnung des Stummen wird sie beredt.“[10] Wie Debord glaubt auch Adorno, dass sich das Kunstwerk nicht mehr mit Methoden der Montage rechtfertigen lässt, denn „[n]achdem dieser

bottom right and upper left-hand corners. At the top a schematic, ovoid face is discernible while at the bottom attempts at figuration have degenerated into a web of tangled lines and isolated drops of paint. The dusky blue tones create a heavy stillness that Jorn's additions, despite their valiant efforts, cannot enliven. Rather than encroaching on the man's contemplative solitude, or disrupting the pictorial space in any significant way, these forms read as what they literally are: impotent paint splotches encrusted on the canvas. Instead of "vandalizing" or "breaking open" the picture plane, Jorn's *non*-alterations testify to the impenetrability of the mute canvas and the failure of immanent deconstructive strategies. Consider also the blatantly humorous *Ainsi on s'ensor* (Out of this World—After Ensor, 1962), a peculiarly mundane painting of a man who has hung himself by a rope in his living room. Here, Jorn's only interventions are a hook-nosed green mask and a message scribbled on the sheet of paper on the table in the foreground that reads: "Merde au Monde"—"Damn the World" or, more vulgarly, "Shit on the World." The strange thing about this work is less the violence of Jorn's words than the fact that the artist has done nothing more than reinforce an already existing condition. In other words, Jorn's additions do not alter the original so much as echo it's already bleak sentiment, a sentiment that appears to confirm the impossibility of positive action in a hopelessly debased world.

Jorn and Debord's degradation of the art object to a position of irrelevance bordering on "self-liquidation" finds a surprising parallel in the writing of Theodor Adorno, that champion of the radical, autonomous artwork. In his *Aesthetic Theory,* Adorno lauds Baudelaire for being the first to acknowledge that art in a mature commodity society is powerless to do anything but look on as that society takes its course. Art can transcend capitalist society's reign only by integrating its own autonomy with society's images. "The modernity of art lies in its mimetic relation to a petrified and alienated reality. This, and not the denial of that mute reality is what makes art speak."[10] Like Debord, Adorno holds that the work of art can no longer justify itself through strategies such as montage for "now that shock has lost its punch, the products of montage revert to being indifferent stuff or substance."[11] In plagiarizing images, themes and ideologies, the Situationist work does not negate these forms, but rather, presents them as "surplus," revealing prior avant-garde strategies to be "indifferent stuff and substance," undone by their own irrelevance within contemporary culture. Jorn's paintings reveal previous critical gestures to be mere crust on the canvas.

"Be modern, collectors, museums," Jorn writes in his 1959 essay. If you have old paintings do not despair. Retain your memories but detourn them so that they correspond with your era [...]. Painting is over. You might as well finish it off. Detourn. Long live painting."[12] It is significant that these works remain paintings because, as such, and through their inert opacity, they become ciphers of their own demise. Jorn stands back as his paintings self-destruct before his eyes: "It is impossible to establish a future without a past. The future is made through relinquishing or sacrificing the past [...]. I solemnly tip my hat and let the blood of my victims flow while intoning Baudelaire's hymn to beauty."[13]

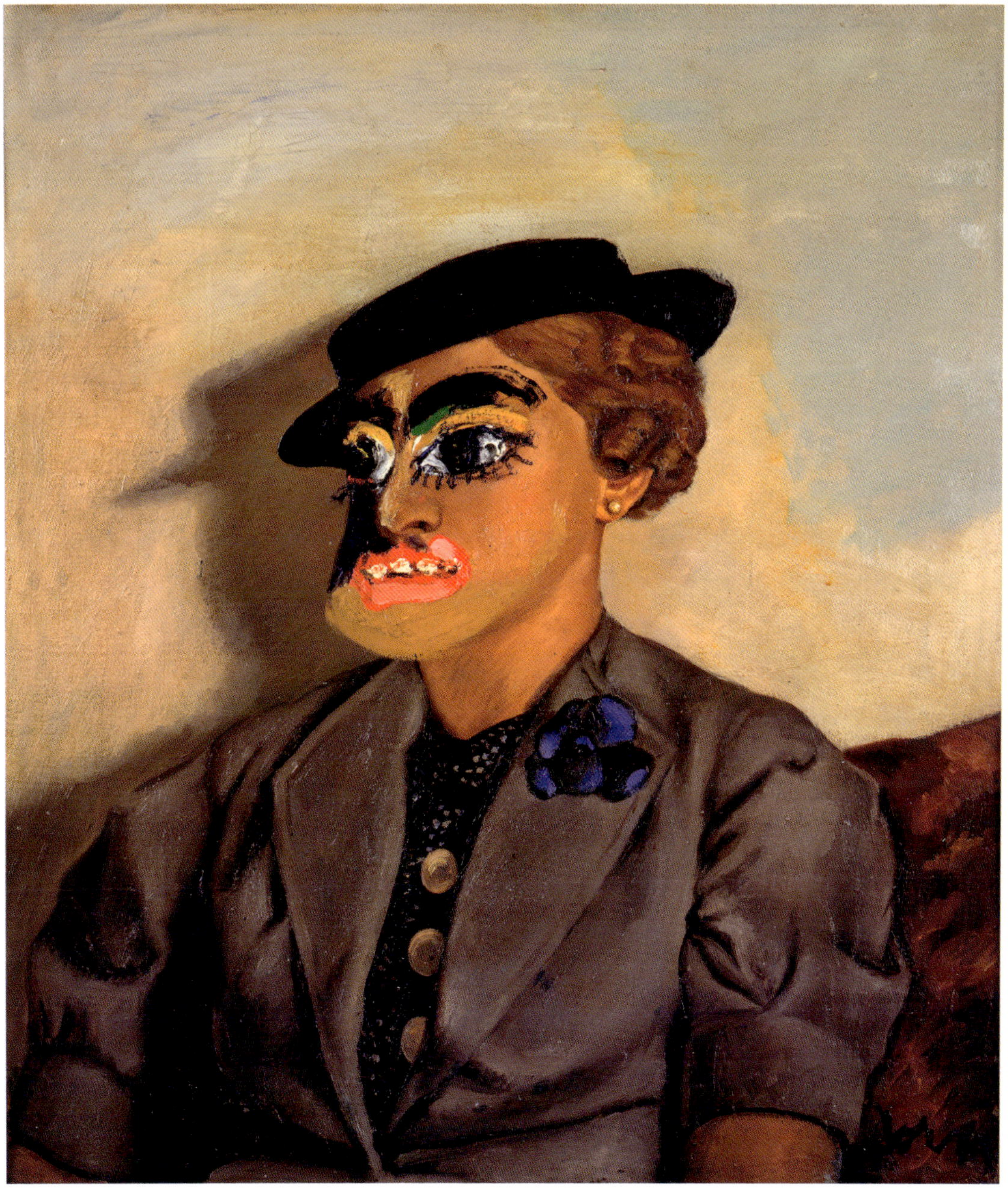

080 **Asger Jorn**
Souriez rue froide
1962
(Lachen Sie kalte Straße / Smile Cold Street)
Öl auf Leinwand / oil on canvas
65 x 54 cm
Pierre et Micky Alechinsky, Bougival

[Schock] sich abgestumpft hat, wird das Montierte abermals zum bloßen indifferenten Stoff".[11] Mit ihren Plagiaten negiert die situationistische Methode die Bilder, Themen und Ideologien nicht, sondern stellt sie vielmehr als „Überfluss" dar. Dadurch werden ehemals avantgardistische Methoden „zum bloßen indifferenten Stoff", der sich durch seine eigene Bedeutungslosigkeit in der zeitgenössischen Kultur selbst aufhebt. Jorns Gemälde enttarnen damit ehedem kritische Methoden als bloße Kruste auf der Leinwand.

„Sammler, Museen, seien Sie modern", schreibt Jorn in seinem Aufsatz aus dem Jahr 1959. „Verzweifeln Sie nicht, wenn Sie alte Bilder haben. Behalten Sie Ihre Erinnerungen, aber leiten Sie sie um, sodass sie Ihrer Zeit entsprechen. [...] Die Malerei ist am Ende. Man kann ihr gleich den

What sort of beauty is Jorn referring to here? Is he speaking of that ephemeral quality that mirrors the age it typifies and, in this way, comes to parallel Adorno's autonomous artwork, or is he instead referencing Baudelaire's other beauty—the eternal and immutable—, and implying that this kind of rigidity must ultimately be rejected? According to Adorno, art's very repulsiveness carries a certain "catastrophic potential" which conjures up the possibility of "the unutterable, which is Utopia."[14] A similar paradox lies at the heart of Jorn's „Modifications" and Debord's writing. For it is important to emphasize that utopian aspirations do not disappear from Situationist art theory. As time went on, the Situationists became more and more adamant that critical action could only exist outside the art object—on the streets, in the city, or, as Debord put it, "underground," beyond spectacle's domain.[15] But it is possible to see a revolutionary impulse in Jorn's insistence on a manifest temporality, in his revelation, that is, of the provisional nature of things.[16] It is this celebration of insufficiency that Jorn appreciates in kitsch painting which never presumes to be complete in and of itself and whose value lies less in what it depicts than in the popular sentiment behind the depiction. Gestures live and die but the desire to create and to forge, as he puts it, "a link between [...] subjects" remains.[17]

By asserting their own bounded materiality—as well as the historicity of the gestures they contain—Jorn's paintings suggest that nothing is given once and for all and that therefore, even if artistic opposition is uncertain or impossible under present circumstances, there is always the future. Or as he puts it somewhat less optimistically: "It is impossible to establish a future without a past."[18]

1 Asger Jorn, "Peinture détourné," in *Vingt peintures modifées par Asger Jorn,* (Paris: Galerie Rive Gauche, 1959). Translated as "Detourned Painting" in On the Passage of a Few People through a Brief Moment in Time: The Situationist International: 1957-1972, ed. Elisabeth Sussman (Boston: The Institute of Contemporary Art, 1989), p. 142.

2 This work does not belong to the original „Modifications" series from 1959, but rather to a group entitled *New Disfigurations,* which was executed after the „Modifications" and, for that matter, shortly after Jorn's resignation from the SI in 1961. In fact, there are three categories of modified paintings, which Jorn produced from 1959 to 1962: the „Modifications", the *New Disfigurations* and *Anecdotal Imagery from Daily Life.* Guy Atkins sees a thematic difference between the groups observing that the New Disfigurations have a "more serious intention" and "lend themselves to sometimes quite sinister psychological adaptations." There may be some truth to this suggestion but it is certainly not uniformly the case given that *The Avant-Garde Doesn't Give Up* is officially part of the second group. Guy Atkins, *Asger Jorn: The Crucial Years,* 1954-1964 (New York: Wittenborn Art Books, 1977), pp. 65-68ff.

3 It is worth noting that Jorn was one of the few people who chose to resign from the SI of his own volition and on amicable terms. He remained friends with Debord throughout his life although their view of art certainly differed as Jorn returned to a more gestural style of painting and Debord became more and more suspicious of artistic interventions of any kind.

4 Guy Debord, *The Society of the Spectacle,* trans. Donald Nicholson-Smith (New York: Zone Books, 1994).

5 « Le détournement comme négation et comme prélude, » Internationale situationiste 3 (1959). Translated as "Détournement as Negation and Prelude," in the *Situationist International Anthology*, ed. and trans. Ken Knabb (Berkeley, CA: Bureau of Public Secrets, 1981), 55-56 (hereafter SIA).

6 Debord and Gil Wolman, "Methods of Détournement," in *Les Lévres Nues 8,* (May 1956). Trans. as "Methods of Détournement," in SIA, p. 12.

7 Debord, *The Society of the Spectacle,* p. 133.

Gnadenstoß versetzen. Leiten Sie um. Es lebe die Malerei."[12] Bezeichnend ist, dass diese Werke dennoch Malerei bleiben, weil sie als solche durch ihre träge Undurchsichtigkeit selbst zu Symbolen ihrer eigenen Abdankung werden. „Ohne Vergangenheit kann man keine Zukunft bauen. Die Zukunft wird gemacht, indem man die Vergangenheit aufgibt oder opfert [...]. Feierlich ziehe ich meinen Hut und lasse das Blut meiner Opfer fließen, während ich Baudelaires Hymne an die Schönheit anstimme".[13]

Welche Schönheit meint er hier? Spricht er von jener ephemeren Qualität, die jenes Zeitalter widerspiegelt, für das sie typisch ist? Dann gäbe es eine Parallele zu Adornos autonomem Kunstwerk. Oder meint er die andere Schönheit Baudelaires, die – ewig und unveränderlich – in ihrer Starrheit abgelehnt werden muss? Adorno zufolge hat genau die Widerständigkeit der Kunst ein gewisses „Katastrophenpotenzial", sie spricht „das Unaussprechliche aus, die Utopie".[14] Ein ähnliches Paradox ist sowohl der Kern von Jorns „Modifications" als auch von Debords Denken. Denn es ist wichtig, darauf hinzuweisen, dass die utopischen Ziele aus der Kunsttheorie der Situationisten niemals verschwunden sind. Mit der Zeit behaupteten sie immer eiserner, dass es kritisches Handeln nur abseits des Kunstgegenstands gäbe – auf den Straßen, in der Stadt oder, wie Debord es ausdrückte, im „Untergrund" unter dem Reich des Spektakels.[15] Man kann in Jorns Beharren auf einer manifesten Zeitlichkeit, das heißt auf der vergänglichen Natur der Dinge, einen revolutionären Impuls erkennen.[16] Das Zelebrieren der eigenen Unfähigkeit schätzt Jorn an der Kitschmalerei, die niemals behauptet, an und in sich schlüssig zu sein, und deren Wert weniger im Dargestellten als im Gefühl des Volks bezüglich des Dargestellten liegt. Gesten von Künstlern kommen und gehen, aber der Schaffens- und Formwille bleibt, wie Jorn sagt, „ein Bindeglied zwischen den Einzelnen".[17]

Indem sie ihre eigene begrenzte Materialität nicht verbergen und auch nicht die Geschichtlichkeit der Gesten, die sie ausmachen, sagen Jorns Bilder, dass nichts ein für alle Mal feststeht und es deshalb immer eine Zukunft gibt, selbst wenn künstlerische Opposition unter gegenwärtigen Umständen unsicher oder unmöglich ist. Oder, wie er es selbst etwas weniger optimistisch ausdrückt: „Man kann keine Zukunft ohne Vergangenheit schaffen."[18]

1 Asger Jorn, „Peinture détournée", in: *Vingt peintures modifiées par Asger Jorn*, Paris, Galerie Rive Gauche, 1959.

2 Dieses Werk gehört nicht zur ursprünglichen Serie der „Modifications" aus dem Jahr 1959, sondern zu einer Werkgruppe namens „New Disfigurations" („Défigurations"), die Jorn nach den „Modifications" kurz nach seinem Austritt aus der SI 1961 ausgeführt hat. Es gibt drei Arten abgewandelter Gemälde, die Jorn zwischen 1959 und 1962 geschaffen hat: die „Modifications", „New Disfigurations" („Défigurations") und die „Anekdotenbilder aus dem Alltag". Guy Atkins hat thematische Unterschiede zwischen diesen Werkgruppen festgestellt: Die „New Disfigurations" („Défigurations") hätten eine „ernsthaftere Intention" und „tendieren bisweilen zu recht dunklen psychologischen Ansichten". Diese Beobachtung könnte etwas Wahres an sich haben, stimmt aber sicher nicht allgemein, wenn man bedenkt, dass *L'avant-garde se rend pas* verbürgt zur zweiten Gruppe gehört. Guy Atkins, *Asger Jorn: The Crucial Years 1954–1964*, New York 1977, S. 65–68 ff.

3 Hier muss angemerkt werden, dass Jorn als einer von wenigen freiwillig und in Freundschaft aus der SI austrat. Er und Debord blieben zeitlebens Freunde, obwohl sich ihre Ansichten, was Kunst betrifft, deutlich unterschieden. Jorn kehrte zu einem eher gestischen Malstil zurück, und Debord misstraute mehr und mehr künstlerischer Intervention jeder Art.

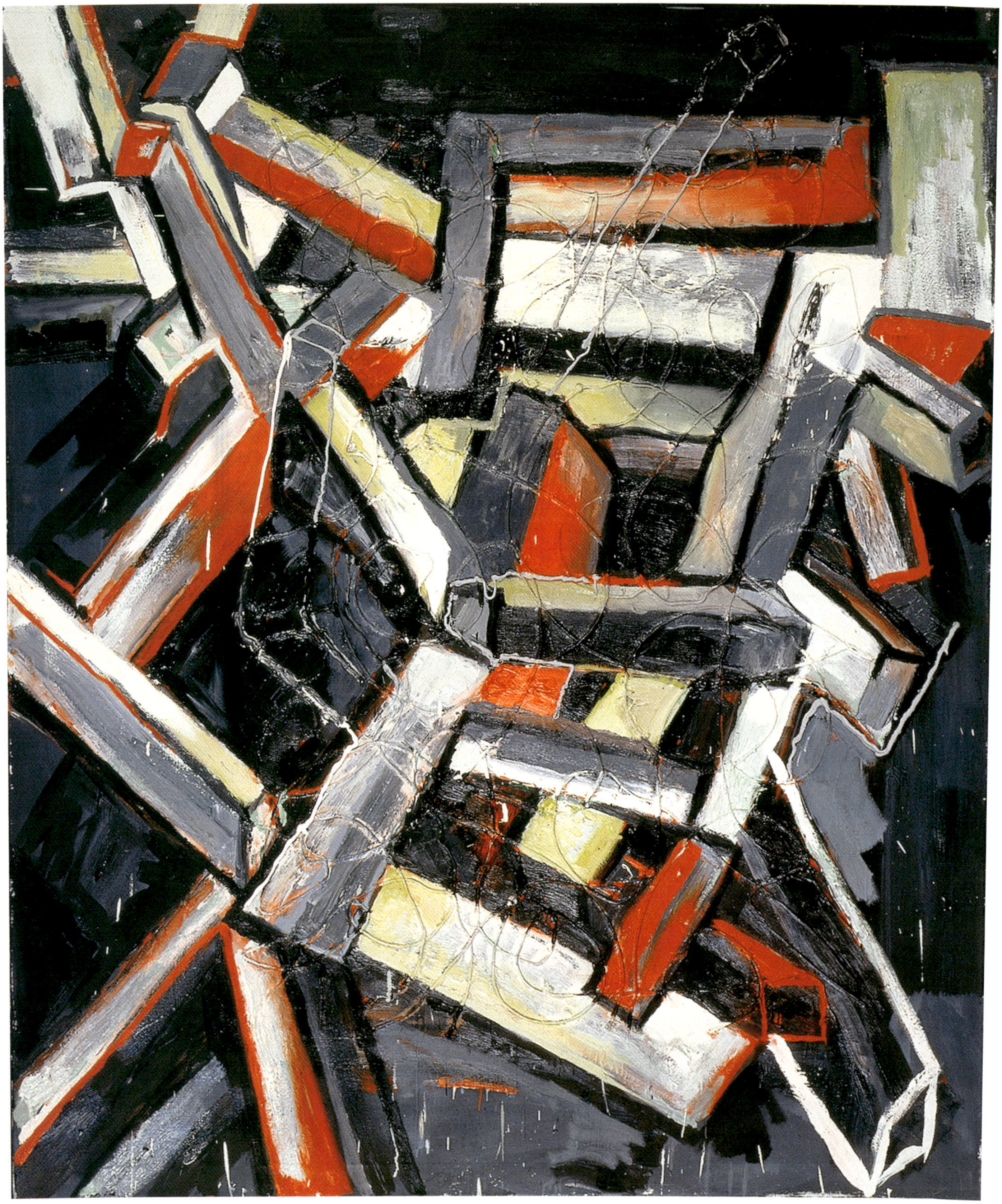

081 **Martin Kippenberger**
Ich kann beim besten Willen kein Hakenkreuz erkennen, 1984
(With the Best Will in the World, I Can't see a Swastika)

Öl und Silikon auf Leinwand / oil, silicon on canvas
160 x 133 cm
Friedrich Christian Flick Collection

Keine schlechten Maler

Ethik und Ästhetik bei Polke und Kippenberger

Julia Gelshorn

Nach dem Tod Martin Kippenbergers am 7. März 1997 in Wien schrieb der Kunstkritiker Harald Fricke in seinem Nachruf in der *tageszeitung* unter dem Titel „Pinkeln gegen den Kunstbetrieb“: „Allzu viele Freunde hat er sich mit seiner Art nicht gemacht. Und da die Feinde seiner Freunde ihm auch Feinde waren, blieb in den letzten Jahren nur ein sehr kleiner Künstlerkreis um Martin Kippenberger zurück. Nun ist der böse ‚Hetzler‘-Boy [...] tot: Kippenberger erlag am Freitag einem Leberversagen.“ Frickes Artikel endete mit den Worten: „Er war kein guter Mensch, er war kein schlechter Maler – irgendwo dazwischen.“[1] Dieser letzte Satz ist nicht nur verwunderlich, weil er auf äußerst unschöne Weise einen Nachruf beschließt, sondern vor allem, weil er eine ästhetische mit einer ethischen Verurteilung vermengt und wie in einer Kategorienverwechslung ein „Irgendwo-Dazwischen“ annimmt. Es ist daher zu fragen, inwiefern Kippenbergers künstlerische Arbeit selbst diese Vermengung von Ethik und Ästhetik provoziert hat und wie die ambivalente Bewertung, er sei „kein schlechter Maler“ gewesen, in Bezug auf seinen eigenen Anspruch an die Malerei zu lesen ist.

Kippenbergers Gemälde *Ich kann beim besten Willen kein Hakenkreuz erkennen* [ABB·081] von 1984 mag am deutlichsten vor Augen führen, wie er die Überlagerung von ästhetischen und ethisch-politischen Aspekten in seiner Kunst zwar unmittelbar einführt, dann aber in Schwebe hält, da das Verhältnis beider Ebenen zueinander ungeklärt bleibt. Zunächst lässt das Gemälde nichts Ungewöhnliches erkennen – im Gegenteil: Kippenberger greift auf ‚Bekanntes‘ zurück, indem er mit einem räumlichen Gebilde aus rot-grau-weiß-gelb-schwarzen Stäben und Winkeln auf kubistische Malerei zu verweisen scheint, ohne den Stil jedoch perfekt nachzuahmen, zumal die Darstellung über ein freies Linienspiel aus Silikonwülsten gelegt ist, das zum Kubismus in keinerlei Bezug steht.

Dass in den Stäben und Kuben keine Gegenstände auszumachen sind, greift Kippenberger denn auch mit dem Bildtitel auf, der mit der Redewendung: „Ich kann beim besten Willen kein ... erkennen“, die klischeehafte populäre Reaktion auf kubistische Malerei karikiert. Obwohl der Titel mit „Ich“ beginnt, ist der umgangssprachliche Ausspruch als Zitat eines fiktiven Rezipienten vor dem Bild zu verstehen und somit nicht als Stimme des Autors zu lesen. Zugleich aber regt der Titel beim Betrachter überhaupt erst einen visuellen Suchvorgang an: Das der Betitelung nach nicht erkennbare

title refers is indeed nowhere to be seen, although the various angles and forms in the painting could certainly be arranged to this effect.[2]

The comment in the title is thus initially confirmed by the visual representation. The use of the emotive term "swastika," however, turns a harmless question about the legibility of an "abstract" painting into a political provocation. Hence a minor verbal addition to the painting dramatically changes its meaning. Whereas, at first sight, the visual representation appears to deal with purely formal problems, the picture title and the word swastika introduce a voice that allows for a new interpretation precisely because of the discrepancy between the voice and the picture. A statement by Albert Oehlen, one of Kippenberger's fellow artists, clearly reveals that this manner of confronting painting styles with tabooed content was a standard procedure for both of them when they sought to replace "good painting" with "good provocations": "The stage we were trying to reach at the time was to torment painting with motifs freighted with the most powerful associations in order to turn people's minds away from all that claptrap about technique."[3]

Art critics, however, accused Kippenberger of both refusing to adopt a serious position with his provocative allusions and of remaining inappropriately vague.[4] Others interpreted his painting as a serious debate on the repression of recent German history in respect of which people did not, "[w]ith the best will in the world," want to see any more swastikas, and as an allusion to the "fascist ideas at the back of some people's minds in Germany."[5] According to Roland Schappert, Kippenberger's painting failed to do justice to its intended socio-political reference because the formal elements retained their painterly autonomy without serving a specific semantic content.[6] This is deliberate: the title chosen by Kippenberger can be read as a conceptual element in the painting in the sense of an "iconotext." Alternately, it can be described as a "skillfully executed trick," a vital stimulus, which ultimately ends up in a carefully staged overtaxing of semantics.[7] No matter how little the form of presentation might lend itself to precise interpretation, the title makes it impossible to view the picture as "pure painting." Indeed, the verbal commentary clearly intervenes in the reception of the work and opens a discussion on German mechanisms of repression whilst refraining from engaging in any further attempts to manipulate that reception and, at the same time, maintaining a cynical distance to forms of painterly representation.

Painting what the viewer sees

Kippenberger's *Ich kann beim besten Willen kein Hakenkreuz erkennen* must also be seen as a dual reference to the work of the painter Sigmar Polke. Polke was twelve years older than Kippenberger and taught at the Hamburg Hochschule für bildende Künste (Hamburg Academy of Fine Arts) at the time Kippenberger was studying there. He did not, however, actually teach Kippenberger himself. As early as 1963, Polke had presented a "bad" imitation of a painting style in his work *Konstruktivistisch* (Constructivist) [ILL·082] by manipulating the modernist Mondrian-style

hatte sich Polke den ‚Konstruktivismus' bereits in ‚vermittelter Form' über Roy Lichtensteins Popvarianten von Mondrian-Gemälden angeeignet, indem er dessen Benday Dots wiederholte und somit sein eigenes Gemälde als Appropriation markierte.

Den rationalen konstruktivistischen Formen wurde durch die Manipulation des Signifikanten eine Ideologie ‚untergeschoben', die ihrer ursprünglichen Konzeption und der zeitgenössischen politischen Rezeption deutlich widersprach. Polke demonstrierte hier eine vehemente Aversion gegenüber jegliche Ideologie, die sich für ihn auch in Stilbegriffen wie dem ‚Konstruktivismus' verbarg. Indem er seine Anklage in einen malerischen Stil ironisch ‚verkleidete', fand er nicht nur eine formalistische Verschleierung für eine provokative politische Aussage, sondern er persiflierte auch geradezu bösartig das stilistische Modell, das er zitierte. Eine derart starke Anklage, deren Vermengung zweier wohl kaum vergleichbarer Phänomene schon fast verfehlt scheint, lässt sich jedoch vor dem Hintergrund der ideologisch gefärbten euphorischen Förderung der abstrakten Malerei in der Nachkriegszeit und dem zunehmenden Skeptizismus und Zynismus der Neoavantgarden gegenüber den Utopien der Moderne erklären.[9]

Kippenberger übernahm zwar Polkes Verfahren einer stilistischen Persiflage, wandte sich jedoch weniger gegen eine modernistische Ideologie, als dass er durch die Redeweise seines Titels die Aufmerksamkeit auf den Habitus des durchschnittlichen Betrachters vor dem Bild lenkte. Auch hierfür hatte Polke 1968 das Vorbild geliefert, indem er in Gemälden wie *Moderne Kunst* [ABB·083] oder *Akt mit Geige* [ABB·017] in absichtlich dilettantischer Malweise vorführte, was das allgemeine Publikum mit derartigen Bildtiteln verband.[10] So vereinte Polke im Gemälde *Moderne Kunst* auf parodistische Weise verschiedene malerische Paradigmen wie den Klecks, den Pinselstrich, die Farbfläche, die geometrische Form und die freie Linie, obwohl diese in der Entwicklung der modernen Kunst ganz unterschiedliche Stile und teilweise gegensätzliche Konzepte verkörperten. Mit der gemalten weißen Rahmung, die das Gemälde wie ein vergrößertes Polaroidfoto erscheinen lässt, kennzeichnete Polke sein Gemälde als scheinbare Wiederholung eines Bildes, wobei der in den Rahmen eingeschriebene Bildtitel als „fremde Rede" fungierte, die die Darstellung als Persiflage, also als stilistische Herabsetzung dessen kennzeichnete, was der Betrachter als ‚moderne Kunst' sah.[11] Die ideologische Codierung der

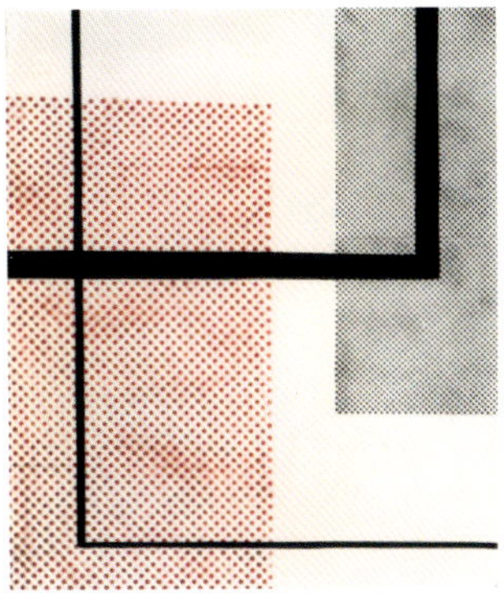

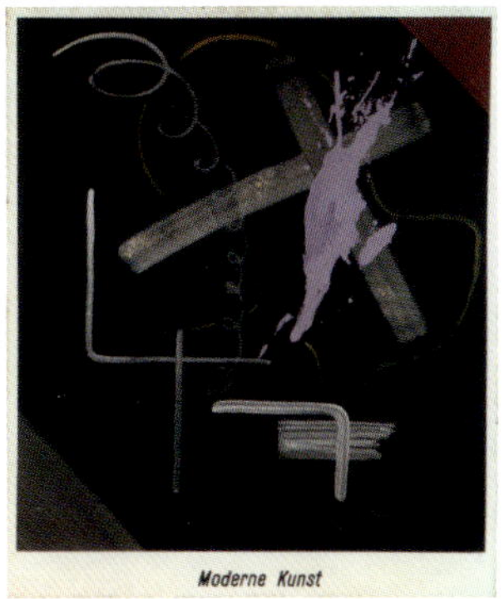

082 Sigmar Polke
Konstruktivistisch, 1968
(Constructivist)
Dispersion auf Leinwand / emulsion on canvas
150 x 125 cm

083 Sigmar Polke
Moderne Kunst, 1968
(Modern Art)
Dispersion auf Leinwand / emulsion on canvas
150 x 125 cm

signifiers, whose signifieds mutually exclude one another by virtue of the historical succession in which the relevant styles appeared, and, on the other hand, in the rhetorical reduction of styles to "brush strokes," "daubs" and "blobs"—as seen through the eyes of the "man on the street."

In *Ich kann beim besten Willen kein Hakenkreuz erkennen*, Kippenberger also imitates the common response of viewers standing before an "abstract" picture. Because his painting reveals what the viewer sees in abstract art—namely, no swastika—he exposes a tactic of repression that takes place within both abstract art and the viewer. Whereas Polke's ironic visual jokes analytically and didactically express a neo-avant-garde skepticism towards the utopias of the modern movement and thereby represent another attempt to legitimate painting, Kippenberger's rhetoric of taboo-breaking serves as a cynical rejection of a form of painting that is divorced from socio-political questions.[12] In so doing, he does not so much build on the medium of painting, as turn the medium against itself.

The desecration of painting

Technically speaking, both Polke and Kippenberger practice a kind of strategic dilettantism that manifests itself in, among other things, an "awkward" mode, which Roland Barthes described, in relation to Cy Twombly, as a contrast to an implicitly "correct" or "right" pictorial manner.[13] On the one hand, Polke's "awkwardness"—as manifested in *Moderne Kunst* or in his *Streifenbilder* (Stripe Paintings) [ILL·084]—serves as a critique of the modernist fetishizing of painterly gestures. On the other hand, however, the intentional "defectiveness" which Polke employs in his early gridworks such as *Ohne Titel (Vase)* (Untitled (Vase)) [ILL·085] can be interpreted as expressing an explicit counter-position of a painter to the pictures and art forms of the so-called "new media."[14] However, Polke's "awkwardness" may also be compared to the early artistic strategies of deskilling of the twentieth-century avant-gardes, as exemplified in their attempts to banish craft skill from art by turning to so-called "primitive art" and to children's drawings.[15] However, whereas modern art sought the exotic and the "Other" precisely because of the "higher truth" they contained, Polke chose to banalize the exotic. *Negerplastik* (or Statue of Negro, as one of Polke's paintings is called) is trivialized as a petty-bourgeois decorative furnishing in exactly the same way as the palm, the vase, the kidney-shaped table,

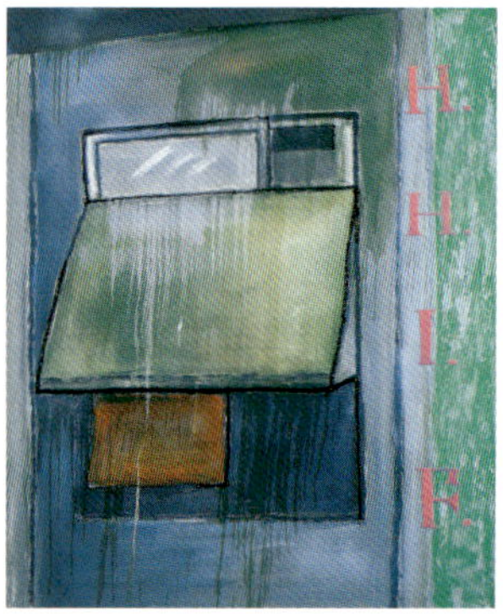

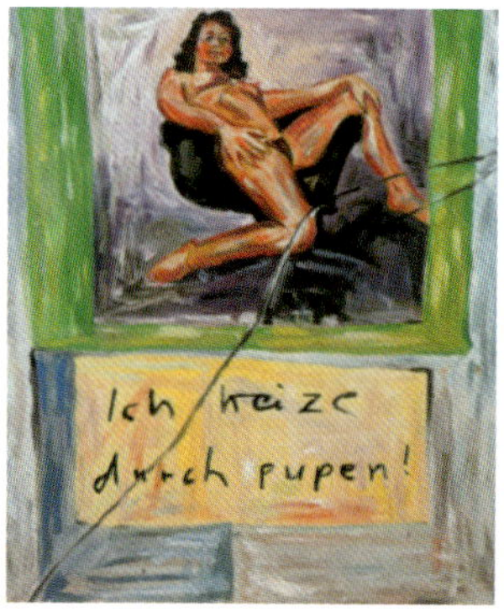

088 Martin Kippenberger
Heil Hitler Ihr Fetischisten, 1984
(Heil Hitler You Fetishists)
Öl, Silikon auf Leinwand /
oil, silicon on canvas
160 x 133 cm

089 Martin Kippenberger
Ich heize durch pupen, 1983
(I Heat by Farting)
Öl auf Leinwand /
oil on canvas
120 x 100 cm

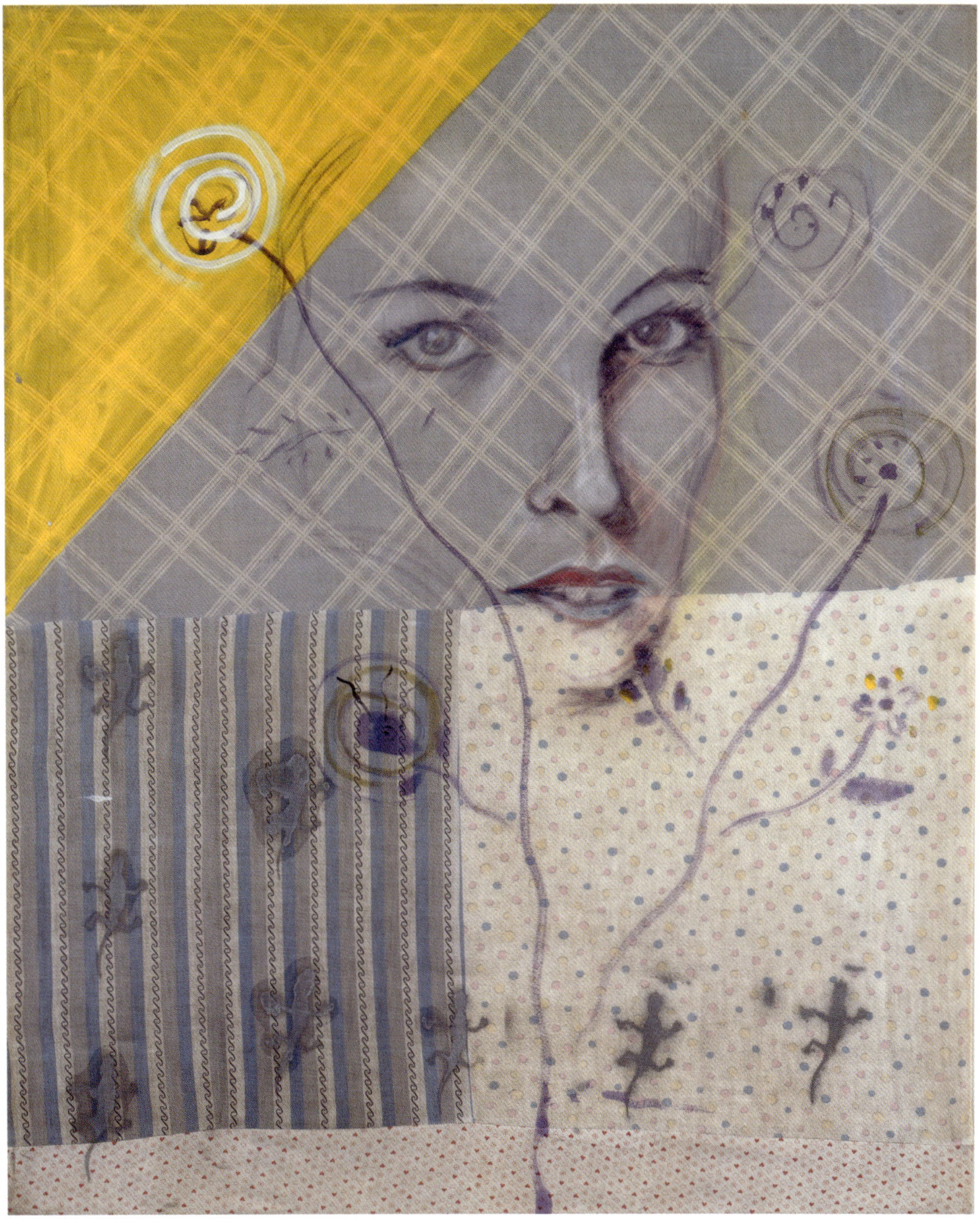

090 Sigmar Polke
Ohne Titel (Porträt)
1966
(Untitled (Portrait))
Pastellkreide, Öl, Dekorstoffe / pastells, oil, furnishing fabrics
115 x 91 cm
Stiftung Museum Kunstpalast, Düsseldorf

verborgenen ‚höheren Wahrheit' suchte, wird genau dies bei Polke in der Banalisierung des Exotischen aufgehoben. Die *Negerplastik*, so ein Werktitel Polkes, wird in seiner Malerei ebenso als kleinbürgerliche Dekorationsausstattung trivialisiert wie die Palme, die Vase, der Nierentisch, die Flamingos oder jene bedruckten Dekorationsstoffe, welche Polke zu Bildträgern umfunktioniert [ABB·090].[16] Während die Avantgarden die handwerklichen Fachkenntnisse gerade als korrumpiert betrachteten, weil sie bei der Produktion von ‚Durchschnittskitsch' zur Anwendung kamen, greift Polke gerade diesen Kitsch auf, grenzt ihn jedoch durch die linkische Malweise von der reinen Dekoration wieder ab. Im Gegensatz zu den Konsumfetischen, mit der die Pop-Art die Hochkunst durchsetzt, quält Polke die Malerei demnach durch das Bildrepertoire und die Wohlstandsikonen des deutschen Kleinbürgertums und

the flamingos and the printed decorative material that Polke converted into supports for his paintings [ILL·090].[16] Whereas the avant-gardes viewed craft skill as corrupt because it was used to produce "mediocre kitsch," Polke takes up this very kitsch, but distinguishes it from pure decoration with the aid of his "awkward mode" of painting. Thus, in contrast to the consumer fetishes with which pop art permeates high art, Polke torments painting with the repertoire of images and icons of the affluence of the German middle class and introduces "bad taste" into painting—just as Gerhard Richter had done in his early paintings *Hirsch* (Deer) [ILL·010] and *Neuschwanstein Castle* [ILL·087].[17]

This was the point of departure for Kippenberger's "desecration" of painting: awkward lines and brush strokes, as well as naive imagery, are the most harmless variants used in intentionally "bad painting," especially when one considers that he repeatedly commissioned professional poster artists or their assistants to do his paintings, thus fully stripping the artist's signature of any weight. Not only did Kippenberger view "Bad Painting" as "resistance to refinement through technical mastery," as Bazon Brock once put it, he also felt that it demonstrated his radical aesthetic indifference both to technique and the motifs he chose.[18]

Polke's petty-bourgeois and banal motifs are thereby raised to the status of breaches of taboo, whether of an ethical, blasphemous, sexist or political nature as in *Heil Hitler Ihr Fetischisten* (Heil Hitler You Fetishists) [ILL·088], which directly addresses the viewer, or in adolescent jokes such as *Ich heize durch pupen* (I heat by Farting) [ILL·089]. Infantilism, incorrect spelling and "political incorrectness" (rather like the punk anarchism) undermine all forms of bourgeois aesthetics and morality and are thus aimed (even if they are not limited to painting in Kippenberger's case) directly at contemporary neo-bourgeois painting hype of the kind celebrated by, for instance, Wolfgang Max Faust as an "appetite for paintings," and elsewhere as a "new spirit in painting or as a "new figuration."[19]

In his essay "Figures of Authority, Ciphers of Regression" (1981), Benjamin Buchloh characterized the return of expressive painting—especially among German painters such as Markus Lüpertz, Anselm Kiefer and George Baselitz—as a form of regression. He went on to criticize the fact that both the supposedly new painting of the 1980s and the "new" realism of the late 1910s and 1920s satisfied a wide range of reactionary and elitist desires for prestige and esteem. Buchloh saw the cliché-ridden pathos-filled formulae and vitalisms used to describe these forms of painting as evidence of the way that art was used to serve the nationalist, authoritarian and neo-liberal ideologies of the elites.[20] Kippenberger's radical subversion of pompous gestures, in which he committed himself to moments of indignity and embarrassment, must be seen as a vehement reaction to the new elitism of this painting hysteria, since he tries in various ways to extend the impact of his art to all spheres of life.

I ♥ Polke + Baselitz: Fooling around and anarchy

Although the "principle of involving" diverse media and levels with equally diverse modes of self-promotion was characteristic of the way Kippenberger broke the rules of an elitist art

führt – ganz ähnlich wie Gerhard Richter in seinen frühen Gemälden *Hirsch* [ABB·010] oder *Schloss Neuschwanstein* [ABB·087] – den ‚schlechten Geschmack' in die Kunst ein.[17]

Genau an diesem Punkt setzen Kippenbergers ‚Schändungen' der Malerei erst an: Linkische Linien- oder Pinselführung oder kindliche Bildsprache sind dabei die harmlosesten Varianten eines absichtsvoll ‚schlechten Malens', zumal die Bilder auch wiederholt bei einem professionellen Plakatmaler oder bei Assistenten in Auftrag gegeben werden und somit die künstlerische Handschrift gänzlich verneinen. Bad Painting versteht sich bei Kippenberger jedoch nicht nur als „Widerstand gegen die Veredelung durch technische Meisterschaft", wie dies Bazon Brock genannt hat, sondern demonstriert technisch und motivisch eine radikale ästhetische Indifferenz.[18]

Polkes kleinbürgerliche und banale Motive werden dabei zu Tabubrüchen ethischer, blasphemischer, sexistischer oder politischer Art gesteigert wie etwa in *Heil Hitler Ihr Fetischisten* [ABB·088], das den Betrachter direkt anspricht, oder in pubertären Witzen wie *Ich heize durch pupen* [ABB·089]. Infantilismus, falsche Orthografie und das ‚politisch Unkorrekte' untergraben – in Analogie zum Anarchismus des Punk – jede bürgerliche Ästhetik und Moral und richten sich damit, auch wenn sie sich bei Kippenberger nicht auf die Malerei beschränken, ganz direkt gegen den zeitgenössischen neobürgerlichen Malereihype, der etwa von Wolfgang Max Faust als „Hunger nach Bildern" und andernorts als „New Spirit in Painting" oder als „Neue Figuration" gefeiert wurde.[19]

Benjamin Buchloh hat 1981 in seinem Aufsatz „Figures of Authority, Ciphers of Regression" diese Wiederkehr der expressiven Malerei – vor allem bei deutschen Malern wie Markus Lüpertz, Anselm Kiefer oder Georg Baselitz – als Regression bezeichnet und kritisiert, dass sowohl die vermeintlich neue Malerei 1980er-Jahre wie auch der ‚neue' Realismus der späten 1910er- und 1920er-Jahre beliebige reaktionäre und elitäre Repräsentationsbedürfnisse befriedigten. Die klischeehaften Pathosformeln und Vitalismen, mit denen die Malerei jeweils beschrieben wurde, sah Buchloh als Beleg für die Verfügbarmachung der Kunst für nationalistische, autoritäre und neoliberalistische Ideologien der Eliten.[20] Kippenbergers radikale Subversion des Pathetischen durch ein Bekenntnis zu Momenten der Würdelosigkeit und Peinlichkeit muss als vehemente Reaktion gegen den neuen Elitismus dieser Malereihysterie verstanden werden, versuchte er doch auf unterschiedlichste Weise, die Wirkung seiner Kunst auf alle Lebensbereiche auszuweiten.

I ♥ Polke + Baselitz: Blödelei und Anarchie

Obwohl gerade das „Prinzip der Verstrickung" unterschiedlicher Medien und Ebenen mit ebenso vielfältigen Modi der Selbstdarstellung für Kippenbergers Durchbrechung der Regeln einer elitären Kunstwelt bezeichnend war, lässt sich auch innerhalb einzelner Werke und vor allem an seinem Umgang mit der Malerei verfolgen, wie der Bezugsrahmen der Kunst systematisch durch – meist sprachlich eingeführte – Tabubrüche erweitert wurde.[21] Dass Kippenbergers Malerei dabei als direkte Gegenposition zum zeitgenössischen Neoexpressionismus verstanden werden muss, zeigt sich bereits

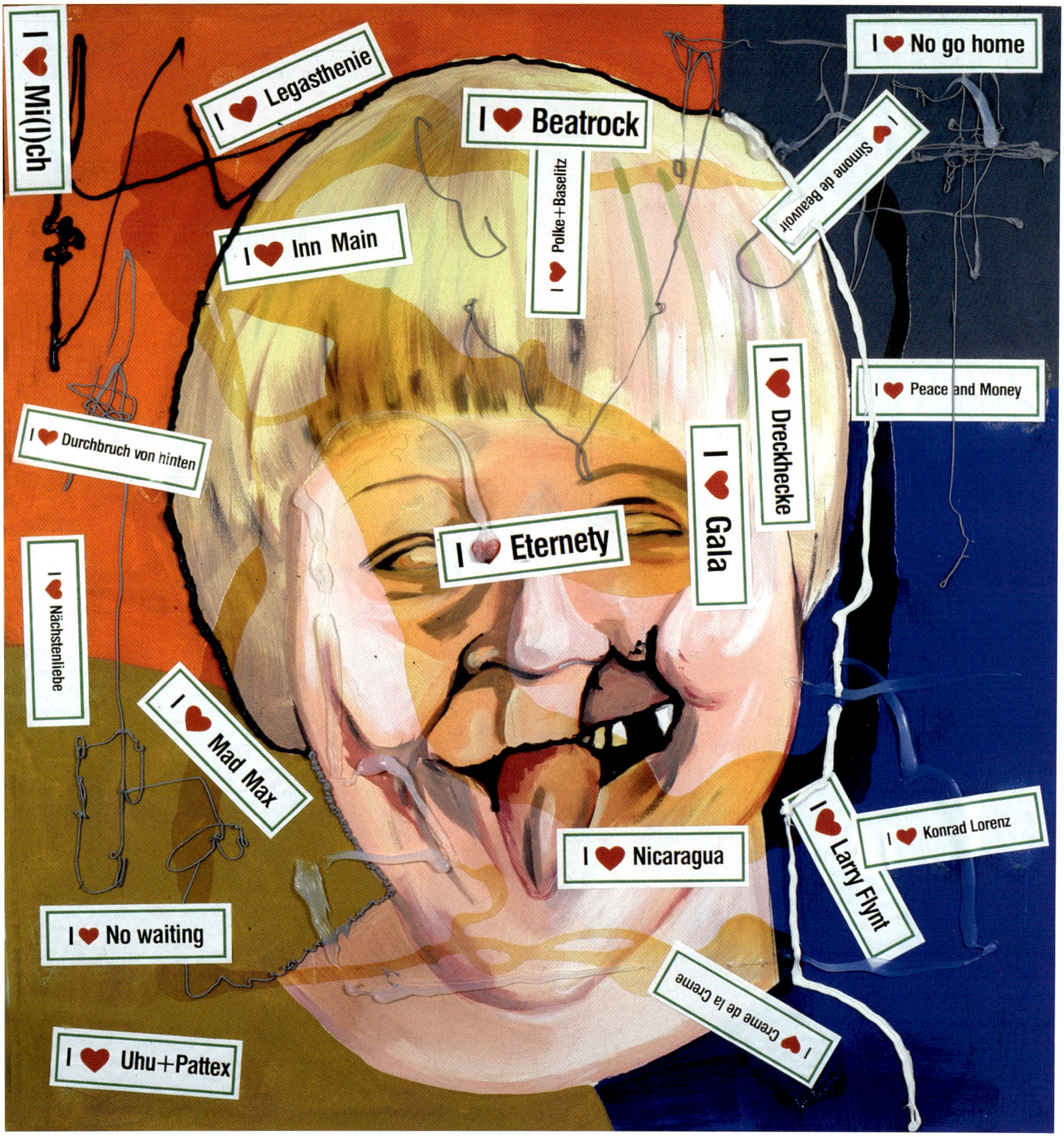

world, one can see in individual works and, above all, in his approach to painting, how he systematically extended the referential framework of art by breaking taboos—generally at a verbal level.[21] The fact that Kippenberger's painting must be understood here as the direct antithesis of contemporary Neo-Expressionism is evident in his painting *Ich kann beim besten Willen kein Hakenkreuz erkennen*, which can also be interpreted as a sideswipe at artists such as Markus Lüpertz and Georg Baselitz, who claimed to reduce militaristic motifs to their purely formal significance. Hence, Gregory Williams noted that Kippenberger's tendency to thrash the anecdotal to death, which gave many of his works a completely hermetic quality, could be understood as a response to Baselitz's dubious claim that he did not want to create "any descriptive, anecdotal pictures" but only deal with "painting problems."[22]

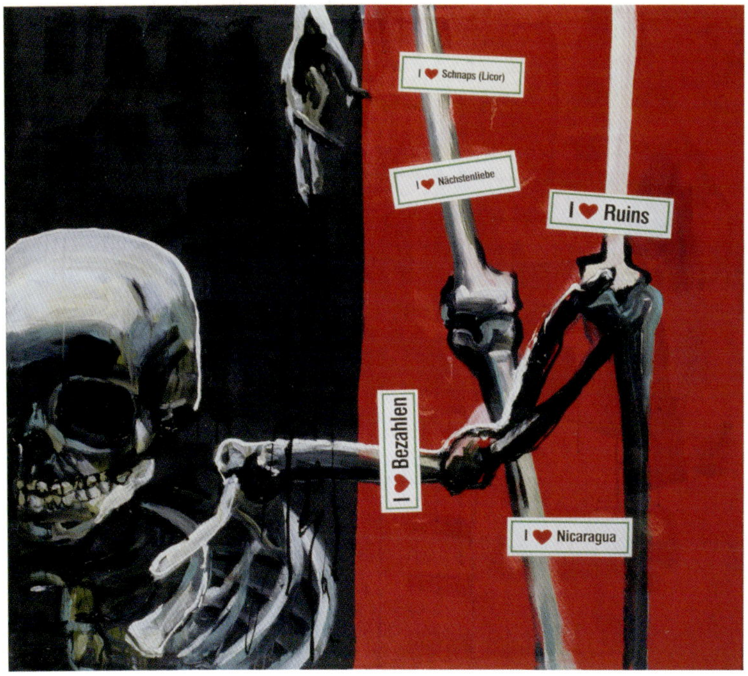

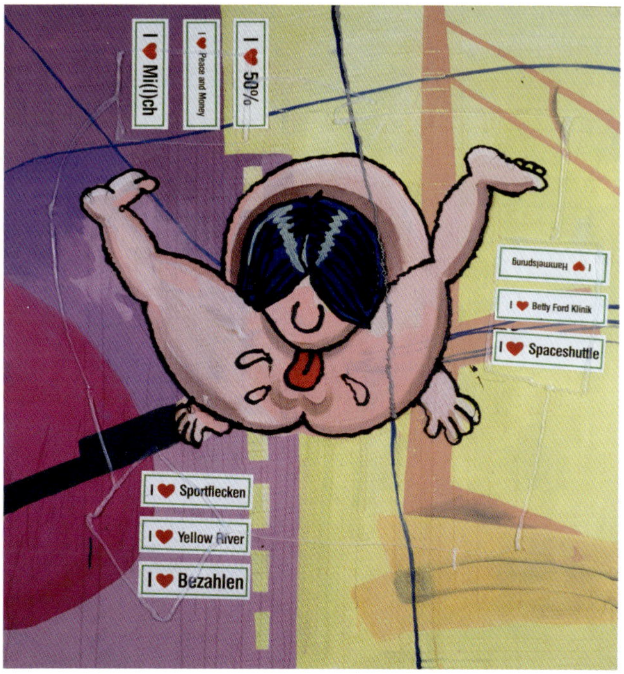

091 **Martin Kippenberger**
Kaputtes Kind, 1985 (Broken Child)
Dispersion, Acryl, Aufkleber auf Leinwand / emulsion, acrylic, sticker on canvas
130 x 120 cm

092 **Martin Kippenberger**
Hinterbliebener Hilfeschreiender in der Gaza Gegend, 1985
(Bereaved Screaming for Succour in Gaza)
Dispersion, Acryl, Aufkleber auf Leinwand / emulsion, acrylic, sticker on canvas
120 x 130 cm
Estate Martin Kippenberger, Galerie Gisela Capitain, Köln

093 **Martin Kippenberger**
Die Bourgeoisie kommt nicht weiter und der Fußball bewegt sich im Mittelfeld, 1985
(The Bourgeoisie aren't Getting Anywhere and the Football's in the Midfield)
Dispersion, Acryl, Aufkleber auf Leinwand / emulsion, acrylic, sticker on canvas
130 x 120 cm
Estate Martin Kippenberger, Galerie Gisela Capitain, Köln

an dem Gemälde *Ich kann beim besten Willen kein Hakenkreuz erkennen*, das auch als Seitenhieb gegen Künstler wie Markus Lüpertz oder Georg Baselitz verstanden werden kann, die vorgaben, ihre militaristischen Motive seien auf rein formale Bedeutungen reduziert. Gregory Williams hat entsprechend festgestellt, dass auch Kippenbergers exzessives Ausreizen des Anekdotischen, das viele seiner Werke völlig hermetisch erscheinen ließ, als Reaktion auf die zweifelhafte Behauptung von Baselitz gelesen werden kann, er wolle „keine anekdotischen, deskriptiven Bilder" schaffen, sondern sich nur mit „malerischen Problemen" auseinander setzen.[22]

‚Malerische Probleme' werden bei Kippenberger nicht nur formal zu ‚geschmacklichen Problemen', sie werden auch konsequent mit Sozialem, Ethischem oder Anekdotischem durchsetzt und dabei in ihrer Semantik zum Scheitern gebracht. Dass darin auch ein direkter Angriff auf die vermeintliche Expressivität zeitgenössischer Malerei angelegt war, zeigt sich in Werken wie *Kaputtes Kind* von 1985 [ABB·091]. In dilettantischer Malweise präsentiert Kippenberger hier ein Kindergesicht, das eine hässliche Grimasse schneidet und die Zunge herausstreckt. Die Darstellung ist in scheinbar willkürlicher Anordnung mit Aufklebern überdeckt, die alle mit dem Statement „I ♥ …" beginnen und deren Typografie allgemein bekannt ist. Statt der bekannten Aussagen wie „I ♥ my dog" oder „I ♥ New York" ist auf Kippenbergers Aufklebern jedoch zu lesen „I ♥ Legasthenie", „I ♥ Polke + Baselitz", „I ♥ Mi(l)ch" oder „I ♥ Uhu + Pattex". Nicht nur exponieren die Selbstbekenntnisse bereits ihre Unsinnigkeit, sondern in ihrer Kombination werden auch diejenigen unglaubwürdig, die zunächst

Kippenberger did not treat "painting problems" solely as "problems of taste" on a purely formal level, but also viewed them as being thoroughly permeated by social, ethical and anecdotal elements which continually foiled their semantic freight. That this approach also contained a direct attack on the alleged expressiveness of contemporary painting can be seen in works such as *Kaputtes Kind* (Broken Child) from 1985 [ILL·091]. Here, Kippenberberger amateurishly paints a child's face as it grimaces and pokes out its tongue. The portrait is covered with adhesive labels seemingly arranged haphazardly and beginning with the words: "I ♥..." in a font familiar to most people. Instead of well-known phrases like "I ♥ my dog" or "I ♥ New York," Kippenberger's adhesive labels display the words "I ♥ dyslexia," "I ♥ Polke + Baselitz," "I ♥ Mi(l)ch" and "I ♥ Uhu + Pattex." Not only do the confessions reveal their absurdity immediately, but the combination in which they appear also renders implausible even those phrases that seemed to make sense initially. Kippenberger thus sabotages a common system of communication by undermining its communication structure by amassing disconnected signifiers and various categories. The moment one grasps the absurd confessions on the adhesive labels as statements issued by the figure represented, one also understands the title *Kaputtes Kind* as a judgment on a "messed-up" expressiveness that is frustrated by its own contradictory and banal character as it seeks recourse to prefabricated demonstrations of identity.

In 1988, Roland Schappert chose a painting with these very same stickers as the starting point for asking whether Kippenberger produces random pictures or presents randomness in a particular way. For Schappert, the fact that the stickers are by no means integrated into the painting as found objects, but have, on the contrary, been professionally made for this purpose, suggests that randomness has been deliberately presented here and that the details therefore already contain a "maximum concentration" of the overall structure. Just as the stickers "I ♥ M(i)lch" demonstrates the randomness of random alternatives to "I ♥ Mich (Myself)" and "I ♥ Milch (Milk)," the overall picture presents seemingly spontaneous associations of motifs whose effect is, however, "calculated" to appear like that.[23]

Schnappert compares Kippenberger's method of reducing the content of an adhesive label (a trivial bearer of information) to the level of absurdity with the structure of an anti-joke, which subverts the natural demand for meaning and identifiable form and thus focuses the viewer's attention on his or her own expectations.[24] Considered from this standpoint, it is not the joke that provides the basis of Kippenberger's paintings, but his strategy of "fooling around," a communication game which literary scholar Dieter Wellershoff calls a "subculture of humor" that tolerates a voluntary "loss of form and of a certain standard" in order to render reality increasingly chaotic and thus escape all forms of control by internalized norms of reason or taste.[25]

Whereas Polke and Richter exposed painting symbols as codifications in the 1960s, and presented the style of modern painting as pure rhetoric, Kippenberger overcodes painting by overloading its semantics. It is with the aid of this "subculture of humor" and the "organization of failure"

noch sinnvoll erscheinen. Kippenberger bringt hier ein gängiges Kommunikationssystem zum Scheitern, indem er dessen Mitteilungsstruktur in der Anhäufung unzusammenhängender Signifikanten und unterschiedlicher Kategorien gerade unterläuft. Versteht man die absurden Bekenntnisse der Aufkleber als Aussagen der dargestellten Figur, so kann der Titel des Bildes *Kaputtes Kind* auch als Bewertung einer ‚kaputten' Expressivität verstanden werden, die im Rückgriff auf vorgefertigte Identitätsbezeugungen an deren Widersprüchlichkeit und Banalität scheitert.

Roland Schappert hat 1998 ein Gemälde mit ebensolchen Aufklebern als Ausgangspunkt für seine Frage gewählt, ob Kippenberger beliebige Bilder produziere oder in besonderer Weise Beliebigkeit darstelle. In der Tatsache, dass die Aufkleber keineswegs als Fundstücke in das Gemälde integriert sind, sondern vielmehr professionell für diesen Zweck angefertigt wurden, sieht Schappert einen Hinweis darauf, dass hier Beliebigkeit gezielt dargestellt werde und demnach auch im Detail bereits eine „maximale Verdichtung" der Gesamtstruktur vorliege: Wie etwa der Aufkleber „I ♥ Mi(l)ch" die Beliebigkeit als beliebige Alternativen von „I ♥ Mich" und „I ♥ Milch" vorführe, inszeniere auch das gesamte Bild scheinbar spontane Motivverbindungen, deren Wirkung jedoch als solche ‚kalkuliert' sei.[23]

Die Art und Weise, in der Kippenberger den Gehalt des trivialen Informationsträgers Aufkleber ad absurdum führt, vergleicht Schappert mit der Struktur eines Antiwitzes, der den selbstverständlichen Anspruch auf Sinnhaftigkeit und Geformtheit unterlaufe und damit den Blick der Rezipienten auf die eigenen Erwartungen lenke.[24] Statt des Witzes liege demnach Kippenbergers Bildern die Strategie des „Blödelns" zugrunde, ein vom Literaturwissenschaftler Dieter Wellershoff als „Subkultur des Humors" bezeichnetes Kommunikationsspiel, das einen freiwilligen „Form- und Niveauverlust" in Kauf nehme, um auf fortschreitende „Chaotisierung" der Realität zu drängen und sich dabei jeder Kontrolle durch verinnerlichte Normen der Vernunft oder des Geschmacks zu entziehen.[25]

Hatten Polke und Richter in den 1960er-Jahren das malerische Zeichen als ein codiertes bloßgelegt und die Stile der modernen Malerei als bloße Rhetorik vorgeführt, wird bei Kippenberger die Malerei gerade übercodiert, indem er ihre Semantik überfrachtet. Es sind diese „Subkultur des Humors" und die „Organisation des Scheiterns", durch die Kippenberger die ironischen Infragestellungen innerbildlicher Logiken, wie sie etwa schon in Polkes „Lösungen" [ABB·086] angelegt waren, in Anarchismus überführt.[26]

„Keiner hilft Keinem" – der Künstler als schlechter Mensch

Während Polke die modernistisch-heroische Künstlerrolle in den 1960er-Jahren durch ironische Parodien und clowneske Auftritte, dann in den 1970er-Jahren durch das kollektive Arbeiten in einer psychedelischen Hippiekommune konterkarierte, gründete Kippenberger in den 1980er-Jahren mit Albert Oehlen, Jörg Schlick und anderen Künstlern die Lord Jim Loge, einen Männerbund, der sich dem Motto „Keiner hilft Keinem" verschrieb und der seine visuelle Manifestation

that Kippenberger converts the ironic questioning of inner-pictorial logic, which already existed in Polke's "solutions" [ILL·086], into anarchism.[26]

"No-one helps anyone"—the artist as a bad person

In the 1960s, Polke countered the modernist-heroic role of the artist with ironic parodies and clown-like appearances, and later—in the 1970s—by engaging in collective work in a psychedelic hippy commune. In the 1980s, however, Kippenberger founded the Lord Jim Lodge, a men's association, together with Albert Oehlen, Jörg Schlick and other artists. Its motto was: "No-one helps anyone" and its visual manifestation the logo—as grotesque as it was sexist—"Sonne Busen Hammer" (Sun Breasts Hammer).[27] Hence, the veiled sexism and elitism that Buchloh identifies within the domain of cultural production in the 1920s and 1980s was exaggerated by Kippenberger in grand publicly displayed gestures. Even though a cynical declaration of belief in asocial behavior, for instance, found no correspondence in Kippenberger's lifestyle, as an artistic activity it did, nevertheless, seriously violate the "rules of art" and—last but not least, as Harald Fricke's obituary demonstrates—found little sympathy among art critics.

In 1989, Wolfgang Max Faust (who only a few years earlier had paid tribute in his own publication to the "contemporary German art" condemned by Buchloh) wrote a short article for the *Wolkenkratzer Art Journal* entitled "The Artist as Exemplary Alcoholic." Lamenting the "new cynicism" emerging within art, he claimed that some artists had gone through "abortive developments" induced by a trauma that barely took them "beyond the state of adolescent emotionality."[28] Above all, he noticed a "decline" of this nature in the case of Martin Kippenberger and Günter Förg, whom he accused of making a show of themselves by coming out with sexist and racist innuendo when they were drunk—"like German proles at their favorite pub." "For several years now, one has been able to see," according to Faust, "how members of a certain art scene, just like the court jesters during the Baroque period, support pet alcoholics who "let their hair down" for them on command and satisfy their inhibited desires."[29] Significantly, the article is based on Kippenberger's own description of the gaffes and discriminating insults that Günther Förg made under the influence of alcohol, and interprets the mild amusement with which Kippenberger speaks of Förg's "insult strategy" as a sign of "admiration." Although there are enough critical and derogatory remarks that one could quote from Kippenberger *opposing* racism and Nazi slogans, Faust wants to expose an "authoritarian character structure" with a tendency towards fascism, embodied in the person of Kippenberger, who has "a small-minded idea of the artist as an extreme outsider who, when things get out of control, has supposedly authentic experiences, which he then transforms into art."[30] This attack was triggered not only by Kippenberger's remarks, cited above, but also by his famous binges and his speeches and jokes, which would often get out of hand at parties or in the pub, and which he always documented with photos as quasi "artistic" activities in catalogs or on posters [ILL·101]. However, whereas these photo-

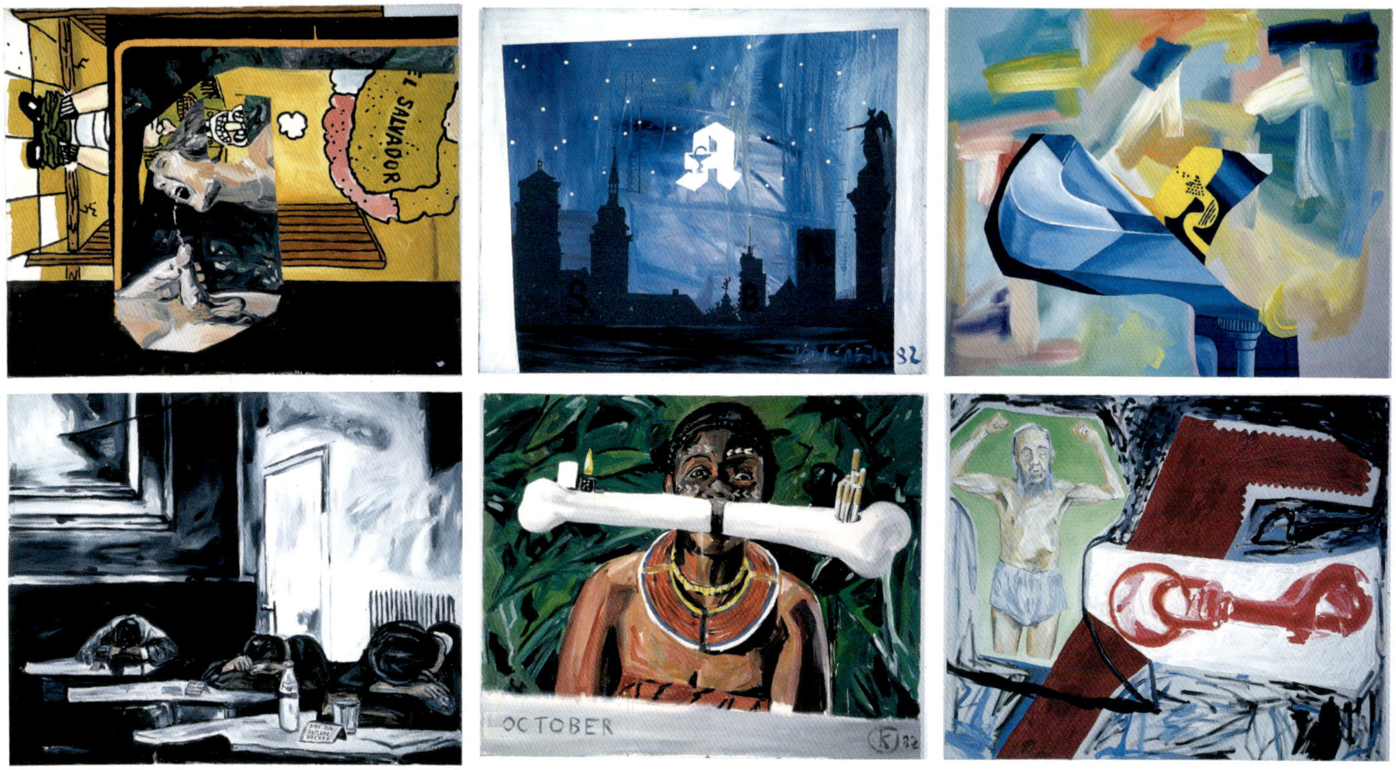

094–099 **Martin Kippenberger**
Ohne Titel, 1982 (Untitled)

6-teilige Serie / 6-parted series
Öl, Acryl auf Leinwand / oil, acrylic on canvas
je / each 100 x 120 cm
Sammlung Falckenberg

in dem ebenso grotesken wie sexistischen Logo „Sonne Busen Hammer“ fand.[27] Der verschleierte Sexismus und Elitismus, den Buchloh in der kulturellen Produktion sowohl der 1920er- wie auch der 1980er-Jahre beschrieben hat, wurde also von Kippenberger in großen Gesten öffentlich übersteigert. Doch auch wenn etwa das zynische Bekenntnis zum Asozialen nicht der Lebensweise Kippenbergers entsprach, verletzte es als künstlerische Aktion auf empfindliche Art die ‚Regeln der Kunst‘ und stieß – wie nicht zuletzt der Nachruf Harald Frickes belegt – auf wenig Verständnis bei der Kunstkritik.

1989 verfasste Wolfgang Max Faust, der wenige Jahre zuvor die von Buchloh verurteilte „deutsche Malerei der Gegenwart“ in einer eigenen Publikation gewürdigt hatte, für das *Wolkenkratzer Art Journal* einen kurzen Artikel unter dem Titel „Der Künstler als exemplarischer Alkoholiker“, in dem er einen „neuen Zynismus“ in der Kunstentwicklung beklagte und einigen Künstlern eine traumatisch bedingte „Fehlentwicklung“ nachsagte, die „über den Zustand pubertärer Emotionalität nur partiell hinausgelange“.[28] Einen solchen „Abstieg“ beobachtete er besonders bei Martin Kippenberger und Günther Förg, die er bezichtigte, sich im Suff – „ganz im Stil deutscher Stammtischproleten“ – mit sexistischen und rassistischen Anspielungen zu produzieren: „Schon seit Jahren lässt sich beobachten“, so Faust, „wie sich eine bestimmte Kunstszene – analog zu den Hofnarren im Barock – ihre Alkoholiker hält, die für sie fast auf Kommando ‚die Sau rauslassen‘ und ihre verklemmten Bedürfnisse befriedigen.“[29] Bezeichnenderweise geht der Artikel von Kippenbergers eigenen Schilderungen der alkoholisierten Entgleisungen und diskriminierenden Beleidigungen Günther Förgs aus und legt die abgeklärte

graphs could appear as an authentic testimony to the life of an artist who had gone off the rails, in works such as *Alkoholfolter* (Alcohol Torture) Kippenberger reflects upon his alcohol consumption with a sense of self-irony [ILL·100·102] With handcuffs made of the plastic seal of a three-pack of beer and putting on a nervous and frightened face, Kippenberger presented himself as the prisoner of his own alcohol addiction: the combination of "torture" and handcuffs characterized him as both victim and perpetrator. He repeatedly staged himself in this way (Faust also indirectly alludes to this) as a social outcast and outsider. On the exhibition poster *1/4 Jhdt. Kippenberger als einer von Euch, unter Euch, mit Euch* (1/4 Century. Kippenberger as One of You, among You, with You) [ILL·101] he even managed to equate the artist as a "bad person" with a saint by casting himself with a halo comprising words such as "squanderer," "show-off," "mega voyeur" and "leader," an allusion to an insult which he himself immediately called into question again with meaningless terms such as "feeder" and "Schonlangemaler" (Long-standing-painter).

Diedrich Diederichsen rightly asked whether, when a contemporary artist dies, people have ever first asked whether the artist was a good person or not. He noted that this type of polemic was specific to the reception accorded Kippenberger.[31] On the one hand, he traces this specific feature back to Kippenberger's enduring tendency to stir up hornets" nests by "simply touching on or naming certain correlations." On the other hand, he recognized the over-stressed connection between art and life as a source of criticism of the nature of the artist. To critics this reflected a lack of seriousness, since there had been neither any separation of "pub and art" nor an emphatic declaration that "art is life," as with Joseph Beuys.[32] The "uniquely close relationship" that Kippenberger maintained "between different levels such as "work," "social," "rumor," "interview statement," "catalog statement," etc. presented a threat whenever the person on the receiving end was no longer able to distinguish between these various levels, and cynicism turned into a form of boredom that proceeded from one dirty joke to the next. According to Diederichsen, one could find pleasure only in greater diversity and heterogeneity when one was stuck with "emulsion," and did not "compound" things.[33]

Kippenberger precluded the danger of "compounding" primarily by rendering the boundary between the production and reception of his work porous, and by not only including all

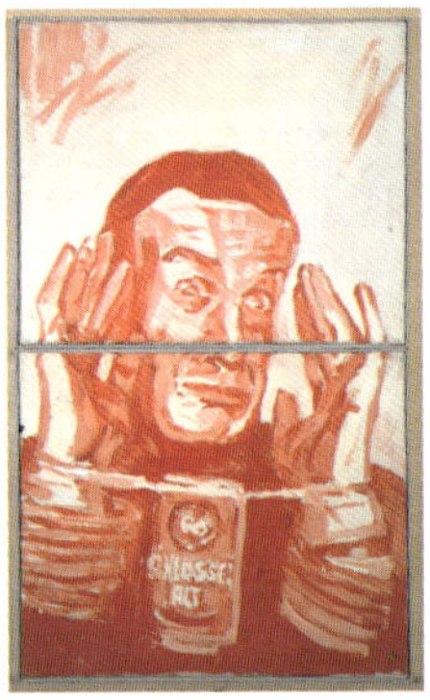

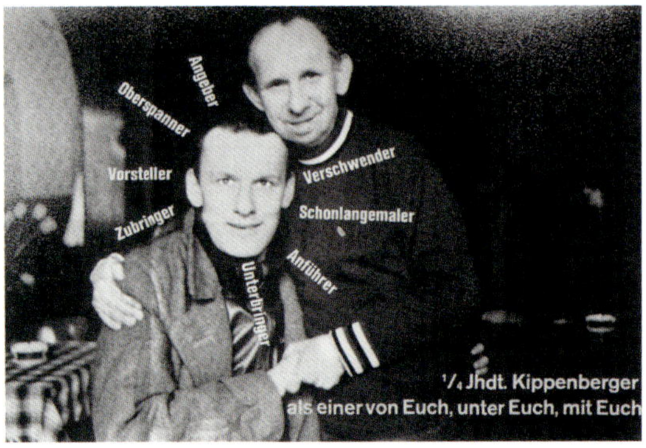

100 Martin Kippenberger
Alkoholfolter, 1981
(Alcohol Torture)
Öl auf Leinwand /
oil on canvas
100 x 60 cm

101 Martin Kippenberger
1/4 Jhdt. Kippenberger als
einer von Euch, unter Euch,
mit Euch, Berlin 1978
(1/4 Century Kippenberger
as One of You, Among
You, With You)
Offset, 59,5 x 84 cm

Belustigung, mit der Kippenberger von Förgs „Beleidigungsprogramm" berichtet, als „Bewunderung" aus. Obwohl es genügend kritische und abfällige Äußerungen Kippenbergers *gegen* Rassismus und Naziparolen zu zitieren gäbe, geht es Faust darum, eine „autoritäre Charakterstruktur" mit Hang zum Faschismus zu entlarven, die sich in der Figur Kippenbergers „mit der kleinkarierten Vorstellung vom Künstler als extremem Außenseiter, der im Exzess zu angeblich authentischen Erfahrungen vorstößt, die er in Kunst transformiert", materialisiere.[30]

Auslöser des Angriffs waren nicht nur Kippenbergers zitierte Äußerungen, sondern auch seine bekannten Alkoholexzesse sowie die ausufernden Reden und Witze auf Partys oder in der Kneipe, die er immer anhand von Fotos als quasi ‚künstlerische' Aktionen in Katalogen oder auf Plakaten dokumentierte [ABB·101]. Während jedoch diese Fotos noch wie das authentische Zeugnis eines entgleisten Künstlerlebens wirken konnten, wird der Alkoholkonsum in Werken wie *Alkoholfolter* von 1981 selbstironisch reflektiert [ABB·100·102]: Mit Handschellen aus der Plastikverschweißung eines Bierdosendreierpacks und gespielt ängstlich-erschrockenem Gesichtsausdruck präsentiert sich der Künstler als Gefangener seiner Alkoholsucht, wobei die Überlagerung von ‚Folter' und Handschellen ihn zugleich als Opfer und Täter kennzeichnet. Immer wieder thematisierte er sich auf diese Weise, worauf ja auch Faust indirekt anspielt, als Verstoßenen und Außenseiter der Gesellschaft. Auf dem Plakat der Ausstellung *1/4 Jhdt. Kippenberger als einer von Euch, unter Euch, mit Euch* [ABB·101] brachte er den Künstler als ‚schlechten Menschen' und Heiligen gar zur Deckungsgleichheit, indem er sich selbst mit einem Heiligenschein aus Begriffen wie „Verschwender", „Angeber", „Oberspanner" und „Anführer" zeigte und damit eine Beschimpfung suggerierte, die er jedoch gleich selbst durch unsinnige Bezeichnungen wie „Zubringer" und „Schonlangemaler" wieder infrage stellte.

Diedrich Diederichsen hat zu Recht die Frage gestellt, ob beim Tod anderer zeitgenössischer Künstler je zuallererst danach gefragt worden sei, ob der Künstler ein guter Menschen gewesen sei, und festgestellt, dass es sich bei dieser Art der Polemik um eine Besonderheit der Kippenberger-Rezeption handle.[31] Einerseits führte er diese Besonderheit auf Kippenbergers ständiges Öffnen von „Wespennestern" durch „bloßes Anschneiden oder Benennen von Zusammenhängen" zurück, andererseits erkannte er die exzessive Verbindung von Kunst und Leben als Quelle der Kritik am Wesen des

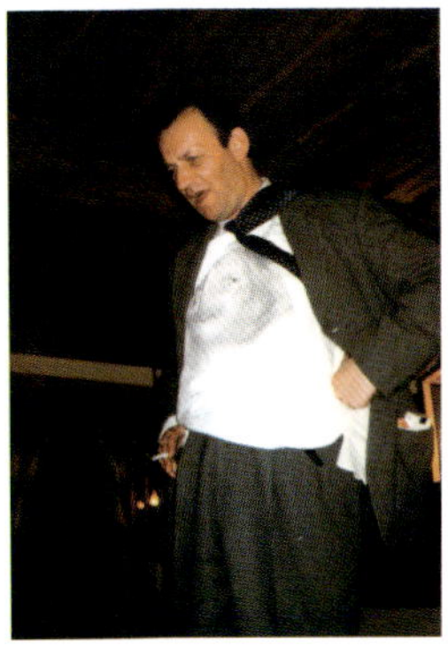

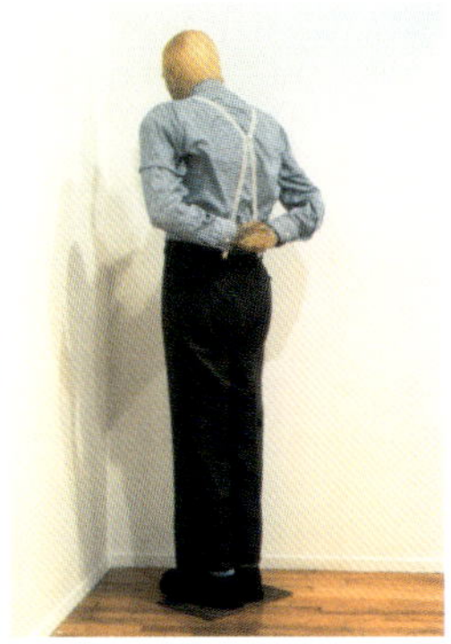

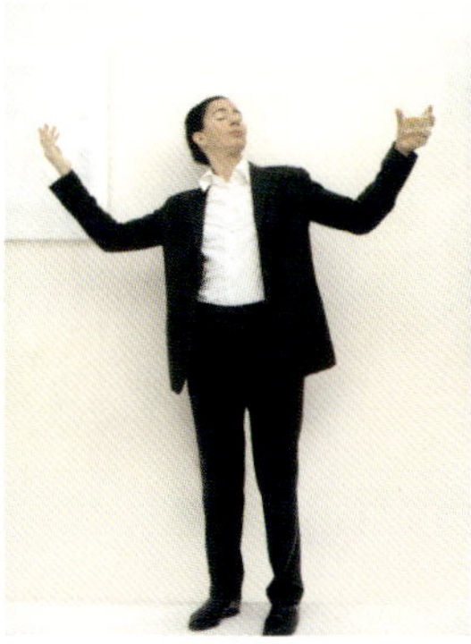

102 Jörg Schlick
Fotografie von Martin Kippenberger, (Photograph of Martin Kippenberger)

103 Martin Kippenberger
Martin, ab in die Ecke und schäm dich, 1989
(Martin, Into the Corner, You Should be Ashamed of Yourself)
Gießharz, Latex, Kleidung / casting resin, latex, clothes
175 x 66 x 40 cm

104 Andrea Fraser
Kunst muss hängen, 2001
(Art must Hang)
Performance, Galerie Christian Nagel, Köln

of the press's responses to his art in subsequent catalogs, but also by structuring his works themselves as a constant—and frequently incomprehensible—dialog. He would develop ideas for paintings and titles from private anecdotes, insider jokes and references to himself that were almost impossible to understand in retrospect. At the same time, his works often proceeded strategically from the reaction that they themselves provoked, as in the series entitled *Ist-Nicht-Peinlich-Bilder* (It's-Not-Embarrasing Pictures) dating from 1984.[34]

In response to the damning criticism expressed by Wolfgang Max Faust, Kippenberger produced different versions of the sculpture *Martin, ab in die Ecke und schäm dich* (Martin, go to the corner. Shame on you) [ILL·103] in wood, bronze and latex, dressing it in his clothes and other intentionally conservative items that added to its already ridiculous appearance.[35] Kippenberger's sculpture thus gave material form to Faust's criticisms as disciplinary measures imposed by a teacher on a cheeky pupil. The conservative clothing and the unmistakable adult figure were Kippenberger's response to the accusation leveled against him by the German petty-bourgeois that he was infantile and that he had failed to move beyond the stage of adolescent emotionality. The fact that Kippenberger had published an artist's book entitled *Durch die Pubertät zum Erfolg* (Through Puberty to Success) in 1981, where he had long since provocatively formulated Faust's accusation that he, Kippenberger, displayed a maldeveloped infantilism, reveals that Faust had been taken in by Kippenberger's well-calculated mixture of ethics and aesthetics.

In a performance entitled *Kunst muss hängen* (Art must Hang), given at the Cologne Galerie Christian Nagel in 2001, the artist Andrea Fraser staged Kippenberger's "art of mixing" as a strategy game played with the art world. Equipped with Kippenberger's famous virility symbol—an expensive suit with a white shirt, and holding a glass in one hand—she delivered Martin Kippenberger's entire spontaneous speech, which she had learned in a rather unsteady German, including all the silly and obscene racist and sexist jokes. [ILL·104][36] In the process, she also faithfully imitated Kippenberger's behavior, with his gestures and facial expressions getting out of control as the quantity of alcohol consumed increased.

In her review of the performance, Isabelle Graw pointed out that it was precisely Fraser's act of appropriation, with its unconvincing roughness and alienation, that revealed her impudence, whilst the audience felt uncomfortable and uneasy in much the same way about the staged embarrassing performance as it had with Kippenberger's.[37] Fraser admitted that, by re-staging his speech, she had wanted to double the "ambivalence" and "ambiguity" in the way in which Kippenberger used to present himself, and to complicate matters by exploiting the gender difference and contrasting two very different positions on art.[38] Nonetheless, Isabelle Graw was able to show convincingly that the differences between Kippenberger and Fraser were not *that* great, especially as they devoted similar attention to the institutional framework and the ways of the art world. Graw interpreted the act of appropriating an artist who had been stylized into a kind of meta-artist since his death as a "powerful

Künstlers. Die Kritik habe es als Unseriosität verbucht, dass es weder eine Zweiteilung von „Kneipe und Kunst" gegeben habe, noch ein emphatisches „Kunst-ist-Leben-Bekenntnis" wie etwa dasjenige von Joseph Beuys.[32] Kippenbergers „spezifisch engmaschige Verbindung zwischen Ebenen wie ‚Werk', ‚Soziales', ‚Gerücht', ‚Interviewstatement', ‚Katalogstatement' etc." berge dort ihre Gefahr, wo der Rezipient nicht mehr zwischen den einzelnen Ebenen unterscheiden könne und der Zynismus in Langeweile umschlage, die sich nur noch von Zote zu Zote hangle. Der Genuss am Zuwachs von Diversität und Heterogenität könne hingegen, so Diederichsen, nur funktionieren, wenn es bei der „Emulsion" bleibe und „nicht zur Verbindung" komme.[33]

Die Gefahr einer Verbindung wurde jedoch von Kippenberger vor allem dadurch gelegt, dass er selbst die Grenzen zwischen Produktion und Rezeption seines Werkes durchlässig machte, indem er nicht nur sämtliche Pressereaktionen auf seine Kunst in die folgenden Kataloge integrierte, sondern seine Werke selbst als einen ständigen – und oft unverständlichen – Dialog anlegte. Einerseits entwickelte er Bildideen und Titel aus nachträglich kaum noch nachvollziehbaren privaten Anekdoten, Insiderwitzen und Selbstbezügen, andererseits gingen seine Werke oft strategisch von der Reaktion aus, die sie selbst provozierten, wie etwa in der Serie der *Ist-Nicht-Peinlich-Bilder* von 1984.[34]

Als Reaktion auf seinen Verriss durch Wolfgang Max Faust entwickelte Kippenberger 1989 unterschiedliche Versionen der Skulptur *Martin, ab in die Ecke und schäm dich* [ABB·103] aus Holz, Bronze oder Latex, die mit seinen Kleidern und zusätzlichen, absichtlich biederen Stücken ausgestattet wurde, die sie umso lächerlicher erscheinen ließen.[35] Kippenbergers Skulptur setzte damit die Kritik Fausts als Maßregelungen eines Lehrers gegenüber einem ungezogenen Schüler um und griff mit der biederen Kleidung und der Figur eines eindeutig Erwachsenen direkt den Vorwurf des deutschen Spießers auf, der infantil sei und über eine pubertäre Emotionalität nicht hinauskomme. Die Tatsache jedoch, dass Kippenberger bereits 1981 ein Künstlerbuch unter dem Titel *Durch die Pubertät zum Erfolg* herausgebracht hatte, das den von Faust geäußerten Vorwurf der fehlentwickelten Infantilität des Künstlers längst selbst provokativ formuliert hatte, belegt, dass Faust der von Kippenberger kalkulierten Vermengung von Ethik und Ästhetik schlicht auf den Leim gegangen war.

2001 führte die Künstlerin Andrea Fraser in einer Performance in der Kölner Galerie Christian Nagel unter dem Titel *Kunst muss hängen* Kippenbergers ‚Kunst der Vermengung' als ein strategisches Spiel mit dem Kunstbetrieb vor: Ausgestattet mit Kippenbergers bekannten Virilitätskennzeichen des teuren Anzugs mit weißem Hemd und einem Glas in der Hand, führte sie eine gesamte Stegreiftischrede Martin Kippenbergers auf, die sie in unsicherem Deutsch auswendig gelernt hatte und mit allen albernen und unflätigen rassistischen und sexistischen Witzen wiederholte [ABB·104].[36] Dabei ahmte sie zudem Kippenbergers gesamten Habitus der durch den Alkoholpegel ausufernden Gestik und Mimik nach.

Isabelle Graw hat in ihrer Besprechung der Performance darauf hingewiesen, dass gerade die misslungene Brüchigkeit und Verfremdung der Aneignung Frasers ihre Anmaßung

statement" and as a "homage."[39] The fact that a conceptual artist and critic of institutions like Fraser was able to physically incarnate the model of the male artist that Kippenberger had embodied seems significant. On the one hand, by repeating every embarrassing situation and every bad joke, she made Kippenberger's behavior as a male artist a subject of debate. On the other hand, however, this incorporated act of repetition also revealed the critical and reflexive potential of both Kippenberger's and Fraser's strategy and their congruence. In her performance, Fraser demonstrated that the apparent spontaneity of the artist during public performances is always artificial—hence, the performance was not only given à la Kippenberger, but was probably also fully in keeping with his intentions.

1 Harald Fricke, "Pinkeln gegen den Kunstbetrieb. Martin Kippenberger," in *taz, die tageszeitung* newspaper, March 11, 1997, no. 5,175, p. 11.

2 In this painting, Manfred Hermes believes he can discern a swastika cut up into "black-red-yellow-and-white bars, although it must be noted here that this allusion to the German flag, or even to the National Socialist flag, is not identifiable with the very best will in the world, because the colors do not match those of the German flag and are, furthermore, dominated by a shade of gray not mentioned by Hermes. Manfred Hermes, "Bilder/Paintings 1984," in *Nach Kippenberger/After Kippenberger*, exhib. cat. Vienna, MUMOK Museum Moderner Kunst Stiftung Ludwig; Eindhoven, Van Abbe Museum, 2003/2004, Eva Meyer-Hermann and Susanne Neuburger (ed.) Vienna 2003, pp. 74–77, here p. 74.

3 Wilfried Dickhoff and Martin Prinzhorn (ed.), *Albert Oehlen im Gespräch mit Wilfried Dickhoff und Martin Prinzhorn* (Kunst heute, vol. 7), Cologne 1991, p. 38.

4 For a critical review of the work, see Roland Schappert, *Martin Kippenberger. Die Organisation des Scheiterns*, Kunstwissenschaftliche Bibliothek, vol. 7, (Cologne: Verlag Walther König, 1998), pp. 77–82.

5 Isabelle Graw, "Reworking History. It is not enough to 'relive' Germany's past," in *Flash Art* 149 (November/December 1989), pp. 107–111, here p 109; Hermes 2003 (see note 2), p. 74.

6 Schappert 1998 (see note 4), p. 79.

7 See Schappert 1998 (see note 4), p. 79 on "trick" and "overtaxing." On the term "Iconotext," see Peter Wagner, *Reading Iconotexts. From Swift to the French Revolution*, London 1995; Peter Wagner (ed.), *Icons – Texts – Iconotexts. Essays on Ekphrasis and Intermediality*, Berlin, New York 1996, esp. pp. 1–40.

8 In addition, a reference was made to the colors black, red and white in the National Socialist flag; see: Barbara Reise, "Wer ... Was ... ist Sigmar Polke," in exhib. cat. *Sigmar Polke*, Zurich, Kunsthaus, 1984, Harald Szeemann (ed.), Zurich 1984, pp. 48–57; Gerlinde Gabriel, "Sigmar Polke's Paganini," in *Sigmar Polke. Back to Postmodernity (Polke Critical Forum)*, David Thistlewood (ed.) (Liverpool, 1996), pp. 81–87.

9 For the growing skepticism of the neo-avant-garde towards the modernists see Benjamin H. D. Buchloh, "Parody and Appropriation in Francis Picabia, Pop, and Sigmar Polke," in *Artforum*, vol. 20, no. 7, 1982, pp. 28–34, esp. pp. 31–32.

10 See Dörte Zbikowski, "Polkes Wege zur Erneuerung der Kunst," in exhib. cat. *Sigmar Polke. Werke aus der Sammlung Froehlich* (Karlsruhe: Museum für neue Kunst, zkm, 2000/2001), Götz Adriani (ed.) (Ostfildern-Ruit: Hatje-Cantz, 2000), pp. 115–128, esp. p. 122; Ellen Heider, "Spiele mit der Tradition. Polkes Kommentare zur Kunst," in ibid., p. 138–145, esp. p. 142. The deliberately dilettantish approach to painting the pictures in cheap emulsion paint also confirms apparent prejudices such as: "Anyone can do that" and "That's not art." See in this context Dieter Scholz, "Ironie, Kontingenz und tiefere Bedeutung," in *Das XX. Jahrhundert. Kunst, Kultur, Politik und Gesellschaft in Deutschland*, Andrea Bärnreuther and Peter-Klaus Schuster (ed.) (Cologne: Verlag Walther König, 1999), p. 352–363, esp. p. 353.

11 On the concept of "reported speech," ("fremde Rede") see Michail M. Bachtin, *Literatur und Karneval. Zur Romantheorie der Lachkultur*, trans. Alexander Kaempfe (Frankfurt/M., 1990), pp. 107–131; Michail M. Bachtin, *Die Ästhetik des Wortes*, trans. Rainer Grübel and Sabine Reese (Frankfurt/M., 1979), pp. 192–219.

gleichsam offen legte, während das Publikum in ähnlicher Weise wie bei Kippenbergers eigenen Auftritten von der selbst inszenierten Peinlichkeit unangenehm berührt war und sich unwohl fühlte.[37] Fraser gab an, sie habe durch die Wiederaufführung der Rede die „Ambivalenz" und „Mehrdeutigkeit" der Selbstdarstellungen Kippenbergers verdoppeln und durch die Gender-Differenz und Gegenüberstellung zweier so verschiedener künstlerischer Positionen verkomplizieren wollen.[38] Isabelle Graw konnte jedoch überzeugend darlegen, dass die Unterschiede zwischen Kippenberger und Fraser gar nicht so ausgeprägt gewesen seien, zumal beide durch ihre Aufmerksamkeit für den institutionellen Rahmen und die Gepflogenheiten des Betriebs vergleichbar würden. Die Aneignung eines Künstlers, der seit seinem Tod zu einer Art Metakünstler stilisiert werde, deutete Graw dabei als eine „massive Setzung" und zugleich als „Hommage".[39]

Dass eine institutionskritische Konzeptkünstlerin wie Fraser sich gerade Kippenbergers männliches Künstlermodell körperlich aneignet, scheint bezeichnend: In der Wiederholung jeder Peinlichkeit und jedes schlechten Witzes stellt sie einerseits das Gebaren Kippenbergers als das eines männlichen Künstlers zur Disposition, legt aber andererseits in der inkorporierten Wiederholung auch das kritische und reflexive Potenzial der Strategie Kippenbergers wie ihrer eigenen offen und bringt sie zur Deckungsgleichheit. Performativ führt Fraser vor Augen, dass die vermeintliche Spontaneität des Künstlers beim öffentlichen Auftritt immer artifiziell ist – der Auftritt war somit nicht nur à la Kippenberger, sondern wäre wohl auch ganz in seinem Sinne gewesen.

1 Harald Fricke, „Pinkeln gegen den Kunstbetrieb. Martin Kippenberger", in: *taz, die tageszeitung*, 11.03.1997, Nr. 5.175, S. 11.

2 Manfred Hermes möchte auf dem Gemälde die Zerlegung des Hakenkreuzes in „schwarz-rot-gelb-weiße Stangen" erkennen, wobei sich anmerken ließe, dass diese Anspielung auf die deutsche Flagge oder gar die NS-Flagge auch ‚beim besten Willen' nicht zu erkennen ist, da die Farbtöne nicht der deutschen Flagge entsprechen und zusätzlich von einem bei Hermes nicht erwähnten Grau dominiert werden; Manfred Hermes, „Bilder/Paintings 1984", in: *Nach Kippenberger/After Kippenberger*, Ausst.-Kat. Wien, MUMOK Museum Moderner Kunst Stiftung Ludwig; Eindhoven, Van Abbe Museum, 2003/2004, Eva Meyer-Hermann und Susanne Neuburger (Hg.), Wien 2003, S. 74–77, hier S. 74.

3 Wilfried Dickhoff und Martin Prinzhorn (Hg.), *Albert Oehlen im Gespräch mit Wilfried Dickhoff und Martin Prinzhorn* (Kunst heute, Bd. 7), Köln 1991, S. 38.

4 Zur kritischen Rezeption des Werks, vgl. Roland Schappert, *Martin Kippenberger. Die Organisation des Scheiterns* (Kunstwissenschaftliche Bibliothek, Bd. 7), Köln 1998, S. 77–82.

5 Isabelle Graw, „Reworking History. It is not enough to 'relive' Germany's past", in: *Flash Art*, Nr. 149, November/Dezember 1989, S. 107–111, hier S. 109; Hermes 2003 (zit. Anm. 2), S. 74.

6 Schappert (zit. Anm. 4), S. 79.

7 Zur „Finte" und „Überforderung", siehe Schappert 1998 (zit. Anm. 4), S. 79. Zum Begriff „Ikonotext", vgl. Peter Wagner, *Reading Iconotexts. From Swift to the French Revolution*, London 1995; Peter Wagner (Hg.), *Icons – Texts – Iconotexts. Essays on Ekphrasis and Intermediality*, Berlin, New York 1996, bes. S. 1–40.

8 Zusätzlich wurde durch die Farben Schwarz, Weiß und Rot auf die NS-Flagge verwiesen; siehe dazu: Barbara Reise, „Wer … Was … ist Sigmar Polke", in: Ausst.-Kat. *Sigmar Polke*, Zürich, Kunsthaus, 1984, Harald Szeemann (Hg.), Zürich 1984, S. 48–57; Gerlinde Gabriel, „Sigmar Polke's Paganini", in: *Sigmar Polke. Back to Postmodernity (Polke Critical Forum)*, David Thistlewood (Hg.), Liverpool 1996, S. 81–87.

12 See Buchloh 1982 (see note 9); Thomas McEvilley, "Flower Power or Trying to Say the Obvious about Sigmar Polke," in *Parkett*, no. 30, 1991, pp. 32–40.

13 Roland Barthes, "Cy Twombly ou ‹ Non multa sed multum ›," in idem, *Œuvres complètes*, vol. 3 (Paris, 1995), pp. 1033–1049, here p. 1037. The reference to Barthes is to be found in Martin Hentschel's *Die Ordnung des Heterogenen. Sigmar Polkes Werk bis 1986* (Cologne: Verlag Walther König, 1991), p. 86; see also Hans Dickel, "Zeichnen gegen den Strich. Das Linkische bei Sigmar Polke und Anselm Kiefer," in *Aspekte deutscher Zeichenkunst*, Iris Lauterbach u. Margaret Stuffmann (ed.), Munich 2006 (Veröffentlichungen des Zentralinstituts für Kunstgeschichte, vol. 16), pp. 199–208. For Kippenberger's "strategic dilettantism" see Schappert 1998 (see note 4), pp. 60–66.

14 On the grid as ideology critique see Benjamin Buchloh, "Sigmar Polke und das große Triviale," in exhib. cat. *Sigmar Polke. Bilder – Tücher – Objekte. Werkauswahl 1962–1971*, Tübingen, Kunsthalle; Düsseldorf, Städtische Kunsthalle and Eindhoven, Stedelijk Van Abbemuseum, 1976, Benjamin Buchloh (ed.) (Cologne: Verlag Walther König, 1976), pp. 135–150, here pp. 140–142. On the ornamental quality of grids in Polke's art see: Hentschel 1991 (see note 13), pp. 152–158. On the intentional "printing errors" and Scotch mist in incorrectly placed stencils see Sabine Hofmeister, "Der beabsichtigte Zufall und die gewollten Veränderungen im malerischen Werk Sigmar Polkes," in *Zeitschrift für Kunsttechnologie und Konservierung*, vol. 9, no. 1, 1995, pp. 50–76, here pp. 64–65.

15 On the subject of deskilling see Ian Burn, "The Sixties: Crisis and Aftermath (Or the Memoir of an Ex-Conceptual Artist)," in *Art & Text*, no. 1, autumn 1981, pp. 49–65; Rosalind Krauss: "Der Tod der Fachkenntnisse und Kunstfertigkeiten," in *Texte zur Kunst*, no. 20, 1995, pp. 60–67.

16 On this matter see Walter Grasskamp, "Sigmar Polke. Kleinbürgerlicher Realismus," in idem, *Der vergeßliche Engel. Künstlerportraits für Fortgeschrittene*, Munich 1986, pp. 36–74; Hentschel 1991 (see note 13), pp. 193 ff.

17 Hentschel 1991 (see note 13), pp. 180 ff.

18 Bazon Brock, "Bildjournalismus als ästhetische Macht/Picture-Journalism as an aesthetic force," in exhib. cat. *Martin Kippenberger. Miete Strom Gas* (Darmstadt: Hessisches Landesmuseum, 1986), (ed.) Wolfgang Beeh (Darmstadt, 1986), pp. 61–77, here p. 65.

19 Wolfgang Max Faust and Gerd de Vries, *Hunger nach Bildern. Deutsche Malerei der Gegenwart*, Cologne 1982; exhib. cat. *A New Spirit in Painting 1981*, London, Royal Academy of Arts, 1981, (ed.) Christos M. Joachimedes, Norman Rosenthal und Nicholas Serota (London, 1981); exhib. cat. *Neue Figuration. Deutsche Malerei 1960–88*, Düsseldorf, Kunstmuseum; Frankfurt, Schirn Kunsthalle; Toledo, Toledo Museum of Art; New York, Solomon R. Guggenheim Museum; Williamstown, Mass., Williams College Museum of Art, 1988–1989, (ed.) Thomas Krens, Michael Govan and Michael Thompson, Munich 1989.

20 Benjamin H. D. Buchloh, "Figures of Authority, Ciphers of Regression: Notes on the Return of Representation," in *October*, no. 16, autumn 1981, pp. 39–69.

21 Diedrich Diederichsen, "Das Prinzip der Verstrickung: Kippenberger und seine Rezeptionen," in *Texte zur Kunst*, vol. 7, no. 26, 1997, pp. 75–83.

22 Gregory Williams, "Jokus interruptus. Martin Kippenbergers fliehende Pointen," in exhib. cat. *Martin Kippenberger* (London: Tate Modern; Düsseldorf: K21 Kunstsammlung Nordrhein-Westfalen, 2006, (ed.) Doris Krystof and Jessica Morgan, Ostfildern-Ruit: Hatje Cantz, 2006), pp. 39–57, here pp. 45–46. See the quotation by Baselitz in Faust 1982 (see note 19), pp. 37.

23 Schappert 1998 (see note 4), pp. 33.

24 Ibid., pp. 34–35.

25 Dieter Wellershoff, "Infantilismus als Revolte oder das ausgeschlagene Erbe – Zur Theorie des Blödelns," in *Das Komische*, (ed.) Wolfgang Preisendanz and Rainer Warning (Munich, 1976), pp. 335–357.

26 Williams (see note 22), pp. 39–57.

27 See, for example, Isabelle Graw, "Der Komplex Kippenberger", in *Texte zur Kunst*, vol. 7, no. 26, 1997, pp. 45–73, esp. pp. 68–70.

28 Wolfgang Max Faust, "Der Künstler als exemplarischer Alkoholiker," in *Wolkenkratzer Art Journal*, 1989, May/June, no. 3, pp. 20–21.

9 Zum zunehmenden Skeptizismus der Neoavantgarden gegenüber der Moderne vgl. Benjamin H. D. Buchloh, „Parody and Appropriation in Francis Picabia, Pop, and Sigmar Polke", in: *Artforum*, Bd. 20, Nr. 7, 1982, S. 28–34, bes. S. 31 f.

10 Vgl. Dörte Zbikowski, „Polkes Wege zur Erneuerung der Kunst", in: Ausst.-Kat. *Sigmar Polke. Werke aus der Sammlung Froehlich*, Karlsruhe, Museum für neue Kunst, zkm, 2000/2001, Götz Adriani (Hg.), Ostfildern-Ruit 2000, S. 115–128, bes. S. 122; Ellen Heider, „Spiele mit der Tradition. Polkes Kommentare zur Kunst", in: ebd., S. 138–145, bes. S. 142. Die absichtsvoll dilettantische Malweise der Bilder in billiger Dispersionsfarbe bestätigt zudem scheinbar Vorurteile wie „Das kann doch jeder" und „Das ist doch keine Kunst", vgl. dazu Dieter Scholz, „Ironie, Kontingenz und tiefere Bedeutung", in: *Das XX. Jahrhundert. Kunst, Kultur, Politik und Gesellschaft in Deutschland*, Andrea Bärnreuther u. Peter-Klaus Schuster (Hg.), Köln 1999, S. 352–363, bes. S. 353.

11 Vgl. zum Begriff der ‚fremden Rede' Michail M. Bachtin, *Literatur und Karneval. Zur Romantheorie der Lachkultur*, übers. von Alexander Kaempfe, Frankfurt/M. 1990, S. 107–131; Michail M. Bachtin, *Die Ästhetik des Wortes*, übers. von Rainer Grübel u. Sabine Reese, Frankfurt/M. 1979, S. 192–219.

12 Vgl. dazu Buchloh (zit. Anm. 9); Thomas McEvilley, „Flower Power or Trying to Say the Obvious about Sigmar Polke", in: *Parkett*, Nr. 30, 1991, S. 32–40.

13 Roland Barthes, „Cy Twombly ou ‹ Non multa sed multum ›", in: ders., *Œuvres complètes*, Bd. 3, Paris 1995, S. 1033–1049, hier S. 1037. Der Hinweis auf Barthes findet sich bei Martin Hentschel, *Die Ordnung des Heterogenen. Sigmar Polkes Werk bis 1986*, Köln: Verlag Walther König, 1991, S. 86; vgl. dazu auch Hans Dickel, „Zeichnen gegen den Strich. Das Linkische bei Sigmar Polke und Anselm Kiefer", in: *Aspekte deutscher Zeichenkunst*, Iris Lauterbach, Margaret Stuffmann (Hg.), München 2006 (Veröffentlichungen des Zentralinstituts für Kunstgeschichte, Bd. 16), S. 199–208. Zum „strategischen Dilettantismus" bei Kippenberger vgl. Schappert (zit. Anm. 4), S. 60–66.

14 Vgl. zum Raster als Ideologiekritik Benjamin Buchloh, „Sigmar Polke und das große Triviale", in: Ausst.-Kat. *Sigmar Polke. Bilder – Tücher – Objekte. Werkauswahl 1962–1971*, Tübingen, Kunsthalle; Düsseldorf, Städtische Kunsthalle und Eindhoven, Stedelijk Van Abbemuseum, 1976, Benjamin Buchloh (Hg.), Köln 1976, S. 135–150, hier S. 140 ff. Zu den ornamentalen Qualitäten des Rasters bei Polke: Hentschel (zit. Anm. 13), S. 152–158. Zu den absichtlichen „Druckfehlern" und Sprühnebeln bei nicht richtig aufliegender Schablone vgl. Sabine Hofmeister, „Der beabsichtigte Zufall und die gewollten Veränderungen im malerischen Werk Sigmar Polkes", in: *Zeitschrift für Kunsttechnologie und Konservierung*, Bd. 9, Nr. 1, 1995, S. 50–76, hier S. 64 f.

15 Zum Deskilling siehe Ian Burn, „The Sixties: Crisis and Aftermath (Or the Memoire of an Ex-Conceptual Artist)", in: *Art & Text*, Nr. 1, Herbst 1981, S. 49–65; Rosalind Krauss: „Der Tod der Fachkenntnisse und Kunstfertigkeiten", in: *Texte zur Kunst*, Nr. 20, 1995, S. 60–67.

16 Vgl. dazu Walter Grasskamp, „Sigmar Polke. Kleinbürgerlicher Realismus", in: ders., *Der vergeßliche Engel. Künstlerportraits für Fortgeschrittene*, München 1986, S. 36–74; Hentschel 1991 (zit. Anm. 13), S. 193 ff.

17 Hentschel (zit. Anm. 13), S. 180 ff.

18 Bazon Brock, „Bildjournalismus als ästhetische Macht/Picture-Journalism as an aesthetic force", in: Ausst.-Kat. *Martin Kippenberger. Miete Strom Gas*, Darmstadt, Hessisches Landesmuseum, 1986, hrsg. von Wolfgang Beeh, Darmstadt 1986, S. 61–77, hier S. 65.

19 Wolfgang Max Faust und Gerd de Vries, *Hunger nach Bildern. Deutsche Malerei der Gegenwart*, Köln 1982; Ausst.-Kat. *A New Spirit in Painting 1981*, London, Royal Academy of Arts, 1981, hg. von Christos M. Joachimedes, Norman Rosenthal und Nicholas Serota, London 1981; Ausst.-Kat. *Neue Figuration. Deutsche Malerei 1960–88*, Düsseldorf, Kunstmuseum; Frankfurt, Schirn Kunsthalle; Toledo, Toledo Museum of Art; New York, Solomon R. Guggenheim Museum; Williamstown, Mass., Williams College Museum of Art, 1988–1989, hrsg. von Thomas Krens, Michael Govan und Michael Thompson, München 1989.

20 Benjamin H. D. Buchloh, „Figures of Authority, Ciphers of Regression: Notes on the Return of Representation", in: *October*, Nr. 16, Herbst 1981, S. 39–69.

21 Diedrich Diederichsen, „Das Prinzip der Verstrickung: Kippenberger und seine Rezeptionen", in: *Texte zur Kunst*, Jg. 7, Nr. 26, 1997, S. 75–83.

22 Gregory Williams, „Jokus interruptus. Martin Kippenbergers fliehende Pointen", in: Ausst.-Kat. *Martin Kippenberger*,

29 Faust 1989 (see note 28), p. 21.

30 Ibid.

31 Diederichsen 1997 (see note 21), pp. 75–83; for the moralistic reception accorded Kippenberger as a person see also Schappert 1998 (see note 4), esp. p.p 17–31.

32 Diederichsen 1997 (see note 21), p. 77.

33 Ibid., p. 76.

34 Diedrich Diederichsen, "Der Selbstdarsteller. Martin Kippenberger zwischen 1977 und 1983/ "Selbstdarsteller": Martin Kippenberger between 1977 und 1983," in Meyer-Hermann/Neuburger 2003 (see note 2), p. 42–61.

35 Susanne Neuburger, "Martin, ab in die Ecke und schäm dich, 1989," in Meyer-Hermann/Neuburger 2003 (see note 2), p. 138.

36 For the entire text see Andrea Fraser, "Kunst muss hängen," in *Witte Raaf*, 2003, November/December, No. 106, pp. 5–6; see also Fraser's own description in exhib. cat. *Andrea Fraser. Works 1984 to 2003* (Hamburg: Kunstverein, 2003), (ed.) Yilmaz Dziewior (Cologne, 2003), pp. 208–211.

37 Isabelle Graw, "I love Kippenberger," in *Texte zur Kunst*, vol. 11, no. 43, 2001, pp. 156–160.

38 Fraser 2003 (see note 36), p. 13.

39 Graw 2003 (see note 37), p. 156–160.

London, Tate Modern; Düsseldorf, K21 Kunstsammlung Nordrhein-Westfalen, 2006, hg. v. Doris Krystof, Jessica Morgan, Ostfildern-Ruit: Hatje Cantz, 2006, S. 39–57, hier S. 45 f. Vgl. dazu das Zitat von Baselitz in: Faust (zit. Anm. 19), S. 37.

23 Schappert (zit. Anm. 4), S. 33.

24 Ebd., S. 34–35.

25 Dieter Wellershoff, „Infantilismus als Revolte oder das ausgeschlagene Erbe – Zur Theorie des Blödelns", in: *Das Komische*, hg. v. Wolfgang Preisendanz und Rainer Warning, München 1976, S. 335–357.

26 Williams (zit. Anm. 22), S. 39–57.

27 Vgl. dazu etwa Isabelle Graw, „Der Komplex Kippenberger", in: *Texte zur Kunst*, Jg. 7, Nr. 26, 1997, S. 45–73, bes. S. 68 ff.

28 Wolfgang Max Faust, „Der Künstler als exemplarischer Alkoholiker", in: *Wolkenkratzer Art Journal*, 1989, Mai/Juni, Nr. 3, S. 20 f.

29 Faust 1989 (zit. Anm. 28), S. 21.

30 Ebd.

31 Diederichsen (zit. Anm. 21), S. 75–83; vgl. zur moralisch wertenden Rezeption der Person Kippenbergers auch Schappert (zit. Anm. 4), bes. S. 17–31.

32 Diederichsen (zit. Anm. 21), S. 77.

33 Ebd., S. 76.

34 Diedrich Diederichsen, „Der Selbstdarsteller. Martin Kippenberger zwischen 1977 und 1983/‚Selbstdarsteller': Martin Kippenberger between 1977 und 1983", in: Meyer-Hermann/Neuburger 2003 (zit. Anm. 2), S. 42–61.

35 Susanne Neuburger, „Martin, ab in die Ecke und schäm dich, 1989", in: Meyer-Hermann/Neuburger (zit. Anm. 2), S. 138.

36 Gesamter Text in: Andrea Fraser, „Kunst muss hängen", in: *Witte Raaf*, 2003, November/Dezember, Nr. 106, S. 5 f.; vgl. auch die eigene Beschreibung Frasers in: Ausst.-Kat. *Andrea Fraser. Works 1984 to 2003*, Hamburg, Kunstverein, 2003, hg. v. Yilmaz Dziewior, Köln 2003, S. 208–211.

37 Isabelle Graw, „I love Kippenberger", in: *Texte zur Kunst*, Bd. 11, Nr. 43, 2001, S. 156–160.

38 Fraser, *Andrea Fraser. Works 1984 to 2003* (zit. Anm. 36), S. 13.

39 Graw (zit. Anm. 37).

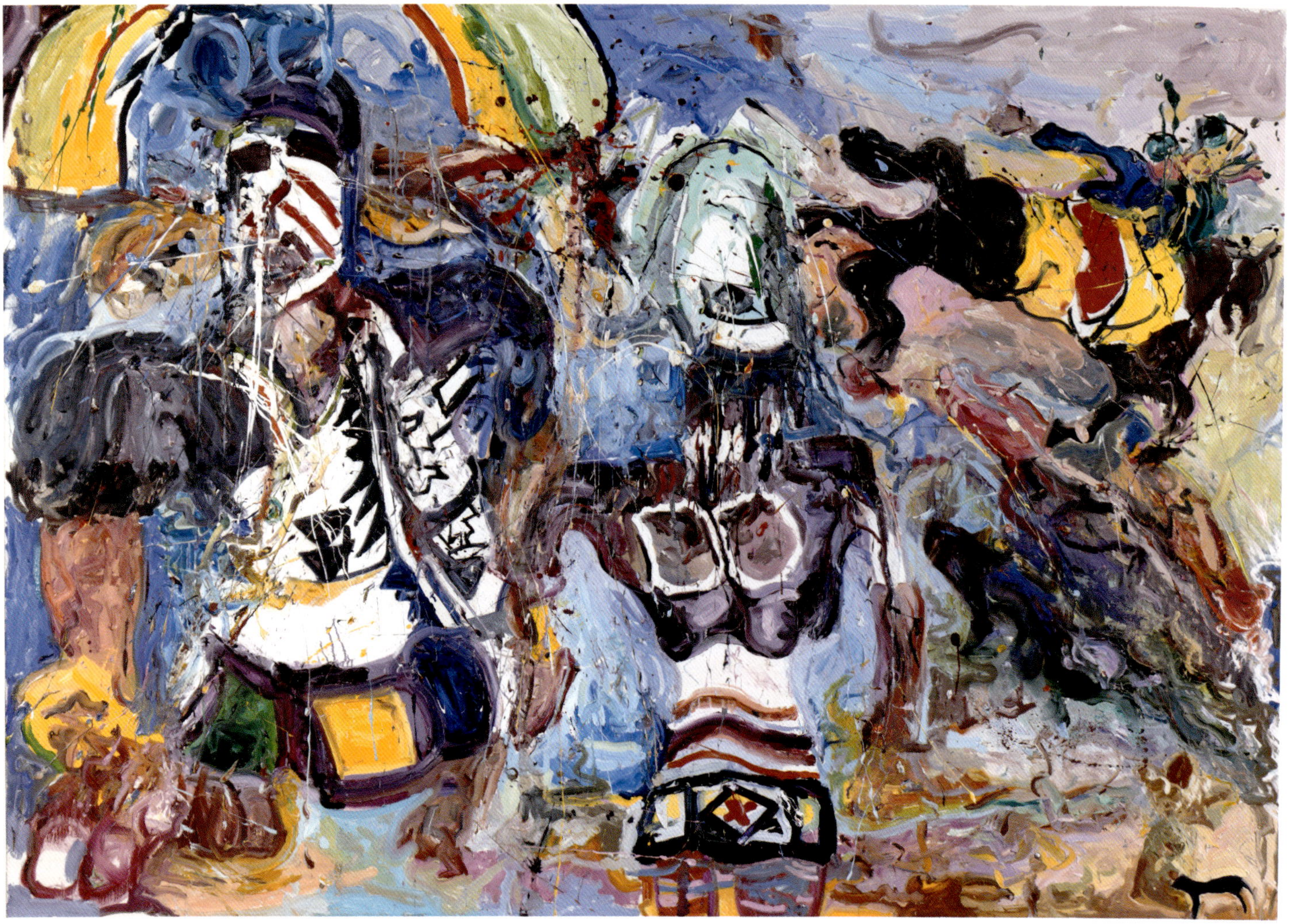

105 **Malcolm Morley**
The Injuns are Cuming, The Officer of the Imperial Guard is Fleeing, 1983
(Die Indianer spritzen ab, der Offizier der kaiserlichen Garde flüchtet)

Öl auf Leinwand / oil on canvas
208 x 284 cm
Astrup Fearnley Collection, Oslo

The Good, the Bad, and the Terrific

Friedrich Petzel

„Mir gefiel die Vorstellung eines schönen gemalten Bildes, das dieses große Problem hat [...], wie eine am Fußgelenk festgekettete Bleikugel. Ein schweres Gewicht, das es hindert, jemals gut zu sein."[1] In diesem kürzlich veröffentlichten Zitat spricht John Currin über seine Gemälde aus den späten 1990er-Jahren wie *The Bra Shop* (Das Büstenhaltergeschäft, 1997) [ABB·106], wo zwei Frauen ihre ungeheuer riesigen Brüste mit einem Maßband vergleichen. Das Gesicht der Blondine ist mit dem Palettenmesser gemalt. Die raue, fast verwitterte Oberfläche ist ein indirektes Malzitat aus der Trickkiste von Courbet, der bekanntlich feinste Oberflächenlasuren neben Partien stehen ließ, die eindeutig mit dem Schrubber gemalt wurden. Diese und andere Frechheiten haben in der Malerei der Moderne und Spätmoderne zu einer fast in sich geschlossenen Tradition geführt. Eine Malerei, die sich mit sich selbst und ihren Regeln beschäftigt, die sich oft im Widerspruch zur jeweiligen Avantgarde der Zeit behauptet. Eine Malerei, die peinlich, reaktionär, stumpfsinnig, transitorisch und gleichzeitig wegweisend, lustig und boshaft sein will.

Unter dem Sammelbegriff „Bad Painting" sind seit den späten 1970er-Jahren eine Reihe von Ausstellungen kuratiert[2] und unzählige Texte geschrieben worden, die diese „attitude" zur Grundlage wählten. Allein das Adjektiv „bad" bleibt immer schwammig, weil man sich nicht einigen kann, ob es mit „schlecht", „böse" oder „hässlich" übersetzt werden soll. „Bad" im Verhältnis zu was? Zum Wahren, Schönen und Guten? Viele andere Strategien haben im 20. Jahrhundert diese klassische Ästhetik mit anderen Mitteln als denen der Malerei unterwandert. In ihrem wegweisenden Text zum Thema Bad Painting verkehrt Marcia Tucker den Begriff „Ikonoklasmus" in sein Gegenteil, wenn sie behauptet, dass Bad Painters wie Neil Jenney und Bill Copley gegen die Konventionen der rationalen Minimal- und Konzeptkunst arbeiten, die dogmatisch den Diskurs der 1960er- und 1970er-Jahre beherrschen. Natürlich sei diese Haltung ironisch gemeint, aber am Beispiel von Philip Gustons Werk ließe sich durchaus eine Rehabilitierung der grotesk-figurativen Malerei erkennen.

Verachtung

Aber soll denn all dies triviale Geschmiere, das seit den frühen 1980er-Jahren mit Riesenerfolg auf die Kunstwelt eindrosch, etwa erkenntnisstiftend sein? Reicht diese inversive ‚ikono-

The Good, the Bad, and the Terrific

Friedrich Petzel

"I liked the idea of a beautiful painting that has this big problem [...] like a lead ball chained to its ankle. A heavy weight that keeps it from ever being good."[1] In this recently published statement, John Currin discusses paintings he did in the 1990s, including *The Bra Shop* (1997) [ILL·106], which shows two women using a tape measure to compare their enormous breasts. The blonde's face has been painted with a palette knife, and the rough, weathered-looking surface is an indirect allusion to Courbet's bag of tricks: as is well known, the Frenchman left finely glazed surfaces next to patches evidently painted with a hard brush. In Modernist and late Modernist painting, these and other bits of cheekiness lead to a nearly self-contained tradition, a school of painting that grapples with itself and its own rules and that has frequently prevailed over the respective avant-garde movements of the age. It aims not only to be embarrassing, reactionary, obtuse and transitory, but also pioneering, humorous and wicked.

Since the 1970s, a series of exhibitions[2] and countless texts have taken up this attitude under the umbrella term "Bad Painting." The adjective "bad" is always a bit unclear since there is never any agreement on whether it's supposed to mean "poor quality," "evil" or "ugly." Bad in relation to what? The true, the beautiful and the good? Numerous twentieth-century strategies employed mediums other than painting to undermine such traditional aesthetics. In her seminal text on "bad painting," Marcia Tucker twists the meaning of the concept of iconoclasm around by claiming that 'bad' painters such as Neil Jenney and Bill Copley work against the conventions of rational-minded Minimal and

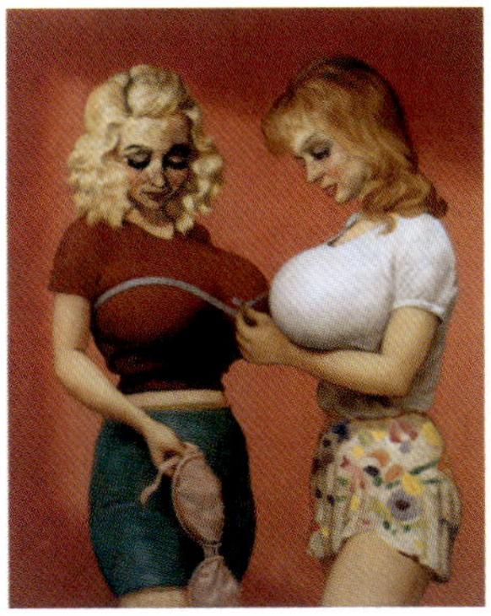

106 John Currin
The Bra Shop, 1997
(Das Büstenhaltergeschäft)
Öl auf Leinwand / oil on canvas
121,9 x 96,5 cm

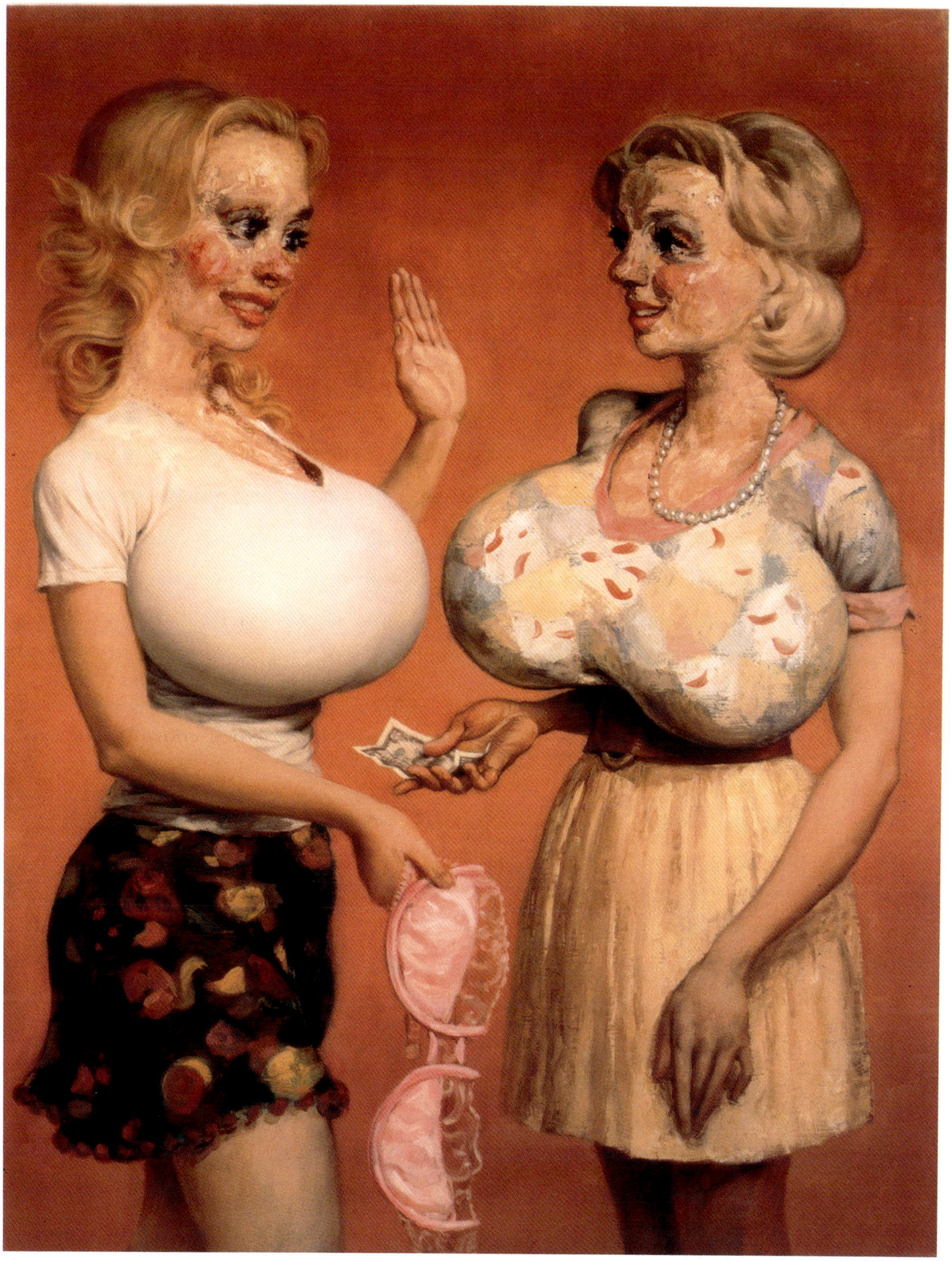

107 **John Currin**
Jaunty and Mame, 1997
Öl auf Leinwand /
oil on canvas
121,9 x 91,4 cm
The Sander Collection

klastische' Gebärde aus, die orthodoxe Sinnsuche der Moderne zu unterwandern? Benjamin Buchloh gibt 1981 seine Totalabsage an die Produktionsmethoden der Malerei als abbildende Darstellung bekannt: „Ihrer historischen Funktion und Bedeutung entleert, verschwinden sie nicht, sondern treiben durch die Geschichte als leere Gefäße, die darauf warten, mit reaktionären Interessen im Bedürfnis kultureller Legitimation befüllt zu werden."[3] Autsch, das hat gesessen. Buchloh mag dieser ganzen Revitalisierung ironisch gemeinter figurativer Malerei gar keinen Humor abgewinnen. In der Presse wurde ohnehin gegen die „Kunstmarktkunst" polemisiert. New Wave Painting oder in Deutschland die Neuen Wilden wurden als vollkommen bedeutungslos verpönt. Es wurden auch kaum Unterschiede hervorgehoben: Albert Oehlen, Werner Büttner und Martin Kippenberger differenzierten sich

Concept art, which dogmatically dominated the 1960s and 1970s discourse. According to Tucker, this stance is naturally meant to be ironic, but if one takes Philip Guston's work as an example one may well say that grotesque figurative painting is being rehabilitated.

Contempt

But are all these trivial smearings, which, beginning in the early 1980s, were stupendously successful in lambasting the art world, supposed to help us arrive at an understanding of existence? Does this sort of inverse "iconoclastic" gesture suffice to undercut Modernity's orthodox search for meaning? In 1981 Benjamin Buchloh totally rejected the production methods of painting as depictive representation: "Emptied of their historical function and meaning, they do not disappear but rather drift in history as empty vessels waiting to be filled with reactionary interests in need of cultural legitimation."[3] Ouch, that hits home! Buchloh finds no humor in all the attempts to revitalize ironic figurative painting. At this time, the press was already railing against "art market art." New Wave painting and Germany's *Neuen Wilden* (New Wild Ones) were looked down upon as utterly insignificant. Furthermore, hardly any differences were made: in the widespread critical reviews, Albert Oehlen, Werner Büttner and Martin Kippenberger, were largely thrown together with the *Neuen Wilden* artists. On the contrary—these three "Hetzler boys" fared far worse in the public tribunals of the day than did their fellow artists in Berlin and Italy. Art criticism has always accused 1980s painters of "radical cynicism" and "decoratively staged banality."[4] Additional criticism has repeatedly been leveled at the "postmodern arbitrariness" and lack of "concrete utopias" that negatively characterize these artists.

But were all the artists who experimented with painting around 1980 similarly dumb? Isn't Buchloh's dialectic historicism, rooted in the progress of Modernism, a reactionary model that does not permit fundamental contradictions? Might we, using a theory of Bad Painting, develop a paradigmatic critique of *art* as a semantic principle that creates meaning? And what differences would we find to Dada? Following all of Dada's campaigns against art (especially art that is beholden to the eye), why should a few cheeky "punk painters" bother picking up their brushes in the postmodern period?

Mockery

When Otto Dix, in *Der Streichholzhändler* (The Match Seller, 1920), makes an allusion to Kokoschka and the appeal not to riddle pictures with bullets, this criticism is *external* to Dix's painting and its artistic composition: while the work is a grotesque that implicitly accuses Austrian expressionism of being kitschy, the result is part of a visual tradition that dates to the late Middle Ages. The painting may be artistic and political invective, but it's not indecent! Despite their drawn-out struggles, the Berlin artists of the Dada movement did in fact have utopian visions that went beyond art or were supposed to help abolish it. In New York, such non-artistic ambitions were viewed rather

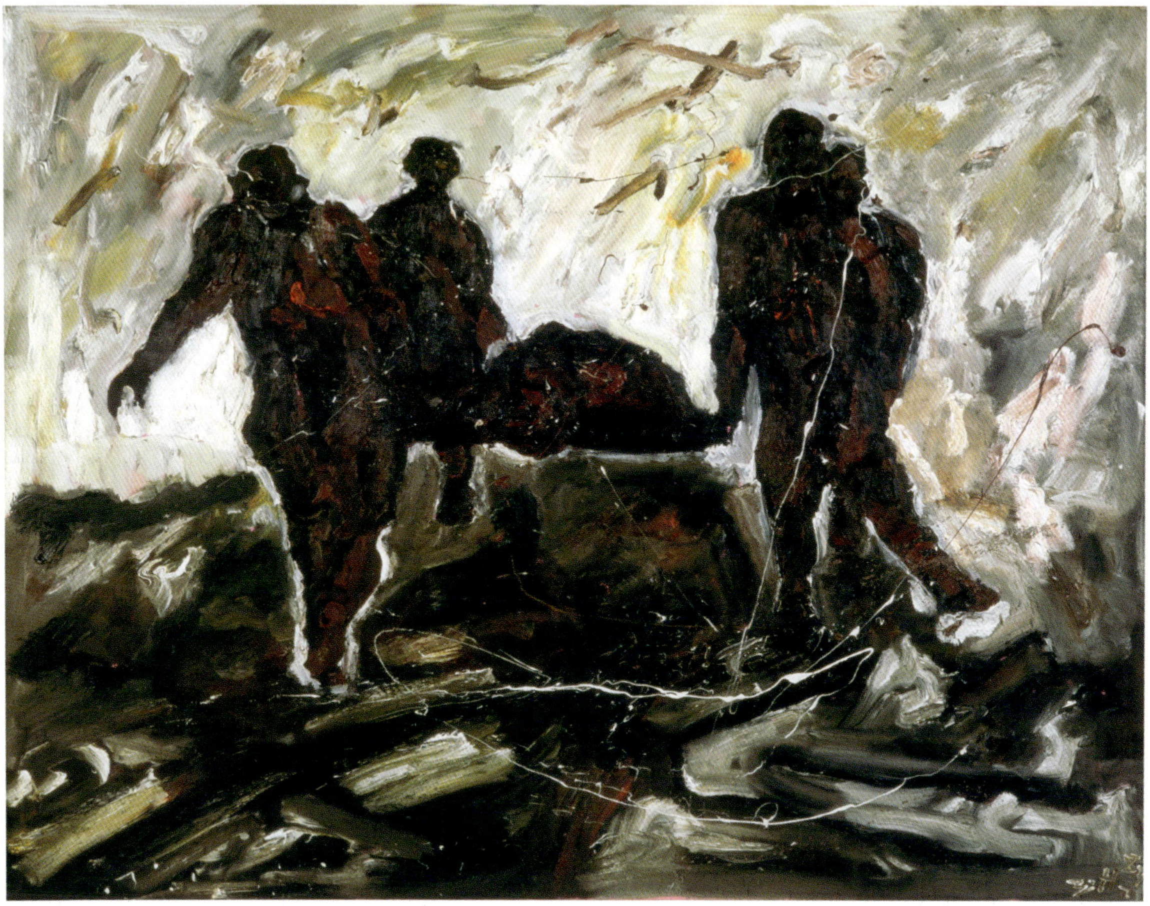

108 **Werner Büttner**
Über das Böse VI, 1983 (On Evil VI)
Öl auf Leinwand / oil on canvas
150 x 190 cm
Sammlung Grässlin, St. Georgen

in der geläufigen Rezeption kaum von den Künstlern der Mülheimer Freiheit. Im Gegenteil, diese drei „Hetzler-Boys" kamen in den öffentlichen Tribunalen noch schlechter weg als ihre Berliner und italienischen Kollegen. Den Malern der 1980er-Jahre warf die Kunstkritik immer wieder „radikalen Zynismus" und „dekorativ inszenierte Banalität" vor.[4] Ein weiterer Vorwurf kehrt immer wieder in dem Zitat der „postmodernen Beliebigkeit" und dem Mangel an „konkreten Utopien", die diese Künstler negativ auszeichneten.

Aber waren alle diese Künstler, die um 1980 mit Malerei experimentieren, wirklich gleich dumm? Ist vielleicht Buchlohs dialektischer Historismus vom Fortschritt der Moderne selbst ein reaktionäres Modell, das keinen fundamentalen Widerspruch zulassen mag? Könnte man mithilfe einer Theorie des Bad Painting eine exemplarische Kritik der *Kunst* als sinnstiftendes Bedeutungsprinzip entwickeln und was wären dann die Unterschiede zu Dada? Was müssen nach allen dadaistischen Aktionen gegen Kunst (besonders der Retina verpflichtete Kunst) noch ein paar freche „Punkmaler" in der Postmoderne ihre Pinsel schwingen?

Verhöhnung

Wenn sich Otto Dix mit seinem Gemälde *Der Streichholzhändler* (1920) auf Kokoschka und dessen Aufruf bezieht, doch nicht mit Gewehrkugeln auf Bilder zu schießen, dann ist diese Kritik in Dix' Bild und seiner malerischen Beschaffenheit jedoch *äußerlich*: Das Gemälde ist zwar

pessimistically. Man Ray and Marcel Duchamp's rejection of oil painting sprang from the conviction that all virtuosity in painting got in the way of intellectual curiosity. Duchamp's *Nu descendant un escalier no. 2* (Nude Descending a Staircase no. 2, 1912–14) is a caricature of Cubism, yet it is executed with such commanding authority that we must see it as an early twentieth-century masterpiece. It is a successful painting against painting pictures! In contrast to the art of Grosz, Dix and others, Duchamp's work criticizes painting using the means of painting. It is not agitation or social criticism.

Disruption

After two world wars and hundreds of revolutionary attempts to exploit and abolish painting — and to transform it into "orgy mysteries"—one question remains: do Buchloh's words set the course, albeit under reverse circumstances? Today more than ever—and despite all the radical attempts to nullify it—painting appears to have emerged victorious in the dispute over paragons. It is for this reason that, as early as 1985, the prophetic artists Albert Oehlen and Werner Büttner sought to justify their decision to use the medium of painting. In the catalog *Tiefe Blicke* (Deep Glances), they write: "[...] at some point came the realization that if you want to achieve anything against art, then you have to go right to the core of it. Which means large-format paintings."[5] They were therefore concerned not only with painting, but with a large-scale attack on the aesthetic principles of Modernity, which ascribed the function of social criticism to art. This is a restatement of the spirit of Dada, cloaked as a critique of the avant-garde, using the means of painting.[6]

Francis Picabia, whom art critics have crowned the founder of Bad Painting, treated the theme of "masterpieces in world art" in a series of nineteen paintings made in 1927. In one, he desecrates Gainsborough's *Musidora* by reducing the original's subtle chiaroscuro to vulgar color contrasts and by maiming her limbs. In contrast to Gainsborough's virtuoso portrait painting, Picabia degrades his *La Danseuse rouge* into a hairless caricature with a red nose.[7] Eighty years later we laugh aloud when viewing these "Monstres" [ILL·058], but the humor is laced with a slight horror, and the bother-some question arises as to what the painter must have been thinking while creating his art. Picabia visibly enjoys corrupting painting as a genre. He wants to put an intellectual distance between himself and his precursors, and he manipulates his motifs to such a degree that they haunt his pictures as debased, interchangeable artifacts. He pursues similarly disruptive maneuvers both with the use of ripolin and confetti in *Nu Fantastique* (which borrows from Michelangelo's Sistine Chapel) and with other malicious deformations from art history.

In contrast to Picasso in his classical period, Picabia simulates the virtuosity of painting in his "Transparences" [ILL·031·056], in which he superimposes amongst others iconographic motifs from Renaissance painting on ancient models, thereby transforming these motifs into arabesques. Yet it is only in his kitschy paintings, made from the late 1930s onwards [ILL·030·068], that he reaches the pinnacle of brashness: "Picabia [...] was now simply copying images from illustrated

eine Groteske mit implizitem Kitschvorwurf an den österreichischen Expressionisten, aber das Resultat reiht sich durchaus in eine Bildtradition seit dem Spätmittelalter ein. Das Gemälde ist eine künstlerische und politische Invektive, aber keine Schweinerei! Die Berliner Künstler aus dem Dada-Umfeld hatten bei allen Grabenkämpfen durchaus utopische Visionen, die über die Kunst hinausführen oder helfen sollten, diese abzuschaffen. In New York wurden solche außerkünstlerischen Ambitionen eher pessimistisch gesehen. Man Rays und Marcel Duchamps Absage an die Ölmalerei entsprang eher der Überzeugung, dass jede Art malerischer Virtuosität die intellektuelle Neugier verhindere. Duchamps *Nu descendant un escalier no. 2* (Akt eine Treppe hinabsteigend Nr. 2, 1912–14) ist eine Karikatur mit Bezug auf den Kubismus, aber mit solch unerhörter Autorität ausgeführt, dass es sich dabei um ein Meisterwerk des frühen 20. Jahrhunderts handelt. Ein erfolgreiches Bild gegen das Bildermalen! Im Unterschied zu Grosz, Dix und anderen handelt es sich bei Duchamp bereits um eine Kritik der Malerei mit den Mitteln der Malerei, nicht um Agitation oder Gesellschaftskritik.

Störung

Nach zwei Weltkriegen, hunderten von revolutionären Versuchen, die Malerei zu instrumentalisieren, abzuschaffen, in Orgienmysterien zu verwandeln – sind etwa Buchlohs Vokabeln vielleicht wegbestimmend, allerdings mit umgekehrten Vorzeichen? Die Malerei erscheint heutzutage mehr denn je – trotz aller radikalen Versuche, sie abzuschaffen – als Siegerin im Paragone-Streit. Die weissagenden Künstler Albert Oehlen und Werner Büttner rechtfertigten daher schon 1985 ihre Entscheidung für das Medium der Malerei im Katalog *Tiefe Blicke*: „[...] irgendwann kam uns die Erkenntnis, wenn man etwas gegen die Kunst ausrichten will, dann muss man genau den Kern treffen. Das sind großformatige Gemälde."[5] Also geht es gar nicht allein um Malerei, sondern um den Großangriff auf die ästhetischen Prinzipien der Moderne, die die Kunst als Gesellschaftskritik funktionalisierten. Eine Reprise aus dem Geist von Dada, verkleidet als eine Kritik der Avantgarde mit den Mitteln der Malerei.[6]

Francis Picabia, der von der Kunstkritik zum Begründer des Bad Painting gemacht wurde, behandelte im Jahr 1927 in einer Serie von 19 Bildern das Thema Meisterwerk in der Weltkunst. Er profaniert beispielsweise Gainsboroughs *Musidora*, indem er das subtile Chiaroscuro des Vorbildes auf vulgäre Farbkontraste reduziert und ihre Gliedmaßen verstümmelt. Im Widerspruch zu Gainsboroughs virtuoser Porträtmalerei hat Picabia seine *Rote Tänzerin* zur haarlosen Karikatur mit roter Nase degradiert.[7] Noch 80 Jahre später lacht man beim Betrachten dieser „Monstres" [ABB·058] laut auf, ein leichtes Grauen mischt sich dazu – und die störende Frage, was der Maler sich dabei wohl gedacht haben mag. Picabia genießt sichtlich, die Malerei als Gattung zu korrumpieren, er wünscht, eine intellektuelle Distanz zu seinen Vorbildern zu schaffen, und er manipuliert seine Motive dergestalt, dass sie als austauschbare Artefakte deklassiert umhergeistern. Ähnliche Störmanöver verfolgt Picabia mit seinem Gebrauch von Ripolin und Konfetti in seinem *Nu Fantastique* (an Michelangelos Sixtinische Kapelle angelehnt) oder mit anderen boshaften Deformationen aus der Kunstgeschichte.

magazines and using a poster artist's technique to turn them into an all-out attack on good taste."[8] Twenty years later, a young Andy Warhol made screen prints of similarly random originals. Picabia's indiscriminate use of iconic material from "high" art and vulgar magazines objectifies the former's claim to transcendence, progress and taste, and converts this purported certainty into the most trivial erotic kitsch.

Here we perhaps come full circle from Courbet to Francis Picabia to Sean Landers and John Currin: all these artists concern themselves not only with sex, voyeurism and arousal, but also with their opposite, their own caricature, as well as with clichés, sexism, Internet pornography and the bottomless idiocy of all attempts to depict such motifs. The degradation of the heterosexual man is an additional motif favored by Richard Prince in his *Joke Paintings* (and the cowboy photos are naturally the most moronic glorification of the American masculinity cult, despite all theories of Appropriation art). It is noteworthy that, while Cindy Sherman accords many of these painters the license to farce, she herself would *never* take a brush in hand. If one wishes to subsume all these names, Bad Painting appears to be an exclusive matter of male artists.

Doubt

Although attempts to describe Bad Painting will inevitably be as variegated as the artists' motivations, one commonality remains. The dubiousness of painting, addressed above by Buchloh, is cultivated as a categorical imperative. The slimy pornographic motif in John Currin's works enters into a dialectical relationship with "sophisticated" high art in much the same way that Albert Oehlen's expressive gesture is related to the purported depths of abstraction. Donald Kuspit writes: "In new German art, expressionism itself is used to demythologize painting. Pictures become a kind of opera bouffe, in which ideas count as much as style."[9]

Magritte's "période vache" in 1947/48 [ILL·008·009·070–076] also speaks in favor of an analytic distance to the topic of painting. Magritte interrupted his own production, offering the cycle as a riposte to the general approval of a late "Fauves" exhibition. His painting *Le Contenu Pictural* (The Content of Painting) [ILL·072] is nothing less than a denunciatory critique of the fauvists' means of representation. It shows a brown-suited figure from whose head additional heads are sprouting as from a gorgon. Streams of green, red, yellow and blue flow from the body. Magritte disdains the fauves' direct wildness, their insistence on primary colors and lack of reflection. In 1948 no one recognized the analytic content of Magritte's caricature paintings, the "Destabilization [...] regarding the art of strong painting and the way that things [...] represented."[10]

Sean Landers and George Condo have made unflinching use of the "période vache"—though it must be noted that Condo absorbs and celebrates Magritte's smearings with incredible technical mastery, while Landers takes the blasphemous criticism directed at the Belgian painter as a reference point for his own career slump.

Im Gegensatz zu Picassos klassischer Periode simuliert Picabia die Virtuosität der Malerei mit seinen „Transparences" [ABB·031·056], wo er etwa ikonografische Motive aus der Renaissancemalerei mit antiken Vorlagen überlagert und zu Arabesken transformiert. Aber erst in seinen Kitschbildern, die ab den späten 1930er-Jahren entstanden [ABB·030·068], erreicht Picabia den Gipfel der Penetranz: „Picabia [...] kopierte nun einfach Bilder aus Illustrierten und verwendete die Technik eines Plakatmalers, um so einen Großangriff auf den guten Geschmack zu starten."[8] Erst 20 Jahre später wird der junge Andy Warhol Siebdrucke nach ähnlich beliebigen Vorlagen machen. Picabias indifferenter Gebrauch des ikonischen Materials aus „Hoch"-Kunst und vulgären Magazinen vergegenständlicht den Anspruch der hohen Kunst auf Transzendenz, Fortschritt, Geschmack und überführt diese vermeintliche Gewissheit in trivialsten Erotikkitsch.

Hier mag sich der Kreis von Courbet über Francis Picabia bis zu Sean Landers und John Currin schließen: Alle diese Künstler beschäftigen sich mit Sex, Voyeurismus, Geilheit, aber auch mit der Umkehrung desselben, ihrer eigenen Karikatur, dem Klischee, Sexismus, Internetpornografie und der abgrundtiefen Blödheit, solche Motive abzubilden. Die Erniedrigung des heterosexuellen Mannes ist auch bei Richard Prince in seinen *Joke Paintings* ein beliebtes Motiv (und die Cowboyfotos sind trotz aller Thesen zur Appropriation-Art natürlich auch die schwachsinnigste Glorifizierung des amerikanischen Männlichkeitskultes). Es fällt auf, dass zwar Cindy Sherman vielen dieser Maler die Lizenz zum Possenspiel gibt, selbst aber *nie* einen Pinsel in die Hand nehmen würde. Bad Painting scheint, wenn man alle diese Namen subsumieren mag, eine Angelegenheit ausschließlich männlicher Künstler.

Zweifel

Wenn auch die Ansätze, Bad Painting zu beschreiben, so unterschiedlich ausfallen mögen, wie Künstler verschiedenen Motivationen verpflichtet sind, so bleibt doch eine Restübereinstimmung: Die Fragwürdigkeit der Malerei, von der Buchloh oben sprach, wird als kategorischer Imperativ gepflegt. Das schleimig-pornografische Bildmotiv in John Currins Werken verhält sich dialektisch zur „sophisticated" Hochkunst wie Albert Oehlens expressive Geste zur vermeintlichen Tiefe der Abstraktion. Donald Kuspit schrieb dazu: „In der neuen deutschen Kunst wird der Expressionismus selbst eingesetzt, um die Malerei zu entmythologisieren. Bilder werden zu einer Art Opera buffa, in der Ideen ebenso viel zählen wie Stil."[9]

Für eine analytische Distanz zum Thema Malerei spricht auch Magrittes „période vache" aus den Jahren 1947/1948 [ABB·008·009·070–076]. Magritte unterbricht seine eigene Produktion, um mit diesem Zyklus auf die allgemeine Zustimmung zu einer späten Werkschau der „fauves" zu reagieren. Sein Bild *Le Contenu Pictural* (Der Inhalt der Malerei) [ABB·072] ist nichts als eine denunzierende Kritik an den Darstellungsmitteln der Fauvisten. Es zeigt eine Figur in braunem Anzug, aus deren Haupt gorgonenhaft immer weitere Köpfe wachsen. Aus dem Körper brechen grüne, rote, gelbe und blaue Farbschwalle aus. Magritte verachtete die unmittelbare Wildheit der „fauves", ihr Insistieren

Difference

It is legitimate to ask: Are the "période vache" paintings "good" Bad Paintings? Are these works contemplative images that point to the stupidity of forerunners? Is the "intellectual method of the contradiction"[11] a mark of Bad Painting?

Grand failure, as both motif and motivation, cannot alone be conceived or regarded as a style or an appropriation of style. Establishing the ugly as a style is not itself proof. Regardless of how pompously this visual rhetoric is presented: when the insight is small, the format must be all the larger, which leads to nothing other than horribly bad art—as the recent past has all too clearly shown.[12] A promise of *improvement* and a revocation of defeatist (or nihilist?) gestures can only stem from permanent change, from experimenting with what a painting can bear in terms of contradiction and dissonance.

Martin Kippenberger always developed his iconography out of a specific exhibition context, out of a place that was linked to a particular cliché. When he received an invitation to an exhibition in Sweden, his first association was IKEA, and the flat pack furniture empire immediately became his leitmotif. Due to Kippenberger's penchant for mixing the latest news from TV and the daily papers, Bazon Brock defined his Bad Paintings as "intellectual distance to the automatic process of the well made, yes, of the perfect."[13] According to Brock, Kippenberger bears witness to the resistance mounted by the artists of the 1980s, who revolted against the "creative mania of modern painting," the perfectionism of utopian Modernism and the dictate of creative authenticity. Martin Kippenberger finds an equivalent in the work of American artist Peter Saul [ILL·041·042·109], who referred to himself as a "walking news magazine," but who also enjoyed crossing expressive, de Kooningesque gestures with Disney cartoons, thereby continuing the tradition of Magritte and his "période vache." "Saul, then, could be characterized as a subjective historist, or maybe social realist in the same confrontational manner that Albert Oehlen and Martin Kippenberger contextualize their disconcertingly awkward content."[14] Robert Storr regards Peter Saul as a historiographer of the vulgar zeitgeist, one who uses painting as an obscene means of communication. According to Storr, the "wrong style" ruins the picture and creates the necessary differentiation in the eyes of the beholder: painting (or rather, art!) is not meant to fulfill

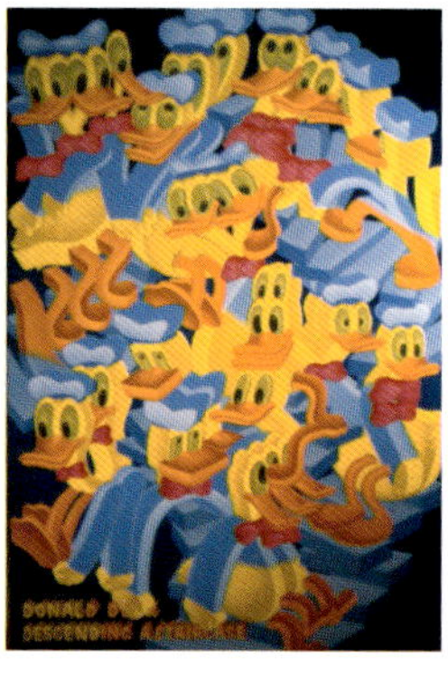

109 Peter Saul
Donald Duck Descending a Staircase, 1979
(Donald Duck eine Treppe hinabsteigend)
Acryl auf Leinwand / acrylic on canvas
198 x 134 cm

auf die Primärfarben und ihren Mangel an Reflexion. Niemand vermochte 1948 in Magrittes Malereikarikaturen den analytischen Gehalt wahrnehmen, die „Destabilisierung […] hinsichtlich der Kunst des kraftvollen Malens und der Art und Weise, die Dinge […] darzustellen".[10]

Sean Landers und George Condo haben sich beherzt der „période vache" bedient, wobei Condo Magrittes Geschmiere mit ungeheurer technischer Meisterschaft auffängt und zelebriert, während Landers die blasphemische Kritik, die dem Belgier entgegenkam, als Bezugspunkt zum eigenen Karriereknick setzt.

Differenz

Die Frage sei nun berechtigt: Sind diese Bilder der „période vache" ‚gute' Bad Paintings? Sind diese Arbeiten Denk-Bilder, die auf die Dummheit anderer Vorläufer verweisen? Funktioniert diese Kritik der Malerei mit den Mitteln der Malerei? Ist die „intellektuelle Methode des Widerspruchs"[11] ein Kennzeichen des Bad Painting?

Das grandiose Scheitern als Motiv und Motivation kann nicht allein als ein Stil oder eine Stilaneignung gedacht und gesehen werden. Im Etablieren des Hässlichen als Stil liegt kein Beweis. Egal, wie aufgeblasen diese Bildrhetorik sich gerieren mag: Ist der Erkenntnisgehalt gering, muss das Format umso größer sein und führt zu nichts anderem als grauenhaft schlechter Kunst, was sich in jüngerer Vergangenheit allzu deutlich zeigen lässt.[12] Erst im permanenten Wechsel, im Ausprobieren, was ein Bild an Widersprüchen aushalten kann, ist ein Versprechen der *Besserung* verborgen, ein Widerruf der defätistischen (oder nihilistischen?) Gebärde.

Martin Kippenberger bezog seine Ikonografie immer aus einem bestimmten Ausstellungszusammenhang, einem Ort, der mit irgendeinem Klischee verbunden war. Eingeladen zu einer Ausstellung in Schweden, fiel ihm als Erstes IKEA ein, und in Windeseile wurde das Selbstbaumöbelimperium sein Leitmotiv. Dazu mixte Kippenberger gern das Neuste aus den Nachrichten und der Tageszeitung, was Bazon Brock veranlasste, Kippenbergers Bad Painting als „intellektuelle Distanzierung vom Selbstlauf des gut Gemachten, ja des Vollendeten" zu verstehen.[13] Kippenberger wird bei Brock zum Zeugen eines Widerstandes der Künstler der 1980er-Jahre, die gegen den „Schöpfungswahn moderner Malerei", den Perfektionsdrang der utopischen Moderne und das Diktat der schöpferischen Authentizität revoltieren. Eine Entsprechung findet Martin Kippenberger im Werk des amerikanischen Künstlers Peter Saul [ABB·041·042·109], der sich als „wandelndes Nachrichtenmagazin" bezeichnet, aber auch gern die expressive Gestik aus dem Inventar von de Kooning mit Disney-Cartoons überkreuzt und damit an Magritte und die „période vache" anschließt. „Saul könnte also charakterisiert werden als subjektiver Historist oder vielleicht als sozialer Realist mit derselben konfrontativen Art und Weise, wie Albert Oehlen und Martin Kippenberger ihre unangenehmen, sperrigen Inhalte kontextualisieren."[14] Robert Storr sieht Peter Saul als Historiografen des vulgären Zeitgeistes, der sich der Malerei als obszönes Vermittlungsmedium bedient. Der „verkehrte Stil" ruiniere das Bild und erzwinge beim

an ersatz function for the transcendental deficits of Postmodernism. Painting must necessarily be as bad as the world itself. In another text on aesthetic theory, Bazon Brock uses the metaphor of the "ruin" as an epistemological model: "Ruining would therefore be a process that creates the distinction needed for all knowledge: between appearance and nature, past and present, desire and effect, plan and realization, design and implementation. [...] The ruin is the objectification of forced difference."[15]

In line with this thinking, difference assumes concrete visual form in "Bad Painting." To be more precise, trashy images articulate the aesthetic promise of a "successful" image as a negatively connoted desire or phantasmagoria. The balancing act performed by the artists who for years have been linked to Bad Painting lies in the intellectual challenge of portraying the non-identity of the depicted subject together with the intended content; and of developing an artistic rhetoric that persuasively expresses the failure of the avant-garde, Modernism, cliché, as well as regression, stupidity and authority. When the artwork focuses on the unrealizable nature of both form and that which is formed, Bad Painting is not a style or anti-style, but a model for naming the non-identical, a product that must necessarily remain unreconciled as a result of its disgusting nature. As Albert Oehlen once said: "Because we now refuse to deny the absolute dependency and responsibility of art in relation to reality, yet do not see any possibility for art in our sense to have an impact, there is but one possibility: failure."[16]

Reconstruction

The modus operandi of the artists gathered here appears to consist of expressing the failure of the artist, the ruins of the image and the collapse of art. The impetus to paint especially horrendous paintings appears to come from an awareness that the intention to have any kind of actual impact on life, history, politics or the present by means of art is basically hopeless. This contradiction is particularly evident in the work of Jörg Immendorff: *Hört auf zu malen* (Stop Painting, 1966) [ILL·110]—its title written in thick oil on canvas—ranks among the icons of Bad Painting. Immendorff's communication of political content was of fundamental importance for Albert Oehlen's paintings. Immendorf reduced the contradiction between aesthetic production and political relevance to a common denominator: "[...] for me, painting was always a schizophrenic undertaking. Working in a

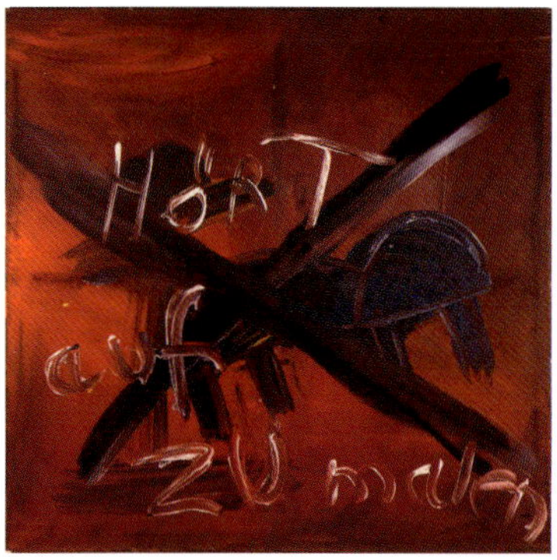

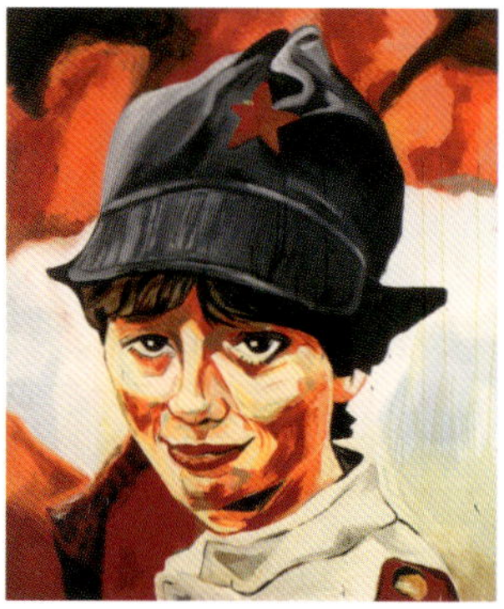

110 Jörg Immendorff
Hört auf zu malen, 1966
(Stop Painting)
Kunstharz auf Leinwand / Resin on canvas
135 x 135 cm

111 Martin Kippenberger
Sympatische Kommunistin, 1983
(Likeable Communist Woman)
Öl auf Leinwand / oil on canvas
180 x 150 cm

Betrachter eine notwendige Differenzierung: Malerei (beziehungsweise Kunst!) soll nicht als Ersatzfunktion für ein postmodernes transzendentes Defizit herhalten. Die Malerei muss zwingend so schlecht wie die Welt sein. In einem weiteren Text zur ästhetischen Theorie bietet Bazon Brock die Metapher der Ruine als erkenntnistheoretisches Modell an: „Das Ruinieren wäre also ein Verfahren, die für jede Erkenntnis notwendige Differenz von Erscheinung und Wesen, von Gegenwart und Vergangenheit, von Wunsch und Wirkung, von Plan und Realisierung, von Entwurf und Verwirklichung herzustellen. [...] die Ruine ist die Vergegenständlichung der erzwungenen Differenz."[15]

Demnach konkretisiert sich im Bad Painting diese Differenz im Bild. Genauer gesagt, im Ramschbild wird das ästhetische Versprechen eines ‚gelungenen' Bildes als negativ besetzter Wunsch oder Phantasmagorie artikuliert. Der Balanceakt der Künstler, die seit vielen Jahren mit Bad Painting in Verbindung gebracht werden, besteht in der intellektuellen Herausforderung, die Nichtidentität des Abgebildeten mit dem Gemeinten zur Darstellung zu bringen, eine bildnerische Rhetorik zu entwickeln, die überzeugend das Scheitern der Avantgarde, der Moderne, der Konfektion, aber auch der Regression, Dummheit, Autorität zum Ausdruck bringt. Indem das Kunstwerk die Unrealisierbarkeit von Form und Geformtem zum Inhalt werden lässt, ist Bad Painting kein Stil, auch kein Antistil, sondern ein Modell zur Benennung des Nichtidentischen, ein Produkt, das durch seinen ekeligen Charakter notwendig unversöhnt bleiben soll. Albert Oehlen meint dazu: „Da wir nun aber die unbedingte Abhängigkeit und Verantwortung der Kunst gegenüber der Realität zu leugnen verbieten, andererseits aber auch keine Möglichkeit sehen, die Kunst in unserem Sinne wirken zu lassen, gibt es nur noch eine Möglichkeit: zu versagen."[16]

Rekonstruktion

Das Scheitern des Künstlers, die Ruine des Bildes, das Versagen der Kunst zum Ausdruck zu bringen scheint der Modus Operandi der hier versammelten Maler zu sein. Der Impuls, besonders gut scheußliche Bilder zu malen, scheint aus dem Bewusstsein zu kommen, dass die Absicht, irgendeine Art von tatsächlicher Wirkung auf Leben, Geschichte, Politik, Gegenwart mit den Mitteln der Kunst auszuüben, grundsätzlich hoffnungslos sei. Dieser Widerspruch wird besonders bei Jörg Immendorff deutlich: *Hört auf zu malen* (1966) [ABB·110], der Bildtitel in fettem Öl auf die Leinwand geschrieben, gehört zu den Ikonen des Bad Painting. Immendorff, dessen Vermittlung politischer Inhalte für Albert Oehlens Malerei fundamentale Bedeutung hatte, brachte den Widerspruch von ästhetischer Produktion und politischer Relevanz auf einen Nenner: „[...] für mich war die Malerei ja immer ein schizophrenes Unterfangen. Gleichzeitig eine Kunstform installieren mit dem Aspekt des Bekämpfens dieser Kunstform, da steckt was drin, was ich immer die konstruktive Schizophrenie nenne."[17]

Albert Oehlen entwickelt diese Diskrepanzen in den 1980er-Jahren zu einer fundamentalen Theorie des Scheiterns. In seinen Werkgruppen *Farbenlehre 1* und *2*, den *Spiegelbildern* [ABB·050·112·113] und den *Schriftbildern* von 1987 lässt er die fundamentalen Grundbedingungen seiner

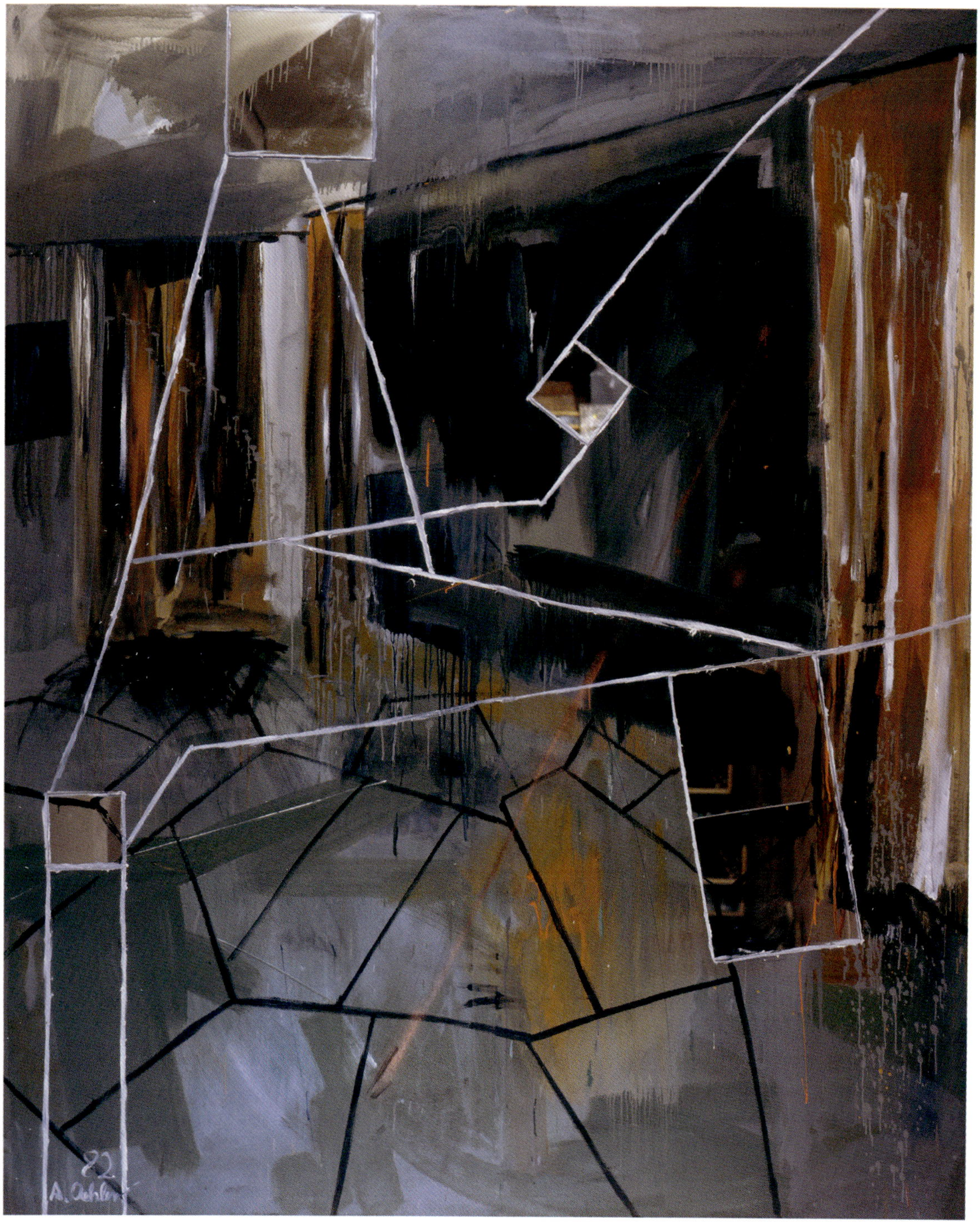

112
Albert Oehlen
Flur, 1982
(Corridor)

Öl, Lack, Spiegel auf Leinwand / oil, lacquer, mirror on canvas, 250 x 200 cm
Sammlung Landesbank Baden-Württemberg, Stuttgart

medium while at the same time fighting it, there's something about that which I always call constructive schizophrenia."[17]

In the 1980s, Albert Oehlen developed these discrepancies into a fundamental theory of failure. In his groups of work *Farbenlehre* (Color Theory) *1* and *2*, as well as in *Spiegelbilder* (Mirror Paintings) [ILL·050·112·113] and *Schriftbilder* (Text Paintings, 1987), he pits the basic conditions of his paintings against one another. Color and object, spatial allusion and abstraction—all contradict the programmatic text scattered across the surfaces of the images. Like Brecht's analytic theater, the "tricks" from the artist-creator's repertoire are shown as such. No alienating effect is too dumb or too clever to seep into one of Oehlen's paintings.

Bilder gegeneinander operieren. Farbe und Gegenstand, Raumillusion und Abstraktion stehen im Widerspruch zu programmatischen Schriftzügen, die kreuz und quer über die Bildfläche verteilt sind. Die ,Tricks' aus der Wundertüte des Künstler-Schöpfers werden – ähnlich wie auf Brechts analytischer Theaterbühne – als solche vorgeführt. Kein Verfremdungseffekt ist dumm oder raffiniert genug, um sich nicht doch in eines von Oehlens Bildern einzuschleichen.

Malcolm Morley verfolgt eine ähnliche Strategie, wenn er seine *SS Amsterdam in front of Rotterdam* nach einer Postkarte des Passagierschiffs malt, wie ein riesig aufgeblasenes Erinnerungsvehikel an eine wie auch immer distinguierte Vergangenheit. Dann rekapituliert Morley 1972 bis 1974 die Reproduktion seines eigenen Gemäldes als *Disaster*: Im oberen Drittel ist dieses Gemälde eine peinlich genaue Übertragung seiner eigenen zerfetzten Vorlage. Noch schöner: *Age of Catastrophe* (Katastrophenzeitalter, 1976) [ABB·114], wo Morley die ohnehin schon verrottete Postkarte mit einem verbeulten Modellflugzeug und einem U-Boot überlagert. Alles Anekdotische dieser Motive wird konterkariert im Farbauftrag und in der Pinselführung; nichts führt zu einer einheitlichen Bildanschauung. Das Monströse im Prozess der Abbildung selbst wird zum Gegenstand des Betrachtens, nicht das Abgebildete. Wo Albert Oehlen Spiegel auf die Bilder klebt, schraubt Morley später ganze Modellflugzeuge auf seine Leinwände. Alles dient der Unterbrechung des Bildgefüges, wobei Julian Schnabel aber doch am weitesten ging mit seinen Hirschgeweihen und Porzellantellern [ABB·051]. Die Geschichte der Malerei wird hier als Travestie vorgeführt, ein unheimliches Gaukelspiel, dessen Referenten und Protagonisten längst von der Bühne verabschiedet worden sind.

Dieser Aspekt der Kunst als einer Gruselgeschichte findet sein Echo auch bei Georg Baselitz: „Die Bilder mit den Deformationen des Gegenstandes haben bis zum abstrakten Bild geführt. Dadurch ist es möglich geworden, ein Anti-Bild zu machen, ein Bild ohne Stil. [...] Für mich bestand das Problem darin, keine anekdotischen, deskriptiven Bilder zu schaffen. Andererseits war mir die nebulöse Willkür der Theorie der gegenstandslosen Malerei immer verhasst."[18]

Sigmar Polke hat sich nie irgendeiner erdig-matschigen Malerei verpflichtet, um damit ästhetischen Widerstand zu demonstrieren. Polke liebt es, seine Urteilskraft als Autor aufzuheben, mal als Medium – *Höhere Wesen befahlen: rechte obere Ecke schwarz malen!* –, dann als Alchemist

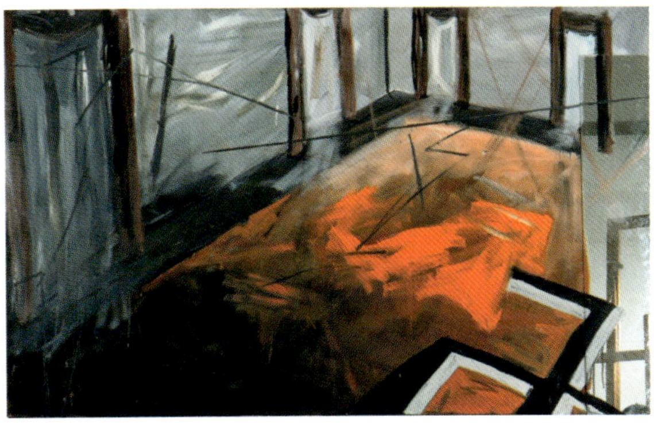

113 Albert Oehlen
Morgenlicht fällt ins Führerhauptquartier, 1982
(Morninglight Falling into the Fuehrer's Headquarters)
Öl, Lack, Spiegel auf Leinwand / oil, lacquer, mirror on canvas
180 x 280 cm

Malcolm Morley uses a similar strategy in *SS Amsterdam in front of Rotterdam*. He painted the work from a postcard image of the passenger ship, creating a huge blown-up vehicle to commemorate some sort of distinguished past. Later, between 1972 and 1974, he recapitulated the reproduction of his own painting as *Disaster*: in the upper third part is a painstakingly accurate depiction of his own painting, but slashed by a knife. Even more taking is *Age of Catastrophe* (1976) [ILL·114], in which he mounts a dented model airplane and submarine over the decaying postcard. All the anecdotal qualities of this motif are negated by the brushwork and application of paint. Nothing leads to a homogenous view. The monstrous aspects of the process of representation become the subject of contemplation, overriding the subject portrayed. Where Albert Oehlen glues mirrors to paintings, Morley screws entire model airplanes onto his canvas. Everything works to disrupt the painting's composition in an approach that Julian Schnabel took to the utmost extreme with his deer antlers and porcelain plates [ILL·051]. Here the history of painting is presented as a travesty, as an eerie circus act whose protagonists have long since left the stage.

This aspect of art as horror story is also echoed in the work of Georg Baselitz: "The paintings with deformed objects led to the abstract image, making it possible to create an anti-image, an image without a style. [...] In my eyes, the problem consisted of not creating anecdotal, descriptive images. On the other hand, I always hated the nebulous randomness of the theory of nonobjective painting."[18]

Sigmar Polke never committed himself to any kind of earthy oozy painting to demonstrate aesthetic resistance. He loves suspending his power of judgment as author, sometimes as a medium —*Höhere Wesen befahlen: rechte obere Ecke schwarz malen!* (Higher Beings ordained: paint the upper right corner black!, 1969)—sometimes as an alchemist (chemistry paintings). Even so, works such as *Schimpftuch* (Cloth of Abuse, 1968) [ILL·018] and *Neid und Habgier* (Envy and Greed, 1985) have earned him the title of "peintre maudit." More than any other artist, Polke has examined and exhausted the capacities of his paintings, motifs and substrates. Nothing is permanent, everything is an experiment and a model. Only when potential is stretched to the extreme—as in a glut of suggested solutions—does the painting collapse, thereby creating something new. But since this collapse is only an exchange

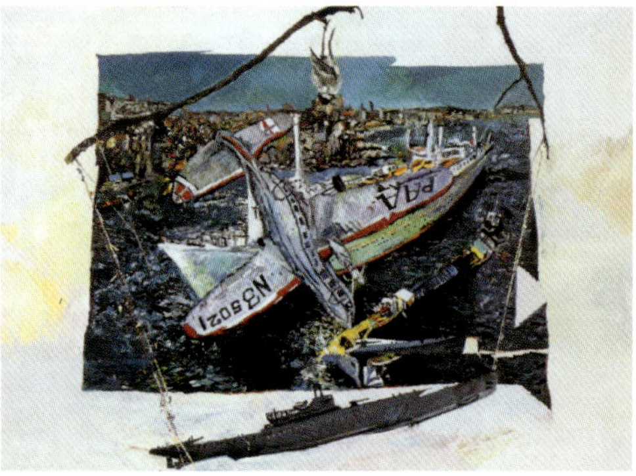

114 Malcolm Morley
Age of Catastophe, 1976
(Katastrophenzeitalter)
Öl auf Leinwand / oil on canvas
152,4 x 243,8 cm

(Chemiebilder), aber doch haben ihm Arbeiten wie das *Schimpftuch* (1968) [ABB·018] und *Neid und Habgier* (1985) den Titel des „peintre maudit" eingebracht. Wie kaum ein anderer Künstler hat Polke die Belastbarkeit seiner Gemälde, seiner Motive, aber auch ihrer Bildträger untersucht und ausgereizt. Nichts hat dauerhaft Bestand, alles sei Experiment und Modell. Erst mit der Dehnung der Leistungskraft an die äußersten Grenzen, wie bei einem Überangebot an Lösungsvorschlägen, bricht das Bild zusammen und schafft dann was Neues. Da dieses Zusammenbrechen aber nur ein Austausch einer Metapher für eine andere ist, sollte man beim Bad Painting wertfrei von experimentellen Modellen sprechen.

Gewissen

Asger Jorn hat in einem vergleichbaren Zusammenhang gesagt, dass die Aufgabe des Künstlers heute sei, das „Können des Nicht-Könnens als Fähigkeit" zu zeigen.[19] Diese experimentelle Fähigkeit sei ein Drittes, welches jedoch nach wissenschaftlichen Gesichtspunkten in ein logisches Dilemma führe. Wenn die Antithesen des Bad Painting gegen alle eingebauten Widerstände doch ein Symbolsystem etablieren könnten, würde das Programm zu einer „uninteressanten Selbstverständlichkeit" (Jorn).

Es gibt also verschiedene Wege, das Scheitern am Bild zum Ausdruck zu bringen. Der ehemalige Assistent von Georg Baselitz und heutzutage einer der einflussreichsten Künstler in Deutschland, Michael Krebber, hat jahrelang den Kunstbetrieb ganz gemieden und pflegt heute noch ein extrem distanziertes Verhältnis zum Thema Bilderfindung. Sein Malprojekt ist vollkommen dem Gewissen des Versagens verschrieben. Jeder Pinselstrich bei Krebber ist bereits die Arabeske einer vermuteten, aber nicht einlösbaren Erwartung an Substanz, Form und Inhalt. Krebber verkleidet seine Bilder (wenn es denn Bad Paintings wären) nicht in gestische Gewaltakte, sondern er dilettiert als Connaisseur in einem fast grillenhaften Gaukelspiel.

Wenn wir aber heute kaum Künstler finden, die seit den 1990er-Jahren eine ähnliche Strategie verfolgen, liegt es dann daran, dass Bad Painting tatsächlich zu einer uninteressanten Selbstverständlichkeit geworden ist? Es fällt auf, dass mit Ausnahme von John Currin nur wenige Maler der Gegenwart skeptische Blicke auf diesen alten Kadaver der Malerei werfen. Fröhliches Gekleckse, wohin man schaut, in den USA und auch in Europa, natürlich mit einer großen Portion ironischer Distanz, denn das ist Teil der Hausaufgaben geworden, die jeder Akademiestudent zu absolvieren hat. Ist es möglich, dass ein wirklich gemeiner Bildentwurf nur unter den gesellschaftlichen Bedingungen von Wim Thoelkes Bundesrepublik beziehungsweise der Allgegenwart von Kunstdiktatoren wie Donald Judd und Clement Greenberg entspringen mag?

Versprechung

Was wäre, wenn das Groteske – nicht mehr nur eine rhetorische oder symbolische Figur, die am Abgrund der Hochkultur steht und diese kommentierend begleitet – von der Peripherie

of one metaphor for another, one ought to speak, in the case of Bad Painting, of experimental models and not make value judgments.

Conscience

In a similar context, Asger Jorn said that today's artist has been tasked with revealing the "ability of inability as a skill."[19] This experimental ability, says Jorn, is the third path, but one that leads to a dilemma from a scientific perspective. If the antitheses of Bad Painting were able to establish a system of symbols despite all the built-in opposition, the program would become an "uninteresting given." (Jorn)

So there are different ways to express the failure of the image. Michael Krebber, former assistant to Georg Baselitz and currently one of the most influential German artists, avoided the art world for years and today cultivates an extremely distant relationship with the subject of image creation. His painting project is completely devoted to the conscience of failure. In Krebber's work, every stroke of the brush is the arabesque of a presumed, yet disappointed, anticipation of substance, form and content. Krebber does not cloak his images (if at all they were Bad Paintings) in gestural acts of violence. He dabbles, as a connoisseur, in a nearly whimsical circus act.

Yet if one hardly encounters any artists today who have been pursuing similar strategies since the 1990s, is it because Bad Painting has in fact devolved into an uninteresting "given"? It is striking that, with the exception of John Currin, only a few contemporary painters have cast skeptical glances at this old cadaver of painting. Wherever the eye falls, there are merry dabs and splashes, in both the United States and Europe, which naturally include a large portion of ironic distance, since this is the assignment given to every art student. Can really nasty painting only evolve under the social conditions of Wim Thoelke's Germany or in response to the omnipresence of art dictators such as Donald Judd und Clement Greenberg?

Promise

What if the grotesque were shifted from the periphery to the center, serving as something more than a rhetorical or symbolic figure that provides commentary at the abyss of high culture?[20] In a situation in which ironic distance has long established itself as the dominant discourse, how can artists offer aesthetic resistance that is not automatically compartmentalized as all-assimilating humor? In the manner of Dieter Roth, Falckenberg has bid farewell to the "grotesque-comical as a counterculture within the framework of social debate." He assumes that, on the level of the individual, the potential for resistance remains, shifted to the subjective sphere. Perhaps the stuttering in Jonathan Meese's performances (in which he screams like crazy the names of Stalin and Heidegger) is more disturbing than his paintings.

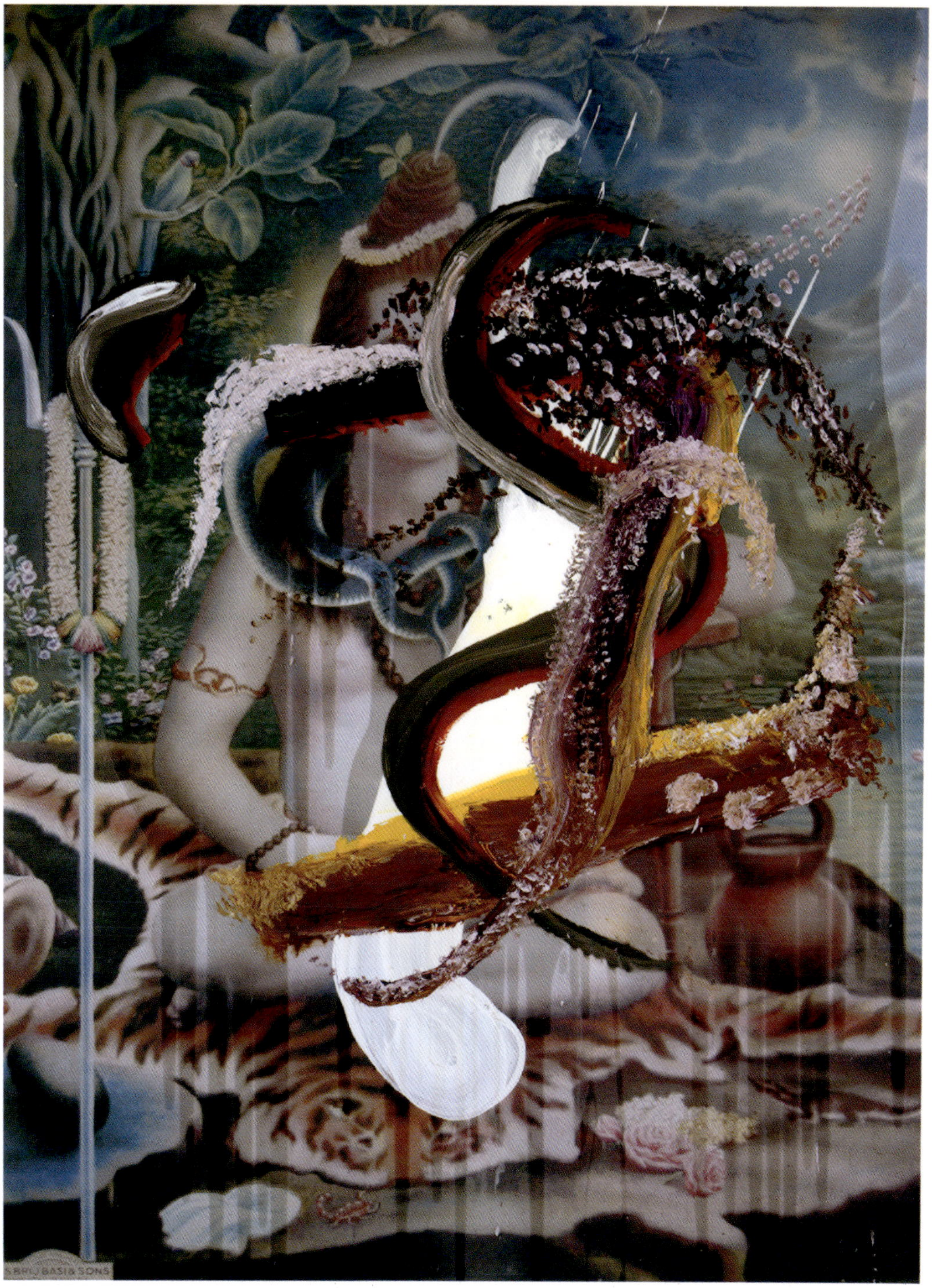

115 **Julian Schnabel**
Eddie Stern, 2007
Öl, Wachs, Gesso auf Polyester / oil, wax, gesso on polyester
271,8 x 195,6
Privatsammlung / Private Collection, New York
Courtesy Sperone Westwater, New York

ins Zentrum gerückt wäre?[20] Wenn die ironische Distanz längst zum herrschenden Diskurs geworden wäre, wie sollten Künstler ästhetischen Widerstand leisten, der nicht automatisch in die alles assimilierende Humorkiste weggelacht wird? In Anlehnung an Dieter Roth verabschiedet Falckenberg das „Grotesk-Komische als Gegenkultur im Rahmen gesellschaftlicher Auseinandersetzung“ und vermutet, dass auf individueller Ebene, ins Subjektive verlagert, noch ein Widerstandspotenzial erhalten bliebe. Vielleicht ist das Gestottere in Jonathan Meeses Performances (wenn er wie am Spieß die Namen Stalin und Heidegger rausbrüllt) viel verstörender als dessen Gemälde.

Natürlich wird es immer ein Reservoir dissidenter, peinlicher und deshalb praktischer (!) Strategien geben, aber von der kritischen Bühne Bad Painting wird in absehbarer Zeit kaum

Dissident, embarrassing and, for this reason, practical (!) strategies will naturally always exist, but in the foreseeable future we can hardly expect any feedback from the critical stage of Bad Painting. This conclusion must nevertheless not be misunderstood as a defeatist *rien-ne-va-plus*. True, beautiful, nasty and contradictory art always exists where criticism least expects it, where concepts fail and pure witchery rules.

1 Calvin Tomkins, "Lifting the Veil: Old Masters, pornography, and the works of John Currin," in *The New Yorker*, January 28, 2008: 65.

2 See also *"Bad" Painting*, exhib. cat. (New York: The New Museum of Contemporary Art, 1978).

3 Benjamin H. D. Buchloh, "Figures of Authority, Ciphers of Regression: Notes on the Return of Representation in European Painting," reprinted in *Art After Modernism: Rethinking Representation*, ed. Brian Wallis, 120 (New York, 1984).

4 Karin Thomas, *Zweimal deutsche Kunst nach 1945* (Cologne: DuMont Buchverlag, 1985), p. 242.

5 Cited from Stephan Schmidt-Wulffen, "Alles in allem – Panorama "wilder" Malerei," in *Tiefe Blicke: Kunst der achtziger Jahre aus der BRD, der DDR, Österreich und der Schweiz* (Cologne: Hessisches Landesmuseum Darmstadt, 1985), p. 56.

6 The master's thesis that I wrote on this topic in 1990 provides a basis for this text: *Die Theorie des Bad Painting am Beispiel von Albert Oehlen* (University of Cologne, 1990, unpublished).

7 See also Maria Lluisa Borras, *Picabia* (London: Thames and Hudson, 1985), 292, and catalog no. 608.

8 Ibid., p. 422.

9 Donald B. Kuspit, "Acts of Aggression: German Painting Today," *Art in America*, September 1982, p. 146.

10 Jacques Meuris, *Magritte* (Paris: Casterman, 1988), 121. « déstabilisation [...] par rapport à l'art de peindre en vigueur et à la manière de représenter [...] les choses ».See also *Westkunst: Zeitgenössische Kunst seit 1939*, ed. Laszlo Glozer, exhib. cat. (Cologne: Kölner Messehallen, 1981), p. 161 f.; and *René Magritte*, exhib. cat. (Munich: Kunsthalle der Hypo-Stiftung München, 1987–1988), p. 70.

11 Vincent Bounoure, "Le Thème de la Contradiction chez Magritte," in *L'œil* 206–207, February/March 1972.

12 The work of Martin Kippenberger, in particular, has served many younger colleagues as a goldmine for dialectically understood "bad" taste. Who would ever have expected thousands of Columbia University graduates to bring such enthusiasm to the terribly slobbery paintings each year and cite "Saint Martin"?

13 Bazon Brock, "Bildjournalismus als ästhetische Macht," in *Martin Kippenberger: Miete Strom Gas*, exhib. cat. (Darmstadt: Hessisches Landesmuseum Darmstadt, 1986), pp. 61–77.

14 Joseph Scanlan, "Peter Saul," in *Artscribe International*, January/February 1990, p. 83; see also Robert Storr, "Peter Saul: Radical Distaste," *Art in America*, January 1985, pp. 92–101.

15 Bazon Brock, "Die Ruine als Modell der Differenz" in *Ästhetik gegen erzwungene Unmittelbarkeit: Die Gottsucherbande. Schriften 1978–1986*, ed. Bazon Brock (Cologne: DuMont Buchverlag, 1986), p. 179.

16 Interview with Diedrich Diederichsen, in Diedrich Diederichsen, *Elektra. Schriften zur Kunst* (Hamburg: Meterverlag, 1986), p. 16.

17 Jörg Immendorff talking to Walter Grasskamp, in *Arbeit in Geschichte, Geschichte in Arbeit*, exhib. cat. (Hamburg: Kunsthaus Hamburg, 1988), p. 157.

18 Georg Baselitz in an interview with Evelyn Weiss at Schloss Derneburg on June 22, 1975, in *Georg Baselitz*, exhib. cat. (Braunschweig: Kunstverein Braunschweig, 1981), p. 64.

19 Asger Jorn, "Die Ordnung der Natur," in *Gedanken eines Künstlers* (Munich: Galerie van de Loo, 1966), p. 314.

20 See also Harald Falckenberg, "Auf Wiedersehen: Zur Rolle des Grotesken in der Gegenwartskunst," in *Aus dem Maschinenraum der Kunst: Aufzeichnungen eines Sammlers* (Hamburg: Fundus, 2007), p. 257.

ein Feedback zu erwarten sein. Dieses Fazit soll aber nicht als ein defätistisches Rien-ne-va-plus missverstanden werden; die wahre, schöne, gemeine, widersprüchliche Kunst ist immer da, wo die Kritik sie gerade nicht vermutet, wo die Begriffe versagen, also dort, wo reine Hexerei herrscht.

1 Calvin Tomkins, „Lifting the Veil. Old Masters, pornography, and the works of John Currin", in: *The New Yorker*, 28.01.2008, S. 65.

2 Vgl. *"Bad" Painting*, Ausst.-Kat., The New Museum of Contemporary Art, New York 1978.

3 Benjamin H. D. Buchloh, „Figures of Authority, Ciphers of Regression. Notes on the Return of Representation in European Painting", wieder abgedruckt in: *Art After Modernism. Rethinking Representation*, hg. v. Brian Wallis, New York 1984, S. 120.

4 Karin Thomas, *Zweimal deutsche Kunst nach 1945*, Köln 1985, S. 242.

5 Zitiert nach Stephan Schmidt-Wulffen, „Alles in allem – Panorama ‚wilder' Malerei", in: *Tiefe Blicke. Kunst der achtziger Jahre aus der BRD, der DDR, Österreich und der Schweiz*, hg. v. Hessisches Landesmuseum Darmstadt, Köln 1985, S. 56.

6 Dazu habe ich 1990 eine Magisterarbeit geschrieben, die eine Grundlage dieses Textes bildet: *Die Theorie des Bad Painting am Beispiel von Albert Oehlen*, Universität Köln, 1990 (unveröffentlicht).

7 Vgl. Maria Lluïsa Borràs, *Picabia*, London 1985, S. 292 u. Kat.-Nr. 608.

8 Ebd., S. 422.

9 Donald B. Kuspit, „Acts of Aggression: German Painting Today", in: *Art in America*, September 1982, S. 146.

10 Jacques Meuris, *Magritte*, Paris 1988, S. 121. « déstabilisation [...] par rapport à l'art de peindre en vigueur et à la manière de représenter [...] les choses ». Vgl. auch: *Westkunst. Zeitgenössische Kunst seit 1939*, hg. v. Laszlo Glozer, Ausst.-Kat., Kölner Messehallen, Köln 1981, S. 161 f., und *René Magritte*, Ausst.-Kat., Kunsthalle der Hypo-Stiftung München, München 1987–1988, S. 70.

11 Vincent Bounoure, „Le Thème de la Contradiction chez Magritte", in: *L'œil*, Nr. 206–207, Februar/März 1972.

12 Besonders das Werk Martin Kippenbergers dient vielen jüngeren Kollegen als Steinbruch des dialektisch verstandenen ‚schlechten' Geschmacks. Wer hätte jemals geahnt, mit welcher Begeisterung tausende Abgänger der Columbia University sich jährlich an furchtbar matschiger Malerei delektieren und dabei den ‚heiligen Martin' zitieren?

13 Bazon Brock, „Bildjournalismus als ästhetische Macht", in: *Martin Kippenberger. Miete Strom Gas*, Ausst.-Kat., Hessisches Landesmuseum Darmstadt, 1986, S. 61–77.

14 Joseph Scanlan, „Peter Saul", in: *Artscribe International*, Januar/Februar 1990, S. 83; vgl. auch Robert Storr, „Peter Saul. Radical Distaste", in: *Art in America*, Januar 1985, S. 92–101.

15 Bazon Brock, „Die Ruine als Modell der Differenz", in: ders., *Ästhetik gegen erzwungene Unmittelbarkeit. Die Gottsucherbande. Schriften 1978–1986*, Köln 1986, S. 179.

16 Interview mit Diedrich Diederichsen, in: Diedrich Diederichsen, *Elektra. Schriften zur Kunst*, Hamburg 1986, S. 16.

17 Jörg Immendorff im Gespräch mit Walter Grasskamp, in: *Arbeit in Geschichte, Geschichte in Arbeit*, Ausst.-Kat., Kunsthaus Hamburg, Hamburg 1988, S. 157.

18 Georg Baselitz im Gespräch mit Evelyn Weiss im Schloss Derneburg am 22.06.1975, in: *Georg Baselitz*, Ausst.-Kat., Kunstverein Braunschweig, Braunschweig 1981, S. 64.

19 Asger Jorn, „Die Ordnung der Natur", in: *Gedanken eines Künstlers*, hg. v. Galerie van de Loo, München 1966, S. 314.

20 Vgl. Harald Falckenberg, „Auf Wiedersehen. Zur Rolle des Grotesken in der Gegenwartskunst", in: ders., *Aus dem Maschinenraum der Kunst. Aufzeichnungen eines Sammlers*, Hamburg 2007, S. 257.

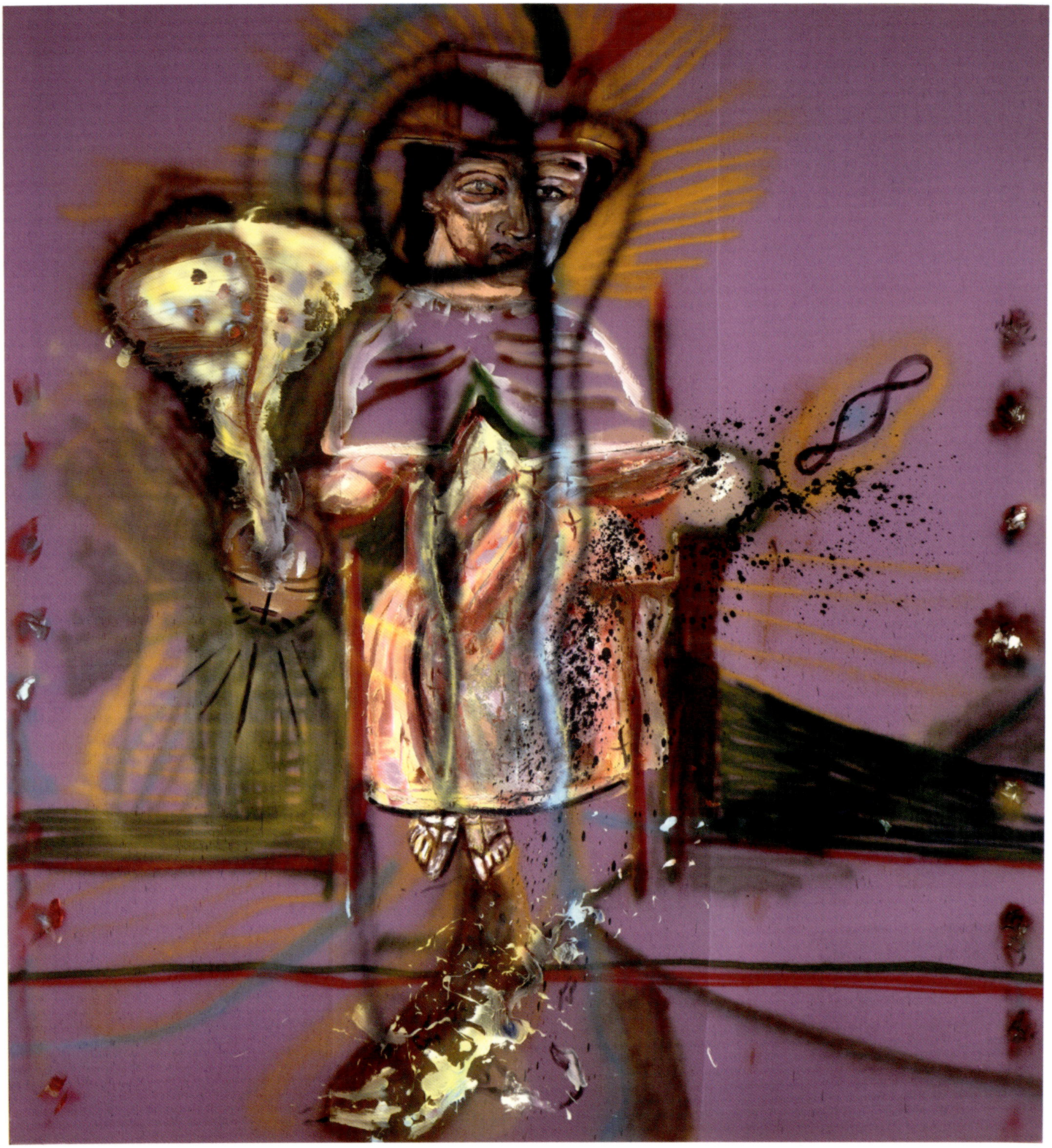

116 **Julian Schnabel**
Resurrection, 1984 (Auferstehung)

Öl, Sprühfarbe, Modellierpaste auf Samt /
oil, spray paint, modeling compound on velvet
304,8 x 271,3 cm
Privatsammlung / Private Collection, New York
Courtesy Sperone Westwater, New York

Falschtöne und Fehlfarben

Über Gemeinsamkeiten von Malerei und Musik, zirka 1975 bis 1985

Christian Höller

Die Malerei, sagte Don Van Vliet einmal, sollte ihre BetrachterInnen „umarmen und kräftig durchschütteln". Und mehr noch: „Wenn ein Bild nicht verstörend auf mich wirkt, landet es auf dem Müll."[1] Van Vliet hatte zum Zeitpunkt dieser Aussage seine aus heutiger Sicht kanonisch verehrte Musikerlaufbahn unter dem Pseudonym Captain Beefheart längst zugunsten einer ungleich lukrativeren Malerkarriere aufgegeben. Seine letzte Plattenaufnahme war 1982 erschienen, groß ins Kunstmarktgeschäft stieg er etwa ab 1985 ein. Und dennoch schwingt in dieser ebenso knappen wie harschen Programmatik eine Art gemeinsamer Nenner mit, der seinen bevorzugten Medien – Musik, Malerei und, nicht zu vergessen, Dichtung (Lyrics) – gleichermaßen zugrunde liegt. Die HörerInnen und SeherInnen gleichsam physisch tangieren, ja, sie nach Möglichkeit in heftige Konvulsionen versetzen und dabei selbstreflexiv die Verstörtheit des Produzenten als Maßstab anlegen, dies war exakt jener Modus, den Beefhearts Blues- und Rockdestruktionen seit seinen ersten Aufnahmen Mitte der 1960er-Jahre vehementest ausagiert hatten. Der Nichteinklang mit der Welt, aber auch mit der Welt der Kunst und den allzu reibungslos deren Konventionen bedienenden eigenen Hervorbringungen – dies waren zentrale Parameter, die Beefhearts Musik zwar in den Kritikerolymp hievten, gleichzeitig aber ihre kommerzielle Erfolglosigkeit besiegelten.

Dennoch ging Van Vliet nicht sequenziell von der Musik zur Malerei über, so als müsste das Versprechen beziehungsweise der erhoffte Erfolg der einen für die mangelnde Akzeptanz oder die vermeintlichen Verirrungen der anderen einstehen. Vielmehr hatte der multidisziplinäre Künstler immer schon in beiden Medien gleichzeitig gearbeitet, wobei die öffentliche Persona gut 15 Jahre lang fast ausschließlich im Zeichen der Musikerfigur stand. Frühe Öl-Dripping-Bilder wie das abgründig-fahrige *Ghost Red Wire* (1967) [ABB·117] legen davon ebenso Zeugnis ab wie sporadisch auf Plattencovers erscheinende Malereien, etwa das abstrakt in die Landschaft gesetzte Vogelinsekt auf der Rückseite von *Lick My Decals Off, Baby* (1970), die animalisch zerzausten Porträts der Bandmitglieder auf *The Spotlight Kid* (1972) oder die beiden rosarot angelaufenen, wildköpfigen Tier-Mensch-Hybriden im Bild *Green Tom* (1976), welches schließlich das Cover von *Shiny Beast (Bat Chain Puller)* (1978) [ABB·118] zieren sollte. Zwar wurde retrospektiv immer wieder auf die Unterschiedlichkeit der beiden Praktiken Van Vliets verwiesen,[2] doch halten die dabei bemühten Kriterien – die eine (Musik)

Wrong Notes and Off-Colors

Common Ground in Painting and Music, circa 1975 to 1985

Christian Höller

Don Van Vliet once remarked that his paintings should "hug and shake" those who look at them, and "If my paintings don't disturb me I scrap them."[1] When he said this Van Vliet had already long given up his career as the musician Captain Beefheart—a figure that enjoys canonic status today—and set upon a far more lucrative career as a painter. His last music recording was published in 1982, and from around 1975 he launched into the art business in a big way. This short and programmatic statement on painting nonetheless stands as a kind of common denominator for his approach to all the media he worked in—music, painting, and poetry (lyrics). His listeners and viewers should be physically affected, and wherever possible subject to violent physical reaction; they should self-reflectively accept and emulate the musician's own deranged state of mind. This was the method that Beefheart had pursued so uncompromisingly with his deconstruction of blues and rock right from his first recordings in the mid-1960s. Disharmony with the world, and in particular the world of art and any own creations that drew too easily on artistic convention—these were the central parameters that assured Beefheart's music both its remarkable critical success and commercial failure.

But Van Vliet did not move seamlessly from music to painting, as if the promise and hope of success in one medium were to make up for the lack of general acceptance and all the aberrations of the other. Van Vliet was a multidisciplinary artist who had already worked in both media simultaneously, even if for some fifteen years his public image rested almost exclusively on his role as a musician. Among early works of art are oil-drip paintings such as the mysterious and erratic *Ghost Red Wire* (1967) [ILL·117], and paintings that occasionally appeared on record covers, like the abstract bird-like insect in a landscape on the back cover of *Lick My Decals Off, Baby* (1970), or the animalistic and ragged portraits of the band members on *The Spotlight Kid* (1972), and the two semi-pink wild-headed human-animal hybrids in the picture *Green Tom* (1976), which later was included on the cover of *Shiny Beast (Bat Chain Puller)* (1978) [ILL·118]. In criticism, it has become standard to highlight the differences between Van Vliet's work in the two media of music and art.[2] The criteria thereby used—the music is composed according to strict rules and therefore conceptual, while the painting is spontaneous and thus instinctive; the painting can always be deleted, while recorded music is permanently fixed—do not stand up to closer scrutiny. The apparent opposites of conceptual versus instinctive can,

sei nach strengen Regeln verfasst und daher konzeptuell, die andere hingegen spontan und gleichsam instinktiv; die eine (Malerei) lasse sich immer wieder löschen, die andere sei nach erfolgter Aufnahme ein für alle Mal fixiert – keiner kategorischen Unterscheidung stand. Vielmehr kehrt das scheinbare Gegensatzpaar „konzeptuell/instinktiv" in der Musik und in den Songtexten, hört man genau genug hin, ebenso wieder wie in der Malerei, deren widersprüchliche Natur Van Vliet folgendermaßen erklärt: „Ich versuche, mein Selbst auf der Leinwand nach außen zu stülpen. Ich versuche, völlig bloßzulegen, was mir in diesem Moment gerade einfällt, und doch mache ich mir viele Gedanken darüber, was ich tue [...] das hört sich wie ein Widerspruch an, aber [...]"[3] Dieses körperliche Denken, das kein Denken sein will beziehungsweise sich jeglichen repräsentativen Gehalts zu entledigen versucht, dieses Sein-Selbst-nach-außen-Stülpen, das keiner Idee von Innerlichkeit geschuldet ist, dieses physische Umarmen und Durchschütteln, das Wert darauf legt, nicht der eigenen Verstörung verlustig zu gehen – all dies sind Symptome respektive Umschreibungen eines künstlerischen Prinzips, das Malerei, Musik und Dichtung gleichermaßen auszeichnet. Dass sie in Beefhearts/Van Vliets Biografie zeitlich auseinander dividiert sind, ist eher der institutionellen Eigengesetzlichkeit und Akzeptanzbereitschaft der jeweiligen Sparten als einer substanziellen medienspezifischen Unterscheidung geschuldet.

Wenn im Folgenden von ausgewählten Episoden solcher medialen Überschneidungen die Rede ist, so soll damit nicht nur einer künstlerischen Genealogie des Rohen, Ungezähmten und Undisziplinierten Geltung verschafft werden. Vielmehr lässt sich darin der Kern eines unhintergehbaren Gemeinsamen erkennen, das – zumindest in der Zeitspanne von 1975 bis 1985 – musikalische, malerische, aber darüber hinaus auch filmische, literarische oder gestalterische Produktionen in bestimmten urbanen Szenen des Westens zentral kennzeichnete und strukturierte. Dass das Hässliche, Brachiale und Widerspenstige, ja, das Widerwärtige und Abstoßende im genannten Zeitraum verstärkt Eingang in Musik *und* Kunst fand, davon gibt Don Van Vliets künstlerisches Doppel- und Dreifachleben einen individuellen Vorgeschmack. Dass der forcierte Einsatz des Disharmonischen, Atonalen oder einfach nur stumpf auf dem eigenen Widerspruchsgeist Beharrenden zu einem feldübergreifenden Szenecharakteristikum wurde, davon künden zahlreiche exemplarische Produktionszusammenhänge, die sich nur schwer einer schematischen Medien- beziehungsweise Spartenunterteilung fügen.

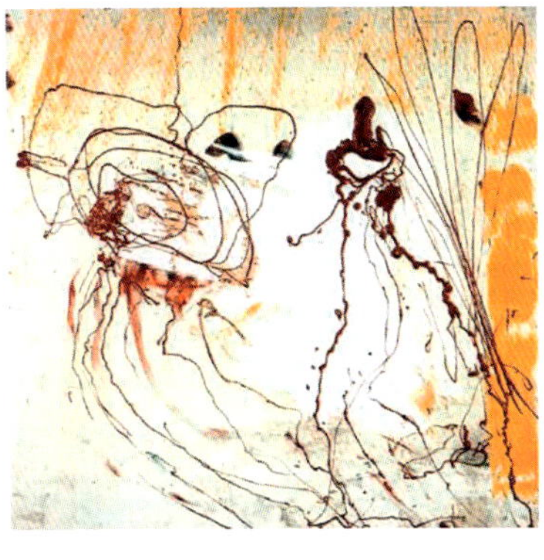

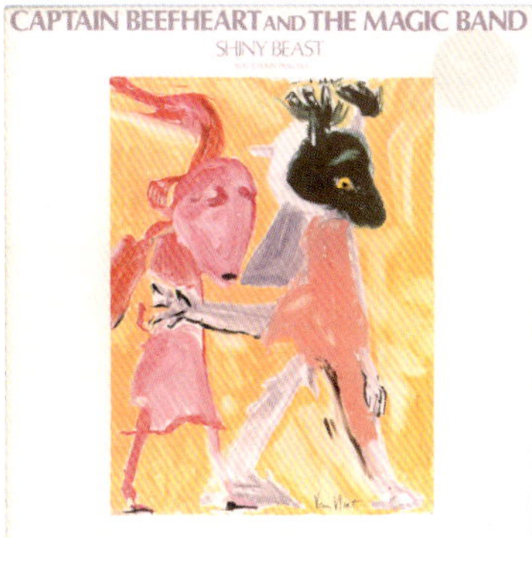

117 **Don Van Vliet**
Ghost Red Wire, 1967
Öl auf Holzfaserplatte / oil on particleboard
61 x 61 cm

118 **Don Van Vliet**
Green Tom, 1976
Cover für / for Captain Beefheart and the Magic Band, *Shiny Beast*, LP, Virgin Records, 1978

paints that others had discarded or the brownish mixture that was left at the bottom of the pots used to wash the paint brushes.[4] This kind of picture making, with the paint applied to old found pieces of material and incorporating all kinds of collaged motifs from advertising, provided a blueprint for a new dimension of trashiness in the music of the 1970s. It was not the old idea of trash as uninhibited dilettantism, obtrusive repetition, or extreme exaggeration, as it had been current in the 1960s (and earlier) that was important here, but rather a confrontational adaptation of found material (B movies, sex ads, pulp novels, etc.) using unconventional techniques that transcended established idioms. This was about rummaging and poking around in cultural trash, not so as to uncover some hidden value there, but rather to meet the tastelessness head on with one's own productions, and even to outdo the trash with noise and din of one's own.

This idea was not only evident in the artistic work of individual band members (in Niagara's gloomy drawings, for example, or Loren's film, photo, and comic work that was strongly influenced by Jack Smith[5]), but also in concentrated form in the Destroy All Monsters sound. The group was active in the configuration mentioned above for about two years (1974 to 1976) and oscillated musically between two poles, which defined the particular fascination of this anti-virtuoso proto-punk outfit. On the one hand there were song-like sketches that mostly drew on dark subjects from B movies and science fiction and demolished these in an overtly disrespectful low-fi manner ("Paranoid of Blondes," "I Love You But You're Dead," "You Can't Kill Kill"), and on the other hand instrumental soundscapes, experiments with drone and collage, using homemade "instruments" and occasional guest performances by free jazz musicians ("Low and Warped," "Crunch Drone," "To the Throne of Chaos Where the Thin Flutes Pipe Mindlessly").[6] The Destroy All Monsters musical "throne of chaos" was by no means just a matter of spontaneity and expressivity (as in a combination of free jazz and Abstract Expressionism in the early 1960s), and nor was it just a case of expanding consciousness with freak-outs or cosmic revelation (as in a combination of acid rock and psychedelic fantasy art). These elements—and many others—were present, but the Monsters sound was based on a different artistic credo that was just as evident in the visual appearance of the group and in its members' parallel works in visual art as in the music: rather one false note and one color too many than fall prey to any

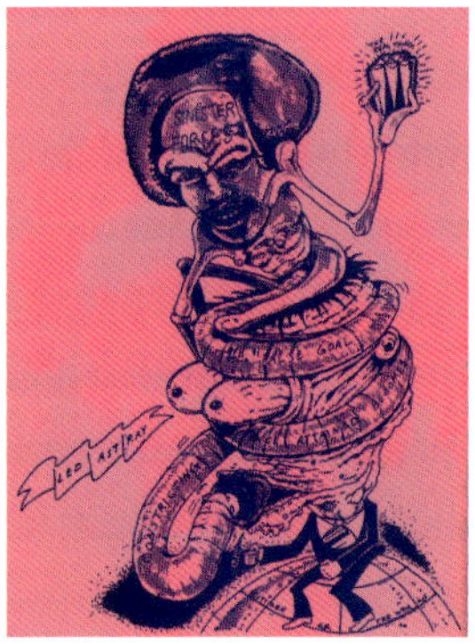

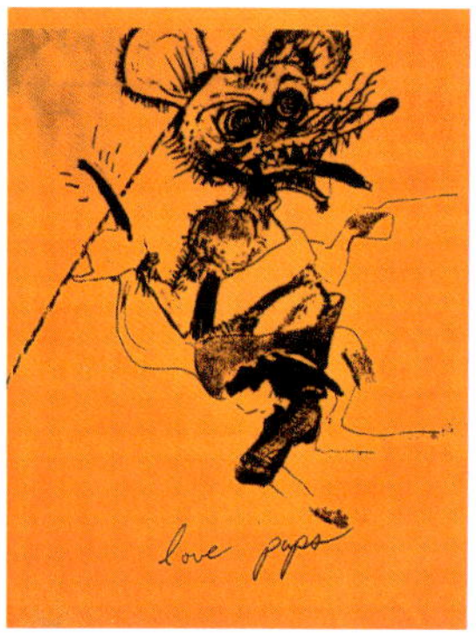

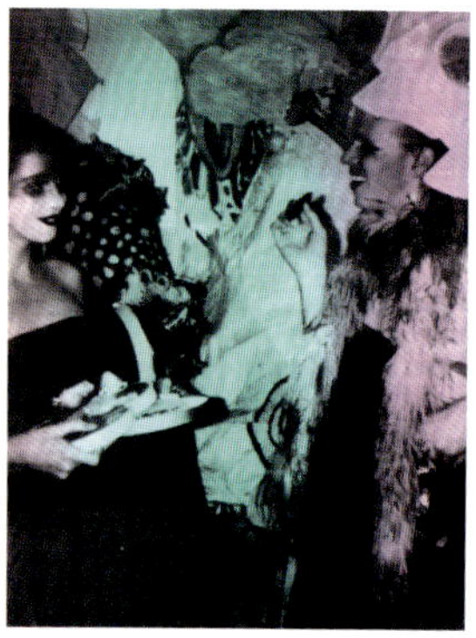

You're Dead", „You Can't Kill Kill"), und instrumentalen Soundschraffuren, Drone- und Collageexperimenten zum anderen, bei denen selbst gebaute Klanggeräte zum Einsatz kamen und gelegentlich Gastauftritte von Free-Jazz-Musikern integriert wurden („Low and Warped", „Crunch Drone", „To the Throne of Chaos Where the Thin Flutes Pipe Mindlessly").[6] Dabei stand das thronende Chaos der Destroy-All-Monsters-Musik keineswegs bloß im Zeichen von Spontaneität und Expressivität (so wie man Free Jazz und abstrakten Expressionismus in den frühen 1960er-Jahren zusammendenken konnte). Ebenso wenig war ihr allein an bewusstseinsüberschreitenden Freak-outs oder kosmischer Wahrheitsschau gelegen (wie dies in der Kombination von Acidrock und psychedelischer Fantasykunst zum Ausdruck kam). Wiewohl er auch diese Elemente nebst vielen anderen enthielt, baute der Monsters-Sound auf einer anderen künstlerischen Grundlage auf, die im visuellen Erscheinungsbild der Gruppe beziehungsweise den parallel entstandenen bildnerischen Arbeiten ebenso zum Tragen kam wie in der musikalischen Umsetzung: lieber ein Ton daneben und eine Farbe zu viel, als in die Fänge einer wie immer gearteten technischen Präzision und Überkontrolliertheit zu geraten. Lieber den ganzen Schrott einer gerümpelartig herumliegenden Populär- und Massenkultur mit dem eigenen Schweißbrenner bearbeiten, als sich von ihm wahlweise zumüllen zu lassen oder sich vermeintlich vor ihm schützen zu müssen. Lieber den Gipfel (respektive die Niederungen) einer geschmacksverworrenen Chaotik ausloten, als sich (hoch-)kulturell erhaben davor in Sicherheit zu wähnen. Selbst wenn dabei das dünne Geflöte „niedrigen" Kulturversatzes endlos in den überstrapazierten Gehirnwindungen nachhallen sollte. [ABB·119–122]

Solcherlei „Medien-Hopping" – Malen mit gleichsam musikalischen Mitteln, Musizieren mit den Mitteln der Malerei – sollte sich gerade in der Vor- und Nachgeschichte dessen, was gemeinhin als die „Punkjahre" gilt (1976/1977), häufig wiederfinden. Neben der eher insularen Laborsituation, welche Mike Kelley und Co. in Ann Arbor für sich eingerichtet hatten, war es in den Jahren 1972 bis 1976 unter anderem Cleveland, Ohio, wo sich ein vergleichbares Szenario ausbilden sollte. Aus der lokalen, im Umfeld diverser Art Departments existierenden Szene rekrutierte sich ein loser Verbund aus renitenten Drop-outs und Misfits, die in der Folge immer mehr zu MusikerInnen mutierten und retrospektiv zu den wichtigsten WegbereiterInnen der Punkästhetik – sowohl in der

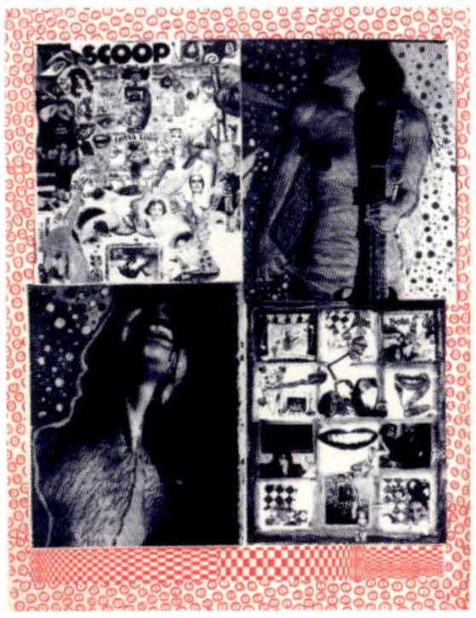

119–122
Destroy All Monsters - Geisha This. A Compilation of the first six issues of Destroy All Monsters magazine, 1975–1979, Book Beat Gallery, Oak Park, Michigan, 1995

kind of technical precision and super-control. Rather have a go with a blow torch at all the pop and mass culture trash lying around in heaps than choose to be smothered by it or try to protect yourself from it. Rather explore the peaks (and the troughs) of a chaos of bad taste than pretend to be immune to it from behind the walls of high culture. Even if this meant that the watered-down flutes of "low" culture's edifices should never cease to echo in the overheated corridors of the mind. [ILL·119–122]

This kind of "media hopping"—painting with what amounts to musical means, making music with the tools of painting—was frequently encountered in the run up to and aftermath of what has come to be seen as the "punk years" of 1976 and 1977. In addition to the rather insular laboratory set-ups that Mike Kelley and co. had created in Ann Arbor, between 1972 and 1976 Cleveland, Ohio, also saw a comparable scenario. From the local scene centered around various art departments there formed a loose group of renitent drop-outs and misfits, who then transformed more and more into musicians and—looking back—can now be numbered among the most important pioneers of punk aesthetics, both in music and in its visual manifestations.[7] Groups like Rocket from the Tombs, Electric Eels, Mirrors, and Pere Ubu were eminently interested in art (the term "artrock" was invented for them some time later), as is evidenced by their being labeled under "anti-music" or "art terrorism," both key signals of a decidedly anti-idealist approach to art. This also frequently comes to the fore in retrospective descriptions of live performances, which must have been extremely confrontational at times, and it is also evident in some cover designs, such as those done by the painter and musician John Morton for his group Electric Eels. The cover of the Eels single *Cyclotron/Agitated* [ILL·123] that was recorded in 1975 and published posthumously in 1978 shows a Fauvist scribble, in which all kinds of everyday objects (a table, a cup, a house etc.) are whirling through space as if there was nothing to hold on to for anything or anyone, and no point of reference for the eye, for the sense of direction, or for what is seen as good taste. As if they had been subjected to the cyclotron of the song title and given broken German titles, the wild and fragmented characters seem to adhere completely to the idea of brutally frank anti-art. Graphic works like these, which could be said to be a kind of "liberation of signs from below"—are a prototype of what was to be openly celebrated only a short time later in the large-format works of Jean-Michel Basquiat and other graffiti-influenced painters. And decades later

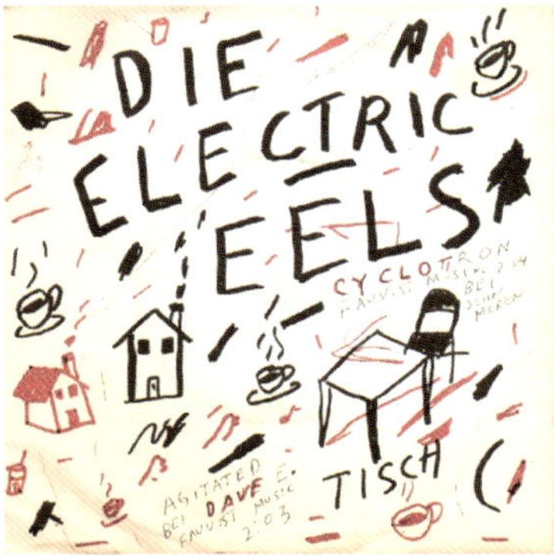

123
The Electric Eels – Cyclotron / Agitated Single, Rough Trade, 1978, Gestaltung / art work: John Morton

Musik als auch deren visuellen Erscheinungsformen – gezählt werden.[7] Wie kunstaffin das Auftreten der Gruppen Rocket from the Tombs, Electric Eels, Mirrors oder Pere Ubu war – nicht umsonst wurde für sie später das Label Artrock geprägt –, lässt sich allein schon an deren Etikettierung als „Antimusik" beziehungsweise „Kunstterrorismus", beides zentrale Wegmarken einer dezidiert antiidealistischen Kunstauffassung, ablesen. Dieses Moment kommt in retrospektiven Beschreibungen der Bandauftritte, die bisweilen äußerst konfrontativ angelegt waren, wiederholt zur Sprache, darüber hinaus ist es auch in den gelegentlichen Covergestaltungen präsent, wie sie etwa der Maler/Musiker John Morton für seine Gruppe Electric Eels vornahm. So zeigt das Cover der 1975 aufgenommenen und posthum veröffentlichten Eeels-Single *Cyclotron/Agitated* (1978) [ABB·123] ein fauvistisches Gekritzel, in dem allerlei Alltagsobjekte (Tisch, Tasse, Haus et cetera) durch den Raum wirbeln, als gäbe es keinen Halt für nichts und niemanden, weder für das Auge noch für den Orientierungssinn oder den vermeintlich guten Geschmack. Wie von dem im Songtitel angeführten Zyklotron erfasst und mit gebrochen deutschen Beschriftungen versehen, wirken die wild hingefetzten Bildzeichen, als wären sie ganz dem Konzept einer nichts beschönigenden Antikunst verpflichtet. Grafiken wie diese – man könnte vom Ansatz her von einer „Zeichenbefreiung von unten" sprechen – sind ein Prototyp dessen, was kurze Zeit später in den Großformaten eines Jean-Michel Basquiat und anderer graffitibeeinflusster MalerInnen regelrecht zelebriert werden sollte. Und noch Dekaden später hat dieser Stil nichts an Faszination eingebüßt, betrachtet man etwa das Cover der 2004 erschienenen Destroy-All-Monsters-CD *Live in Tokyo & Osaka 1996* [ABB·124]. Unbestreitbar entsprechen das betont Grobe und bewusst Naive dieser Formgebung dem, was Musikstücke wie das besagte „Cyclotron" oder einen Gutteil der Destroy-All-Monsters-Experimente in all ihrer ungestümen, antivirtuosen Vehemenz auszeichnet.

Antivirtuosität bei gleichzeitiger Betonung einer besonderen kulturellen Dringlichkeit – dem Insistieren darauf, dass das eigene Anliegen beziehungsweise Lebensgefühl im öffentlichen und sozialen Leben schlichtweg kein Ventil fand –, diese Koppelung sollte schließlich ein Markenzeichen dessen werden, was unter diversen Signets wie „New York Noise", „Downtown Scene" oder „No Wave"-Bewegung bis heute nachwirkt und eine zentrale Stelle in der Genealogie der „Falschton- und Fehlfarbenkunst" einnimmt.[8] Dabei stellt No Wave einen umfassenden Komplex dar, der heute

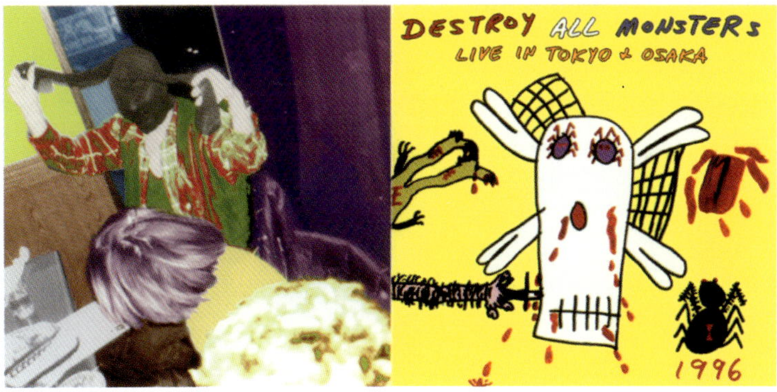

124
Destroy All Monsters – Live in Tokyo & Osaka 1996, Compound Annex Records, 2004, Malerei / painting: Sevan Boosinger

this style has lost none of its fascination, as the cover of the 2004 Destroy All Monsters CD *Live in Tokyo & Osaka 1996* [ILL·124] shows. Without doubt the exaggeratedly raw and the deliberately naive form of these artworks corresponds to the characteristically energetic, rough and anti-virtuoso music like "Cyclotron" and a large number of the Destroy All Monsters experiments.

Anti-virtuosity coupled with an emphasis on a special cultural urgency—an insistence that your key concerns and way of life found no outlet in public and social contexts—was ultimately to become a key feature of a movement that went under names like "New York Noise," "Downtown Scene," and "No Wave." This is still influential to this day, and occupies a central place in the genealogy of the "art of false notes and off-colors."[8] No Wave stands for a comprehensive phenomenon, which is often wrongly identified with punk today. Its specific New York manifestation, concentrated around a few concert bars in the years 1973 to 1977,[9] had by 1978 long left the emergent noise movement behind and moved in the direction of an even more radical confrontation with the atonal and disharmonic. The fine arts, performance, poetry, music, and film were the genres involved, with more or less equal status, although there seems to have been a slight preference for music and film, especially among fine artists.[10] A classical example of this kind of work across different fields is seen in a compressed form in the short film *Black Box* (1978) [ILL·125–127] made by the couple Beth B & Scott B. Here, too, the issue is an exorcism of monsters, using especially monstrous means and all of the artistic genres named above. Inspired by an Amnesty International report on torture chambers that were made in the USA and exported to totalitarian regimes, the film stages the kidnapping of a youth and his subsequent "treatment" in one of these torture boxes. The room where all this takes place is only decorated with large paintings done in rough strokes, showing bodies stretched out on instruments of torture. Slowly the victim is brought ever closer to resembling these images, and becomes the signifier of a brutal torture himself. Finally he finds himself in the actual "black box," an isolation cell, where an ugly and exaggerated cacophony of electronic noise introduces the actual torture. The soundtrack is like pure No Wave, and the torturess is Lydia Lunch, at the time a member of her first band Teenage Jesus & The Jerks and influential on the style of the whole scene and here a brilliant embodiment of everything evil and malignant. The "painterly" quality of *Black Box* consists to some degree in the fact that the film

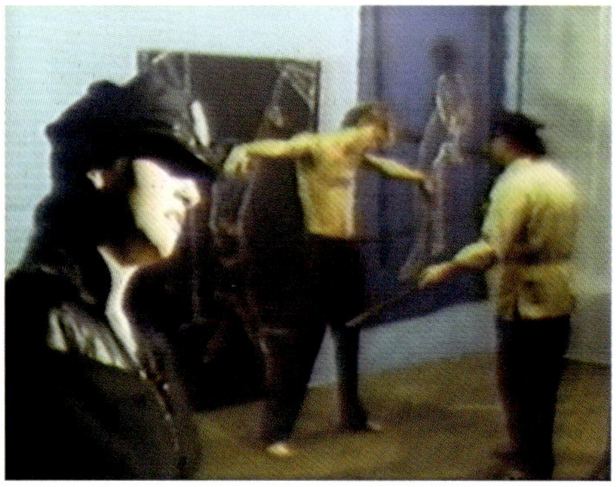

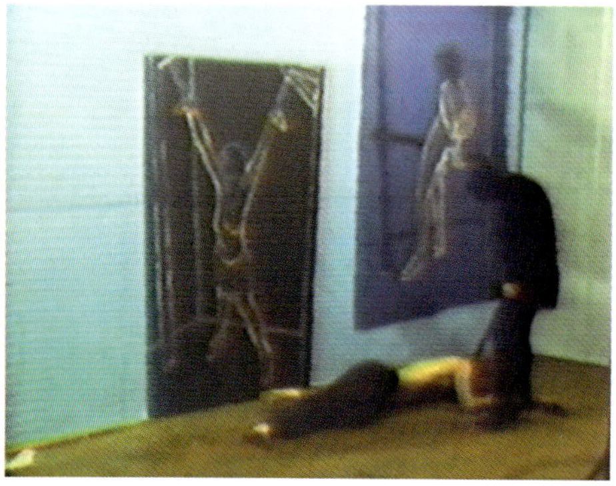

fälschlicherweise oft mit Punk identifiziert wird. Dessen spezifische New-Yorker Ausprägung, wie sie in den Jahren 1973 bis 1977 rund um einige wenige Konzertbars bestand,[9] hatte die ab 1978 auftauchende Noisebewegung längst hinter sich gelassen beziehungsweise in Richtung einer noch unversöhnlicheren Konfrontation mit dem Atonalen und Disharmonischen weiterentwickelt. Bildende Kunst, Performance, Poetry, Musik und Film bildeten weitgehend egalitäre Sparten dieses Komplexes, wobei ein leichter Hang, vor allem vonseiten bildender KünstlerInnen, in Richtung Musik und Film zu existieren schien.[10] Ein klassisches Beispiel solch feldübergreifenden Arbeitens findet sich komprimiert im Kurzfilm *Black Box* (1978) [ABB·125–127] des Paares Beth B & Scott B. Auch darin geht es um einen Fall von Monsteraustreibung – mit durchaus monströsen Mitteln, die sich sämtlicher genannter Kunstsparten bedienen. Inspiriert von einem Amnesty-Report über Folterkammern, die in den USA gefertigt und an totalitäre Regime exportiert wurden, inszeniert der Film das Kidnapping eines Jugendlichen und seine anschließende „Behandlung" in einer dieser Folterboxen. Der Raum, in dem das ganze stattfindet, enthält als einzige Ausstattung großformatige, mit groben Strichen operierende Malereien von auf Folterinstrumente gespannten Körpern. Langsam wird das Opfer immer mehr diesen Bildinhalten anverwandelt, wird selbst zum Signifikanten einer gröblichen Zurichtung. Schließlich findet er sich in der eigentlichen „Black Box", einer Isolierzelle, wieder, wo eine grässlich übersteuerte Kakofonie aus elektronischen Störgeräuschen die eigentliche Tortur einleitet. Der Soundtrack ist gleichsam No Wave pur, die Foltermagd Lydia Lunch, damals gerade mit ihrer ersten Band Teenage Jesus & The Jerks stilprägend für die ganze Szene, eine kongeniale Verkörperung alles Bösen und Schlechten. Die „malerische" Qualität von *Black Box* besteht nicht zuletzt darin, dass der Film seine BetrachterInnen (wie sein „reales" Opfer) auf immer engmaschigere Weise einzufangen beginnt und schließlich kräftig durchschüttelt – so wie Don Van Vliet dies später für seine Bilder behaupten sollte.

Black Box ist nur eines von dutzenden Beispielen aus dem No-Wave-Zusammenhang, worin ein Moment der medialen Übertragung und Verschaltung – von Musik und Film, aber auch von Malerei und Dichtung – wirksam wird.[11] Drei Jahre später (1981) sollte Jean-Michel Basquiat in dem Film *Downtown 81* als junger, brotloser Künstler durch die wie ausgebombt wirkende New-Yorker Lower East Side wandern.[12] Ein Gemälde mit sich tragend, das er schließlich einer wohlgesonnenen

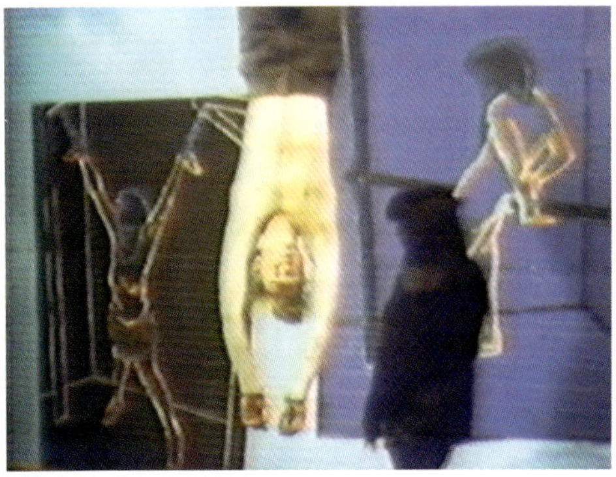

125–127
Black Box
Regie / director: Beth B & Scott B,
USA 1978, Filmstills

gradually sucks in its viewers (just like the "real" victim) and takes control of them, then shakes them up good and proper—as Don Van Vliet later said his paintings should do.

Black Box is only one of dozens of examples from No Wave in which an element of media crossover and interweaving—of music and film, and also painting and poetry—takes effect.[11] Three years later, in 1981, Jean-Michel Basquiat was to stroll through the New York Lower East Side—looking as if it had been bombed out—as a young penniless artist in the film *Downtown 81*.[12] Carrying a painting, which he finally sells to a well-meaning rich collector, Basquiat visits various locations in a cultural scene where it is primarily music that is being made (James White & The Blacks, DNA). As an artist he is clearly able to pointedly identify the excessive nature of his own approach: "When I tell people that I am an artist, they usually say, 'What's your medium?' I usually say, 'Extra-large.'" Many of his paintings to come would be indeed extra large, and their rather bare images and characters—a mix of children's drawings, borrowings from Primitivism, and street graffiti—can be best compared to the rough and shrill guitar music of Arto Lindsay (DNA). Lydia Lunch's crude short bursts on an untuned guitar may also have been a model for Basquiat's scribbly speed painting, as also the saxophone hypertrophy of James White and the obsession of early hip-hop culture [ILL·128] with break beat that was just emerging at the time. Like many other painters in this scene, Basquiat also had his own band project (called Gray) and also worked as a music producer, which can certainly be seen as an extension of his production of images.[13] The expansion of his audacious signs and characters, which seem as if taken straight off the street, into a four-dimensional space and the appertaining scene was logical enough, since painting and music, as Basquiat went about them, were based on a common milieu and the shift from one to the other amounted to a kind of return or retranslation into an original context. Visual-acoustic experience, having gone through all kinds of artistic processors, was to be fed back into the very place where it originated—as a stimulant drawn from everyday life: the studio (which was also a dilapidated place to live), the street (which was also a devastated panorama of society), the club (which was a self-selected milieu and provided a kind of link between the other two).[14]

At the time of the making of *Downtown 81*, Basquiat's artistic life was still fairly evenly distributed between these areas (studio and painting, street and graffiti, club and music and poetry), but this quickly changed after his first large gallery shows and his participation in Documenta 1982. It is interesting that in general in the early 1980s the whole field of the "downtown" scene underwent a dynamic of change, similar to that which music and painting had first been subjected to. In the case of music, either the explosive vehemence and experimental stylistic diversity of the pioneering years 1978 to 1981 had lost steam—as had happened in post-punk in a larger context and other places,[15] or the energy that had been released in this intensive phase was now channeled into more straightforward and ultimately domesticated genre definitions: sleek and plain club music, or hip-hop, which was now slowly gaining a global dimension, and, on the other hand, also the equally marketable and

reichen Sammlerin verkauft, klappert Basquiat diverse Orte seines kulturellen Umfeldes ab, wo in erster Linie rabiate Musik fabriziert wird (James White & The Blacks, DNA). Als Künstler weiß er die Maßlosigkeit seines eigenen Anspruchs durchaus pointiert einzuschätzen: „Wenn ich erzähle, dass ich Künstler bin, fragen mich die Leute meistens: ‚Welches Medium?' Ich antworte für gewöhnlich: ‚Extra large.'" Extragroß sollten in der Folge zahlreiche seiner Malereien ausfallen, deren lapidar hingeworfene Bildzeichen – eine Mischung aus Kinderzeichnung, primitivistischen Anleihen und Straßengraffiti – bestens den schroff geformten und schrill kolorierten Gitarrenfiguren eines Arto Lindsay (DNA) entsprachen. Auch Lydia Lunchs rüde Kürzestattacken auf einer ungestimmten Gitarre mögen Pate gestanden haben bei Basquiats krakeliger Schnellmalerei, aber ebenso die Saxofonhypertrophie von James White oder die zeitgleich einsetzende Breakbeatobsession der frühen Hip-Hop-Kultur. [ABB·128] Wie viele andere MalerInnen dieser Szene hatte auch Basquiat sein eigenes Bandprojekt[13] (namens Gray) und trat zudem als Musikproduzent in Erscheinung, was sich durchaus als Verlängerung seiner bildnerischen Produktion betrachten lässt. Die Expansion der widerständigen, gleichsam auf der Straße aufgelesenen Zeichen in den vierdimensionalen Raum und dessen Szeneagglomerate lag hier insofern auf der Hand, als Malerei und Musik, wie Basquiat sie betrieb, auf einer gemeinsamen milieuhaften Basis fußten, es also um eine Art Rückerstattung respektive Rückübersetzung in den Ausgangskontext ging. Die visuell-akustische Erfahrung, nachdem sie durch allerlei künstlerische Prozessoren hindurchgegangen war, sollte also genau dorthin zurückgefüttert werden, wo sie sich als lebensweltliche Stimulanz herleitete: Studio (das zugleich heruntergekommene Wohnstätte war), Straße (die zugleich ein devastiertes Sozialpanorama bot), Club (der als selbst gewähltes Milieu sozusagen der Link zwischen den anderen beiden darstellte)[14].

War Basquiats künstlerisches Leben zur Zeit der Dreharbeiten von *Downtown 81* noch relativ gleichmäßig zwischen diesen Bereichen (Studio – Malerei, Straße – Graffiti, Club – Musik/Poetry) verteilt, so sollte sich dies mit seinen ersten großen Galerienausstellungen beziehungsweise der Documenta-Teilnahme 1982 rasch ändern. Insgesamt scheint interessant, dass das gesamte Feld der so genannten Downtown-Szene zu Beginn der 1980er-Jahre von einer Dynamik erfasst wurde, der Musik und Malerei zunächst auf durchaus vergleichbare Weise ausgesetzt waren. Was Erstere

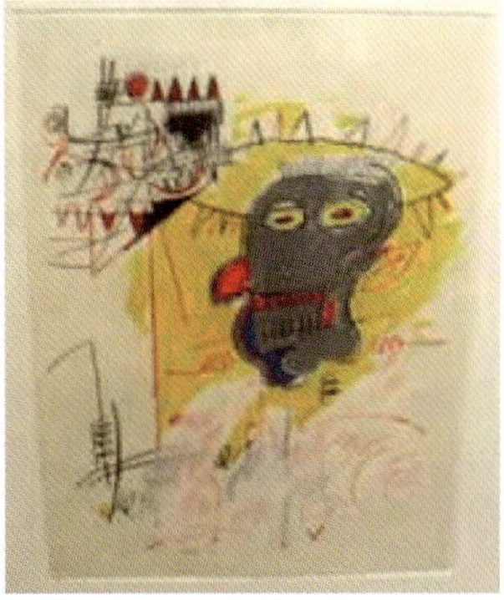

128 **Jean-Michel Basquiat**
Famous Negro Athletes # 4, 1981
(berühmte schwarze Athleten #4)
Kreide auf Papier / crayon on paper

commercial "noise scene." Painting developed in a similar way, but rather more one-dimensionally. Whereas the "bad painting" of Basquiat, Kenny Scharf, Lee Quinones, Julian Schnabel, and many others, initially aimed to ironically subvert accepted art conventions, now the label "bad" became a signifier in the marketplace, in which all the traces of association with the Afro-American "cool" had been removed, and which, as a sign of taste, stood for a higher level of beauty.[16] The negative, the dark, and the distant, which the artistic "bad" had first intended to bring to light, was soon transformed into a new and positive, vital and expressive energy inherent to an increasingly bombastic kind of art, which then finally triumphed under the label of "Neo-Expressionism."[17]

From British to Continental Post-Punk

Ultimately the increase in categorization and marketing that began to take hold of the cultural field in the early 1980s also contributed to a stronger distinction between the two areas of art and music (and numerous sub-areas within these two). In other scenes in the West the kind of cross-over between fields described above had also already taken place, with music, performance, painting, film, graphic design, and other genres beginning to draw their ideas from one and the same source. Certain examples of this from the British and continental European context serve to show that this phenomenon was not media-immanent, but—and decisively—derived from an approach that cut across all these areas with an explosive "external energy." The English artist and musician Linder (full name Linder Sterling) is an exemplary case for the interconnection of media and genres. She hardly ever entered the public arena as a "painter," and worked in graphic design and photomontage in Manchester in the mid-1970s, but she saw her materials—photos from magazines and a scalpel—as her very own "painting tools."[18] This painting with graphic and found materials led to a number of exciting cut-up montages that became influential for punk and post-punk aesthetics—a good example is the famous picture of a naked female torso with an electric iron instead of a head that the Buzzcocks used on the cover of their single *Orgasm Addict* (1977). Moreover, the montage technique was translated into the "angular" style of Linder's band Ludus, which powerfully dismantled any notion of pleasant harmony with broken rhythms and shrill vocal bursts. Programmatic titles like "Anatomy is

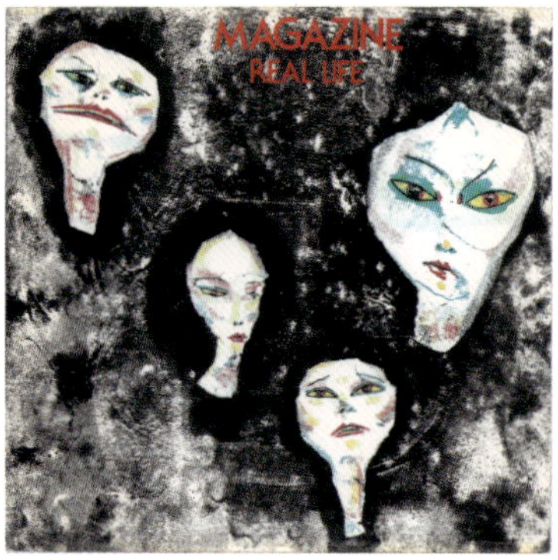

129
Magazine – Real Life
LP, Virgin Records, 1978
Gestaltung / art work: Linder (Sterling)

betrifft, so hatte sich die explosive Vehemenz und experimentelle Stilvielfalt der Aufbruchsjahre 1978 bis 1981 entweder erschöpft – so wie dies bei Postpunk im größeren Zusammenhang respektive auch andernorts der Fall war[15] –, oder aber die in dieser Ballungsphase freigesetzte Energie kanalisierte sich entlang einer überschaubaren und letztlich domestizierenden Genreeinteilung: zur immer glatter werdenden Clubmusik hier, dem langsam in globale Dimensionen vordringenden Hip-Hop da, schließlich zur ebenfalls höchst verkaufsträchtig etikettierbaren Noiseszene dort. Nicht unähnlich, obgleich viel eindimensionaler ging der historische Prozess aufseiten der Malerei vonstatten: War die „schlechte Malerei" eines Basquiat, Kenny Scharf, Lee Quinones, Julian Schnabel und vieler anderer zunächst auf die ironische Subvertierung geltender Kunstkonventionen angelegt gewesen, so verfestigte sich das Label „bad" alsbald zu einem marktgängigen Signifikanten, in dem jegliche assoziative Spur mit dem afroamerikanischen „cool" getilgt war und sich geschmacklich eine höhere Stufe von Schönheit ankündigte.[16] Das Negative, Abgründige und Distanzierende, welches das künstlerisch „Schlechte" anfangs noch zutage fördern sollte, fand sich alsbald in die neue positive, vitale und ausdrucksstarke Kraft einer immer protzigeren Kunst verwandelt, deren Triumph schließlich mit dem Label „Neoexpressionismus" besiegelt wurde.[17]

Von britischem zu kontinentalem Postpunk

Letztlich trug der Kategorisierungs- und Vermarktungsschub, der das kulturelle Feld ab Beginn der 1980er-Jahre zu erfassen begann, mit dazu bei, dass die Bereiche Kunst und Musik (und innerhalb von beiden zahlreiche Subbereiche) wieder stärker voneinander getrennt wurden. Dabei hatten zuvor auch in anderen westlichen Szenen Feldüberlagerungen der beschriebenen Art stattgefunden, wonach Musik, Performance, Malerei, Film, Grafikdesign und andere Sparten begannen, sich aus ein und derselben Antriebsquelle zu speisen. Wie wenig medienimmanent diese zu fassen ist, sondern – viel entscheidender – auf eine all diese Bereiche durchkreuzende und mit „externer Energie" aufsprengende Haltung zurückgeht, dies lässt sich auch an ausgewählten Beispielen aus dem britischen und kontinentaleuropäischen Kontext ablesen. Die englische Künstlerin und Musikerin Linder (mit vollem Namen Linder Sterling) mag exemplarisch für den Zusammenhang der genannten Medien und Sparten stehen. Wiewohl sie kaum je als Malerin in Erscheinung trat, betrachtete die im Manchester der mittleren 1970er-Jahre vorwiegend mit Grafikdesign und Fotocollage befasste Künstlerin ihre Materialien – Zeitschriftenfotos und Skalpell – als ihre ureigensten „Malwerkzeuge".[18] Diese Malerei mit grafischen beziehungsweise vorgefundenen Mitteln produzierte eine Reihe spannungsgeladener Cut-up-Montagen, die stilbildend für die Punk- und Postpunkästhetik wurden – man denke nur an das berühmte Bild eines nackten Frauenkörpers mit einem Bügeleisen anstelle des Kopfes, das als Covermotiv der Single *Orgasm Addict* (1977) der Buzzcocks Verwendung fand. Darüber hinaus übersetzte sich diese Verschnitttechnik auch in den „angularen" Stil ihrer Band Ludus, die mit gebrochenen Rhythmen und schrillen Vokaleruptionen jede Wohlfühlharmonik nachhaltig demontierte. Program-

not Destiny" and the ironic "My Cherry is in Sherry" helped to create a pop-feminist space, in which a general skepticism toward the world was coupled with undomesticated exuberance. One of Linder's most absurd works is found on the front cover (again as a cover design) of the record *Real Life* (1978) by the group Magazine [ILL·129]. This is not painting in the strict sense of the word, but rather a monoprint. It shows four strangely misshapen heads that emerge like nightmarish ghosts from a patchy black-and-white maelstrom-like background. The faces are overly made up with garish colors (turquoise, green, yellow) and seem like they had been ripped off the heads of their wearers like larvae—as if something real were being revealed that can only be made accessible via the use of distorted and discolored masks. This ensemble of grimaces is shockingly diffuse, and it touches a reality that can only be identified by means of "bad," deformed, and "disturbed" images. An image of off-colors and false notes that is characteristic of the post-punk constellation.

Similarly crude and disparate forms are found on the cover designs of various British post-punk acts, often made by band members themselves or close associates, whereby graphic work clearly outnumbers painting. Nonetheless, a range of "unpainterly" paintings can be discerned in the images of groups like the Raincoats, The Slits, Delta 5, The Fall and Pop Group, all of which made a kind of scribbled and abstruse graphic art and painting a trademark of the visual packaging. On the debut single *She is Beyond Good and Evil* (1979) [ILL·130] by Pop Group there are Arnulf-Rainer-like streaks and scratches, in black and white and bright red, that evoke an abstract and domed all-consuming Hades. On the back cover there is a bold pieta, with sharp angles like in a woodcut, which could hardly be more out of place. The record *Kangaroo?* (1981) [ILL·131] by Red Crayola with Art & Language offers an even more prominent example of this kind of fiery and bold painting. A Baselitz-like motif of an animal standing on its head seems comparatively friendly and warm, at least as far as the colors are concerned, and it is like an emblem of the relatively harmonious music made by Crayola at this time. Mayo Thompson, who had already worked with Art & Language previously, had come to London in 1976, where he became impresario and regular producer for the Rough Trade labels and also played a key role in bringing together music and the fine arts. From 1979 the new band Red Crayola began to publish its music—to distinguish it from Thompson's first psychedelic formation

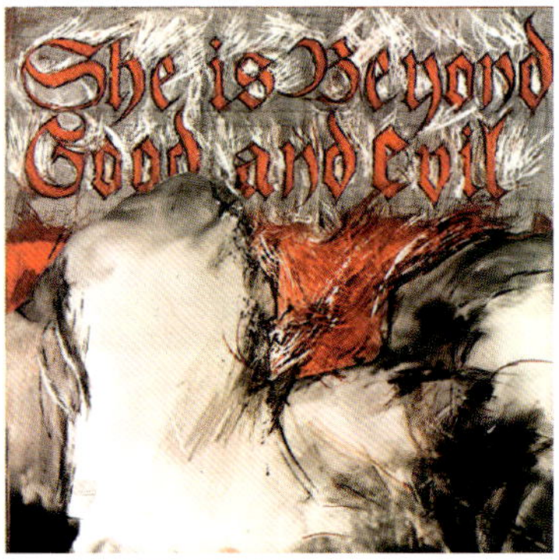

130
Pop Group – She is Beyond Good and Evil, Single, Radarscope Records, 1979

matische Stücke wie „Anatomy is not Destiny“ oder das ironische „My Cherry is in Sherry“ halfen mit, einen popfeministischen Resonanzraum zu kreieren, in dem sich eine generelle Weltdistanz und undomestizierter Überschwang miteinander verbanden. Eine von Linders abwegigsten Arbeiten findet sich – einmal mehr als Coverdesignerin in Erscheinung tretend – auf der Vorderseite der Platte *Real Life* (1978) der Gruppe Magazine [ABB·129]. Keine Malerei im strengen Sinn, sondern ein so genannter Monoprint, zeigt das Bild vier merkwürdig verunstaltete Köpfe, die wie albtraumhafte Chimären aus einem schwarz-weiß gefleckten, strudelartigen Hintergrund auftauchen. Die mit grellen Farbspuren (türkis/grün, gelb) überschminkten Gesichter wirken, als wären sie ihren TrägerInnen wie Larven vom Kopf gerissen – als sollte dadurch ein Reales enthüllt werden, das nur über den Umweg verzerrter und verfärbter Masken zugänglich ist. Das in seiner Diffusität erschreckende Fratzenensemble rührt an eine Wirklichkeit, die nur über „schlechte“, deformierte, ja, „gestörte“ Abbilder greifbar wird. Ein Fehlfarben- und Falschtonbild, wie es für die Postpunkkonstellation charakteristisch ist.

Ähnlich krud-disparate Formgebungen finden sich in zahlreichen Covergestaltungen diverser britischer Postpunkacts, vielfach ausgeführt von Bandmitgliedern selbst oder ihrem engeren Umfeld, wobei ein deutlicher Überhang von grafischen gegenüber malerischen Verfahren existiert. Dennoch lässt sich eine ganze Reihe von „unmalerischen“ Malereien im Erscheinungsbild von Gruppen wie The Raincoats, The Slits, Delta 5, The Fall oder The Pop Group finden, welche allesamt eine Art von krakelig-abstrusem Grafik- und Malstil zum Markenzeichen ihres visuellen Packaging machten. Auf der Debütsingle *She is Beyond Good and Evil* (1979) [ABB·130] von The Pop Group ist es ein Arnulf-Rainer-haftes Gewische und Gekratze, das, ganz in Schwarz-Weiß und knalligem Rot gehalten, einen abstrakt gewölbten, alles verschlingenden Orkus evoziert. Auf der Rückseite prangt dazu, holzschnittartig und scharfkantig, eine Pietà, die in diesem Zusammenhang deplatzierter nicht sein könnte. Die Platte *Kangaroo?* (1981) [ABB·131] von The Red Crayola with Art & Language bietet ein noch prominenteres Beispiel solch feurig-dreister Malerei. Vergleichsweise freundlich und warm, zumindest was die Farbgebung betrifft, wirkt das Motiv des Baselitz-haft auf dem Kopf stehenden Tieres wie ein Emblem der zu diesem Zeitpunkt relativ versöhnlich klingenden Crayola-Musik. Mayo Thompson, der zuvor schon mit Art & Language zusammengearbeitet hatte, war 1976 nach London gekommen,

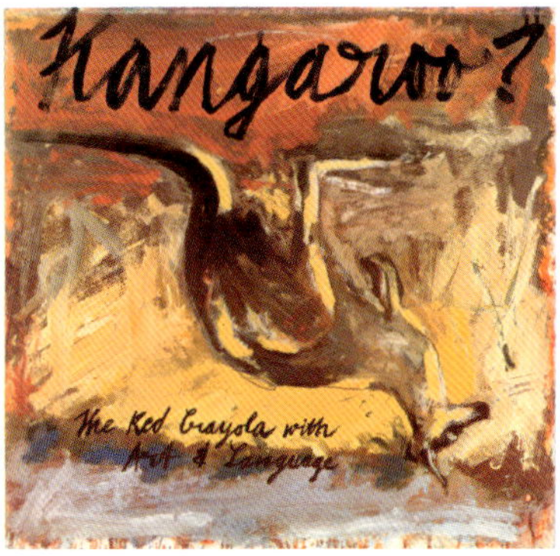

131
The Red Crayola – Kangaroo?
LP, Rough Trade, 1981

of the late 1960s (The Red Krayola) the name was now written with a C. In the Art & Language context, which was conceptual and concerned with the philosophy of language, it was all the more surprising to find an early 1980s Red-Crayola record adorned with the epitome of a neo-expressionist picture. But perhaps this was just an appropriate contemporary comment on a style that was then just starting to conquer the art market, or a tongue-in-cheek reflection of the music, which was now much more harmonious and even sugar sweet (although the texts were even more forceful Marxist critiques —"The Mistakes of Trotzky," "The Principles of Party Organisation," and "A Portrait of V. I. Lenin in the Style of Jackson Pollock"). In any case, music and painting here began to move away from each other again and now did no more than to mutually refer to and comment on each other, which had certainly not been the case in the earlier phases of No Wave and anti-aesthetics. And it was not long before the British post-punk context saw a far sleeker and more attractive approach to both sound and visual design, as happened increasingly from 1982.

But before all this, and elsewhere, there were significant and intensive phases of deliberate and experimental overlapping and transgression across the artistic genres. A link between New York and Berlin played an important role in this. Martin Kippenberger had just opened Kippenbergers Büro in Berlin, a kind of Factory, and he was also the co-manager of the music club S.O.36, when he met the New York No Wave film maker Eric Mitchell and the musician Christine Hahn, who played in Glenn Branca's band The Static, among others. Together they recorded a double single in April 1979, using the band name Luxus. They were extremely tasteless and provocative, as the first title on the record, "New York – Auschwitz," shows. With street noises in the background, the piece includes fragments of a conversation featuring linguistic barriers between Germans and Americans and absurd misunderstandings, here with a pun on Auschwitz and "my arse sweats": "[K:] Die Hose. Lederhose. – [H:] Lederhose? – [K:] Mein Arsch schwitzt. – [H:] Auschwitz?" In the piece entitled "Love Song" a subdued voice stubbornly repeats the line "Can't Buy Me Love" a capella, whilst "Pretty Good" is a ragged strumming instrumental, and "Falsch verbunden" (Wrong Number) mocks the German nursery rhyme "Alle meine Entlein." Kippenberger performed several times with this group, which later was joined by his partner at S.O.36, Achim Schächtele, and he saw music-making without doubt as an

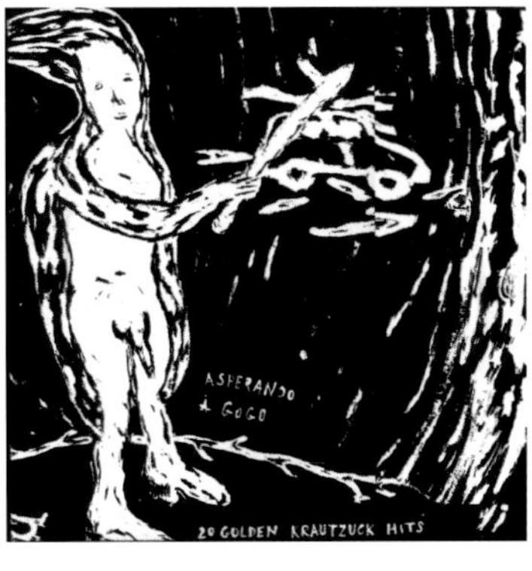

132 Peter Bömmels
Der heilige Wolfsburg, 1982
Cover für / for Asperando a Gogo – 20 Krautzuck Hits, LP, Styrophon Records 1997

um dort nicht nur zum Impresario und Hausproduzenten des Rough-Trade-Labels zu werden, sondern auch an der Engführung von Musik und bildender Kunst maßgeblichen Anteil zu haben. Ab 1979 erschienen eigene Veröffentlichungen der neu formierten The Red Crayola – im Unterschied zu Thompsons erster psychedelischer Formation Ende der 1960er-Jahre (The Red Krayola) nunmehr mit C geschrieben. Im Umfeld der konzeptuell und sprachphilosophisch orientierten Art & Language überraschte es zu Beginn der 1980er-Jahre umso mehr, den Inbegriff eines neoexpressionistischen Bildes auf einer Red-Crayola-Platte vorzufinden. Aber vielleicht war dies auch nur der zeitgemäße Kommentar auf den damals gerade den Kunstmarkt erobernden Stil; oder das augenzwinkernde Pendant zu der nunmehr ungleich harmonischer und teils süßlich wirkenden Musik – wobei die Texte umso eindringlicher im Zeichen marxistischer Analyse standen („The Mistakes of Trotzky", „The Principles of Party Organisation" oder „A Portrait of V. I. Lenin in the Style of Jackson Pollock"). Jedenfalls begannen sich Musik und Malerei hier bereits wieder voneinander zu lösen und ließen sich allenfalls im Sinne einer wechselseitigen Kommentierung aufeinander beziehen, so wie dies in den zuvor beschriebenen Phasen von No Wave und Antiästhetik genau nicht der Fall gewesen war. Auch im britischen Postpunkumfeld sollte es schließlich nicht mehr lange dauern, bis – sukzessive ab 1982 – ein ungleich glätterer und gefälligerer Erscheinungsmodus Einzug in Sounddesign und visuelle Gestaltung hielt.

Doch zuvor kam es auch andernorts noch zu signifikanten Ballungsphasen, was das forcierte Übertragungs- und Überschreitungsspiel zwischen den Kunstsparten betraf. Die Achse New York–Berlin spielte dabei keine unwesentliche Rolle: Martin Kippenberger hatte in Berlin gerade Kippenbergers Büro, eine Art Factory, eröffnet und war Kobetreiber des Musikclubs S.O.36 geworden, als er den New-Yorker No-Wave-Filmemacher Eric Mitchell und die Musikerin Christine Hahn – sie spielte unter anderem in Glenn Brancas Band The Static – kennen lernte. Gemeinsam nahmen sie im April 1979 eine Doppelsingle unter dem Bandnamen Luxus auf. Wie abgeschmackt und provokant das Ensemble agierte, lässt sich am ersten Stück der Platte, „New York – Auschwitz", ermessen. Zu Straßenlärm im Hintergrund hört man Gesprächsfetzen, in denen deutsch-amerikanische Sprachbarrieren und abseitige Missverständnisse im Mittelpunkt stehen: „[K:] Die Hose. Lederhose. – [H:] Lederhose? – [K:] Mein Arsch schwitzt. – [H:] Auschwitz?" Im Stück „Love Song" wird mit gepresster Stimme und a cappella stur die Zeile „Can't Buy Me Love" wiederholt, während es in „Pretty Good" dann instrumental – zackig schrummend – zur Sache geht und schließlich in „Falsch verbunden" das Kinderlied „Alle meine Entlein" zerschrammt wird. Kippenberger, der mit dieser Formation – später gehörte ihr auch sein Kompagnon im S.O.36, Achim Schächtele, an – mehrfach auftrat, sah im Musikmachen zweifellos eine Art von verlängertem Arm seiner Malerei. Keinen Schauplatzwechsel oder eine abgekoppelte Parallelbeschäftigung, sondern ein Ausagieren von Motorik, Showgehabe und nicht zuletzt Peinlichkeit, wie sie die Malerei nur bedingt in sich aufnehmen konnte. Als selbstverständlicher „Teil der künstlerischen Produktion" war die Musik „wie die Einladungskarten, Plakate und Kataloge"[19] –

extension of his painting. This was not a change of scene or a distinct parallel interest, but rather the acting out of movement, show, and not least a kind of embarrassment, that could only be done up to a point in painting. As a natural "part of artistic production," music, "like the invitation cards, posters, and catalogs,"[19] was neither subordinate nor superior to any other areas Kippenberger worked in—and he was to come back to music again and again in various ensembles and with various stylistic interests from jazz to German beat music. "The pleasure and fostering of one's own alienation and redirecting it as a strength,"[20] as this kind of self-subdivision into a myriad of experimental stages was once appropriately described, was evident at the time in many other painters/musicians. The artistic priority may have been in the visual medium (or at least retrospectively and one-sidedly been concentrated there), and yet painting and music in the years 1978 to 1982 worked on one and the same level of immanence—a horizon in which a drastic, confrontational approach and anti-virtuosity within a form of self-appointed praxis were far more dominant than any reflection on medium or material.

It is possible to see the special relations of exchange between painting and music in the German post-punk context in numerous band projects of the time. These include Der Plan, whose stage sets—reminiscent of Milan Kunc's large format works—were made by the band founder Moritz Reichelt; the oversexed electronic duo Geile Tiere, which had been set up by the Berlin "wild" painter Salome; and Nachdenkliche Wehrpflichtige (Contemplative Conscripts) or the project LSDAP/AO, with the key actors Diedrich Diederichsen and the brothers Markus and Albert Oehlen. Albert Oehlen was not only the cover designer for the Wehrpflichtige single *Politik für junge Leute* (Politics for Young People, 1980) [ILL·133]—on the cover is a groovy group of soldiers showing the soles of their boots to the viewer—but was also the band's saxophonist. The group's mix of intellectualistic soldiers', football, and workers' songs ("Hundert Mann und ein Befehl" (Hundred Men and One Command), "Heutiger Soldaten Tun und Lassen" (Today's Soldiers do Whatever They Please), etc.[21]) is imbued with exactly the same spirit of destruction and disharmony that Oehlen would later declare programmatic for his painting: "Pictures should not be authentic, but tactically correct." And: "The destructive prevents consumption, but not market success."[22] The latter—commercial success—was denied Oehlen's many band projects (and he probably thought rightly so), ranging from Nachdenkliche Wehrpflichtige to

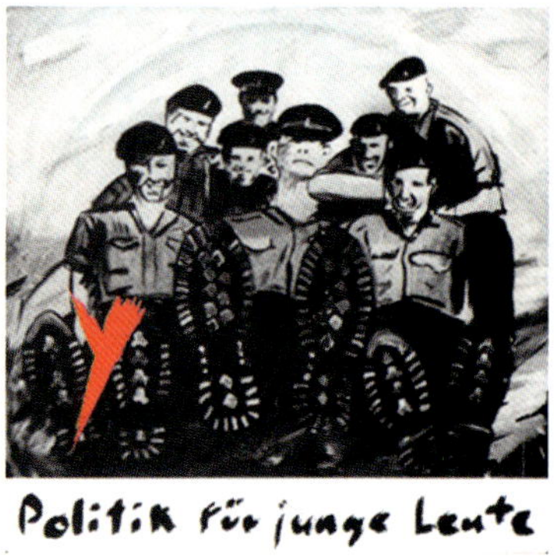

133
Nachdenkliche Wehrpflichtige –
Politik für junge Leute, EP, Zickzack
1980
Cover: Albert Oehlen

und Kippenberger sollte immer wieder in unterschiedlichen Ensembles und mit verschiedentlichen stilistischen Vorlieben von Jazz bis Schlager darauf zurückkommen – den übrigen Bereichen seiner Arbeit weder vor- noch nachgeordnet. „Genuss und Ausbau der eigenen Entfremdung und [deren] Umlenkung in eine Stärke“[20], wie dieser Modus der Selbstaufspaltung in vielfältigste Experimentierstadien einmal treffend genannt wurde, fand sich zeitgleich noch bei vielen anderen MalerInnen/MusikerInnen. Mag deren künstlerische Priorität auch im visuellen Medium gelegen haben (oder sich retrospektiv einseitig darin verfestigt haben), so bewegten sich Malerei und Musik in den Jahren 1978 bis 1982 auf ein und derselben Immanenzebene – einem Horizont, in dem Drastik, konfrontative Haltung und Antivirtuosität im Zuge einer selbstermächtigenden Praxis mehr als jede Medien- oder Materialreflexion dominierten.

Das besondere Austauschverhältnis, in dem Mal- und Musikpraxis im deutschen Postpunkkontext standen, lässt sich an vielerlei Bandprojekten der Zeit ablesen: an Der Plan (dessen Bühnendekoration die an Milan Kunc anschließenden Großformate des Bandgründers Moritz Reichelt bildeten), am übersexualisierten Elektronikduo Geile Tiere, das der Berliner „Wilde“ Salome ins Leben gerufen hatte, oder an den Nachdenklichen Wehrpflichtigen beziehungsweise dem Projekt LSDAP/AO, an denen neben Diedrich Diederichsen die Brüder Markus und Albert Oehlen maßgeblich beteiligt waren. Letzterer trat nicht nur als Covergestalter der Wehrpflichtigen-Single *Politik für junge Leute* (1980) [ABB·133] in Erscheinung – man sieht darauf eine fetzig hingemalte Gruppe von Soldaten, die den BetrachterInnen die Stiefel entgegenstrecken –, sondern auch als Saxofonist der Gruppe. Die Mischung aus intellektualisierten Soldaten-, Fußballer- und Arbeiterliedern („Hundert Mann und ein Befehl“, „Heutiger Soldaten Tun und Lassen“[21] et cetera) atmet exakt jenen Geist der Destruktion und Disharmonie, den Oehlen später programmatisch für seine Malerei formulieren sollte: „Bilder sollen nicht authentisch sein, sondern taktisch richtig.“ Und: „Das Destruktive verhindert Konsumierbarkeit, aber nicht den Markterfolg.“[22] Dieser mag den vielen Bandprojekten, denen Oehlen angehörte – von den Nachdenklichen Wehrpflichtigen über die Alma Band und The Golden Kot Quartett bis hin zur dritten Reinkarnation von The Red Krayola (ab 1993) und deren Ableger Van Oehlen –, wohlweislich versagt geblieben sein. Dafür löste er sich auf dem Kunstmarkt geradezu self-fulfilling-mäßig ein, wo das

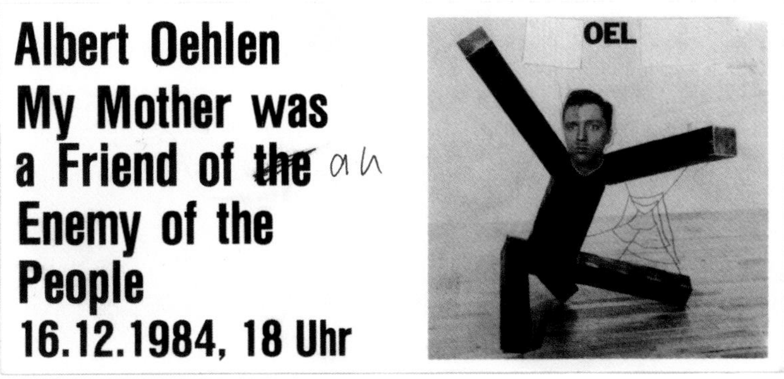

134 Albert Oehlen My Mother was a Friend of the [an] Enemy of the People, (Meine Mutter war eine Freundin des [eines] Volksfeindes), Galerie Peter Pakesch Wien, 1984, Einladungskarte

Alma Band and The Golden Kot Quartett to the third reincarnation of The Red Krayola (from 1993) and their offshoots. By contrast his remarkable success on the art market was like a self-fulfilling prophecy, with the uncultivated ugliness of his earlier pictures receiving the highest praise. In an early review, Jutta Koether described this well, and also noted that there remained something that was hard to stomach: "The nasty taste might have gone, and a few days later all the ugliness seems acceptable, although some of the leftovers are still quietly fermenting deep down in your stomach, once again forming a rebellious front."[23] It was precisely this rebellion that was at work in both Oehlen's painting and his various music projects, as an apodictic and cacophonic impetus that went against any kind of tonal balance, harmony in sound and color, and formal consistency.[24] In the following years this principle was to be pursued with vigor, as shown by exhibition titles like *The Enemies of Our Enemies Are also Our Friends* (Galerie Rudolf Zwirner, Cologne, 1983) and *My Mother Was a Friend of the Enemy of the People* (Galerie Peter Pakesch, Vienna, 1984) [ILL·134], which was borrowed from the British post-punk band Blurt.

The crossover between painting and music in the work of Martin Kippenberger and Albert Oehlen is typical of the special proximity between these media that was evident at the same time between the post-punk sound and the newly emerging *wilde Malerei* (Wild Painting). Imi Knoebel's brilliant cover picture for the record PST! (1980) [ILL·135] by the group S.Y.P.H., in which all musicality becomes a question of gesture, should be mentioned here, as also the sometimes blunt and sometimes humorous paintings of Jiri Georg Dokoupil for the publications of the group Wirtschaftswunder (Economic Boom) [ILL·136], of which his brother Tom Dokoupil was a member. Young, neo-Fauvist painting was characteristic of the Vienna band Molto Brutto too, whose first work (1982) was decorated by Gunter Damisch's and Gerwald Rockenschaub's pictogram-like thick-brush paintings [ILL·137]. Here, too, there was a jerky and erratic sound that was determined to undermine any conventional notion of melody and a corresponding pictorial language, with both of them derived from one and the same heady urgency that worked across very different media. The same can be said of many of the protagonists of the Vienna scene at the time, such as Konrad Becker's *Monotonprodukte* (Monotonous Products), which began in a way that was still strongly linked to the excessive painting of his

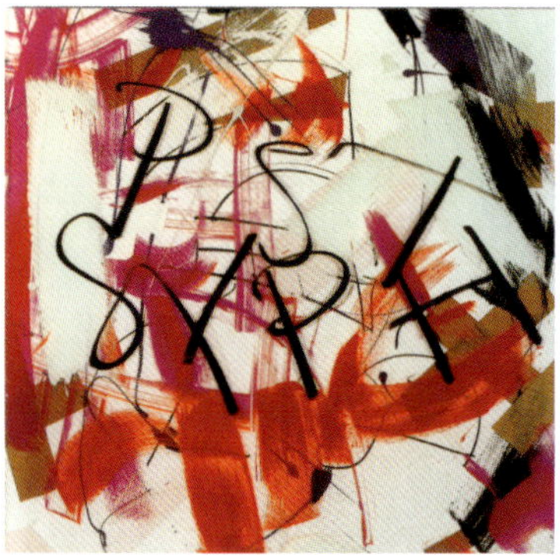

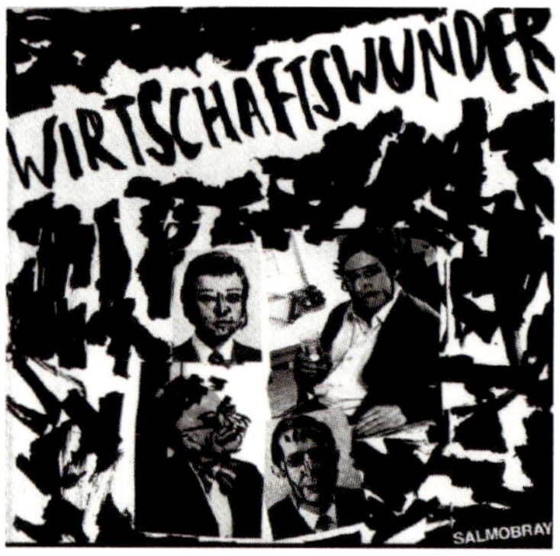

135
S.Y.P.H. – PST!
LP, Pure Freude, 1980
(Pure Pleasure)
Cover: Imi Knoebel

136
The Wirtschaftswunder – Salmobray,
LP, Zickzack, 1981
Cover: Jiri Georg Dokoupil

unkultiviert Hässliche der frühen Bilder bald schon höchst positive Resonanz erfuhr. Jutta Koether brachte dies in einer frühen Besprechung auf den Punkt, wobei sie eine gewisse Latenz des Unverdaulichen nicht in Abrede stellte: „Der unappetitliche Geschmack mag verschwunden sein, mit den Hässlichkeiten versöhnt man sich einige Tage später, auch wenn es – tief im Bauch – leise gärt und brodelt, da gewisse Rückstände erneut Front machen.“[23] Genau dieses Frontmachen war es gewesen, was in Oehlens Malerei und den diversen Musikprojekten gleichermaßen am Werk war – als jener apodiktisch vorgetragene, vom Ansatz her kakofone Impetus, der jeder tonalen Balance, (klang-) farblichen Harmonie und formellen Stimmigkeit zuwiderlief.[24] Wie sehr dieses Prinzip in den folgenden Jahren noch zum Tragen kommen sollte, zeigen alleine schon Ausstellungstitel wie *Die Feinde unserer Feinde sind auch unsere Feinde* (Galerie Rudolf Zwirner, Köln, 1983) beziehungsweise das von der britischen Postpunkband Blurt entlehnte Motto *My Mother Was a Friend of the Enemy of the People* (Galerie Peter Pakesch, Wien, 1984) [ABB·134] an.

Wenn hier exemplarisch von den Malerei-Musik-Übergängen bei Martin Kippenberger und Albert Oehlen die Rede ist, so sollte das besondere Naheverhältnis, das gleichzeitig auch anderswo zwischen Postpunksound und neu aufkeimender wilder Malerei existierte, dabei nicht ausgeblendet werden. Imi Knoebels kongeniales Coverbild für die Platte *PST!* (1980) [ABB·135] der Gruppe S.Y.P.H., auf der alle Musikalität zu einer Frage des Gestischen wird, sei hier ebenso erwähnt wie die teils stumpfen, teils humorigen Malereien von Jiri Georg Dokoupil für die Veröffentlichungen der Gruppe Wirtschaftswunder [ABB·136], in der sein Bruder Tom Dokoupil zugange war. Junge, neofauvistische Malerei prägte auch das Erscheinungsbild der Wiener Band Molto Brutto, deren Erstlingswerk (1982) Gunter Damischs und Gerwald Rockenschaubs dickpinselige, piktogrammartige Malkürzel zieren [ABB·137]. Auch hier fand sich dem nervös-scheppernden, jede geläufigere Melodik konsequent unterlaufenden Sound eine adäquate Bildsprache zur Seite gestellt oder, besser, leiteten sich beide von der gleichen ungestümen Dringlichkeit her, die quer durch unterschiedlichste Medien wirkte. Ähnliches gilt für viele weitere ProtagonistInnen der damaligen Wiener Szene, für Konrad Beckers *Monotonprodukte* etwa, die anfangs noch stark auf die Malereiexzesse seiner Partnerin Eugenia Rochas abgestimmt waren, oder Hans Weigands feldübergreifende Praxis, die zwischen Skulptur, Malerei,

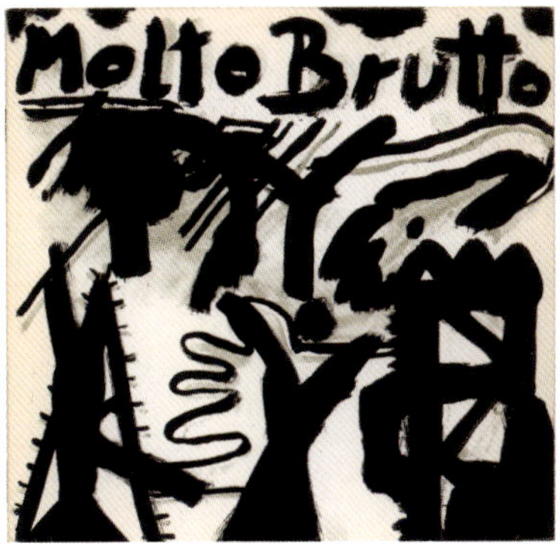

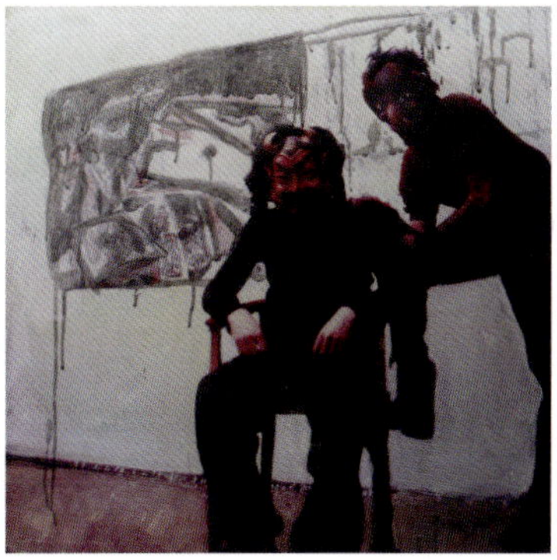

137
Molto Brutto,
LP, Schallter, 1982,
Cover: Gunter Damisch
& Gerwald Rockenschaub

138 **Hans Weigand**
Malteufel, 1978/94
(Painting Maniac) Druck,
verschiedene Materialien
auf Leinwand / print,
mixed media on canvas
50 x 60 cm

partner Eugenia Rochas, or Hans Weigand's praxis across various fields, which alternated between sculpture, painting, photography, and music. Weigand's group Pas Paravent was never really able to decide on finished products, as the music was far too caught up in an experimental stage.[25] By contrast, many of his paintings or photo products were all the more final, like *Malteufel* (Painting Maniac, 1978/1994) [ILL·138], where, as in a high low poker game, the bet is for something like the "worst possible picture."

Like many other of the painters/musicians mentioned here, Weigand was a confessed Captain Beefheart fan. As a result of this particular musical affinity, like many of his contemporaries he was quick to internalize Van Vliet's credo, according to which really successful—or "bad"—painting had to be disturbing, like a physical attack. The fact that there were so many people working in this way in the years 1975 to 1985 may simply be a chance of history. But that much of what they did is still fermenting today is due alone to a way of seeing that is not concerned with restricting their approach to just one medium.

1 Interview with John Yau, in *Interview*, 10 (1991), cited in Mike Barnes, *Captain Beefheart. The Biography* (London: Omnibus Press, 2004), p. 323.

2 See for example Luca Ferrari, "Perlen vor die Säue. Eiscreme für Krähen. Zum Verhältnis von Musik und Malerei im Werk von Captain Beefheart," in *Stand Up To Be Discontinued. Die Malerei von Don Van Vliet* (Ostfildern: Hatje-Cantz, 1993), pp. 23–26.

3 Telephone interview with Lars Movin, in *Copyright*, 5 (1991), cited in Barnes, p. 315.

4 See Mike Kelley, "To the Throne of Chaos Where the Thin Flutes Pipe Mindlessly," accompanying text with the triple CD *Destroy All Monsters 1974–1976*, Ecstatic Peace! 1995; accessible online under http://www.mikekelley.com/DAMthrone.html [2008-03-21].

5 See Brandon W. Joseph, "Son of a Creature: An Interview with Carey Loren," in *Grey Room*, 12 (2003), pp. 166–125.

6 See the above-mentioned triple CD *Destroy All Monsters 1974–1976*, the compendium on the band's history *Destroy All Monsters: Geisha This* (Detroit: Book Beat, 1995), (further editions 1996 and 1998), and the DVD compilation *Grow Live Monsters*, MVDvisual 2006.

7 On the Cleveland scene see Clinton Heylin, *From the Velvets to the Voidoids. A Pre-Punk History for a Post-Punk World* (London, New York: Penguin Books, 1993), pp. 50 ff. and pp. 142 ff.; Charlotte Pressler, "Those Were Different Times. A Memoir of Cleveland Life 1967–1973 (Part One)," online [http://www.scatrecords.com/eels/twdt.htm], 2008-03-21.

8 See the overviews of the scene in Marvin J. Taylor (ed.), *The Downtown Book. The New York Art Scene 1974–1984* (Princeton, Oxford: Princeton University Press, 2006); Marc Masters, *No Wave* (London, 2007); *New York Noise. Photographs by Paula Court*, London 2007, and *East Village USA*, New York, New Museum of Contemporary Art 2004.

9 See Heylin, pp. 93 ff., and Legs McNeil, Gillian McCain, *Please Kill Me. The Uncensored Oral History of Punk* (New York: Grove Press, 1996).

10 See the quotations from Robert Longo, Glenn Branca, and Sal Principato (Liquid Liquid) in *New York Noise*, p. 3, p. 54 and p. 161.

11 On the special features of No Wave cinema see Matthew Yokobosky, "Not a Part of Any Wave: No Wave Cinema," in Taylor, pp. 117–128, and Marc Masters, "The Offenders: No Wave Cinema," in *No Wave*, pp. 139–163.

12 The film was begun in 1981 under the title *New York Beat* by the director Edo Bertoglio, but not finished until 2000 with a new voice-over to replace Basquiat's voice—he had died in 1988.

Fotografie und Musik changierte. Weigands Gruppe Pas Paravent konnte sich nie so recht zu fertigen Produkten durchringen, zu sehr war die Musik im Experimentierstadium verhangen.[25] Dafür nahmen sich viele seiner Mal- und Fotozurichtungen umso finaler aus, etwa *Malteufel* (1978/1994) [ABB·138], bei dem – wie in einem Pokerspiel der Marke „High/Low" – der Einsatz auf so etwas wie dem „schlechtestmöglichen Bild" liegt.

Weigand war wie viele andere der hier erwähnten MalerInnen-MusikerInnen bekennender Captain-Beefheart-Fan. Dessen Credo, wonach wirklich gelungene, sprich: „schlechte" Malerei verstörend, ja, eine Art körperliche Attacke sein sollte, hatte er wie viele seiner KollegInnen aufgrund seiner speziellen Musikaffinität früh internalisiert. Dass in den Jahren 1975 bis 1985 eine Vielzahl von Ansätzen in dieser Richtung bestand, mag ein historischer Glücksfall gewesen sein. Dass heute noch etliches davon brodelt und gärt, verdankt sich einzig einer Betrachtungsweise, der nicht daran gelegen ist, die zugrunde liegende Haltung in einem einzelnen Medium einzufrieden.

1 Interview mit John Yau, in: *Interview*, 10 (1991), zitiert nach: Mike Barnes, *Captain Beefheart. The Biography*, London 2004, S. 323.

2 Vgl. etwa Luca Ferrari, „Perlen vor die Säue. Eiscreme für Krähen. Zum Verhältnis von Musik und Malerei im Werk von Captain Beefheart", in: *Stand Up To Be Discontinued. Die Malerei von Don Van Vliet*, Ostfildern 1993, S. 23–26.

3 Telefoninterview mit Lars Movin, in: *Copyright*, 5 (1991), zitiert nach: Barnes (zit. Anm. 1), S. 315.

4 Vgl. Mike Kelley, „To the Throne of Chaos Where the Thin Flutes Pipe Mindlessly", Begleittext der Tripel-CD *Destroy All Monsters 1974–1976*, Ecstatic Peace! 1995; online zu finden unter http://www.mikekelley.com/DAMthrone.html [2008-03-21].

5 Vgl. Brandon W. Joseph, „Son of a Creature: An Interview with Carey Loren", in: *Grey Room*, 12 (2003), S. 166–125.

6 Vgl. die bereits erwähnte Tripel-CD *Destroy All Monsters 1974–1976*, das Kompendium zur Bandgeschichte *Destroy All Monsters: Geisha This*, Detroit 1995 (Folgeauflagen 1996 und 1998), sowie die DVD-Kompilation *Grow Live Monsters*, MVDvisual 2006.

7 Zur Cleveland-Szene vgl. Clinton Heylin, *From the Velvets to the Voidoids. A Pre-Punk History for a Post-Punk World*, London, New York 1993, S. 50 ff. u. S. 142 ff.; Charlotte Pressler, „Those Were Different Times. A Memoir of Cleveland Life 1967–1973 (Part One)", Onlinedokument [http://www.scatrecords.com/eels/twdt.htm], 2008-03-21.

8 Vgl. die Szeneüberblicke in: Marvin J. Taylor (Hg.), *The Downtown Book. The New York Art Scene 1974–1984*, Princeton, Oxford 2006; Marc Masters, *No Wave*, London 2007; *New York Noise. Photographs by Paula Court*, London 2007, sowie *East Village USA*, New York, New Museum of Contemporary Art 2004.

9 Vgl. Heylin (zit. Anm. 7), S. 93 ff., sowie Legs McNeil, Gillian McCain, *Please Kill Me. The Uncensored Oral History of Punk*, New York 1996.

10 Vgl. die Zitate von Robert Longo, Glenn Branca und Sal Principato (Liquid Liquid) in: *New York Noise* (zit. Anm. 8), S. 3, S. 54 bzw. S. 161.

11 Zu den Besonderheiten des No Wave Cinema vgl. Matthew Yokobosky, „Not a Part of Any Wave: No Wave Cinema", in: Taylor (zit. Anm. 8), S. 117–128, sowie Marc Masters, „The Offenders: No Wave Cinema", in: ders., *No Wave* (zit. Anm. 8), S. 139–163.

12 Der Film wurde 1981 unter dem Titel *New York Beat* von Regisseur Edo Bertoglio begonnen, aber erst 2000 mit neuem Voice-over anstelle des 1988 verstorbenen Basquiat fertig gestellt.

13 Angeführt seien hier auch die Band von Robert Longo und Richard Prince, Menthol Wars, sowie die Gruppe des in unterschiedlichsten Sparten aktiven David Wojnarowicz namens 3 Teens Kill 4.

14 Zur Rolle des „interdisziplinären Clubs" in der East-Village-Szene der 1980er-Jahre vgl. Dan Cameron,

13 Other artists' bands included Robert Longo und Richard Prince's band, Menthol Wars, and the group 3 Teens Kill 4, with David Wojnarowicz who was active in a number of genres.

14 On the role of the "interdisciplinary club" in the East Village scene of the 1980s see Dan Cameron, "It Takes a Village," in *East Village USA*, pp. 57 f., and Liza Kirwin, "Hybrid Spaces, Polymorphous Creativity,", in ibid., pp. 85 f.

15 See Simon Reynolds, *Rip It Up and Start Again. Post-Punk 1978–1984*, London: Faber&Faber, 2005).

16 See Carlo McCormick, "A Crack in Time," in Taylor, p. 88.

17 See Craig Owens, "Honor, Power, and the Love of Women," in *Art in America*, January 1983, pp. 7–13, reprinted in Craig Owens, *Beyond Recognition*, Berkeley, Los Angeles, Oxford 1992, pp. 143–155; and, referring to Europe, Benjamin H. D. Buchloh, "Figures of Authority, Ciphers of Regression: Notes on the Return of Representation in European Painting," in *October*, 16 (1981), pp. 39–68.

18 See *Linder – Works 1976–2006*, Zurich 2006, p. 17 ("When I began to work solely in photomontage [_] I used simply a surgeon's scalpel as my paintbrush and magazines became my new palette.").

19 Susanne Kippenberger, *Kippenberger. Der Künstler und seine Familien* (Berlin: Berlin Verlag, 2007), p. 174 (translated).

20 Diedrich Diederichsen, "Der Selbstdarsteller. Martin Kippenberger zwischen 1977 und 1983," in Eva Meyer-Hermann, Susanne Neuburger (ed.), *Nach Kippenberger*, Vienna 2003, p. 56 (translated). It is noteworthy that the first (and impressive) report on the "Neue Deutsche Welle," published by Alfred Hilsberg in fall 1979, already spoke of Kippenberger as an infamous *"Selbstdarsteller"* (showy extrovert) well known in Hamburg; see "Aus grauer Städte Mauern" (parts 1 to 3), in *Sounds*, October to December 1979, online under http://mitglied.lycos.de/RaFuchs/ndw/sounds/sounds3.htm, http://mitglied.lycos.de/RaFuchs/ndw/sounds/sounds4.htm sowie http://mitglied.lycos.de/RaFuchs/ndw/sounds/sounds5.htm [2008-03-21]; reference from part 3.

21 This piece is on the double EP *Kirche der Ununterschiedlichkeit* (1982), which includes Nachdenkliche Wehrpflichtige and LSDAP/AO as well as Markus Oehlen's Vielleichtors and Albert Oehlen's project "Männer in nassen Kleidern" (Men in Wet Clothes).

22 Cited from Jutta Koether, "Schlimme Zeiten sind immer zu lang. Werner Büttner und Albert Oehlen," in *Spex – Musik zur Zeit*, November 1983, p. 29 (translated).

23 ibid (translated).

24 The common basis of music and painting in the German post-punk context is also emphasized by Diedrich Diederichsen, see "Intensität – Negation – Klartext," in *Zurück zum Beton. Die Anfänge von Punk und New Wave in Deutschland 1977–'82*, (Cologne: Walther König, 2002), above all pp. 143 f.

25 For an overview of Weigand's music see Thomas Edlinger, "The Beat Goes On. Zum künstlerischen Umgang mit dem Kommunikationsmedium Musik," in *Hans Weigand*, (Cologne: Walther König, 2005), pp. 112–119.

„It Takes a Village", in: *East Village USA* (zit. Anm. 8), S. 57 f., sowie Liza Kirwin, „Hybrid Spaces, Polymorphous Creativity", ebd., S. 85 f.

15 Vgl. Simon Reynolds, *Rip It Up and Start Again. Post-Punk 1978–1984*, London 2005.

16 Vgl. Carlo McCormick, „A Crack in Time", in: Taylor (zit. Anm. 8), S. 88.

17 Vgl. Craig Owens, „Honor, Power, and the Love of Women", in: *Art in America*, Januar 1983, S. 7–13, wieder abgedruckt in: ders., *Beyond Recognition*, Berkeley, Los Angeles, Oxford 1992, S. 143–155, sowie, auf Europa bezogen, Benjamin H. D. Buchloh, „Figures of Authority, Ciphers of Regression: Notes on the Return of Representation in European Painting", in: *October*, 16 (1981), S. 39–68.

18 Vgl. *Linder – Works 1976–2006*, Zürich 2006, S. 17. ("When I began to work solely in photomontage [...] I used simply a surgeon's scalpel as my paintbrush and magazines became my new palette.")

19 Susanne Kippenberger, *Kippenberger. Der Künstler und seine Familien*, Berlin 2007, S. 174.

20 Diedrich Diederichsen, „Der Selbstdarsteller. Martin Kippenberger zwischen 1977 und 1983", in: Eva Meyer-Hermann, Susanne Neuburger (Hg.), *Nach Kippenberger*, Wien 2003, S. 56. Bezeichnend ist, dass bereits in der ersten, äußerst eindrücklichen „Neue Deutsche Welle"-Reportage von Alfred Hilsberg im Herbst 1979 von dem „auch schon von Hamburg her berüchtigte[n] Selbstdarsteller Kippenberger" die Rede ist; vgl. „Aus grauer Städte Mauern" (Teil 1 bis 3), in: *Sounds*, Oktober bis Dezember 1979, online zu finden unter http://mitglied.lycos.de/RaFuchs/ndw/sounds/sounds3.htm, http://mitglied.lycos.de/RaFuchs/ndw/sounds/sounds4.htm sowie http://mitglied.lycos.de/RaFuchs/ndw/sounds/sounds5.htm [2008-03-21]; Zitat aus Teil 3.

21 Dieses Stück findet sich auf der Doppel-EP *Kirche der Ununterschiedlichkeit* (1982), auf der neben den Nachdenklichen Wehrpflichtigen und LSDAP/AO auch Markus Oehlens Vielleichtors sowie Albert Oehlens Projekt Männer in nassen Kleidern vertreten sind.

22 Zitiert nach Jutta Koether, „Schlimme Zeiten sind immer zu lang. Werner Büttner und Albert Oehlen", in: *Spex – Musik zur Zeit*, November 1983, S. 29.

23 Ebd.

24 Die gemeinsame Basis von Musik und Malerei im deutschen Postpunkkontext betont auch Diedrich Diederichsen, vgl. „Intensität – Negation – Klartext", in: *Zurück zum Beton. Die Anfänge von Punk und New Wave in Deutschland 1977–'82*, Köln 2002, vor allem S. 143 f.

25 Zum Überblick über Weigands Musikschaffen vgl. Thomas Edlinger, „The Beat Goes On. Zum künstlerischen Umgang mit dem Kommunikationsmedium Musik", in: *Hans Weigand*, Köln 2005, S. 112–119.

Anhang / *Appendix*

Biografien / *Biographies*

Eva Badura-Triska ist Kunsthistorikerin und Kuratorin am Museum Moderner Kunst Stiftung Ludwig Wien. Publikationen u. a.: Herausgabe der Stuttgarter und Wiener Tagebücher von Johannes Itten (1990), monografische Publikationen über Rudolf Schwarzkogler (1992, zusammen mit Hubert Klocker), Franz West (1996) und Heimo Zobernig (2003). Jüngste Veröffentlichungen: Kat. *Entdecken und Besitzen. Einblicke in österreichische Privatsammlungen*, MUMOK, Wien (2005), „Yves Klein in Relation zum Wiener Aktionismus", in: Kat. *Yves Klein*, Centre Pompidou, Paris (2006)/MUMOK, Wien (2007)

Eva Badura-Triska is art historian and curator at the Museum Moderner Kunst Stiftung Ludwig Vienna. She has edited the diaries Johannes Itten wrote in Stuttgart and Vienna (1990), monographic publications on Rudolf Schwarzkogler (1992, together with Hubert Klocker), *Franz West*, MUMOK Vienna (1996) and *Heimo Zobernig*, MUMOK Vienna (2003). Her latest publications include exhib. cat. *Entdecken und Besitzen. Einblicke in österreichische Privatsammlungen*, MUMOK Vienna (2005), Yves Klein in relation to the Vienna Actionism, in exhib. cat. *Yves Klein*, Centre Pompidou Paris (2006) / MUMOK Vienna (2007)

Julia Gelshorn ist Kunsthistorikerin und hat an den Universitäten Köln und Bern studiert. Promotion zum Thema „Aneignung der Kunstgeschichte. Strategien der Wiederholung bei Gerhard Richter und Sigmar Polke". Seit 2001 wissenschaftliche Assistentin am Institut für Kunstgeschichte der Universität Bern und seit 2005 wissenschaftliche Assistentin am Kunsthistorischen Institut der Universität Zürich. 2006 bis 2008 Research Fellow am Deutschen Forum für Kunstgeschichte, Paris. Publikationen zur zeitgenössischen Kunst (Appropriation-Art, Konzepte der Autorschaft, Künstlerschriften, Intermedialität von Bild und Text, Künstleridentität und Kunstbetrieb). Forschungsprojekt zu ästhetischen und sozialen Normen in Kunst und Kultur des 18. Jahrhunderts.

Julia Gelshorn is art historian; she studied at the University of Cologne and Bern. Her graduation thesis was "Aneignung der Kunstgeschichte. Strategien der Wiederholung bei Gerhard Richter und Sigmar Polke" (Appropriation of art history. Strategies of repetition in the work of Gerhard Richter and Sigmar Polke). Since 2001, she is scientific assistant at the Institute of Art History at the University of Bern and since 2005 research associate at the University of Zurich; from 2006–2008, Research Fellow at the German Forum for Art History, Paris. Her many publications on contemporary art themes include those on Appropriation Art, concepts of authorship, artists' writings, the intermediality of image and text, identity of the artist and the art industry, etc. She is currently working on a research project on aesthetics and social norms in eighteenth-century art and culture.

Claire Gilman ist eine in New York lebende Wissenschaftlerin und Kuratorin. Im Moment stellt sie ein Buchmanuskript mit dem Titel *Arte Povera's Theater: Artifice and Anti-Modernism in Italian Art of the 1960s* fertig. Sie ist neben Margaret Sundell Kokuratorin von *The Storyteller*, einer Ausstellung zeitgenössischer Kunst, welche die Form der Erzählung von Künstlern in Hinsicht auf aktuelle soziale und politische Ereignisse untersucht und von ICI (Independent Curators International) organisiert und vertrieben wird. 2002 kuratierte sie *Arte Povera: Selections from the Sonnabend Collection* an der Wallach Art Gallery der Columbia University. Ihre Texte werden u. a. in *October*, *Documents*, *CAA Reviews* und *Frieze* veröffentlicht.

Claire Gilman is a New York based independent scholar and curator, and is currently completing a book manuscript entitled *Arte Povera's Theater: Artifice and Anti-Modernism in Italian Art of the 1960s*. She is co-curating (with Margaret Sundell) *The Storyteller*, an exhibition of contemporary art, organized and circulated by ICI (Independent Curators International), which explores the use of the story form in art as a way of dealing with recent social and political events. In 2002, she curated *Arte Povera: Selections from the Sonnabend Collection* at Columbia University's Wallach Art Gallery. Her writings have appeared in *October*, *Documents*, *CAA Reviews* and *Frieze*.

Christian Höller ist Redakteur und Mitherausgeber der Zeitschrift *springerin – Hefte für Gegenwartskunst*; seit 1994 umfassende Publikationstätigkeit im Bereich Kunst- und Kulturtheorie; Kurator des Sonderprogramms *Pop Unlimited? Imagetransfers und Bildproduktion in der aktuellen Popkultur* bei den 46. Internationalen Kurzfilmtagen Oberhausen, Mai 2000; Herausgeber der Sammelbände *Pop Unlimited?* (Verlag Turia + Kant, Wien, 2001), *Techno-Visionen* (Folio Verlag, Wien, Bozen, 2005; mit Sandro Droschl und Harald A. Wiltsche) sowie des Kataloges *Hans Weigand* (Verlag der Buchhandlung Walther König, Köln, 2005); Autor des Interviewbandes *Time Action Vision: Conversations in Cultural Studies, Theory, and Activism* (JRP Ringier, Zürich, in Vorbereitung); 2006/2007 wissenschaftlicher Editor von *documenta 12 magazines*; seit 2002 Gastprofessor an der École supérieure des beaux-arts in Genf.

Christian Höller is editor and co-publisher of *springerin – Hefte für Gegenwartskunst* magazine; since1994, he has published extensively in the field of art and culture theory; he curated the spezial program *Pop Unlimited? Imagetransfers und Bildproduktion in der aktuellen Popkultur* at the 46. Internationalen Kurzfilmtagen Oberhausen (46th International Short Film Festival), held in May 2000. He publishes the anthology *Pop Unlimited?* (Vienna: Verlag Turia + Kant, 2001), *Techno-Visionen* (Vienna, Bolzano: Folio Verlag, 2005), with Sandro Droschl and Harald A. Wiltsche, as well as the catalog *Hans Weigand* (Cologne: Verlag der Buchhandlung Walther König, 2005); he is author of the interview volume *Time Action Vision: Conversations in Cultural Studies, Theory, and Activism* (Zurich: JRP Ringier, in preparation); From 2006–2007, he was scientific editor of *documenta 12 magazines*, and since 2002 is visiting professor at École supérieure des beaux-arts in Geneva.

Susanne Neuburger ist Kunsthistorikerin und Kuratorin am Museum Moderner Kunst Stiftung Ludwig Wien. Ausstellungen, Projekte und Texte, zuletzt *Nouveau Réalisme*, MUMOK, Wien (2005), *Konzept. Aktion. Sprache. Pop-Art, Fluxus und Konzeptkunst aus der Sammlung* (mit Achim Hochdörfer), MUMOK, Wien (2006), *Laboratorium Moderne. Bildende Kunst, Film und Fotografie im Aufbruch*, MUMOK, Wien (2007).

Susanne Neuburger is art historian and curator at Museum Moderner Kunst Stiftung Ludwig Wien. Her latest exhibitions, projects and texts include *Nouveau Réalisme*, MUMOK, Vienna (2005), *Konzept. Aktion. Sprache. Pop-Art, Fluxus und Konzeptkunst aus der Sammlung* (together with Achim Hochdörfer), MUMOK, Vienna (2006), *Laboratorium Moderne. Bildende Kunst, Film und Fotografie im Aufbruch*, MUMOK, Vienna (2007).

Stefan Neuner Kunsthistoriker, Musikwissenschaftler, hat an der Universität Wien studiert. Seit 2005 wissenschaftlicher Assistent am Kunsthistorischen Institut der Universität Zürich sowie seit Mai 2007 wissenschaftlicher Mitarbeiter am Institut für Theorie der Gestaltung und Kunst an der Zürcher Hochschule der Künste. Jüngste Publikationen: „Order from Noise. Bild, Pop und Kontingenz in Jeff Walls ‚The Guitarist'", in: *Gestalten der Kontingenz – Ein Bilderbuch*, hrsg. von Jörg Huber u. Philipp Stoellger (T:G 06), Wien, New York: Springer 2008, S. 167–191 (zusammen mit Simone Mathys); *Maskierung der Malerei. Jasper Johns nach Willem de Kooning*, München: Fink 2008.

Stefan Neuner is art historian and musicologist. He studied at the University of Vienna. Since 2005, he is research associate at the Institute of Art History, University of Zurich, and since 2007 also research associate at the Institute for Critical Theory at the University of the Arts, Zurich. He has recently published: "Order from Noise. Bild, Pop und Kontingenz in Jeff Walls 'The Guitarist,'" in *Gestalten der Kontingenz – Ein Bilderbuch*, ed. Jörg Huber, Philipp Stoellger (T:G 06), Vienna / New York: Springer 2008, S. 167–191 (together with Simone Mathys); *Maskierung der Malerei. Jasper Johns nach Willem de Kooning*, Munich: Fink 2008.

Friedrich Petzel ist seit 1994 Mitarbeiter der Friedrich Petzel Gallery in New York und bald Partner bei Capitain & Petzel in Berlin. Abschluss des Kunstgeschichtestudiums in Köln, sporadische Veröffentlichungen in *Texte zur Kunst*. Seit 1991 verschiedene Katalogtexte.

Friedrich Petzel is at the Friedrich Petzel Gallery in New York since 1994, and soon partner of Capitain & Petzel in Berlin. He studied art history in Cologne, occasionally publishing in *Texte zur Kunst*. Since 1991, he has written several essays for various catalogs.

Werkliste / *List of Works*

Georg Baselitz

— Der Kummerkopf, 1962
(Sorrow Head)
Öl auf Leinwand / oil on canvas
100 x 80 cm
Privatsammlung / Private Collection, Berlin
© Georg Baselitz
Foto / photo: Privatsammlung, Berlin / Frank Oleski, Köln

— Der Zwerg, 1962
(The Dwarf)
Öl auf Leinwand / oil on canvas
136 x 101 cm
Bayerische Staatsgemäldesammlungen, München, Pinakothek der Moderne, Wittelsbacher Ausgleichsfonds Sammlung Prinz Franz von Bayern
© Georg Baselitz
Foto / photo: Bayerische Staatsgemäldesammlungen, München, Pinakothek der Moderne (Baselitz, Sammlung WAF, Sammlung Prinz Franz von Bayern)

— Erster P.D. – Der Fuß, 1963
(First P.D. – The Foot)
Öl auf Leinwand / oil on canvas
101 x 82 cm
Sammlung Crex, Zürich
© Georg Baselitz
Foto / photo: Sammlung Crex, Zürich

— Sechster P.D. Fuß, 1963
(Sixth P.D. Foot)
Öl auf Leinwand / oil on canvas
100,7 x 82 cm
Sammlung Crex, Zürich
© Georg Baselitz
Foto / photo: Sammlung Crex, Zürich

— P.D. Fuss – Kelte, 1963
(P.D. Foot – Celt)
Öl auf Leinwand / oil on canvas
100 x 82,2 cm
Sammlung Crex, Zürich
© Georg Baselitz
Foto / photo: Sammlung Crex, Zürich

— Achter P.D. – Die Hand, 1963
(Eighth P.D. – The Hand)
Öl auf Leinwand / oil on canvas
100,9 x 82,1 cm
Sammlung Crex, Zürich
© Georg Baselitz
Foto / photo: Sammlung Crex, Zürich

— P.D. Stengel, 1963
(P.D. Stem)
Öl auf Leinwand / oil on canvas
130 x 90 cm
Sammlung Schmidt-Drenhaus, Köln / Dresden
© Georg Baselitz
Foto / photo: Sammlung Schmidt-Drenhaus, Köln / Dresden

Werner Büttner

— Über das Böse VI, 1983
(On Evil VI)
Öl auf Leinwand / oil on canvas
150 x 190 cm
Sammlung Grässlin, St. Georgen
© Werner Büttner
Foto / photo: Sammlung Grässlin, St. Georgen

— Die Paarung des Grundgesetzes mit Farbe ergibt kein Grundgesetz sondern Farbe (Art. 14: Das Erbrecht und das Eigentum werden gewährleistet), 1983
(The Copulation of Basic Law with Color Totals no Basic Law but Color [art. 14: Property and the Right of Inheritance Shall be Guaranteed])
Öl auf Leinwand / oil on canvas
120 x 120 cm
Sammlung Grässlin, St. Georgen
© Werner Büttner
Foto / photo: Sammlung Grässlin, St. Georgen

— Die Paarung des Grundgesetzes mit Farbe ergibt kein Grundgesetz sondern Farbe; Art. 15: Grund und Boden anderes könnten, 1983
(The Copulation of Basic Law with Color Totals no Basic Law but Color [art. 15: Land, Natural Resources, and others May])
Öl auf Leinwand / oil on canvas
90 x 75 cm
Sammlung Grässlin, St. Georgen
© Werner Büttner
Foto / photo: Sammlung Grässlin, St. Georgen

— Die Paarung des Grundgesetzes mit Farbe ergibt kein Grundgesetz sondern Farbe (Art. 17: Jeder Deutsche hat das Recht, sich zu beschweren), 1983
(The Copulation of Basic Law with Color Totals no Basic Law but Color [art. 17: Every German Shall Have the Right to Address Complaints])
Öl auf Leinwand / oil on canvas
100 x 79 cm
Sammlung Grässlin, St. Georgen
© Werner Büttner
Foto / photo: Sammlung Grässlin, St. Georgen

— Die Paarung des Grundgesetzes mit Farbe ergibt kein Grundgesetz sondern Farbe (Art. 18: Wer die Grundordnung missbraucht, verwirkt dieselbe), 1983
(The Copulation of Basic Law with Color Totals no Basic Law but Color [art. 18: Whoever Abuses the Freedom of Expression, Shall Forfeit these Basic Rights])
Öl auf Leinwand / oil on canvas
75 x 75 cm
Sammlung Grässlin, St. Georgen
© Werner Büttner
Foto / photo: Sammlung Grässlin, St. Georgen

André Butzer
— Pluton, 2002
Öl auf Leinwand / oil on canvas
250 x 200 cm
Privatsammlung / Private Collection
© André Butzer
Foto / photo: Galerie Max Hetzler, Berlin

— Frau, 2002
(Woman)
Öl auf Leinwand / oil on canvas
250 x 200 cm
Privatsammlung / Private Collection
© André Butzer
Foto / photo: Galerie Max Hetzler, Berlin

John Currin
— Jaunty and Mame, 1997
Öl auf Leinwand / oil on canvas
121,9 x 91,4 cm
The Sander Collection
© John Currin
Foto / photo: The Sander Collection

— The Invalids, 1997
(Die Invaliden)
Öl auf Leinwand / oil on canvas
121,9 x 91,4 cm
Hauser & Wirth, Zürich / London
© John Currin
Foto / photo: Hauser & Wirth, Zürich / London

— Sheree North, 2003
Öl auf Leinwand / oil on canvas
66 x 50,8 cm
Courtesy Sadie Coles HQ, London
© John Currin
Foto / photo: Courtesy Sadie Coles HQ, London

— Thanksgiving, 2003
(Erntedankfest)
Öl auf Leinwand / oil on canvas
172,9 x 132,3 cm
Tate London, Leihgabe / on loan from the American Fund for the Tate Gallery, courtesy of Marc Jacobs, 2004
© John Currin
Foto / photo: Tate London

Giorgio de Chirico
— Gladiateurs s'amusant à l'école, 1927
(Sich in der Schule amüsierende Gladiatoren / Gladiators Amusing Themselves at School)
Öl auf Leinwand / oil on canvas
55 x 46 cm
Privatsammlung, Venedig / Private Collection, Venice
© VBK Wien
Foto / photo: Private Collection, Venice

— Au bord de la mer, 1925
(Am Meer / At the Sea)
Öl auf Leinwand / oil on canvas
100 x 80 cm
Museum Moderner Kunst Stiftung Ludwig Wien, erworben / acquired 1985
© VBK Wien
Foto / photo: MUMOK, Lisa Rastl / Lena Deinhardstein, Wien

Pinot Gallizio
— Il muro della mia casa, 1958
(Die Wand meines Hauses / The Wall of my House)
Öl auf Leinwand / oil on canvas
95 x 1073 cm
Galerie van de Loo, München
© Estate Pinot Gallizio
Foto / photo: Galerie van de Loo, München / Hans Döring, München

Philip Guston
— Monument, 1976
Öl auf Leinwand / oil on canvas
203,2 x 279,4 cm
Tate London, erworben mit Unterstützung des / purchased with assistance of the American Fund for the Tate Gallery, 1991
© Estate of Philip Guston
Foto / photo: Tate London

— Black Sea, 1977
(Schwarzes Meer)
Öl auf Leinwand / oil on canvas
173 x 297 cm
Tate London, erworben / purchased 1982
© Estate of Philip Guston
Foto / photo: Tate London

Neil Jenney
— Man and Mirage, 1969
(Mann und Fata Morgana)
Öl auf Leinwand / oil on canvas
gerahmt / framed 147,5 x 193 cm
Privatsammlung / Private Collection
© Neil Jenney
Foto / photo: Thomas Ammann Fine Art, Zürich

— Girl and Doll, 1969
(Mädchen und Puppe)
Acryl auf Leinwand / acrylic on canvas
gerahmt / framed 147,5 x 193 cm
Privatsammlung / Private Collection
© Neil Jenney
Foto / photo: Thomas Ammann Fine Art, Zürich

Asger Jorn
— Paris by Night, 1959
(Paris bei Nacht)
Öl auf Leinwand / oil on canvas
53 x 37 cm
Pierre et Micky Alechinsky, Bougival
© VBK Wien
Foto / photo: Pierre et Micky Alechinsky, Bougival

— Hirschbrunft im Wilden Kaiser, 1960
(Stag Rut at the Wilder Kaiser)
Öl auf Leinwand / oil on canvas
90 x 120 cm
Staatliche Museen zu Berlin, Nationalgalerie
© VBK Wien
Foto / photo: Staatliche Museen zu Berlin / Jörg P. Anders, Berlin

— Choux, 1961
(Kohlkopf / Cabbage)
Öl auf Leinwand / oil on canvas
210 x 117 cm
Kunsthalle zu Kiel, Dauerleihgabe Stifterkreis
© VBK Wien
Foto / photo: Kunsthalle zu Kiel

— Souriez rue froide, 1962
(Lachen Sie kalte Straße / Smile Cold Street)
Öl auf Leinwand / oil on canvas
65 x 54 cm
Pierre et Micky Alechinsky, Bougival
© VBK Wien
Foto / photo: Pierre et Micky Alechinsky, Bougival

— Grand Baiser au Cardinal d'Amerique, 1962
(Dicker Kuss an den Kardinal von Amerika / Big Kiss to the Cardinal of America)
Öl auf Leinwand / oil on canvas
92 x 73 cm
Pierre et Micky Alechinsky, Bougival
© VBK Wien
Foto / photo: Pierre et Micky Alechinsky, Bougival / Andre Morain, Paris

— Il faut porter la fortune du bonheur, 1962
(Wir müssen die Zufälligkeit des Glücks ertragen / We Have to Carry the Fortuity of Bliss)
Öl auf Leinwand / oil on canvas
81 x 55 cm
Pierre et Micky Alechinsky, Bougival
© VBK Wien
Foto / photo: Pierre et Micky Alechinsky, Bougival

— L'Avantgarde se rend pas, 1962
(Die Avantgarde gibt nicht auf / The Avant-garde Does not Give up)
Öl auf Leinwand / oil on canvas
73 x 60 cm
Pierre et Micky Alechinsky, Bougival
© VBK Wien
Foto / photo: Pierre et Micky Alechinsky, Bougival / André Morain, Paris

Martin Kippenberger
— Ohne Titel, 1982
(Untitled)
6-teilige Serie / 6-parted series
Öl, Acryl auf Leinwand /
oil, acrylic on canvas
je / each100 x 120 cm
Sammlung Falckenberg
© Estate Martin Kippenberger
Foto / photo: Sammlung Falckenberg

* Ich kann beim besten Willen kein Hakenkreuz erkennen, 1984
(With the Best Will in the World I Can't See a Swastika)
Öl und Silikon auf Leinwand /
oil, silicon on canvas
160 x 133 cm
Friedrich Christian Flick Collection
© Estate Martin Kippenberger
Foto: Galerie Gisela Capitain, Cologne

— Die Bourgeoisie kommt nicht weiter und der Fußball bewegt sich im Mittelfeld, 1985
(The Bourgeoisie aren't Getting Any-where and the Football's in the Midfield)
Dispersion, Acryl, Aufkleber auf Leinwand / emulsion, acrylic, sticker on canvas
130 x 120 cm
Estate Martin Kippenberger,
Galerie Gisela Capitain, Cologne
© Estate Martin Kippenberger
Foto / photo: Galerie Gisela Capitain, Cologne

— Hinterbliebener Hilfeschreiender in der Gaza Gegend, 1985
(Bereaved Screaming for Succour in Gaza)
Dispersion, Acryl, Aufkleber auf Leinwand / emulsion, acrylic, sticker on canvas
120 x 130 cm
Estate Martin Kippenberger,
Galerie Gisela Capitain, Cologne
© Estate Martin Kippenberger
Foto / photo: Galerie Gisela Capitain, Cologne

* Kaputtes Kind, 1985, (Broken Child)
Dispersion, Acryl, Aufkleber auf Leinwand / emulsion, acrylic, sticker on canvas
130 x 120 cm
© Estate Martin Kippenberger
Foto / photo: Galerie Gisela Capitain, Cologne

René Magritte
— Le Stropiat, 1948
(Verkrüppelter / Mangled)
Öl auf Leinwand / oil on canvas
59,5 x 49,5 cm
Paris, musée national d'Art moderne – Centre Georges Pompidou
© VBK Wien
Foto / photo: CNAC/MNAM, Dist. RMN / © Jean-Claude Planche

Malcolm Morley
— The Injuns are Cuming, The Officer of the Imperial Guard is Fleeing, 1983
(Die Indianer spritzen ab, der Offizier der kaiserlichen Garde flüchtet)
Öl auf Leinwand / oil on canvas
208 x 284 cm
Astrup Fearnley Collection, Oslo
© Malcolm Morley
Foto / photo: Astrup Fearnley Collection Oslo / Tore H. Røyneland

Albert Oehlen
— Flur, 1982, (Corridor)
Öl, Lack, Spiegel auf Leinwand /
oil, lacquer, mirror on canvas
250 x 200 cm
Sammlung Landesbank
Baden-Württemberg, Stuttgart
© Albert Oehlen
Foto / photo: © Landesbank
Baden-Württemberg, Stuttgart

— Krefelder Appell, 1983
(Muster of Krefeld)
Öl, Bastringe auf Leinwand /
bast fiber coils, oil on canvas
122,2 x 133,4 cm
Museum Moderner Kunst Stiftung Ludwig Wien, Leihgabe der Österreichischen Ludwig Stiftung / on loan from the Austrian Ludwig Foundation, seit / since 2007
© Albert Oehlen
Foto / photo: MUMOK, Lisa Rastl / Lena Deinhardstein, Wien

— Ohne Titel, 1983, (Untitled)
Öl, Spiegel auf Leinwand /
oil, mirror on canvas
60 x 60 cm
Sammlung Stolitzka, Graz
© Albert Oehlen
Foto / photo: © Galerie Bärbel Grässlin, Frankfurt a. M. / Wolfgang Günzel, Offenbach a. M.

— Ohne Titel, 1992, (Untitled)
Öl auf Leinwand / oil on canvas
200 x 200 cm
Essl Museum Klosterneuburg / Wien
© Albert Oehlen
Foto / photo: © Sammlung Essl Privatstiftung / Archiv Sammlung Essl

Francis Picabia
* Première rencontre (Les Amoureux), 1925–1926
(Erste Begegnung [Die Liebenden] / First Encounter [The Lovers])
Öl, Lack auf Weichfaserplatte /
oil, varnish on fiber board
93 x 73 cm
Moderna Museet Stockholm
© VBK Wien
Foto / photo: Moderna Museet Stockholm

— Ganga, 1927
Öl auf Leinwand / oil on canvas
116,5 x 87 cm
Museum Moderner Kunst Stiftung Ludwig Wien, Leihgabe der Österreichischen Ludwig Stiftung / on loan from the Austrian Ludwig Foundation, seit / since 1988
© VBK Wien
Foto / photo: MUMOK, Lisa Rastl / Lena Deinhardstein, Wien

— Aello, 1930
Öl auf Leinwand / oil on canvas
169 x 169 cm
Privatsammlung /
Private Collection, Paris
© VBK Wien
Foto / photo: Private Collection, Paris

— Maternité, 1935/36
(Mutterschaft / Maternity)
Öl auf Leinwand / oil on canvas
163 x 130,7 cm
Paris, musée national d'Art moderne – Centre Georges Pompidou
© VBK Wien
Foto / photo: © CNAC/MNAM, Dist. RMN – © Philippe Migeat

— Portrait de Femme, 1935
(Porträt einer Frau / Portrait of a Woman)
Öl auf Karton / oil on cardboard
73 x 60 cm
Galerie Bruno Bischofberger, Zürich
© VBK Wien
Foto / photo: Werner Schnüringer, Wädenswil

— L'Espagnole, 1938
(Spanierin / Spanish Woman)
Öl auf Leinwand / oil on canvas
73 x 60 cm
Galerie Bruno Bischofberger, Zürich
© VBK Wien
Foto / photo: Werner Schnüringer, Wädenswil

— Noi, 1938
Öl auf Leinwand / oil on canvas
80 x 60 cm
Privatsammlung / Private Collection Wien
© VBK Wien
Foto / photo: MUMOK, Lisa Rastl / Lena Deinhardstein, Wien

— Nu devant un paysage, 1938
(Akt vor einer Landschaft /
Nude in Front of a Landscape)
Öl auf Leinwand / oil on canvas
81 x 100 cm
Musée Magnelli, musée de la céramique, Vallauris, France
© VBK Wien
Foto / photo: Musée Magnelli, musée de la céramique, Vallauris, France

Sigmar Polke
— Akt mit Geige, 1968
(Nude with Violin)
Dispersion auf Holzfaserplatte / emulsion on particleboard
100,1 x 79,8 cm
Bayerische Staatsgemäldesammlungen, Pinakothek der Moderne, Wittelsbacher Ausgleichsfonds Sammlung Prinz Franz von Bayern
© VBK Wien
Foto / photo: Pinakothek der Moderne / ARTOTHEK

— Schimpftuch, 1968
(Cloth of Abuse)
Acryl auf Bibertuch / acrylic on flannelette
400 x 437 cm
Daros Collection, Zürich
© VBK Wien
Foto / photo: Daros Collection, Zürich

— Reiherbild IV, 1969
(Heron Painting IV)
Dispersion auf Bibertuch / emulsion on flannelette
Städtische Galerie Karlsruhe, Sammlung Garnatz
190 x 150 cm
© VBK Wien
Foto / photo: Städtische Galerie Karlsruhe

— Ohne Titel (Porträt), 1966
(Untitled [Portrait])
Pastellkreide, Öl, Dekostoffe / pastells, oil, furnishing fabrics
115 x 91 cm
Stiftung Museum Kunstpalast, Düsseldorf
© VBK Wien
Foto / photo: Stiftung Museum Kunstpalast, Düsseldorf

Peter Saul
— Tokyo Rose, 1961
(Rose von Tokio)
Öl auf Leinwand / oil on canvas
140 x 109 cm
BAM, Collection de la Communauté française de Belgique, Mons, Donation Maurice Duvivier
© Peter Saul
Foto / photo: BAM, Collection de la Communauté française de Belgique, Mons

— Communist Hideout, 1963
(Kommunistisches Versteck)
Öl auf Leinwand / oil on canvas
160 x 120 cm
Ludwig Museum, Köln
© Peter Saul
Foto / photo: Ludwig Museum, Köln

Julian Schnabel
— Painting without Mercy, 1981
(Malerei ohne Erbarmen)
Teller, Kitt, Ölfarbe, Wachs, Epoxy auf Holz / Plates, plaster, oil paint, wax, epoxy on wood
240 x 336 cm
Museum Moderner Kunst Stiftung Ludwig Wien, Leihgabe der Österreichischen Ludwig Stiftung / on loan from the Austrian Ludwig Foundation, seit / since 1981
© Julian Schnabel
Foto / photo: MUMOK, Lisa Rastl / Lena Deinhardstein, Wien

— Resurrection, 1984
(Auferstehung)
Öl, Sprühfarbe, Modellierpaste auf Samt / oil, spray paint, modeling compound on velvet
Privatsammlung / Private Collection, New York, Courtesy Sperone Westwater, New York
304,8 x 271,3 cm
© Julian Schnabel
Foto / photo: Courtesy Sperone Westwater, New York

— Eddie Stern, 2007
Öl, Wachs, Gesso auf Polyester / oil, wax, gesso on polyester
271,8 x 195,6
Privatsammlung / Private Collection, New York, Courtesy Sperone Westwater, New York
© Julian Schnabel
Foto / photo: Courtesy Sperone Westwater, New York

SPUR / HP Zimmer
— Die behaarte Pforte der Sehnsucht, 1961/62
(Hairy Gate of Desire)
Öl auf Leinwand / oil on canvas
140 x 100 cm
Galerie van de Loo, München
© HP Zimmer
Foto / photo: Galerie van de Loo, München

SPUR / Helmut Sturm
— Ländlicher Konflikt (Ländliches Scharmützel), 1962
(Rural Conflict – Rural Skirmish)
Öl auf Leinwand / oil on canvas
150 x 120 cm
Sammlung Niggl, Feldafing
© VBK Wien
Foto / photo: Sammlung Niggl, Richard Beer

SPUR / Heimrad Prem
— Trampers Nachtlied, 1962
(Tramper's Nightsong)
Öl auf Leinwand / oil on canvas
125 x 100 cm
Sammlung Niggl, Feldafing
© VBK Wien
Foto / photo: Sammlung Niggl, Freiherr von Werthern

— Roding. Strafgesetz (Weg-Männer), 1959
(Roding. Penal Law)
Öl, verschiedene Materialien auf Leinwand / oil, various materials on canvas
100 x 100 cm
Museum Lothar Fischer, Neumarkt i.d. OPf
© VBK Wien
Foto / photo: Archiv Museum Lothar Fischer, Neumarkt i.d. OPf

Lisa Yuskavage
— Brood, 2005–2006
(Brut)
Öl auf Leinwand / oil on canvas
190,5 x 175 cm
Sammlung / Collection of Mr. Alberto Cortina
© Lisa Yuskavage
Foto / photo: Courtesy David Zwirner, New York

— Cliff, 2007
(Klippe)
Öl auf Leinwand / oil on canvas
195,6 x 157,5 cm
Sammlung Titze
© Lisa Yuskavage
Foto / photo: MUMOK, Lisa Rastl / Lena Deinhardstein, Wien

* Nicht in der Ausstellung / not in the exhibition

Referenzabbildungen / *List of References*

Jean-Michel Basquiat
— Famous Negro Athletes # 4, 1981
[www.studiovisit.net/SV.EastVillage.pdf]

Black Box
— Regie: Beth B & Scott B, USA 1978, Filmstills

Peter Bömmels
— Der heilige Wolfsburg, 1982 (Cover der LP Asperando a Gogo – 20 Krautzuck Hits, Styrophon Records 1997), [http://xraybarbecue.blogspot.com/2007/12/asperando-gogo-20-golden-krautzuck-hits.html]

Sandro Botticelli
— Madonna della melagrana, ca. 1487, [in: Sandro Botticelli. Complete Catalog, Bd. II, University of California Press, Berkeley 1978, Nr. B48]

Michelangelo Buonarroti
— Il sogno, ca. 1533
[in: The Drawings of Michelangelo, London 1971, Nr. 359]

John Currin
— The Bra Shop, 1997
[in: John Currin, Gagosian Gallery/Rizzoli, London/New York 2006, S. 193]

Destroy All Monsters
— Auszüge aus Geisha This. A Compilation of the first six issues of Destroy All Monsters magazine, 1975–1979, Book Beat Gallery, Oak Park, Michigan, 1995

— Live in Tokyo & Osaka 1996, Compound Annex Records, 2004, Sevan Boosinger, [http://www.popsyndicate.com/site/story/destroy_all_monsters_live_in_tokyo_osaka]

Jean Fautrier
— Tête d'otage no.1, 1943
[in: Jean Fautrier 1898–1964, Yale University Press, New Haven and London, 2002 S. 109]

Andrea Fraser
— Kunst muss hängen, 2001
[in: Andrea Fraser – Works 1984 to 2003, DuMont, Köln 2003, Coverrückseite]

Pinot Gallizio
— Versteigerung der "pittura industriale" Pinot Gallizios in der Galerie van de Loo, München 15. April,1959
© Archivio Gallizio Torino
Foto / photo: Felicitas Timpe

Jörg Immendorff
— Hört auf zu malen, 1966, (Stop Painting) Collection Van Abbemuseum, Eindhoven, The Netherlands
Foto / photo: Peter Cox Eindhoven

Martin Kippenberger
— Heavy Burschi, 1989/90
Installationsansicht
Tate London 2006
© Estate Martin Kippenberger,
Foto / photo: Galerie Gisela Capitain, Cologne

— Heil Hitler Ihr Fetischisten, 1984
[in: Nach Kippenberger, MUMOK / schlebrügge.editor, Wien 2003, S. 76]

— Ich heize durch pupen, 1983
[in: Martin Kippenberger (Collector's Choice. Künstlermonographien Friedrich Christian Flick Collection Band 4), DuMont, Köln 2005, S. 38]

— Alkoholfolter, 1981
[in: Nach Kippenberger, MUMOK / schlebrügge.editor, Wien 2003, S. 55]

— 1/4 Jhdt. Kippenberger als einer von Euch, unter Euch, mit Euch, Berlin 1978
[in: Martin Kippenberger. Die gesamten Plakate 1977–1997, König, Köln 1998, S. 32]

— Martin, ab in die Ecke und schäm dich, 1989, [in: Martin Kippenberger, Hatje Cantz Ostfildern 2006, S. 109]

— Sympatische Kommunistin, 1983
[in: Modell Martin Kippenberger – Utopien für alle, Kunsthaus Graz, Graz 2008, S.101]

René Magritte
— Le Contenu Pictural, 1947
[in: Magritte – La Période Vache, Musée de Marseille, Ludion SA, 1992, p. 71]

— Le mal de mer, 1947
[in: Magritte – La Période Vache, Reunion des Musées Nationaux, Musée de Marseille, Ludion SA, 1992, S. 76]

— Le Psychologue, 1948
[in: Magritte, The Royal Museum of Fine Arts, Belgium, Brussels, 2005, S. 77]

— L'Etape, 1948
[in: Magritte – La Période Vache, Reunion des Musées Nationaux, Musée de Marseille, Ludion SA, 1992, S. 87]

— L'Ellipse, 1948
[in: Magritte, The Royal Museum of Fine Arts, Belgium, Brussels, 2005, S. 74]

— Titania, 1948
[in: Magritte, The Royal Museum of Fine Arts, Belgium, Brussels, 2005, S. 118]

— La Famine, 1948
[in: Magritte – La Période Vache, Reunion des Musées Nationaux, Musée de Marseille, Ludion SA, 1992, S. 92]

— Le Galet, 1948
[in: Magritte – La Période Vache, Reunion des Musées Nationaux, Musée de Marseille, Ludion SA, 1992, S. 125]

— Le Lyrisme, 1948
[in: Magritte, The Royal Museum of Fine Arts, Belgium, Brussels, 2005, S. 62]

Malcolm Morley
— Age of Catastophe, 1976
[in: Malcolm Morley – in Full Colour, Hayward Gallery, London 2001, S. 73]

Nachdenkliche Wehrpflichtige
– Politik für junge Leute, EP, Zickzack, 1980, Cover: Albert Oehlen [http://www.fc45.de/store.cgi?&shop=football&L=eng&P=971]

Albert Oehlen
– My Mother was a Friend of the [an] Enemy of the People, Galerie Peter Pakesch Wien, 1984, Einladungskarte

– Morgenlicht fällt ins Führerhauptquartier, 1982, [in: Das Bild an der Schwelle: Motivische Studien zum Fenster in der Kunst nach 1945, S. 273]

Francis Picabia
– Crucifixion, 1912, [in: Picabia, Rizzoli, New York 1985, S. 135, Fig. 240]

– Voilà Haviland, 1915, [in: Picabia. Le saint masque. Essai sur la peinture érotique de Francis Picabia, Paris 1998, S. 15.]

– Espagnole à la rose, 1916, [in: Francis Picabia. Drawings 1902-1950, Galerie Michael Werner: New York/Köln, Köln 2006, Kat. Nr. 7]

– La Sainte Vierge, 1920, [in: Francis Picabia. Singulier idéal, Editions des Musées de la Ville de Paris, Paris 2003, S. 214]

– Eröffnung der Ausstellung / Exhibition opening Francis Picabia, Galerie Dalmau, Barcelona, 18. November 1922. [in: The Artwork Caught by the Tail. Francis Picabia and Dada in Paris, MIT Cambridge (Mass.)/London 2007, S. 216]

– Nu, ca. 1942, [in: Francis Picabia. Les Nus et la méthode, Musée de Grenoble, Paris 1998, Kat.-Nr. 29, S. 76]

– Mon Paris, Nr. 5, März 1936 [in: Francis Picabia. Les Nus et la méthode, Musée de Grenoble, Paris 1998, S. 7]

Sigmar Polke
– Ohne Titel (Vase), 1965, [in: Sigmar Polke, Die drei Lügen der Malerei, Hatje Cantz, Ostfildern-Ruit 1997, S. 29]

– Lösungen V, 1967, [in: Polke – eine Retrospektive, Hatje Cantz, Ostfildern-Ruit 2008, S. 30]

– Streifenbild I, 1967, [in: Sigmar Polke, Die drei Lügen der Malerei, Hatje Cantz, Ostfildern-Ruit 1997, S. 119]

– Konstruktivistisch, 1968, [in: Sigmar Polke, Die drei Lügen der Malerei, Hatje Cantz, Ostfildern-Ruit 1997, S. 176]

– Moderne Kunst, 1968, [in: Sigmar Polke, Werke aus der Sammlung Froehlich, Hatje Cantz, Ostfildern-Ruit 2000, S. 51]

Pop Group
– She is Beyond Good and Evil, Single, Radarscope Records, 1979

Richard Prince
– I'm Lucky, 2001/02, © Richard Prince, Foto / photo: courtesy Gladstone Gallery, New York

Gerhard Richter
– Schloss Neuschwanstein, 1963 [in: Sigmar Polke, Sammlung Frieder Burda, Hatje Cantz, Ostfildern 2004, S. 159]

– Hirsch, 1963, [in: http://www.gerhard-richter.com/art/search/detail.php?5476] courtesy of the artist

– Vorgartenausstellung der Galerie Parnass, 1964, Courtesy Zentralarchiv des Internationalen Kunsthandels E.V. Zadik

Peter Saul
– Donald Duck Descending a Staircase, 1979, © Peter Saul
Foto / photo: Courtesy of the artist

Jörg Schlick
– Fotografie von Martin Kippenberger, (Photograph of Martin Kippenberger) [in: Martin Kippenberger, Wolfgang Bauer, Jörg Schlick und Peter Weibel, hg. steirischer herbst 98, König, Köln, 1998]

S.Y.P.H.
– PST!, LP, Pure Freude, 1980 (Pure Pleasure) Cover: Imi Knoebel [http://www.indigo.de/unser_programm/cover/88339/]

The Electric Eels
– Cyclotron/Agitated, Single, Rough Trade, 1978, Gestaltung: John Morton [http://www.discogs.com/release/899485]

The Red Crayola
– Kangaroo?, LP, Rough Trade, 1981 [http://commercialzone.blogspot.com/2007/07/red-krayola-with-art-language-kangaroo.html]

The Wirtschaftswunder
– Salmobray, LP, Zickzack, 1981
Cover: Jiri Georg Dokoupil) [http://ndw-wiki.org/index.php?title=Bild:Wirtschaftswunder-LP-A.gif]

Don Van Vliet
– Ghost Red Wire, 1967 [http://www.beefheart.com/runpaint/ghost.htm]

– Green Tom, 1976
Cover von Captain Beefheart and the Magic Band, Shiny Beast (Bat Chain Puller), LP, Virgin Records, 1978 [http://www.freewebs.com/teejo/disco/13beast.html]

Hans Weigand
– Malteufel, 1978/94
© Hans Weigand
Foto / photo: Courtesy of the artist

Dank / *Acknowledgement*

Dank an alle KünstlerInnen und AutorInnen ebenso an alle LeihgeberInnen /
Thanks to all artists and authors as well as to all lenders

sowie an / *as well to:*
Pierre Alechinsky, Grete Årbu, Paolo Baldacci, Maryse Brand, Gisela Capitain, Lutz Casper, Tomaso Corvi-Mora, Michel Dereymaeker, Diedrich Diederichsen, Claudia Dohr, Pia Dornacher, Silvia Eiblmayr, Lisa Franzen, Georg Frei, Bärbel Grässlin, Detlef Gretenkort, Thomas Grötz, Christine und Andy Hall, Eva Sabine Hänsel, Rebecca Heald, Erna Hécey, Günter Herzog, Galerie Max Hetzler, Marinne Holtermann, Xavier Hufkens, Eva Kernbauer, Gabriele Knapstein, Eva Köhler, Jutta Koether, Gretchen Kraus, Jean-Jacques Lebel, Sylvie Liska, Olga Makhroff, Porfirio Munoz, Selima Niggl, David Nolan, Alfred Pacquement, Jana Peltier, Patrick Peternader, Friedrich Petzel, Stephan Ratibor, Ines Ratz, Madeleine Richardson, Sally Saul, Aurel Scheibler, Hanna Schouwink, Carla Schulz-Hoffmann, Franz Seilern, Gabriele Senn, Marie-José van de Loo, Johan Vansteenkiste, Nicola von Velsen, David Zwirner

Museum Moderner Kunst Stiftung Ludwig Wien
Direktor / *Director:* Edelbert Köb

Ausstellung / *Exhibition*
Kuratorinnen / *Curators:* Eva Badura-Triska, Susanne Neuburger
Ausstellungsorganisation / *Exhibition manager:* Dagmar Steyrer
Ausstellungsarchitektur / *Exhibition architecture:* Walter Kirpicsenko
Presse / *Press:* Eva Engelberger
Marketing: Daniela Birk, Wolfgang Schreiner
Fundraising: Bärbel Holaus
Kooperationen / *Corporate involvement:* Yvonne Katzenberger
Ausstellungsaufbau / *Exhibition installation:* Olli Aigner & Team, MUMOK-Team
Kunstvermittlungsprogramm / *Art education program:* Claudia Ehgartner, Johanna Gudden, Jörg Wolfert & Team (Moni Ankele, Maria Bucher, Ivan Jurica)

Publikation / *Publication*
Diese Publikation erscheint anlässlich der Ausstellung *Bad Painting – good art* im Museum Moderner Kunst Stiftung Ludwig Wien (6. Juni–12. Oktober 2008).
This catalogue has been published on the occasion of the exhibition Bad Painting – good art *at Museum Moderner Kunst Stiftung Ludwig Wien (June 6–October 12, 2008).*

Herausgegeben von / *Edited by*
Museum Moderner Kunst Stiftung Ludwig Wien
Eva Badura-Triska, Susanne Neuburger
Museumsplatz 1
A–1070 Wien
T: +43 1 52500
F: +43 1 52500 1300
I: www.mumok.at
ISBN 978-3-902490-44-5

Produktionsleitung / *Head of production:* Nina Krick
Gestaltung / *Graphic design:* Stephan Pfeffer
Deutsches Lektorat / *German copy editor:* m∞bius
Englisches Lektorat / *English copy editor:* Nita Tandon
Übersetzungen / *Translations:* Robin Benson (Gelshorn, Biografien),
Adam Blauhut (Petzel), Greg Bond (Höller, Neuner),
Nicholas Grindell (Köb, Badura-Triska), Christina Oberstebrink (Neuburger),
Thomas Raab (Gilman), transparent (Blistène)
Texte / *Texts:* Eva Badura-Triska, Bernhard Blistène, Julia Gelshorn, Claire Gilman,
Christian Höller, Susanne Neuburger, Stefan Neuner, Friedrich Petzel
Lithografie / *Lithograph:* pixelstorm, Wien / *Vienna*
Druck / *Printed by:* Remaprint, Wien / *Vienna*
Schrift / *Typeface:* Minion, DTLArgo
Papier / *Paper:* Garda matt 170 g, 300 g
Auflage / *Print run:* 2.750

Bildnachweis siehe Werkliste und Referenzabbildungen /
Photo Credits see List of Works and List of References

Gestaltet und gedruckt in Österreich / *Designed and Printed in Austria*

Erschienen im / *Published by*
DuMont Buchverlag GmbH & Co. KG
Amsterdamer Straße 192
D–50735 Köln
T: +49 221 224 1877
F: +49 221 224 1973
www.dumontliteraturundkunst.de
Buchhandelsausgabe / *Publisher's edition*
ISBN 978-3-8321-9112-2

Bad Painting
good art